A Guide and Reference with Readi...

P9-BJB-272

reference

reader

HOW TO
WRITE
ANYTHING

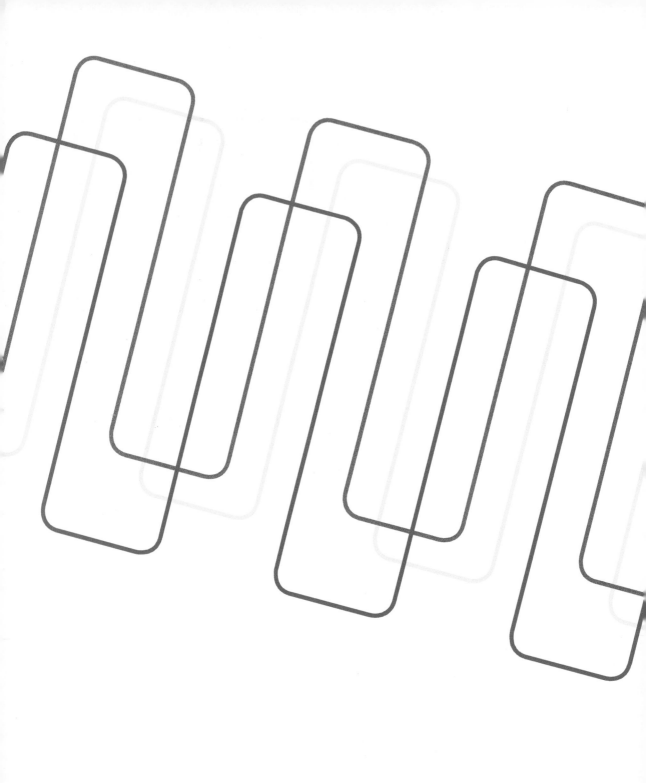

FOURTH EDITION

HOW TO WRITE ANYTHING

A Guide and Reference
with Readings

John J. Ruszkiewicz
UNIVERSITY OF TEXAS AT AUSTIN

Jay T. Dolmage
UNIVERSITY OF WATERLOO

bedford/st.martin's
Macmillan Learning

Boston | New York

For Bedford/St. Martin's

Vice President, Editorial, Macmillan Learning Humanities: Edwin Hill

Executive Program Director for English: Leasa Burton

Senior Program Manager: Laura Arcari

Marketing Manager: Vivian Garcia

Director of Content Development, Humanities: Jane Knetzger

Executive Development Editor: Christina Gerogiannis

Senior Content Project Manager: Kerri A. Cardone

Senior Workflow Project Manager: Jennifer L. Wetzel

Production Supervisor: Brianna Lester

Associate Editor: Suzanne Chouljian

Editorial Assistant: Annie Campbell

Media Project Manager: Jodi Isman

Media Editor: Angela Beckett

Editorial Services: Lumina Datamatics, Inc.

Composition: Lumina Datamatics, Inc.

Text Permissions Manager: Kalina Ingham

Photo Permissions Editor: Angela Boehler

Photo Researcher: Krystyna Borgen, Lumina Datamatics, Inc.

Director of Design, Content Management: Diana Blume

Text Design: Rick Koarb, Rick Koarb Design

Cover Design: William Boardman

Cover Image: Moritz Wolf/Getty Images

Printing and Binding: King Printing Co., Inc.

Manufactured in the United States of America.

1 2 3 4 5   23 22 21 20 19

For information, write: Bedford/St. Martin's, 75 Arlington Street, Boston, MA 02116

ISBN: 978-1-319-28233-2 (Student Edition)

Acknowledgments

Text acknowledgments and copyrights appear at the back of the book on pages A-1–A-6, which constitute an extension of the copyright page. Art acknowledgments and copyrights appear on the same page as the art selections they cover.

A textbook called *How to Write Anything* needs to deliver on an ambitious title. Its first edition was built upon the premise that introducing college students to the powerful concept of genres would give them control over a wide range of writing projects: Two subsequent editions refined this approach and responded to instructors' requests for coverage of more specialized academic assignments, including annotated bibliographies, synthesis papers, and portfolios.

But writers matter every bit as much as the theories that guide their writing, especially when these writers come from ever more varied backgrounds and with more diverse ambitions. So this fourth edition has been purposefully designed to give more attention to the students who will use it—their goals, expectations, and anxieties, as they begin a composition class.

Most noticeably, *How to Write Anything*, Fourth Edition, opens with a new section entitled "Strategies for College Writing." Its seven brief chapters on foundational topics such as "Defining Genres and Purpose" and "Organizing Ideas" offer practical advice for students wanting to succeed in college writing courses. Then the book follows up with materials refined for greater clarity and impact, especially in the "Key Academic Genres" (Part 2) and "Special College Assignments" chapters (Part 3). There are more summary boxes and helpful lists too, and readings have been chosen to represent a broader range of student interests and concerns. Even the grammar, mechanics, and usage sections have been restructured to make them more thorough and yet easier to navigate. And, in a nod to its audience, some of the best writing in *How to Write Anything*, Fourth Edition, comes from students who have used earlier editions.

Like those earlier editions, the fourth edition doesn't define a single course structure or imagine that all students using it will have the same skills or academic ambitions. Instead, a modular chapter organization and an innovative system of cross-references enables writers to find exactly the information they want at the level of specificity they need. Thus in retaining its familiar guide/reference structure, *How to Write Anything* marries the resources of a full rhetoric to the efficiency of a compact handbook.

A Guide, a Reference, and a Reader

Parts 1, 2, and 3 of *How to Write Anything* make up the Guide. An entirely new opening chapter in Part 1, "Academic Goals and Expectations," outlines what students should expect in composition courses and encourages them to take advantage of writing centers and faculty office hours. To prompt them to think of themselves as writers, Chapter 1 concludes with a literacy narrative assignment, supported by a model. Six subsequent chapters then briefly outline the specific rhetorical choices they'll explore within each of the genre chapters in Part 2: Defining Genres and Purpose; Claiming Topics; Imagining Audiences; Gathering Materials; Organizing Ideas; and Choosing Style and Design.

In effect, Part 1 is the overture to the book, explaining how genres define expectations for writers to consider whenever they compose.

For each of the genres in Parts 2 and 3, writers are offered a framework presented as a flexible series of the rhetorical choices first introduced in Part 1. The explanations here are direct, practical, and economical, encouraging students to explore a range of options within genres. If writers do need more help with a particular topic, targeted cross-references make it easy to find in the Reference section. Part 2, "Key Academic Genres," explores eight essential types of writing in depth, breaking each into its significant subgenres and then walking writers through the process of composing them. Each chapter opens with an annotated example of its genre and closes with additional models and carefully coordinated assignments. Part 3, "Special College Assignments," covers nine essential subgenres of writing (and, in some cases, speaking) in the academic and professional world. Each of these chapters is newly introduced with an "At a Glance" overview.

The Reference section (Parts 4 through 8) covers key aspects of the writing process. Writers might turn to these sections to find techniques for generating arguments, improving their sentences, or overcoming writer's block. The organization of *How to Write Anything* lets students find preceisely what they need without getting bogged down in other material.

Materials in the Reference section have been reorganized as well, to make better sense to college writers. Part 4, "A Writer's Routines," now examines eight essential elements of the writing process. Taken together, the chapters imply a sequence, but they don't have to be approached that way. Part 5 on "Style" offers strategies for writers to use when composing effective sentences, paragraphs, and more—even titles. It leads logically to Part 6 on "Design and Digital Media," its three chapters presenting options for enhancing the look and power of documents, especially those in electronic environments. The ten chapters in Part 7, "Academic Research and Sources," provide detailed guidance for students new to college research and a refresher for those who've written term papers or research reports before. Finally, a substantially augmented Part 8, reimagined as a "Handbook," offers separate chapters on MLA documentation, APA documentation, grammar, mechanics, sentence structure, and troublesome pairs. Those final four chapters are selective, but address matters that bedevil writers throughout their careers. Most students will find these chapters are just about what they need for college projects.

Part 9, the Reader, is an anthology of thirty-nine additional contemporary selections organized by genres covered in the Guide. Drawn from a variety of sources such as print and online journals, books, scholarly and popular magazines, blogs, and graphic novels, the readings offer both solid models for writing as well as compelling topics for students to respond to. The readings advocate for the power of unlikeable characters, superheroes, and Beyoncé; consider alien invasions, bans on plastics, and how to survive as a low-income college student; and argue that we should lock up our phones and wear only jumpsuits. The Reader includes fresh content from established authors such as Zadie Smith, Patton Oswalt, Neil Degrasse-Tyson, and Lynda Barry, as well as from newer voices such as Roxane Gay, Ta-Nehisi Coates, and Teju Cole. Headnotes provide context for all readings in the text, and selections in the Reader are followed by analysis questions and writing assignments, which feature cross-references from the questions back to the Guide and Reference sections of the book. These readings, and the questions that follow them, are intended to help students more deeply consider and use the major genres in *How to Write Anything*.

Key Features

A Flexible Writing Process and Design that Works

How to Write Anything works hard to make its materials accessible and attractive to writers accustomed to intuitive design. For instance, "How to Start" questions at the opening of each chapter in Parts 2 and 3 anticipate where writers get stuck and direct them to exactly what they need: One writer might seek advice about finding a topic for a report, while another with a topic already in hand wants prompts for developing that idea.

Similarly, frequent cross-references between the Guide and Reference sections call attention to topics that students are likely to want to know more about. The simple language and unobtrusive design of the cross-references make it easy for students to stay focused on their own writing while finding where related material is located—no explanations necessary and minimal clutter on the page.

Readings and images throughout the book are similarly highlighted and variously annotated so that writers, once again, find information they need precisely when they require it.

Media savvy students know that learning occurs in more than just words, so this edition preserves one of the favorite design features of *How To Write Anything*: its context-rich "How To" visual tutorials. Through drawings, photographs, and screenshots, these items offer step-by-step instructions for topics, such as "How to Use the Writing Center" and "How to Browse for Ideas." In this fourth edition, the Writing Center graphic has been moved into Chapter 1 where it will get immediate attention. Other tutorials focus on how to revise texts and how to cite selected materials in both MLA and APA formats.

Writing Worth Reading—From Professionals and Students

How to Write Anything contains an ample selection of readings, more than twenty in the Guide chapters alone, representing a wide range of genres. Selections illustrate key principles and show how genres change in response to different contexts, audiences, and—increasingly important—media. Every chapter in Parts 2 and 3 includes complete examples of the genres under discussion, most of these texts are annotated to show how they meet criteria set down in *How to Write Anything*. The assignments at the end of these chapters are closely tied to the chapter readings so students can use the sample texts both as models and as springboards for discussion and exploration.

Just as important, the models in *How to Write Anything* are approachable. The readings—some by published professionals and others by students—reveal the diversity of contemporary writing being done in various genres. The student samples are especially inventive—chosen to motivate undergraduates to take comparable risks with their own writing. Together, the readings and exercises suggest to writers the creative possibilities within a wide range of genres and sub-genres.

New to This Edition

How to Write Anything was designed from the outset to be a practical, highly readable guide to writing for a generation used to exploring texts actively. The fourth edition adds many new features that enhance its practicality and accessibility:

- **A new opening part on "Strategies for College Writing."** Seven lean and carefully cross-referenced chapters describe what goes on in college writing courses with appealing frankness. The tips and advice, including *don't make writing harder than it is*; *take advantage of office hours*; and *use the writing center*, provide an encouraging roadmap to the writing process for writers. A sample literacy narrative in Chapter 1 introduces students to a common first assignment.

- **A stand-alone chapter on genres.** Genres and subgenres are now explained in a chapter of their own. Chapter 2, "Defining Genres and Purpose," explains why learning about genres really does make composing easier. It's not just theory.

- **Brainstorming is now explained upfront.** Because writers need advice about finding and developing ideas right away, techniques of invention are now explored in Chapter 3, "Claiming Topics." It includes a visual tutorial.

- **Organization is now explained upfront.** College writers struggling to organize papers too often fall back on the five-paragraph essay learned in middle school. Chapter 6, "Organizing Ideas," explains why that's not the best strategy even before students compose their first papers and then offers alternatives.

- **Part 2, "Key Academic Genres," has been refined.** The section now begins with "Reports" instead of narratives because instructors preferred an initial assignment more typical of college work. The former chapter on "Causal Analyses" has been renamed "Explanations" to broaden the kinds of writing that it might cover or encourage.

- **A new chapter on "Essays."** Replacing "Narratives" in the previous editions, is a more sophisticated and intriguing chapter on "Essays," informed by the genre Michel de Montaigne created in the sixteenth century and updated by writers ever since. Students can still compose narratives, but now with more focus on exploring ideas and issues. The new chapter is introduced by selections from Paul Graham's "The Age of the Essay" and concludes, fittingly, with two vastly different personal essays by college undergraduates.

- **Lively new readings or visual texts in every "Key Academic Genres" chapter.** The new selections, more than a dozen, include intriguing and surprising pieces such as "Grocery Store Economics: Why Are Rotisserie Chickens So Cheap? (report); "We're the Only Animals With Chins, and No One Knows Why" (explanation); "Serena Williams Is Not the Best Tennis Player" (evaluation); and "Join the Revolution: Eat More Bugs" (proposal).

- **New graphics to highlight writing processes.** In Chapter 20, a PowerPoint presentation is used to show how to handle an oral report; in Chapter 41, an infographic explains how to make an infographic.

- **Helpful summary charts.** Writers will find thoughtful new charts throughout the Reference sections (Parts 4–8): key terms in essay examination questions (Chapter 16); data required in bibliographic citations (Chapter 17); guidelines for formal outlines (Chapter 29); items to proofread carefully in college papers (Chapter 30); items to consider when evaluating sources (Chapter 46); style guides used in academic disciplines (Chapter 52).

- **Refreshed and updated chapter on professional correspondence.** Chapter 21 merges formerly separate coverage of business letters and email into an up-to-date discussion of how to communicate clearly in both academic and business situations. It still explains how to format that rare, but sometimes essential, paper letter.

- **Dynamic new material on Outlining.** Chapter 29 better illustrates how outlines can actually generate ideas and help writers discover new perspectives on topics, and continues to provide examples of scratch, informal, and formal outlines.

- **Expanded and thoroughly revised take on grammar, mechanics, and usage.** Eleven chapters on "Common Errors" in the previous edition provide the core for four more carefully structured chapters in this latest version. The new and much-enlarged chapters make up a new "Handbook" section and do much more than correct errors. They set questions about grammar, mechanics, and sentence rhetoric in fuller contexts than before, with many more topics addressed. There's even a brief chapter on "troublesome pairs"—explaining the differences between words often confused, such as *its and it's*, *affect and effect*, and *rein and reign*.

- **New selections in the Reader** highlight the ways that text, images, and informational graphics and figures work together; and the questions and prompts that accompany each reading push students to consider how they can create their own multimodal texts.

- A new *Student's Companion for How to Write Anything*, authored by Elizabeth Catanese (Community College of Philadelphia), offers thorough support for students in ALP/corequisite courses. The text includes coverage of college success strategies; activities to help students develop thoughtful, college-level essays; and additional practice in correcting writing problems, from revising topic sentences and developing paragraphs to correcting fragments. This handy resource is available at a significant discount when packaged with the book, and it can be found in the book's LaunchPad.

Acknowledgments

The following reviewers were very helpful through several drafts of this book:

Lisa Arnold, North Dakota State University; Deborah Bertsch, Columbus State Community College; Patricia Bostian, Central Piedmont Community College; Erin Breaux, South Louisiana Community College; Daniel Compton, Midlands Technical College Beltline; Natasha David-Walker, Columbus State University; Melanie Dusseau, Northwest State Community College; Amy Eggert, Bradley University; Bart Ganzert, Forsyth Technical Community College; Courtney George, Columbus State University; Priscilla Glanville, State College of Florida; Maura Grady, Ashland University; Lauren Hahn, DePaul University; Jo Hallawell, Ivy Tech Community College; Anne Helms, Alamance Community College; Judy Hevener, Blue Ridge Community College and Stuarts Draft High School; Peggy Karsten, Ridgewater College; Wolfgang Lepschy, Tallahassee Community College; Maryann Lesert, Grand Rapids Community College; Darby Lewes, Lycoming College; Trina Litteral, Ashland Community and Technical College; Rachel Lutwick-Deaner, Grand Rapids Community College; Bonni Miller, University of Massachusetts - Boston; Melissa Mohlere, Central Piedmont Community College; Lisa Muir, Wilkes Community College; Amy Nawrocki, University of Bridgeport; Marguerite Newcomb, Wayland Baptist University; Nichole Peacock, Marion Military Institute; Deidre Price, Northwest Florida State College; Michelle Pultorak, Tarrant County College District; Paula Rash, Caldwell Community College & Technical Institute; Brian Reeves, Lone Star College-University Park; Arleen Reinhardt, John Tyler Community College; Alison Reynolds, University of Florida; Karin Rhodes, Salem State University; Courtney Schoolmaster, South Louisiana Community College; Marilyn Senter, Johnson County Community College; Patrick Shaw, University of South; Guy Shebat, Youngstown State University; Hailey Sheets, Southwestern Michigan College; Joyce Staples, Patrick Henry Community College; Alabama; Jennifer Steigerwalt, University of Pikeville; Joel Thomas, Ancilla Domini College; Shelley Tuttle, Lakeview Christian Academy; Mari-jo Ulbricht, University of Maryland - Eastern Shore; Stephanie Williams, University of Arkansas at Little Rock; and Marilyn Yamin, Pellissippi State Community College.

All textbooks are collaborations, but we have never before worked on a project that more creatively drew upon the resources of an editorial team and publisher. *How to Write Anything* began with the confidence of Joan Feinberg, co-founder of Bedford/St. Martin's, that we could develop a groundbreaking brief rhetoric. She had the patience to allow the idea to develop at its own pace and then assembled an incredible team to support it. We are grateful for the contributions of Edwin Hill, Vice President of Editorial for the Humanities; Leasa Burton, Executive Program Director for Bedford/St. Martin's English; and Laura Arcari, Senior Program Manager. We are also indebted to Kerri Cardone, Senior Content Project Manager. For her marketing efforts, we are grateful for the guidance offered by Vivian Garcia and, of course, for the efforts of the incomparable Bedford/St. Martin's sales team. For her contributions to the fourth edition, we thank Christina Gerogiannis, Executive Development Editor. Christina has given thoughtful attention to every corner of the book, helping to ensure that this edition is tight, lively, and imaginative. It has been a pleasure to work with her, as well as with Molly Parke, Jill Gallagher, Stephanie Thomas, Stephanie Cohen, Suzanne Chouljian, and Annie Campbell.

Finally, we are extraordinarily grateful to our former students whose papers or paragraphs appear in *How to Write Anything*. Their writing speaks for itself, but we have been inspired, too, by their personal dedication and character. These are the sort of students who motivate teachers, and so we are very proud to see their work published in *How to Write Anything*: Ellen Airhart, Alysha Behn, Marissa Dahlstrom, Manasi Deshpande, Micah T. Eades, Laura Grisham, Wade Lamb, Desiree Lopez, Cheryl Lovelady, Soup Martinez, Matthew Nance, Lily Parish, Heidi Rogers, Kanaka Sathasivan, Leah Vann, Scott L. Walker, Susan Wilcox, and Ryan Young.

John J. Ruszkiewicz
Jay T. Dolmage

We're all in. As always.

Bedford/St. Martin's is as passionately committed to the discipline of English as ever, working hard to provide support and services that make it easier for you to teach your course your way.

Find **community support** at the Bedford/St. Martin's English Community (community.macmillan.com), where you can follow our *Bits* blog for new teaching ideas, download titles from our professional resource series, and review projects in the pipeline.

Choose **curriculum solutions** that offer flexible custom options, combining our carefully developed print and digital resources, acclaimed works from Macmillan's trade imprints, and your own course or program materials to provide the exact resources your students need. Our approach to customization makes it possible to create a customized project uniquely suited for your students, and based on your enrollment size, return money to your department and raise your institutional profile with a high-impact author visit through the Macmillan Author Program ("MAP").

Rely on **outstanding service** from your Bedford/St. Martin's sales representative and editorial team. Contact us or visit macmillanlearning.com to learn more about any of the options below.

LaunchPad for *How to Write Anything:* Where Students Learn

LaunchPad provides engaging content and new ways to get the most out of your book. Get an interactive e-book combined with assessment tools in a fully customizable course space; then assign and mix our resources with yours.

- **Book-specific quizzes** test students' comprehension for every full selection in the Reader.

- **Diagnostics** provide opportunities to assess areas for improvement and assign additional exercises based on students' needs. Visual reports show performance by topic, class, and student as well as improvement over time.

- **Pre-built units**—including readings, videos, quizzes, and more—are easy to adapt and assign by adding your own materials and mixing them with our high-quality multimedia content and ready-made assessment options, such as **LearningCurve** adaptive quizzing and Exercise Central.

- *A Student's Companion for How to Write Anything* helps students build a strong foundation, particularly in ALP/corequisite courses.

- Use LaunchPad on its own or **integrate it** with your school's learning management system so that your class is always on the same page.

LaunchPad for *How to Write Anything* can be purchased on its own or packaged with the print book at a significant discount. An activation code is required. To order LaunchPad for *How to Write Anything* with the print book, use ISBN 978-1-319-22188-1. For more information, go to **launchpadworks.com**

Choose from Alternative Formats of *How to Write Anything*

Bedford/St. Martin's offers a range of formats. Choose what works best for you and your students:

- *Paperback* To order the paperback edition, use ISBN 978-1-319-05853-1.

- *Popular e-book formats* For details of our e-book partners, visit **macmillanlearning .com/ebooks**.

- *Version without readings* To order the version without readings, use ISBN 978-1-319-10397-2.

- To package with *A Student's Companion for How to Write Anything*, our new ALP supplement, use ISBN 978-1-319-22810-1.

- To package with *LaunchPad for How to Write Anything*, use ISBN 978-1-319-22188-1.

Instructor Resources

You have a lot to do in your course. We want to make it easy for you to find the support you need—and to get it quickly.

Resources for Teaching How to Write Anything is available as a PDF that can be downloaded from macmillanlearning.com. Visit the instructor resources tab for *How to Write Anything*. In addition to chapter overviews and teaching tips, the instructor's manual includes sample syllabi and classroom activities.

Correlation to the Council of Writing Program Administrators' (WPA) Outcomes Statement

How to Write Anything helps students build proficiency in the five categories of learning that writing programs across the country use to assess their work: rhetorical knowledge; critical thinking, reading, and writing; writing processes; knowledge of conventions; and composing in electronic environments. A detailed correlation follows.

Features of *How to Write Anything: A Guide and Reference with Readings*, Fourth Edition, Correlated to the WPA Outcomes Statement

Note: This chart aligns with the latest WPA Outcomes Statement, ratified in July 2014.

WPA Outcomes	Relevant Features of *How to Write Anything*
Rhetorical Knowledge	
Learn and use key rhetorical concepts through analyzing and composing a variety of texts.	Each assignment chapter in the Guide includes three texts in a wide variety of genres. Questions, headnotes, and "Reading the Genre" prompts encourage students to examine and understand the key rhetorical concepts behind each genre of writing. Writing activities and prompts guide students through composing a range of texts. In addition, the Reader includes more than 40 more texts for student analysis.
Gain experience reading and composing in several genres to understand how genre conventions shape and are shaped by readers' and writers' practices and purposes.	The Introduction provides a foundation for thinking about genre, while each assignment chapter in the Guide offers a thorough look at each genre's conventions and how those conventions have developed and changed, as well as how to apply them to students' own writing situations.
	Each chapter in the Reader includes a "Genre Moves" feature, which analyzes a classic model to highlight a specific genre convention and suggest ways students might make use of it.
Develop facility in responding to a variety of situations and contexts, calling for purposeful shifts in voice, tone, level of formality, design, medium, and/or structure.	Each assignment chapter in the Guide offers detailed advice on responding to a particular rhetorical situation, from arguing a claim and proposing a solution to writing an e-mail or a résumé.
	See "Choosing a Style and Design" sections in Part 1 chapters, and the "Getting the Details Right" sections in Part 2 chapters for advice on situation-specific style and design.
	Part 5 features chapters on "Levels of Style" (33); "Inclusive Writing" (35); and "Clear and Vigorous Writing" (34).

WPA Outcomes	Relevant Features of *How to Write Anything*
Rhetorical Knowledge (*continued*)	
Understand and use a variety of technologies to address a range of audiences.	Chapter 40 covers digital media, including blogs, social networks, Web sites, wikis, podcasts, maps, and videos. Chapter 41 covers creating and using visuals to present data and ideas.
	Each assignment chapter includes at least one visual example of the genre that the chapter focuses on, and several of the reference chapters include Visual Tutorials featuring photographs and illustrations that provide students with step-by-step instructions for challenging topics, such as using the Web to browse for ideas. This emphasis on visuals, media, and design helps students develop visual and technological literacy they can use in their own work.
	Chapter 21 covers e-mail; Chapters 24 and 20 address portfolio and presentation software; and Chapters 45 and 46 cover finding, evaluating, and using print and electronic resources for research.
Match the capacities of different environments (e.g., print and electronic) to varying rhetorical situations.	The text and LaunchPad include a wide range of print and multimodal genres from essays and scholarly articles to photographs, infographics, Web sites, and audio and video presentations. Rhetorical choices that students make in each genre are covered in the Guide chapters and appear in discussions of the writing context and in abundant models in the book.
Critical Thinking, Reading, and Composing	
Use composing and reading for inquiry, learning, thinking, and communicating in various rhetorical contexts.	The assignment chapters in the Guide emphasize the connection between reading and writing a particular genre: Each chapter includes model readings with annotations that address the key features of the genre. Each Part 1 chapter shows students the rhetorical choices they need to consider when writing their own papers in these genres and offers assignments to actively engage them in these choices.
	Chapter 26, "Critical Thinking," explains rhetorical appeals and logical fallacies.
	Reference chapters in Parts 4 through 8 cover invention, reading, writing, research, and design strategies that work across all genres.
Read a diverse range of texts, attending especially to relationships between assertion and evidence, to patterns of organization, to interplay between verbal and nonverbal elements, and how these features function for different audiences and situations.	Each assignment chapter in the Guide includes three texts in a wide variety of genres. In addition, the Reader includes more than 40 more texts for student analysis.
	Each of the Guide chapters also includes sections on understanding audience, creating a structure, finding and developing material (including evidence), and choosing a style and design that best reflect the genre of writing.
	Chapter 25, "Smart Reading," helps students read deeply and "against the grain," while in Chapter 26, "Critical Thinking," students learn about claims, assumptions, and evidence. Chapter 6, "Organizing Ideas" gives advice on devising a structure for a piece of writing.

WPA Outcomes	Relevant Features of *How to Write Anything*
Critical Thinking, Reading, and Composing (*continued*)	
Locate and evaluate primary and secondary research materials, including journal articles, essays, books, databases, and informal Internet sources.	Part 7 covers research and sources in depth, with chapters on beginning your research, finding print and online sources, doing field research, evaluating and annotating sources, and documenting sources.
Use strategies — such as interpretation, synthesis, response, critique, and design/redesign — to compose texts that integrate the writer's ideas with those from appropriate sources.	Chapters 48 ("Annotating Sources"), 50 ("Paraphrasing Sources"), and 51 ("Incorporating Sources into Your Work") explore a variety of strategies for integrating the writer's ideas with ideas and information from sources. Chapter 18, "Synthesis Papers," shows students how to summarize, compare, and assess the views offered by different sources.
Processes	
Develop a writing project through multiple drafts.	Chapter 35, "Revising, Editing and Proofreading" discusses the importance of revising and gives detailed advice on how to approach different types of revision. Targeted cross-references throughout the text help students get the revision help they need when they need it.
Develop flexible strategies for reading, drafting, reviewing, collaboration, revising, rewriting, rereading, and editing.	The Reference's brief, targeted chapters and cross-references lend themselves to a flexible approach to writing process, with an array of strategies for students to choose from whether they're crafting an introduction or preparing to revise a first draft.
	Genre-specific advice in the Guide chapters helps students tailor each step of the writing process to their writing situation, while process-based chapters in the Reference offer guidance that can be applied to any type of writing.
Use composing processes and tools as a means to discover and reconsider ideas.	Each Part 1 chapter includes two sections that encourage students to use the composing process as a means of discovery. "Deciding to write . . ." covers the reasons a writer might choose a specific form of writing, while "Exploring purpose and topic" prompts students to challenge their own ideas about a subject and write to discover what they think when they look more deeply at it.
Experience the collaborative and social aspects of writing processes.	Several chapters in the Reference send students out into their worlds for advice, information, and feedback. Chapter 44, "Consulting Experts," talks about the kinds of experts — such as librarians, instructors, peers, and writing center tutors — that students can call on for help. Chapter 47, "Doing Field Research," discusses the whys and hows of interviewing and observing people as part of the research process. Chapter 31, "Peer Editing," offers advice for helping peers improve their work.
Learn to give and act on productive feedback to works in progress.	Chapter 31, "Peer Editing," encourages students to give specific , helpful advice to peers and think about peer editing in the same way they revise their own work.

WPA Outcomes	Relevant Features of *How to Write Anything*
Processes (*continued*)	
Adapt composing processes for a variety of technologies and modalities.	Chapter 40 focuses on digital media, including blogs, Web sites, wikis, podcasts, maps, and videos.
	Chapter 21 covers e-mail; Chapters 24 and 20 address portfolio and presentation software; and Chapters 45 and 46 cover finding, evaluating, and using print and electronic resources for research.
Reflect on the development of composing practices and how those practices influence their work.	The new Introduction invites students to consider their writing practices and how the choices they make during invention, drafting, research, and revision shape their process and their work.
Knowledge of Conventions	
Develop knowledge of linguistic structures, including grammar, punctuation, and spelling, through practice in composing and revising.	Part 8 (Handbook) includes chapters on grammar, punctuation, and mechanics, while Chapter 30 provide editing and proofreading advice. Targeted cross-references throughout the text send students to these chapters as needed.
Understand why genre conventions for structure, paragraphing, tone, and mechanics vary.	Each Part 2 chapter includes a section on choosing style and design to help students understand how their choice of style, structure, tone, and mechanics is shaped by the genre in which they're writing.
Gain experience negotiating variations in genre conventions.	Models of work from several subgenres within the book's main genres show students the variations that exist within the confines of a given genre. In addition, "Reading the Genre" prompts help students identify and understand the genre conventions at work in each selection.
Learn common formats and/or design features for different kinds of texts.	Each assignment chapter in the Guide covers a format specific to the genre covered there; see "Choosing a Style and Design" in the Part 1 chapters and "Getting the Details Right" in the Part 2 chapters.
Explore the concepts of intellectual property (such as fair use and copyright) that motivate documentation conventions.	Chapter 52, "Documenting Sources," helps students understand why documentation is important and what's at stake in properly identifying and citing material used from sources.
Practice applying citation conventions systematically in their own work.	Chapters 53, "MLA Documentation and Format," and 54, "APA Documentation and Format," include detailed guidance for citing sources according to each style's conventions. Visual Tutorials in each chapter help students identify and find the information they need in order to create accurate citations.

Contents

guide

9   Explanations   65

14   **Rhetorical Analyses**   **197**

Part 3   Special College Assignments   242

16   Essay Examinations   244

reference

Part 4   **A Writer's Routines**   322

57 Sentence Issues   566

reader

Genres and Subgenres in *How to Write Anything*

Narratives

- Literacy narrative
- Memoir/reflection
- Graphic narrative
- Personal statement

Reports

- Research report
- Feature story
- Infographic
- Essay examination
- Annotated bibliography
- Synthesis paper
- E-mail
- Business letter
- Résumé
- Oral report

Arguments

- Support of a thesis
- Refutation
- Visual argument
- Position paper

Evaluations

- Arts review
- Satire
- Product review
- Parody
- Portfolio review
- Peer review

Causal Analyses

- Causal argument
- Research analysis
- Cultural analysis

Proposals

- Trial balloon
- Manifesto
- Visual proposal
- Topic proposal

Literary Analysis

- Thematic analysis
- Close reading
- Photographs as literary texts

Rhetorical Analysis

- Rhetorical analysis
- Close analysis of an argument
- Film analysis

guide

Strategies for College Writing

1

Need a form you don't see here? Try "Key Academic Genres," p. 36

1

Academic Goals and Expectations

You may not look forward to writing in college, worrying perhaps about the high expectations, the range of assignments, and your inability to recall obscure rules of mechanics and usage. Maybe you haven't written much recently or English is your second or third language? Yet suddenly, you'll be responsible for term papers, arguments, essays, lab reports, and more—and you've never produced work quite like this before. Even if you've been writing most of your life and correspond via electronic media all the time, the prospect of sharing words and ideas with college audiences scares you.

Maybe it should. After all, writing today isn't just for English majors: If you expect a career in business, sales, government, nursing, science, even engineering, you'll spend a lot of time pounding out sentences in school and on the job. Writing has always been an essential professional skill, maybe *the* essential one, so being able to communicate your insights, impressions, or opinions with clarity matters. Instructors, colleagues, and employers will expect that. More reason to panic?

Far from it. The problem many people have with writing is that they see it as a knack they don't possess when it is, in fact, a set of practical skills that can be learned and refined. It surely doesn't mean gazing at your navel until inspiration strikes. Once you realize that, writing becomes manageable. So the seven brief chapters in this opening section of *How To Write Anything* introduce you to basic moves and principles you'll need to handle many types of college writing. The next two parts of the book go into detail about specific writing assignments and projects. Then the remaining sections function as a "reference guide," explaining technical details about the writing process, everything from how to do college-level research to choosing a good title. There's even a brief guide to grammar and mechanics.

To get you started, here's some general counsel about writing and writing courses.

Know that writing is more than avoiding grammar errors. Grammar, mechanics, usage, and correct spelling *are* important of course and will be on your mind whenever you compose, especially if English isn't your first language. You can't ignore these matters, especially in the final stages of preparing a writing project, and the handbook section at the end of this book should help with the details—as will online grammar sites or a full grammar handbook. Chapter 30, "Revising, Editing, and Proofreading," offers specific tips for polishing your writing, and Chapter 31, "Peer Editing," will help when you are called to comment on a colleague's work.

But you're getting off on the wrong foot in a college writing course if you believe you won't do well because you missed the rigorous training in grammar all your classmates somehow got. Here's the truth: almost no one took such courses in elementary school or high school—except maybe colleagues who studied English as a second language. (And, if you're in that category, you likely *do* know more about English tenses and pronoun usage than most native speakers.)

Predictably, college courses focus more on the content, structure, and style of written work than they do on "correctness" because that's what's new and challenging. You'll be assigned specific types of projects requiring both research and reading, and you'll need to respond coherently, sometimes persuasively, and in an appropriate format—these days that may involve working in media other than print alone. Grammar and mechanics remain in the mix, but you'll be exercising new muscles in these writing courses—which is the whole point of being in school.

Don't make writing harder than it is. Now if you're still wondering whether you can succeed in writing class, be assured the skills required aren't arcane or esoteric—fancy words for *hard*. The chapters in this book will walk you through a wide range of projects, all of them explained in detail. The work you produce won't be fill-in-the-blank easy because you face choices and make judgment calls whenever you write. But you'll be following well-worn paths, not hacking through the brush every time you're given a new assignment.

You'll also receive lots of commonsensical advice to make writing projects manageable. Worried about essay exams, for instance, or oral reports, or all those personal statements you know you'll have to write when applying for jobs or internships? You're not on your own: Specific strategies will enhance your success. You don't have to reinvent the wheel. And if just getting started is an issue for you, you might detour briefly to read Chapter 32, "Overcoming Writer's Block."

It *is* important to pay attention to advice, study model papers, and take the technicalities of specific types of writing seriously. You can't treat a college paper like a tweet, but you know that already—which means you understand a key concept of this book: genres. You'll learn all about them in Chapter 2, "Defining Genres and Purpose."

Take advantage of your instructor's office hours.

This advice might seem like a jump, but it's timely: Talking about writing with your instructor (occasionally) can bring you up to speed. Really. So whether you're confused by course policies or excited by particular assignments, consult with your instructor or teaching assistant. Run topic ideas by them, ask for advice about best sources for a report or argument, or discuss an assignment that puzzles you. Don't plaintively ask, "What do you want?" or complain about your previous instructors. Instead, use an office appointment to let your teacher know who you are and what your ambitions might be. Most instructors will be happy to see you, and some may even remember your name when it's time to ask for a letter of recommendation. Everyone eventually needs one.

Use the writing center.

Let's get this straight: The college writing centers now common across two- and four-year schools are *not* editing services or fix-it shops. Tutors in these facilities are actually trained *not* to revise your prose or correct your grammar. And that's a good thing. You won't learn anything if someone else does your writing for you.

Nor should you think that writing centers are for weak writers only—a place where you should be ashamed to be seen. That's old-school thinking. Writing centers today typically offer support to writers at any stage in the writing process and at every level of expertise. Their mission is not only to improve specific papers and projects, but also to create more confident and capable writers.

Writing centers *will* help you work through issues you may have with grammar and mechanics. Tutors will understand and support you if English isn't your first language and its verb tenses or its rules for documenting papers seem strange to you. But they'll also be glad to help you find a topic, develop it, or support it with reputable sources. They'll give you advice about the format of a lab report or résumé. They'll react to your brainstorming or to an off-the-cuff draft. They might even read your sonnets or the first chapter of the graphic novel you've been drawing.

That's because the best thing about writing centers—especially those staffed by your peers—is that they provide opportunities for heart-to-heart conversations about writing. Perhaps you're wondering *what can I learn from another student?* The answer is plenty because peer-to-peer discussions are much less intimidating than most sessions with instructors. Conversations with peers allow you to push back, ask dumb questions, and work out issues together. You might be surprised by how much you enjoy writing center consultations.

Think of writing as a process.

Throughout this book, you'll find maps to guide you through various stages of writing. In particular, you'll find that the eight chapters in Part 2, "Key Academic Genres," are organized by six principles representing important decisions you'll make in writing everything from a report to a personal essay:

- Defining the Genre
- Claiming a Topic
- Imagining Your Audience
- Gathering Materials
- Organizing Ideas
- Choosing Style and Design

The remaining chapters in this section each discuss one of those aspects of writing in more detail.

Think of yourself as a writer.

Writing is a way of learning. As you encounter new ideas in courses that require responses, you'll find yourself instinctively looking for ways to focus and organize that material. How do these data, ideas, or arguments fit together, and how might I communicate what I'm learning to others? In doing such work—writing reports, constructing arguments, designing infographics—your academic confidence will grow. Thinking like a writer—that is, as someone responsible for shaping and expressing ideas—will make you a more active and critical student. In other words, a smarter person. Yes, writing can do that. For an example of this process, see "Literacy Narrative Model" on the following page.

Literacy Narrative Model

In many composition courses, students are asked to write a short initial piece describing their prior experiences with reading, literature, and writing. If you have this opportunity, you'll discover that such an assignment can also function as an icebreaker in a course, allowing you to introduce yourself to your peers with whom you'll be sharing ideas, drafts, and editing suggestions for an entire semester. Laura Grisham, a student at the University of Texas at Austin, wrote her literary narrative in response to a prompt that included this advice:

> Tell us about your successes and failures and the teachers who made a difference to you—or those who never appreciated your talent. In the course of the essay, consider sharing the best advice you have ever received about writing—or the worst. Your audience for this item will obviously be your classmates in this class, but imagine a wider readership as well. Your language should be precise, lively, and, of course, mechanically correct. And you may include photos.

Reading the Genre   Laura Grisham is someone who expects to write all her life because of the fiction she read as a child. Your literacy narrative—if you compose one—might talk of other genres, everything from video games, graphic novels, and movies to social media, sports columns, social media, even math books. Not everyone in a composition class thinks of writing as a career.

Not a reader initially, Grisham explains her transition from would-be athlete to Harry Potter fan.

In third grade I dreamed of becoming a professional athlete. Despite mildly severe scoliosis and limited depth perception, my imagined future likely included a Gatorade sponsorship. However, one fateful day in third grade, as the result of an unfortunate face plant in P.E. class that knocked out my front teeth, I humbly opted to change my future area of expertise from athletics to a more academic concentration.

I decided to start taking reading seriously. I memorized the Dewey Decimal System. I convinced the librarian to allow me to check out multiple books at a time. I became curious about the stories on the pages and dove headfirst into their worlds. My curiosity pushed me so far into the literary abyss until suddenly Harry was trying to win over an emotionally unstable Cho Chang in *Harry Potter and the Order of the Phoenix*.

I became a sponge. I soaked up the sharp wit of Lemony Snicket in *A Series of Unfortunate Events* and consequently developed a harsh sarcasm that has stuck with me ever since *The Bad Beginning*. Christopher John Frances Boone, with refreshing objectivity, taught me the value in having an earnest desire to do the right thing in *The Curious Incident of the Dog in the Night-Time*. I learned that our actions, despite our intentions, deeply affect those around us in *A Separate Peace*.

As I read and absorbed, the stories provoked self-reflective questions: Why can't I drink from the fountain of youth alongside Jesse Tuck? Why can't I love people the way Gatsby loved Daisy? Why do the Pevensie children find adventure through a wardrobe on a rainy day while I am stuck watching raindrops hit the window as my teacher drones on about the difference between sedimentary and igneous rocks?

These thoughts bounced around relentlessly in my head, but I lacked both the confidence and eloquence to express my musings aloud. Then, in eighth grade my English teacher taught me to put my thoughts in words.

She spent long, painful hours drilling grammar rules into my head, pushing me to hate writing. That is, until she presented the class with a creative writing prompt and I realized that understanding proper grammatical structures enabled me to express my thoughts more clearly and concisely than ever before. Since then, I have rarely been found without a black Pilot G-2 pen clipped to my shirt and a thin notebook of thoughts in my backpack.

I am taking this writing class to revitalize and redefine my love for words. I don't know if I want to write for a living, but I know myself well enough to know that in order to live I have to write. And who knows; maybe, someday, good writers will all be rewarded with Gatorade sponsorships.

> Grisham counts on readers recognizing at least some of the books and characters who influenced her.

> Reading and an influential teacher turn Grisham into a writer, represented by the pen and notebook she routinely carries.

Assignment

Compose a Literacy Narrative: After reading Laura Grisham's literacy narrative (p. 8), write one of your own, perhaps recalling how you learned to read or write and teachers who influenced you during the process. Describe books that changed you or any ambitions you might now have to pursue a writing or media career. However, you don't have to be an aspiring writer to make sense of this assignment. Remember that there are many kinds of literacy. The narrative you compose may be about your encounters with paintings, films, music, fashion, architecture, or maybe even video games. Or it may explore any intellectual passion—from mathematics to foreign policy.

1

Bring materials with you, including the assignment, previous drafts or outlines, comments from your instructor if you have any, a pen, and a notebook.

2

Be actively involved during the session, and arrive with specific goals in mind. Your tutor may ask questions about your writing process and your paper. Be prepared to think about and respond to your tutor's suggestions.

3

Keep revising. While the tutor may be able to help you with some aspects of your writing, you are ultimately responsible for the finished paper — and your grade.

2

understand
genres and
subgenres

Defining Genres and Purpose

If a blank page or empty screen scares you, join the club. Even professional writers freeze up when facing unfamiliar assignments. So what do you do when asked to submit, say, a literacy narrative or causal analysis or even an infographic in a college course? Exactly what experienced authors do: look at models and examine strategies others have used to meet similar assignments. That's not very creative, you might object. But in fact, it's the way inventive people in many fields operate, from video game producers to automobile designers. They get a feel for the design and features, structures and strategies, materials and styles of whatever they hope to construct themselves, and then they work to create fresh products. They become masters of their *genre*. This book will show you how to take the same approach with academic and professional writing.

Appreciate what genres are. You're already familiar with the concept because you encounter it daily, though the terms you might hear for it include *class*, *category*, *type*, *species*, *model*. If you have your phone or tablet with you, just open Netflix, click the three bars in the upper left-hand corner, and examine the categories listed in the menu: everything from TV shows, documentaries, and originals to action and adventure, comedies, horror movies, and so on. Each item represents a genre of entertainment. Although Netflix's categories overlap, they help you find what you're looking for if you recognize the differences between, for example, romantic movies and horror movies. And Netflix is pretty sure you do.

Now click one of Netflix's general categories and you get even more specific options—what might be called "sub-genres": gory horror

Francis Vachon/Alamy Stock Photo

movies, monster movies, supernatural horror movies, teen screams. Chances are you've watched enough films to explain what to expect from each of these subgenres. You might be disappointed when a particular film doesn't meet your expectations or, alternatively, delighted when a director pushes the genre envelope and surprises you. That's how genres work. Think about the concept, and you'll appreciate how often you encounter genres and subgenres every day—they are a part of everything from your trip to the grocery store to your selection of courses for next term.

Understand why writers rely on genres. Genres provide a road map or template for academic work. You'll come to recognize such models for what they do and for their distinctive features. For instance, a work that fits into the genre of *report* conveys information, drawing upon careful research to provide readers with reliable facts and information. Similarly, an *argument* employs a wide range of strategies to persuade audiences to accept claims—everything from reams of data to appeals to the heart. The eight chapters in Part 2 of *How to Write Anything* introduce you to these two familiar genres (reports and arguments), along with six others you'll run up against in your academic and professional life: *evaluations, explanations, proposals, literary analyses, rhetorical analyses,* and *personal essays.*

However, if you expect simple formulas, templates, and step-by-step instructions for each of these categories, think again. No one learns to write by filling in boxes or cloning five-paragraph essays. Serious genres reflect real-life responses to ever-changing writing situations, so they can't be either simple or simplistic. You'll come to appreciate that a genre approach to writing isn't arbitrary, inflexible, predictable, or dull because genres change constantly—maybe the better term is *evolve*—to serve both writers *and* readers.

Using genres to meet assignments.

Although it makes sense to become familiar with academic genres in the abstract, that's only half the process of learning to write. First you figure out what specific genres do (and that's a lot). Then you bend those genres to fit actual assignments you get in school and, later in life, the kind of work you'll do on your own. You figure out what to say within a genre, tailor its features to the people you hope to influence, organize your ideas strategically, and state them powerfully in appropriate media—including visual, oral, and online formats. That's what all the chapters in Part 2 of *How to Write Anything* are about. They walk you through a full range of choices you face in making academic assignments work for you—and not the other way around.

So think of genres as shortcuts to success. When you learn a new genre, you don't acquire a hard-and-fast set of rules for writing; instead, you gain control over that genre's *possibilities*. Who knows where such insights might take you?

Understand subgenres.

Quite often you'll be asked to compose projects so narrowly focused that a *genre* turns into a *subgenre*. A subgenre is simply a specialized version of a genre, one that adapts broad principles to very specific purposes.

For example, only rarely will you be asked to compose a nonspecific report; more typically, you'll be given a focus—for instance, a history term paper detailing some aspect of the Cuban Missile Crisis of 1961 or a newspaper column explaining NCAA recruitment policies. In day-to-day writing, you won't argue just for the fun of it; instead you may dash off a purposeful letter-to-the-editor to persuade student government at your school to fix its broken election code. In effect, you tune a genre to meet immediate needs. And that usually makes your task easier.

Fortunately, models of hard-working subgenres are readily available in print and online today for you to study and emulate as needed. In *How to Write Anything*, for instance, the chapter on "Evaluations" in Part 2 presents basic strategies for making informed judgments about people and things, explaining in detail how to create and apply the criteria of evaluation. Fair enough.

But your purpose in reading and writing evaluations is often more focused. You want to know whether a book is worth reading, a restaurant deserves your dollar, a professional school will get you a job. So you'll consult book, restaurant, or program reviews you've learned to regard as trustworthy, likely because of how well they themselves handle the criteria of evaluation and evidence. When you know how a genre works, you'll appreciate how its subgenres refine its moves.

Like genres, subgenres present an array of specific features and strategies for you to use. For that reason, you'll find connections between genre and subgenres throughout *How to Write Anything*. For example, each of the major readings in Part 2 is identified by its subgenre, and all the major writing assignments at the end of chapters suggest that you take one of those items as a pattern to help you with a project of your own.

Part 3, "Special Assignments," is entirely about subgenres crucial to people in school or entering the job market—items such as essay examinations, résumés, personal statements, and oral reports. In this section, you'll see how practical and action-oriented writing can be. Just as important, you'll learn one strategy for managing any writing task you are assigned: Find a good model to emulate.

Genres and Subgenres in *How to Write Anything*

Reports
- Research report
- Feature story
- Infographic
- Essay examination
- Annotated bibliography
- Synthesis paper
- E-mail
- Professional correspondence
- Résumé
- Personal statement
- Oral report

Explanations
- Causal analysis
- Research study
- Flow diagram

Arguments
- Proof
- Refutation
- Visual argument
- Position paper

Evaluations
- Critical assessment
- Product review
- Arts review
- Social satire
- Portfolio review
- Peer review

Proposals
- Trial balloon
- Manifesto
- Visual proposal

Literary Analyses
- Cultural reflection
- Close reading
- Literacy narrative

Rhetorical Analyses
- Discourse analysis
- Critical analysis
- Cultural assessment
- Analysis of an argument

Essays
- Exploratory essay
- Argumentative essay
- Personal essay

3

find a topic /
get an idea

Claiming Topics

You've been assigned a paper and have some sense what you're supposed to do. But you still have to decide on a topic. Asked to offer an argument, evaluation, or proposal, for instance, the question quickly becomes, *what will I actually argue, evaluate, or propose?* Suddenly, you're on your own. You could write about so many things—though nothing comes to mind. What to do?

Brainstorm a bit. Put some possibilities on the table and assess their potential. If a topic has been on your mind, run with it now. Here's your chance to think about ideas seriously—or maybe even apply what you've been learning in your major to real-world situations. Following are some general techniques of "invention," a term the ancient Greeks used to describe how to come up with topic ideas and arguments.

Follow routines that support invention. Some people do their best brainstorming while jogging, cycling, knitting, or sipping brew at a coffeehouse—especially once they've focused on a topic area. Such routine activities keep the body occupied, allowing insights to emerge. Be sure to capture and record those ideas in notes or, perhaps, voice memos. One warning: Passive routines like those mentioned can easily slip into procrastination. That comfortable corner at Starbucks might become a spot too collegial for much thinking or writing. If your productivity drops, change tactics.

"It's great for multicrastinating."

Paul Noth/The New Yorker Collection/The Cartoon Bank

Browse course materials. Don't be surprised when topics for academic papers emerge from course activities and materials. It makes perfect sense. So review course textbooks, readings, and Web sites for ideas to explore in more detail, especially in areas not covered explicitly in class. Or take an idea an instructor or classmate briefly mentions in a discussion and follow up on its implications. Or look for connections between the course and the world outside—in the local community, in the workforce, or in political or cultural environments. See Chapter 25, "Smart Reading," for effective reading strategies.

Search online. You can generate many ideas simply by exploring topics online (or in a library catalog). Identify a few keywords that describe a subject area that interests you and then see what they uncover. Then follow up with additional terms, concepts, or names you discover while browsing. But remember that at this point you are searching only for topic ideas. Your research on any subject will always involve far more than a quick online search.

Build from lists. Write down any plausible topic possibility that emerges or, if you already have a subject, the major points you might cover. Don't be picky at this stage: Record everything that comes to mind. One idea might generate another, then another. (Even grocery lists work this way.)

For instance, considering a report on collegiate sports, you might note the controversies or issues you've discussed with friends or have thought about yourself. Write down, too, all names, circumstances, or events that might harbor a possible subject. When you have a page of possibilities, pick out the more intriguing ones and rank them. Which topics show potential? Which do you want to learn more about? Which would you want to write about?

Map your ideas. If you find a list too static as a prompt for writing, explore the relationships between your ideas *visually*. Some writers use logic trees to represent their thinking, starting with a single general concept and breaking it into smaller and smaller parts. Others begin with a key concept (just a word or two), circle it, and then begin to free-associate, quickly writing down more circled concepts and linking them by lines of relationship. When a page is full of lines and circles, writers look for patterns and connections that might turn into topics.

Try freewriting. This is a technique of nonstop composing designed to loosen restraints we sometimes impose on our own thinking. Typically, freewriting sessions begin slowly, with a few disconnected phrases and words. But, suddenly, there's a spark and words stream onto the page. Although freewriting comes in many forms, the basic formula is simple.

Ideas won't keep; something must be done about them.
—Alfred North Whitehead

Cultura Creative (RF)/Alamy Stock Photo

STAGE ONE

- Start with a blank screen or sheet of paper.
- Put your subject or title at the top of the page.
- Write on that subject *nonstop* for ten minutes.
- Don't stop typing or lift your pen from the paper during that time.
- Write nonsense if you must, but keep writing.

STAGE TWO

- Stop at ten minutes and review what you have composed.
- Underscore or highlight the most intriguing idea, phrase, or sentence.
- Put the highlighted idea at the top of a new screen or sheet.
- Freewrite for another ten minutes on the more focused topic.

Like other brainstorming techniques, freewriting works best when you already know something about potential topics. For obvious reasons then, freewriting is a potent starting point for personal narratives, personal statements, arguments, and proposals.

Use memory prompts. When writing personal essays, arguments, or even résumés, you might trigger topic ideas with photographs, yearbooks, even social media like Facebook, Twitter, or Instagram. An image from a vacation may recover events worth writing about. Even checkbooks or credit card statements may help you reconstruct past experiences or see patterns in your life worth exploring in writing.

Don't, however, forget one of the best prompts for writing projects—talking about your work with your friends, colleagues, or your instructors. Most writing centers are eager to help you at the invention or brainstorming stages too.

Writing about Writing   If you have never used freewriting as a brainstorming activity, give it a try. Pick a general topic from among courses you are currently studying, news events that interest you, or activities you are deeply involved in: for example, the Japanese concept of Bushido, immigration reform, or unpaid internships. (You want a topic about which you have *some* knowledge or opinions.) Then follow the preceding directions. See what happens.

Uncle Bob, who's a cop, complains about the *"CSI* effect." What is that?

I found a study by professors of law and psychology. What do they think?

Google | CSI effect

About 20,600,000 results (0.15 seconds)

▶ Scholarly articles for **CSI effect**

CSI Effect: Popular Fiction about Forensic Scien
... Concerning Scientific Evidence: Does the "**CS**
The **CSI effect**: fact or fiction - Thomas - Cited b

CSI effect - Wikipedia, the free encyclopedia
en.wikipedia.org/wiki/**CSI_effect** - Cached
The **CSI effect**, also known as the CSI syndrome and th
in which the exaggerated portrayal of forensic science o
Background - Manifestations - Trials - References

The '**CSI Effect**': Does It Really Exist? | Natio
www.nij.gov/journals/259/**csi-effect**.htm - Cached
by DE Shelton - Cited by 12 - Related articles
Mar 17, 2008 - Do law-related television shows like '**CS**
influence juror expectations and demands for forensic e

/archive/csieffect.pdf

108% ▾ | 🖶 | | Find ▾

ARTICLE

THE *CSI* EFFECT: POPULAR FICTION ABOUT FORENSIC SCIENCE AFFECTS THE PUBLIC'S EXPECTATIONS ABOUT REAL FORENSIC SCIENCE

N.J. Schweitzer
Michael J. Saks*

ABSTRACT: Two of a number of hypotheses loosely referred to as the CSI Effect suggest that the television program and its spin-offs, which wildly exaggerate and glorify forensic science, affect the public, and in turn affect trials either by (a) burdening the prosecution by creating greater expectations about forensic science than can be delivered or (b) burdening the defense by creating exaggerated faith in the capabilities and reliability of the forensic sciences. The present study tested these hypotheses by presenting to mock jurors a simulated trial transcript that included the testimony of a forensic scientist. The case for conviction was relatively weak, unless the expert testimony could carry the case across the threshold of reasonable doubt. In addition to reacting to the trial evidence, respondents were asked about their television viewing habits. Compared to non-CSI viewers, CSI viewers were more critical of the forensic evidence presented at the trial, finding it less believable. Regarding their verdicts, 29% of non-CSI viewers said they would convict, compared to 18% of CSI viewers (not a statistically significant difference). Forensic science viewers expressed more confidence in their verdicts than did non-viewers. Viewers of general crime programs, however, did not differ significantly from their non-viewing counterparts on any of the other dependent measures, suggesting that skepticism toward the forensic science testimony was specific to those whose diet consisted of heavy doses of forensic science television programs.

*N.J. Schweitzer is a Ph.D. candidate, Department of Psychology, Arizona State University. Michael J. Saks is Professor of Law and Psychology and Faculty Fellow, Center for the Study of Law, Science, and Technology, Sandra Day O'Connor College of Law, Arizona State University. The authors wish to thank Dawn McQuiston-Surrett for her assistance with this project and for the development of the experimental materials. Correspondence can be sent to N.J. Schweitzer, Department of Psychology, Arizona State University, Tempe, AZ 85287-1104 or njs@asu.edu.

1

Find reliable sources.

Wikipedia isn't an academic source, but it will help me get a sense of the big picture.

This article comes from a government publication—does that automatically mean it's not biased?

WIKIPEDIA
The Free Encyclopedia

Main page
Contents
Featured content
Current events
Random article
Donate to Wikipedia

▾ Interaction
  Help
  About Wikipedia
  Community portal
  Recent changes
  Contact Wikipedia

▸ Toolbox

▸ Print/export

▾ Languages
  Česky
  Deutsch
  Español
  Français
  Italiano

Article   Discussion

CSI effect

From Wikipedia, the free encyclopedia

The **CSI effect**, also known as the **CSI syndrome**[1] and the **CSI**
public perception. The term most often refers to the belief that jur
American legal professionals, several studies have shown that cr

There are several other manifestations of the CSI effect. Greater
and popularity of forensic science programs at the university leve
forensic science shows teach criminals how to conceal evidence

Contents [hide]
1 Background
2 Manifestations
2.1 Trials
2.2 Academia
2.3 Crimes
2.4 Police investigations
3 References

Background

The CSI effect is named for *CSI: Crime Scene Investigation*, a te
discovery of a dead body leads to a criminal investigation by mer
which debuted in 2002, and *CSI: NY*, first aired in 2004. The *CSI*
Bones, Cold Case, Cold Case Files, Cold Squad, Criminal Minds

OFFICE OF JUSTICE PROGRAMS

NATIONAL INSTITUTE OF JUSTICE
Research • Development • Evaluation

HOME | FUNDING | PUBLICATIONS & MULTIMEDIA | EVENTS | TRAINING |

NIJ Home Page > NIJ Journal > NIJ Journal No. 259

NIJ JOURNAL NO. 259

Director's Message

The 'CSI Effect': Does It
Really Exist?

Voice Stress Analysis: Only
15 Percent of Lies About
Drug Use Detected in Field
Test

Shopping Malls: Are They
Prepared to Prevent and
Respond to Attack?

Software Defined Radios
Help Agencies
Communicate

The 'CSI Effect': Does It Really Exist?

by Honorable Donald E. Shelton

Crime and courtroom proceedings have long been fodder f
scriptwriters. In recent years, however, the media's use of
for drama has not only proliferated, it has changed focus.
our criminal justice process, many of today's courtroom dr
cases. *Court TV* offers live gavel-to-gavel coverage of trial
month. Now, that's "reality television"!

Reality and fiction have begun to blur with crime magazine
Hours Mystery, American Justice, and even, on occasion, *L*
portray actual cases, but only after extensively editing the
narration for dramatic effect. Presenting one 35-year-old c
Hours Mystery filmed for months to capture all pretrial hea
trial; the program, however, was ultimately edited to a 1-
the crime remained a "mystery" . . . notwithstanding the j

2
Stay alert to differing perspectives.

3
Question claims.

4 Imagining Audiences

It's common sense: Writing is all about satisfying readers. Yet students can be so concerned by the technical requirements of course assignments that they forget someone will actually read what they compose. Even teachers appreciate engaging papers. So you'll find specific advice for winning over audiences in every chapter in Part 2, Key Academic Genres, and elsewhere throughout *How to Write Anything*. Following is a preview of important audience concerns.

Consider what your audiences expect. Readers of your work—whoever they are—assume you'll address them appropriately and they'll be surprised or disappointed if you don't. Different genres often mean different audiences. Readers of literary analyses, for example, anticipate a challenging thesis backed by thoughtful evidence: They expect to be taken seriously, and they may even welcome technical language and footnotes. People you address on social media are different—they'll prefer colloquial language that resembles speech. Yet even informal online posts require all sorts of adjustments to sound right to potential readers. (Just consider how dicey messages on Twitter can be.) Audiences are rarely simple.

In academic situations, you can usually anticipate what an instructor expects. Term papers or essay exams, for example, are usually quite formal, so you likely know not to be chummy or flippant—unless an instructor signals otherwise. What *will* impress most instructors (and teaching assistants) is the accuracy, clarity, and competence of your work. They'll notice how you handle important course concepts, the way you sequence your materials, the sources you use, and, crucially sometimes, the way your words echo what you've read and heard during the class.

So study the directions your instructors provide with their assignments closely. Sometimes they may even ask you to direct your writing to particular groups: to colleagues in your course, administrators on campus, or leaders in the state legislature. When that's the case, expect them to evaluate the strategies you use to address these groups.

Consider who else your readers might be. In some ways, imagining the readers of traditional academic reports or presentations is easier than writing for broader and less well-defined audiences. Once a project goes public, your task grows more complicated. After all, an instructor or TA *has* to read your paper. Other readers don't—which is an especially good reason to have drafts of important work reviewed at a writing center. Tutors there will signal when an editorial or proposal might not be reaching audiences as well as you hoped. Similarly, if you have the advantage of work-shopping drafts of your papers in a class, ask colleagues to be frank about where they might stop reading your work if they weren't required to review the entire essay.

Tougher still are writing situations in which you have to imagine unknown but consequential readers. Consider the personal statements now routinely part of most job, scholarship, or internship applications: Someone you don't know will weigh your words carefully, yet you can't anticipate what they're looking for exactly. Should you play it safe and be serious and professional? Can you risk being amusing or emotional? Would a personal anecdote be riveting or cheesy? So much is at stake that just getting started on such tasks can be daunting. Yet these are exactly the kind of questions you need to ask.

Make adjustments for your readers. Consider how different a report on bullying originally aimed at tenth-graders would be if it were rewritten for parents or public officials.

STUDENT VERSION

- Emotional paragraphs about how bullying harms everyone
- Images of bullying situations
- List of specific dos and don'ts

ADULT VERSION

- Legal side of bullying, framed in technical language
- Specific, possibly graphic, examples
- Advice for handling children who are either bullies or being bullied

The adult version—almost certainly longer—would likely be phrased with greater urgency and emphasize legal consequences. That's common sense, you say. Exactly. Children and adults are different audiences. But writers do sometimes forget to make such adjustments for readers they hope to influence.

That may be because writers get so wrapped up in their subjects that they forget what readers don't know about it, or alternatively, explain too much, or use specialized terminology without defining it, or fail to consider how images or charts might clarify ideas. In other words, they write for themselves, not their intended audience. That's fine—perhaps—in a first draft. But when revising always pause to ask *how can I make this work better for my readers?*

Define who your readers should be. As a writer, you sometimes have the option to define or summon specific audiences to your work. After all, not every item you write has to appeal to every reader. The authors of academic books and articles—many of which you'll encounter in doing your work in school—usually get right down to business, assuming expert readers already interested in highly specialized material. They make little or no effort to win readers from outside their immediate circle and don't need to.

Technical writing—even some that reaches the general public—also makes few concessions to nonexpert readers. Open up a prescription medicine and you'll often find an insert describing the item in highly complex and specialized ways. The insert may help medical professionals (and meet legal requirements), but most patients won't learn much from its pharmacological details or molecular charts. Even the fine type and small print on such documents signal that this material is not for everyday readers.

What's the lesson here for you? It's that the need you have to serve audiences is balanced by the power you sometimes have to choose them.

Thinking about Writing   Below is a list of audiences for academic writing. Can you add three more audiences to the list?

POTENTIAL AUDIENCES FOR COLLEGE WRITING

- Individual instructors and teaching assistants
- Colleagues in a project group
- Classmates within a course
- Specific school organizations
- Students at specific academic levels
- Student body as a whole
- Administrators of programs, departments, service units
- University community
- Local businesses
- Parents

5 Gathering Materials

In college, you'll read, observe, and think about subjects as abstract as physics and philosophy or as down-to-earth as nutrition and civil engineering. And you'll be expected to write about them intelligently. Writing off the top of your head or drawing only upon common knowledge won't be viable options. Instead, you'll be expected to find and use the best available information and sources in whatever you write.

In subsequent sections of this book, you'll get *very* specific advice about how and where to gather such stuff, how to read these materials appropriately, how to take notes, and how to prove to readers you've actually done all these things. For now, let's get you up to speed with some general principles for using source materials.

Gather information from reputable and appropriate sources. Today when it's so easy to go online for information on almost any topic, it's worth restating the obvious: Not all information is created equal. So you will need to learn what counts as a serious source. Librarians and your instructor can lead you to materials more authoritative than you'll find in a casual online search or a quick visit to Wikipedia. There's a hierarchy for ranking the quality and reputation of everything from newspapers and popular magazines to publishers and academic journals.

So when you complete a paper, expect readers to pay attention to the sources you cite and where they come from. You'll gain credibility simply by knowing how to find trustworthy materials. The first items that pop up in a routine Web search are rarely good enough for serious academic papers. Nor will tweets impress readers interested in serious discussions of a topic—unless, maybe, if your subject is social media.

Use the research tools your school provides. For much college work, you'll be expected to use information drawn from academic or professional publications—that is, scholarly books and journals that carefully vet whatever they publish. You'll also need to recognize what the hallmarks of good research and reporting are—which is why you should take a look at Part 7, Academic Research and Sources, soon. But research *is* a completely manageable process. Once you get the hang of it, you'll have a tool that will serve you all your life.

If you have access to a traditional library, visit it early and often and exploit its resources. You may be surprised by what you find there, but the most valuable resource could be the librarians themselves. They know what's in their collections, they are experts at research, and they enjoy helping writers. Get to know one or two by name.

Also take advantage of any research tools available to you as a registered student— such as online databases, articles, study guides, and more. Your school likely pays good money to give you access to truly professional academic materials, especially collections of highly searchable online journals and news sources, all of them easy to document when it's time to write your papers. With such tools, you can do serious work on a project at any time of the day and from any place you can sit down with a laptop.

Look for diverse sources representing a respected range of opinion. When the topics you're writing are controversial or disputed—and they often will be in college—be sure to read more than just articles or authors you agree with. Here's what President Obama had to say in a town meeting with Iowa high school students when questioned about the issue of intellectual diversity:

> When I went to college, suddenly there were some folks who didn't think at all like me. And if I had an opinion about something they'd look at me and say, "Well, that's stupid." And then they'd describe how they saw the world. And they might have had a different sense of politics. Or they might have a different view about poverty. Or they might have a different perspective on race. And sometimes their views would be infuriating to me. But it was because there was this space where you could interact with people who didn't agree with you and had different backgrounds than you, that I then started testing my own assumptions. And sometimes I changed my mind. Sometimes I realized, you know what, maybe I'd been too narrow-minded. Maybe I didn't take this into account. Maybe I should see this person's perspective. So that's what college, in part, is all about.
>
> —September 14, 2015

Steve Pope/Getty Images

Good advice here. In your college writing, look for materials that complicate issues rather than simplify them, that acknowledge nuances rather than rush to good/bad, right/wrong judgments. Instructors will notice when the bibliography at the end of a paper is robust and interesting. They'll likely think your writing is too.

Pay attention to dates. In some academic areas, especially the sciences, you'll be expected to cite the most recent research on a given topic—and researchers in those areas make that easy to do. But currency matters in just about any field, so pay attention to the dates when you are citing. It's perfectly fine sometimes to base your writing on older or "classic" sources as long as you know when they were written and that they are still timely. (You should see them mentioned respectfully in later research materials.) But, too often, writers seem oblivious to the fact—until it is pointed out to them—that data or books they've relied on are seriously out of date, even irrelevant or wrong. When you have doubts about a source, ask your instructor or a librarian.

Use an adequate number of sources. Writers have an understandable tendency to base academic papers on two or three strong sources. If you've done a good search for materials, chances are you *will* find pieces that are genuinely admirable. Your inclination to rely on them makes sense. But make an effort to add more voices to your writing to confirm or expand what you've learned from your best sources. Otherwise your writing may slip into paraphrase and your instructor—who likely knows those key resources already—will find your efforts barely adequate.

Be sure to collect and document your sources systematically.
Your eyes may roll back in your head when your instructor mentions the virtue in annotating, paraphrasing, summarizing, and incorporating materials into your work. (See Chapters 48–50.) But these research techniques make your life easier in the long run. That's because doing research and finding good sources is only half the job—you've also got to use them efficiently and well. You'll discover that a little work up front can pay impressive dividends later, especially on longer projects, when you can quickly call up exactly the authors, ideas, quotations, and data you need for a project. You'll look like an expert to your instructor and colleagues and for the best of reasons: You are.

Thinking about Writing   Different schools have different tools and resources. Find out early what your institution offers in terms of research support and how to access it, especially any online tools. Consider, too, what may be available in your community—at other schools, libraries, museums, or government offices.

Organizing Ideas

Remember the five-paragraph essay? If you attended American schools, this "pattern of organization" was almost certainly drilled into your head early and often in composition classes and may even have played a role in your preparation for a standardized test or two. The recipe for a successful paper was simple. Begin with an *introductory paragraph* that introduces your topic and then, in its final sentence, narrows to a *thesis statement* that makes three points about the topic, each to be developed in a subsequent paragraph.

For the *body* of the paper, compose those three paragraphs, making sure each opens with a topic sentence derived from the thesis. Be sure, too, to insert *transitions* between these paragraphs: *first*, *second*, and *third* are usually adequate, with the third point the most important and fully developed. Then, in a *concluding paragraph*, restate the thesis you've just proved (varying its words a bit) and draw out an implication or two. Mission complete.

Sound familiar now? Unfortunately, the five-paragraph essay is a formula with few uses outside of high school because it is so generic and dull. Moreover, you'll look hard to find examples of the structure in public or popular writing. But it *is* easy to teach and grade, and the pattern certainly helps novices who don't have a clue how to begin a paper. Better than nothing—but just barely.

In college, you'll be offered more sophisticated structures for your writing, derived from purposeful genres—each chapter in Parts 2 and 3 deals with organization. You'll still encounter thesis statements, topic sentences, introductory/concluding paragraphs, and transitions because those are useful concepts. But you'll also discover that just about every form of writing works within a range of possible structures—which you can imitate or modify. The point to remember, perhaps, is that effective organization makes writing easier for you and reading easier for your audiences. Here are some key points to consider when composing an academic or professional piece.

Examine model documents.
Many types of writing *are* highly conventional —which implies that they follow patterns and formulas that can be conveniently learned and modified. So when asked to compose in a new genre, it makes sense to review successful examples and figure how they are constructed: what parts they have and what order they follow. Some structural features are immediately obvious, such as headings or introductory and concluding sections. But look for more subtle moves too—for example, many proposals first describe a problem, then review failed attempts to solve it, then offer a better solution, and finally defend the feasibility of the recommended approach. Makes sense, doesn't it? Successful models will point you in the right direction.

Sketch out a plan or sequence.
To give direction to a new project, try starting with a scratch or informal outline. Even a list of possible potential topics can jump-start your work. You may uncover unforeseen relationships between ideas or quickly discover gaps in your thinking. Just as important, creating a simple structure makes a writing project suddenly seem more feasible because you've broken a complex task into smaller, more manageable parts.

With a lengthy project, you might want to move up from a scratch outline to something more formal, a detailed plan covering your major sections and key supporting points or arguments, including examples. Although a formal outline like this might seem old-fashioned, it can resolve many issues before you get deep into a paper and thus prevent time-consuming rewrites. Be sure to check out Chapter 29, "Outlining."

Try reverse outlining.
When you suspect a draft isn't working, try a technique employed in many writing centers: reverse outlining. Simply go through your paper and extract the main point or topic sentence from each paragraph. (You might use a highlighter pen for emphasis rather than physically rewriting the key sentences.) Then ask yourself if the ideas you present lay out a sequence that readers can follow easily: Does your report or argument make sense? Any structural problems will show up quickly, and you'll know where to revise. As you might guess, reverse outlining works particularly well when you review a draft with the help of a colleague or writing center tutor.

Provide cues or signals for readers.
Just because you understand how the parts of your project fit together, don't assume readers will. You have to give them cues—which come in various forms, including titles, headings, captions, and, especially, transitional words and phrases. Consider numbers and lists too. For example, in a narrative you might include transitional words to mark the passage

of time (*next, then, before, afterward*). Or, if you organize a project according to a principle of magnitude, you might give readers signals that clearly show a change from *best* to *worst, cheapest* to *most expensive, most common species* to *endangered species*. And if you are writing to inform or report or persuade, you might also rely heavily on visuals to help make your point. (See Chapters 37–39 for more about transitions, effective openings and closings, and titles.)

Deliver on your commitments.   This is a basic principle of organization. If, for example, you offer a thesis statement in an introductory paragraph promising to offer two reasons in support of a claim, you need to offer two clearly identifiable reasons in that paper or readers will feel that they missed something. A thesis raises expectations that you have to meet. But commitments are broader than that: Narratives ordinarily lead somewhere, perhaps to a climax; editorials offer opinions; proposals offer and defend new ideas; evaluations make judgments. You can depart from these structural expectations, but you should do so knowing what readers expect and anticipating how they might react to your straying from a formula. For much more on thesis statements see Chapter 27, "Shaping a Thesis."

Appreciate the value in varying structure.   There are times when being predictable is essential. No one will complain if your write a proposal argument or résumé that follows successful patterns used by countless other writers. But neither do you have an obligation to repeat a formula just because it has worked for you before. Not every argument that you compose needs to end with a concession, nor must a thesis statement appear in the first paragraph of every report you write—even if instructors have praised you when you've done that. Once you gain skill in particular genres, feel free to explore alternatives: Write a literacy narrative that doesn't begin in kindergarten; compose an evaluation that doesn't pick a winner. For other ways of imagining a topic, see Chapter 28, "Strategies of Development."

Writing about Writing   Take a paper you've already composed—perhaps one already graded—and apply the reverse outline technique to it, perhaps using just a highlighting pen. Can you identify some equivalent of a thesis statement or main point? Helpful topic sentences in most paragraphs? Sensible transitions? A concluding sentence or concluding point? Taken together, do the highlighted items provide the structure for a coherent paper? Would you revise the paper, based on what you discovered—or can you justify the structure you actually used?

Choosing Style and Design

We all have an ear for the way words work in sentences and paragraphs, for the distinctive melding of voice, tone, rhythm, and texture some call *style*. You might not be able to explain exactly why one paragraph sparkles and another seems flat as day-old soda. But you recognize when writing feels energetic, precise, and clear—or stodgy, lifeless, and plodding. Choices you make about sentence type, sentence length, vocabulary, pronouns, and punctuation really *do* send distinct signals that shape particular types of writing. So, you will find advice on appropriate style throughout the genre chapters in this book (Parts 2 and 3).

Following are a few matters to take seriously right from the start to help you gain control over this essential dimension of academic writing.

Appreciate the choices you have. Many writers don't think much about how their words work—they assume they have one voice and always sound the same when writing. But of course they don't, no more than they speak the same way in every situation. Even small adjustments in phrasing make a difference. You greet a teacher with "Good morning" while it's "What's up?" to friends.

As you might expect, you have numerous options for adapting your written language (or "prose") to different subjects, genres, and audiences.

- Vocabulary: from abstract, formal, and denotative to concrete, colloquial, and connotative
- Point of view: first person (I, we), second person (you), third person (he, she, it, they)

"I'm not certain what the author means here, professor."

Hero Images Inc./Alamy Stock Photo

- Tone: factual, analytical, reportorial, argumentative, persuasive, serious, ironic, satiric, comic
- Sentence structure: simple, compound, complex, parallel, balanced, cumulative
- Sentence type: declarative, interrogative, exclamatory, complete, fragment, lists
- Sentence length: from very short (Yes!) to extremely long
- Special punctuation and markers: quotation marks, semicolons, colons, dashes, ellipses, italics, boldface
- Paragraphs: length, shape, formatting (standard, block)

"Enough already!" you might object, "That's just about everything." And you would be right. Choices about style and voice reach into almost every line of writing.

Moreover, appropriate style will range widely from the formality of academic articles and objectivity of technical reports to the passion of arguments or playfulness of satire.

Academic: unintelligent, vapid, obtuse

Informal: stupid, dumb, pea-brained

"Y'all won't believe what went down in class today!"

Richard G. Bingham II/Alamy Stock Photo

Be prepared to make lots of adjustments. See Chapter 33, "Levels of Style," for a more detailed discussion of your options.

Strive for clarity in academic writing.

For all the complexity of academic and professional styles, one virtue rules them all: *clarity*. Enthusiasm for clear writing is not universal—some theorists argue that a simple style itself can be a rhetorical ploy to disguise the nuances in difficult issues. And some subjects can indeed be so abstract and technical that even the sweetest sentences won't make them easy to understand.

That said, you could do worse than to make clarity a goal for most of your prose. Readers will appreciate your efforts to choose tangible subjects enlivened by action verbs. They'll admire the parallel phrases you used to connect related ideas and the clever way you varied sentence lengths to focus on key ideas. And they sure won't miss any wordy phrases you deleted. How'd you manage to do all this? Here's the good news: Clarity is an aspect of writing that *can* be reduced to user-friendly guidelines and techniques. You actually can learn to be a lucid writer. The suggestions are waiting for you in Chapter 34, "Clear and Vigorous Writing." Check them out before you compose your next college paper.

Use language that respects audiences. Because language is powerful, it has to be used carefully, particularly in academic settings where people from vastly different communities interact. You might encounter issues, for example, when writing arguments about politics or culture. How you describe individuals, the work they do, the choices they make, or the things they believe can ruffle the feathers of readers. So be willing to reconsider your language when words or phrases you use might reasonably be construed as disrespectful or offensive. In most cases, such adjustments are easy. For more advice, see the recommendations in Chapter 35, "Inclusive Writing."

But control of language can be a political tool, a deliberate means to silence those with whom one disagrees. "You can't say that" may be just another way of saying "Shut up." Understand that you may not always need or want to placate everyone in an audience.

Appreciate that design is part of style. Design is the visual counterpart of style. What readers see on a page, screen, poster, or infographic can be just as important as the words they find there. While many of your academic assignments will still be print-based, you may have opportunities to use media tools to enhance your work, and you should take advantage of them. Here again, your best mentors may be existing models of multimodal works you admire and would like to emulate. What design elements do they use—fonts, colors, backgrounds, photos? How do they make use of audio or clips? How do they present or arrange ideas? How are sources introduced and connected? What devices do they use to encourage audience participation or reaction?

When more than words are expected, think of that requirement as an opportunity to learn another aspect of style.

Writing about Writing Can the brief messages on social media, such as Twitter and Facebook, have style? Pick a few items from these sites or other sites and describe how the language influences you—if it does. If you don't do social media, examine the style of any brief communication, maybe from an advertisement or a letter to the editor.

Key Academic Genres

part two

Need a form you don't see here? Try "Special Assignments," p. 242.

How to start

- Need a **topic**? See page 44.
- Need to **find information**? See page 46.
- Need to **organize that information**? See page 47.

8

provide readers with reliable information

Reports

You've been preparing reports since the second grade, when you probably used an encyclopedia to explain why volcanoes erupt or who Eleanor Roosevelt was. Today, any reports you write will be more ambitious.

RESEARCH REPORT   You write a *research report* drawing from a music archive on campus to document the influence of two important blues pioneers.

FEATURE STORY   You do a *feature story* on countries that are competing for international attention by building skyscrapers or other signature buildings.

INFOGRAPHIC   You design an *infographic* to present recent data on the gender and ethnic makeup of students graduating from local high schools.

Defining the genre

As you might guess, reports make up one of the broadest genres of writing. If you use Google to search the term online, you will turn up an unwieldy 4.3 billion items, opening with dictionary entries and the Wikipedia entry on the subject, then moving on to sites that cover everything from financial news to morbidity studies. Such sites may not resemble the term papers, presentations, and lab reports you'll prepare for school. But they'll share at least some of the same goals (for more on choosing a genre, see Chapter 2).

This report was issued by the EPA's Office of Inspector General, in response to a congressional inquiry about an EPA emergency order against a gas drilling company. The report includes an "At a Glance" page describing the report's background and results, before the detailed full report that includes visual aids, such as a map and a chemical analysis chart. U.S. Environmental Protection Agency and the Office of the Inspector General/Cover photo: Outside the Range Resources' Butler and Teal hydraulic fracturing well sites. EPA OIG photo.

U.S. ENVIRONMENTAL PROTECTION AGENCY

OFFICE OF INSPECTOR GENERAL

**Response to
Congressional Inquiry
Regarding the EPA's
Emergency Order to the
Range Resources
Gas Drilling Company**

Report No. 14-P-0044   December 20, 2013

Present information. People read reports to discover what they don't already know or to confirm what they do. So they'll expect whatever you offer to be timely and accurate. Sometimes, information you present *will*, in fact, be new (as in *news*), built upon recent events or fresh data. But just as often, your academic reports will repackage research from existing sources. *Are dogs really color-blind?* The answer to such a question is already out there for you to find—if you know where to look.

Find reliable sources. The heart and soul of any report will be reliable sources that provide or confirm information—whether they are "high government officials" quoted anonymously in news stories or scholarly articles listed in the bibliographies of college term papers. If asked to write a report about a topic new to you, immediately plan to do library and online research. **O**

The information in reports may also come from careful experiments and observations—as would be the case when you prepare a lab report for a biology or chemistry course. Even personal experience may provide material for reports, though observations and anecdotes of this kind usually need corroboration to be convincing.

Aim for objectivity. Writers and institutions (such as newspapers or government agencies) know that they lose credibility when their factual presentations seem incomplete, biased, or fake. Of course, smart readers understand that reports on contentious subjects—climate change, energy policy, or health-care reform, for example—may lean one way or another. In fact, you may develop strong opinions based on the research you've done and be inclined to favor certain ideas. But most readers of reports prefer to draw their own conclusions.

Present information clearly. Readers expect material in reports and reference material to be arranged (and perhaps illustrated) for their benefit. **O** So when you put forward information, state your claims quickly and support them with data. You'll gain no points for surprises, twists, or suspense in most reports. In fact, you'll usually give away the game on the first page by announcing not only the thesis of your report but also perhaps your conclusions.

find a topic
p. 44

think visually
p. 417

Feature Story

In a lively feature item that starts off like a personal narrative, Cat Vasko shares what she discovered about those rotisserie chickens you see under warming lights in deli sections of most grocery stores. *Rotisserie chickens*? What could possibly be interesting about them? You're about to find out in a lively and informative piece that originally appeared on the Web site of KCET, an independent educational TV station and media site.

Reading the Genre   Reports work especially well when they have "surprise value"—that is, they explain something new to you. Take note of any new information you learn from Cat Vasko's report for consumers. What details keep you reading? Do you feel like part of the audience for this essay? Will you now try rotisserie chickens, if you haven't already?

Grocery Store Economics: Why Are Rotisserie Chickens So Cheap?

CAT VASKO

March 4, 2014

The report uses a personal anecdote to introduce its subject, a strategy more common in feature stories than academic reports.

A couple of years ago, I got it into my head that I wanted to roast a whole chicken, just because. I wandered around my local Ralphs for a few minutes looking for poultry that hadn't already been turned into individually shrink-wrapped meat units before asking for help. The gentleman I flagged down blinked a few times at my question. "Um," he answered finally, "You know we have chickens for sale up at the front of the store that have already been cooked, right?"

I bought the raw chicken anyway. I took it home, rubbed it in butter and herbs, shoved a lemon half up its butt, and roasted it low and slow for the majority of the day. It turned out okay. For all the work it took, it certainly wasn't notably better than a store-bought rotisserie chicken, and with the other ingredients factored in, it cost significantly more. Right now, an uncooked chicken at Ralphs runs you $9.87, but a rotisserie chicken is $6.99; at Gelson's, you'll pay $8.99 for a cooked chicken or $12.67 for the raw version;

and at that beloved emporium of insanity Whole Foods, a rotisserie chicken is $8.99, while a whole chicken from the butcher counter is $12.79 . . . per pound.

In retrospect, it's not hard to understand why the fellow at Ralphs thought I was weird. But in most cases, preparing meals from scratch is significantly cheaper than buying them premade. What makes rotisserie chickens the exception?

Grocery Store Economics

The answer lies in the curious economics of the full-service supermarket. For instance, the Gelson's by me offers, among other amenities, a hot bar, a salad bar, a bakery, a gelateria, a full-service deli, and an olive bar, because we live in L.A. so why not. But how can it afford to put out all of this food fresh every day?

It can't. Neither can Ralphs. Even Whole Foods' notoriously inflated prices don't offset that level of production. Instead, much like hunters who strive to use every part of the animal, grocery stores attempt to sell every modicum of fresh food they stock. Produce past its prime is chopped up for the salad bar; meat that's overdue for sale is cooked up and sold hot. Some mega-grocers like Costco have dedicated rotisserie chicken programs, but employees report that standard supermarkets routinely pop unsold chickens from the butcher into the ol' rotisserie oven.

Although supermarkets are loath to admit as much, likely for fear of turning off the squeamish, the former CEO of Trader Joe's cheerfully confirmed in a recent interview that meat and produce are recycled into prepared foods. And the vendor of one of the leading commercial rotisserie ovens offers, as a complement to its wares, "culinary support" that, among other things, aims to "develop programs to minimize food shrinkage and waste" and "improve production planning to optimize the amount of fresh food that is available during both peak and down times."

Rotisserie chickens aren't even the end of the line. When unsold, fresh meats, fruits, and veggies that have passed their sell-by points can be "cooked up for in-store deli and salad counters before they spoil," per no less a source than a consultant to the supermarket industry.

> Vasko explains why grocery chains like Ralphs can sell already roasted chicken for less than unprocessed ones.

> The informal and personal style used throughout likely keeps readers engaged.

Thinking back with horror on all the times you picked up a prepared meal on the way home from a long day of work, then demolished it within ten minutes of walking through the door? Don't panic just yet.

Safe as Milk

It's worth noting, first of all, that sell-by, use-by, and best-by dates were never intended as indicators of food safety, but rather as estimates of food quality. The USDA itself says that food product dating is intended to "help the purchaser to know the time limit to purchase or use the product at its best quality. It is not a safety date."

Further, it's pretty well documented that these estimates are no substitute for boring old human discretion. Sites like StillTasty.com aim to help consumers get the most out of their groceries by educating them on the real shelf lives of thousands of foods as well as ways to ascertain quality that have nothing to do with the numbers stamped on the package. And a recent report from Harvard's Food Law and Policy Clinic suggests that because date labels are wildly inaccurate a lot of the time, they're pretty much directly responsible for 60 billion pounds of wasted food every year. Even more disturbingly (especially for we Californians), the report estimates that 25 percent of the fresh water used in the United States is "squandered on the production of wasted food." Awesome.

In fact, in spite of their creative uses of items that have passed their sell-by dates, grocery stores are still being conservative enough when it comes to food safety to waste plenty of usable meat and produce—around $900 million in inventory annually, according to a 2001 study. And as the Harvard report points out, major retailers aren't generally wont to take a loss, meaning their waste "ultimately could be a cost borne by consumers in the price of goods."

So not only do you have nothing to fear from that grocery store rotisserie chicken, you could actually be doing a triple good deed by purchasing it—making your life easier, keeping prices down for your fellow shoppers, and helping the environment.

Vasko offers critical information about "sell-by" dates, anticipating concerns readers might have.

Vasko's sources are less fully documented than those in an academic paper would be.

Concluding paragraph offers a conventional summary of main points.

Claiming the topic

▶ topic

When you are assigned a report, carefully identify the subgenre (psychology term paper, physics lab report, article for a sports blog) and the kinds of information your report will require. Will your report merely answer a factual question about a topic and deliver basic information? Or are you expected to do a more in-depth study or compare different points of view, as you would in an investigative report? Or might the report deliver information based on your own research or experiments? Consider your various options as you select a topic.

Answer questions. For this kind of report, include basic facts and, perhaps, an overview of key features, issues, or problems. Think of an encyclopedia entry as a model: Facts are laid out cleanly, usually under a series of headings. The discussions are generally efficient and basic, not exhaustive.

Assigned an informative piece like this, you can choose topics that might otherwise seem overly ambitious. When readers expect an overview, not expertise, you can easily write two or three fact-filled pages on "Atonal Music" or "The Zoot Suit Riots" by focusing on just a few key figures, events, or concepts. So look for a topic that introduces you to new ideas or perspectives.

Review what is already known about a subject. Instructors who ask you to write five- or ten-page reports on specific subjects within a field—for example, to compare banking practices in Japan and the European Union or to describe current trends in museum architecture—doubtless know plenty about those subjects already. They want you to look at the topic in some depth to increase what *you* know. But the subject may also be one evolving rapidly because of current events, technological changes, or ongoing research.

Field research is one way to acquire new information.

So consider updating an idea introduced in a lecture or textbook: You might be surprised by how much you can add to what an instructor has presented. If workers are striking in Greece again, make that a focal point of your general report on European Union economic policies; if your course covers globalism, consider how a world community made smaller by jet travel complicates the response to epidemic diseases. In considering topics for in-depth reports, you'll find library "research guides" especially helpful. ○ You may also want to consult librarians or experts in the field you're writing about. ○

Images & Stories/Alamy Stock Photo

Report new knowledge. Many schools encourage undergraduates to conduct original research in college. In most cases, this work is done

plan a project
p. 426

ask for help
p. 433

under the supervision of an instructor in your major field, and you'll probably choose a topic only after developing expertise in some area. For a sampling of research topics students from different schools have explored, search "undergraduate research journal" on the Web.

If you have trouble finding a subject for a report, try the brainstorming techniques suggested in Chapter 3, both to identify topic ideas and to narrow them to manageable size.

> **Writing about Writing**   Having trouble finding a fresh topic for a report? Let curiosity motivate you—as Cat Vasko does in her essay on roast chickens. Make a list of things you'd simply like to know more about within the general area of your topic. If you need general prompts, check out HowStuffWorks .com, especially its blogs and podcasts, such as the "Stuff You Missed in History Class" archive. You'll see that almost any subject or topic area is filled with interesting nooks and crannies.

Imagining your audience

You know that you should attune any report to its potential readers: for example, well-informed audiences will expect sophisticated papers that use technical language. But when you anticipate a wider range of readers—from experts to amateurs—you need to design your report to engage them all. Perhaps you can use headings to ease novices through your report while simultaneously signaling to more knowledgeable readers what sections they might skip. ⭕ Make audience-sensitive moves like this routinely, whenever you are composing.

However, sometimes it's not the content that you must modify for potential readers but their perceptions of you. They'll look at you differently according to the expertise you bring to the project. What are the options?

Suppose you are the expert. This may be the typical stance of most writers of professional reports, who confidently present material they know well enough to teach. But knowledgeable people often make two common mistakes in presenting information. Either they assume that an audience is as informed as they are and so omit the very details and helpful transitions that many readers need, or they underestimate the intelligence of their readers and consequently bore them with trivial and unnecessary explanations. ⭕ Readers want an expert guide but also one who knows when—*and when not*—to define a term, provide a graph, or supply some context.

| think visually | respect your readers |
| p. 417 | p. 366 |

Tips for Writing Credible Reports
- Choose a serious subject you know you can research.
- Model the project on professional reports in that area.
- Select sources recognized in the field.
- Document those sources correctly.
- Use the discipline's technical vocabulary and conventions.

Suppose you are the novice. In a typical report for school, you're often dealing with material relatively new to you. Your expertise on language acquisition in childhood may be only a book chapter and two journal articles thick, but you may still have to write ten pages on the topic to pass a psychology course. Moreover, not only do you have to provide information in a report, but you also have to convince an expert reader—your instructor—that you have earned the credentials to write about this subject.

Suppose you are the peer. For some reports, your peers may be your primary audience. That's especially true of oral presentations in class. You know that an instructor is watching your presentation and is probably grading the content—including your topic, organization, and sources. But that instructor may also be watching how well you adapt that material to the interests and capabilities of your classmates. **O**

Gathering materials

▶ find information

Once you have settled on a research topic and thesis, plan to spend time accumulating data. You can start with reference works, such as dictionaries and encyclopedias, but you need to move quickly to resources created or used by experts in the field, including scholarly books published by university presses, articles in academic journals, government reports (also known as white papers), oral histories, and so on. Look for materials that push you well beyond what you knew at the outset of the project. Such works may intimidate you at first, but that's a signal that you are learning something new—an outcome your instructor probably intended.

To get reports right, follow these basic principles.

Base reports on the best available sources. You will embarrass yourself quickly if you don't develop procedures and instincts for evaluating sources. Look for materials—including data such as statistics and photographic reproductions—presented by reliable authors and experts and supported by major institutions in government, business, and the media. For academic papers, take your information whenever possible from journals and books published by university presses and professional organizations. **O** Not sure how to find this information? Ask librarians for assistance.

With Web materials, track them back to their original sources and then evaluate them. Use the Google search engine for "Korean War," for instance, and you might find an item that seems generic—except that its URL indicates a military location (.mil).

understand oral reports
p. 275

find reliable sources
p. 442

Opening the URL, you discover that a government institution—the Naval Historical Center—supports the site. So its information is likely to be credible but will reflect the perspectives of the Department of the Navy. That's information you need to know as you read material from the site.

Base reports on diverse sources. Don't rely on a limited or biased selection of material. You need not give equal weight to all ideas or points of view, but neither should you ignore important perspectives you disagree with. Above all, avoid the temptation to base a report on a single source, even one that is genuinely excellent. You may find yourself merely paraphrasing the material, not writing a report of your own. **O**

Need help finding relevant sources? See "How to Browse for Ideas" on pp. 20–21.

Fact-check your report. It's a shame to get the big picture in focus in a report and then lose credibility because you slip up on a few easily verifiable facts. In a lengthy project, minor errors might seem inevitable or just a nuisance. But misstatements can take on a life of their own and become lore—consider the controversy over fake news that surrounded the 2016 presidential election in the United States. So take the extra few minutes required to get the details right.

Some Online Sites for Locating Facts and Information

- **Biography.com** A collection of twenty-five thousand brief biographies, from Julius Caesar to Miley Cyrus.
- **FedStats** The site for finding information gathered by the federal government. Also check out USA.gov.
- **The World Factbook** Check here for data about any country—compiled by the CIA.

Organizing ideas

How does a report work? Not like a shopping mall—where the escalators and aisles are designed to keep you wandering and buying, deliberately confused. Not like a mystery novel that leads up to an unexpected climax, or even like an argument, which steadily builds in power to a memorable conclusion. Instead, reports lay all their cards on the table right at the start and harbor no secrets. They announce what they intend to do and then do it, providing clear markers all along the way.

organize ◀
information

restate ideas
p. 460

Clarity doesn't come easily; it only seems that way when a writer has been successful. You have to know a topic in depth to explain it to others. Then you need to choose a structure that supports what you want to say. Among patterns you might choose for drafting a report are the following, some of which overlap. **O**

Organize by date, time, or sequence. Drafting a history report, it makes sense to arrange your material chronologically: In 1958, the Soviet Union launched *Sputnik*, the first earth satellite; in 1961, the Soviets launched a cosmonaut into earth's orbit; in 1969, the United States landed two men on the moon. This structure puts information into a relationship readers understand immediately as a competition. You'd still have blanks to fill in with facts and details to tell the story of the race to the moon, but a chronological structure helps readers keep complicated events in perspective.

By presenting a simple sequence of events, you can use time to organize reports involving many kinds of information, from the scores in football games to the movement of stock markets to the flow of blood through the human heart. **O**

Organize by magnitude or order of importance. Many reports present their subjects in sequence, ranked from biggest to smallest (or vice versa), most important to least important, most common/frequent to least, and so on. Such structures assume, naturally, that you have already done the research to position the items you expect to present. At first glance, reports of this kind might seem tailored to the popular media: "Ten Best Restaurants in Seattle," "One Hundred Coolest American Cities." But you might also use such a framework to report on the disputed causes of a war, the multiple effects of a stock market crash, or even the factors responsible for a disease.

Organize by division. It's natural to arrange some reports by simply breaking a subject into its major parts. A report on the federal government, for example, might be organized by treating each of its three branches in turn: executive, legislative, and judicial. A report on the Elizabethan stage might examine the individual parts of a typical theater: the "heavens," the balcony, the stage wall, the stage, the pit, and so on. Of course, you'd then have to decide in what order to present the items, perhaps spatially or in order of importance. For example, you might use an illustration to clarify your report, working from top to bottom. Simple but effective.

Organize by classification. Classification is the division of a group of concepts or items according to specified and consistent principles. Reports organized by classification

develop a draft   shape your work
p. 338   p. 345

are easy to set up when you borrow a structure that is already well established—such as those that follow.

- **Psychology** (by type of study): abnormal, clinical, comparative, developmental, educational, industrial, social
- **Plays** (by type): tragedy, comedy, tragicomedy, epic, pastoral, musical
- **Nations** (by form of government): monarchy, oligarchy, democracy, dictatorship
- **Passenger cars** (by engine placement): front engine, mid-engine, rear engine
- **Dogs** (by breed group): sporting, hound, working, terrier, toy, non-sporting, herding

A project becomes more challenging when you try to create a new system—perhaps to classify the various political groups on your campus or to describe the behavior of workers at a fast-food restaurant. But such inventiveness can be worth the effort.

Organize by position, location, or space.

Organizing a report spatially is a powerful strategy for arranging ideas—even more so today, given the ease with which material can be illustrated. O A map, for example, is a report organized by position and location. But it is only one type of spatial structure.

You use spatial organization in describing a painting from left to right, a building from top to bottom, a cell from nucleus to membrane. A poster session or report on medical conditions might be presented most effectively via cutaways that expose different layers of tissues and organs. Or a report on an art exhibition might follow a viewer through a virtual 3-D gallery.

The Swan Theatre. The architectural layout of this Elizabethan theater, shown in this 1596 sketch by Johannes de Witt, might suggest the structure of a report describing the theater.

Universal History Archive/Universal Images Group/REX/Shutterstock

think visually
p. 417

Portrait of a young man holding a papyrus scroll, 55-79 AD (fresco)/Roman (1st century AD)/DE AGOSTINI EDITORE/Museo Archeologico Nazionale, Naples, Campania, Italy/Bridgeman Images

Interior of a Scriptorium, School of Segovia (oil on panel)/Spanish School (16th century)/Museo Lazaro Galdiano, Madrid, Spain/Bridgeman Images

The images here compare two important "technologies" for reading, the scroll (top) and the codex (bottom).

Organize by definition. Typically, definitions begin by identifying an object by its "genus" and "species" and then listing its distinguishing features, functions, or variations. This useful structure is the pattern behind most entries in dictionaries, encyclopedias, and other reference works. Once the genus and species have been established, you can expand a definition through explanatory details: *Ontario* is a *province of Canada* between Hudson Bay and the Great Lakes. That's a good start, but what are its geographical features, history, products, and major cities—all the things that distinguish it from other provinces? You could write a book, let alone a report, based on this simple structure.

Organize by comparison/contrast. You probably learned this pattern in the fourth grade, but that doesn't make comparison/contrast any less potent for college-level reports. ○ You compare and contrast to highlight distinctions that might otherwise not be readily apparent. Items are often compared one at a time or feature by feature.

Organize by thesis statement. Obviously, you have many options for organizing a report; moreover, a single report might use several structural patterns. So it helps if you explain early in a report what its method of organization will be. That idea may be announced in a single thesis sentence, a full paragraph (or section), or even a PowerPoint slide. ○

SENTENCE ANNOUNCES STRUCTURE

In the late thirteenth century, Native Puebloans may have abandoned their cliff dwellings for several related reasons, including an exhaustion of natural resources, political disintegration, and, most likely, a prolonged drought.

— Kendrick Frazier, *People of Chaco: A Canyon and Its Culture*

understand evaluation   develop a statement
p. 120   p. 333

PARAGRAPH EXPLAINS STRUCTURE

In order to detect a problem in the beginning of life, medical professionals and caregivers must be knowledgeable about normal development and potential warning signs. Research provides this knowledge. In most cases, research also allows for accurate diagnosis and effective intervention. Such is the case with cri du chat syndrome (CDCS), also commonly known as cat cry syndrome.

— Marissa Dahlstrom, "Developmental Disorders: Cri du Chat Syndrome"

Choosing style and design

Reports are typically written in a formal or *high* style—free of contentious language that might make them sound like arguments. ❍ To separate fact from opinion, scientific and professional reports usually avoid personal reflections as well as devices such as contractions and dialogue. Reports in newspapers, magazines, and even encyclopedias may be less formal: You might detect a person behind the prose. But the style will still strive for impartiality, signaling that the writer's opinions are (or, at least, *should* be) less important than the facts reported.

Why tone down the emotional, personal, or argumentative temper of the language in reports? It's a matter of audience. The moment readers suspect that you are twisting language to advocate an agenda or moving away from a sober presentation of facts, they will question the accuracy of your report. So review your drafts to see if a word or phrase might be sending the wrong signals to readers. Give your language the appearance of neutrality, balance, and thoughtfulness.

Present the facts cleanly. Get right to the point and answer key questions directly: *Who? What? Where? When? How? Why?* Organize paragraphs around topic sentences so readers know what will follow. Don't go off on tangents. Keep the exposition controlled and focus on data. When you do, the prose will seem coolly efficient and trustworthy.

Keep out of it. Write from a neutral, third-person perspective, avoiding the pronouns *I* and *you.* When perusing a report, readers usually don't care about the writer's personal opinion unless that writer's individual experiences are part of the story.

define your style
p. 366

But like all guidelines, this one has exceptions, and it certainly doesn't apply across the board to other genres of writing. Increasingly, even scientific and scholarly reports in some fields allow researchers to explain themselves directly to readers—as you'll see in a model report on page 53.

Avoid connotative language.
Maintaining objectivity is not easy because language is rife with *connotations*—the powerful cultural associations that may surround words, enlarging their meanings and sometimes imposing value judgments. Connotations make *shadowy* and *gloomy* differ from *dark*; *porcine* and *tubby*, from *overweight*. What's more, the connotations of individual words are not the same for every reader. One person may have no problem with a term like *slums*, but another person living in *low-income housing* may beg to differ.

Given the hotbed of protest that writing can be, don't use loaded words when more neutral terms are available and just as accurate. Choose *confident*, not *overweening* or *pompous*; try *corporate official* rather than *robber baron*—unless, of course, the more colorful term fits the context. ○

Pay attention to elements of design.
Clear and effective design is particularly important in reports. ○ If your paper runs more than a few pages and can be divided into coherent parts, consider inserting headings to help readers appreciate its structure or locate information they need. Documents such as term papers and lab reports may even follow patterns and templates you are required to use.

Many types of factual information are best presented graphically. This is especially the case with numbers and statistics. So don't hesitate to use charts, graphs, photos, illustrations, and also captions in your work. Software such as Microsoft Word allows you to create modest tables and simple graphics; you can generate more complex tables and graphs with software such as Excel or OmniGraffle. And remember that any visual items should be purposeful, not ornamental.

Many reports these days are, in fact, oral presentations that rely on presentation software such as PowerPoint, Keynote, or Prezi. You'll want to learn how to use these tools effectively. ○

improve your sentences
p. 366

think visually
p. 417

prepare oral reports
p. 275

Examining models

ACADEMIC RESEARCH REPORT   When Susan Wilcox received an open-ended assignment to write a report, she responded with a traditionally researched academic essay on a subject important to her, one that she wanted her classmates to learn more about. The essay is formally documented in MLA style.

Reading the Genre   Wilcox's report prepared for an academic course draws on a wide range of sources, from personal interviews to books. What impact might this list of sources have on a reader's reception of the report?

Wilcox 1

Susan Wilcox

Professor Longmire

Rhetoric 325M

March 7, 20--

Marathons for Women

Today in America, five women are running. Two of them live in Minnesota, one in Virginia, and two in Texas. Their careers are different, their political views are divergent, and their other hobbies are irrelevant, for it is running that draws these women together. They are marathoners. Between them, they are eighteen-time veterans of the 26.2-mile march of exhaustion and exhilaration.

These five women are not alone; over 205,000 women in the United States alone ran a marathon in 2010 ("Annual Marathon Report"). They sacrifice sleeping late, watching TV, and

> Opening paragraph establishes a context for a report on women marathon runners, engaging readers.

Wilcox 2

sometimes even toenails (lost toenails are a common malady among marathon runners) for the sake of their sport. Why do these women do this to themselves? Karin Warren explains, "It started out being about losing weight and getting fit again. But I enjoyed running so much—not just how physically fit I felt afterward, but the actual act of running and how it cleared my mind and made me feel better about myself in all aspects of my life—that it became a part of who I am." The other women agree, using words like "conquer," "powerful," and "confident" to describe how running makes them feel.

However, these women know that only a generation ago, marathons weren't considered suitable for women. Tammy Moriearty and Wendy Anderson remember hearing that running could make a woman's uterus fall out; Tammy adds, "It floors me that medical professionals used to believe that." Michelle Gibson says that her friends cautioned her against running when she was pregnant (she ran anyway; it's safe). Naomi Olson has never heard a specific caution, but "lots of people think I am crazy," she says. Female runners, like their male counterparts, do have to maintain adequate nutrition during training (Matheson), but "there are no inherent health risks involved with marathon preparation and participation" (Dilworth). Unfortunately, scientists were not researching running health for women when the marathon was born, and

> Author uses interviews with runners to dispel myths about women and marathoning.

Wilcox 3

most people thought women were too fragile to run that far. The myth that marathoning is dangerous for women was allowed to fester in the minds of race organizers around the world.

Legend holds that the original marathon runner, Pheidippides, ran from the Battle of Marathon to Athens to bring news of the Athenian victory over Persia. Pheidippides died of exhaustion after giving the news, and the marathon race today is held in honor of his final journey (Lovett x). Historians doubt all the details of this legend, including that a professional runner in Greece would die after what would have been a relatively short distance for him (x–xi). Nevertheless, the myth remains. When the Olympic Games were revived in Athens in 1896, a race covering Pheidippides's route from Marathon to Athens was scheduled as the final Olympic event (xii). Even though no women were permitted to compete, a Greek woman known as Melpomene arrived on the day of the race, ready to run. Race officials denied her access to the course, so she ran alongside it, eventually finishing an hour and a half after the winner. However, the first woman known to have run the marathon distance was a different Greek woman, Stamatis Rovithi, who ran the course from Marathon to Athens in March of 1896, a few months before the Olympic Games (Lovett 126). Even without proper medical research, these two women were proof that the marathon was not too far for a woman to run.

The report is organized by time and sequence.

Wilcox 4

The occasional woman would run a marathon throughout the first half of the twentieth century (Lovett 126), but never with sufficient fanfare to attract attention to her accomplishment. That changed in 1966, when Roberta Gibb decided to enter the Boston Marathon. At the time, Gibb would sometimes cover forty miles on a training run, so she was shocked when her entry was returned with a note informing her that "women [are] not physiologically capable of running twenty-six miles" (Gibb). Gibb was not put off by such assertions; she hid in the bushes at the starting line and wore her brother's clothes to hide her gender. It was obvious to the men running around her that she was a woman, though, and buoyed by their support, Gibb took off the bulky sweatshirt she was wearing, delighting the crowd who hadn't expected to see a woman running Boston.

By the time Gibb reached the finish, the governor of Massachusetts was there to greet her. *Sports Illustrated* reported of Gibb's achievement: "[The] performance should do much to phase out the old-fashioned notion that a female is too frail for distance running" (Brown). Race officials were less pleased, insisting that Gibb "merely covered the same route as the official race while it was in progress. No girl has ever run in the Boston Marathon" (Brown). The fight was on.

Wilcox 5

Bettmann/Getty Images

An official attempts to remove Kathrine Switzer from the 1967 Boston Marathon.

> Photo in the report provides visual evidence.

The following year, another woman took on Boston, this time as an official entrant. Kathrine Switzer's coach, like so many others, thought that women couldn't handle the marathon distance (Switzer 49). He had insisted that she prove her ability before he would allow her to enter the race, and once she did so, he also insisted that she be an official registrant to avoid being suspended from collegiate athletics (70). Switzer registered using her initials, not revealing her gender. On the day of the race, once word spread that a woman was running with a race number, officials tried to remove Switzer from the course. Her teammates protected her from the attack in full view of the press truck; once again, a woman running Boston was front-page news (Lovett 127).

Wilcox 6

Women continued to run Boston unofficially for the next four years, but it was the New York City Marathon that first moved toward equality, allowing women runners for the first time in 1971. In the face of this inclusion by the neighbor race, Boston officials relented and allowed women to enter in 1972 (Run Like a Girl). The Boston Marathon is popular enough to require qualifying times for competitors, so it holds a mystique in the minds of many runners. On any given marathon day, many runners cross the start line hoping to finish in a Boston qualifying time.

Even after the prestigious New York and Boston races accepted women, the fight raged on for a women's Olympic marathon. Other race distances for women were also on the Olympic wish list, and Lovett notes, "Some lobbyists felt that the addition of women's races should be made gradually" (128), a notion that did not sit well with many women who were longing to compete on the world's largest stage. Marathoner Jacqueline Hansen pointed out, "They didn't ask [two-time Olympic marathon gold medalist] Frank Shorter to wait another four years" ("History"). After years of lobbying from supporters, including Nike and the now-famous Switzer, the International Olympic Committee agreed. Joan Benoit from Maine launched herself into stardom and gained iconic status when she finished first at the inaugural Olympic marathon in 1984 (Lovett 136).

The report champions women runners, although its style generally avoids connotative language.

Wilcox 7

The evolution of women's running is not over. In September 2011, the governing body of running (the International Association of Athletics Federations, or IAAF) announced that beginning in 2012, women's finishing times can only be considered for world records if they are set in women-only races. The rule is in the interest of fairness: Women running with men have faster competitors to pace themselves with, while men have no such pacers (Associated Press). Runners worldwide reacted with shock, since current women's marathon world-record-holder Paula Radcliffe would lose her time of 2:15.25, set at the 2003 London Marathon. That record would now be called a "world best," and the new official record would be shifted to 2:17.42, Radcliffe's time in the 2005 women-only London Marathon (Longman). However, under "the vehemence of protests," the IAAF has insisted that Radcliffe's faster time will be allowed to stand as the world record (Associated Press) and that this rule only applies to future races. The controversy is ongoing, and IAAF has been known to change policy before.

Thousands of women run today, competitively and recreationally, at distances ranging from across the front lawn to 100-mile ultramarathons. Our five women all agree that running makes their lives better, no matter what the distance. And they agree on one more thing: No one has ever told any of them that

Wilcox 8

they shouldn't run just because they are women. The fight for running equality was a generation before these women, but they do not fail to be grateful for the benefits. Women run marathons because they can.

In a college paper, the list of Works Cited begins on a separate page.

Works Cited

Anderson, Wendy. Facebook interview, 25 Feb. 2012.

"Annual Marathon Report." *Running USA*, 16 Mar. 2011,
     www.runningusa.org/index.cfm?fuseaction=news
     .details&ArticleId=332.

Associated Press. "Paula Radcliffe to Keep Marathon Record."
     ESPN Olympic Sports, 9 Nov. 2011, espn.go.com/olympics/
     trackandfield/story/_/id/7212726/paula-radcliffe-keep
     -women-marathon-record-iaaf-reverses-decision.

Brown, Gwilym S. "A Game Girl in a Man's Game." *Sports
     Illustrated Vault,* 2 May 1966, www.si.com/
     vault/1966/05/02/609229/a-game-girl-in-a-mans-game.

Dilworth, Mark. "Women Running Marathons: Health Risks."
     EmpowHER, 23 Apr. 2010, www.empowher.com/fitness/
     content/women-running-marathons-health-risks.

Gibb, Roberta. "A Run of One's Own." *Running Past*, 2011,
     www.runningpast.com/gibb_story.htm.

Gibson, Michelle. Facebook interview, 20 Feb. 2012.

"History of Women's Distance Running." *Run Like a Girl*,
    runlikeagirlfilm.com/history.php.

Longman, Jeré. "Still Playing Catch-Up." *The New York Times*,
    5 Nov. 2011, www.nytimes.com/2011/11/06/sports/
    radcliffes-womens-record-for-marathon-looks
    -unbreakable.html.

Lovett, Charles C. *Olympic Marathon: A Centennial History of
    the Games' Most Storied Race*. Praeger Publishers, 1997.

Matheson, Christie. "Women Running Marathons: Do Benefits
    Outweigh Risks?" *Lifescript*, 2012, www.lifescript.com/
    diet-fitness/articles/w/women_running_marathons_do
    _benefits_outweigh_risks.aspx.

Moriearty, Tammy. Facebook interview, 21 Feb. 2012.

Olson, Naomi. Facebook interview, 21 Feb. 2012.

Switzer, Kathrine. *Marathon Woman: Running the Race to
    Revolutionize Women's Sports*. Da Capo Press, 2007.

Warren, Karin. Facebook interview, 21 Feb. 2012.

INFOGRAPHIC   Infographics are visual reports designed to present data memorably and powerfully. Government agencies use them routinely, sometimes to report on the progress of particular programs. Following is an example from the Office of Disease Prevention and Health Promotion, which uses infographics to report regularly on its Healthy People initiative. The topic of this 2015 item is a look at who was smoking in the United States in 2015.

Reading the Genre   Note that this infographic has two parts. The top section presents data on the relationship between smoking and educational attainment. The bottom items measure adult and adolescent smoking rates in terms of specific 2020 goals for reduction in this habit. How does this second half of the graphic relate to the top half? What does the information suggest about the potential for long-term reduction in smoking rates? What role will keeping children in school have on smoking rates?

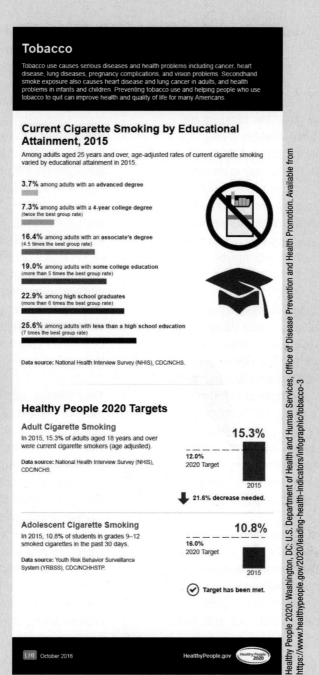

Tobacco

Tobacco use causes serious diseases and health problems including cancer, heart disease, lung diseases, pregnancy complications, and vision problems. Secondhand smoke exposure also causes heart disease and lung cancer in adults, and health problems in infants and children. Preventing tobacco use and helping people who use tobacco to quit can improve health and quality of life for many Americans.

Current Cigarette Smoking by Educational Attainment, 2015

Among adults aged 25 years and over, age-adjusted rates of current cigarette smoking varied by educational attainment in 2015.

3.7% among adults with an **advanced degree**

7.3% among adults with a **4-year college degree**
(twice the best group rate)

16.4% among adults with an **associate's degree**
(4.5 times the best group rate)

19.0% among adults with **some college education**
(more than 5 times the best group rate)

22.9% among **high school graduates**
(more than 6 times the best group rate)

25.6% among adults with **less than a high school education**
(7 times the best group rate)

Data source: National Health Interview Survey (NHIS), CDC/NCHS.

Healthy People 2020 Targets

Adult Cigarette Smoking

In 2015, 15.3% of adults aged 18 years and over were current cigarette smokers (age adjusted).

Data source: National Health Interview Survey (NHIS), CDC/NCHS.

15.3%

12.0%
2020 Target

2015

⬇ 21.6% decrease needed.

Adolescent Cigarette Smoking

In 2015, 10.8% of students in grades 9–12 smoked cigarettes in the past 30 days.

Data source: Youth Risk Behavior Surveillance System (YRBSS), CDC/NCHHSTP.

10.8%

16.0%
2020 Target

2015

✓ Target has been met.

LHI October 2016

HealthyPeople.gov

Healthy People 2020

Healthy People 2020. Washington, DC: U.S. Department of Health and Human Services, Office of Disease Prevention and Health Promotion. Available from https://www.healthypeople.gov/2020/leading-health-indicators/infographic/tobacco-3

Source: Current Cigarette Smoking by Educational Attainment, 2015. Healthypeople.gov. October 2016.

1. **Feature Story:** Cat Vasko, the author of "Why Are Rotisserie Chickens So Cheap?" (p. 41) defines herself as a "professional word nerd, amateur francophile, home cook, carbohydrate enthusiast, and person who is obnoxious about yoga." Her interests are obviously in play throughout her report. Identify a topic that intrigues you in a similar way and write a fact-filled story of interest to general readers modeled upon Vasko's report. It can be from any area of concern, academic or not. Perhaps you wonder just how coffeeshops get people to pay so much for the products they offer. Or maybe you wonder whether apprenticeship programs in technical subjects might make more sense than a traditional college degree. Do the necessary research on your subject and present what you learn to a general audience. Like Vasko, you may use first person in this report and, if you are adventurous, you might try holding off on your thesis or point until the final section or paragraph as she does. Present any sources you use responsibly, mentioning them in the body of the paper or (if your instructor prefers) citing them in traditional academic form—see Susan Wilcox's research report on page 53.

2. **Research Report:** Susan Wilcox, author of "Marathons for Women" (p. 53), is a runner who turned a subject personally important to her into a fully documented academic paper of general interest. Write a similar factual report based on a serious topic from your major or on a subject you would like more people to know about. Narrow your subject to a specific claim you can explore in several pages. Use trustworthy sources and document them correctly.

3. **Infographic:** "Current Cigarette Smoking by Educational Attainment, 2015" (p. 63) not only conveys information but presents the data with some sense of looking toward long-term health goals. Using a data source such as FedStats, The World Factbook (see p. 47), or SportsStats.com, create a factual report based upon interesting, important, or surprising data or information. Be creative, perhaps using statistics pertinent to your local environment or community. You can write a paper, create a slide presentation, or even try your hand at designing an infographic.

4. **Your Choice:** Identify a *controversial* topic you would love to know more about, choosing one that has at least two clearly defined and disputed sides. Do the necessary research to find out much more about the controversy, narrowing the matter down to manageable size for a paper or oral presentation. Then either prepare a written version of the report to submit to your instructor or an oral version to share with a wider audience, perhaps your classmates if you have the opportunity. In your report, explain the controversy *without taking sides*.

How to start

- Need a **topic**? See page 70.
- Need to identify **possible causes**? See page 73.
- Need to **organize your analysis**? See page 75.

Explanations

9

explain how, why, or what if something happens

We all analyze and explain things daily. Someone asks, "Why?" We reply, "Because . . ." and then offer reasons and rationales. Such a response comes naturally.

CAUSAL ANALYSIS
An instructor asks for a ten-page *causal analysis* of the political or economic forces responsible for a major armed conflict during the twentieth century. You choose to write about Operation Desert Shield (1990–91) because you know almost nothing about that war.

RESEARCH STUDY
You notice that most students now walk across campus chatting on cell phones or listening to music. You develop a *research study* to examine whether this phenomenon has any relationship to a recent drop in the numbers of students joining campus clubs and activities across the country.

FLOW DIAGRAM
To explain why so few students are taking advantage of study-abroad opportunities at your school, you create a *flow diagram* to show how complicated that application and approval process is.

Defining the genre

Explanations are a species of report with a special concern for issues defined by *how*, *why*, and *what if* questions—matters ranging, for example, from the effects of climate change to the causes of childhood obesity or high school students' poor performance on standardized tests. These are often described as issues of *cause and effect*, terms we'll use frequently in this chapter. Take childhood obesity. The public wants to know why we have a generation of overweight kids. Too much fast food? Not enough dodge ball? People worry, too, about the consequences of the trend. Will overweight children grow into obese adults with major medical problems? Will they be happy?

We're intrigued by such questions and read and write about them constantly because they matter, and we'd like to find explanations and answers—sometimes even solutions. Inquiries like these usually require persistence, precision, research, and openness to new ideas (for more on choosing a genre, see Chapter 2). Not every problem or issue can—or should—be explained simply. **O**

Don't jump to conclusions. Think you know why American attitudes toward same-sex marriage changed so quickly or why people have started to resist Hollywood's summer blockbusters? Guess again. Nothing's as straightforward as it seems and trying to explain such phenomena to other people will quickly teach you humility—even if you *don't* jump to hasty conclusions. It's just plain hard to identify which factors, separately or working together, account for particular events, activities, or behaviors. It is tougher still to predict how what's happening today might affect the future. So approach explanatory arguments cautiously and prepare to use qualifiers (*sometimes*, *perhaps*, *possibly*)—lots of them. **O**

Appreciate your limits. There are rarely easy answers when investigating why things happen the way they do. In 2003, the space shuttle *Columbia* burned up on reentry because a 1.67-pound piece of foam hit the wing of the 240,000-pound craft on liftoff. Who could have imagined so unlikely a sequence of events? Yet investigators had to follow the evidence relentlessly to its conclusion, in this case working backwards—from effect to cause.

The fact is that you'll often have to settle for explanations for events or phenomena that are merely plausible or probable because—outside of the hard sciences—you are often dealing with imprecise and unpredictable forces (especially *people*).

Offer sufficient evidence for claims. Academic and professional analyses of cause and effect will be held to high standards of proof—particularly in the sciences. The evidence you provide may be a little looser when you write for popular media, where some readers will tolerate anecdotal and personal examples. But even then, give readers ample reasons to believe you. Avoid hearsay, qualify your claims, and admit when you are merely speculating.

analyze claims and evidence p. 327   develop a statement p. 333

Causal Analysis

Not every phenomenon has a simple and certain explanation, nor is every analysis of cause and effect argumentative. Take, for example, an article that appeared in the *Atlantic* with the oddly provocative title: "We're the Only Animals with Chins, and No One Knows Why." You'd probably read it even if, as is likely, you've never given any thought to the subject.

Reading the Genre Ed Yong's exploration of chins doesn't uncover a simple solution to the question he raises. Can you think of another topic that might similarly resist a simple causal explanation?

We're the Only Animals with Chins, and No One Knows Why

ED YONG

January 28, 2016

"Little pig, little pig, let me come in," says the big, bad wolf. "No, no, not by the hair on my chinny chin chin," say the three little pigs. This scene is deeply unrealistic and not just because of the pigs' architectural competence, the wolf's implausible lung capacity, and everyone's ability to talk.

The thing is: Pigs don't have chins. Nor do any animals, except for us.

> Readers are introduced to the oddity of the human chin.

The lower jaw of a chimpanzee or gorilla slopes backwards from the front teeth. So did the jaw of other hominids like Homo erectus. Even Neanderthal jaws ended in a flat vertical plane. Only in modern humans does the lower jaw end in a protruding strut of bone. A sticky-outy bit. A chin.

"It's really strange that only humans have chins," says James Pampush from Duke University. "When we're looking at things that are uniquely human, we can't look to big brains or bipedalism because our extinct relatives had those. But they didn't have chins. That makes this immediately relevant to everyone." Indeed, except in rare cases involving birth defects, everyone has chins. Sure, some people have less pronounced ones than others, perhaps because their lower jaws are small or they have more flesh around the area. But if you peeled back that flesh and exposed their jawbones—and maybe don't do that—you'd still see a chin.

> Key question is posed, initiating a search for an answer.

So, why do chins exist?

There are no firm answers, which isn't for lack of effort. Evolutionary biologists have been proposing hypotheses for more than a century, and

Pampush has recently reviewed all the major ideas, together with David Daegling. "We kept showing, for one reason or another, that these hypotheses are not very good," he says.

The most heavily promoted explanation is that chins are adaptations for chewing—that they help to reduce the physical stresses acting upon a masticating jaw. But Pampush found that, if anything, the chin makes things worse. The lower jaw consists of two halves that are joined in the middle; when we chew, we compress the bone on the outer face of this join (near the lips) and pull on the bone on the inner face (near the tongue). Since bone is much stronger when compressed than pulled, you'd ideally want to reinforce the inner face of the join and not the outer one. In other words, you'd want the opposite of a chin.

<aside>First major theory is presented.</aside>

Others have suggested that the chin is an adaptation for chin-wags: It resists the forces we create when speaking. After all, speech is certainly a feature that separates us from other living animals. But there's no good evidence that the tongue exerts substantial enough forces to warrant a thick chunk of reinforcing bone. "And any mammal that also communicates vocally or suckles or engages in complex feeding behaviors that involve the tongue are probably experiencing similar stresses and strains, and they're not getting chins," says Pampush.

<aside>A second plausible explanation</aside>

Maybe it's about sex, then? Men typically have bigger chins than women, and stronger chins are often equated with attractiveness. Perhaps the chin is a sexual ornament, the human equivalent of a stag's antlers or a peacock's tail, a way of attracting mates or perhaps even signaling one's health and quality. "But if that's the case, we'd be the only mammal ever where both sexes have selected for the exact same ornament," says Pampush. In other words, women have chins, too. Chin shape may well be relevant to sex, but that doesn't explain chin presence. "They must have been there for some other reason before we started looking at the shape of them."

<aside>Additional theories offered and questioned</aside>

Then, there are hypotheses that "stretch the concept of natural selection," says Pampush. For example, one century-old idea says that chins are adaptations for deflecting punches to the face. That is, they helped early humans to take one on the chin. "That would require humans to hit each other so often and to suffer such dire consequences from being hit without a chin . . . it's unrealistic," says Pampush. Also, chins are terrible for deflecting blows. They don't disperse the incoming forces very evenly, which results in broken jaws. Even if our ancestors were constantly pummeling each other in the face, they would have fared better by reinforcing their jaws all the way round.

Pampush doubts that chins are adaptations at all. He thinks it's more likely that they are spandrels—incidental features that have no benefits in themselves, but are by-products of evolution acting upon something else.

For example, during human evolution, our faces shortened and our posture straightened. These changes made our mouths more cramped. To give our tongues and soft tissues more room and to avoid constricting our airways, the lower jaw developed a forward slope, of which the chin was a side effect. The problem with this idea is that the chin's outer face doesn't follow the contours of its inner face and has an exceptionally thick knob of bone. None of that screams "space-saving measure."

A different explanation portrays the chin as a bit of the jaw that got left behind while the rest shrunk back. As early humans started cooking and processing food, we made fewer demands upon our teeth, which started shrinking as a result. They gradually retracted into the face, while the part of the lower jaw that held them did not (or, at least, did so more slowly). Hence: chin.

Stephen Jay Gould and Richard Lewontin, who coined the concept of evolutionary spandrels, liked this hypothesis. So does Nathan Holton from the University of Iowa, who studies facial evolution. "It seems that the appearance of the chin itself is probably related to patterns of facial reduction in humans during the Pleistocene," he says. "In this sense, understanding why faces became smaller is important to explaining why we have chins."

"But why did the lower border of the jaw also not shrink?" Pampush asks. "What happened that left that last little bit sticking out?" This is the problem with spandrel hypotheses more generally: They're often very hard to test.

It may seem frustrating to have so many imperfect competing hypotheses, but that's part of the joy of chins: They reveal something about how scientists think about evolution. Some see the sculpting power of natural selection in everything and view chins as surely some kind of adaptation. Others see natural selection as just one of many evolutionary forces, and so they gravitate toward a spandrel-based explanation. "The chin is one of these rare phenomena in evolutionary biology that really exposes the deep philosophical differences between researchers in the field," says Pampush.

And, indeed, between people outside the field. "I always get entertaining e-mails from lay people trying to help me, so let me thank you in advance for what I'm about to receive," he tells me.

Because if there's one trait that is more universally human than the chin, it's having opinions.

> Supporters and doubters for every theory

> The unsettled debate illustrates how scientists deal with evolutionary theory.

Claiming a topic

▶ topic

To find a topic for an explanatory paper or causal analysis, begin a sentence with *why*, *how*, or *what if* and then finish it, drawing on what you may already know about an issue, trend, or problem. **O**

> Why are fewer young Americans marrying?
>
> Why is the occurrence of juvenile asthma spiking?
>
> Why do so few men study nursing or so few women study petroleum engineering?

There are, of course, many other ways to phrase questions about cause and effect in order to attach important conditions and qualifications.

> What if scientists figure out how to stop the human aging process—as now seems plausible within twenty years? What are the consequences for society?
>
> Is it more likely than ever that a successful third political party might develop in the United States to end the deadlock between Republicans and Democrats?

As you can see, none of these topics would just drop from a tree. They require cultural or technical knowledge and a willingness to speculate. Look for such cause-and-effect issues in your academic courses or professional life. Or search for them in the media—although you should shy away from worn-out subjects, such as plagiarism, credit card debt, and celebrity scandals, unless you can offer fresh insights.

To find a subject, try the following approaches.

A satirical info-graphic suggests that Twitter is destroying the environment.

Twitter is destroying our environment.

FOR EVERY
1 TWEET
128 TONS OF CO₂ ARE RELEASED INTO THE ATMOSPHERE
That's 29.9 billion tons of CO₂ a year, and over 82 million tons each day.

FOR EVERY
18,000 TWEETS
1 HECTARE OF FOREST IS LOST
That's nearly 13,000 hectares of lost forest everyday, yet we can't stop tweeting.

FOR EVERY
27 TWEETS
WE RELEASE 1 TON OF TOXIC CHEMICALS INTO THE ENVIRONMENT
That's 8.7 million tons of toxic chemicals we choke on every year as we continue to tweet.

FOR EVERY
14,000 TWEETS
WE LOSE 1 HECTARE OF SOIL
We lose more than 17,127 hectares of soil every day. That's over 6.2 million hectares of land lost each year.

Courtesy of CableTV.com

find a topic p. 16

Look again at a subject you know well. It may be one that has affected you personally or might in the future. For instance, you may have experienced firsthand the effects of high-stakes testing in high school, or you may have theories about why people your age still smoke despite the risks. Offer a hypothesis.

Look for an issue new to you. Choose a subject you've always wanted to know more about (for example, the long-term cultural effects of video gaming). You probably won't be able to venture a thesis or hypothesis until you've done some research, but that's the appeal of this strategy. The material is novel and you are energized. **O**

Examine a local issue. Look for recent changes on campus, in the community, or at work and examine why they happened or what their consequences may be. Talk to the people responsible or affected. **O** Admissions standards changed? More small restaurants opening? Local proposals for a minimum wage increase? Why, or what if?

Choose a challenging subject. An issue that is complicated or vexed will push you to think harder. Don't rush to judgment; remain open-minded about contrary evidence, conflicting motives, and different points of view.

Tackle an issue that seems settled. If you have guts, look for a phenomenon that most people assume has been adequately explained. Tired of the way Republicans, Wall Street economists, vegans, fundamentalists, or the hosts of *The View* smugly explain the way things are? Pick one sore point and offer a different—and better—analysis.

Thinking about Writing   After Richard Nixon won forty-nine states in the 1972 presidential election, a distinguished film critic for *The New Yorker*, Pauline Kael, is reported to have said, "How can he have won? I don't know anyone who voted for him." This phenomenon repeated itself in many places in 2016. Can you think of any times when you have similarly misread a situation because you did not have a perspective broad enough to understand all the forces in play? Identify such a situation and consider whether it might provide you with a topic for an explanatory paper. Alternatively, consider some of the times—maybe even beginning in childhood—when you have heard explanations for phenomena that you recognized as wildly implausible because they were superstitions, stereotypes, or simply errors. Consider whether you might turn one of these misconceptions into a topic for an explanatory paper.

find a topic   interview and observe
p. 70   p. 448

Imagining your audience

Readers for cause-and-effect analyses and explanations are diverse, but you might notice a difference between audiences you create yourself by drawing attention to a neglected subject and readers who come to your work because your topic already interests them.

Create an audience. In some situations, you must convince readers to pay attention to the phenomenon you intend to explore. Assume they are smart enough to care about subjects that might affect their lives. So make your case for the subject aggressively. That's exactly what the editors of the *Wall Street Journal* do in an editorial noting the steady *decrease* in traffic deaths that followed a congressional decision ten years earlier to do away with a national 55-mph speed limit.

Anticipates readers who might ask, "Why does this issue matter?"

> This may seem noncontroversial now, but at the time the debate was shrill and filled with predictions of doom. Ralph Nader claimed that "history will never forgive Congress for this assault on the sanctity of human life." Judith Stone, president of the Advocates for Highway and Auto Safety, predicted to Katie Couric on NBC's *Today Show* that there would be "6,400 added highway fatalities a year and millions of more injuries." Federico Peña, the Clinton administration's secretary of transportation, declared: "Allowing speed limits to rise above 55 simply means that more Americans will die and be injured on our highways."
>
> — "Safe at Any Speed," July 7, 2006

Write to an existing audience. In most cases, you'll enter cause-and-effect debates already in progress. Whether you intend to uphold what most people already believe or, more controversially, ask them to rethink their positions, you'll probably face readers as knowledgeable (and opinionated) as you are. In the following paragraphs, for example, from deep in an article exploring the downsides of Americans' obsession with electronic communication, notice how cultural critic Andrew Sullivan assumes an intelligent audience already affected by his topic, and possibly offended by its title: "I Used to Be a Human Being." Readers today, he laments, are pummeled by materials fed to them relentlessly by blogs, Facebook, Tumblr, Twitter, and more.

Sullivan insists on "we" in this paragraph and even speaks directly to readers: "Do not flatter yourself."

> We absorb this "content" (as writing or video or photography is now called) no longer primarily by buying a magazine or paper, by bookmarking our favorite website, or by actively choosing to read or watch. We are instead guided to these infonuggets by myriad little interruptions on social media, all cascading at us with individually tailored relevance and accuracy. Do not flatter yourself in thinking that you have much control over which temptations you click on. Silicon Valley's technologists and their ever-perfecting algorithms have discovered the form of bait that will have you jumping like a witless minnow. No information technology ever had this depth of knowledge of its consumers—or greater capacity to tweak their synapses to keep them engaged.

And the engagement never ends. Not long ago, surfing the web, however addictive, was a stationary activity. At your desk at work, or at home on your laptop, you disappeared down a rabbit hole of links and resurfaced minutes (or hours) later to reencounter the world. But the smartphone then went and made the rabbit hole portable, inviting us to get lost in it anywhere, at any time, whatever else we might be doing. Information soon penetrated every waking moment of our lives.

He describes what his audience likely knows: We are all in the thrall of technology.

And it did so with staggering swiftness. We almost forget that ten years ago, there were no smartphones, and as recently as 2011, only a third of Americans owned one. Now nearly two = thirds do. That figure reaches 85 percent when you're only counting young adults. And 46 percent of Americans told Pew surveyors last year a simple but remarkable thing: They could not live without one. The device went from unknown to indispensable in less than a decade. The handful of spaces where it was once impossible to be connected—the airplane, the subway, the wilderness—are dwindling fast. Even hiker backpacks now come fitted with battery power for smartphones. Perhaps the only "safe space" that still exists is the shower.

Sullivan asks his readers to consider how their lives have changed.

— "I Used to Be a Human Being," *New York Magazine*, September 23, 2016

Gathering materials

Expect to do as much research for an explanation as for any fact-based report or argument. You need to be careful to show that you have thoughtfully considered what others have written on a subject. **O**

consider ◀
causes

In particular, it is important to learn how exactly causal relationships work so that any claims you make about them are accurate. Causality is intriguing because it demands precision and subtlety—as the categories explained in this section demonstrate. But once you grasp them, you'll also be better able to identify faulty explanations when you come across them. (Exposing faulty causality makes for notably powerful and winning arguments.) **O**

Understand necessary causes. A *necessary cause* is any factor that must be in place for something to occur. For example, sunlight, chlorophyll, and water are all necessary for photosynthesis to happen. Remove one of these elements from the equation and the natural process simply doesn't take place. But since none of them could cause photosynthesis on its own, they are necessary causes, yet not sufficient (see *sufficient causes* below).

refine your search
p. 436

read closely
p. 321

On a less scientific level, necessary causes are those that seem so crucial that we can't imagine something happening without them. For example, you might argue that a baseball team could not win a World Series without a specific pitcher on the roster: Remove him and the team doesn't even get to the playoffs. Or you might claim that, while fanaticism doesn't itself cause terrorism, terrorism doesn't exist without fanaticism. In any such analysis, it helps to separate necessary causes from those that may be merely contributing factors.

Understand sufficient causes. A *sufficient cause*, by itself, is enough to bring on a particular effect. Driving drunk or shoplifting are two sufficient causes for being arrested in the United States. In a causal argument, you might need to figure out which of several plausible sufficient causes is responsible for a specific phenomenon— assuming that a single explanation exists. A plane might have crashed because it was overloaded, ran out of fuel, had a structural failure, encountered severe wind shear, and so on.

Understand precipitating causes. Think of a *precipitating cause* as the proverbial straw that breaks a camel's back. In itself, the factor may seem trivial. But it becomes the spark that sets a field gone dry for months ablaze. By refusing to give up her bus seat to a white passenger in Montgomery, Alabama, Rosa Parks triggered a civil rights movement in 1955, but she didn't actually cause it: The necessary conditions had been accumulating for generations.

Understand proximate causes. A *proximate cause* is nearby and often easy to spot. A corporation declares bankruptcy when it can no longer meet its massive debt obligations; a minivan crashes because a front tire explodes; a student fails a course because she plagiarizes a paper. But in a causal analysis, getting the facts right about such proximate causes may just be your starting point. You need to work toward a deeper understanding of a situation. As you might guess, proximate causes may sometimes also be sufficient causes.

Understand remote causes. A *remote cause*, as the term suggests, may act at some distance from an event but be closely tied to it. That bankrupt corporation may have defaulted on its loans because of a full decade of bad management decisions; the tire exploded because it was underinflated and its tread was worn; the student resorted to plagiarism *because* she ran out of time *because* she was working two jobs to pay for a Hawaiian vacation *because* she wanted a memorable spring break to impress her friends—a string of remote causes. Remote causes make many causal explanations challenging and interesting: Figuring them out is like detective work.

Understand reciprocal causes. You have a *reciprocal* situation when a cause leads to an effect that, in turn, strengthens the cause. Consider how creating science internships for college women might encourage more women to become scientists, who then sponsor more internships, creating yet more female scientists. Many analyses of global warming describe reciprocal relationships, with CO_2 emissions leading to warming, which increases plant growth or alters ocean currents, which in turn releases more CO_2 or heat, and so on.

> Need help assessing your own work? See "How to Use the Writing Center" on pp. 10–11.

Organizing ideas

The introduction to a cause-and-effect argument should provide enough details for readers to see the point of your project. Spend as many paragraphs as you need to offer background information. The following brief paragraph might seem like an adequate opening for an essay on the failures of dog training by Jon Katz.

> organize ◀
> ideas

> For thousands of years, humans have been training dogs to be hunters, herders, searchers, guards, and companions. Why are we doing so badly? The problem may lie more with our methods than with us.
>
> —"Train in Vain," *Slate.com*, January 14, 2005

In fact, *seven* paragraphs precede this one to set up the causal claim. Those additional paragraphs help readers (especially dog owners) fully appreciate a problem many will find familiar. The actual first paragraph has the author narrating a typical dog owner's dilemma.

> Sam was distressed. His West Highland terrier, aptly named Lightning, was constantly darting out of doors and dashing into busy suburban Connecticut streets. Sam owned three acres behind his house, and he was afraid to let the dog roam any of it.

By paragraph seven, Katz has offered enough corroborating evidence to describe a crisis in dogdom, a problem that leaves readers hoping for an explanation.

> The results of this failure are everywhere: Neurotic and compulsive dog behaviors like barking, biting, chasing cars, and chewing furniture—sometimes severe enough to warrant antidepressants—are growing. Lesser training problems—an inability to sit, stop begging, come, or stay—are epidemic.

△

Like Katz, you'll want to take the time necessary to introduce your subject and get readers invested in the issue. **O** Then you have a number of options for developing your explanation or causal analysis.

Explain why something happened.
When simply suggesting reasons to explain a phenomenon, you can move quickly from an introduction that explains the phenomenon to a thesis or hypothesis. Then work through your list of factors toward a conclusion. Build toward the most convincing explanation.

> **Introduction leading to an explanatory or causal claim**
>
> **First cause explored + reasons/evidence**
>
> **Next cause explored + reasons/evidence**
>
> **Best cause explored + reasons/evidence**
>
> **Conclusion**

Explain the consequences of a phenomenon.
When exploring effects that follow from some cause, event, policy, or change in the status quo, open by describing the situation you believe will have serious consequences. Then work through those effects, connecting them as you need to. Draw out the implications of your analysis in the conclusion.

> **Introduction describing a significant cause**
>
> **First effect likely to follow + reasons**
>
> **Other effect(s) likely to follow + reasons**
>
> **Conclusion and discussion of implications**

Suggest an alternative explanation.
A natural strategy is to open a causal analysis by refuting someone else's faulty theory and then offering a better one of your own. After all, we often think about causality when someone makes a claim we disagree with.

> **Introduction questioning a causal claim**
>
> **Reasons to doubt claim offered + evidence**
>
> **Alternative cause(s) explored**
>
> **Best cause examined + reasons/evidence**
>
> **Conclusion**

shape a beginning p. 395

Explain a chain of causes. Sometimes you'll describe causes that operate in order, one by one: A causes B, B leads to C, C trips D, and so on. In such cases, use a sequential or narrative pattern of organization, giving special attention to the links (or transitions) within the chain. ⭕

> Introduction suggesting a chain of causes/consequences

> First link presented + reasons/evidence

> Next link(s) presented + reasons/evidence

> Final link presented + reasons/evidence

> Conclusion

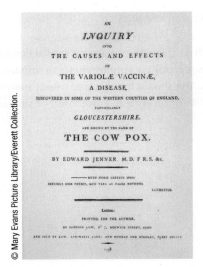

People have been writing such analyses for centuries. Here is the title page of Edward Jenner's 1798 publication, *An Inquiry into the Causes and Effects of the Variolae Vaccinae*. Jenner's research led to a vaccine that protected human beings from smallpox.

Choosing style and design

When you try to explain something clearly, you may sometimes have to work at keeping readers interested. You can do that through both style and design.

Consider a middle style. Even explanations written for fairly academic audiences lean toward the middle style because of its flexibility: It can be both familiar and serious. O Here Robert Bruegmann, discussing the causes of urban sprawl, uses language that is simple, clear, and colloquial—and almost entirely free of technical jargon.

> When asked, most americans declare themselves to be against sprawl, just as they say they are against pollution or the destruction of historic buildings. But the very development that one individual targets as sprawl is often another family's much-loved community. Very few people believe that they themselves live in sprawl or contribute to sprawl. Sprawl is where other people live, particularly people with less good taste. Much antisprawl activism is based on a desire to reform these other people's lives.
>
> — "How Sprawl Got a Bad Name," *American Enterprise*, June 2006

Use appropriate supporting media. Explanations have no special design features. But, like reports and arguments, they routinely employ charts to summarize information and graphics to illustrate ideas. You should too. Because causal analyses usually have distinct sections or parts, they do fit nicely into PowerPoint or similar presentations. O

define your style
p. 366

think visually
p. 425

Examining models

RESEARCH STUDY   In a college research paper, Alysha Behn explores the reasons that women, despite talent and interest, so rarely pursue careers in technology and, more specifically, computer programming. Drawing heavily on research studies, Behn's causal analysis is detailed, complicated, and challenging.

Reading the Genre   You may be surprised that Behn's causal argument ends on a pessimistic note, pointing out that no one-size-fits-all solution will resolve the complex issues keeping women out of technical careers. Does so tentative a conclusion weaken or add authority to the author's ethos? Does it affect how credibly she comes across to readers? (Notice that *I* does not occur in this academic paper.)

Alysha Behn

Professor Ruszkiewicz

Rhetoric 325M

February 20, 20--

Where Have All the Women Gone?

Opening uses statistics to identify the point of the paper.

In 1984, 37.1 percent of computer science graduates were women. In 2009, around 11 percent of computer science graduates were women. What happened?

It's important to make clear what hasn't gone wrong. Experts dismiss the idea that men are more capable than women of succeeding at computer science, and there are no institutional barriers preventing women from pursuing a computer science degree or a tech career. In fact, rather than discriminating against women, colleges and corporations are competing desperately for female applicants. They just can't

Behn 2

find any. Women aren't pursuing careers in computer science anymore, and two decades of research hasn't found a way to stop the exodus.

The root of the problem may be the flawed way sociologists and computer scientists are researching the problem, according to Katrina Markwick, a former researcher at the Monash University Department of Education. If researchers are asking the wrong questions, it follows that the solutions they suggest are going to be ineffective.

Much of the research Markwick criticizes focused on increasing women's access to technological education through equal opportunity (EO) strategies, which try to increase women's participation in a male-dominated field without questioning the culture that made that field male dominated (Markwick 258). Equal opportunity programs focus on removing institutional barriers or encouraging a group to participate more—for example, you could instruct math teachers on how to avoid treating girls differently from boys in class, or you could organize a math- and science-oriented summer camp just for girls in order to generate interest in those fields. The problem with the EO approach is that "[these] policies were predicated on the assumption of ontological equality, a belief in the fundamental sameness of individuals, and the EO mind-set produced an acceptance that white, nondisabled, heterosexual men's experiences and interpretations of organizational life

Behn quickly dismisses some conventional explanations.

Behn 3

were universally applicable" (Moss and Gunn 448). In other words, EO programs and strategies implicitly ask women to conform—to be more like men—in order to have a career in computer science.

There's a fascinating body of research that suggests that the equal opportunity paradigm can't address all the factors turning women away from pursuing technology careers. For example, a 2008 study demonstrated that men prefer the aesthetics of Web sites designed by men, and women prefer the aesthetics of Web sites designed by women (Moss and Gunn 457–58)—and, as a result, people tend to spend more time browsing Web sites designed by a member of their own gender. Given that most computer games are made by men, it similarly follows that "young men are more attracted to playing computer games and . . . young women tend to prefer more passive, purposeful games, and game playing is not a major part of their leisure activities (Lang, 1999)" (Lang 221).

What's problematic about all this is that both playing with video games and tooling around on the Internet indirectly teach computer literacy. What's more, kids who don't enjoy playing with computers aren't likely to pursue careers devoted to tinkering with them. All this points to a positive feedback loop that's responsible for turning men on to technology careers and pushing women away: As more men and fewer women are responsible for designing software and hardware, fewer

A research-based paragraph explains why EO-based strategies don't attract women to tech fields. Although this paper is documented in MLA style, the quotes include APA citations.

Behn 4

technological products (even products intended to look gender neutral, like the Apple iPad) will be designed with women's interests and aesthetic preferences in mind. Thus, fewer women will be interested in using these products, so fewer women will become skilled at using these technologies or drawn toward a career in making them.

Academic socialization steers students toward and away from tech careers.

Equal opportunity programs also don't take into account the process of socialization of gender—that is, learning from others what our gender role is—and aren't always well equipped to combat the negative lessons most women learn about themselves:

> The role socialization plays . . . cannot be underemphasized in explaining the continued presence of the gender gap. . . . By the end of middle school, students develop the notion that mathematics, sciences, and computing fields are for white males (Clewell & Braddock, 2000). Furthermore, these perceptions are found to exist more often for girls than for boys (Trauth, 2002). (Varma 302)

Often the process of socialization is so subtle and pervasive that many women do not even notice it themselves (Varma 308). The perception that "boys are good at math" often leads counselors, parents, and teachers to subtly steer boys toward challenging math and science and away from liberal arts

Behn 5

courses in high school, while for women the reverse holds true (Varma 306; Cheryan and Plaut). The result is that many women enter college less prepared for a computer science program than their male peers. Even when male and female students are equally prepared, male students generally express more confidence in their skills, while women take as long as two years to feel that they are competent. In study after study, women have cited anxiety about performance and loss of self-confidence as a primary reason for leaving the field; in fact, some have suggested that professors have a lower opinion of female students' ability to do well than they do of their male students' (Varma 303). Thus, "Irani (2004) has argued that the act of establishing an 'identity of competence' is necessary for women to situate themselves in CS culture and verify legitimacy" (Varma 303).

In some cases the gendered socialization is a little less subtle. The anonymity afforded by online gaming and the Internet has made unapologetic misogyny disturbingly common in gaming and Internet culture. "The Rules of the Internet," a popular document created by an anonymous poster on the online forum 4chan, include the following: "28. Always question a person's gender—just in case it's really a man. 29. In the Internet all girls are men and all kids are undercover FBI agents" (Lolrus). Such rules establish that it is the norm to be male on the Internet and to be a woman is to be the exception

Behn uses research studies to clarify and support her causal argument.

Behn 6

Behn offers a cultural reason that women avoid tech careers and suggests a way around the problem.

to the rule. Online gaming and participation in popular Web sites like 4chan and Reddit are frequently cited as factors that attract men to computing careers, so an online culture in which women are explicitly made to feel unwelcome is undoubtedly part of the problem.

Let's describe the last gendered assumption this way: Close your eyes and picture a programmer.

You probably pictured a nerdy-looking guy, perhaps with glasses, alone at his computer in a dark basement. Right? Here's the thing: The basement might be passé but the "alone" bit definitely isn't. And women show a marked aversion to programming alone (Lang 220–21). Fortunately, this is a problem we do have a solution for, and it's one that's catching on fast. Pair programming—a programming style where one partner types at the keyboard and the other partner watches closely, making suggestions and watching for errors—is an attractive solution not only because women prefer it but because the resulting code is consistently better than code written alone (Simon and Hanks 73–82). While younger companies have been eager to adopt pair programming practices, older giants like Microsoft and IBM have shown more reluctance. Furthermore, the success of pair programming will remain irrelevant until tech companies and colleges do a little PR to combat the isolated-nerd-in-a-basement image. Until then, the pair programming shift is more likely to aid retention of women in tech majors than to attract more of them to computing careers.

Behn 7

Markwick also criticized a second paradigm for increasing women's interest in technical fields, one emphasizing the values of femininity and suggesting solutions like a "girl friendly" curriculum (Markwick 258–59): "This entailed 'celebrating the female side' of the gender binary and revaluing 'women's ways of knowing' (Belenky, Clinchy, Goldberger, & Tarule, 1986) . . . but it treated girls as an essentialized category, neglecting differences between girls" (Markwick 260). While this is without question a step forward from asking women to conform to the masculine norms of the computing industry, it also substitutes one false assumption—that men and women are basically the same—for another: in this case, that all women are fundamentally the same.

Few studies take into account the fact that women are not a homogeneous group (Varma 306). A solution that tries to attract women to technology careers by designing machines that appeal to women will not have much impact on minority women who can't afford that technology in the first place. Nor would a solution oriented around changing the culture of computer science classrooms do much to attract women who want a career that is known to be compatible with raising a family. A solution that tries to combat the "math is for boys" perception isn't going to make it easier for a woman to go to college if she needs to care for a young child. The list goes on. Too frequently, researchers have tried to pinpoint a single issue and define a one-size-fits-all solution, but moving women into tech careers is much more complicated than that.

> Behn resists any simple solution, noting a flaw in assumptions about women's participation in tech careers.

Behn 8

Works Cited

Cheryan, Sapna, and Victoria C. Plaut. "Explaining Underrep-
    resentation: A Theory of Precluded Interest." *Sex Roles*,
    vol. 63, no. 7–8, Oct. 2010, pp. 475–88.

Lang, Catherine. "Twenty-First Century Australian Women
    and IT." *Computer Science Education*, vol. 17, no. 3,
    May 2007, pp. 215–26.

Lolrus. "Rules of the Internet." *Know Your Meme*, Cheezburger,
    2010, knowyourmeme.com/photos/30662-rules-of-the
    -internet.

Markwick, Katrina. "Under the Feminist Post-structuralist Lens:
    Women in Computing Education." *Journal of Educational
    Computing Research*, vol. 34, no. 3, Apr. 2006, pp. 257–79.

Moss, G. A., and R. W. Gunn. "Gender Differences in Website
    Production and Preference Aesthetics: Preliminary Implica-
    tions for ICT in Education and Beyond." *Behaviour &
    Information Technology*, vol. 28, no. 5, Aug. 2009, pp. 447–60.
    Computer Source, doi:10.1080/01449290802332662.

Simon, Beth, and Brian Hanks. "First Year Students' Impres-
    sions of Pair Programming in CS1." *Proceedings of the
    Third International Workshop on Computing Education
    Research*, Sept. 2007, Atlanta, GA. Association for Com-
    puting Machinery, 2007, pp. 73–85. *ACM Digital Library*,
    doi:10.1145/1288580.1288591.

Varma, Roli. "Why So Few Women Enroll in Computing? Gender
    and Ethnic Differences in Students' Perception." *Computer
    Science Education*, vol. 20, no. 4, Dec. 2010, pp. 301–16.

Documen-
tation style
used is MLA.

Flow Diagram

Reading the Genre A flow diagram or chart like "Traffic Mystery: 'The Shockwave'" can illustrate the movements of people, ideas, physical processes and more, thereby helping audiences to visualize how or why something happens. In this item, why is the separate explanation of the "funnel" effect necessary? Can you think of any process you have to explain routinely that might benefit from a flow diagram?

We've all ground to a halt on freeways without obstacles in sight—no weather issues, no collisions, no ducks crossing the pavement. What gives? Highway engineers know and Stephen J. Beard and Rich Exner at the *Cleveland Plain Dealer* use a flow diagram to illustrate, step by step, cause and effect, how traffic jams just spontaneously occur.

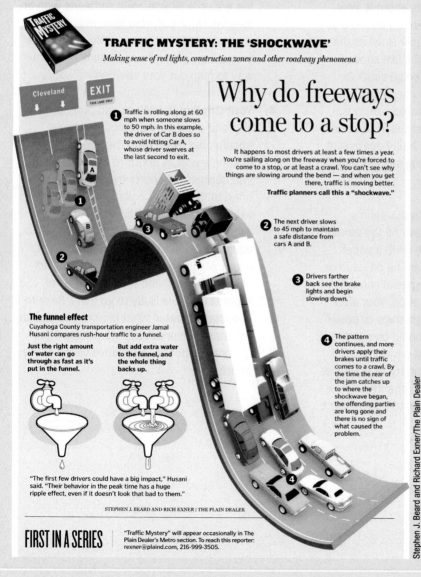

TRAFFIC MYSTERY

TRAFFIC MYSTERY: THE 'SHOCKWAVE'
Making sense of red lights, construction zones and other roadway phenomena

Cleveland

EXIT
THIS LANE ONLY

Why do freeways come to a stop?

1 Traffic is rolling along at 60 mph when someone slows to 50 mph. In this example, the driver of Car B does so to avoid hitting Car A, whose driver swerves at the last second to exit.

It happens to most drivers at least a few times a year. You're sailing along on the freeway when you're forced to come to a stop, or at least a crawl. You can't see why things are slowing around the bend — and when you get there, traffic is moving better.

Traffic planners call this a "shockwave."

2 The next driver slows to 45 mph to maintain a safe distance from cars A and B.

3 Drivers farther back see the brake lights and begin slowing down.

4 The pattern continues, and more drivers apply their brakes until traffic comes to a crawl. By the time the rear of the jam catches up to where the shockwave began, the offending parties are long gone and there is no sign of what caused the problem.

The funnel effect
Cuyahoga County transportation engineer Jamal Husani compares rush-hour traffic to a funnel.

Just the right amount of water can go through as fast as it's put in the funnel.

But add extra water to the funnel, and the whole thing backs up.

"The first few drivers could have a big impact," Husani said. "Their behavior in the peak time has a huge ripple effect, even if it doesn't look that bad to them."

STEPHEN J. BEARD AND RICH EXNER | THE PLAIN DEALER

FIRST IN A SERIES "Traffic Mystery" will appear occasionally in The Plain Dealer's Metro section. To reach this reporter: rexner@plaind.com, 216-999-3505.

Stephen J. Beard and Richard Exner/The Plain Dealer

1. **Causal Analysis:** Like the scientists Ed Yon describes in "We're the Only Animals With Chins, and No One Knows Why" (p. 67), you may have encountered phenomena with multiple, plausible explanations, although perhaps in less technical areas than evolutionary biology. Pick a subject that genuinely puzzles you and write about it. Why, for example, have commercials become as important a part of the Super Bowl as the game itself? Why do women like shoes? What exactly makes a video go viral? Or, more seriously, maybe you belong to a group that has been the subject of causal analyses verging on prejudicial. If so, refute what you regard as some faulty analysis of cause and effect by offering more plausible explanations.

2. **Research Study:** Using Alysha Behn's research essay "Where Have All the Women Gone?" (p. 79) as a model, write a paper based on sources that examine an issue or problem in some area of special concern to you—your job or profession, your area of study, your social relationships or political concerns. The issue should be one that involves questions of how, why, or what if. Base your analysis on a variety of academic or public sources, fully documented. Draw on interviews if appropriate to your subject.

3. **Flow Diagram:** Here's your chance to fix some problem by analyzing what exactly causes it and then illustrating that process, hoping your flow chart or diagram might provide a fix. Maybe it takes too many steps for a novice to acquire a campus parking permit or create a course schedule or fix a flat tire on a bicycle. Help someone with an imaginative visual. Your item might be as simple as "Traffic Mystery: The Shockwave" on p. 87 or maybe you can think of another way to map out your solution.

4. **Your Choice:** Politicians and pundits alike are fond of offering predictions, some hopeful, but many dire. The economy, they might suggest, is about to boom or slide into depression; sports dynasties are destined to blossom or collapse; printed books will disappear; American teens will grow even fonder of vinyl records and old audio equipment. Identify one such prediction about which you have some doubts and develop a cause-and-effect analysis to suggest why it is likely to go awry. Be sure to explain in detail what factors you expect will make the prediction go wrong. If you are brave, offer an alternative vision of the future.

How to start ▶
- Need a **topic**? See page 95.
- Need **support for your argument**? See page 99.
- Need to **organize your ideas**? See page 102.

Arguments

10

ask readers
to consider
debatable
ideas

It doesn't take much to spark an argument these days—a casual remark, a political observation, a dumb joke that hurts someone's feelings. Loud voices and angry Twitter postings may follow, leaving observers upset and frustrated. But arguments aren't polarizing or hostile by nature, not when offered by people genuinely more interested in generating light than heat. It's a lesson worthy of relearning: Arguments should make us smarter and better able to deal with problems in the world. In fact, you probably make such constructive arguments all the time without raising blood pressures, at least not too much.

ARGUMENT TO ADVANCE A THESIS
In an op-ed for the local paper, you *argue for the thesis* that people who talk on cell phones while driving are a greater hazard than drunk drivers because they are more numerous and more callous.

REFUTATION ARGUMENT
In a term paper, you use facts and logic to *refute the argument* that students with college degrees will probably earn more in their lifetimes than students with only high school diplomas.

VISUAL ARGUMENT
Rather than write a letter to the editor about out-of-control salaries for NCAA football coaches, you create a *visual argument*—an editorial cartoon—suggesting that a local coach is paid more than the entire faculty.

Defining the genre

Arguments come in many shapes to serve different purposes. Subsequent chapters in this section cover specialized genres of argument often assigned in the classroom, including *evaluations, proposals,* and *literary analyses* (for more on choosing a genre, see Chapter 2, "Defining Genres and Purpose"). But even less formal arguments have distinctive features. In your projects, you'll aim to do the following.

Offer levelheaded and disputable claims. You won't influence audiences by making points no one cares about. Something consequential should be at stake in an argument you offer for public consumption. Maybe you want to change readers' minds about an issue that everyone else thinks has been settled. Or maybe you want to shore up what people already believe. In either case, you need a well-defined point, either stated or implied, if you hope to influence the kind of readers worth impressing: thoughtful, levelheaded people.

Offer good reasons to support a claim. Without evidence and supporting reasons, a claim is just an assertion—and little better than a shout or a slogan. Slogans do have their appeal in advertising and politics. But they don't become arguments until they are backed by solid reasoning and a paper trail of evidence. No one said writing arguments is easy. Allow time for finding the facts.

Understand opposing claims and points of view. You won't make a strong case of your own until you can *honestly* paraphrase the logic of those who see matters differently. Many people find that tough to do because it forces them to consider alternative perspectives. But you will seem more credible when you

Utah Department of Highway Safety. Creative Director/Art Director: Ryan Anderson, Creative Director/Copywriter: Gary Sume, Account Supervisor: Peggy Lander, Agency Richter7.

What claim does this ad from the Utah Department of Public Safety actually make? Might anyone dispute it? Do you find the ad effective visually?

acknowledge these other *reasonable* opinions even as you refute them. When you face less than rational claims, rebut them calmly but firmly. Avoid the impulse to respond with an insult or a petty comment of your own.

Frame arguments powerfully—and not in words only. Sensible opinions still have to dress for the occasion: You need the right words and images to move a case forward. Fortunately, strategies for making effective arguments also cue you in to appeals that are less legitimate. We've all been seduced by claims just because they are stylish, hip, or repeated so often that they begin to seem true. But if such persuasion doesn't seem fair or sensible, that's all the more reason to reach for a higher standard in your own appeals.

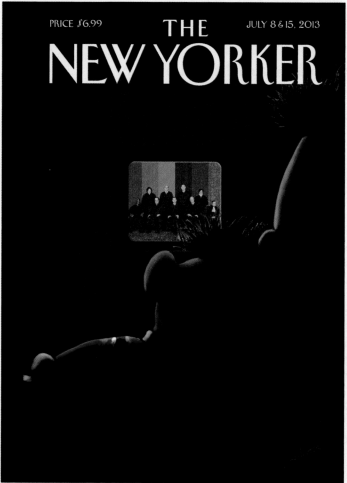

Jack Hunter/The New Yorker © Condé Nast.

Immediately following a 2013 U.S. Supreme Court decision striking down federal prohibitions against same-sex marriage, the *New Yorker*—famous for its memorable covers—added another to its collection. Without a word, the magazine expressed its opinion of the ruling. What elements in the cover make it an argument? How might you phrase the claim it makes visually?

Argument to Advance a Thesis

Here's a deceptively simple argument about what many readers might not perceive (initially, at least) as a problem at all. So Robyn Martin, a senior lecturer at North Arizona University, must briefly describe the growing phenomenon of cairn-building in wilderness areas and then offer good reasons why the practice should stop. The point of view is personal, with the author appealing to the common sense and decency of her readers.

Reading the Genre   As you read Martin's essay, identify some of the strategies you find engaging. Where are its appeals logical and where are they emotional? How would you describe the style of the piece, especially the conclusion?

Stop the Rock-stacking: A Writer Calls for an End to Cairns

ROBYN MARTIN

July 7, 2015

Stones: We've built pyramids and castles with them and painstakingly cleared them out of farm fields, using them to build low walls for fencing. We marvel at the rocks in the Grand Canyon, Arches, and Grand Teton national parks. Yet a perplexing practice has been gaining ground in our wild spaces: People have begun stacking rocks on top of one another, balancing them carefully and doing this for unknown reasons, though probably as some kind of personal or "spiritual" statement.

> Why is rock-stacking a problem? Martin will need to explain.

These piles aren't true cairns, the official term for deliberately stacked rocks. From middle Gaelic, the word means "mound of stones built as a memorial or landmark." There are plenty of those in Celtic territories, that's for sure, as well as in other cultures; indigenous peoples in the United States often used cairns to cover and bury their dead. Those of us who like to hike through wilderness areas are glad to see the occasional cairn, as long as it's indicating the right way to go at critical junctions in the backcountry.

Stone piles have their uses, but the many rock stacks that I'm seeing on our public lands are increasingly problematic. First, if they're set in a

The author describes two issues, one practical, the second cultural.

random place, they can lead an unsuspecting hiker into trouble, away from the trail and into a potentially dangerous place. Second, we go to wilderness to remove ourselves from the human saturation of our lives, not to see mementoes from other people's lives.

We hike, we mountain bike, we run, we backpack, we boat in wilderness areas to retreat from civilization. We need undeveloped places to find quiet in our lives. A stack of rocks left by someone who preceded us on the trail does nothing more than remind us that other people were there before us. It is an unnecessary marker of humanity, like leaving graffiti—no different from finding a tissue bleached and decaying against the earth that a previous traveler didn't pack out, or a forgotten water bottle. Pointless cairns are simply pointless reminders of the human ego.

Note the analogy: In the wilderness, cairns are graffiti or garbage, a human defacement of the environment.

I'm not sure exactly when the practice of stacking stones began in the West. But the so-called Harmonic Convergence in 1987, a globally synchronized meditation event, brought a tighter focus on New Age practices to Sedona, Arizona, just south of my home. Vortexes, those places where spiritual and metaphysical energy are reputed to be found, began to figure prominently on national forests and other public lands surrounding Sedona. Hikers near these vortexes couldn't miss seeing so many new lines of rocks or stacks of stones.

Since then, the cairns, referred to as "prayer stone stacks" by some, have been multiplying on our public lands. Where there were just a dozen or so stone stacks at a much-visited state park on Sedona's Oak Creek ten years ago, now there are hundreds. What's more, the cairn craze has mushroomed, invading wilderness areas everywhere in the West.

Martin characterizes cairns negatively: a craze.

Why should we care about a practice that can be dismantled with a simple foot-push, that uses natural materials that can be returned quickly to the earth, and that some say nature will remove eventually anyway?

Because it's not a harmless practice: Moving rocks increases erosion by exposing the soil underneath, allowing it to wash away the thin soil cover for native plants. Every time a rock is disturbed, an animal loses a potential home, since many insects and mammals burrow under rocks for protection and reproduction.

But the craze is not without environmental and ethical implications.

But mainly, pointless cairns change the value of the wilderness experience by degrading an already beautiful landscape. Building cairns where none are needed for route finding is antithetical to Leave-No-Trace ethics. Move a stone, and you've changed the environment from something that it wasn't to something manmade. Cairn building might also be illegal, since erecting structures or moving natural materials on public lands often comes with fines and/or jail time. Of course, I doubt the Forest Service will hunt down someone who decided that his or her self-expression required erecting a balanced stone sculpture on a sandstone ridge. Yet it is an unwelcome reminder of humanity, something we strive to avoid as we enjoy our wild spaces.

Let's end this invasive practice. Fight the urge to stack rocks and make your mark. Consider deconstructing them when you find them, unless they're marking a critical trail junction. If you must worship in the wild, repress that urge to rearrange the rocks and just say a silent prayer to yourself. Or bring along a journal or sketchpad to recall what you felt in the wild.

Let's check our egos at the trailheads and boat launches, and leave the earth's natural beauty alone. Her geology, as it stands, is already perfect.

The argument turns to a call for action.

Claiming a topic

In a college assignment, you could be asked to write arguments about topics related to courses, but you probably won't be told what your claims should be. When that's the case, choose subjects you genuinely care about—not issues the media or someone else defines as controversial. You'll likely do a more credible job defending your questionable choice *not* to wear a helmet when motorcycling than explaining, one more time, why the environment should concern us all. And if environmental matters do roil you, stake your claim, as Robyn Martin does above, on a well-defined ecological problem, perhaps from within your community—that you might actually influence by the power of your rhetoric.

topic ◄

If you are hard-pressed to find a topic, consider talking with your instructor or a research librarian. Many libraries offer study guides covering various topics. Just browsing these general materials might steer you toward particular subjects you hadn't considered. Or ponder the courses you're taking. What issues have challenged your perspectives or engaged you to such a degree that you want to learn more about them and add your voice to the conversation?

State a preliminary claim, if only for yourself. Some arguments fail because writers never focus their thinking. They wander around broad topics, throwing out ideas or making contradictory assertions and leaving it to readers to assemble the random parts. To avoid this blunder, begin with a claim—a *complete* sentence that states a position you hope to defend. Such a statement will keep you on track as you explore a topic. Even a simple sentence helps:

> The college rankings published annually by *U.S. News & World Report* do more harm than good.

Qualify your claim to make it reasonable. As you learn more about a subject, revise your topic idea to reflect the complications you encounter. Your thesis will probably grow

Cultura Creative (RF) / Alamy Stock Photo.

Courtesy of Dr. Susan Farrell.

Arguments take many different forms, but finger-pointing is rarely a good persuasive tool.

longer or take several sentences to explain, but the topic itself will actually narrow because of the specific issues you've identified. You'll also have less work to do, thanks to qualifying expressions such as *some, most, a few, often, under certain conditions, occasionally, when necessary,* and so on. Other qualifying expressions are highlighted below.

> The **statistically unreliable** college ratings published by *U.S. News & World Report* **usually** do more harm than good to students **because** some claim that they lead admissions officers to award scholarships on the basis of merit rather than need.

Examine your core assumptions.
Claims may be supported by reasons and evidence, but they are based on assumptions. *Assumptions* are the principles and values upon which we build our beliefs and actions. Sometimes these assumptions are controversial and stand right out. At other times, they're so close to us, they seem invisible—they are part of the air we breathe. Expect to spend a paragraph defending any assumptions your readers might find questionable or controversial.

CLAIM:	The statistically unreliable college ratings published by *U.S. News & World Report* usually do more harm than good to students because some claim that they lead admissions officers to award scholarships on the basis of merit rather than need.
ASSUMPTION:	Alleviating need in our society is more important than rewarding merit. [Probably controversial]
CLAIM:	Western countries should favor open border policies because embracing people from different cultures will make societies more diverse.
ASSUMPTION:	Cultural diversity strengthens nations. [Possibly controversial for some audiences]
CLAIM:	Elections should again be decided by paper ballots because they cannot be as easily hacked or tampered with as voting machines.
ASSUMPTION:	Voters should be able to trust the security of their ballots. [Probably not controversial]

> **Writing about Writing**   Many writers have a tough time expressing their topic in a complete sentence. They will offer a tentative word or phrase or sentence fragment instead of making the commitment that a full sentence demands, especially one with subordinators and qualifiers that begin to tie their ideas together. So give it a try. Take a topic you might write about and turn it into a full-bore sentence that tells readers exactly what your claim is and how you intend to support it.

Imagining your audience

Retailers know audiences. In fact, they go to great lengths to pinpoint the groups most likely to buy their soft drinks or running shoes. They then tailor their brand images and Web advertising to precisely those customers. You'll play to audiences the same way when you write arguments—if maybe a little less cynically.

Understand that you won't ever please everyone in a general audience, even if you write bland, colorless mush—because some readers will then regard you as craven and spineless. In fact, how readers imagine you, *as the person presenting an argument*, may determine their willingness to consider your claims at all.

Consider and control your ethos. People who study persuasion describe the identity that writers create for themselves within an argument as their *ethos*—the voice and attitude they fashion to enhance their appeal. It is a powerful concept, worth remembering. Surely you notice when writers are coming across as, let's say, ingratiatingly confident or stupidly obnoxious. And don't you respond in kind, giving ear to the likable voice and dismissing the malicious one? A few audiences—like those for political blogs or tweets—may actually prefer a writer with a snarky ethos. But most readers at least claim to prefer writers who seem reasonable, knowledgeable, and fair—neither insulting those who disagree with them nor making those who share their views embarrassed to have them on their side.

You can shape your ethos by adjusting the style, tone, and vocabulary of your argument: For instance, contractions can make you seem friendly (or too casual); an impressive vocabulary suggests that you are smart (or maybe just pompous); lots of name-dropping makes you seem plugged-in (or perhaps pretentious). You may have to write several drafts to find a suitable ethos for a particular argument. And, yes, your ethos may change from paper to paper, audience to audience.

> **Thinking about Writing**   Chances are you have some favorite Web sites or blogs you consult daily. Choose one of those sites, find an entry in it that expresses the ethos of the contributor(s) or the site itself, and then analyze that ethos. Is the character of the site friendly and down-to-earth? Arrogant and authoritative? Serious and politically concerned? Point to specific features of the site that help create its ethos. If you don't consult blogs or Web sites, apply your analysis to a printed or oral text, perhaps an op-ed by a favorite columnist or a political speech by a public figure.

Need help supporting your argument? See "How to Use the Writing Center" on pp. 10–11.

Consider self-imposed limits.   If you read newspapers and follow social media sites that mostly confirm your own political and social views, you might be in for a wake-up call when you venture outside your circle of friends. Tread softly. There were good reasons why, in the past at least, people didn't talk politics at parties. When you do argue about social, political, or religious issues, give due consideration to those who operate from premises different from your own.

Consider the worlds of your readers.   When arguing about topics such as education, politics, art, economics, ethics, or even athletics, you'll quickly realize that people bring their entire lives into the discussion of such issues. Their views are shaped, in part, by their gender, race, ethnicity, sexual orientation, religion, and upbringing—and in ever-varying combinations. But don't assume that people in any group will all think the same way—or should.

People's lives are, for instance, defined in part by their economic situations and the assumptions that follow from privilege, poverty, or something in between. Think it would be cool to have an outdoor pool on campus or a convenient new parking garage? You may find other students less willing than you to absorb the impact such proposals might have on their tuition. And if you intend to complain about fat cats, ridicule soccer moms, or poke fun at rednecks, is it because you can't imagine people different from you among your readers?

Obviously, age matters too: You'd write differently for children than for their parents on almost any subject, changing your style, vocabulary, and allusions. But consider too that people of different ages really have lived different lives. It matters that each generation grows up with distinctive historical experiences, values, heroes, villains—even music. As a writer, you may have to factor such considerations into arguments you write.

Gathering materials

You could write a book from the materials you'll collect researching some arguments. Since opinion pieces often address current events and topics, start with deep general reading in your subject area, pushing well beyond social media. If you begin with a general Web search, be sure to look beyond just the first few items listed because that's what everyone else reads. You may do better to explore your subject via search tools such as *Academic Source Complete*, *LexisNexis Academic*, or other specialized databases if your library subscribes to them. Again, research librarians will gladly direct you to relevant resources.

As you gather materials, though, consider how much space you have to make your argument. Sometimes a claim has to fit within the confines of a letter to the editor, an op-ed column in a local paper, or a fifteen-minute PowerPoint talk. Aristotle, still one of the best theorists on persuasion, thought arguments *should* be brief, with speakers limiting examples to the *minimum* necessary to make a case—no extra points for piling on. So gather big, and then select only the best stuff for your argument.

List your reasons. You'll come up with reasons to support your claim almost as soon as you choose a subject. Write those down. Then start reading and continue to list new reasons as they arise, not being too fussy at this point. Be careful to paraphrase these ideas so that you don't inadvertently plagiarize your sources later.

Then, when your reading and research are complete, review your notes and try to group the arguments that support your position. You'll likely detect patterns and relationships among these claims: an unwieldy initial list of potential arguments may be trimmed to just three or four—which could become the key reasons supporting your claim. Study these points and look for logical connections or sequences. Readers will expect your ideas to converge on a single claim or lead logically toward it.

Assemble your hard evidence. Gather examples, illustrations, quotations, and numbers to support each main point. Record these items as you read in some reliable way, keeping track of all bibliographical information (author, title, publication info, URL) just as you would when preparing a term paper—even if you aren't required to document your argument. You want that data on hand in case your credibility is challenged later.

If you borrow facts from a Web site, do your best to trace the information to its actual source. For example, if a blogger quotes statistics from the U.S. Department of Agriculture, find that table or graph on the USDA Web site itself and make sure the numbers reported are accurate.

develop ◄
support

■■

The whole
is greater than
the sum of its
parts.

■■

Popperfoto/Getty Images.

—Aristotle

Cull the best quotations. Let's assume you've done your homework for an assignment, reading the most credible sources. Now prove it in your argument by quoting from them intelligently. Choose quotations that do one or more of the following:

- Put your issue in focus or context.
- Make a point with style or clarity.
- Support a claim or piece of evidence that readers might doubt.
- State an opposing point especially well.

Copy passages that appeal to you, but don't figure on using all of them. An argument that is a patchwork of quotations reads like a patchwork of quotations—which is to say, *boring.* Be sure to copy the quotations accurately and be certain you can document them.

Find counterarguments. If you study a subject thoroughly, you'll come across plenty of honest disagreement. List all reasonable objections you can find to your claim, either to your basic argument or to any controversial evidence you expect to cite. When possible, cluster these objections to reduce them to a manageable few. Decide which you must refute in detail, which you might handle briefly, and which you can afford to dismiss.

Watch, for example, how in an editorial, the *New York Times* anticipates objections to its defense of a *Rolling Stone* magazine cover (August 2013) featuring accused Boston Marathon bomber Dzhokhar Tsarnaev. The *Times* concedes that merchants and consumers alike might resist the cover, but then it counterpunches:

> Stores have a right to refuse to sell products because, say, they are unhealthy, like cigarettes. . . . Consumers have every right to avoid buying a magazine that offends them, like *Guns & Ammo* or *Rolling Stone.*
>
> But singling out one magazine issue for shunning is over the top, especially since the photo has already appeared in a lot of prominent places, including the front page of this newspaper, without an outcry. As any seasoned reader should know, magazine covers are not endorsements.
>
> —The Editorial Board, "Judging Rolling Stone by Its Cover," *New York Times*, July 18, 2013

Consider emotional appeals. Feelings play a powerful role in many arguments, a fact you cannot afford to ignore when a claim you make stirs people up. Questions to answer about possible emotional appeals include the following:

- What emotions might be effectively raised to support my point?

- How might I responsibly introduce such feelings: through words, images, color, sound?

- How might any feelings my subject arouses work contrary to my claims or reasons?

Well-chosen visuals add power to an argument. A writer trying to persuade readers not to buy fur might include this photo in an article. How would this image influence you, as a reader?

Jeff Foott/Getty Images.

Organizing ideas

▶ organize
ideas

It's easy to sketch a standard structure for arguments: one that leads from claim to supporting reasons to evidence and even accommodates a counterargument or two.

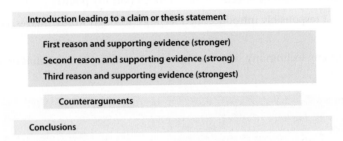

The problem is that you won't read many effective arguments, either in or out of school, that follow this template—which closely resembles the familiar five-paragraph essay.

The structure isn't defective, just too simple to describe the way arguments really move when ideas matter. You won't write a horrible paper if you use the traditional model because all the parts will be in place. Thesis? Check. Three supporting reasons? Check. Counterarguments? Check. But you will sound exactly like what you are: A writer going through the motions instead of engaging with ideas. Here's how to get your ideas to breathe in an argument—while still hitting all the marks.

Make a point or build toward one. Arguments can unfurl just as reports do, with unmistakable claims followed by reams of supporting evidence. But they can also work like crime dramas, in which the evidence in a case builds toward a compelling conclusion—your thesis perhaps. This is your call. But don't just jump into a claim: Take a few sentences or paragraphs to set up the situation. Quote a nasty bureaucrat or tell an eye-popping story or two. Get readers invested in what's to come.

Spell out what's at stake. When you write an argument, you open a controversy, so you'd better explain it clearly. Do you hope to fix a looming problem? Then describe your concern and make readers share it. Do you intend to correct a false notion or bad reporting? Then tell readers why setting the record straight matters. Appalled by the apathy of voters, the dangers of global warming, the infringements of free speech on campus? Explain exactly why readers should care.

Address counterpoints when necessary, not in a separate

section. *Necessary* is when your readers start thinking to themselves, "Yeah, but what about . . . ?" Such doubts will probably surface approximately where your own do—and, admit it, you have some misgivings about your argument. So take them on. Strategically, it rarely makes sense to consign all objections to a lengthy section near the end of a paper. That's asking for trouble. Do you really want to offer a case for the opposition just when your readers are finishing up? On the plus side, dealing with opposing arguments (or writing a refutation itself—see p. 107) can be like caffeine for your prose, sharpening your attention and reflexes.

Save your best arguments for the end. Of course, you want strong points
throughout the paper. But you need a high note early on to get readers interested and then another choral moment as you finish to send them out the door humming. If you must summarize an argument, don't let a dull recap of your main points squander an important opportunity to influence readers. End with a rhetorical flourish that reminds readers how compelling your ideas are.

A pithy phrase, an ironic twist, and a question to contemplate can also lock down your case. Here, for instance, is Ted Gup, a professor at Emerson College, using carefully balanced and parallel phrasing to conclude an essay defending the importance of free speech in the college classroom:

> . . . Nonfiction writing is not just about accuracy but honesty, not just about the grace notes of American life but its open sores as well. The control of language smothers any such undertaking.
>
> It is through speech—the expression of ideas and feelings, noble and ignoble—that we make progress as a culture, that we demonstrate our faith in each other and the body politic, and that we can promote the democratic and artistic principles that we cherish. The only words more powerful than those expressed are those that are repressed.
>
> So say what you will, and welcome to class.
>
> —"A Different Kind of Safe Space," *Chronicle of Higher Education*, August 30, 2016

Choosing style and design

Arguments vary widely in style. An unsigned editorial you write to represent the opinion of a student newspaper might sound formal and serious. Composing an op-ed under your own name, you'd probably ease up on the dramatic metaphors and allow yourself more personal pronouns. Arguing a point in an alternative magazine, you might even slip into the lingo of its vegan or survivalist subscribers. Routine adjustments like these really matter when you need to attract and hold readers.

You should also write with sensitivity since some people reading arguments may well be wavering, defensive, or eager to be offended. There's no reason to distract them with fighting words if you want to offer a serious argument. Recent examples of politically charged or provocative language by public officials and news media are too numerous to mention—and rarely add much to discussions or serious arguments.

Fortunately, there are many powerful ways to advance ideas without resorting to offensive language or fallacies of argument. Some of these strategies follow.

Invite readers with a strong opening. Arguments—like advertisements— are usually discretionary reading. People can turn away the moment they grow irritated or bored. So you may need to open with a little surprise or drama. Try a blunt statement, an anecdote, or a striking example if it helps—maybe an image too. Or consider personalizing the lead-in, giving readers a stake in the claim you are about to make. The following is a remarkable opening paragraph from an argument by Malcolm Gladwell on the wisdom of banning dogs by breed. When you finish, ask yourself whether Gladwell has earned your attention. Would you read the rest of the piece?

> One afternoon last February, Guy Clairoux picked up his two-and-a-half-year-old son, Jayden, from day care and walked him back to their house in the west end of Ottawa, Ontario. They were almost home. Jayden was straggling behind, and, as his father's back was turned, a pit bull jumped over a backyard fence and lunged at Jayden. "The dog had his head in its mouth and started to do this shake," Clairoux's wife, JoAnn Hartley, said later. As she watched in horror, two more pit bulls jumped over the fence, joining in the assault. She and Clairoux came running, and he punched the first of the dogs in the head, until it dropped Jayden, and then he threw the boy toward his mother. Hartley fell on her son, protecting him with her body. "JoAnn!" Clairoux cried out, as all three dogs descended on his wife. "Cover your neck, cover your neck." A neighbor, sitting by her window, screamed for help. Her partner and a friend, Mario Gauthier, ran outside. A neighborhood boy grabbed his hockey stick and threw it to Gauthier. He began hitting one of the dogs over the head, until the stick broke.

"They wouldn't stop," Gauthier said. "As soon as you'd stop, they'd attack again. I've never seen a dog go so crazy. They were like Tasmanian devils." The police came. The dogs were pulled away, and the Clairouxes and one of the rescuers were taken to the hospital. Five days later, the Ontario legislature banned the ownership of pit bulls. "Just as we wouldn't let a great white shark in a swimming pool," the province's attorney general, Michael Bryant, had said, "maybe we shouldn't have these animals on the civilized streets."

—"Troublemakers," *New Yorker*, February 6, 2006

Write vibrant sentences. You can write arguments full throttle, using a complete range of rhetorical devices, from deliberate repetition and parallelism to dialogue and quotation. Metaphors, similes, and analogies fit right in too. The trick is to create sentences rich enough to keep readers hooked, yet lean enough to advance an argument. In the following slightly edited paragraph, student Soup Martinez uses a string of parallel examples to argue that young people today have too little incentive to take risks or follow dreams:

There's also less and less incentive to chase dreams than there once was. It's not worth risking failure in attempting to become great at anything because becoming good at *almost* anything is so accessible. No longer do I have to spend money on the latest camera and photo editing software when I can just snap a shot on my phone and download a free app. No longer do I need to live out in the woods because I can just pitch a tent at a premade campsite and get all my necessities from a convenience store down the road. No longer do I need access to a great music producer to make music because I can just record in my own bedroom. No longer do I need to be a great artist because everything is cool. No longer does anything I create and share with the world have to be original or witty because my Facebook friends and Instagram followers will just blindly like it in hopes I'll return the favor on their next post. There's no more point in standing out because *everyone* is special. By making "good enough" such an accessible choice, we are killing dreams before they even begin.

—"Dreamer's Disease," November 14, 2016

Ask rhetorical questions. The danger of rhetorical questions is that they can seem stagy and readers might not answer them the way you want. But the device can be very powerful in hammering a point home. Good questions also invite readers to think about an issue in exactly the terms that a writer prefers. Here, for example, are John Heubusch and former attorney general Ed Meese using a string of rhetorical questions to refute a central claim of Bill O'Reilly and Martin Dugard's book

Killing Reagan—that the forty-fourth president was seriously incapacitated after an assassination attempt:

> Is there any new evidence cited by O'Reilly of continued or abusive use of pain medications that could affect one's judgment post-surgery? None. Is there evidence cited in the health records of Reagan's annual physicals or workups related to his various surgeries (prostate, precancerous lesions, etc.) showing deterioration in the president's health longer-term due to his wounds? None. The Reagan Library archives contain over 66 million documents. His records have been reviewed by reputable doctors, and no such evidence has come to light. What then is the basis for O'Reilly's statements that President Reagan suffered long-term physical problems associated with the assassination?
>
> — "O'Reilly's *Killing Reagan*: Fiction, Posing as Biography," *Real Clear Politics*, October 21, 2015

Use images and design to make a point. If we didn't know it already (and we did), recent images of political and social upheaval from around the world, from photographs of terrorist attacks to video from political campaigns, clearly demonstrate that persuasion doesn't occur by words only. We react powerfully to what we see with our own eyes. Consider this Reuters image of American presidential candidates Donald Trump and Hillary Clinton at an October 9, 2016, town hall debate in St. Louis.

The image alone is striking and memorable. And yet it calls out for a caption to become a *focused* argument—as pundits and social media routinely demonstrate when they put a spin on news photographs or video. And because digital technology now makes it so easy to incorporate nonverbal media into texts, whether on a page, screen, or Prezi whiteboard, you should always consider how just the right image might enhance the case you want to make.

RICK WILKING/REUTERS/Newscom.

Examining models

REFUTATION ARGUMENT   An important subgenre of arguments is the refutation, a piece that critiques someone else's claims and sometimes seeks to correct them. In the following example of this important and challenging form, Ryan Young uses careful reasoning and ample documentation to argue that claims for the inevitability of autonomous cars and driving might be exaggerated. Needless to say, a refutation is, itself, an argument that deserves careful scrutiny.

Reading the Genre   A columnist for a campus newspaper and a computer science major, Ryan Young wrote "Self-Driving Cars: A Reality Check" for an upper-division rhetoric and writing course. As you read his arguments, which aspects of its organization, content, style, and use of sources mark it as an academic rather than a journalistic piece?

Young

Ryan Young

Professor Coel

27 April 2017

Self-Driving Cars: A Reality Check

Today, the media is awash with buzz about the inevitable arrival of autonomous automobiles, personal vehicles that could transport passengers under complete computer control. Writing for *Forbes*, David Galland predicts that ten million autonomous cars will be on American streets by 2020 (Galland). He expects the adoption of autonomous cars to have profound, transformative effects on our society, by "reducing the number of traffic accidents by upward of 90%," offering new mobility options for seniors and people with disabilities, eliminating the need for expensive and scarce downtown parking, and "[banishing] the whole idea of rush hour . . . to the history

Young 2

books" (Galland). Ford plans to sell "true self-driving cars" without controls for human drivers, such as pedals or steering wheels, by 2021 (Isidore). Not to be left behind, U.S. Senators Gary Peters and John Thune have announced they plan to introduce new legislation to foster the development of autonomous vehicles that will "[leave] room for innovators to reach their full potential" ("Joint Effort"). They believe that autonomous cars "have the potential to dramatically reduce the . . . lives lost on our roads and highways every year and fundamentally transform the way we get around" ("Joint Effort").

But before we speculate on the long-term impacts of autonomous cars, and especially before we formulate sweeping national policies concerning them, we ought to consider just how soon they will become reality. There are difficult ethical, technical, and human interface challenges that the industry has not yet addressed and hard questions that our society has not yet answered. Should autonomous vehicles favor the survival of passengers or pedestrians in the event of an accident? How will we produce and maintain high-resolution maps of every road on which autonomous vehicles will be expected to operate? How will we keep passengers alert and prepared to retake control in the event of an emergency? We are not five years away from autonomous cars, as Ford claims, much less six months away

Opening paragraph reviews claims for self-driving cars.

Young offers a clear thesis: Self-driving cars are not just around the corner, as proponents claim.

Young 3

from "full self-driving" Tesla vehicles, as CEO Elon Musk boasts (@elonmusk). The barriers to designing safe and reliable autonomous cars are so massive that they will preclude their mainstream introduction for many decades, if not indefinitely.

SAE International, an automobile standards organization, has developed a widely used scale that categorizes vehicles by their level of automation. Level 1 and 2 vehicles are capable of limited control of steering, acceleration, or both under the constant supervision of human drivers, as is the case in some of today's luxury cars. "Conditional automation" in level 3 vehicles can perform all driving tasks, including steering, accelerating, changing lanes, and making turns, but must request intervention by human drivers in exceptional situations. "High automation" in level 4 vehicles can perform these tasks in most situations without falling back on human intervention. "Full automation" in level 5 vehicles includes the ability to navigate anywhere, anytime, throughout all phases of a trip. This represents the pinnacle of autonomy ("Automated Driving").

Clearly, achieving level 4 automation or better is necessary to bring about the happily autonomous world that Galland envisions, in which seniors catch self-driving rides across town and travelers are "delivered to their destination in comfort by a self-driving Uber and wave goodbye to the car as it drives off" (Galland). It's also a perquisite for Ford's cars of the future if

Young 4

they will indeed lack steering wheels and brake pedals. But while much effort has been expended to make level 4 and 5 autonomous vehicles technically feasible, the ethical implications of such systems have received little consideration. A study led by Thierry Fraichard, a research scientist in robotics, suggests that autonomous vehicles, no matter how sophisticated, could never prevent all possible collisions. "It appears that absolute motion safety (in the sense that no collision will ever take place whatever happens in the environment) is impossible to guarantee in the real world," he explains. "Today, most autonomous vehicles relies [sic] upon probabilistic modeling and reasoning to drive themselves. Probabilities are ideal to handle uncertainty but they will never allow strict motion safety guarantees" (11). In other words, it is impossible to know the future with absolute certainty. The computer programs that will drive autonomous vehicles may be more precise and perceive events faster than humans, but they must still contend with the physics and unpredictability of the real world, which no mathematical or computational model can forecast.

After explaining the levels of autonomous driving, Young cites a writer who raises questions about the likelihood of reaching the advanced stages.

Given that fully autonomous vehicles will eventually hit something, questions arise over how they should seek to minimize damages, injuries, and loss of life. It is easy to imagine unfortunate situations, such as total loss of control or an imminent crash, in which tragedy is unavoidable—but

Young 5

computer algorithms, not humans with free wills, will be making the life-changing decisions. In "Why Ethics Matters for Autonomous Cars," Patrick Lin, a California Polytechnic State University philosophy professor, presents a variety of frightening scenarios in which autonomous vehicles may be forced to pick and choose victims and survivors. For example, if an autonomous car were on course to strike either a young girl or an old grandmother, the girl's "entire life in front of her—a first love, a family of her own, a career, and other adventures and happiness" would be weighed against the grandmother's "right to life and as valuable a life as the little girl's" (Lin 70). Or an autonomous car might make use of "crash-optimization strategies" by targeting lighter vehicles or vehicles with better safety reputations in the event of a collision (72). Is it right to choose the grandmother over the girl (or vice versa) or to systematically punish bicyclists and SUV riders? How autonomous cars should act in such situations is a question of ethics and what we value, not smarter code or sharper sensors. As Lin aptly notes, "If ethics is ignored and the robotic car behaves badly, a powerful case could be made that auto manufacturers were negligent . . . and that opens them up to tremendous legal liability" (82). Until our society resolves these thorny ethical dilemmas and clarifies how it expects autonomous cars to behave, level 4 or 5 autonomous cars will not be suitable for general use.

Young argues that complex moral and legal issues may delay the debut of truly self-driving vehicles.

Young 6

These scenarios will seem abstract until level 4 or 5 vehicles become reality. Recent years have born witness to much high-profile progress and media hype about the development of autonomous cars, but such reports routinely overstate and grossly exaggerate the state of the art. In reality, the industry has a dirty little secret: Autonomous cars will not be able to travel everywhere, on every road. We hear constantly about advances in sensor and camera technology that promise a breakthrough in autonomous vehicle technology; for example, Tesla recently announced that all of its electric cars in production have the 360-degree cameras and ultrasonic sensors necessary for "full self-driving capability" ("All Tesla Cars"). But the hardware on the car is only one side of the equation.

Autonomous cars also require immensely detailed three-dimensional scans of the roads and environments in which they operate (Boudette). These digital maps include the locations of every road sign, building, and traffic signal along the way, because current technology is not sophisticated enough to recognize every road feature on the fly. In principle, they're similar to digital collections of street imagery, such as Google Street View, except much more complicated and intricate. To produce its maps, Google uses specialized laser scanning equipment that costs upwards of $100,000 per outfitted vehicle (Boudette). Even then, human classifiers must pore over all the

Young 7

data, tagging signs and features by hand in a time-consuming and laborious process (Boudette).

The autonomous vehicle industry admits that such maps will be indispensable for the foreseeable future. "If we want to have autonomous cars everywhere, we have to have digital maps everywhere," says Amnon Shashua, chief technology officer at Mobileye (Boudette). But every moment, accidents damage infrastructure, construction disrupts traffic, and bad weather renders roads dangerous or impassable. If we're going to have the autonomous cars, we face the daunting challenge of creating these maps for every road and keeping them up to date. This may be manageable in large urban areas where autonomous cars will be common, but may be cost-prohibitive for small towns and rural byways. Eventually, we could have level 4 and 5 autonomous cars, but we might not be able to ride them everywhere.

So truly autonomous vehicles present significant ethical problems that remain unsolved and their need for detailed road maps may confine their use to select locations. But what about level 3 automation, in which computers drive vehicles most of the time, but human drivers intervene in exceptional situations? Although it may seem easier to design a level 3 autonomous car, level 3 vehicles would face the serious problem of maintaining the attention of human supervisors. "A car with any level of

Tone of the essay to this point is analytical and unemotional.

Young 8

autonomy that relies upon a human to save the day in an emergency poses almost insurmountable engineering, design, and safety challenges, simply because humans are for the most part horrible backups," writes Alex Davies, a transportation reporter for *Wired*. "They are inattentive, easily distracted, and slow to respond" (Davies). Ford faces this exact problem testing its experimental autonomous cars. Ford engineers, despite specialized training, cannot help but fall asleep and lose focus while monitoring the cars, even when partners are introduced to watch the watchmen (Naughton). Moreover, it's simply not reasonable to ask a human passenger who has been relaxing in an autonomous car for hours to be prepared to retake control at a moment's notice. As a result, Google, Uber, Ford, and other key players in the autonomous vehicle industry have effectively given up on practical level 3 automation (Davies). Autonomous cars will not gradually evolve from level 2 to level 3 to levels 4 and 5; we'll have limited driver assistance one day, then full automation the next. Making that transition will be challenging, to say the least, given the ethical and technical issues inherent to fully autonomous vehicles. It will be an all or nothing proposition.

Autonomous cars *are* coming. But as citizens and lawmakers, we should be skeptical about the grandiose claims made by the autonomous vehicle industry that have "gotten totally out of sync with reality," according to University of

Young uses direct quotations frequently to bolster his case—a strategy expected in academic arguments.

Young 9

California autonomous driving researcher Steven Shladover (Simonite). By 2021, we might be able to ride a level 4 Ford autonomous car, but it will be a "low-speed taxi service limited to certain roads" that Shladover says we should "[not] expect . . . to come in the rain" (Simonite). Galland's self-driving utopia, in which mobility is painless and traffic congestion is nonexistent, will remain a fantasy for some time. But the grand delusion that the arrival of autonomous cars is imminent is not just a harmless misconception; it's having very real consequences for public policy. Senators Peters and Thune are pursuing the deregulation of the autonomous vehicle industry under the guise that the "slow pace of regulation could become a significant obstacle to the development of new and safer vehicle technology" ("Joint Effort"). Transportation commentators like Randal O'Toole argue that investments in public transit "are likely to soon be obsolete" because "self-driving cars will dominate the roads sooner than most people think" (O'Toole). Planning for a future filled with white elephants is foolish.

Conclusion grows more aggressive, even in vocabulary: *white elephants, foolish, gamble, wreak havoc.*

If we gamble it all on the advent of autonomous vehicles, allowing the industry to wreak havoc on our roads and communities and neglecting pressing transportation investments, we will be much like the passengers of Ford's autonomous cars of 2021: going nowhere fast and left out in the rain.

Young 10

Works Cited

"All Tesla Cars Being Produced Now Have Full Self-Driving
    Hardware." *Tesla*, 19 Oct. 2016, www.tesla.com/blog/
    all-tesla-cars-being-produced-now-have-full-self-driving
    -hardware. Accessed 8 Mar. 2017.

"Automated Driving: Levels of Driving Automation Are
    Defined in New SAE International Standard J3016." *SAE
    International*, 2014, www.sae.org/misc/pdfs/automated
    _driving.pdf. Accessed 28 Feb. 2017.

Boudette, Neal. "Building a Road Map for the Self-Driving
    Car." *New York Times*, 2 Mar. 2017, www.nytimes
    .com/2017/03/02/automobiles/wheels/self-driving-cars
    -gps-maps.html. Accessed 7 Mar. 2017.

Davies, Alex. "The Very Human Problem Blocking the Path to
    Self-Driving Cars." *Wired*, 1 Jan. 2017, www.wired
    .com/2017/01/human-problem-blocking-path-self-driving
    -cars. Accessed 9 Mar. 2017.

@elonmusk. "@tsrandall 3 months maybe, 6 months definitely."
    Twitter, 23 Jan. 2017, 7:00 p.m., twitter.com/
    elonmusk/status/823727035088416768.

Fraichard, Thierry. "Will the Driver Seat Ever Be Empty?"
    *Institut National de Recherche en Informatique et en
    Automatique*, research report RR-8493, 2014, hal.inria.fr/
    hal-00965176v2/document. Accessed 28 Feb. 2017.

Young 11

Galland, David. "10 Million Self-Driving Cars Will Hit
    The Road By 2020—Here's How To Profit." *Forbes*,
    3 Mar. 2017, www.forbes.com/sites/oliviergarret/
    2017/03/03/10-million-self-driving-cars-will-hit
    -the-road-by-2020-heres-how-to-profit. Accessed 7
    Mar. 2017.

Gomes, Lee. "Hidden Obstacles for Google's Self-Driving
    Cars." *MIT Technology Review*, 28 Aug. 2014,
    www.technologyreview.com/s/530276/hidden
    -obstacles-for-googles-self-driving-cars. Accessed 28
    Feb. 2017.

Isidore, Chris. "True self-driving cars will arrive in 5 years,
    says Ford." *CNN*, 16 Aug. 2016, money.cnn
    .com/2016/08/16/technology/ford-self-driving-cars
    -five-years. Accessed 7 Mar. 2017.

Lin, Patrick. "Why Ethics Matters for Autonomous Cars."
    Autonomes Fahren, edited by Markus Maurer, et al.,
    Springer, 2015, pp. 69–85.

Naughton, Keith. "Ford's Dozing Engineers Side With
    Google in Full Autonomy Push." *Bloomberg*, 17 Feb.
    2017, www.bloomberg.com/news/articles/2017-02-17/
    ford-s-dozing-engineers-side-with-google-in-full
    -autonomy-push. Accessed 28 Feb. 2017.

Young 12

O'Toole, Randal. "Transit Is Dead. Let's Prepare for the Next
    Mobility Revolution." *Washington Post*, 1 Mar. 2016,
    www.washingtonpost.com/news/in-theory/
    wp/2016/03/01/transit-is-dead-lets-prepare-for-the-next
    -mobility-revolution. Accessed 27 Apr. 2017.

"Sens. Peters and Thune Announce Joint Effort on Self-
    Driving Vehicles." *Gary Peters: United States Senator for
    Michigan*, 13 Feb. 2017, www.peters.senate.gov/
    newsroom/press-releases/sens-peters-and-thune
    -announce-joint-effort-on-self-driving-vehicles. Accessed
    7 Mar. 2017.

Simonite, Tom. "Prepare to be Underwhelmed by 2021's
    Autonomous Cars." *MIT Technology Review*, 23 Aug.
    2016, www.technologyreview.com/s/602210/prepare-to
    -be-underwhelmed-by-2021s-autonomous-cars. Accessed
    28 Feb. 2017.

1. **Argument to Advance a Thesis:** Review the various ways Robyn Martin supports her low-key and very specific thesis in "Stop the Rock-stacking" (p. 92). Then write an argument that similarly provides support for a claim or issue that readers might not have considered deeply before or regarded as consequential. Like Martin, be sure to take time to explain the issue you are addressing and then defend your thesis with ample evidence.

2. **Refutation Argument:** Find an argument or a specific text with which you strongly disagree and then systematically refute it, as Ryan Young does in "Self-Driving Cars: A Reality Check" (p. 107). The text can be a position or policy promoted by politicians or public or corporate officials, or it can be an argument in itself—a column, an editorial, or even a section in a textbook. Make your opposition clear, but also be fair to the position you are attempting to refute. It is especially important that your readers be able to understand whatever you are analyzing, even if they aren't familiar with it. That's a real challenge, so don't hesitate to summarize, paraphrase, or quote from the material, as Young does routinely.

3. **Your Choice:** These days, most serious arguments explode across interactive online environments, where they often take on a life of their own. Working with a group, design a media project (blog, Web site, mash-up, video, etc.) to focus on an issue that members of your group believe deserves more attention. Pool your talents to develop the site technically, rhetorically, and visually. Be sure your project introduces the subject, explains its purpose, encourages interaction, and includes relevant images and, if possible, links.

How to start ▶
- Need a **topic**? See page 126.
- Need **criteria for your evaluation**? See page 127.
- Need to **organize your criteria and evidence**? See page 130.

11

make a claim about the merit of something

Evaluations

Evaluations and reviews are so much a part of our lives that you might wonder whether people even need to learn how to write them. Commentary and criticism of all sorts just happen.

CRITICAL ASSESSMENT
You just can't believe that football fans have forgotten the glory days of the Cleveland Browns. You decide to remind them of how formidable the team once was.

PRODUCT REVIEW
Your bike was stolen and now you need another. You consult several cycling magazines to find which low-cost street bike will get you to work dependably without attracting attention.

ARTS REVIEW
Surprised by the latest blockbuster in the Marvel Cinematic Universe franchise, you draft a full-length critique of the film for the campus arts magazine rather than just your usual few lines for IMDb.

SOCIAL SATIRE/ VISUAL ARGUMENT
Tired of self-righteous cyclists who preach eco-fundamentalism and then clog traffic monthly with Critical Mass rides, you do what any irate citizen would—you mock them in a social satire.

Defining the genre

It's one thing to offer opinions about movies, athletes, consumer products, or even people—and another matter entirely to back up such evaluative claims with good reasons and compelling evidence. Only when you do will readers (or listeners) take you seriously. But you may have to convince them first that you know *how* to evaluate items as different as, let's say, a book, a social policy, a cultural trend, or even a bar of chocolate by reasonable criteria. It helps when you can use objective standards to make judgments, counting or measuring varying degrees of excellence. But perhaps more often, evaluations involve people debating matters of opinion and taste—an activity that requires perception, good sense, and wit. Here's how to frame this kind of argument (for more on choosing a genre, see Chapter 2).

Explain your mission. Just what do you intend to evaluate and for whom? Maybe you'll assess or rank particular products, productions, or performances or raise questions about the wisdom of policies or actions of governments, businesses, or bureaucracies. Or maybe you want to turn social critic, making people aware of their failures or foibles. Or perhaps you see yourself as a sports pundit or fashion guru, addressing fellow enthusiasts. You need to share your opinions, intentions, and credentials with readers.

Every four years at the Summer Olympics, judges decide who gets a medal in gymnastics.

AP Photo/Gregory Bull

Establish and defend criteria.

Criteria are the standards by which objects are measured: *Successful presidents leave office with the country in better shape than when they entered. A good smart home platform like Amazon Alexa or Apple Homekit requires superb voice recognition and seamless integration of its components.* When readers are likely to accept your criteria, you don't need to explain much about them. But when readers might object, prepare to defend your principles. ○ And sometimes you'll break new ground—as happened when critics first asked, *What is good Web design?* or *Which are the most politically influential social networks?* In such cases, criteria of evaluation had to be invented, explained, and defended.

Offer convincing evidence.

Evidence makes the connection between an opinion and the criteria of evaluation that support it. It comes in many forms: facts, statistics, testimony, photographs, and even good sense and keen observations. Proving that a president left the country in better shape than when he or she took office would take reams of data, backed by lots of savvy interpretation. (And you still might not be able to persuade skeptical readers.)

Offer worthwhile advice.

Some evaluations are just for fun: Consider all the hoopla that arguments about sports rankings or accomplishments generate—an example of which follows below. But done right, most evaluations and reviews provide usable information, beneficial criticism, or even ranked choices—just think how often you consult restaurant or entertainment reviews on Yelp or other sites.

develop ideas p. 387

Assessment

On any given day, perhaps only politics provokes more heated arguments than sports. Megan McArdle stepped right into it in defending former tennis champion John McEnroe's assessment of Serena Williams as maybe not the best tennis player in the world. What makes McArdle's piece worth reading is that her piece is as much about how evaluations work as about the accuracy of McEnroe's opinion. McArdle writes for Bloomberg View and has published in the *Atlantic* and the *Economist*.

Reading the Genre Notice how important it is for McArdle to explain her criteria of evaluation in this essay: "The best tennis player is the person who can most regularly defeat the other players under those rules." If you are not familiar with Serena Williams, go online to review her career accomplishments. Then consider whether a counterargument might be offered to McArdle's criterion.

Serena Williams Is Not the Best Tennis Player

MEGAN MCARDLE

June 29, 2017

Who's the best tennis player in the world? I couldn't say. However, I'm pretty sure of one thing: It's not Serena Williams.

John McEnroe has gotten himself in big trouble for saying pretty much exactly the same thing. In an interview with NPR, McEnroe was asked why he called Williams the best female tennis player, rather than simply the best tennis player. McEnroe seemed confused by the question and finally replied "Well, because if she was in, if she played the men's circuit she'd be like 700 in the world."

Cue the outrage. How dare he! How dare he?

I'm going to go out on a limb here and suggest that he dared to say it because it's true.

This is not to take anything away from Williams, whose athleticism stuns me into a near-faint. But even McEnroe's detractors have had to grudgingly acknowledge that if Williams were playing with the men, at best, her superb

> McArdle makes it clear from the outset that she more than agrees with McEnroe's assessment of Williams.

athleticism and mental strength might occasionally earn her a win. That's a pretty strange definition of "best tennis player in the world."

"Best" is a relative value, of course, not an absolute; Tyrannosaurus rex was one of the best in its field, 65 million years ago, but when conditions changed, poor T. rex went from industry leader to the ash heap of history. When we say that someone or something is "the best," we always have to acknowledge that this judgment is highly dependent on the criteria we're using to define excellence.

This is approximately the argument many of McEnroe's critics seem to be making. Unable to refute his core point—that Serena Williams could not be a world champion if she were regularly competing against men—instead they're asking why he would make that the standard for judging whether she's the world's best tennis player.

This leaves me just as confused as McEnroe was when the NPR interviewer asked him essentially the same question. Tennis, after all, is a court, a moderate amount of equipment, and some highly detailed rules for determining who wins. The best tennis player is the person who can most regularly defeat the other players under those rules. Unless some sort of terrible plague wipes out hundreds of top men's tennis players, that person will never be Serena Williams.

I mean, we can wax lyrical about style or mental strength or any other of the nebulous joys of watching sports . . . but at the end of the day, no one ever says "Well, sure, the Yankees may have gotten more runs, but did you see how graceful the Red Sox looked while they were striking out? Such poise! Such panache!" The team that wins a baseball game is the team that gets more runs, whether they lumber across home plate or dance there on angel's wings, because that's what's written in the detailed criteria that govern the sport. If we want different criteria to judge by, then we're no longer talking about who's "the best" at this sport, but about something else, like which team makes best use of its assets. And, of course, people do think about athletes and teams in this way. Consider the Oakland A's, which through the genius of "Moneyball" in the early 2000s came to be considered a great team. But no one therefore proclaimed that really, they had actually won the World Series.

Serena Williams is fantastically talented, and I am in awe of the amount of discipline and sheer labor it must take to get as far as she has. I can see why people are reluctant to refuse her the honor of "best in the world," simply

Judgments often hinge on how evaluative terms like *best* are defined or understood.

McArdle offers her definition of "best tennis player" and then defends it with examples.

The essay includes repeated acknowledgments of Serena Williams's accomplishments.

because biology did not endow her with the same physical potential with which it endowed many males. Most males also were not endowed with the potential to win Grand Slams in men's tennis. But we don't go scouring the lower ranks of amateur tennis circuits seeking out the player who works hardest or plays smartest. We look for a combination of potential and realized potential. We look for that by seeing who can defeat the most other players.

There are, of course, a few sports where men and women compete on par, like equestrian events, where the strength required comes primarily from the horse, not the rider. (Equestrianism is also, it's worth noting, one of the few sports at which older people can continue to compete at top levels.) There are also sports where you really can't compare male and female performances, notably gymnastics, where they compete in distinct events that cater to the relative strengths of the male and female bodies. But where men and women are playing by the same rules, in most cases, the women are doomed to second place. That is, after all, why we have had to set up special women's leagues so that some of them can win.

None of this denigrates women's athletics or the broader feminist project of getting women the opportunities to compete in every field of endeavor. And feminists are right that unequal outcomes are often evidence of lingering discrimination, not proof that women don't have what it takes. So it's understandable that they tend to bridle when they hear language like that.

Anticipating counterarguments, McArdle acknowledges the impact of discrimination against women.

But demanding equal opportunity—and demanding that people take residual discrimination seriously—does not require us to go to the absurd lengths of declaring that there are no important differences at all between men and women. Men are, in general, simply better athletically endowed than women. And while there are outliers within their respective distributions, the male outliers are going to best the female outliers in most physical fields of endeavor. This is not fair, but unfortunately, nature doesn't care about fair.

We should all applaud Serena Williams for becoming the world's best female tennis player. That's a stunning achievement—a testament to her physical gifts and how hard she has worked to develop as a player. Williams has earned her titles, her money, and her fame, and she deserves to bask in all of it. It is a compliment, and a true statement, to call her the best female tennis player. We won't add anything to her achievement by subtracting "female" and turning the true accolade into false flattery.

Claiming a topic

▶ topic

Most evaluations you're required to prepare for school or work come with assigned topics. But here are strategies to follow when you have a choice. **O**

Evaluate a subject you know well. This is the safest option, built on the assumption that everyone is an expert on something. Years of reading *Cook's Illustrated* magazine or playing video games might make it natural for you to review restaurants or a new gaming platform. You've accumulated not only basic facts but also lots of hands-on knowledge—the sort that gives you the confidence to offer an opinion. So go ahead and demonstrate your expertise.

Evaluate a subject you need to investigate. Perhaps you are applying to law schools, looking for family-friendly companies to work for, or thinking about purchasing a reliable used car. To make such choices, you'll need information. So kill two birds with a single assignment: Use the school project to explore personal or professional choices you face, find the necessary facts and data, and make a case for (or against) Arizona State, Whole Foods, or Honda.

Evaluate a subject you'd like to know more about. How do coffee connoisseurs tell one brew from another and rank them so confidently? Why do some apprenticeships or job-training programs turn out more successful job-seekers than others? How would a college football championship team from the 1950s match up against more recent winning teams? Use an assignment to settle questions like these that you and your friends may have debated late into the evening.

Evaluate a subject that's been on your mind. Not all evaluations are driven by decisions of the moment. Instead, you may want to make a point about social, cultural, or political matters: You believe, for instance, that a particular piece of student loan or immigration legislation is bad policy or find yourself disturbed by specific trends in society. An evaluation is often the appropriate genre for giving voice to such thoughts, whether you compose a conventional piece or venture into the realms of satire or parody.

Imagining your audience

Your job as a reviewer is easier when readers care about your opinions. Fortunately, most people consult evaluations and reviews routinely, often hoping to find specific information: *Is the latest Stephen L. Carter novel up to snuff? Who's the most important American architect working today? Red Sox or Yankees in the American League*

find a topic p. 120

East this year? But you'll still have to make accommodations for differing audiences.

Write for experts. Knowledgeable readers can be a tough group because they may bring strong, maybe inflexible, opinions to a topic. But if you know your stuff, you can take on the experts precisely because they know their stuff too. For such readers, you may not need to rehash basic background information or explain criteria of evaluation in detail. You can also use technical vocabulary and make quick allusions to people and concepts experts will recognize. **O** But be sure to get your details right because knowledgeable readers pay attention to them.

Write for a general audience. General audiences need more hand-holding than specialists. You may have to spell out the criteria of evaluation, provide some background information, and define key terms. But general readers usually are willing to learn more about a topic. And they certainly won't mind if your prose is crisp and entertaining.

Write for novices. You have a lot of explaining to do when readers are absolutely fresh to a subject. Prepare to give them context and background information. Define important words and concepts and

John J. Ruszkiewicz

Are buffalo dangerous? For some audiences, you have to explain everything.

prepare to explain the criteria of evaluation in detail. Simple charts and graphs will be appreciated too. Smart reviewers anticipate the needs of their audiences.

Gathering materials

When you are assigned a review, investigate your subject thoroughly. Online research is easy: To figure out what others are thinking, just type the name of whatever you are evaluating into a browser, followed by the word *review* or *critique* or *assessment* **O**. Read what you find carefully, giving especially close attention to reviews from reputable

improve your sentences
p. 375　　refine your search p. 436

▶ develop
criteria

sources. But don't just repeat the opinions you turn up. Feel free to challenge prevailing views whenever you can make a better argument or offer a fresh perspective. To do that, focus on criteria and evidence.

Decide on your criteria. Make readers understand why your subject matters and then clarify your criteria, even if your topic is pie. Here's Megan McArdle (again) on that subject, waxing enthusiastic about her subject.

> Properly made, pie is delicious. Fruit pie is especially delicious, because it has fruit in it. A thin layer of light, flaky crust, stretched across tender fruit that is softly melding with its own sugar-laced juices . . . ah, paradise.

But she gets down to business, explaining exactly *why* the pie you pick up at a bakery or grocery store is likely going to be bad.

> Good pie crust seems to be too labor-intensive to make on a commercial scale; it requires skilled hand-work, and you can't get enough money for a pie to make that worthwhile. Too, commercial bakeries have to worry more about consistent appearance than home bakers. To keep the filling from being too runny, they often load it up with thickeners like cornstarch or tapioca flour, which gives it a beautiful, shiny appearance and, also, a mouthfeel like an oil slick. Then they cover it with a very thick layer of crust that looks gorgeous in the display case, but either crumbles in your mouth like shortbread, or requires fierce chewing, like a sort of flour jerky.

All of her explanation—the *why* of this review—is important: You really don't have criteria until you share them with readers who may not be familiar with your subject. **O** The rationale should be clear even if you state them negatively, as McArdle does: *Great fruit pie shouldn't have fillings thickened with starch and flour; the texture of the crust shouldn't be thick or crumbly.*

Look for hard criteria. You'll seem objective when your criteria at least seem grounded in numbers or corroborated observations. Think, for example, of how instructors set measurable standards for your performance in their courses, translating all sorts of activities, from papers to class participation, into numbers. Teachers aren't alone in deferring to numbers. Reviews, for instance, relies heavily on precise measurements in evaluating televisions and explains those criteria in excruciating detail on its Web site. The following is how CNET assesses just one aspect of an HDTV's performance:

> **Black luminance (0%)** *Example result: 0.0140*
> . . . The measurement is taken of a completely black screen (except for a 5% stripe on or near the bottom), created by using the Quantum Data's 0% window pattern.

develop a statement p. 333

Good: +/− less than 0.009
Average: +/− 0.009 to 0.019
Poor: +/− 0.02 or higher

Got that? Probably not, but aren't you now inclined to take a CNET product review seriously?

Argue for criteria that can't be measured. How do you measure the
success or failure of something that can't be objectively calculated—a student dance recital, Bruno Mars's latest track, or that controversial abstract sculpture just hauled onto campus? Look into how such topics are evaluated and discussed in public media. Get familiar with what sensible critics have to say about whatever you're evaluating and how they say it—whether it's contemporary art, fine saddles, good teaching, or successful foreign policy. If you read carefully, you'll find values and criteria embedded in all your sources. O

In the following excerpt, for example, James Morris explains why he believes American television is often better than Hollywood films—an opinion much seconded in the decade since he wrote his comments. Morris's implied criteria are highlighted.

> What I admire most about these shows, and most deplore about contemporary movies, is the quality of the scripts. The TV series are devised and written by smart people who seem to be allowed to let their intelligence show. Yes, the individual and ensemble performances on several of the series are superb, but would the actors be as good as they are if they were miming the action? TV shows are designed for the small screen and cannot rely, as movies do, on visual and aural effects to distract audiences. If what's being said on TV isn't interesting, why bother to watch? Television is rigorous, right down to the confinement of hour or half-hour time slots, further reduced by commercials. There's no room for the narrative bloat that inflates so many Hollywood movies from their natural party-balloon size to Thanksgiving-parade dimensions.
>
> — "My Favorite Wasteland," *Wilson Quarterly,* Autumn 2005

Stated directly, Morris's criteria might sound like this: Good entertainment is intelligent; it is tailored to its medium; it does not require special effects to keep people interested; it is disciplined.

Stand by your values. Make sure you define criteria that apply to more than just
the case you are examining at the moment. For instance, you might admire particular performers who overcame great personal tragedies on their paths to stardom. But to make such heroics a necessary criterion for artistic achievement might look like special pleading. Think instead about what distinguishes first-rate acting, singing, or writing, for instance, from merely serviceable work.

read closely p. 321

Gather your evidence. Some materials for a review will necessarily come from secondary sources. Before judging the merits of the European Union's immigration policies or Harry Truman's decision to drop atomic bombs to end World War II, expect to do a lot of critical reading in a range of expert sources. Then weigh the evidence before offering your opinion—being sure to credit those sources in your review. ⭕

Other evidence might come from keen observation. Sometimes you just need to be attuned to the world around you. When reviewing a book, cell phone, restaurant, or similar item, take notes. If appropriate, measure, weigh, photograph, or interview your subjects. Gather data. When it matters, survey what others think about an issue (a campus political flap, for example) and record such opinions. Finally, keep an open mind. Be willing to change an opinion when evidence points in directions you hadn't expected.

Organizing ideas

▶ organize
criteria

Like other arguments, evaluations have distinct parts that can be arranged into patterns or structures.

Choose a simple structure when your criteria and categories are predictable. A straightforward review might announce its subject and claim, list criteria of evaluation, present evidence to show whether the subject meets those standards, and draw conclusions. Here's one version of that pattern with the criteria discussed all at once, at the opening of the piece:

> Introduction leading to an evaluative claim
>
> Criteria of evaluation stated and, if necessary, defended
>
> Subject measured by first criterion + evidence
> Subject measured by second criterion + evidence
> Subject measured by additional criteria + evidence
>
> Conclusion

read closely p. 321

And here's a template with the criteria of evaluation introduced one at a time:

> Introduction leading to an evaluative claim
>
>   First criterion of evaluation stated and, if necessary, defended
>
>   Subject measured by first criterion + evidence
>
>   Second criterion stated/defended
>
>   Subject measured by second criterion + evidence
>
>   Additional criteria stated/defended
>
>   Subject measured by additional criteria + evidence
>
> Conclusion

You might find structures this formulaic in job-performance reviews at work or in consumer magazines. Once a pattern is established for assessing computers, paint sprayers, video games, or even teachers (consider those forms you fill in at the end of the term), it can be repeated for each new subject and results can be compared.

Yet what works for hardware and tech products is less convincing when applied to music, books, political policies, or societal behaviors that are more than the sum of their parts. Imagine a film critic whose *every* review marched through the same predictable set of criteria: acting, directing, writing, cinematography, and special effects. When a subject can't (or shouldn't) be reviewed via simple categories, you decide which of its aspects and elements deserve attention. **O**

Choose a focal point. You could, in fact, organize an entire review around one shrewd insight, and many reviewers do. The trick is to support any stellar perceptions with specific and (preferably) lively evidence. Consider, for example, why Megan McArdle spends so much time exploring what "best" means when applied to athletes in her evaluation on Serena Williams. She knows that convincing readers that her definition of *best* is crucial to her argument. Or look how carefully Megan Giller defines the complex issue at the heart of her piece on Mast chocolate:

> But utter the words *Mast, Brooklyn,* or even *beards* to anyone in the chocolate industry—makers, professional tasters, and specialty shop owners—and you'll get a ranty earful about why he or she would never recommend it. How can the most popular craft chocolate in America be so disliked by chocolate experts? The answer to that question says as much about our changing tastes in chocolate as it does about the very definition of an expert.

You can guess that this question will become the focal point for readers of the essay too. (The full essay appears on p. 137.)

shape your work p. 345

Compare and contrast. Another obvious way to organize an evaluation is to examine differences. ⊙ Strengths and weaknesses stand out especially well when similar subjects are examined critically. When *Automobile* columnist Jamie Kitman, for example, wants to make a tongue-in-cheek case that the best American police car is one that looks most intimidating, he first has to explain his odd criterion of evaluation:

> Here [in the United States], police cars aren't meant to make us feel all fuzzy but to instill powerful sensations of fear. . . . At their best, police cars look strong, stout, capable, and most of all, mean. To the extent that they make bad people feel scared, they make those of us who ought to feel safe (because we have done nothing wrong) feel safer, while still feeling scared.

After that, it's a simple way of comparing candidates. He dismisses Ford Tauruses and Explorers because they "don't scare enough, even with light bars on top and armed with police-academy graduates inside." GM police cruisers are even less able to terrify the citizenry: They have "the scare factor of unspoiled rice pudding." Fortunately, he has found a winner, a model already described in the column as "malevolent" and looking "pissed off, angry, and unreasonable":

> That leaves the Dodge Charger, America's indisputable reigning champion cop car, to reign longer. It's the distilled automotive essence of every TV cop who ever drove a car, from Broderick Crawford on, all rolled into one angry, authoritarian appliance. No wonder countless agencies across the country favor Chargers. They're not kidding around, and you might as well know it.

Kitman's comparison is fun, but it makes sense—scary sense—especially when visual evidence is attached.

Courtesy of the Chrysler Foundation

use comparison and
contrast p. 120

Choosing a style and design

Evaluations can be composed in any style, from high to low—depending, as always, on aim and audience. ○ Look for opportunities to present evaluations visually too. They can simplify your task.

Use a high or formal style. Technical reviews tend to be formal and impersonal: They may be almost indistinguishable from reports, describing their findings in plain, unemotional language. Such a style gives the impression of scientific objectivity, even though the work may reflect someone's agenda. For instance, here's a paragraph in formal /technical style from the National Assessment of Educational Progress summarizing the performance of American students in mathematics:

> In 2015, twelfth-grade students had an average score of 152 on the NAEP 0–300 mathematics scale. This was lower compared to the average score in 2013, but was not significantly different in comparison to 2005. No significant change from 2013 was seen in the average mathematics score for any racial/ethnic group. For male and female students and for twelfth-grade students attending public schools, the average score in 2015 was lower compared to 2013.
>
> — *Nation's Report Card*, 2015 Mathematics and Reading Assessment (nationsreportcard.gov)

Use a middle style. When a writer has a more direct stake in the work—as is typical in book or movie reviews, for example—the style moves more decisively toward the middle. You sense a person behind the writing, making judgments and offering opinions. That's certainly the case in these two paragraphs by Clive Crook, written shortly after the death of noted economist John Kenneth Galbraith: Words, phrases, and even sentence fragments that humanize the assessment are highlighted, while a contrast to economist Milton Friedman also sharpens the portrait.

> Galbraith, despite the Harvard professorship, was never really an economist in the ordinary sense in the first place. In one of countless well-turned pronouncements, he said, "Economics is extremely useful as a form of employment for economists." He disdained the scientific pretensions and formal apparatus of modern economics—all that math and number crunching—believing that it missed the point. This view did not spring from mastery of the techniques: Galbraith disdained them from the outset, which saved time.
>
> Friedman, in contrast, devoted his career to grinding out top-quality scholarly work, while publishing the occasional best seller as a sideline. He too was no math whiz, but he was painstakingly scientific in his methods (when engaged in scholarly research) and devoted to data. All that was rather beneath Galbraith. Brilliant, yes; productive, certainly. But he was a bureaucrat, a diplomat, a political pundit, and a popular economics writer of commanding presence more than a serious economic thinker, let alone a great one.
>
> — "John Kenneth Galbraith, Revisited," *National Journal*, May 15, 2006

Use a low style. Many reviewers get personal with readers, some so direct that they verge on rudeness. Consider the product reviews on Amazon.com, Yelp, or almost any

define your style p. 366

comment section online. In contrast, the evaluations you write for academic or work as-signments should be (relatively) polite and low-key in style. But you do have an enormous range of options—especially when offering social and political commentary. Then, if your evaluations turn into satire or parody, all the gloves come off. In such situations, humor or sarcasm can become powerful tools, full of insider humor, colloquial turns of phrase, bizarre allusions, and grammar on the edge. But no style is more difficult to manage. So look for models of the kinds of evaluation you want to compose. Study the ones you admire for lessons in using language effectively.

Present evaluations visually. Evaluations work especially well when their claims are illustrated by tables, charts, graphs, or other visual elements. These allow readers to see relationships that could not be conveyed quite as efficiently in words alone. ○ Here, for ex-ample, is a summary chart that Digital Photography Review includes in its cameras reviews, enabling readers to quickly assess the strengths and weaknesses of particular products:

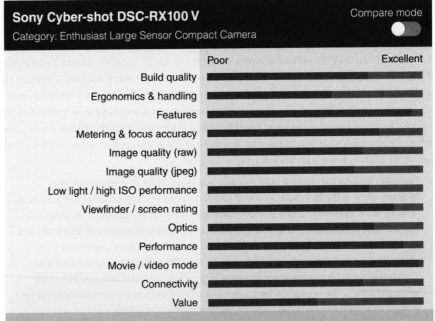

Sony Cyber-shot DSC-RX100 V   Compare mode

Category: Enthusiast Large Sensor Compact Camera

Poor   Excellent

Build quality
Ergonomics & handling
Features
Metering & focus accuracy
Image quality (raw)
Image quality (jpeg)
Low light / high ISO performance
Viewfinder / screen rating
Optics
Performance
Movie / video mode
Connectivity
Value

Conclusion

The Sony RX100 V builds on a camera that was already class-leading in many respects and crams 24fps burst shooting, oversampled 4K video and a 315-point autofocus system into this new pocket-sized companion. But there are no updates to its design, ergonomics or user interface that would ease direct control of its immense feature set. It's the most expensive pocket zoom camera on the market today, and there are other models that we find nicer to use in practice, but the RX100 V remains the highest-specced and most capable camera in its class.

display data p. 411

Sometimes, too, images simply have more impact than text. Consider your response to images of real fast-food items similar to those posted on an offbeat Web site called the West Virginia Surf Report. Here's the description of the feature that appeared on the site:

> **"Fast Food: Ads vs. Reality** Each item was purchased, taken home, and photographed immediately. Nothing was tampered with, run over by a car, or anything of the sort. It is an accurate representation in every case. Shiny, neon-orange, liquefied pump-cheese, and all."

Here are three images, much like those the site presented, of products purchased from well-known national chains:

Fish sandwich

Jellopy/Shutterstock

Taco

P Maxwell Photography/Shutterstock

Michael Neelon(misc)/Alamy Stock Photo

Breakfast burrito

All you need to do is recall the carefully crafted professional photographs of these items you've seen posted in the fast-food restaurants and you can draw your own conclusion: *Caveat emptor!*

Writing about Writing   Almost everyone reads at least one critic or type of review regularly—of restaurants, movies, TV shows, sports teams, gizmos, video games, and so on. Pick a review by your favorite critic or, alternatively, a review you have read recently and noted. Then examine its style closely. Is it formal, informal, or casual? Technical or general? Serious or humorous? Full of allusions to stuff regular readers would get? What features of the style do you like? Do you have any reservations about its style? In a detailed paragraph, evaluate only the style of the reviewer or review (not the substance of the opinion piece), organizing your work to support a clear thesis.

Examining models

PRODUCT REVIEW   Negative assessments of Mast's premium-priced chocolate bars caused a stir among chocolate lovers in 2015. Food writer and self-described "chocolate eater" Megan Giller responds to that controversy in an article on *Slate*. Rather than merely evaluate the controversial products, Giller looks into who Mast's critics are and what their expectations of good chocolate are.

Reading the Genre   Pay particular attention to the insight Giller provides into how chocolate is made, classified, and assessed. What did you learn from the piece and would it influence you if you are someone who routinely eats chocolate?

Chocolate Experts Hate Mast Brothers

By Megan Giller

March 16, 2015

Beards. If you've heard of the Mast brothers, that's probably the first word you came across, even before *chocolate*. Yes, Rick and Michael Mast make craft chocolate in Brooklyn's Williamsburg neighborhood, and they have big, bushy beards. With features in magazines like *Bon Appétit*, a popular cookbook, and three retail stores, the Mast Brothers brand has become synonymous with artisan chocolate in the popular imagination.

But utter the words *Mast, Brooklyn*, or even *beards* to anyone in the chocolate industry—makers, professional tasters, and specialty shop owners—and you'll get a ranty earful about why he or she would never recommend it. How can the most popular craft chocolate in America be so disliked by chocolate experts? The answer to that question says as much about our changing tastes in chocolate as it does about the very definition of an expert.

On a relatively warm day in December, I ventured into the Mast Brothers factory, right behind a tour group. "This is the good stuff," the guide told the twentysomething visitors who gazed hungrily at the display table of bars wrapped in brightly colored, patterned paper. They quickly downed platters of samples: a single-origin bar from Papua New Guinea, a blend with sea salt, and another blend with vanilla and smoke. Behind a glass partition, workers wearing Gant sweaters and Wolverine boots were unbagging, roasting, and grinding cacao beans, then tempering the resulting chocolate into bars. It was a modern-day, hipster

Giller uses a question to lead into the paradox at the heart of the review.

In describing the tour, tourists, and history of Mast, Giller provides a context for her analysis.

Willy Wonka factory, with all the sense of wonder and delight that the fictional king of candy enjoyed.

When they started making chocolate in 2006, the Mast brothers were among the first bean-to-bar chocolate manufacturers in America. (They incorporated in 2007.) Most chocolate comes from cheap, over-roasted beans that big corporations sell in bulk to smaller companies for them to process into individual bars. But bean-to-bar makers start with different varieties of raw, high-quality cacao beans to create handmade, artisanal products that are a league above the chocolate most of us grew up eating. Now there are dozens of bean-to-bar makers in the United States, but Mast remains an ambassador of the bean-to-bar movement, educating the country about high-quality chocolate by making it hip, beautiful, and delectable. Chefs and restaurants have responded, especially in New York; places like Eleven Madison Park and OddFellows Ice Cream cite Mast's local presence as one of the major reasons they use its chocolate.

A simple question focuses the essay.

But does Mast Brothers' chocolate live up to its reputation? Many skeptical specialists contend that Mast's Brooklyn location, hipster image, and beautiful packaging are the real reasons for its popularity— not its taste. "If you were to ask the world's top chocolate reviewers to rate bars, Mast Brothers would hit in the bottom 5 percentile," said Clay Gordon, a Good Food Awards judge and the author of *Discover Chocolate*. "There are defects in every bar, and the chocolate is bad." Writer, chocolate educator, and International Chocolate Awards judge Eagranie Yuh said she's tried Mast bars that tasted stale or moldy. Both Yuh and Lauren Adler, the owner of Seattle-based specialty shop Chocolopolis, commented that some Mast bars have an unpleasant chalky texture.

Though Mast is sold at hundreds of independently owned shops and big-name grocery stores around the world, almost every specialty chocolate store refuses to carry the brand: Cacao in Portland, Oregon; the Chocolate Garage in Palo Alto, California; Bittersweet Café and Fog City News in San Francisco; and La Tablette de Miss Choco in Montreal. The Meadow, in Portland and New York, was the only spot I could find that both specializes in chocolate and carries Mast bars.

Having talked to experts and surveyed specialty shops, Giller explains how chocolate is evaluated.

Most specialty chocolate shops rely on panels of judges to determine which bars to carry, so the straightforward explanation for Mast's exclusion from these stores is that Mast's chocolate didn't wow the judges. But Rick Mast has an alternative theory of why most specialty stores don't carry his brand. When I asked him about experts' criticism of his bars, he replied,

"We are a dangerous company because we are outsiders to the chocolate industry, never leaning on industry norms." Mast went on, "We have achieved incredible success without paying the self-proclaimed industry chocolate experts that you have cited a penny for their 'expertise.'"

It's true that the Mast brothers haven't forged relationships within the craft chocolate industry, despite their strong connections with restaurateurs and consumers. Their absence is noticeable at events and in groups like the Fine Chocolate Industry Association. At a recent brunch for the FCIA at Dandelion Chocolate in San Francisco, makers and experts noshed on bagels and brownies while chatting about their favorite beans and catching up on one another's personal lives. The community is small and tightly knit, and most people in it have never even spoken to the brothers. That makes it easy for Mast to become, in Yuh's words, "the villain in the industry," serving as a scapegoat for the chocolate world's frustration with mediocre products.

> Even the world of chocolate is political.

Most consumers are not in a good position to distinguish mediocre chocolate from non-mediocre chocolate, having been raised on milk chocolate bars that contain more sugar and vanilla than cacao. Hershey's somewhat waxy texture and milky flavor defines chocolate for many Americans, even though it's something of its own creation. But now shelves burst with high-end dark chocolate bars. It's as though we've been drinking wine coolers for years and suddenly have access to a cellar of cabernet sauvignons.

> Wine/chocolate comparison here helps readers understand the growing attention to specialty chocolates.

When expert tasters bite into bars, they look to see if the chocolate is, in Yuh's words, "true to the bean." As with wine grapes, each country's cacao has its own flavor profile. For example, Madagascar's beans are known for their fruity notes—but in the wrong hands, those berry and citric undertones can thunder. For that reason, professional tasters also consider whether a chocolate is well-balanced. Are there off flavors, like that of a No. 2 pencil? Or is it a rich chocolate taste with just a hint of, for example, fruitiness or nuttiness? "Enjoyment is part of it," Yuh noted, "but it also has to match up with my mental checklist." And Mast's chalky, off-balance bars do not.

Gordon is worried that just as Hershey's trained us to think chocolate tasted like Hershey bars, Mast is training us to think good chocolate tastes like Mast bars. Because it's the most popular craft brand in the country, carried at niche stores and in restaurants across America, consumers think that's what craft chocolate should taste like. As a craft chocolate aficionado, Adler said, "It's rare that I try something that blows my mind," but for the rest of us, *any* craft chocolate blows our minds, because it's so different from what we're used to eating. We don't have a good frame of reference yet.

> Giller cites experts throughout the essay to explain what's at stake in the debate.

To be fair, neither do the experts. "There aren't standards like in the wine industry," said Adler. "There's not a sommelier test, and everyone has a different palate." Her advice to craft chocolate newbies is simply to try a lot of different bars to find out what you like.

I've taken Adler's advice, and I'm inclined to agree (mostly) with the experts: Mast Brothers' bars are average. They're not bad, but they're not great, either, when you compare them with the top makers in the field of craft chocolate. The crème de la crème of the industry includes Rogue Chocolatier, almost universally agreed to make the best bars in the country, with big names like David Lebovitz and Martha Stewart praising its single-origin chocolate. (Be forewarned that Rogue's bars are on back order almost everywhere.) Amano also turns out astonishingly good bars from all over Central and South America and has won a slew of awards. Patric makes epic single-origin bars as well as interesting combinations like PBJ OMG (a dark chocolate with peanut butter). And Fruition's dark chocolate with milk (yes, dark milk chocolate) might just change your worldview.

And if, after trying the gamut of bean-to-bar chocolate made in America today, you still prefer Mast Brothers, at least one person won't be surprised: Rick Mast. "Thousands of chocolate lovers make the journey to visit our factory every week," says Mast. "These are our chocolate experts. If it is the perspective of an expert that you seek, I encourage you to become that expert."

Giller concludes by offering her own assessment of premium chocolates.

ARTS/CULTURE REVIEW   People regularly consult reviews of books, movies, plays, concert exhibitions, and so one—indeed, almost any cultural event. Following is a very short book review that offers an appreciation—almost celebration—of a breakthrough novel. The review demonstrates some key elements of the genre.

Reading the Genre   Soup Martinez's brief review of *Catcher in the Rye*, limited to just several hundred words, implies (rather than discusses) its criteria of evaluation. What would you say he values in this book? What should a novel do?

Review of *Catcher in the Rye* by J. D. Salinger

Soup Martinez

October 2, 2016

The Catcher in the Rye (1951) by J. D. Salinger gives voice to what many adolescent boys really think, but are too civil to say. Holden Caulfield, the main character, is a precocious seventeen-year-old, writing about a time when he was sixteen, though he claims to act like he's thirteen—a fact that becomes clear as the audience listens to his observations on reading ("I'm quite illiterate, but I read a lot"), on roommates ("It's really hard to be roommates with people if your suitcases are much better than theirs"), on movies ("I can understand somebody going out to the movies because there's nothing else to do, but when somebody really wants to go, then it depresses the hell out of me"), and on teachers ("You don't have to think too hard when you talk to a teacher").

> Martinez identifies (and dates) his subject and uses quotations to describe its famous antihero.

Holden's irrational ramblings and Salinger's "showy" writing style are what caused so many publishers to pause when first looking at this book. The *New Yorker* refused to publish it despite having published in 1946 Salinger's story "Slight Rebellion off Madison," which presented the earliest known version of Holden Caulfield. The story was later reworked by Salinger and included in *Catcher* as Chapter 17. An executive at another esteemed publishing house would not publish it because he couldn't tell if the main character of the story was supposed to be crazy. Crazy or not, Holden and his story of a lonely three-night stay in New York City came to be read and loved by millions.

> The novel is set in its critical context—publishers were leery.

Critics argue that Salinger's novel has no structure and contains unpleasant prose. What proponents of these arguments fail to realize is that the life of a teenager has no structure, and teenagers speak in unpleasant ways. Salinger was the first to capture the rambling beauty of the teenage mind. He gave permission to teenagers who wanted to do things because they just felt like it for once.

Catcher in the Rye is a book about a boy who is sad and wants to find someone who won't let him down. It's about the way he has seen consumerism begin to steal relationships from him, calling his brother a

> In two brief paragraphs, Martinez explains the appeal of Salinger's book and makes a claim.

"prostitute" after he moves to Hollywood. It's about the way he has grown tired of grownups being "phony," for not being genuine. It's an honest anthem for those who are willing to embrace the emotion that has secretly plagued Americans for generations: sadness.

SOCIAL SATIRE/VISUAL ARGUMENT   Satires, which poke fun at the foibles of society in order to correct them, often require writers to draw exaggerated but recognizable portraits of people and situations. That's their job too if they are cartoonists like Andy Singer. His targets are wide ranging. In the subtle, one-panel item here entitled "Intravenous Smartphones," he makes an evaluative judgment about a very common phenomenon.

Reading the Genre   Study the cartoon closely. Then in a paragraph discuss the assessment Andy Singer makes. What exactly is being evaluated and criticized? What evidence does Singer offer? Pay attention to every detail.

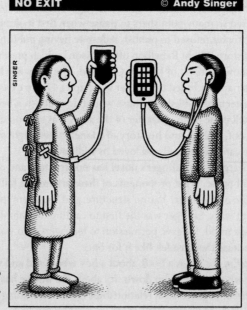

1. **Critical Assessment:** Step into a controversy as boldly as Megan McArdle does in "Serena Williams Is Not the Best Tennis Player" (p. 123)—and write a critique of some disputable claim within the public arena. You can address sports, as McArdle does, or look for a topic in other areas where evaluative claims are common and controversial—politics, business, technology, arts, fashion, and so on. (If necessary, look to your Twitter feed for topic ideas.) Write an assessment strong enough to change someone's mind.

2. **Product Review:** Choose an item that you own, buy, or use regularly, anything from a Coleman Lantern and Dunkin' Donuts coffee to a Web site, phone app, or social network you couldn't live without. Then write a fully developed review, making sure to discuss your criteria of evaluation as thoroughly as Megan Giller does in "Chocolate Experts Hate Mast Brothers" (p. 137). Choose a specific audience if you want and be generous with the supporting details. Use graphics if appropriate.

3. **Arts Review:** Drawing on your experience with the arts, review a movie, book, television series, musical piece, video game, work of art, or artist for a publication that you specify—print or online. It can be as brief as Soup Martinez's review of *Catcher in the Rye* (p. 141). Perhaps write your review for a local or student publication. Or consider writing a substantive piece for an online site that takes reviews—such as Amazon or IMDb.

4. **Social Satire/Visual Argument:** Take a critical look at some aspect of contemporary society the way Andy Singer does in his "No Exit" (p. 142). Use either prose or an image to critique a public policy, social movement, or cultural trend you believe deserves censure. But don't create an item that simply marks your subject as dangerous, pathetic, or unsuccessful. Instead, make people laugh at your target while perhaps offering a plausible alternative.

5. **Your Choice:** Evaluate a program or facility in some institution you know well (school, work, church, recreation center) that you believe works either especially efficiently or remarkably poorly. Prepare a presentation in the medium of your choice and imagine that your audience is an administrator with the power to reward or shut down the operation.

How to start ▶
- Need a **topic**? See page 150.
- Need to come up with a **solution**? See page 154.
- Need to **organize your ideas**? See page 155.

12

define a problem and suggest a solution

Proposals

Proposals are written to solve problems. Typically, you'll make a proposal to initiate an action or change. At a minimum, you hope to alter someone's thinking—even if only to recommend leaving things as they are.

TRIAL BALLOON
Degree programs at your school have so many complicated requirements that most students take far more time to graduate than they expect—adding thousands of dollars to their loans. As a *trial balloon*, you suggest that the catalog include accurate "time-to-degree" estimates for all degree programs and certificates.

MANIFESTO
Packaging is getting out of hand and you've had enough. People can barely open the products they buy because everything is zipped up, shrink-wrapped, blister-packed, containerized, or child-protected. So you write a *manifesto* calling for saner and more eco-friendly approaches to product protection.

VISUAL PROPOSAL
You create a PowerPoint so members of your co-op can visualize how much better your building's study area would look with a few inexpensive tweaks in furniture, paint, and lighting. Your *visual proposal* gets you the job of implementing the changes.

Defining the genre

Got an issue or a problem? Good—let's deal with it. That's the logic driving most proposals, both the professional types that pursue grant money and the less formal propositions that are part of everyday life, academic or otherwise. Like evaluations and some explanations, proposals are another form of argument (for more on choosing a genre, see Chapter 2).

Although it shares some elements of informal proposals, grant writing is driven by rigid formulas set by foundations and government agencies, usually covering things like budgets, personnel, evaluations, outcomes, and so on. Informal proposals are much easier. Although they may not funnel large sums of cash your way, they're still important tools for addressing problems. A sensible proposal can make a difference in any situation—be it academic, personal, or political.

In offering a proposal, you'll need to make many of the moves outlined below. In a first-round pitch, for example, you might launch a trial balloon to test whether an idea will work at all, roughing out a scheme with the details to follow. A more serious plan headed for public debate and scrutiny would have to punch the ticket on more of the items.

These bikes are for YOU. How do you persuade people in a community to find alternatives to cars? The city of Boston makes a different choice easy to use—and easy to understand.

Radharc Images/Alamy Stock Photo

Define a problem. Set the stage for a proposal by describing the specific situation, problem, or opportunity in enough detail that readers *get it*: They see a compelling need for action. In many cases, a proposal needs to explain what's wrong with the status quo.

Make specific recommendations. This is the trial balloon. Don't just complain that someone else has botched a situation or opportunity: Explain what exactly you propose to do about the problem. The more concrete your solution is, the better.

Target the proposal. To make a difference, you have to reach people with the power to change a situation. That means first identifying such individuals (or groups) and then tailoring your proposal to their expectations. Use the Web or library, for example, to get the names and contact information of government or corporate officials. **O** When the people in power *are* the problem, go over their heads to more general audiences with clout of their own: voters, consumers, women, fellow citizens, the elderly, and so on.

Consider plausible alternatives. Your proposal won't be taken seriously unless it's clear that you have weighed other workable possibilities, explaining their advantages and downsides. Only then will you be prepared to make a case for your own ideas. You can, of course, fully describe the problem you hope to address immediately or present the related aspects of your problem/solution case, point by point.

Make realistic recommendations. You typically need to address two related issues in any proposal: *feasibility* and *implementation*. A proposition is feasible if it can be achieved with available resources and is acceptable to the parties involved. But, of course, a feasible plan still needs a pathway to completion that seems plausible: *First we do this; then we do this; finally we do this.*

plan a project p. 428

Trial Balloon

In the following opinion piece from *USA Today*, author Glenn Harlan Reynolds tips his hand early when he uses the phrase "a modest proposal" in his second paragraph. He is alluding to Jonathan Swift's famous satire of the same name, which in 1729 offered a famously outrageous solution to the dire poverty the Irish people suffered under English rule. Reynolds, a professor of law, active blogger, and columnist, was similarly tweaking the nation's elites in 2015—late in the Obama Administration—to live up to their frequent political calls for greater equality by taking a sizeable whack at their own bastions of privilege. He probably doesn't expect them to take his suggestions seriously, but a trial balloon like this might at least make them squirm.

Reading the Genre One of the major tasks in writing a proposal argument is defining the problem. How much of Reynolds's essay is concerned with explaining how the Ivy League's financial status is sustained by average taxpayers? Should he have explained what the Ivy League is for readers unfamiliar with the term? Why or why not?

To Reduce Inequality, Abolish Ivy League

GLENN HARLAN REYNOLDS

November 2, 2015

The problem of "inequality" looms over America like a storm cloud. According to our political and journalistic class, inequality is the single biggest problem facing our nation, with the possible exception of climate change. It is a desperate problem demanding sweeping solutions. President Obama called it the "defining challenge of our time." Hillary Clinton said we're living in a throwback to the elitist age of "robber barons." Bernie Sanders says inequality is the result of a "rigged economy" that favors those at the top while holding down those at the bottom.

In that spirit, I have a modest proposal: Abolish the Ivy League. Because if you're worried about inequality among Americans, I can think of no single institution that does more to contribute to the problem.

By citing Obama, Clinton, and Sanders, Reynolds signals some political targets.

As former Labor Secretary Robert Reich recently noted, Ivy League schools are government-subsidized playgrounds for the rich: "Imagine a system of college education supported by high and growing government spending on elite private universities that mainly educate children of the wealthy and upper-middle class and low and declining government spending on public universities that educate large numbers of children from the working class and the poor.

"You can stop imagining," Reich wrote. "That's the American system right now. . . . Private university endowments are now around $550 billion, centered in a handful of prestigious institutions. Harvard's endowment is over $32 billion, followed by Yale at $20.8 billion, Stanford at $18.6 billion, and Princeton at $18.2 billion. Each of these endowments increased last year by more than $1 billion, and these universities are actively seeking additional support. Last year, Harvard launched a capital campaign for another $6.5 billion. Because of the charitable tax deduction, the amount of government subsidy to these institutions in the form of tax deductions is about one out of every $3 contributed."

The result? "The annual government subsidy to Princeton University, for example, is about $54,000 per student, according to an estimate by economist Richard Vedder," Reich pointed out. "Other elite privates aren't far behind. Public universities, by contrast, have little or no endowment income. They get almost all their funding from state governments. But these subsidies have been shrinking."

Nor does all this money go to enhance opportunities for the nonelites. Ivy League admissions are mostly tilted toward the upper-middle class and the wealthy. As Ross Douthat wrote in *The New York Times*, there is "a truth that everyone who's come up through Ivy League culture knows intuitively— that elite universities are about connecting more than learning, that the social world matters far more than the classroom to undergraduates, and that rather than an escalator elevating the best and brightest from every walk of life, the meritocracy as we know it mostly works to perpetuate the existing upper class."

Nor does the problem end there. Once you're out of college, your chances of making it to the top are much, much greater if you're an Ivy League graduate. Take the Obama administration. A *National Journal* survey

Reynolds extensively uses a secretary of labor under President Clinton to describe the problem he wants to fix.

Reynolds cites numbers to demonstrate the power of the eight Ivy League schools.

A full academic proposal argument might offer more evidence than the "quick survey of headlines" Reynolds presents in his column.

of 250 top decision-makers found that 40 percent of them were Ivy League graduates. Only a quarter had earned graduate degrees from a public university. In fact, more Obama administration officials had degrees from England's Oxford University than from any American public university. Worse yet, more than sixty of them—roughly a fourth—had attended a single Ivy League school, Harvard.

If all of this were making America a better place, maybe the elitism would be justified. But a quick survey of the headlines suggests that while we might be governed by the best credentialed, we're not being governed by the brightest and most competent. What is to be done?

Well, in the name of ending inequality, I have a few modest proposals.

1. We should eliminate the tax deductibility of contributions to schools having endowments in excess of $1 billion. At some point, as our president has said, you've made enough money. That won't end all major donations to the Ivy League, but it will doubtless encourage donors to look at less wealthy and more deserving schools, such as Northern Kentucky University, recently deemed "more inspirational than Harvard" in the *London Times Higher Education* magazine.
2. We should require that all schools with endowments over $1 billion spend at least 10 percent of their endowment annually on student financial aid. That will make it easier for less wealthy students to attend elite institutions.
3. We should require that university admissions be based strictly on objective criteria, such as grades and SAT/ACT scores, with random drawings used to cull the herd further if necessary. That will eliminate the Ivy League's documented discrimination against Asians.

The actual proposals are more plausible than outright abolition of the influential schools.

These are strong measures, which might not actually end the Ivy League, but which would certainly end the Ivy League as we know it, and I can imagine many elite university administrators objecting. Even so, if inequality is as serious a problem in America as our leaders say it is, strong medicine is called for. Let's take these important steps now. For equality!

Claiming a topic

▶ topic

Most people will agree to a reasonable proposal—as long as it doesn't cost them anything. But moving audiences from *I agree* to *I'll actually do something about it* takes a powerful act of persuasion. And for that reason, proposals are typically structured as arguments, requiring many of the strategies used in that genre. **O**

Occasionally, you'll be asked to solve a particular problem in school or on the job. Having an assigned topic makes your task a little easier, but you can bet that any such problem will be complex and open to multiple solutions. Otherwise, there would be no challenge to it.

When choosing a proposal topic on your own, keep in mind the following concerns. **O**

Need help deciding what to write about? See "How to Browse for Ideas" on pp. 20–21.

Look for a genuine issue. Spend the first part of your project determining a problem readers will recognize and care about. You may think it's a shame no one retails Prada close to campus, but your classmates probably worry more about out-of-control student fees or the high price of housing. Reach beyond your own concerns in settling on a problem.

Look for a challenging problem. It helps if others have tried to fix it in the past but failed—and you are able to figure out why. Times change, attitudes shift, technology improves: Factors like these might make what once seemed like an intractable problem more manageable now. Choose a serious topic to which you can bring fresh perspectives and novel solutions.

Look for a soluble problem. Challenges *are* good, but impossible dreams are for Broadway musicals. Parking on campus is the classic impasse—always present, always frustrating. Steer clear of problems no one has ever solved, unless you have a *really* good idea.

Look for a local issue. It's best to leave "world peace" to beauty pageant contestants. Instead, tackle a problem in your community, where you can interview affected people or search local newspapers or archives. **O** Doing so also makes it easier to find an audience you can influence, including people potentially able to improve the situation. You're far more likely to get the attention of your dean of students than the secretary of state.

understand argument p. 89   find a topic p. 16   interview and observe p. 448

FISCAL CLIFF FIX

THE COLUMBUS DISPATCH
CAGLECARTOONS.com

CONGRESS

Nate Beeler/Cagle Cartoons

Columbus Dispatch editorial cartoonist Nate Beeler offers a proposal for solving the country's budget woes.

Thinking about Writing   In 46 BCE, Julius Caesar used his authority as dictator to impose a new calendar on Rome because the old one had fallen five months out of sync with the seasons. Play Caesar today by imagining what problems you would fix if you could simply impose your will. Make a list. Narrow your more grandiose schemes (free pizza for all) to more plausible ones (more night courses for working students), and then consider which items on your roster could be argued rationally and compellingly in a short paper. Compare your list with those of other students and discuss workable proposal topics.

Understanding your audience

While preparing a proposal, keep two audiences in mind—one fairly narrow and the other more broad. The first group includes people who could possibly do something about a problem; the second consists of general readers who could influence those in the first group by bringing the weight of public opinion upon them. And public opinion makes a difference.

Writers calibrate proposals for specific readers all the time. Grant writers, especially, make it a point to learn what agencies and institutions expect in applications. Quite often, it takes two or three tries to figure out how to present a winning grant submission. You won't have that luxury with most academic or political pieces, but you can look for examples of successful proposals and study them.

Appeal to people who can make a difference. For example, a personal letter you prepare for the dean of students to protest her policies against displaying political posters in campus buildings (including dormitories) should have a respectful and perhaps legalistic tone, pointing to case law on the subject and university policies on freedom of speech. You'd also want to assure the dean of your goodwill and provide her with sound reasons for loosening the restrictions.

Rally people who represent public opinion. No response from the dean of students on the political poster proposal you made? Then take the issue to the public, perhaps via an op-ed or letter in a local paper. Keeping the dean still firmly in mind, you'd now also write to stir up student and community opinion. Your new piece could be more emotional than your letter and less burdened by legal points—though still citing facts and presenting solid reasons for giving students more leeway in expressing political beliefs on campus. O

The fact is that people often need a spur to move them—that is, a persuasive strategy that helps them imagine their role in solving a problem. Again, you'd be in good company in leading an audience to your position. As shown on page 153, when President John F. Kennedy proposed a mission to the moon in 1962, he did it in language that stirred a public skeptical about the cost and challenges of such an implausible undertaking.

refine your tone p. 368

JFK Aims High In 1962, the president challenged Americans to go to the moon.

Corbis Historical/Getty Images

There is no strife, no prejudice, no national conflict in outer space as yet. Its hazards are hostile to us all. Its conquest deserves the best of all mankind, and its opportunity for peaceful cooperation may never come again. But why, some say, the moon? Why choose this as our goal? And they may well ask why climb the highest mountain? Why, thirty-five years ago, fly the Atlantic? Why does Rice play Texas?

We choose to go to the moon. We choose to go to the moon in this decade and do the other things, not because they are easy, but because they are hard, because that goal will serve to organize and measure the best of our energies and skills, because that challenge is one that we are willing to accept, one we are unwilling to postpone, and one which we intend to win, and the others, too.

— speech from Rice Stadium, "Moon Speech," September 12, 1962

Gathering materials

► consider
  solutions

Proposals might begin with whining and complaining (*I want easier parking!*), but they can't stay in that mode long. They require sober thought and research. What makes proposals distinctive, however, is the sheer variety of strategies a single document might employ. To write a convincing proposal, you may need to narrate, report, argue, evaluate, and analyze. Here's how to develop those various parts.

Define the problem. Research the existing situation thoroughly enough to explain it concisely to readers. To be sure you've got the basics of your topic down cold, run through the traditional journalist's questions—*Who? What? Where? When? Why? How?* When appropriate, interview experts or people involved with an issue; for instance, in college communities, the best repositories of institutional memory will usually be the staff. O Search for any documents with hard facts on the matter that might convince skeptical readers. For instance, if you propose to change a long-standing policy, find out when it was created, by whom, and for what reasons.

*The Journalist's
Questions*

Who?   What?
Where?   Why?
When?   How?

Examine prior solutions. If a problem is persistent, other people have tried to solve it—or maybe they even caused it. In either case, do the research necessary to figure out, as best you can, what happened in these previous efforts. But expect controversy. You may have to sort through contentious and contradictory narratives. Once you know the history of an issue, shift into an evaluative mode to figure out why earlier strategies faltered. O Then explain them to readers so that they can later compare these failed approaches to your own proposal and appreciate its ingenuity.

Outline a proposal. Coming up with a sensible proposal may take more creativity than you can muster. So consider working collaboratively, when that's an option. Brainstorm aggressively with classmates and be sure to keep track of good ideas as they emerge. Be specific about details, especially numbers and costs.

Defend the proposal. Any ideas that threaten the status quo will surely raise hackles. That's half the fun of proposing change. So advance your position by using all the tools of argument available to you—logical, factual, and, yes, emotional. Present yourself as smart and competent. Anticipate objections, because readers invested in the status quo will offer them in spades. Above all, show that your idea will work and that it is *feasible*—that it can be achieved with existing or new resources you can identify. For example, you might actually solve your school's traffic problems by proposing a

interview and observe
p. 448

understand evaluation
p. 120

monorail linking the central campus to huge new parking garages. But who would pay for the multimillion-dollar system?

And yet, you shouldn't be put off too easily by the objection that *we can't possibly do that*. A little chutzpah is not out of line—it's part of the problem-solving process.

Figure out how to implement the proposal. Readers will need assurances that your ideas can be put into action: Show them how. O Figure out exactly what will happen: where new resources will come from, how personnel can be recruited and hired, where brochures or manuals will be printed, and so on. Provide a timetable if you can.

Organizing ideas

Proposals follow the thought processes most people go through in dealing with issues, and some of these problems raise more complications than others. O Generally, the less formal the proposal, the fewer structural elements it will have. So adapt the following template to your needs, using it as a checklist of *possible* issues to consider in framing a proposal.

organize ideas ◀

> **Introduction defining a problem or an issue**
>
> > **Nature of the problem**
> > **Prior solution(s) + reason(s) for inadequacy**
>
> **New proposal**
>
> > **Explanation**
> > **Rationale**
> > **Comparisons and/or counterarguments**
> > **Feasibility**
> > **Implementation**
>
> **Conclusion**

think critically p. 327   shape your work p. 345

You might use a similar structure whenever you need to examine what effects—good or bad—might follow some action, event, policy, or change in the status quo. Once again, you'd begin with an introduction that fully describes the action you believe will have significant consequences; then you explain those consequences to readers, showing how they are connected. Finally, a conclusion could draw out the implications of your analysis.

Choosing style and design

Proposals do come in many forms and, occasionally, they may be frivolous or satiric. But whenever you suggest changing people's lives or spending someone else's money, show a little respect and humility.

Use a formal style. Professional proposals—especially those seeking grant money—are typically written in a high style, formal and impersonal, almost as if the project would be jeopardized by reviewers detecting the slightest hint of enthusiasm or personality. O Academic audiences are often just as poker-faced. So use a formal style in proposals you write for school when your intended readers are formidable and "official"—professors, deans, and provosts, or administrators (and pay attention to their titles!).

    Observe, for example, the no-nonsense tone that Thao Tran adopts early in an academic essay whose title alone suggests its sober intentions: "Coping with Population Aging in the Industrialized World."

Leaders of industrialized nations and children of baby boomers must understand the consequences of population aging and minimize its economic effects. This report will recommend steps for coping with aging in the industrialized world and will assess counterarguments to those steps. With a dwindling workforce and a rising elderly population, industrialized countries must take a multistep approach to expand the workforce and support the elderly. Governments should attempt to attract immigrants, women, and elderly people into the workforce. Supporting an increasing elderly population will require reforming pension systems and raising indirect taxes. It will also require developing pronatalist

Point of view is impersonal: *This report* rather than *I*.

Purpose of proposal is clearly explained.

define your style p. 368

policies, in which governments subsidize child-rearing costs to encourage births. Many of these strategies will challenge traditional cultural notions and require a change in cultural attitudes. While change will not be easy, industrialized nations must recognize and address this trend quickly in order to reduce its effects.

Premises and assumptions of the proposal are offered in abstract language.

Use a middle style, when appropriate. Shift to a middle style when you need to persuade a general audience or whenever establishing a personal relationship with readers might help your proposal.

It is possible, too, for styles to vary within a document. Your language might be coldly efficient as you scrutinize previous failures or tick off the advantages of your specific proposal. But as you near the end of the piece, you might decide another style would better reflect your vision for the future or your enthusiasm for an idea. Environmentalist David R. Brower offered many technical arguments to explain why his radical proposal for draining Lake Powell would make commercial sense. But he concluded his appeal on a more emotional note:

> The sooner we begin, the sooner lost paradises will begin to recover— Cathedral in the Desert, Music Temple, Hidden Passage, Dove Canyon, Little Arch, Dungeon, and a hundred others. Glen Canyon itself can probably lose its ugly white sidewalls in two or three decades. The tapestries can reemerge, along with the desert varnish, the exiled species of plants and animals, the pictographs, and other mementos of people long gone. The canyon's music will be known again, and "the sudden poetry of springs," Wallace Stegner's beautiful phrase, will be revealed again below the sculptured walls of Navajo sandstone. The phrase, "as long as the rivers shall run and the grasses grow," will regain its meaning.

Place names listed have poetic effect.

Lush details add to emotional appeal of proposal.

Final quotation summarizes the mission of proposal.

Pay attention to elements of design. Writers often incorporate images, charts, tables, graphs, and flowcharts to illustrate what is at stake in a proposal or to make comparisons easy. Images also help readers imagine solutions or proposals and make those ideas attractive. The SmartArt Graphics icon in the Microsoft Word Gallery opens up a range of templates you might use to help readers visualize a project. **○**

think visually p. 417

Thinking about Writing   The style of proposals varies dramatically, depending on audience and purpose. Review the proposals in this chapter offered as models—including the visual items. Then explain in some detail exactly how the language of one of those items works to make its case. You can focus on a whole piece, but you may find it more interesting just to explicate a few sentences or paragraphs or one or two visual details. For example, when does Glenn Harlan Reynolds (p. 147), Ellen Airhart (p. 159), or Jen Sorensen (p. 167) score style points with you? Be ready to explain your observation orally.

Examining models

MANIFESTO   Ellen Airhart believes we'd all be better off if we ate more bugs. She even brought cricket bars to class the day she workshopped the draft of the proposal argument below with her classmates—most of whom were willing to sample the delicacies. Airhart uses a journalistic style to engage her readers, but she backs up her claims with sources cited in conventional APA form.

Reading the Genre   Airhart has the advantage of an attention-grabbing topic. But notice how carefully she develops it, first presenting a character reluctantly eating weevils, then explaining entomophagy, and only then unfolding the logical reasons for embracing this practice—one by one. Can you imagine the argument with its structure reversed—beginning with the environmental crises being caused by eating meat and only then offering insects as a food alternative? Might that approach work just as well?

Eat More Bugs 1

Join the Revolution: Eat More Bugs

Ellen Airhart

The University of Texas at Austin

Join the Revolution: Eat More Bugs

    Ysabel Bello ate her first insect when she was in medical school, volunteering with Native Amazonians in southern Venezuela. After she arrived in a canoe, the locals welcomed her with a plate of South American palm weevil grubs that grow in the dark recesses of palm trees. The Amazonians must delicately coax these rare larvae from inside the trees, and since this work takes so much time and energy, they prize the grubs as delicacies appropriate for distinguished guests. Bello felt obligated to gulp down the insects while her new hosts watched. She said they felt like

Eat More Bugs 2

The title might tip readers off, but the opening paragraph should attract attention.

"spoonfuls of oil" going down her throat, but she swallowed, smiled, and said they were delicious.

North Americans like Bello should get used to entomophagy, the human consumption of insects. Some of them already are. In 2014, Exo, a New York–based nutrition company, created protein bars with an unusual key ingredient—crickets. They are slow-roasted and ground in fine flour, but they're still the chirping, hopping bugs that haunt urban stairwells in the summertime. The cricket bars have been commercially successful: Exo sold out of its first 50,000-bar shipment within a few weeks and quickly raised more than $1.2 million in venture capital (Helmer, 2015). And while the idea might be off-putting at first, you might consider joining the entomophagy revolution by purchasing some insect-based foods. In fact, we would all benefit from munching on arthropods—they're healthy, inexpensive, and, maybe most important, make environmental sense.

Second paragraph ends with a conventional thesis sentence.

Insects could serve as a substitute for red meat, which is an important source of protein for many adults in the United States. Red meat increases risks for stomach, colon, lung, and esophageal cancers, as well as heart disease ("Health & Environmental Implications," 2016). Insect consumption would nibble away at our waistlines and chances of getting these chronic diseases. For example, mealworms have nearly as much protein as beef, with less fat and more vitamins (Van Huis et al., 2013).

Not only will entomophagy decrease cancer and heart disease in the United States; it could remedy malnutrition all

Eat More Bugs 3

over the world. Only twelve species of plants make up three-quarters of the world's food supply (Van Huis et al., 2013). Since our diets are so homogenous, we could be missing out on important nutrients. For instance, about 35 percent of all people around the world rely on a wheat-based diet, which can lead to a deficiency in the crucial amino acids: lysine, tryptophan, and threonine (IDRC Communications, 2016). Without these amino acids, our bodies may struggle to create necessary proteins. Many cultures already take advantage of insects to supplement missing amino acids.

Airhart explains the health benefits of eating bugs.

In the Democratic Republic of Congo, staple protein sources include fish, nuts, and legumes, all of which lack lysine (Dioula, 2014). Therefore, the Congolese eat lysine-rich Cirina forda caterpillars to compensate. Many landlocked countries lack access to fish, and therefore healthy omega-3 and omega-6 fatty acids, which are important for brain development. These communities could use insects to compensate. For example, adult termites contain about the same amount of protein as mackerel, with a similar healthy fat content (Van Huis et al., 2013).

Better yet, termites and weevils have an advantage over fish or meat—they are much cheaper. According to the Food and Agriculture Organization of the United Nations, fish prices went up 15 percent between 2011 and 2013 (2016). With the appetite for meat growing in developing countries, such as China and India, producers are struggling to meet demand. Hence, overall meat prices have also risen nearly 60 percent since 2004

Eat More Bugs 4

Economic reasons for eating insects.

(International Meat Price Indices, 2016). Insect consumption can provide a high-protein alternative. While sanitary insect farming would require an initial investment in capital, there are already facilities designed to produce dietary insects. Many manufacturers in the United States already breed crickets, mealworms, and other insects, but mainly for animal feed. Since these insects are omnivores, they're not picky. Crickets will eat flowers, other insect eggs, fruit, aphids, leaves, decaying plants, other insect larvae, seedlings, and dog food. And, since insects are cold-blooded, they are more effective at converting energy from their food into protein. Crickets need twelve times less feed than cattle to produce the same amount of protein (Van Huis et al., 2013).

Insects are also less particular about their personal space than mammals or birds. For example, a young broiler chicken needs about a foot of turf, and this requirement increases as the chicken gets older ("Animal Welfare for Broiler Chickens," 2012). Livestock currently takes up about 70 percent of all agricultural land, and the efficiency of insect farming could create the space necessary to feed our exponentially expanding population (Steinfeld et al., 2006). It will also cut down on deforestation, since most previously forested areas around the world are now used for livestock production.

Insect farming is better for the environment too.

Meat from mammals, birds, and fish is not only expensive and space-intensive. It contributes to climate change in big ways. Livestock farming alone is responsible for 18 percent

Eat More Bugs 5

of the world's greenhouse gas emissions, which is more than cars, planes, and boats combined (Steinfeld et al., 2006). These greenhouse gases include the usual carbon dioxide, but also methane and nitrous oxide from flatulence, manure, and urine. Most insect species do not produce these greenhouse gases.

The manure of cows, pigs, and other livestock also contains ammonia. Fine dust particles absorb this ammonia, which workers and livestock breathe in, causing respiratory problems such as asthma (Kim et al., 2008). These ammonia particles also smell bad and cause farm equipment to deteriorate faster. This manure spreads across land and seeps into the water system, causing the entire ecosystem to be more acidic and oxygen deficient. As a result, shellfish now struggle to create shells, and coral reefs erode. Fish have to use extra energy to maintain the right blood chemistry, which affects their brains. Clownfish normally avoid predators, but in acidic environments, they have trouble hearing the threat and bumble the escape (Simpson et al., 2011). Insect farming would remedy much of the growing acidification problems—it produces about a tenth of the ammonia of pig and beef ranching.

Most people's main objection to entomophagy is simple disgust—think of Ysabel Bello, cringing as she put grubs down her throat. However, this attitude will change. After all, lobster and shrimp consumption was once a shameful mark of poverty, but they eventually became an expensive delicacy in the United

Eat More Bugs 6

People can
learn to love
insects.

States. We also thought raw fish was disgusting, but wrap it in rice and seaweed and we eat it up—literally. So products such as Exo's protein bars or Sylvain Musquar's delicate French chocolates may similarly bring insects into vogue.

Clearly then, it makes sense to change our eating habits: entomophagy would benefit our hearts, waistlines, wallets, and consciences. The sooner we supplement our current livestock and poultry diets with creepy-crawlies, the healthier and more sustainable our society will be. With all its health and environmental advantages, entomophagy will soon join the mainstream. As more grocery stores and restaurants stock insects, you could join the revolution with just a few crunchy bites.

References

Adult obesity facts. (2015). Centers for Disease Control and
     Prevention. Retrieved from https://www.cdc.gov/nchs/
     data/databriefs/db219.pdf

Animal welfare for broiler chickens. (2012). The National
     Chicken Council. Retrieved from http://www
     .nationalchickencouncil.org/industry-issues/
     animal-welfare-for-broiler-chickens/

Dioula, M.B.M. (2014). Caterpillars in diets. Food and
     Agriculture Organization of the United Nations. Retrieved
     from http://www.fao.org/fileadmin/user_upload/
     nutrition/docs/policies_programmes/Good_practices/12

Eat More Bugs 7

FAO fish price index. (2015). Globefish. Retrieved from http://
test3.2openlab.it/fao_globefish/fao-fish-price-index-jan-2015
.html

FSNL Factsheet_Caterpillars_in_DRC.pdf

Facts & figures on food and biodiversity. (2015). IDRC
Communications. Retrieved from https://www.idrc.ca/en/
article/facts-figures-food-and-biodiversity

Health & environmental implications of U.S. meat
consumption & production. (2016). Center for a Livable
Future. Johns Hopkins Bloomberg School of Public
Health. Retrieved from http://www.jhsph.edu/research/
centers-and-institutes/johns-hopkins-center-for
-a-livable-future/projects/meatless_monday/resources/
meat_consumption.html

Helmer, J. (2015, May). Mmmm, crickets: How Exo protein
bars found its wings. Entrepreneur. Retrieved from
https://www.scribd.com/article/327136065/
Mmmm-Crickets-How-Exo-Protein-Bars-Found-Its-Wings

Kim, K. Y., Jong Ko H., Tae Kim, H., Shin Kim, Y., Man Roh, Y.,
Min Lee, C., & Nyon Kim, C. (2008). Quantification of
ammonia and hydrogen sulfide emitted from pig
buildings in Korea. Journal of Environmental
Management 88(2) (2008), 195–202.

Ocean Portal Team. (2014) Ocean acidification. Smithsonian
Ocean Portal. Retrieved from http://ocean.si.edu/
ocean-acidification

Eat More Bugs 8

Simpson, S. D., Munday, P. L., Wittenrich, M. L., Manassa, R., Dixson, D. L., Gagliano, M., & Yan, H. Y. (2011). Ocean acidification erodes crucial auditory behaviour in a marine fish. Biology Letters 7(6) (2011), 917–20. Retrieved from http://rsbl.royalsocietypublishing.org/content/early/2011/05/25/rsbl.2011.0293

Steinfeld, H., Gerber, P., Wassenaar, T., Castel, V., Rosales, M., & De Haan, C. (2006). Livestock's long shadow: Environmental issues and options. Food and Agriculture Organization of the United Nations. Retrieved from ftp://ftp.fao.org/docrep/fao/010/a0701e/a0701e00.pdf

Van Huis, A., Van Itterbeeck, J., Klunder, H., Mertens, E., Halloran, A., Muir, G., Vantomme, P. (2013). Edible insects: Future prospects for food and feed security. Food and Agriculture Organization of the United States. Retrieved from http://www.fao.org/docrep/018/i3253e/i3253e.pdf

VISUAL PROPOSAL   Jen Sorensen is an editorial cartoonist fond of four-panel spreads with political messages. The medium requires that messages be expressed economically, so Sorensen uses broad strokes to suggest that people might think twice about the logic of convenience. Who really benefits?

Reading the Genre   Notice that each of the panels could stand on its own as a critique of some consumer desire exploited by industries eager to market new products. What happens if you reorder the panels?

1. **Trial Balloon:** Glenn Reynolds no doubt knows that his proposal to abolish the Ivy League isn't ever going to happen (p. 147). too many Ivy Leaguers in Congress and the White House. But he makes a point that's hard to ignore. Choose an issue that you think needs as radical a rethinking as the inequity Reynolds finds in the funding of public colleges (compared to elite private ones) and write a research-based proposal of your own. Like Reynolds, be sure to offer your ideas in language clever and persuasive enough to make responsible adults at least consider them.

2. **Manifesto:** In "Eat More Bugs" (p. 159), Ellen Airhart asks you to alter your life in a small way to benefit society at large. Or is it a small change? Argue for a comparable proposal that others might consider beyond the pale—give up your car; give up your cell phone; give up your privileged career ambitions—and then offer good reasons to eat the bug.

3. **Visual Proposal:** Jen Sorensen's editorial cartoonist offers enough memorable "data" in her four panels (p. 166) to lead readers to recognize a problem and draw their own conclusions. But it's not as easy as it looks. Try your hand at creating a visual proposal of your own that accomplishes as much.

4. **Your Choice:** Proposals are often practical documents, serving a specific need. Identify such a need in your life and address it through a clear, fact-based proposal. For example, you might write to your academic adviser or dean suggesting that a service-learning experience would be a better senior project for you than a traditional written thesis—given your talents and interests. Or perhaps you might write to a banker (or wealthy relative) explaining why loaning you money to open a barbecue restaurant would make sound fiscal sense, especially since no one else in town serves decent brisket and ribs. In other words, write a paper to make your life better.

How to start ▶
- Need to **find texts to analyze**? See page 176.
- Need to come up with **ideas**? See page 179.
- Need to **organize your ideas**? See page 183.

Literary Analyses

13

respond
thoughtfully
to cultural
works

Unless you're an English major, the papers you write for Literature 101 may seem as mechanical as chemistry lab reports—something done just to get a degree. But hardly a day goes by when you don't respond strongly to some literary or cultural experience, sharing your insights and opinions about the books, concerts, movies, and other entertainments you love. It's worth learning to do this well.

CULTURAL REFLECTION
Noticing how influential novels composed in series—and their movie versions—have been recently, you write a paper exploring the cultural significance of the Redwall, Harry Potter, and Hunger Games books for young readers.

CLOSE READING
Unconvinced by a teacher's casual suggestion that the Anglo-Saxon author of "The Wanderer" (c. tenth century CE) was experiencing what we now call "alienation," you write a *close reading* of the poem to show why the modern concept doesn't fit the poem.

LITERACY NARRATIVE
On the first day of a writing course, your instructor asks you to describe your experiences with books and writing. Your narrative opens with recollections of Junie B. Jones and Lemony Snicket's *A Series of Unfortunate Events*. For more on literacy narratives, see Chapter 1.

Defining the genre

In a traditional literary analysis, you respond to a poem, novel, play, or short story. That response can be interpretive, looking at theme, plot, structure, characters, genre, style, and so on. Or it can be critical, theoretical, evaluative, or even personal—locating works within their social, political, or philosophic neighborhoods. Or you might approach a literary work expressively, describing how you connected with it intellectually and emotionally in the present or past. Or you can combine these approaches or imagine alternatives—reflecting new attitudes and assumptions about media.

Other potential media for analysis include films, TV shows, popular music, comic books, and games (for more on choosing a genre, see Chapter 2). Distinctions between high and popular culture have not so much dissolved as ceased to be interesting. After all, you can say dumb things about *Hamlet* and smart things about *Game of Thrones*. Moreover, every genre of artistic expression—from sonnets to opera to graphic novels—at some point struggled for respectability. What matters is the quality of a

***Duvor Cloth* (*Communal Cloth*)** The Ghanaian artist El Anatsui builds his remarkable abstract sculptures from street materials, including metal fragments and bottle caps. He explains, "I believe that artists are better off working with whatever their environment throws up." El Anatsui (Ghanaian, born 1944), *Duvor Cloth (Communal Cloth)*, 2007, aluminum and copper wire, 13 × 17 ft. Indianapolis Museum of Art, Ann M. Stack Fund for Contemporary Art, 2007.25. © El Anatsui/ The Bridgeman Art Library.

literary analysis and whether you help readers appreciate the novel *Pride and Prejudice* or, maybe, the video game *Bayonetta*. Expect your literary or cultural analyses to do *some* of the following.

Begin with a close reading. In traditional analyses of creative works, you slow the pace at which people in a 24/7 world operate to examine a text or object meticulously, sometimes line by line or frame by frame. You may study the way individual words and images connect in a poem, or how plot evolves in a novel, or how creative editing shapes the character of a movie. In short, you study the *calculated* choices writers and artists make in creating their works. **O**

Make a claim or an observation. The point you want to make about a work or cultural trends won't always be argumentative or controversial: You may be amazed at the simplicity of Wordsworth's Lucy poems or blown away by Jimi Hendrix's take on "All Along the Watchtower." But more typically, you'll make an observation you believe is worth proving either by research or by evidence you discover within the work itself.

Use texts for evidence. Reflections and analyses help readers appreciate the complexities in creative works or cultural trends: You direct them to the neat stuff in a poem, novel, drama, or song or ask them to ponder the significance of changes in the cultural environment. For that reason, you have to pay attention to the details—words, images, textures, trends, phenomena, memories—that support your claims about a literary or cultural experience.

Present literature in context. Works of art respond to the world; that's what we like about them and why they sometimes change our lives. Your analysis can explore these relationships among texts, people, and society. Help readers understand the political, cultural, or moral dimensions of literary works.

Draw on previous research. Your response to a work need not match what others have felt. But you should be willing to learn from previous scholarship and criticism—readily available in libraries or online. **O**

read closely
p. 324

plan a project
p. 428

Cultural Reflection

You may have encountered Dana Gioia's "Why Literature Matters" in prepping for college entrance exams: It's a highly readable, much-discussed defense of reading, a phenomenon that seemed in decline in 2005 when Gioia was serving as Chair of the National Endowment for the Arts. He doesn't mention that position in his essay (or even use the pronoun *I*), but his title gives him a soapbox to stand on.

Reading the Genre   Gioia argues that skills learned from serious reading of literature transfer to other spheres of life—even the most practical ones. Thinking about the literary reading you have done in recent years, would you be inclined to support Gioia's analysis? Could other artistic or entertainment genres—movies, TV series, video games—confer similar skills?

Why Literature Matters: Good Books Help Make a Civil Society

BY DANA GIOIA

April 10, 2005

In 1780 Massachusetts patriot John Adams wrote to his wife, Abigail, outlining his vision of how American culture might evolve. "I must study politics and war," he prophesied, so "that our sons may have liberty to study mathematics and philosophy." They will add to their studies geography, navigation, commerce, and agriculture, he continued, so that their children may enjoy the "right to study painting, poetry, music . . ."

Adams's bold prophecy proved correct. By the mid-twentieth century, America boasted internationally preeminent traditions in literature, art, music, dance, theater, and cinema.

But a strange thing has happened in the American arts during the past quarter century. While income rose to unforeseen levels, college attendance ballooned and access to information increased enormously, the interest young Americans showed in the arts—and especially literature—actually diminished.

According to the 2002 Survey of Public Participation in the Arts, a population study designed and commissioned by the National Endowment for the Arts (and executed by the U.S. Bureau of the Census), arts participation by Americans has declined for eight of the nine major forms that are measured. (Only jazz has shown a tiny increase—thank you, Ken Burns.) The declines have been most severe among younger adults (ages 18–24). The most worrisome finding in the 2002 study, however, is the declining percentage of Americans, especially young adults, reading literature.

That individuals at a time of crucial intellectual and emotional development bypass the joys and challenges of literature is a troubling trend. If it were true that they substituted histories, biographies, or political works for literature, one might not worry. But book reading of any kind is falling as well.

That such a longstanding and fundamental cultural activity should slip so swiftly, especially among young adults, signifies deep transformations in contemporary life. To call attention to the trend, the Arts Endowment issued the reading portion of the survey as a separate report, "Reading at Risk: A Survey of Literary Reading in America."

The decline in reading has consequences that go beyond literature. The significance of reading has become a persistent theme in the business world. The February issue of *Wired* magazine, for example, sketches a new set of mental skills and habits proper to the twenty-first century, aptitudes decidedly literary in character: not "linear, logical, analytical talents," author Daniel Pink states, but "the ability to create artistic and emotional beauty, to detect patterns and opportunities, to craft a satisfying narrative." When asked what kind of talents they like to see in management positions, business leaders consistently set imagination, creativity, and higher-order thinking at the top.

Ironically, the value of reading and the intellectual faculties that it inculcates appear most clearly as active and engaged literacy declines. There is now a growing awareness of the consequences of nonreading to the workplace. In 2001 the National Association of Manufacturers polled its members on skill deficiencies among employees. Among hourly workers, poor reading skills ranked second, and 38 percent of employers complained that local schools inadequately taught reading comprehension.

Gioia focuses on evidence that young people are doing less "literary" reading.

Gioia uses an essay by Daniel Pink to define skills cultivated by literary reading.

Corporate America makes similar complaints about a skill intimately related to reading—writing. Last year, the College Board reported that corporations spend some $3.1 billion a year on remedial writing instruction for employees, adding that they "express a fair degree of dissatisfaction with the writing of recent college graduates." If the twenty-first-century American economy requires innovation and creativity, solid reading skills and the imaginative growth fostered by literary reading are central elements in that program.

> Gioia argues that serious reading skills are valued in the corporate and civic spheres.

The decline of reading is also taking its toll in the civic sphere. In a 2000 survey of college seniors from the top fifty-five colleges, the Roper Organization found that 81 percent could not earn a grade of C on a high-school-level history test. A 2003 study of 15- to 26-year-olds' civic knowledge by the National Conference of State Legislatures concluded, "Young people do not understand the ideals of citizenship . . . and their appreciation and support of American democracy is limited."

It is probably no surprise that declining rates of literary reading coincide with declining levels of historical and political awareness among young people. One of the surprising findings of "Reading at Risk" was that literary readers are markedly more civically engaged than nonreaders, scoring two to four times more likely to perform charity work, visit a museum, or attend a sporting event. One reason for their higher social and cultural interactions may lie in the kind of civic and historical knowledge that comes with literary reading.

> Does literary reading cause civic/social engagement or merely correlate with it?

Unlike the passive activities of watching television and DVDs or surfing the Web, reading is actually a highly active enterprise. Reading requires sustained and focused attention as well as active use of memory and imagination. Literary reading also enhances and enlarges our humility by helping us imagine and understand lives quite different from our own.

Indeed, we sometimes underestimate how large a role literature has played in the evolution of our national identity, especially in that literature often has served to introduce young people to events from the past and principles of civil society and governance. Just as more ancient Greeks learned about moral and political conduct from the epics of Homer than from the dialogues of Plato, so the most important work in the abolitionist movement was the novel *Uncle Tom's Cabin*.

Consider your own recent engagement with literary works like those named by Gioia. Do literary works influence you more than entertainments that don't require reading?

Likewise our notions of American populism come more from Walt Whitman's poetic vision than from any political tracts. Today when people recall the Depression, the images that most come to mind are of the travails of John Steinbeck's Joad family from *The Grapes of Wrath*. Without a literary inheritance, the historical past is impoverished.

In focusing on the social advantages of a literary education, however, we should not overlook the personal impact. Every day authors receive letters from readers that say, "Your book changed my life." History reveals case after case of famous people whose lives were transformed by literature. When the great Victorian thinker John Stuart Mill suffered a crippling depression in late-adolescence, the poetry of Wordsworth restored his optimism and self-confidence—a "medicine for my state of mind," he called it.

A few decades later, W. E. B. Du Bois found a different tonic in literature, an escape from the indignities of Jim Crow into a world of equality. "I sit with Shakespeare and he winces not," Du Bois observed. "Across the color line I move arm in arm with Balzac and Dumas, where smiling men and welcoming women glide in gilded halls." Literature is a catalyst for education and culture.

The evidence of literature's importance to civic, personal, and economic health is too strong to ignore. The decline of literary reading foreshadows serious long-term social and economic problems, and it is time to bring literature and the other arts into discussions of public policy. Libraries, schools, and public agencies do noble work, but addressing the reading issue will require the leadership of politicians and the business community as well.

Could politicians, entertainers, or entrepreneurs convince young people especially to read more? Has the trend away from reading continued in the years since Gioia wrote this reflection?

Literature now competes with an enormous array of electronic media. While no single activity is responsible for the decline in reading, the cumulative presence and availability of electronic alternatives increasingly have drawn Americans away from reading.

Reading is not a timeless, universal capability. Advanced literacy is a specific intellectual skill and social habit that depends on a great many educational, cultural, and economic factors. As more Americans lose this capability, our nation becomes less informed, active, and independent-minded. These are not the qualities that a free, innovative, or productive society can afford to lose.

Claiming a topic

▶ find a text

In most cases, you write a literary reflection or analysis to meet a course requirement, a paper usually designed to improve your skills as a reader of literature and art. Such a lofty goal, however, doesn't mean you can't enjoy the project or put your own spin on it.

Your first priority is to read any assignment sheet closely to find out exactly what you are asked to do. Underline any key words in the project description and take them seriously. Typically, you will see terms such as *compare and contrast*, *classify*, *analyze*, or *interpret*. They mean different things, and each entails a different strategy.

Once you know your goal in writing an analysis, you may have to choose a subject—though occasionally it may even be yourself. ○ It's not unusual to have your instructor assign a work (*Three pages on* The House on Mango Street *by Friday*). But just as often, you'll select a work to study from within a range defined by the title of the course: Mexican American Literature; Major Works of Dostoyevsky; Banned Books; Theater and Cultural Diversity. Which should you choose?

Choose a text, genre, or literary/cultural perspective you connect with. It makes sense to spend time writing about works or ideas that move you, perhaps because they touch on an aspect of your life or identity. You may feel more confident studying them because of who you are and what you've experienced.

Choose a topic you want to learn more about. In the backs of their minds, most people have lists of works and artists they've always wanted to explore. So turn an assignment into an opportunity to sample one of them: *Beowulf*; *The Chronicles of Narnia*; or the work of William Gibson, Leslie Marmon Silko, or the Clash. Or use an assignment to push beyond the works that are from within your comfort zone or familiar to your own experience: Examine writers and artists from cultures different from your own and with challenging points of view.

get an idea
p. 387

Choose a text or topic you don't understand. Most students write about accessible works that are relatively new: Why struggle with a hoary epic poem when you can just watch *The Lord of the Rings* on Blu-ray? One obvious reason may be to figure out how works from unfamiliar times still powerfully connect to our own; the very strangeness of older and more mysterious texts may even rouse you to ask better questions. You'll pay more attention to literary texts or issues that puzzle you.

Imagining your audience

Unless you post book reviews on Amazon or write essays for a campus literary magazine, the people reading your analyses of works of art and culture are most likely a professor and other students in your course. But in either situation, assume a degree of expertise among your readers. Understand, too, that people who read literary and cultural analyses on their own expect to learn something. So make good use of their time.

Clearly identify the author and works you are analyzing. It seems like common sense, but this courtesy is neglected in many academic papers because students assume that *the teacher must know what I'm doing.* Don't make this mistake. Also briefly recap what happens in the works you are discussing—especially with texts not everyone has read recently. ○ Follow the model of good reviewers, who typically review key story elements before commenting on them. Such summaries give readers their bearings at the beginning of a paper. Here's James Wood introducing a novel by Marilynne Robinson that he will be reviewing for the *New York Times*.

> *Gilead* is set in 1956 in the small town of Gilead, Iowa, and is narrated by a seventy-six-year-old pastor named John Ames, who has recently been told he has angina pectoris and believes he is facing imminent death. In this terminal spirit, he decides to write a long letter to his seven-year-old son, the fruit of a recent marriage to a much younger woman. This novel is that letter, set down in the easy, discontinuous form of a diary, mixing long and short entries, reminiscences, moral advice, and so on.

Define key terms. Literary analyses use many specialized and technical expressions. Your instructor will doubtless know what an *epithet*, *peripeteia*, or *rondel* might be, but you need to define terms like these for wider audiences—your classmates, for instance. Alternatively, you can look for more familiar synonyms.

Don't aim to please professional critics. Are you tempted to imitate the style of serious academic theorists you've encountered while researching your paper? No need—your instructor probably won't expect you to write in that way, at least not until graduate school.

> **Thinking about Writing** You may not browse academic journals on literary subjects, but you probably read about cultural texts you enjoy—book series, current movies, television series, video games, popular music, and so on. What is it you are looking for when you read about these entertainments, especially online? Basic information? Critical opinions? Evaluations and reviews? What might you like to contribute to such conversations? Could you turn any such conversation into a serious academic piece?

sum up ideas
p. 457

Gathering materials

develop ◀
ideas

With an academic assignment in hand and works to analyze, the next step—and it's a necessary one—is to establish that you have reliable "texts" of whatever you'll be studying. In a course, a professor may assign a particular edition or literary anthology for you to use, making your job easier.

This Bedford/St. Martin's edition of *Frankenstein* provides important textual information and background. Look for texts with such material when studying classic novels, poems, and plays.

Be aware that many texts are available in multiple editions. (For instance, the novel *Frankenstein* first appeared in 1818, but the revised third edition of 1831 is the one most widely read today.) For classical works, such as the plays of Shakespeare, choose an edition from a major publisher, preferably one that includes thorough notes and perhaps some critical essays. When in doubt, ask your professor which texts to use.

Other kinds of media pose interesting problems as well. For instance, you may have to decide which version of a movie to study—the one seen by audiences in theaters or the "director's cut" on Blu-ray. Similarly, you might find multiple recordings of classical music: Look for widely respected performances. Even popular music may come in several versions: studio (*American Idiot*), live (*Bullet in a Bible*), alternative recording (*American Idiot: The Original Broadway Cast Recording*). Then there is the question of drama: Do you read a play on the page, watch a video when one is available, or see it in a theater? Perhaps you do all three. But whatever versions of a text you choose for study, be sure to identify them in your project, either in the text itself or on the Works Cited page. **○**

Establishing a text is the easy part. Once that's done, how do you find an angle on the subject? **○** Try the following strategies and approaches.

Examine the "text" closely. Guided by your assignment, carefully read, watch, or examine the selected work(s) and take notes. Obviously, you'll treat some works

understand citation styles p. 463

find a topic p. 16

179

differently from others. You can read a Seamus Heaney sonnet a dozen times to absorb its nuances, but it's unlikely you'd push through Rudolfo Anaya's novel *Bless Me, Ultima* more than once or twice for a paper. But, in either case, you'll need to keep notes or to annotate what you're studying.

Honestly, you should count on a minimum of two readings or viewings of any text, the first one to get familiar with the work and find a potential approach, the second and subsequent ones to confirm your thesis and to find evidence for it. And do read the actual novel or play, not some slimmed-down synopsis, modernized, or "no fear" version.

Focus on the text itself. Your earliest literature papers probably tackled basic questions about plot, character, setting, theme, and language—but you needn't cringe. These are still issues that fascinate many readers. Just be sure to look for moments when the plot of the novel you're analyzing establishes its themes or study how characters develop in response to specific events. Even the setting of a short story or film might be worth writing about when it becomes a factor in the story: Can you imagine the film *Casablanca* taking place in any other location?

Questions about language always loom large in literary analyses. How does word choice shape the mood of a poem? How does a writer create irony through diction or dialogue? Indeed, any technical feature of a work might be studied and researched, from the narrators in novels to the rhyme schemes in poetry to the editing of a scene within a movie.

Focus on meanings, themes, and interpretations. Although tracing themes in literary works seems like an occupation mostly for English majors, the impulse to find meanings is irresistible. If you take any work seriously, you'll discover angles and ideas worth sharing with readers. Maybe *Seinfeld* is a modern version of *Everyman*, or you see elements of *The Breakfast Club* in *13 Reasons Why*, or maybe not. Open your mind to possible connections: What have you seen like this before? What structural patterns do you detect? What ideas are supported or undercut?

Focus on authorship and history. Some artists stand apart from their creations, while others cannot be separated from them. So you might explore closely how a work mirrors the life, education, and attitudes of its author. Is the author writing to represent his or her gender, race, ethnicity, or class? Or does the work repudiate its author's identity, social standing, or religion? What psychological forces or religious perspectives drive the work's characters or themes?

Similarly, consider how a text embodies the assumptions, attitudes, politics, fashions, and even technology of the times during which it was composed. A work as familiar as Jonathan Swift's "A Modest Proposal" still requires readers to know at least a *little* about Irish and English politics in the eighteenth century. How does Swift's satire expand in scope when you learn more about its environment?

Focus on genre. Literary genres are formulas. Take noble characters, give them a catastrophic flaw, have them make bad choices, and then kill them off: That's tragedy—or, in the wrong hands, melodrama. With a little brainstorming, you could identify dozens of other genres and subcategories: epics, sonnets, historical novels, superhero comics, grand opera, soap opera, and so on. Artists often create works that fall between genres, sometimes producing new ones. Readers, too, bring clear-cut expectations to a text: Try to turn a 007 action-spy thriller into a three-hankie teen angst flick, and you've got trouble in River City.

You can analyze genre in various ways. For instance, track a text backward to discover its literary forebears—the works an author used for models. Even works that revolt against older genres bear traces of what their authors have rejected. It's also possible to study the way artists combine different genres or play with or against the expectations of audiences. Needless to say, you can also explore the relationships of works within a genre. For example, what do twentieth-century coming-of-age stories, such as *A Separate Peace*, *The Catcher in the Rye*, and *Lord of the Flies*, have in common?

Focus on influences. Some works have an obvious impact on life or society, changing how people think or behave: *Uncle Tom's Cabin*, *To Kill a Mockingbird*, *Roots*, *Schindler's List*. TV shows have broadened people's notions of family; musical genres, such as jazz and gospel, have created and sustained entire communities.

But impact doesn't always occur on such a grand scale or express itself through social movements. Books influence other books, films other films, and so on—with not a few texts crossing genres. For better or worse, books, movies, and other cultural productions influence styles, fashions, and even the way people speak. Consider *Breaking Bad*, *The Simpsons*, or *Game of Thrones*. You may have to think outside the box, but projects that trace and study cultural influences can shake things up.

Focus on social connections. In recent decades, many texts have been studied for what they reveal about relationships between genders, races, ethnicities, and social classes. Works by newer writers are now more widely read in schools, and hard questions are asked about texts traditionally taught: What do they reveal about the treatment of women, minorities, immigrants, homosexual or transgender people? Whose lives have been ignored in "canonical" texts? What responsibility do such texts have for maintaining repressive political or social arrangements? Critical analyses of this sort have changed how many people view literature and art, and you can follow up on such studies and extend them to texts you believe deserve more (or less) attention.

Find good sources. Developing a literary paper provides you with many opportunities and choices. Fortunately, you needn't make all the decisions on your own. Ample commentary and research are available on almost any literary subject or method, both in print and online. ○ Your instructor and local librarians can help you focus on the best resources for your project, but the following boxes list some possibilities.

Literary Resources in Print

Beacham, Walton, editor. *Research Guide to Biography and Criticism*. Beacham Publishing, 1990.

Birch, Dinah, editor. *The Oxford Companion to English Literature*. 7th ed., Oxford UP, 2009.

Crystal, David. *The Cambridge Encyclopedia of Language*. 3rd ed., Cambridge UP, 2010.

Encyclopedia of World Literature in the 20th Century. 3rd ed., St. James Press, 1999.

Gates, Henry Louis, Jr., et al. *The Norton Anthology of African American Literature*. 3rd ed., W. W. Norton, 2014.

Gilbert, Sandra M., and Susan Gubar. *The Norton Anthology of Literature by Women: The Traditions in English*. 3rd ed., W. W. Norton, 2007.

Greene, Roland, et al. *The Princeton Encyclopedia of Poetry and Poetics*. 4th ed., Princeton UP, 2012.

Harmon, William, and Hugh Holman. *A Handbook to Literature*. 12th ed., Prentice Hall, 2012.

Harner, James L. *Literary Research Guide: A Guide to Reference Sources for the Study of Literature in English and Related Topics*. 6th ed., Modern Language Association of America, 2014.

Hart, James D., and Phillip W. Leininger. *The Oxford Companion to American Literature*. 6th ed., Oxford UP, 1995. Online edition 2013.

Howatson, M. C. *The Oxford Companion to Classical Literature*. 3rd ed., Oxford UP, 2011.

Leitch, Vincent, et al. *The Norton Anthology of Theory and Criticism*. 2nd ed., Norton, 2010.

Murfin, Ross, and Supryia M. Ray. *The Bedford Glossary of Critical and Literary Terms*. 4th ed., Macmillan Learning, 2018.

Sage, Lorna. *The Cambridge Guide to Women's Writing in English*. Cambridge UP, 1999.

refine your search
p. 436

Literary Resources Online

Annual Bibliography of English Language and Literature (ABELL) (subscription)

The Atlantic (theatlantic.com) (for culture and reviews)

Browne Popular Culture Library (bgsu.edu/colleges/library/pcl)

The Complete Works of William Shakespeare (shakespeare.mit.edu)

Eserver.org: Accessible Writing (eserver.org)

A Handbook of Rhetorical Devices (virtualsalt.com/rhetoric.htm)

Literature Resource Center (Gale Group) (subscription)

New York Review of Books (nybooks.com/)

New York Times Book Review (nytimes.com/pages/books)

The Online Books Page (onlinebooks.library.upenn.edu)

Organizing ideas

Build the structure for your literary analysis around the particular observation, claim, or point you hope to make. Your project will be organized like a report if you're interested in sharing information and explaining what is already known. It will develop like an argument if your thesis offers fresh claims or veers toward controversy. ○ Or it may read like a narrative or personal essay if it is a reflection on your own experiences as a reader or writer. What matters most, however, is that you organize your work in ways that make sense to readers.

organize ◀
ideas

Imagine a structure. Analyses of literature and culture can head in various directions. One analysis might present a string of evidence to support a thematic claim; another might examine similarities and differences between two or more works; yet another might explore an open-ended question, with ideas emerging expressively,

○
understand argument
p. 89

rather than demonstrating a single point. Consider how the following claims might lead to very different structures:

STUDY OF THEME

In *Bless Me, Ultima*, the youngster Antonio has to reconcile his mystical beliefs with Ultima's prediction that he will become a "man of learning."

CONTRAST OF GENRES

The movie version of Annie Proulx's short story "Brokeback Mountain" actually improves on the original work, making the narrative more appealing, moving, and believable.

CULTURAL ANALYSIS

One likely impact of digital technology will be to eliminate traditional barriers between art, entertainment, and business—with books becoming films that morph into games that inspire commercial art and even music.

Here are three simple forms a literary analysis might take, the first developing from a thesis stated early on, the second comparing two works to make a point, and the third building toward a conclusion rather than opening with a traditional thesis. **O**

Introduction leading to a claim

    First supporting reason + textual evidence
    Second supporting reason + textual evidence
    Additional supporting reasons + textual evidence

Conclusion

Introduction leading to a claim about Texts 1 and 2

    First supporting reason

        Evidence from Text 1
        Evidence from Text 2

    Next supporting reason

        Evidence from Text 1
        Evidence from Text 2

develop a statement
p. 333

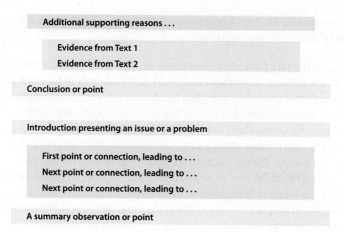

Work on your opening. Be sure that the introductory paragraphs of your literary or cultural analyses identify the works you are examining, explain what you hope to accomplish, and provide necessary background information (including brief plot summaries, for example). ○ Always provide enough context so that the project stands on its own and would make sense to someone other than the instructor who assigned it.

Choosing style and design

Literary analyses are often traditional assignments still typically done in an academic style and following specific conventions of language and MLA documentation. ○ But such analyses also lend themselves surprisingly well to new media, especially when their topics focus on video or aural texts. So style and media can be important issues in both literary and cultural projects.

Use a formal style for most assignments. As the student example in this chapter suggests, literary analyses you write for courses will be serious in tone, formal in vocabulary, and, for the most part, impersonal—all markers of a formal or high style. ○ Elements of that style can be identified in this paragraph from an academic paper in

shape a beginning
p. 395

cite in MLA
p. 470

define your style
p. 368

which Manasi Deshpande analyzes Emily Brontë's *Wuthering Heights*. Here she explores the character of its Byronic hero, Heathcliff:

Examines Heathcliff from the perspective of potential readers.

Complex sentences smoothly incorporate quotations and documentation.

Related points are expressed in parallel clauses.

Vocabulary throughout is accessible but formal. No contractions are used.

In witnessing Heathcliff's blatantly violent behavior, the reader is caught between sympathy for the tormented Heathcliff and shock at the intensity of his cruelty and mistreatment of others. Intent on avenging Hindley's treatment of him, Heathcliff turns his wrath toward Hareton by keeping him in such an uneducated and dependent state that young Cathy becomes "upset at the bare notion of relationship with such a clown" (193). Living first under Hindley's neglect and later under Heathcliff's wrath, Hareton escapes his situation only when Catherine befriends him and Heathcliff dies. In addition, Heathcliff marries Isabella only because Catherine wants to "'torture [him] to death for [her] amusement'" and must "'allow [him] to amuse [himself] a little in the same style'" (111). Heathcliff's sole objective in seducing and running away with Isabella is to take revenge on Catherine for abandoning him. Heathcliff's sadism is so strong that he is willing to harm innocent third parties in order to punish those who have caused his misery. He even forces young Cathy and Linton to marry by locking them in Wuthering Heights and keeping Cathy from her dying father until she has married Linton, further illustrating his willingness to torture others out of spite and vengeance.

Use a middle style for informal or literacy narratives.

Occasionally, for example, you may have to write brief essays called *response* or *position papers*, in which you record your immediate reactions to poems, short stories, or other readings. Or an instructor may ask for a paper in which you discuss the influence reading or literature has on you. In these assignments, an instructor may want to hear your voice and may even encourage exploratory reactions. Here is Cheryl Lovelady responding somewhat personally to a proposal to revive the Broadway musical *Fiddler on the Roof*:

Question focuses paragraph. Reply suggests strong personal opinion.

Basic style remains serious and quite formal: Note series of roughly parallel clauses that follow colon.

How can a play set in a small, tradition-bound Jewish village during the Russian Revolution be modernized? I would argue that *Fiddler on the Roof* is actually an apt portrayal of our own time. Throughout the show, the conflicted main character, Tevye, is on the brink of pivotal decisions. Perplexed by his daughters' increasingly modern choices, Tevye prays aloud, "Where do they think they are, America?" Tevye identifies America as a symbol of personal freedom—the antithesis of the tradition that keeps his life from being "as shaky as a fiddler on the roof." Forty years after the play's debut, America has become startlingly more like the Anatevka Tevye knows than the America he envisions. Post-9/11 America parallels Anatevka in a multitude of ways: Political agendas ideologically separate the United States from most of the world; public safety and conventional wisdom are valued over individual freedoms; Americans have felt the shock of violence brought onto their own soil; minority groups are isolated or isolate themselves in closed communities; and societal taboos dictate whom people may marry.

Sara Krulwich/The New York Times/Redux Pictures

A 2015 Broadway revival of the musical *Fiddler on the Roof*.

Follow the conventions of academic literary analysis. One of the norms of such pieces is to set the action in a novel, poem, or movie in the present tense when you describe or summarize it: "Hamlet kills his uncle just moments before he himself dies."

Another convention is to furnish the dates of birth and death for any major authors or artists you mention in an analysis. Similarly, give a year of publication or release date for any major works of art you mention. The dates usually appear in parentheses.

> Joan Didion (b. 1934) is the author of *Play It as It Lays* (1970), *Slouching Towards Bethlehem* (1968), and *The Year of Magical Thinking* (2005).

Finally, since you'll be frequently citing passages from literary works as well as quoting critics and reviewers, thoroughly review the rules for handling quotations. ○ All quoted materials need to be appropriately introduced and, if necessary, modified to fit smoothly into your sentences and paragraphs.

○
use quotations
p. 463

△

Cite plays correctly. Plays are cited by act, scene, and line number. In the past, passages from Shakespeare were routinely identified using a combination of Roman and Arabic numerals. But currently, MLA recommends Arabic numerals only for such references.

FORMER STYLE

Hamlet's final words are "The rest is silence" (*Ham.* V.ii.358).

CURRENT STYLE

Hamlet's final words are "The rest is silence" (*Ham.* 5.2.358).

Explore alternative media. You can be creative with literary and cultural projects, depending on the tools and media available to you. ○ For example, an oral presentation on a literary text can be handled impressively using presentation software, such as PowerPoint or Prezi. Or Google Maps might be used to trace the physical locations or journeys in literary works. Naturally, if your project is to be submitted in electronic form, you can incorporate photographs, images, or the spoken word into your project, as appropriate. "Appropriate" means that the media elements genuinely enrich your analysis.

go multimodal
p. 404

Examining models

In "Insanity: Two Women," Kanaka Sathasivan examines a poem (Emily Dickinson's "I felt a Funeral, in my Brain") and a short story (Charlotte Perkins Gilman's "The Yellow Wallpaper") to discover a disturbing common theme in the work of these two American women writers. The essay, written in a formal academic style, uses a structure that examines the works individually, drawing comparisons in a final paragraph. Note, in particular, how Sathasivan manages the close reading of the poem by Emily Dickinson, moving through it almost line by line to draw out its themes and meanings. Here's the text of "I felt a Funeral, in my Brain."

> I felt a Funeral, in my Brain,
> And Mourners to and fro
> Kept treading—treading—till it seemed
> That Sense was breaking through—
> And when they all were seated,
> A Service, like a Drum—
> Kept beating—beating—till I thought
> My Mind was going numb—
> And then I heard them lift a Box
> And creak across my Soul
> With those same Boots of Lead, again,
> Then Space—began to toll,
> As all the Heavens were a Bell,
> And Being, but an Ear,
> And I, and Silence, some strange Race
> Wrecked, solitary, here—
> And then a Plank in Reason, broke,
> And I dropped down, and down—
> And hit a World, at every plunge,
> And Finished knowing—then—

You can find the full text of "The Yellow Wallpaper" by searching online by the title. One such text is available at the University of Virginia Library Electronic Text Center.

Reading the Genre   Like any skillful academic paper, Sathasivan's "Insanity: Two Women" follows a great many conventions in structure, style, and mechanics. Go through the essay paragraph by paragraph and list as many of these moves as you can identify—right through the Works Cited page. Compare your list with those produced by several classmates.

Sathasivan 1

Kanaka Sathasivan

Professor Box

English 102

March 3, 20--

Insanity: Two Women

The societal expectations of women in the late nineteenth century served to keep women demure, submissive, and dumb. Although women's rights had begun to improve as more people rejected these stereotypes, many women remained trapped in their roles because of the pressures placed on them by men. Their suppression had deep impacts not only on their lives but also on their art. At a time when women writers often published under male aliases to gain respect, two of America's well-known authors, Emily Dickinson (1830–1886) and Charlotte Perkins Gilman (1860–1935), both wrote disturbing pieces describing the spiritual and mental imprisonment of women. In verse, Dickinson uses a funeral as a metaphor for the silencing of women and the insanity it subsequently causes. Gilman's prose piece "The Yellow Wallpaper" (1899) gives us a firsthand look into the mental degradation of a suppressed woman. These two works use vivid sensory images and rhythmic narration to describe sequential declines into madness.

Works to be analyzed are set in context: late nineteenth century.

Identifies authors and sets works in thematic relationship.

States thesis for the comparison.

Sathasivan 2

In "I felt a Funeral, in my Brain" (first published in 1896), Dickinson outlines the stages of a burial ceremony, using them as metaphors for a silenced woman's departure from sanity. The first verse, the arrival of Mourners, symbolizes the imposition of men and society on her mind. They are "treading" "to and fro," breaking down her thoughts and principles, until even she is convinced of their ideas (lines 3, 2). The Service comes next, representing the closure—the acceptance of fate. Her "Mind was going numb" as the sounds of the service force her to stop thinking and begin accepting her doomed life. These first two verses use repetition at parallel points as they describe the Mourners as "treading—treading" and the service as a drum "beating—beating" (3, 7). The repetition emphasizes the incessant insistence of men; they try to control threatening women with such vigor and persistence that eventually even the women themselves begin to believe men's ideas and allow their minds to be silenced.

As the funeral progresses, the Mourners carry her casket from the service. Here Dickinson describes how they scar her very Soul using the "same Boots of Lead" that destroyed her mind (11). From the rest of the poem, one can infer that the service took place inside a church, and the act of parting from a house of God places another level of finality on the loss of her spirituality. While the figures in the poem transport her, the church's chimes begin to ring, and, as if "all the Heavens were a Bell / And Being, but an Ear," the noise consumes her (13–14).

Offers close reading of Dickinson's poem.

Sathasivan 3

In this tremendous sound, her voice finally dissolves forever; her race with Silence has ended, "Wrecked," and Silence has won (16). Finally, after the loss of her mind, her soul, and her voice, she loses her sanity as they lower her casket into the grave and bury her. She "hit a World, at every plunge, / And Finished knowing" (19–20). The worlds she hits represent further stages of psychosis, and she plunges deeper until she hits the bottom, completely broken.

Like Dickinson, Gilman in "The Yellow Wallpaper" also segments her character's descent into madness. The narrator of the story expresses her thoughts in a diary written while she takes a vacation for her health. Each journal entry represents another step toward insanity, and Gilman reveals the woman's psychosis with subtle hints and clues placed discreetly within the entries. These often take the form of new information about the yellow room the woman has been confined to, such as the peeled wallpaper or bite marks on the bedpost. The inconspicuous presentation of such details leads the reader to think that these artifacts have long existed, created by someone else, and only now does the narrator share them with us. "I wonder how it was done and who did it, and what they did it for," she says, speaking of a groove that follows the perimeter of the walls (400). Here, Gilman reuses specific words at crucial points in the narration to allude to the state of her character's mental health. In this particular example, both the narrator and

With simple transition, turns to Gilman's short story.

Sathasivan 4

the maid use the word "smooch" to describe, respectively, the groove in the wall and yellow smudges on the narrator's clothes (400). This repetition indicates that she created the groove in the room, a fact affirmed at the end of the story.

Uses present tense to describe action in "The Yellow Wallpaper."

Gilman's narrator not only seems to believe other people have caused the damage she sees, but also imagines that a woman lives trapped within the paper, shaking the pattern in her attempts to escape. "I think that woman gets out in the daytime!" the narrator exclaims, recounting her memories of a woman "creeping" about the garden (400, 401). Again, Gilman uses repetition to make associations for the reader as the narrator uses "creeping" to describe her own exploits. As in the previous example, the end of the story reveals that the woman in the paper is none other than the narrator, tricked by her insanity. This connection also symbolizes the narrator's oppression. The design of the wallpaper trapping the woman represents the spiritual bars placed on the narrator by her husband and doctor, who prescribes mental rest, forbidding her from working or thinking. Even the description of the room lends itself to the image of a dungeon or cell, with "barred" windows and "rings and things in the walls" (392). Just as the woman escapes during the daytime, so, too, does the narrator, giving in to her sickness and disobeying her husband by writing. Finally, like the woman in the paper breaking free, the narrator succumbs to her insanity.

Sathasivan 5

Both Dickinson's and Gilman's works explore society's influence on a woman's mental health. Like Dickinson's character, Gilman's narrator has also been compelled into silence by a man. Although she knows she is sick, her husband insists it isn't so and that she, a fragile woman, simply needs to avoid intellectual stimulation. Like a Mourner, "treading—treading," he continually assures her he knows best and that she shouldn't socialize or work. This advice, however, only leads to further degradation as her solitude allows her to indulge her mental delusions. When the narrator attempts to argue with her husband, she is silenced, losing the same race as Dickinson's character.

In both these pieces, the characters remain mildly aware of their declining mental health, but neither tries to fight it. In Dickinson's poem, the woman passively observes her funeral, commenting objectively on her suppression and burial. Dickinson uses sound to describe every step, creating the feel of secondary sensory images—images that cannot create a picture alone and require interpretation to do so. Gilman's narrator also talks of her sickness passively, showing her decline only by describing mental fatigue. In these moments she often comments that her husband "loves [her] very dearly" and she usually accepts the advice he offers (Gilman 396). Even on those rare occasions when she disagrees, she remains submissive and

Draws attention to common themes and strategies in the two works.

Notes difference in technique between authors.

allows her suppression to continue. In contrast to Dickinson, Gilman uses visual images to create this portrait, describing most of all how the narrator sees the yellow wallpaper, an approach that allows insight into the narrator's mental state.

Both Dickinson and Gilman used their writing to make profound statements about the painful lives led by many women in the nineteenth century. Through repetition, metaphor, symbolism, and sensory images, both "I felt a Funeral, in my Brain" and "The Yellow Wallpaper" describe a woman's mental breakdown, as caused by societal expectations and oppression. The poetry and prose parallel one another and together give insight into a horrific picture of insanity.

Concludes that writers use similar techniques to explore a common theme in two very different works.

Works Cited

Dickinson, Emily. "I felt a Funeral, in my Brain." *Concise Anthology of American Literature*, edited by George McMichael, 7th ed., Longman Publishing, 2011, p. 1139.

Gilman, Charlotte Perkins. "The Yellow Wallpaper." *The American Short Story and Its Writer: An Anthology*, edited by Ann Charters, Bedford/St. Martin's, 2000, pp. 391–403.

MLA documentation style used for in-text notes and works cited.

1. **Cultural Analysis**: Review Dana Gioia's "Why Literature Matters" (p. 172). Then try your hand at writing an essay or argument about some aspect of literacy or culture you believe more people should take seriously—or, alternatively, already take too seriously. Feel free to define "culture or literacy" broadly. Essays like this work best when you draw on expertise you already have. Sing the praises of *Empire* or *Downton Abbey* or the Houston rap scene—but do it with authority and do some reading. Gioia's essay is relatively short and has no documentation. Your essay might follow the same format, but be respectful in acknowledging any sources you use.

2. **Close Reading**: In "Insanity: Two Women" (p. 190), Kanaka Sathasivan does a close, almost line-by-line analysis of Emily Dickinson's "I felt a Funeral, in my Brain"; then she compares the themes and strategies of the poem to those she finds in Charlotte Perkins Gilman's "The Yellow Wallpaper." For a project of your own, do *either* a close reading of a favorite short poem or song *or* a comparison of two works from different genres or media.

   For the close reading, tease out all the meanings and strategies you can uncover and show readers how the text works. For the comparison, be sure to begin with works that interest you because of some important similarity: They may share a theme or plot, or even be the *same* work in two different media—*Game of Thrones* in novel and television forms, for instance.

3. **Your Choice**: Write a paper about any work of poetry or fiction that you wish more people would read. Use your essay to explain (or, if necessary, defend) the qualities of the work that make it worth someone's serious attention.

How to start

- Need to **find a text to analyze**? See page 203.
- Need to come up with **ideas**? See page 205.
- Need to **organize your ideas**? See page 208.

Rhetorical Analyses

14

examine in
detail the
way texts
work

Rhetorical analysis is a fancy term for paying careful attention to how texts of all kinds (not just written communications) influence and sometimes manipulate you. These days, it seems everyone wants to shape your opinion, get you to "like" them, or open your wallet. Recognizing the strategies behind these endless appeals has become a survival skill worth cultivating. You can acquire that talent by observing how exactly rhetorical appeals work in editorials, political commentary of all sorts, and, especially, social media—and then reacting prudently whenever you see (or feel) them. Analyses of arguments have become common academic assignments, especially in these times when almost everyone pays attention to politics.

DISCOURSE/ CRITICAL ANALYSIS

For an assignment in a writing class, you do a close reading of an argument a politician makes in an important campaign speech. You want to identify the rhetorical strategies she uses and why she manages to sound so much more persuasive than most Washington pols.

ANALYSIS OF CULTURE

You can't help but notice the way political rhetoric, much of it partisan and belligerent, now spreads virally from social media, to online sources and then to TV and print news outlets. Finding the phenomenon disturbing, you explore the long-term ramifications of this trend.

ANALYSIS OF AN ARGUMENT

You find an extended story in a national news magazine so persuasive that you study it carefully to find out exactly what features contribute to its clarity and credibility.

Defining the genre

You react to what others say or write all the time. Sometimes it's an advertisement, a speech, or maybe an Instagram photograph that grabs you so hard that you want to take it apart to see how it works. Put those discoveries into words and you've composed a *rhetorical analysis* (for more on choosing a genre, see Chapter 2).

"Graduation Speaker" To some readers, this editorial cartoon by Nate Beeler of the *Columbus Dispatch* might seem like a harmless jab at cowardly college administrators unwilling to face protests at graduations. But why are those puppies wearing mortarboards? What exactly is going on here—rhetorically?

Rhetoric is the art of using language and media to achieve particular ends. When you want to identify and maybe imitate the specific techniques that writers, speakers, artists, or advertisers use to be persuasive, you can do what is called a discourse analysis—an objective study of how language and other media work in specific situations or texts. ◘ Taking such an analysis one step further, you might cast neutrality aside and offer good reasons for endorsing or disagreeing with a particular technique or argument and even stake out a position of your own. Such a detailed inspection of a text is sometimes called a *critical analysis*.

Whatever type of rhetorical analysis you choose to pursue (and the subgenres often merge), you'll find the following advice helpful.

understand argument
p. 89

Take words and images seriously. When you compose rhetorical analyses, hold writers to high standards because their choices have consequences. Fair and effective techniques of persuasion deserve to be identified and applauded. And crooked ones should be exposed and sent packing. It takes practice to distinguish one from the other—which is what rhetorical analyses provide.

Spend time with texts. We blow through most of what we read (and see) without much thought. But you cannot assess the techniques of a writer, speaker, or artist until you know them inside out. So serious rhetorical analysis requires that you sometimes read line-by-line and pixel-by-pixel, asking questions all the time: *Why did the writer choose this word? Emphasize this example? Employ this metaphor? What impact on the audience did images projected behind the speaker have? What's the significance of the musical themes used in the convention hall?* A rhetorical analysis makes texts move like bullets in *The Matrix*—their motion slowed and their trajectories traced for careful study. **O**

Pay attention to audiences. When you do a rhetorical analysis, understanding for *whom* a text is written can be as important as *what* it says. In fact, audiences determine the content, shape, and language of most arguments. You'll see this principle in action on p. 200.

Mine texts and rhetorical occasions for evidence. Take nothing for granted. Point to subtle or ironic language, overblown emotional appeals, intricate logic, or covert bigotry. Give special emphasis to any rhetorical moves that casual readers of a text (or participants in a rhetorical event, such as a rally, demonstration, or speech) are likely to miss. Moves such as these will be the best support for your claims in a rhetorical analysis. Expect to quote often. **O**

read closely p. 324   use quotations p. 463

Discourse/Critical Analysis

David E. Bernstein, a professor of law at George Mason University constructed the following comparison between Chanukah messages sent by President Barack Obama and Texas Senator Ted Cruz in 2015. (The Jewish holiday is explained in one of the messages.) Bernstein's discourse analysis makes it clear how purposefully different the rhetoric of the two men was. In effect, Obama and Cruz were reaching out to different audiences within the Jewish community with contrasting worldviews. The analysis is reprinted here without commentary so as not to disrupt Bernstein's original structure and typography. Note that his commentary after each part is italicized and his conclusion is boldfaced.

Reading the Genre   Could you do a rhetorical analysis of Bernstein's rhetorical analysis itself? How does its structure influence your response? Why the boldfaced conclusion? Does the analysis seem fair, or do you detect a bias? Do you need to know more about the author? (The piece originally appeared online on the Volokh Conspiracy, a blog allied with the *Washington Post*, but editorially independent. Contributors to the blog describe themselves this way: "We're generally libertarian, conservative, centrist, or some mixture of these, though we don't toe any party line and sometimes disagree even with each other.")

The Fascinating Contrast between President Obama's and Sen. Cruz's Hanukkah (Chanukah) Greetings

BY DAVID BERNSTEIN

December 6, 2015

First part:
   President Obama: "Tonight, Jews in America, Israel, and around the world come together to light the first candle of the Festival of Lights. At its heart, Hanukkah is about the struggle for justice in the face of overwhelming obstacles."
   Sen. Ted Cruz (R-Tex.): "Today Heidi and I wish the Jewish Community a very Happy Chanukah. On this holiday, we remember the miracle that enabled a freedom-loving people—led by the heroic Maccabees—to defeat the oppressive dictator Antiochus so that they could once again freely

worship the God of Abraham, Isaac, and Jacob. For the eight days of Chanukah, the Jewish people commemorate their liberation from oppression and the rededication of the Temple in Jerusalem. As the Talmud teaches, God delivered 'many into the hands of the few, strong into the hands of the weak, and evildoers into the hands of the righteous.'"

> *Obama's Hanukkah is universalist, about a "struggle for justice." There is no mention of God. Cruz's Chanukah (note the less common, but more traditional spelling) is about the Jewish people, with God's help, winning the right to worship against an oppressive dictatorship.*

Second part:

Obama: "It's a chance to reflect on the triumph of liberty over tyranny, the rejection of persecution, and on the miracles that can happen even in our darkest hours. It renews our commitment as Americans—as people who live by faith and conscience—to lead the way and act as unyielding advocates for the fundamental dignity of every human being."

Cruz: "Today, the Jewish people, together with freedom-loving people around the world, once again find their religious faith and liberty under attack from radical forces of oppression and intolerance. Whether it is the BDS movement on college campuses, anti-Semitic attacks in Europe, or radical Islamic terror in Israel and around the world, we need modern-day Maccabees to stand together and push back against the forces of evil. As a nation founded by a people seeking religious liberty, America stands with the Jewish people both at home and abroad in protecting the light of faith and liberty."

> *The lesson from Obama's Hanukkah is that Americans should advocate for "the fundamental dignity of every human being." Jews as such are incidental to the holiday, as is religious freedom. Cruz's Chanukah lesson is that Jews must be protected from their modern enemies.*

Third part:

Obama: "During these eight days, let us be inspired by the light that can overcome darkness. As we recall the Maccabees' struggle to free a people from oppression, let us rededicate ourselves to being the engine of the miracles we seek. May the lights of the menorah brighten your home and warm your heart, and from my family to yours, Chag Sameach."

Cruz: "The victory of the people of Israel is a testament to God's providence. On these nights when Jewish families around the country and the world celebrate with latkes, lighting the menorah, and playing dreidel, Heidi and I join with you to recognize 'Nes Gadol Hayah Sham,' a great miracle happened there. We only need to look at our nation's heritage to know that great miracles have happened here too, 'Nes Gadol Hayah Po,' and will continue to happen with God's blessing. We are grateful for the Divine tradition and we give thanks for the blessings of liberty. Happy Chanukah."

> *Obama's Hanukkah teaches the sort of vague, and vaguely agnostic, and universalistic Sunday school platitudes one might find in theologically liberal congregations around the country, that we should "be the engine of the miracles we seek." And he doesn't even identify which "people" the Maccabees sought to free from oppression. Cruz's Chanukah is both a specifically Jewish celebration and a "testament to God's providence," to which Cruz, evoking Ronald Reagan, also attributes the wonders of the United States.*

Conclusion: Each politicians' [sic] Hanukkah appeals to the sort of Jews (and non-Jews) most likely to support them. For Obama, it's the culturally Jewish, universalist, theologically liberal or atheistic Jews who see in Judaism primarily a call to pursue "social justice," and who often believe that Jews, as "white people," don't come within modern liberalism's concern for marginalized groups.

For Cruz, it's the religiously Jewish, theologically more conservative Jews, along with Jews who think that the Jewish position in the world is hardly so secure that they can ignore the fate of the Jewish people in favor of a purely universalistic ethic.

Given that each politician undoubtedly had aides responsible for their "Jewish portfolio" prepare their greetings, it's a fascinating insight into their competing perspectives. I think it may also tell us a lot about the emerging worldviews of liberal Democratic and conservative Republicans more generally.

Claiming a topic

Make a difference. Done right, rhetorical analyses can be as important as the texts they examine. They may change readers' opinions, open their eyes to new ideas, or keep an important argument going. They may also draw attention to rhetorical strategies and techniques worth imitating or avoiding. But cast your net widely because almost any kind of text—not just political ones—can have consequences. For example, an insurance form so deliberately complex that it might discourage legitimate claims would be ripe for a rhetorical analysis. So would almost any advertisement or Web site. Even events like rallies or public ceremonies could be worth scrutiny.

Choose a text you can work with. When responding to a course assignment and you can choose a text on your own to analyze rhetorically, find a gutsy piece that makes a claim you or someone else might actually disagree with. It helps too if you have a stake in the issue and already know something about it. The text should also be of a manageable length so that you can explore it coherently within the limits of the assignment.

Choose a text you can learn more about. Some items won't make much sense out of context. So choose a text or series of texts that you are willing to study and research. O It will obviously help to know who created an item; where it first appeared; and when it was written, presented, or produced. This information—which you'll certainly want to share with readers—is just as important for visual texts, such as advertisements, posters, and films, as for traditional speeches or articles.

Choose a text with handles. Investigate arguments that do interesting things. Maybe a speech uses lots of anecdotes or repetition to generate emotional appeals; perhaps a photo-essay's commentary is more provocative than the images; a print ad may arrest attention by its simplicity but still be full of cultural significance. You've got to write about the piece. Make sure it offers you adventurous things to say.

Choose a text you know how to analyze. Stick to printed texts if you aren't sure how to write about ads or films or even speeches. But don't sell yourself short. You can pick up the necessary vocabulary by reading models of rhetorical and critical analysis. Moreover, you don't always need highly technical terms to describe poor logic, inept design, or offensive strategies, wherever they appear. Nor do you need special expertise to describe cultural trends or detect political motives.

find a text ◀

Need help deciding what to write about? See "How to Browse for Ideas" on pp. 20–21.

plan your research p. 426

> **Thinking about Writing**   A highbrow or sophisticated topic isn't
> required for a successful rhetorical analysis. If you analyze a text that genuinely
> interests you (Chanukah messages, for example; see p. 200), chances are good
> readers will feel the same way. So begin an open-ended assignment by listing
> the sorts of texts you encounter and react to regularly. Even text messages and
> tweets can be studied rhetorically—as readers have learned in recent years.

Imagining your audience

The Shelter Pet Project
Advertisements featuring animals appeal to audiences, especially when they involve animal care or welfare. Here's a thought-provoking pitch to adopt shelter pets.

Some published rhetorical analyses are written for audiences already inclined to agree with their authors' opinions. Riled up by an offensive editorial or tweet, people these days even seek out and enjoy mean-spirited, over-the-top criticism, especially on the Web. But rhetorical and critical analyses you write for class should be relatively restrained because you can't predict how your readers might feel about the arguments you are critiquing. Always assume that you are writing for a diverse and thoughtful group, full of readers who prefer reflective analysis to clever put-downs. You don't have to be dull or passionless. Just avoid the easy slide into rudeness. ○

The Humane Society of the United States, Maddie's Fund ® and the Ad Council

respect your readers
p. 383

Gathering materials

Before you analyze a text of any kind, do some background research. Discover all you can about its author, creator, publisher, sponsor, and so on. For example, you would need to know if a TV commercial you intend to examine has aired only on sports networks or lifestyle programs on cable. Figure out, too, the contexts in which an argument occurs. If you reply to a *Wall Street Journal* editorial, know what events sparked that item and investigate the paper's editorial slant.

ideas ◄

Then read the piece carefully just for information, highlighting names or allusions you need to look up: there's very little you can't uncover these days via a Web search. When you think you understand the basics, you are prepared to approach the text rhetorically. Persuasive texts are often analyzed according to how they use three types of rhetorical appeal. Typically, a text may establish the character and credibility of its author (*ethos*), generate emotions in order to move audiences (*pathos*), and use evidence and logic to make its case (*logos*).

Consider the ethos of the author. Ethos—the appeal to character—may be the toughest argumentative strategy to understand. Every text and argument is presented by someone, whether an individual, a group, or an institution. Consciously or not, audiences are influenced by that self-presentation: They are swayed by writers or speakers who come across as knowledgeable, honest, fair-minded, and believable. They are less friendly to people or institutions that seem to be deceptive, untrustworthy, or incompetent.

> Here Michael Ruse describes a witness whose frank words established his ethos in a 1981 court case dealing with requiring creation science in Arkansas schools.
>
> The assistant attorney general was trying to tie him into knots over some technical point in evolutionary biology. Finally, the man blurted out, "Mr. Williams, I'm not a scientist. . . . I am an educator, and I have my pride and professional responsibilities. And I just can't teach that stuff [meaning creationism] to my kids."
>
> — "Science for Science Teachers," *Chronicle of Higher Education*, January 13, 2010

Look for such moments in texts—although such plain-spoken testimony will be rare. Instead, you may find indications of writers' authority and competence (or lack thereof) in how they describe their credentials, how they use sources, how they address readers, or how they use language. Even the absence of a "self" in a piece, as is typically the case in a scientific paper or academic article, can suggest a persuasive objectivity and rigor. Writers also bring their careers and reputations to a piece, and that stature may be enhanced (or diminished) by where they publish, yet another aspect of ethos. An article about climate change in a respected scientific journal will simply have more clout than a report on its results on a blog.

Consider how a writer plays to emotions. *Pathos*—the emotional appeal—is usually easy to detect but sometimes difficult to assess. Look for places where a text generates strong feelings to support its points, win over readers, or influence them in other ways. Then consider how appropriate the tactic is for advancing a particular argument. The strategy is legitimate so long as raising emotions, such as pity, fear, pride, outrage, and the like, fits the moment and doesn't move audiences to make choices based upon distorted perceptions of the facts. Pulitzer Prize-winning columnist Peggy Noonan, for example, routinely uses emotions to make her political points.

> We fought a war to free slaves. We sent millions of white men to battle and destroyed a portion of our nation to free millions of black men. What kind of nation does this? We went to Europe, fought, died, and won, and then taxed ourselves to save our enemies with the Marshall Plan. What kind of nation does this? Soviet communism stalked the world, and we were the ones who steeled ourselves and taxed ourselves to stop it. Again: What kind of nation does this?
>   Only a very great one.
>
> — "Patriots, Then and Now," *Wall Street Journal*, March 30, 2006

Obviously, patriotic sentiments like these can be a smoke screen in some political debates. Your challenge in a rhetorical analysis is to point out emotional appeals and to determine whether they move audiences to act humanely or manipulate them into making bad or even stupid choices.

Consider how well reasoned a text is. *Logos*—the appeal to reason and evidence—is most favored in academic pieces. In a rhetorical analysis, you look carefully at the claims a text makes and whether they are supported by facts, data, testimony, and good reasons. What assumptions lie beneath the argument? That's a crucial query.

Ask questions about evidence too. Does it come from reliable sources or valid research? Is it up to date? Has it been reported accurately and fully? Has due attention been given to alternative points of view and explanations? Has enough evidence been offered to make a valid point? You might raise such objections, for example, when Peter Bregman, an expert on leadership training in business, makes an especially controversial argument:

> A study of 829 companies over thirty-one years showed that diversity training had "no positive effects in the average workplace." Millions of dollars a year were spent on the training resulting in, well, nothing. Attitudes—and the diversity of the organizations—remained the same.

It gets worse. The researchers—Frank Dobbin of Harvard, Alexandra Kalev of Berkeley, and Erin Kelly of the University of Minnesota—concluded that "In firms where training is mandatory or emphasizes the threat of lawsuits, training actually has negative effects on management diversity."

— "Diversity Training Doesn't Work," *Harvard Business Review Blog Network*, March 12, 2012

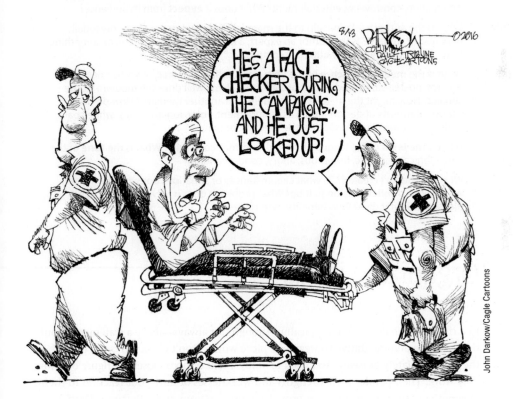

John Darkow/Cagle Cartoons

Clearly, you have your work cut out for you: Suddenly you are dealing not solely with Bregman but also with the study he cites (and a link in his blog posting takes you right to it). The bottom line is that the logic of every major claim in a text may need such scrutiny in a rhetorical analysis. You are simultaneously fact-checker and skeptic.

Questions for a Rhetorical Analysis

Consider the topic.	What is **fresh** or striking about the topic? How well defined is it? **Does the piece make a point?** Could it be clearer? Is **the topic** important? Relevant? Controversial? Is the subject covered comprehensively or selectively and **with obvious biases**? What is the level of detail?
Consider the audiences of the text.	To whom is the piece addressed? How **well** is the text **adapted** to its audience? Who is **excluded** from the audience, and how can you tell? What does the text offer its audience: information, controversy, entertainment? What does it **expect** from its audience?
Consider the author.	What is the author's relationship to the material? Is the writer or creator personally **invested** or **distant**? Is the author an expert, a knowledgeable amateur, or something else? What does the author **aim** to accomplish?
Consider the medium and design.	What is the medium or **genre** of the text: essay, article, editorial, advertisement, book excerpt, poster, video, podcast, or other format? How well does the medium **fit** the subject? How might the material look different in another medium? How do the various **elements** of design—such as arrangement, color, fonts, images, white space, audio, video, and so on—support the medium or genre?
Examine the language.	What is the **level** of the language: formal, informal, colloquial? What is the **tone** of the text—logical, sarcastic, humorous, angry, condescending?
Consider the occasion.	Why was the text created? To what circumstances or situations does it respond, and what might **public reaction** to it be? What problems does it solve or create? What pleasure might it give? Who benefits from the text?

Organizing ideas

▶ organize
   ideas

In a rhetorical analysis, you'll typically—though not always—make a statement about how well the argumentative strategy of a piece works. Don't expect to come up with a thesis immediately or easily: You need to study a text or texts closely to figure out how they work. Then ponder their strengths and weaknesses or note your reaction to them. Obviously, rhetorical analyses can provoke many reactions and reflections. Draft a tentative thesis and then refine it throughout the process of writing until you have a thought-provoking claim you can prove. ○

Your thesis should certainly do more than just list rhetorical features: *This ad has good logical arguments and uses emotions and rhetorical questions.* Why would someone want to read (or write) a paper with such an empty claim? The following thesis promises a far more potent rhetorical analysis:

> The latest government antidrug posters offer good reasons for avoiding steroids but do it in a visual style so bland that most students will ignore them.

develop a statement
p. 333

Once you have a thesis or hypothesis, try sketching a design based on a thesis/supporting reason/evidence plan. Focus on those features of the text that illustrate the points you wish to make. You don't have to discuss every facet of the text.

Introduction leading to a claim

> First supporting reason + textual evidence
> Second supporting reason + textual evidence
> Additional supporting reasons + textual evidence

Conclusion

In some cases, you might perform a line-by-line or paragraph-by-paragraph deconstruction of a text. This structure shows up frequently online. Such analyses practically organize themselves, but your commentary must be smart, accurate, and stylish to keep readers on board.

Introduction leading to a claim

> First section/paragraph + detailed analysis
> Next section/paragraph + detailed analysis
> Additional section/paragraph + detailed analysis

Conclusion

Choosing style and design

The style of your rhetorical analyses will vary depending on the audience, but you always face one problem that can sometimes be overcome by clever design: sharing the work you are analyzing with readers. They have to know what you are talking about.

Consider a high style.   Rhetorical and critical analyses for school usually need a formal or high style. ○ Keep the tone respectful, the vocabulary technical, and the perspective impersonal—avoiding *I* and *you*. Such a style gives the impression of objectivity and seriousness and enhances your ethos as a critic.

define your style p. 368

Consider a middle style. Rhetorical and critical analyses appearing in the public arena—rather than in the classroom—are often less formal. To win over readers not compelled to read their stuff, writers turn to the middle style, which gives them ample options for expressing strong opinions and feelings (sometimes including anger, outrage, and contempt). Public writing is full of distinctive personal voices—from Stephen Carter and Paul Krugman to Naomi Klein and Peggy Noonan—offering opinions, making judgments, and advancing agendas. The ethos of middle style is often more cordial and sympathetic than that of high style, if somewhat less authoritative and commanding. You win the assent of readers by making them like and trust you.

Make the text accessible to readers. Your rhetorical analysis should be written *as if readers do not have the text you are analyzing in hand or in front of them.* One way to achieve that clarity is to summarize and quote selectively from the text as you examine it or to provide visual images that are captioned or annotated. You can see examples of this technique in Matthew James Nance's essay on pages 214–19. Of course, you can always also attach photocopies or images of any items you are analyzing or provide Web links to them. With other types of subjects—such as movies, advertising campaigns, and so on—simply describe or summarize the content of the work. Or consider whether an analysis in another format might work better—you could use presentation software or create a video to present your analysis. Whatever you examine, always be sure to identify authors (or creators), titles, places/modes of publication, and dates in your paper.

Examining models

ANALYSIS OF CULTURE   Rather than just looking at the rhetoric of specific texts (as David Bernstein does on p. 200), Joe Weisenthal, writing for Bloomberg View, considers how persuasive language in general was changed by the presidential election of 2016. As you'll see, his thesis is sweeping and provocative, even though the specific evidence he can offer in a short piece is minimal. Yet Weisenthal is probably counting on readers to draw upon their own experiences with social media during recent election seasons to confirm (or refute) his theory.

Reading the Genre   Not all rhetoric is political. Persuasion occurs in all walks of life—including education, law, advertising, marketing, and even religion. Consider whether and how Weisenthal's thesis might apply to one of these other areas. Has, for example, education moved away from its traditional emphasis on texts and careful reading toward a reliance on Web sites, poster board sessions, and Powerpoint presentations—and, if so, does it matter?

Donald Trump, the First President of Our Post-Literate Age

By Joe Weisenthal

November 29, 2016

Introductory paragraphs suggest fake news was not the real media issue in the 2016 U.S. presidential election.

In the wake of the 2016 presidential election, the media has worked itself into a panic about the rise of fake news on social media. Reporters have examined the subject from dozens of angles—profiling misinformation peddlers from California to the Caucasus, analyzing how hoaxes spread, raising red flags about media literacy, and much more.

You can understand why journalists are so worried. For one thing, most reporters genuinely want the public to be well-informed. For another, there's a matter of self-interest: Fake news undermines journalists' authority as arbiters of truth. Also—and I'll let you in on a little secret here—most mainstream journalists probably preferred Clinton to Trump, so the idea that fake news swung the election is a tantalizing story.

But all this focus on fake Facebook news obscures a much bigger story about the way social media—the endless public opining and sharing of information—is reshaping politics. Even if you've never given much thought to its meaning, you've probably heard someone say "the medium is the message," the famous dictum of media theorist Marshall McLuhan.

To give context to his forthcoming claim, Weisenthal introduces readers to the language theories of Marshall McLuhan and Walter J. Ong.

But what does that mean, and what does it mean specifically for the 2016 election? A possible answer can be found in the work of Walter J. Ong, a Jesuit priest and a former student of McLuhan's at St. Louis University. In his most famous work, "Orality and Literacy," Ong examined how the invention of reading and writing fundamentally changed human consciousness. He argued that the written word wasn't just an extension of the spoken word, but something that opened up new ways of thinking—something that created a whole new world.

The easiest way to grasp the difference between the written world and the oral world is that in the latter, there's no way to look up anything. Before the invention of writing, knowledge existed in the present tense between two or more people; when information was forgotten, it disappeared forever. That state of affairs created a special need for ideas that were easily memorized and repeatable (so, in a way, they could go viral). The immediacy of the oral world did not favor complicated, abstract ideas that need to be thought through. Instead, it elevated individuals who passed along memorable stories, wisdom and good news.

And here we begin to see how the age of social media resembles the pre-literate, oral world. Facebook, Twitter, Snapchat, and other platforms are fostering an emerging linguistic economy that places a high premium on ideas that are pithy, clear, memorable, and repeatable (that is to say, viral). Complicated, nuanced thoughts that require context don't play very well on most social platforms, but a resonant hashtag can have extraordinary influence. Evan Spiegel, the chief executive officer of Snap Inc., grasped the new oral dynamics of social media when he told the Wall Street Journal: "People wonder why their daughter is taking 10,000 photos a day. What they don't realize is that she isn't preserving images. She's talking."

In "Orality and Literacy," Ong laid out several key differences between the oral and literate worlds, and through these, you can see why someone like Donald Trump would thrive in this new oral context. Here are a few examples:

- In the oral world, thoughts and expressions were, in Ong's words, "aggregative, not analytic"—which is to say that language was for-mulaic. Ong, who studied ancient oral epics like "The Odyssey" as well as pre-literate traditions that survived into the modern age, wrote that old masters of the oral tradition preferred to speak of "not

An oral culture uses language differently than a literate one.

Social media, Weisenthal argues, have shifted public language toward orality.

the soldier, but the brave soldier; not the princess, but the beautiful princess; not the oak, but the sturdy oak." That sounds familiar, right? Thus with Trump, it was never "Ted Cruz," "Marco Rubio," or "Hillary Clinton"; it was "Lyin' Ted," "Little Marco" and "Crooked Hillary." These endlessly repeated epithets packed extra information into small, instantly memorable packets.

- Oral culture rewards redundancy, because when an audience can't go back and consult a text, speakers must guard against distraction and confusion. Repetition is one useful technique, and Trump is a master of it. Consider the remarks he made during a March debate: "I'm a leader. I'm a leader. I've always been a leader. I've never had any problem leading people. If I say do it, they're going to do it. That's what leadership is all about." Oral traditions are all about hammering the point home.

- Because all communication in a pre-literate culture takes place face to face, there's a greater emphasis on verbal jousting. As Ong puts it, oral communication often resembles a "polite duel, a contest of wits"—in contrast to literature, which promotes abstraction by severing the link between author and text. Jeet Heer at the New Republic has made this point as well. Of course, aggression and argumentativeness are key to Trump's communication style.

> Political language in an oral culture becomes formulaic, repetitive, and combative.

None of this is totally novel in politics, of course. Politicians have always had slogans. Repetition is a standard rhetorical technique. And in general, the political world has always valued the ability to make a good speech.

Furthermore, the world is still an extremely long way from eliminating classical, written literacy. We can still look up something in a dictionary or Wikipedia. You can still experience solitude, getting lost in the deep stacks of a library, meticulously poring over authoritative documents word for word. But as information gets more social—taking on the immediate, short-form characteristics of Facebook and Twitter—it acquires more qualities of the oral world. And that lends itself particularly well to politicians who think and communicate like Donald Trump.

ANALYSIS OF AN ARGUMENT   For a class assignment on rhetorical analysis, Matthew James Nance chose as his subject the award-winning feature article "Can't Die for Trying" by journalist Laura Miller—who later would serve as mayor of Dallas. In the essay, Nance explains in detail how Miller manages to present the story of a convicted killer who wants to be executed to readers who might have contrary views about capital punishment. Nance's analysis is both technical and objective. He does an especially good job of helping readers follow the argument of "Can't Die for Trying," a fairly long and complicated article.

Reading the Genre   Nance skillfully handles an important technical feature of many rhetorical analyses: quotations. Read this piece with a focus on the ways he introduces material from Laura Miller's "Can't Die for Trying." Note how smoothly he merges her words with his and how strategically he introduces quotations to make or confirm his analyses.

Nance 1

Matthew James Nance

Professor Doss

English 2

June 14, 20--

A Mockery of Justice

In 1987, David Martin Long was convicted of double homicide and sentenced to death. He made no attempt to appeal this sentence and, surprisingly, did everything he could to expedite his execution. Nonetheless, due to an automatic appeals process, Long remained on Texas's Death Row for twelve years before he was finally executed. For various reasons, including investigations into whether he was mentally ill, the state of Texas had continued to postpone his execution date. In 1994, when David Long was still in the middle of his

Sets scene carefully and provides necessary background information.

Nance 2

appeals process, *Dallas Observer* columnist Laura Miller took
up his case in the award-winning article "Can't Die for Trying."
In this article, Miller explores the enigma of a legal system in
which a sociopath willing to die continues to be mired in the
legal process. The article is no typical plea on behalf of a
death-row inmate, and Miller manages to avoid a facile
political stance on capital punishment. Instead, Miller uses an
effective combination of logical reasoning and emotional
appeal to evoke from readers a sense of frustration at the
system's absurdity.

> Miller defies expectations and Nance explains why in his thesis.

   To show that David Martin Long's execution should be
carried out as soon as possible, Miller offers a reasoned
argument based on two premises: that he wants death and that
he deserves it. Miller cites Long's statement from the day he
was arrested: "I realize what I did was wrong. I don't belong in
this society. I never have. . . . I'd just wish they'd hurry up and
get this over with" (5). She emphasizes that this desire has not
changed, by quoting Long's correspondence from 1988, 1991,
and 1992. In this way, Miller makes Long's argument seem
reasoned and well thought out, not simply a temporary gesture
of desperation. "'Yes, there are innocent men here, retarded
men, insane men, and men who just plain deserve another
chance,' Long wrote [State District Judge Larry] Baraka in April
1992, 'But I am none of these!'" (5). Miller also points out his
guilty plea and the jury's remarkably short deliberation: "The

Nance 3

jury took only an hour to find Long guilty of capital murder—and forty-five minutes to give him the death penalty" (5). Miller does not stop there, however. She gives a grisly description of the murders themselves, followed by Long's calculated behavior in the aftermath:

> He hacked away at Laura twenty-one times before going back inside where he gave Donna fourteen chops. The blind woman, who lay in bed screaming while he savaged Donna, got five chops. Long washed the hatchet, stuck it in the kitchen sink, and headed out of town in Donna's brown station wagon. (5)

Miller's juxtaposition of reasoned deliberation with the bloody narrative of the murders allows her to show that Long, in refusing to appeal, is reacting justly to his own sociopathy. Not only is it right that he die; it is also right that he does not object to his death.

In the midst of this reasoned argument, Miller expresses frustration at the bureaucratic inefficiency that is at odds with her logic. She offers a pragmatic, resource-based view of the situation:

> Of course, in the handful of instances where a person is wrongly accused . . . this [death-penalty activism] is noble, important work. But I would argue that in others—David Martin Long in particular—it is a sheer waste of taxpayer dollars. And a mockery of justice. (6)

Long paragraph furnishes detailed evidence for Miller's two premises.

Provides both summaries and quotations from the article so that readers can follow Miller's argument.

To clarify Miller's point, Nance adds a phrase in brackets to the quotation.

Nance 4

Miller portrays the system as being practically incompatible with her brand of pragmatism. The figures involved in Long's case are painted as invisible, equivocal, or both. For instance, in spite of Long's plea, Judge Baraka was forced to appoint one of Long's attorneys to start the appeals process. "The judge didn't have a choice. Texas law requires that a death-penalty verdict be automatically appealed. . . . [This] is supposed to expedite the process. But the court sat on Long's case for four long years" (5). Miller also mentions Danny Burn, a Fort Worth lawyer in association with the Texas Resource Center, one of the "do-good . . . organizations whose sole feverish purpose is to get people off Death Row. . . . No matter how airtight the cases" (6). Burn filed on Long's behalf, though he never met Long in person. This fact underscores Miller's notion of the death-row bureaucracy as being inaccessible and, by extension, incomprehensible.

This parade of equivocal incompetence culminates in Miller's interview with John Blume, another activist who argued on Long's behalf. Miller paints Blume as so equivocal that he comes across as a straw man. "As a general rule," says Blume, "I tend to think most people who are telling you that are telling you something else, and that's their way of expressing it. There's something else they're depressed or upset about" (6). The article ends with Miller's rejoinder: "Well, I'd wager, Mr. Blume, that something is a lawyer like you" (6). Whereas the

> Notice how smoothly quotations merge into Nance's sentences.

Nance 5

article up to this point has maintained a balance between reason and frustration, here Miller seems to let gradually building frustration get the best of her. She does not adequately address whether Blume might be correct in implying that Long is insane, mentally ill, or otherwise misguided. She attempts to dismiss this idea by repeatedly pointing out Long's consistency in his stance and his own statements that he is not retarded, but her fallacy is obvious: Consistency does not imply sanity. Clearly, Miller would have benefited from citing Long's medical history and comparing his case with those of other death-row inmates, both mentally ill and well. Then her frustrated attack on Blume would seem more justified.

Miller also evokes frustration through her empathetic portrayal of Long. Although the article is essentially a plea for Long to get what he wants, this fact itself prevents Miller from portraying Long sympathetically. Miller is stuck in a rhetorical bind; if her readers become sympathetic toward Long, they won't want him to die. However, the audience needs an emotional connection with Long to accept the argument on his behalf. Miller gets around this problem by abandoning sympathy altogether, portraying Long as a cold-blooded killer. The quotation "I've never seen a more cold-blooded, steel-eyed sociopath ever" (5) is set apart from the text in a large font, and Miller notes, "This is a case of a really bad dude, plain and

---

Nance makes a clear judgment about Miller's objectivity— then offers evidence for his claim.

Nance examines the way Miller deals with the problem she has portraying a cold-blooded killer to readers.

simple. . . Use any cliché you want. It fits" (5). Miller here opts
for a weak appeal, evoking from the audience the same negative
emotion that Long feels. She gives voice to Long's frustration
over his interminable appeals: "Long stewed. . . . Long steamed.
. . . Long fumes . . ." (6). She also points out Long's fear of
himself: "I fear I'll kill again" (6). Clearly, the audience is meant
to echo these feelings of frustration and fear. This may seem like
a weak emotional connection with Long, but perhaps it is the
best Miller could do, given that a primary goal of hers was to
show that Long deserves death.

Laura Miller won the H. L. Mencken Award for this article,
which raises important questions about the legal process. Part
of its appeal is that it approaches capital punishment without
taking a simplistic position. It can appeal to people on both
sides of the capital punishment debate. The argument is
logically valid, and, for the most part, the emotional appeal is
effective. Its deficiencies, including the weak emotional appeal
for Long, are ultimately outweighed by Miller's overarching
rationale, which calls for pragmatism in the face of absurdity.

Work Cited

Miller, Laura. "Can't Die for Trying." *Dallas Observer*, 12 Jan.
    1994, pp. 5–6.

1. **Discourse/Critical Analysis:** Note how cleverly David Bernstein uses contrasting Chanukah messages from President Barack Obama and Senator Ted Cruz to explain the rhetorical choices each man made to reach an intended audience (see p. 200). Then try a similar discourse analysis of your own, comparing or contrasting how two (or more) texts in any media adapt their messages to particular audiences or situations. You might even contrast the rhetorical strategies needed to deliver *similar* messages in two or three different media—say an editorial, a cartoon, and a Facebook post. You may not find materials quite so apt to compare as Bernstein did, but consider borrowing—if you wish—the structure he uses for his analysis.

2. **Analysis of Culture:** In "Donald Trump, the First President of Our Post-Literate Age" (see p. 211), Joe Wisenthal argues that the repetitive, formulaic, and combative nature of recent political language indicates a return to older forms of communication. Study some other aspect of contemporary communication or media and, like Wisenthal, speculate about what it may mean for the future. Might the popularity of superhero-themed film series indicate that societies need new myths? Does the influence of Twitter (and similar media) indicate that we have lost patience for complex ideas or are increasingly unable to create them? Have video games become a substitute for real competition or enterprise? Have the rise of new gendered or gender-free pronouns mean that society is becoming more or less tolerant? Try to keep this paper focused on language, texts, and media, if possible.

3. **Close Reading of an Argument:** Browse recent news or popular-interest magazines or Web sites (such as *Time*, *The Atlantic*, *GQ*, the *New Yorker*, and so on) to locate a serious article you find especially well argued. Then, as Matthew James Nance does in "A Mockery of Justice" (p. 214), study the piece carefully enough to understand the precise techniques it uses to influence readers. Finally, write a rhetorical analysis in which you make and support a specific claim about the rhetorical strategies of the article.

4. **Your Choice:** Fed up by the blustering of a talk-show host, Twitter user, sports commentator, op-ed columnist, local editorialist, or stupid advertiser? Try an item-by-item or paragraph-by-paragraph refutation of such a target, taking on his or her poorly reasoned claims, inadequate evidence, emotional excesses, or lack of credibility. If possible, locate a transcript or reproduction of the text you want to refute so that you can work from the facts just as they have been offered. If you are examining a visual text you can reproduce electronically, experiment with using callouts to annotate the problems as you find them.

How to start

- Need a **topic**? See page 226.
- Need to recall the right **details**? See page 227.
- Need to **organize your ideas**? See page 229.

Essays

15

chronicle events in people's lives

explore ideas

You probably use the term *essay* simply as a synonym for academic *paper: I have to write an essay on the American Civil War.* But the essay is a distinct genre with a distinguished and remarkable pedigree. It was, in fact, invented by French author Michel de Montaigne (1533–92) when he published his personal reflections on a wide range of subjects under the title *Essais*. Appearing in three editions between 1580 and 1595, Montaigne's highly influential work established a pattern for writers ever since who choose to examine ideas through the lens of their own experiences. And his title stuck, defining a new open-minded and humanistic genre of writing.

Essays assigned in school generally follow the tradition when they encourage you to explore subjects from an individual (but well-informed) point of view.

EXPLORATORY ESSAY	On a long road trip from Connecticut to California, you keep a video diary. Reviewing it afterward, you wonder if "one nation, indivisible" still aptly defines the people you have encountered.
ARGUMENTATIVE ESSAY	Unable to afford a prestigious, but unpaid internship, you write an essay wondering whether the blue-collar labor of working-class students gives them more valuable and honest real-world experience.
PERSONAL ESSAY	Realizing that you mark time by the passage of sporting seasons, you write an essay pondering the influence these games and players have on your life and those of people around the world.

Defining the genre

Essays begin with an itch to use words to understand something better—that's the purpose of the genre. It gives you an opportunity to examine any aspect of life—as you've come to know it through encounters with people, places, and ideas. Of course, you could just ponder any subject on your own, study it online, or talk an issue to death with friends. But words committed to paper or screen put you face-to-face with your perceptions, exposing any contradictions or inconsistencies. *Do I really believe that? Do I want to believe that?* Fortunately, writing an essay also gives you the opportunity to change your mind. Essays you compose might do any of the following.

Make a point—usually. There's typically a reason for writing an essay, beyond the obvious one of fulfilling a school assignment. Your essays can convey information, explain phenomena, or make arguments—just as other genres do—but they also invite readers to watch how your mind works, to follow the processes of thought that lead to your conclusions. Think of essays as narratives, reports, or arguments with a heart—creative pieces that connect with readers to amuse, enlighten, and, perhaps, even change them. ○ Essays can be therapeutic too, helping you confront personal issues or get a load off your chest.

Tell a story. Essays often have a narrative dimension, their authors sharing personal experiences to illustrate points they wish to make. You could use an essay to recall a moment that altered your point of view or even changed your life. Or you might narrate a sequence of events that seem unrelated at first—the classic road-trip script—but that come together in a surprising or illuminating way. Or you might spin a tale as complicated as a mystery and invite readers to draw their own conclusions.

Offer details. They bring contemporary essays to life—providing evidence that your essay, whatever its topic, is authentic. Readers need assurance that you are knowledgeable enough about a subject or close enough to an experience to have an insider's perspective worthy of their consideration. You are their guide in an essay, and they expect a good one.

Focus on people. The personal dimension of many essays lends itself to portraits of people connected to your subject. In an essay, you might find yourself quoting individuals you've interviewed, offering anecdotes about people's lives and careers to underscore a point, or even making a single individual the focus of an entire piece. And that individual could be you.

> ❚❚
> When I play with my cat, who knows whether she is not amusing herself with me more than I with her.
> ❚❚

Sophie Bassouls/Sygma/Getty Images

—Michel de Montaigne

developing a statement
p. 333

Exploratory Essay

What better way to introduce this genre than to present an essay about essays, particularly a recent one that has garnered attention for criticizing the way writing is taught in school? Like Montaigne, its author Paul Graham is a bit of a Renaissance man, a Harvard PhD (in computer science) with business credentials and interests in painting and writing. Graham's "The Age of the Essay" is too lengthy to reprint in its entirety, so we offer its third and fourth sections "Trying" and "The River" (edited slightly for continuity). The full essay is available online.

Reading the Genre   Graham reflects on both the history of the essay as a genre and on his own experience writing pieces that don't follow the structure of more traditional legal or academic arguments, especially the kind driven by a thesis statement. What observations do you find most interesting or perhaps subversive in Graham's sections? What risks might you take submitting an essay as Graham describes it in an academic course?

The Age of the Essay (Excerpts)

PAUL GRAHAM

September 2004

Trying

To understand what a real essay is, we have to reach back into history . . . [t]o Michel de Montaigne, who in 1580 published a book of what he called "essais." He was doing something quite different from what lawyers do, and the difference is embodied in the name. *Essayer* is the French verb meaning "to try" and an *essai* is an attempt. An essay is something you write to try to figure something out.

Figure out what? You don't know yet. And so you can't begin with a thesis, because you don't have one and may never have one. An essay doesn't begin with a statement, but with a question. In a real essay, you don't take a position and defend it. You notice a door that's ajar, and you open it and walk in to see what's inside.

If all you want to do is figure things out, why do you need to write anything, though? Why not just sit and think? Well, there precisely is

> Notice the metaphor here comparing an essay to a not-quite-open door.

Montaigne's great discovery. Expressing ideas helps to form them. Indeed, helps is far too weak a word. Most of what ends up in my essays I only thought of when I sat down to write them. That's why I write them.

In the things you write in school, you are, in theory, merely explaining yourself to the reader. In a real essay you're writing for yourself. You're thinking out loud.

Writing for yourself distances you from potential readers.

But not quite. Just as inviting people over forces you to clean up your apartment, writing something that other people will read forces you to think well. So it does matter to have an audience. The things I've written just for myself are no good. They tend to peter out. When I run into difficulties, I find I conclude with a few vague questions and then drift off to get a cup of tea.

Many published essays peter out in the same way. Particularly the sort written by the staff writers of newsmagazines. Outside writers tend to supply editorials of the defend-a-position variety that make a beeline toward a rousing (and foreordained) conclusion. But the staff writers feel obliged to write something "balanced." Since they're writing for a popular magazine, they start with the most radioactively controversial questions, from which—because they're writing for a popular magazine—they then proceed to recoil in terror. Abortion, for or against? This group says one thing. That group says another. One thing is certain: the question is a complex one. (But don't get mad at us. We didn't draw any conclusions.)

The River

Questions aren't enough. An essay has to come up with answers. They don't always, of course. Sometimes you start with a promising question and get nowhere. But those you don't publish. Those are like experiments that get inconclusive results. An essay you publish ought to tell the reader something he didn't already know.

For Graham, essays are all about questions and answers.

But what you tell him doesn't matter, so long as it's interesting. I'm sometimes accused of meandering. In defend-a-position writing that would be a flaw. There you're not concerned with truth. You already know where you're going, and you want to go straight there, blustering through obstacles, and hand-waving your way across swampy ground. But that's not what you're trying to do in an essay. An essay is supposed to be a search for truth. It would be suspicious if it didn't meander.

The Meander (aka Menderes) is a river in Turkey. As you might expect, it winds all over the place. But it doesn't do this out of frivolity. The path it has discovered is the most economical route to the sea.

The river's algorithm is simple. At each step, flow down. For the essayist this translates to: flow interesting. Of all the places to go next, choose the most interesting. One can't have quite as little foresight as a river. I always know generally what I want to write about. But not the specific conclusions I want to reach; from paragraph to paragraph I let the ideas take their course.

This doesn't always work. Sometimes, like a river, one runs up against a wall. Then I do the same thing the river does: backtrack. At one point in this essay I found that after following a certain thread I ran out of ideas. I had to go back seven paragraphs and start over in another direction.

Fundamentally an essay is a train of thought—but a cleaned-up train of thought, as dialogue is cleaned-up conversation. Real thought, like real conversation, is full of false starts. It would be exhausting to read. You need to cut and fill to emphasize the central thread, like an illustrator inking over a pencil drawing. But don't change so much that you lose the spontaneity of the original.

Err on the side of the river. An essay is not a reference work. It's not something you read looking for a specific answer and feel cheated if you don't find it. I'd much rather read an essay that went off in an unexpected but interesting direction than one that plodded dutifully along a prescribed course.

> Unlike most academic reports and arguments, essays can wander like a river or conversation.

Claiming a topic

▶ topic

Montaigne was no specialist. His more than one hundred essays explore an amazing range of subjects: Of Fear, Of Friendship, Of Cannibals, Of the Custom of Wearing Clothes, Of the Inequality Among Us, Of War Horses, Of Smells, Of Drunkenness, Of Conscience. What holds his collections together is the author himself curious about all aspects of life.

You may face narrower choices when asked to write an essay for school. Typically, such an assignment invites you to ponder a specific facet of a broader subject you have been studying. Or perhaps an instructor wants a paper that gives historical and critical context to a particular phenomenon, such as a musical trend, a technological advancement, a political change. When no topic idea suggests itself, consider the following strategies.

Brainstorm, freewrite, build lists, and use memory prompts. To find a personal topic worth developing, pick up a yearbook, scroll through photographs, or browse your social media sites. Details you find there may jog your memory or set you to thinking about how your life is changing. Talk too with others about their choices of subjects and share ideas on a class Web site. For more details, see Chapter 3, p. 14.

Choose a manageable subject. You might be tempted to focus an essay on life-changing events so dramatic that they can seem clichéd: deaths, graduations, car wrecks, first job, or first love. For such topics to work, you have to make them fresh for readers who've probably undergone similar experiences—or seen the movie. If you can offer a fresh perspective on a common event (it may be a satiric or ironic one), take the risk. ○

Choose a consequential subject. Consequential doesn't necessarily mean long, ponderous, and boring. It means a subject that will resonate with readers who might share concerns you have about money, jobs, professions, families, relationships, race, sexuality, education, religion, technology, business, pop culture, sports. But here's the key—you don't tackle the topic in the abstract. Instead, you come at it from what you know or what you care about or maybe what surprises you. Write an essay about how awful Michael Bay films are, or what your grandmother's gift of a dollhouse meant to you, or how makeup makes your life better, or why we should take the Kardashians seriously. Explain to readers why a topic that intrigues you should interest them too.

Choose a puzzling subject. Recall Paul Graham's comparison of an essay with a meandering river (p. 224)? You don't have to begin an essay with a thesis or with every point nailed down. This paper may require several drafts to work through all its puzzles because you either don't quite understand something yourself at the outset or, maybe, most of your readers may not get what you are trying to accomplish. (After all, they might like Michael Bay films.)

get an idea p. 387

Imagining your audience

People like to read essays because when they are personal, thoughtful, and full of surprising insights, so audiences for the genre can be diverse and receptive—if that's what you want. Essays can also be addressed to special audiences of enthusiasts and experts, likely to care about, for example, FIFA, video game platforms, or *Stranger Things*. Readers of essays do expect their authors to make some point or share an insight. They hope to be moved by what they read, learn something from it, or perhaps be amused by it.

You can even use an essay to cajole readers into considering subjects they've never thought much about before. Here's Megan McArdle (again, see p. 123) making a case for taking pie seriously:

> Pie is not a dessert well suited to our modern era, but that is our loss, not pie's. Its very difficulty and imperfections of form are part of its charm. They remind us that appearance is not everything and that some of the most worthwhile things in life can only be attained through our own hard work.

Until McArdle raises the issue, few readers may have taken the fruit and pastry confection so seriously. And notice how the author connects with readers, talking about *our* modern era and *our* own hard work. The essay is a genre that encourages connections between writer and readers and hence relies heavily on first person *I*. Readers (and most instructors) will not have a problem hearing your voice or opinions in a personal essay. In fact, they'll expect it.

Of course, you might sometimes decide that the target audience of an essay is really yourself: You can write about personal experiences to get a handle on them. Even then, be demanding. Think about how your story might sound ten or twenty years from now.

Gathering materials

Any source materials you present in an essay—whether facts, research, or opinion pieces—should be as rigorously summarized and documented (formally or informally) as those you'd use in reports, arguments, or other academic essays (See Chapter 5 p. 28). However, given the exploratory nature of the genre, you might find yourself gathering pertinent materials as you go along. In other words, research won't necessarily precede writing, and you needn't feel guilty about that since you may be working *toward* a conclusion rather than *from* a thesis.

▶ develop details

What's different about writing essays is how often you'll supplement traditional research with personal information, recollections, and memories. Of course, when you write about issues or events soon after they occur—for instance, your reaction to a concert or a political issue on campus—you'll have some facts fresh in your mind. Yet even in such cases, physical evidence, such as news stories, editorials, programs, published reviews, might rouse your thinking.

Talk to the people involved. A phone call home or a posting on social media might provide fresh information about any personal issue or event you intend to treat in an essay. Family, friends, classmates, and coworkers might recall details of a situation you've forgotten (or suppressed). They might also see events from perspectives you haven't considered.

For informative or argumentative essays, you'll likely want to interview knowledgeable people in a community, experts in a field, or enthusiasts who share your own passion about a subject. Adding voices other than your own to an essay may broaden its appeal and, depending on the subject, enhance its credibility.

Trust your experiences. Assigned a personal essay, lots of people wonder, "What have I done worth writing about?" ○ They underestimate the quality of their own perceptions. College students, for example, are incredibly knowledgeable about high school or the local music scene or working minimum-wage jobs or dealing with narrow-minded parents. You don't have to be a salaried professional to observe life or have something to say about it.

Here's humorist David Sedaris—who has made a career writing essays about his very middle-class life from his unique personal perspective—describing the insecurity of many writers:

> When I was teaching—I taught for a while—my students would write as if they were raised by wolves. Or raised on the streets. They were middle-class kids, and they were ashamed of their background. They felt like unless they grew up in poverty, they had nothing to write about. Which was interesting because I had always thought that poor people were the ones who were ashamed. But it's not. It's middle-class people who are ashamed of their lives. And it doesn't really matter what your life was like, you can write about anything. It's just the writing of it that is the challenge. I felt sorry for these kids, that they thought that their whole past was absolutely worthless because it was less than remarkable.
>
> — David Sedaris, interviewed in *January Magazine*, June 2000

Consult personal documents. A journal, if you keep one, may be a valuable resource for essays. But even a yearbook, daily planner, or electronic calendar might hold just the facts you need to reconstruct a sequence of events or remind you of people you've met or dealt with. Social media, especially Facebook and Instagram, may similarly contribute material for some types of essays. Visual images especially contain physical details—clothing, hairstyles, locals—that can add authenticity to an essay.

❚❚ ▬▬▬▬

If every picture tells a story, what narrative does this image suggest? Consider the missing windmill blade, the worker's posture, the quiet sky, and any other details that seem important.

❚❚

John J. Ruszkiewicz

find a topic p. 16

Organizing ideas

organize ◀
events

Now might be the time to reread "The River" section of Paul Graham's essay on p. 224. But don't let yourself be intimidated by a genre without a predictable or preferred structure. You already know a lot about the shape of essays from your own navigation of op-eds, magazine pieces, and endless blog posts. They go where they need to. And they aren't confusing, or people wouldn't read them.

Maybe the biggest hurdle is, as Graham suggests, giving up the notion of writing a paper built around a formal thesis announced somewhere in its introduction. Of course, many essays *do* present their arguments up front. It's right in the title of Leah Vann's essay reprinted later in this chapter: "Bald Is NOT Beautiful" (p. 233). Yet you'll have to read the entire piece to learn exactly why the issue matters so much to the author.

In this respect, Vann's paper resembles the alternative strategy: essays that build *toward* a thesis or point revealed—directly or indirectly—only near the end of the piece. That's certainly the design Scott Walker uses in the final sample essay in this chapter, "Who Do You Want to Be When You Grow Up?" Neither of these essays rambles nor seems out of control, but they do ask readers to pay attention and follow along.

Following are structural options to consider when drafting an essay.

Consider a conventional structure. It's not wrong for an essay to open with an observation or thesis statement and follow up with supporting (or contrary) details or events. Readers won't get lost, but you may have to work to keep them engaged.

> **Initial point(s) or thesis**
>
> > **Supporting evidence**
> > **Supporting evidence**
> > **Contradicting evidence**
>
> **Reaffirmation of point or thesis**

Build toward a climax. Essays become more complicated when you present a series of observations that lead up to a *main point* or even an *epiphany*. A main point is the moment when the essay strikes home, takes an important turn, or resolves the issue it raises: Leah Vann explains exactly why bald is not beautiful (p. 233). An epiphany is a moment of revelation or insight, when a writer or reader suddenly sees things in a new way: Scott Walker figures out that he's been asking the wrong question about his life (p. 237).

| Initial point(s) or issue |
| First observation |
| Next observation |
| Next observation |
| Main point and/or epiphany |

Give your readers directions. In the five-paragraph essay you might have learned in middle school (see p. 27), the transitions between sections can be as simple as *one, two, three* because you're just running through a list of related points. Readers know exactly where you are taking them, and the piece is predictable. They might just skip to the conclusion.

Essays in the mode of Montaigne and Graham typically are not. Composing one of those, you're asking readers to follow the twists and turns of your thinking as you grapple with serious matters. So you'll need to talk to them and give them signals to follow you.

One way is through what some describe as *meta-discourse*—language that tells readers what you are up to. It can be as simple as words and phrases that push readers to pay attention (*it is important to note, contrary to what you might believe*); to note a shift in emphasis (*to the contrary, on the other hand*); to signal shifts in direction (*to begin, to illustrate further, to summarize*), to indicate qualified positions (*I suppose, I would guess, I would venture*), and so on.

But meta-discourse can also be more extended and directive. Here, for example, are the opening sentences of Paul Graham's "The Age of the Essay" where he speaks directly to readers and suggests why they might want to read his essay:

> Remember the essays you had to write in high school? Topic sentence, introductory paragraph, supporting paragraphs, conclusion. The conclusion being, say, that Ahab in *Moby Dick* was a Christ-like figure.
>
> Oy. So I'm going to try to give the other side of the story: what an essay really is and how you write one. Or at least, how I write one.

Most academic essays won't open quite this directly, but you can see how useful the technique can be. So don't be afraid of talking to your readers—just don't be chatty.

Use headings and transitions. If essays get lengthy, you might consider headings as a way of keeping readers on track, signaling the major divisions of your piece. Laura Vann, for example, uses two headings in her piece to emphasize an important shift backward in time. And don't ignore the power of conventional transitions, discussed in detail in Chapter 37 (p. 391). They are especially important in essays as you move between paragraphs.

Choosing a style and design

Essays are usually written in approachable middle or low styles because they nicely mimic the human voice through devices, such as contractions, and even dialogue when the piece has sections of narrative. Both styles are also comfortable with *I*, the point of view of many essays. A middle style may be perfect for reaching academic or professional audiences. But a low style, dipping into slang and unconventional speech, may sometimes feel more authentic to general readers. It's your choice.

Essays do benefit from tight but expressive language—*tight* to keep the argument moving, *expressive* to convey emotions and textures. Here's a suggestion: In the first draft of an essay, run with your ideas and don't do much editing. Flesh out the argument as you have imagined it and then go back to see if it works technically: issues should be raised, people identified, any events clearly explained and sequenced, key ideas and arguments expressed memorably and emphatically. You may need several drafts to get all these elements into shape.

Then look to your language and allow plenty of time to revise it. You might begin by reviewing Chapter 34, "Clear and Vigorous Writing." Here are some additional recommendations for essays.

Don't hesitate to use first person—*I*. Most personal essays begin with the concerns of the writer, so first-person pronouns are used without apology. A narrative often takes readers to where the *I* has been, so using first-person makes writing authentic. Consider online journalist Michael Yon's explanation of why he reported on the Iraq War using *I* rather than a more objective third-person perspective:

> I write in first person because I am actually there at the events I write about. When I write about the bombs exploding, or the smell of blood, or the bullets snapping by, and I say *I*, it's because I was there. Yesterday a sniper shot at us, and seven of my neighbors were injured by a large bomb. These are my neighbors. These are soldiers. . . . I feel the fire from the explosions, and am lucky, very lucky, still to be alive. Everything here is first person.

— From Glenn Reynolds, *An Army of Davids*

And yet don't focus only on yourself in essays. Bring readers in with a "you" or a "we." Scott Walker, for instance, makes an important transition from *I* to *we* very late in his essay (see p. 237).

Use figures of speech, such as similes, metaphors, and analogies, to make memorable comparisons. *Similes* make comparisons by using *like* or *as*: *He used his camera like a rifle*. *Metaphors* drop the *like* or *as* to gain even more power: *His camera was a rifle aimed at enemies*. An *analogy* extends the comparison: *His camera became a rifle aimed at his imaginary enemies, their private lives in his crosshairs.*

The difference between the almost right word and the right word is really a large matter—it's the difference between the lightning bug and the lightning.

—Mark Twain

Need help seeing the big picture? See "How to Revise Your Work" on pp. 354–55.

People make comparisons habitually. Some are so common they've been reduced to invisible clichés: *hit me like a ton of bricks; dumb as an ox; clear as a bell*. In your own essays, you want similes and metaphors fresher than these and yet not contrived or strained. Here's science writer Michael Chorost effortlessly deploying both a metaphor (*spins up*) and a simile (*like riding a roller coaster*) to describe what he experiences as he awaits surgery.

I can feel the bustle and clatter around me as the surgical team spins up to take-off speed. It is like riding a roller coaster upward to the first great plunge, strapped in and committed.

— *Rebuilt: How Becoming Part Computer Made Me More Human*

Thinking about Writing   In "The Age of the Essay," Graham shows a fondest for similes, metaphors, and especially analogies. Review the selections from that piece above (p. 223), list as many of these figures of speech as you can find, and discuss their function. Do they help you to understand his concept of the essay?

In choosing verbs, favor active rather than passive voice.   Active verbs propel the action (*Montaigne invented the essay*), while passive verbs slow it down by an unneeded word or two (*The essay was invented by Montaigne*). ○

Since essays are all about movement of thought, build sentences around strong verbs that do things. Edit until you get down to the nub of the action. You will produce sentences as effortless as these from Joseph Epstein, from an essay describing the pleasures of catching plagiarists. ○ Verbs are highlighted in this passage; only one (*is followed*) is passive.

In thirty years of teaching university students, I never encountered a case of plagiarism or even one that I suspected. Teachers I've known who have caught students in this sad act report that the capture gives one an odd sense of power. The power derives from the authority that resides behind the word *gotcha*. This is followed by that awful moment—a veritable sadist's Mardi Gras—when one calls the student into one's office and points out the odd coincidence that he seems to have written about existentialism in precisely the same words Jean-Paul Sartre used fifty-two years earlier.

— "Plagiary, It's Crawling All Over Me," *Weekly Standard*, March 6, 2006

Keep the language simple.   Your language need not be elaborate when it is fresh and authentic. Look for concrete expressions that help readers visualize ideas or concepts. And when it comes to modifiers, one strong word is usually better than several weaker ones (*freezing* rather than *very cold; doltish* rather than *not very bright*).

improve your sentences p. 375 | avoid plagiarism p. 463

Examining models

ARGUMENTATIVE ESSAY   It is easy to imagine Leah Vann writing a purely argumentative version of "Bald Is NOT Beautiful," one that offers a string of good reasons to support the thesis already asserted in the title. Instead, as you will see, she makes her case more memorable by setting the argument within a two-part narrative structure, signaled by dates in headings she provides. The narrative would be compelling on its own, but becomes something more as an essay that makes a powerful point in its very last line.

Reading the Genre   An epiphany is a sudden moment of insight that may occur at some moment in a personal narrative, often in the conclusion. Would you describe Vann's final paragraphs as an epiphany? What feelings in you does the conclusion of the essay generate?

Bald Is NOT Beautiful

By Leah Vann

December 8, 2016

April 2014

It was like reliving a nightmare.

I could hear the sound of the razor from one hundred yards away. That familiar, sudden click and buzz. A circle of students stood around her, most with freshly shaved heads.

"Don't do it. Stop it," I thought.

The girl smiled as the razor skimmed the bottom, then sides of her head, letting her hair fall gently on the tarp beneath her. The students clapped and cheered. She still smiled, with tears streaming down her face.

I was frozen. Stone-cold on a sunny day, standing in front of the University of Texas tower, where a sign read "Brave the Shave for St. Baldrick's" in large, green letters.

The "beauty." The "glamour." The "bravery."

How admirable it must be to shave your head when you don't have to. When you have a choice to keep your hair.

"Bald is beautiful," they tell you.

But it's not so beautiful to me.

> Vann assumes readers are familiar with "Brave the Shave." You can find out more about the fundraising campaign for child cancer research online.

> Readers here will likely want to know why— although they might be able to guess.

November 28th, 2010

"Good morning, Leah. I have your pills," one of my nurses says.

They wake me up at 8:00 every morning to take my cup of twelve pills. It's only been a month and I can already swallow them all at once, including Bactrim, the gigantic horse-pill. I scratch my head and collect a clump of hair to throw in the trash can next to me. My hair started falling out a week ago, but since it's so thick, I still look normal.

The nurse walks in the bathroom to check my toilet.

"Um, I think the last time you peed was around 3:00 am. Let me know if you're having trouble, okay?" she says.

Lord, can I wake up first? I'm 15; my ideal wake-up time is noon.

"I'll go soon. It's just really early and I want to sleep," I say. I'm trying to make her go away.

In the hospital, I don't have privacy. Care partners check my blood pressure and temperature every four hours. There are two containers in the toilet that measure my pee and poop for the nurses to collect. Doctors pop in for daily checkups, visitors come to bring food I won't eat, and the nutritionist comes in to scare me into eating.

"Leah, it's really important to eat during chemotherapy because your organs will get damaged. You don't want to have an appendectomy while your platelets are this low. It's dangerous," the nutritionist says.

"I know."

"Now, I have these Carnation instant breakfasts you can drink. They have all kinds of vitamins and protein and you can mix it with milk or water. There's vanilla, chocolate, strawberry . . ."

I cringe. She rolls her eyes.

Mom strides in. There's no way I will sleep now, so I climb out of bed to pee into the measuring bucket.

"Thank you," the nurse says, still typing away on her computer.

Mom gasps.

"Oh my God!" she shouts.

"What?" I ask.

"Can we get some fresh sheets for her?" mom asks the nurse.

"Yes, of course. I'll be right back," she says, taking my bucket of pee.

I look at my bed. It's coated with a blanket of red hair. I carefully scratch my head again, throwing another mass of hair in my trash can.

Deliberately graphic details contrast with *beauty, glamour, bravery* noted in the opening section.

Dialogue enhances the reality of the narrative.

I feel as if thousands of needles are brushing the surface of my head at once.

"Honey, isn't this uncomfortable for you?" mom asks. The nurses come in to change the sheets. I remain standing by the mirror, washing my hands.

"I mean, I'm itchy, but I told you I don't want to shave it until I have my wigs." I've been putting this off for over a week. It keeps me restless. I lie awake at night trying not to scratch hair off my head. I've tried rubbing and applying icepacks to my scalp, but nothing makes it better. Unfortunately, the medicine fighting for my life is what causes it.

"Honey, you could cut your head scratching it. I don't want you to bleed. It's dangerous and it's gross. Look at all this hair."

I stare into the mirror, surveying my head for bald spots. I do this every morning just in case it stops falling out. But in the top right corner, just behind where my hairline begins, is a tiny bald spot on my part. It's the first one. I flip my bangs over the opposite direction and cover it with a clip. The flipping of my bangs sends a tingling burn across my scalp. I wince.

"Um . . . I guess . . . Can we call Cheryl and ask when my wigs will be ready?" I ask, only half-admitting defeat.

"Okay, honey," mom says.

My nurse comes in with visitors. My youth group was coming today to give me a present. Our youth group advisor hands me a University of Michigan football, signed by head coach Rich Rodriguez and athletic director Dave Brandon. She explains that she had a few friends who worked in the athletic department to help make it happen.

The University of Michigan has been a dream of mine since my dad died. He went there and used to sing me the fight song as a lullaby. Brandon wrote a message saying he couldn't wait for me to be a student. I hope that happens . . .

My friends leave and my mom sits on the edge of my bed.

"So, I talked to Cheryl. She has a temporary wig you can wear until the other ones come in. So, what do you want to do? She can come today," Mom says.

I pause. I look behind me, where a freshly woven sweater of hair from the past few hours covers my pillow. I can't put this off any longer. I'm disgusting.

> Visitors here perhaps parallel the students clapping and cheering in the first part.

Δ

"I think you would feel a lot better," mom says.

"Okay," I say.

Cheryl comes in a few hours later, followed by my stepdad and his hairstylist of twenty years. The hairstylist has a special razor that is gentle enough to prevent open wounds. The last thing I need is to bleed when I don't have the platelets to stop it.

She sits me in front of the mirror.

"You're going to feel so much better, honey. It's just itchy and uncomfortable. All my friends I've shaved say they feel better." I'm silent.

Click. Buzz. She starts under my right ear and strokes backwards.

I have a love-hate relationship with my red hair. I hate how curly it is, so I always straighten it. People stop me in grocery stores or shopping malls to tell me how beautiful my hair is. How thick it is. And how do I grow it out so long? To the point it falls almost down to my hips in the back? I'm so damn lucky.

She starts fresh above the first stroke, combing a new bald path down the back of my head. Every stroke is instant relief. But within seconds, she's at the top of my head, near my bald spot. Buzz. Only half of my head of hair remains, and I shut my eyes. I can't watch it anymore. Buzz. Suddenly I love it. I love all of my hair, every inch of it. I promise I won't straighten it. Ever. Buzz. I shiver, it's getting colder. Buzz. It's gone.

"Remember honey, bald is beautiful," the stylist says.

I open my eyes to look in the mirror. The grey lighting illuminates a pale-faced figure staring at me with large, light blue eyes. Clothes hang on the figure like a coat hanger, loose and slightly crinkled.

I don't recognize her.

She looks like a 5' 5" underweight infant, which is ironic, because she's dying, the exact opposite of youth.

She's dying. No, Leah, *you're* dying.

I look around. A long tube attaches the arteries in my heart to a bag of chemotherapy hanging from an IV pole. My wrist is covered in plastic bracelets of different colors that read, "Vann, Leah, Leukemia." The walls are covered with autographed signs telling me to "Beat Cancer" or "Get Well Soon."

I run into the bathroom with my IV pole trailing behind me. I fall to my knees, kneeling before the ledge of the bathtub and I scream.

"I'M SO UGLY!"

This is bald.

The medical details here emphasize the seriousness of Vann's condition. She has no choice.

Final lines are lean, dramatic, purposeful, repudiating "bald is beautiful."

PERSONAL ESSAY In "Who Do You Want to Be When You Grow Up?" Scott Walker explores a question many students wrestle with as they select courses and their majors, compete for internships, and plan for the future. But his personal essay is far from clichéd or even predictable. Nor does it come to an easy resolution—and the genre doesn't require that he find one.

Reading the genre Do you find yourself identifying with Walker's dilemma? If so, why? If not, where does he lose you? Briefly imagine what an essay of your own on his subject might cover.

Who Do You Want to Be When You Grow Up?

Scott Walker

May 15, 2017

A policeman. The first person I wanted to be was a policeman. I don't know why, but when I was six that's who I wanted to be. I couldn't have known anything about what a policeman did—the paperwork involved or the risks and dangers. But a policeman was someone I could imagine being—a policeman fights crime, a policeman is good, a policeman is a hero. There was something grand about a policeman, and I wanted to be a hero.

A fireman. The policeman obsession didn't last long; firemen fight fire, and giant fires were the scariest things I could imagine. Firemen were good, firemen were heroes. I wanted to be a hero.

A pilot. Pilots fly all over the world, a magical feat for an elementary school student who proudly wears the Continental wings distributed by a smiling flight attendant.

A farmer—probably not who most middle-school students aspire to be. This ambition was a recurring one, but not because of noble aspirations to husband the land or provide for a family by my own hands. I was certain, despite corrections from my parents, that farmers didn't have to go to school. I would be a farmer; therefore, I didn't have to go to school, or so I thought.

An Olympic runner. I ran cross-country and track-and-field in middle school, then in high school, and for a year-and-a-half in college.

Highly rhetorical in structure, the six opening paragraphs probably remind readers of their own childhood dreams.

People all over the world watch the Olympics, and I wanted them to watch me. Athletes perform incredible feats, and Olympic athletes perform the greatest feats. When I didn't want to be a farmer in middle school, I wanted to be an Olympic runner.

A writer—and not just any writer, a writer of fantasy. Sophomore year of high school I would go to the library for the first half of lunch to read R.A. Salvatore's tales of the Dark Elf Drizzt Do'urden and his friends. After cross-country and track practice, I would come home and read a chapter alongside a plate of two grilled tuna fish sandwiches before starting my homework.

> *Where do you want to go to college?*
> *What do you want to study in college?*
> *What do you want to do after college?*

As college came around, I felt pressured to discover where I wanted to go and what I wanted to study. I had to think about what I wanted to do. It's a subtle shift, from *who* you want to be to *what* you want to do, but it changed my life.

I never really answered the three questions. I never could. I think it's because I'd stopped asking the more fundamental one.

At least whenever someone had asked who I wanted to be, I could imagine the police officer fighting crime, the firefighter fighting fire, the plane flying in the sky, the farmer in a field (not at school), the Olympic runner sprinting across the finish line, the writer at work creating a fantasy where high school boys might find an escape among elves and magic. But when people ask me what I want to do, there are no images.

I chose to study classics because I didn't know what else to do. I attended Colgate University for a year-and-a-half and studied economics and math to grab a Wall Street job. But I didn't find a niche there. I transferred to the University of Texas's Jackson School of Geosciences and chose a geophysics degree, hoping to land a job with a large oil company. But again I drifted, finding friends and letting them go.

After a year, I transferred to the classics department because I loved words, and I enjoyed studying their etymologies. I felt drawn to studying the languages where many of the words I know come from. But it also felt safe

---

Three familiar questions signal a shift in the essay, leading to a focus on the present and the question in the title.

The essay becomes more openly exploratory. Walker is looking for answers in different majors.

to choose a degree that would get me away from practical majors designed to land their students in careers. I dreaded any path littered with résumés, interviews, and networking—and the stress of classmate conversations about big companies, how many students they're hiring, what expectations they have, what tasks you need to check off for an acceptable résumé.

These are all practical concerns, but I don't think they're the most pressing questions—not for the many college students who don't know either who they are or who they want to be.

We make decisions, sometimes life-shaping ones, according to some internal compass. For many, that compass points in the most profitable and prestigious directions. And that's only logical, since for years they've only been asked what they plan to do, not who they really want to be.

Studying classics has protected me from that terrifying question. I've buried my head in texts two millennia old and accompanied heroes like Aeneas on journeys seeking their destiny. His story begins after Troy, his home, is sacked by the Greeks, and he leads the Trojan survivors on a circuitous Mediterranean journey. Early on, Aeneas receives prophecies that he will lead the Trojan race to Italy, where his progeny will establish Rome and rule the known world. Aeneas responds to every obstacle by enduring it and overcoming it. He chooses not to fold. For Aeneas, that is his answer to the question: *What will you do?*

But he can only answer it so valiantly because he knows who he is—he's been told by the gods in oracles and prophecies. Unfortunately (or perhaps luckily), no gods or God have informed me who I am. I imagine you also haven't received any recent divine revelation. It seems we're tasked with asking ourselves who we want to be in order to answer life's recurring question: *What will we do?*

A student recently came to me in the writing center where I work with a paper on the Bhagavad Gita, a sacred Hindu text. His essay discussed Karmic yoga and Bhakti yoga, comparing and contrasting the two. I learned that Karmic yoga is selfless work, a means available to all human beings—regardless of their religion or occupation—to purify their karma and escape the endless cycle of Samsara. And Bhakti yoga involves holding an image or conception of your chosen deity in your mind, forfeiting all benefits of your actions to that deity.

> Walker now brings other college students into the essay as his pronouns shift from "I" to "we."

> The essay shifts again as Walker describes an encounter that offers him a potential answer to his quest.

I imagine that, through Bhakti yoga, practitioners seek to live their lives as meditations on their chosen deities. Life becomes a sort of dialogue. When we ask ourselves who we want to be, we conceive of that person in our minds. That person is no one other than the deity we've chosen. And by fixing that image in our minds, we set a path to become that person, that deity. No longer do we have to choose among so many options and directions. There is one path, and obstacles on that path have only to be overcome.

Still, I don't exactly know who I hope to be, not yet. But though the image is hazy, it's there. Like a steady rhythm, I have a question for each day: *Who do I want to be?*

Assignments

1. **Exploratory Essay:** Have you given as much thought to any subject as Paul Graham gives to writing essays in "The Age of the Essay" (p. 223)? If so, turn your knowledge, expertise, or enthusiasm into an exploratory essay that, like Graham's, corrects misconceptions people have about the topic or helps readers understand it better. Your subject could be related to an area of academic interest, but it need not be. Good essays can be written about almost any subject.

2. **Personal essay.** In "Who Do You Want to Be When You Grow Up?" (p. 237), Scott Walker uses an essay to explore a problem he can't avoid—choosing a career path. Consider writing an essay about some aspect of your life that might similarly resonate with others, perhaps recalling how you learned to adapt to hostile environments, or figured out how to deal with sibling rivalry, or made your way into the workforce. Or you might explore conflicts in your life that you may never quite resolve—personal, athletic, artistic, cultural. As Walker's piece demonstrates, a personal essay doesn't have to settle matters.

3. **Argumentative Essay:** Using Leah Vann's "Bald Is NOT Beautiful" (p. 233) as a model, compose an argumentative essay that draws heavily upon your personal experiences. Your piece need not necessarily tell a story (as Vann's does), but it should convince readers that you have the knowledge and experiences to back up your claims. Make this a paper you might want to keep.

4. **Your Choice:** In this chapter, Paul Graham aims his essay at people who hope to be writers; Leah Vann and Scott Walker seem to be addressing fellow students. Compose an essay of your own (exploratory, argumentative, or personal) on a subject of your choice *and for a specific audience* who might benefit from what you've come to know. Maybe you've discovered that travel on your own is a powerful way to build self-confidence? Maybe your part-time job at a fast-food restaurant convinces you that more people need comparable work experience? Maybe you wish more teachers could remember what it's like to be a student? Write an essay that expresses what you know or what you've been thinking.

Special College Assignments

part three

Need a form of writing you don't see here? See chart on p. 15 in Chapter 2.

16

Essay Examinations

Essay examinations test what you know about a subject and your ability to write about it coherently and professionally.

At a glance . . .

- Size up the examination when it is announced. Ask questions about its content and form.
- Review texts, notes, and other materials, highlighting crucial names, dates, and concepts.
- Exam in hand, formulate a plan and stick to it—watching the clock.
- Leave no question unanswered.
- Frontload your answers so you get credit even if you run out of time.
- Budget time to review your answer and correct obvious gaffes.

UNDERSTANDING ESSAY EXAMS. You've probably taken enough essay exams to know that there are no magic bullets to slay this dragon and that the best approach is to know the material well enough to make credible points within the time limit. You must also write—*under pressure*—coherent sentences and paragraphs. ○ Here are some strategies to increase your odds of success.

got a test ◄ tomorrow?

Anticipate the types of questions to be asked. What occurs in class—

the concepts presented, issues raised, assignments given—is like a coming-attractions trailer for an exam. Attend class regularly and do the required readings, and you'll figure out many of an instructor's habitual moves and learn something to boot. Read over your notes, study PowerPoints and handouts, attend any review sessions, and look over sample essay exams—they may even be available on a course Web site. Pay attention to your instructor's description of the examination and don't hesitate to ask questions: *How many items on the exam? Short answer or long? Covering what material, chapters, or pages? Open book or closed? Access to class notes permitted? How much time available for exam? Blue books necessary? Laptops allowed? Sample exams available?*

Read exam questions carefully. Highlight key words, as shown on chart on

following page, and then respect the differences between these strategies.

Exam questions may be like short essays themselves, furnishing contextual information or offering materials to read before the actual query appears. Respond to that specific question and not to your own take on the introductory materials.

Sketch out a plan for your essay(s). The first part of the plan should deal

with *time*. Read all the exam questions carefully and then estimate how many minutes to spend on each—understanding that some will require more work than others. ○ (Pay attention to point totals too: Focus on essay questions that count more, but don't ignore any. Five points is five points.) Then allot time for organizing, writing, and briefly editing each answer. Above all, stick to your time limits.

Organize your answers strategically. As quickly as possible, create a scratch

outline and thesis for longer answers. ○ In the first paragraph, state this main point and then preview the structure of the whole essay. That way, even if you cannot finish, a reader will know where you were heading and possibly give you partial credit for incomplete work.

improve your sentences p. 375 | develop a draft p. 338 | develop a thesis p. 333

Analyze/Examine	Look at a subject systematically, doing a careful reading of it or breaking it into components and then discussing them.
Argue	Take a position on whatever issue or topic the question specifies. Offer good reasons and evidence, drawing on principles learned in the class if possible. You might argue for or against a specific immigration policy.
Assess/Evaluate/ Critique	Make a judgment and defend it on whatever the question specifies: an idea, principle, book, political policy, etc. Offer reasons and evidence.
Classify/Divide	Explain by what consistent principles you might group whatever the question specifies. Or explain what existing categories might be applied to the subjects: liberal/ conservative; dwarf planet/Kuiper object.
Compare	Look for and explain similarities in whatever a question specifies: different authors, principles, policies, concepts, theories, etc.
Compare and Contrast	Look for *both* similarities and differences between whatever a question specifies.
Explain	Account for how or why something has happened. List plausible reasons in some significant order or offer competing theories—for example, for the outbreak of World War I.
Interpret/Do a Close Reading	Explain what you think a work of art, a speech, a government document, or other text or object means. Analyze the language or particular features of the assigned text in detail. In a close reading, you might exam how a sonnet or soliloquy from a play works line by line.
Justify	Offer a specific defense for whatever action, policy, or position that the question specifies. Your response might differ if the question is *Can you justify?*
Outline/Summarize	Offer a point-by-point or general overview of a text, concept, policy, etc., respecting the original organization of the item specified. Do not offer an assessment or evaluation unless directed by the exam question.
Speculate	Offer your own best judgment about the implications, directions, or prospects of whatever the question specifies.
Synthesize	Compare, briefly paraphrase (if specified), and assess a variety of opinions, authors, or sources specified in the exam.
Trace	Account for the development of a concept, idea, trend, political or social movement, etc. over time, specifying if possible a point of origin.

Offer strong evidence for your claims. The overall pattern of your responses to exam questions should convey your grasp of ideas—your ability to see the big picture. Within that structure, provide details and evidence to demonstrate your command of the subject. Use memorable examples culled from class reading to make key points: Mention important names, concepts, and dates; touch on all critical issues and terms; rattle off the accurate titles of books and articles.

Come to a conclusion. Even if you run short on time, find a moment to write a paragraph (or even a sentence) that brings your essay together. Don't just repeat the topic sentences of your paragraphs. A reader will already have those ideas firmly in mind. So add something new at the end—an implication or extrapolation that suggests you could write more about the subject. ○

Keep the tone serious. Write essay examinations in a high or middle style. ○ Avoid a personal point of view unless the question invites your opinions. Given the time constraints, you can probably get away with contractions and standard abbreviations. But make sure the essay reads like prose, not a text message or tweet.

Keep your eye on the clock. But *don't panic*. Everyone is working under the same constraints and can produce only so much prose in an hour or two. If you have prepared for the test and start with a plan, ideas will come. Even if they don't, keep writing or typing. You'll get no credit for blank pages.

Thinking about writing   Preparing for an examination now? Take a moment to list *from memory* as many as you can of the key names, titles, and concepts likely to appear on that exam—terms you are certain to need when you compose your answers. Then check these terms as you have written them down against the way they appear in your notes or textbooks or on the course Web site. Have you gotten important names and titles right? Have you phrased the concepts correctly, and can you explain what they mean? Just as important, do you notice any important ideas that should have made your list but didn't?

---

shape an ending p. 395 | refine your tone p. 368

Getting the details right

Save a few minutes near the end of the exam period to reread your essays and insert corrections and emendations. You won't have time to fix large-scale problems: If you've confused the Spanish Armada with Torquemada, you're toast. But a quick edit may catch embarrassing gaffes or omissions. When you write quickly, you may leave out or transpose some words or simply use the wrong expressions (*it's* for *its* or *there* for *their*). Edit these fixable errors. In the process, you may also amplify or repair an idea or two. Here are some other useful strategies.

Use topic sentences and transitions. Get right to the point in answering questions, stating what you know and then proving it, paragraph by paragraph, as efficiently as you can. Essay examinations are the perfect place to deploy conspicuous transitions, such as *first, second,* and *third,* or *next, nonetheless, even more important, in contrast, in conclusion,* and so on. Don't be subtle: Transitions keep you on track as you compose, and they help your instructor follow what you have to say. ○ You will seem in charge of the material.

Do a quick check of grammar, mechanics, and spelling. Some instructors take great offense at mechanical slips, even minor ones. At a minimum, avoid the common errors covered in Part 8 of this book. ○ Also be sure to spell correctly any names and concepts you've been reviewing in preparation for the examination. It's Macbeth, not McBeth.

Write legibly or print. Few people do much writing by hand anymore. But paper or blue books are still sometimes used for essay examinations. If your handwriting is flat-out illegible, then print and use a pen, as pencil can be faint and hard to read. Printing takes more time, but instructors appreciate the clarity. Also consider double-spacing your essays to allow room for corrections and additions. But don't spread your words too far apart. A blue book with just a few sentences per page undermines your ethos: It looks juvenile.

transitions p. 391

help with common errors p. 550

Examining a model

Wade Lamb offered the following response to this essay question on a midterm essay examination in a course titled Classical to Modern Rhetoric:

> The structure of Plato's *Phaedrus* is dominated by three speeches about the lover and non-lover—one by Lysias and two by Socrates. How do these speeches differ in their themes and strategies, and what point do they make about rhetoric and truth?

Lamb 1

Wade Lamb

Professor Barber

Rhetoric 101

September 19, 20--

Plato's *Phaedrus* is unique among Platonic dialogues because it takes place in a rural setting between only two characters— Socrates and the youth Phaedrus. It is, however, like Plato's *Gorgias* in that it is "based on a distinction between knowledge and belief" and focuses on some of the ways we can use rhetoric to seek the truth.

The first speech presented in *Phaedrus*, written by Lysias and read aloud by Phaedrus, is the simplest of the three. Composed by Lysias to demonstrate the power of rhetoric to persuade an audience, it claims perversely that it is better to have a sexual relationship with someone who doesn't love you than someone who does.

Socrates responds with a speech of his own, making the same point, which he composes on the spot, but which he describes as "a greater lie than Lysias's." Unlike Lysias, however, Socrates begins by carefully defining his terms and

Opening focuses directly on issues posed in question.

Short quotation functions as a piece of evidence.

Sensibly organized around three speeches to be examined: one paragraph per speech.

Lamb 2

organizes his speech more effectively. He does so to teach Phaedrus that in order to persuade an audience, an orator must first understand the subject and divide it into its appropriate parts. However, Socrates delivers this speech with a veil over his head because he knows that what he and Lysias have claimed about love is false.

The third speech—again composed by Socrates—is the most important. In it, Socrates demonstrates that persuasion that leads merely to belief (not truth) damages both the orator and the audience. He compares rhetoric, such as that used by Lysias, to the unconcerned and harmful lust of a non-lover. Good rhetoric, on the other hand—which Socrates says is persuasion that leads to knowledge—is like the true lover who seeks to lead his beloved to transcendent truth. Socrates shows that he believes good rhetoric should ultimately be concerned with finding and teaching truth, not just with making a clever argument someone might falsely believe, as Lysias's speech does.

By comparing the three speeches in *Phaedrus*, Plato shows that he gives some value to rhetoric, but not in the form practiced by orators such as Lysias. Plato emphasizes the importance of the distinction between belief and knowledge and argues that rhetoric should search for and communicate the truth.

Most important speech gets lengthiest and most detailed treatment.

Conclusion states Lamb's thesis, describing the point he believes Plato wished to make about rhetoric in *Phaedrus*.

How to start

● **Need to write a summary?** Check Chapter 49 for more details. See page 457.

Annotated Bibliographies

17

summarize
and assess
sources

When you are preparing a term paper, senior thesis, or other lengthy research project, an instructor may expect you to submit an annotated bibliography. The bibliography may be due weeks before you turn in the paper, or it may be turned in with the finished project.

At a glance . . .

● For academic projects, keep track of all your sources from Day 1.

● Choose a system of documentation early and learn how to record every item you use in the proper form.

● Use a database, software, or note cards to compile all necessary bibliographic data on the materials you use—author(s), title, publication date, publisher, medium (book, journal article, Web site), URL.

● Write down your comments on sources as you read them. Record two types of comments separately, those that describe the source and those that evaluate it.

● Examine models of annotated bibliographies in the field you are working to get a feel for proper content and form. Most documentation systems list sources alphabetically by author.

UNDERSTANDING ANNOTATED BIBLIOGRAPHIES. An annotated bibliography is an alphabetical list of the sources and documents you have used in developing a research project, with each item in the list summarized and, very often, evaluated. Annotations can be brief or very lengthy, depending on an assignment. You might prepare such a bibliography to confirm the depth and appropriateness of your research, the range of the sources you used (for example, handwritten documents, letters, electronic resources), or the reliability of the materials you encountered—information potentially useful to readers of a research project.

Instructors may ask you to attach a bibliography to the final version of a project so that they can determine at a glance how well you've investigated your subject. But some may ask you to submit a list of sources earlier in the writing process—sometimes even as part of a topic proposal—to be sure you're on track, poring over reputable materials, and getting the most out of them. **O**

Begin with an accurate record of research materials. Items recorded
in the alphabetical list should follow the guidelines of some documentation system, typically MLA or APA. (If instructors don't specify what documentation systems to use in a paper, ask—many fields and professions use specialized systems, some listed later in this chapter on p. 255.)

For instance, in a paper using MLA documentation (common in humanities courses), the list of sources used is labeled "Works Cited" and includes only books, articles, and other source materials actually mentioned in the project; it is labeled "Works Consulted" if you also want to include materials you've read but not actually cited in the body of the paper. In a project using APA style (used in psychology and related scientific and health fields), the list is called "References." **O**

Make certain to record every item you will need to create
an accurate citation. If you are working with online sources or documentation software, some of the work may be done for you. But always check that you have the correct data. The information needed will vary slightly, depending on the documentation system you use. And sources will have unique features and characteristics. **O** But the core items you may need for bibliography entries are the following:

plan a project p. 428   cite in APA p. 510   understand citation styles p. 467

Authors/ Contributors	Record full names, though APA style uses only initials of first names. Also pay attention to any important contributors to the work. They may be identified by phrases such as *edited by, introduced by, translated by*, etc.
Titles	Titles will be complicated because there are many variations: books, articles, movies, encyclopedia entries, Web pages, songs, etc. In general, cite titles and any significant subtitles, usually separated by a colon.
Publication Details	Note when a work has been updated, expanded, or revised. With academic journals, record volume numbers; with works like TV shows, specify series and episode numbers, etc.
Publisher or Container	Identify who published the work or where an item can be found. It can be within a book, journal, magazine, newspaper, network, digital platform, or other container.
Date of Publication	Record the year for books. With articles and newspapers you may need more specific information: month, day, year, volume, issue or number.
Location	Location can range from page numbers to a full URL or digital object identifier (DOI).

Describe or summarize the content of each item in the bibliography. These summaries can be very brief, often just one or two sentences. Begin with a concise description of the work if it isn't self-evident (*a review of; an interview with; a CIA report on*). Then, in your own words, describe its contents, scope, audience, perspective, or other features relevant to your project. Keep your language in this section descriptive and impartial. Be sure to follow any special guidelines offered by your instructor. For more about summarizing, see Chapter 49, "Summarizing Sources."

need to ◄
write a
summary?

Assess the significance or quality of the work. Immediately following the summary, offer a brief appraisal of the item, responding to its authority, thoroughness, length, relevance, usefulness, age (for example, *up-to-date/dated*), reputation in field (if known), and so on. Your remarks should be professional and academic: You aren't writing a Yelp review.

Explain the role the work plays in your research. When an annotated bibliography is part of a topic proposal, size up the materials you have located so far and describe how you expect to use them in your project. Emphasize works that provide creative or fresh ideas, authoritative coverage, up-to-date research, diverse perspectives, or ample bibliographies.

Lauren Nicole/Getty Images

When the bibliography is part of a completed paper or thesis, explain how exactly the source influenced or shaped the project, if it did. Also assess the quality, relevance, thoroughness, and currency of the source—this information may help other readers decide whether an item deserves their attention. When you find items that did not contribute significantly to your work, say so.

Getting the details right

You will grasp the value of annotated bibliographies the moment you find a trustworthy one covering a subject you are researching. So consider how any bibliography you prepare might assist other readers and researchers. An instructor reading your bibliography will certainly appreciate your effort, recognizing too that you have grasped a topic well enough to evaluate the work of others.

Follow a single documentation style. Documentation systems like MLA and APA can seem fussy, but they make life easier for researchers by standardizing the way all the identifying features of a source are treated. O So when you get an entry right in your annotated bibliography, you make life easier for the next person who needs to cite that item. Following is a list of documentation manuals commonly used in various professions and fields: Always check with an instructor about the preferred style in a given course since more than one may be acceptable.

Anthropology, Art, Business, Computer Science, History, Music, Religion, Theater	*Chicago Manual of Style* · 17th edition · **Chicago style** · See also Kate L. Turabian's *Manual for Writers of Research Papers, Theses, and Dissertations* · 9th edition · **Turabian**
Chemistry	*The ACS Style Guide: Effective Communication of Scientific Information* · 3rd edition · **ACS style**
Earth Science	*Geowriting: A Guide to Writing, Editing, and Printing in Earth Science* · 5th edition
Journalism	*The Associated Press Stylebook* · Updated annually · **AP style**
Law	*Uniform System of Citations: The Bluebook* · 20th edition
Literature, Language, Linguistics, Communications, Religion, Theater	*MLA Handbook* · 8th edition · **MLA style**
Mathematics	*American Mathematical Society Handbook* · **AMS style**

understand citation styles
p. 467

Music	*Writing About Music: An Introductory Guide* • 4th edition
Nursing	*Writing for Publication in Nursing* • 4th edition
Political Science	*Style Manual for Political Science* • 2nd edition • **APSA style**
Psychology, Education	*Publication Manual of the American Psychological Association* • 6th edition • **APA style**
Sciences	*Scientific Style and Format: The CSE Manual for Authors, Editors, and Publishers* • 8th edition • **CSE style**
U.S. Government	*United States Government Publishing Office Style Manual* • 31st edition • **GPO style**

Record the information on your sources accurately.

As you format the items in your list, be sure that the titles, authors, page numbers, and dates are error-free so that users can quickly locate the materials you have used. Proofread aggressively.

Keep summaries and assessments brief.

Don't get carried away. In most cases, instructors and other readers will want an annotated bibliography they can scan. They'll appreciate writing that is both precise and succinct. If they want especially detailed annotations, they will likely explain that expectation when making the assignment.

Follow directions carefully.

Some instructors may provide specific directions for annotated bibliographies, depending on the field or subject of your research. For example, they may ask you to supply the volume numbers, locations, and physical dimensions of books; describe illustrations; provide URLs; and so on. Don't hesitate to ask an instructor to explain any such requirements—or talk them over with a reference librarian.

Examining a model

The following three items are from an annotated bibliography offered as part of a topic proposal on the cultural impact of the iPod. Note the clarity and brevity of these items—making them particularly useful to readers deciding whether they might examine these pieces themselves.

Full bibliographical citation in MLA style.

Stephenson, Seth. "You and Your Shadow." *Slate*, 2 Mar. 2004, www.slate.com/articles/business/ad_report_card/2004/03/you_and_your_shadow.html. This article from *Slate*'s "Ad Report Card" series argues that the original iPod ads featuring silhouetted dancers may alienate viewers by suggesting that the product is cooler than the people who buy it. Stephenson explains why some people may resent the advertisements. The piece may be useful for explaining early reactions to the iPod as a cultural phenomenon.

Summary of Stephenson's argument.

Potential role source might play in paper.

Sullivan, Andrew. "Society Is Dead: We Have Retreated into the iWorld." *The Sunday Times*, 20 Feb. 2005, www.thesundaytimes.co.uk/sto/news/Features/Focus/article132446.ece. In this opinion piece, Sullivan examines how people in cities use iPods to isolate themselves. The author makes a highly personal but plausible case for turning off the machines and demonstrates how quickly the iPod changed society.

Evaluation of Sullivan's opinion piece.

Walker, Rob. "The Guts of a New Machine." *The New York Times Magazine*, 30 Nov. 2003. *General OneFile*, web.b.ebscohost.com.ezproxy.bpl.org. This lengthy report describes in detail how Apple developed the concept and technology of the iPod. Walker not only provides a detailed early look at the product but also shows how badly Apple's competitors underestimated its market strength. May help explain Apple's later dominance in smartphones as well.

Citation demonstrates how to cite an article from a database—in this case, *General OneFile*.

Writing about Writing   For a quick exercise in preparing an annotated bibliography, choose a film that has opened very recently, locate five or six reviews or news articles about it, and then prepare an annotated bibliography using these items. Imagine that you'll be writing a research paper about the public and critical reception the film received when it debuted. (Public and critical reaction may be quite different.) Be sure to choose a documentation system for your bibliography and to use it consistently.

How to start ▸ ● **Need to write a synthesis paper?**
Summarize and paraphrase what you have
read. See page 259.

18

require a
response
to multiple
sources

Synthesis Papers

In some classes, you may be asked to write a synthesis paper, in which
you summarize, compare, or assess the views of a variety of authors on
a specific topic. The assignment might also require that you respond
with a thesis of your own on that subject, based on what you've
learned from your research. A synthesis paper (also sometimes called a
"review of literature") gives you practice in using sources in academic
papers.

At a glance . . .

● Determine the exact nature and structure of your synthesis
assignment.

● Locate and read reputable sources critical to your project.

● Analyze the positions taken by authors you have read.

● Respond in writing to the authors you have read.

UNDERSTANDING SYNTHESIS PAPERS. In a synthesis, you typically survey a range of opinions on a topic, sometimes a controversial one. For example, you might be asked to review the positions of authors who both support and challenge the view that we have no choice but to adapt to new media and technology. Or for a chemistry course, you could prepare a literature review covering the most recently published research on lithium-ion polymer batteries.

need to ◄
write a
synthesis
paper?

Always pay close attention to the actual assignment: Note what types of sources you must review, whether you may quote from them, how to document them, **O** and whether you are, in fact, expected to develop a thesis of your own after reviewing all the material. Sometimes a synthesis will be part of another project: A prospectus you write for an end-of-semester research paper might require a section in which you summarize the sources you expect to use and explain the different positions they represent.

When your assignment is to prepare a review of literature, you will identify and report on the most important books and articles on a subject, usually over a specified period of time: *currently, from the last five years, over the past three decades*. The topic of the review may be assigned to you or it may be one you must prepare as part of a thesis, term paper, or capstone project. In either case, check whether your summary must follow a specific pattern of organization: Most literature reviews are chronological, though some are thematic, and still others are arranged by comparison and contrast. **O**

Identify reputable sources on your subject.

Expect to find multiple articles, books, and research studies on any significant topic. You can locate relevant material using library catalogs, research guides, or online tools (see Chapter 45). Work with your instructor or a research librarian to separate mainstream and essential works from outliers, which may or may not deserve a closer look.

Summarize and paraphrase the works you have identified.

Take these notes carefully. Summaries capture the gist of every source you read, even those that don't pan out. Paraphrases are lengthier notes you take when you expect to refer to sources extensively or quote from them directly. (Review these skills, as necessary, in Chapters 48–50.)

understand citation
styles p. 467

develop a draft p. 338

Look for connections between your sources. Once you have summarized and paraphrased a range of sources, examine them *in relationship to each other* to determine where they come down on your issue. Think about categories to describe their stances: *similarity/difference, congruence/divergence, consistency/inconsistency, conventional/radical,* and so on. Look for sources, too, that explain how a controversy has evolved and where it stands now. Introduce such materials with verbs of attribution such as *describes, reports, points out, asserts, argues, claims, agrees, concurs.*

Acknowledge disagreements and rebuttals. Describe accurately all the opinions you encounter, introducing them with verbs of attribution such as *questions, denies, disagrees, contradicts, undermines, disputes, calls into question, takes issue with.* Your synthesis should represent a full range of opinions.

Don't rush to judgment. In synthesizing, writers sometimes divide their sources too conveniently between those that merely support a claim and those that oppose it, ignoring complications and subtleties. Quite often, the most interesting relationships are to be found in places where belligerent authors unexpectedly agree or orthodox research generates unexpected results. Don't precook the results or try to fit your materials into an existing framework.

Cite materials that both support and challenge your own thesis. Any thesis you develop yourself as a result of your synthesis (as seen in the sample essay on p. 265) should reflect the inclusiveness of your research. Of course, you will draw on, quote from, and amplify the materials that help define your position. But be sure to acknowledge materials that run counter to your thesis too. In academic and professional writing, you must not only acknowledge these dissenters but also outline their ideas objectively and introduce any quotations from them fairly (Rosen *says,* not Rosen *whines*). **O**

use quotations p. 463

Getting the details right

Although synthesis assignments vary enormously, certain organizational strategies and conventions are worth noting.

Provide a context for your topic. Open a synthesis paper by identifying your subject and placing it in a historical or cultural context. Identify writers or sources that have defined the topic, and explain the rationale for your project. Help readers appreciate why an issue is important.

Tell a story. Whether your synthesis merely summarizes varying points of view or defends a thesis statement, it's often a good strategy to create a narrative readers can follow. O Help them understand the issues as you have come to appreciate them yourself. Separate major issues from minor ones, and use transitions as necessary to establish connections (*consequently*), highlight contrasts (*on the other hand*), show parallels (*similarly*), and so on.

Pay attention to language. Keep the style of your synthesis objective, neutral, and fairly formal. In most cases, avoid *I* when summarizing and paraphrasing. O Remember that the summaries of materials you cite should be in your own words; some synthesis assignments may even prohibit direct quotations. If you do quote from sources, choose statements that cogently represent the positions of your sources.

Be sure to document your sources. Record full bibliographic information for all the materials you read. You'll need it for the works cited or references page required at the end of most synthesis papers.

> **Writing about Writing** On pages 262–64, you'll find paragraphs from sources used in the model synthesis paper on page 265. All these articles are available online. Choose two or three, find and read them, and then write a detailed synthesis of their authors' full positions, being sure to highlight the similarities and/or differences. Keep your analysis as neutral and objective as you can, *especially* if you find yourself taking sides. When you are done, a reader should have some sense of the overall media controversy that these pieces address, but have no idea where you might stand.

understand narratives p. 169

refine your tone p. 366

Examining a model

To give you an idea of how to bring sources together, we'll build a brief synthesis paper from selections drawn from essays that focus on one topic: whether new media technologies like the Web pose a threat to literacy and culture. Ideas that play a role in the synthesis essay are highlighted. Here are the sources, presented alphabetically by the author:

I ask my students about their reading habits, and though I'm not surprised to find that few read newspapers or print magazines, many check in with online news sources, aggregate sites, incessantly. They are seldom away from their screens for long, but that's true of us, their parents, as well.

— Sven Birkerts, "Reading in a Digital Age"

The picture emerging from the research is deeply troubling, at least to anyone who values the depth, rather than just the velocity, of human thought. People who read text studded with links, the studies show, comprehend less than those who read traditional linear text. People who watch busy multimedia presentations remember less than those who take in information in a more sedate and focused manner. People who are continually distracted by e-mails, alerts, and other messages understand less than those who are able to concentrate. And people who juggle many tasks are less creative and less productive than those who do one thing at a time.

It is this control, this mental discipline that we are at risk of losing as we spend ever more time scanning and skimming online. If the slow progression of words across printed pages damped our craving to be inundated by mental stimulation, the Internet indulges it. It returns us to our native state of distractedness, while presenting us with far more distractions than our ancestors ever had to contend with.

Top: Jackie Ricciardi/*The Augusta Chronicle*/ZUMA PRESS.
Bottom: Will Vragovis/*St. Petersburg Times*/ZUMA PRESS.

— Nicholas Carr, "Does the Internet Make You Dumber?"

Today some 4.5 billion digital screens illuminate our lives. Words have migrated from wood pulp to pixels on computers, phones, laptops, game consoles, televisions, billboards, and tablets. Letters are no longer fixed in black ink on paper, but flitter on a glass surface in a rainbow of colors as fast as our eyes can blink.

Screens fill our pockets, briefcases, dashboards, living room walls, and the sides of buildings. They sit in front of us when we work—regardless of what we do. We are now people of the screen. And of course, these newly ubiquitous screens have changed how we read and write.

— Kevin Kelly, "Reading in a Whole New Way"

I have been reading a lot on my iPad recently, and I have some complaints—not about the iPad but about the state of digital reading generally. Reading is a subtle thing, and its subtleties are artifacts of a venerable medium: words printed in ink on paper. Glass and pixels aren't the same.

— Verlyn Klinkenborg, "Further Thoughts of a Novice E-reader"

Top: DPA/ZUMA Press
Bottom: Lannis Waters/*The Palm Beach Post*/ZUMA PRESS.

The new media have caught on for a reason. Knowledge is increasing exponentially; human brainpower and waking hours are not. Fortunately, the Internet and information technologies are helping us manage, search, and retrieve our collective intellectual output at different scales, from Twitter and previews to e-books and online encyclopedias. Far from making us stupid, these technologies are the only things that will keep us smart.

— Steven Pinker, "Mind over Mass Media"

No teenager that I know of regularly reads a newspaper, as most do not have the time and cannot be bothered to read pages and pages of text while they could watch the news summarized on the Internet or on TV.

— Matthew Robson, "How Teenagers Consume Media"

Then again, perhaps we will simply adjust and come to accept what James called "acquired inattention." E-mails pouring in, cell phones ringing, televisions blaring, podcasts streaming—all this may become background noise, like the "din of a foundry or factory" that James observed workers could scarcely avoid at first, but which eventually became just another part of their daily routine. For the younger generation of multitaskers, the great electronic din is an expected part of everyday life. And given what neuroscience and anecdotal evidence have shown us, this state of constant intentional self-distraction could well be of profound detriment to individual and cultural well-being. When people do their work only in the "interstices of their mind-wandering," with crumbs of attention rationed out among many competing tasks, their culture may gain in information, but it will surely weaken in wisdom.

— Christine Rosen, "The Myth of Multitasking"

The past was not as golden, nor is the present as tawdry, as the pessimists suggest, but the only thing really worth arguing about is the future. It is our misfortune, as a historical generation, to live through the largest expansion in expressive capability in human history, a misfortune because abundance breaks more things than scarcity. We are now witnessing the rapid stress of older institutions accompanied by the slow and fitful development of cultural alternatives. Just as required education was a response to print, using the Internet well will require new cultural institutions as well, not just new technologies.

— Clay Shirky, "Does the Internet Make You Smarter?"

Both Carr and Rosen are right about one thing: The changeover to digital reading brings challenges and changes, requiring a reconsideration of what books are and what they're supposed to do. That doesn't mean the shift won't be worth it. The change will also bring innovations impossible on Gutenberg's printed page, from text mixed with multimedia to components that allow readers to interact with the author and fellow consumers.

— Peter Suderman, "Don't Fear the E-reader"

Here is a brief paper that synthesizes the positions represented in the preceding materials, quoting extensively from them and leading up to a thesis. We have boldfaced the authors' names the first time they appear to emphasize the number of sources used in this short example.

Chiu 1

Lauren Chiu

Professor Chappell

Writing 203

September 28, 2017

Time to Adapt?

There is considerable agreement that the Internet and other electronic media are changing the way people read, write, think, and behave. Scholars such as **Sven Birkerts** report that their students do not seem to read printed materials anymore, a fact confirmed by fifteen-year-old intern **Matthew Robson**, when asked by his employer Morgan Stanley to describe the media habits of teenagers in England: "No teenager that I know of regularly reads a newspaper, as most do not have the time and cannot be bothered to read pages and pages of text."

But the changes we are experiencing may be more significant than just students abandoning the printed word. Working with an iPad, for instance, makes **Verlyn Klinkenborg** wonder whether reading on a screen may actually be a different and less perceptive experience than reading on paper. More worrisome, **Nicholas Carr** points to a growing body of research suggesting that the cognitive abilities of those who use media frequently may actually be degraded, weakening their comprehension and concentration. Yet, according to **Clay Shirky**, the Internet is increasing our ability to communicate immeasurably, and so we simply have to deal with whatever

Two sources are cited to support a general claim about the media.

Chiu 2

Other authorities amplify and complicate the issue.

consequences follow from such a major shift in technology. Thinkers like Shirky argue that we do not, in fact, have any choice but to adapt to such changes.

Even **Christine Rosen**, a critic of technology, acknowledges that people will probably have to adjust to their diminished attention spans (110). After all, are there really any alternatives to the speed, convenience, and power of the new technologies when we have become what **Kevin Kelly** describes as "people of the screen" and are no more likely to return to paper for reading than we are to vinyl for music recordings? Fears of the Internet may be overblown too. **Peter Suderman** observes that changes in media allow us to do vastly more than we can with print alone. Moreover, because the sheer amount of knowledge is increasing so quickly, **Steven Pinker** argues that we absolutely need the new ways of communicating: "[T]hese technologies are the only things that will keep us smart."

Carr and Shirky are well-known authors with opposing views of the Web.

In a full-length essay, this section would be much longer and quote more sources.

We cannot, however, ignore voices of caution. The differences Carr describes between habits of deep reading and skimming are especially troubling because so many users of the Web have experienced them. And who can doubt the loss of seriousness and goodwill in our public and political discussions these days? Maybe Rosen *is* right when she worries that our culture is trading wisdom for a glut of information. But it seems more likely that society will be better off trying to fix the problems electronic media are causing than imagining that we can return to simpler technologies that have already just about vanished.

Concerns about the Web are portrayed as reasonable.

The writer states a thesis that might guide a longer analysis.

Chiu 3

Works Cited

Birkerts, Sven. "Reading in a Digital Age." *The American Scholar*, Phi Beta Kappa, Spring 2010, theamericanscholar.org/reading-in-a-digital-age/.

Carr, Nicholas. "Does the Internet Make You Dumber?" *The Wall Street Journal*, 5 June 2010, www.wsj.com/articles/ SB10001424052748704025304575284981644790098.

Kelly, Kevin. "Reading in a Whole New Way." *Smithsonian*, Aug. 2010, www.smithsonianmag.com/40th-anniversary/ reading-in-a-whole-new-way-1144822/?no-ist.

Klinkenborg, Verlyn. "Further Thoughts of a Novice E-reader." *The New York Times*, 28 May 2010, www.nytimes .com/2010/05/30/opinion/30sun4.html?_r=0.

Pinker, Steven. "Mind over Mass Media." *The New York Times*, 10 June 2010, www.nytimes.com/2010/06/11/ opinion/11Pinker.html.

Robson, Matthew. "How Teenagers Consume Media." *The Guardian*, 13 July 2009, www.theguardian.com/ business/2009/jul/13/teenage-media-habits-morgan-stanley.

Rosen, Christine. "The Myth of Multitasking." *The New Atlantis*, no. 20, Spring 2008, pp. 105–10.

Shirky, Clay. "Does the Internet Make You Smarter?" *The Wall Street Journal*, 4 June 2010, www.wsj.com/articles/ SB10001424052748704025304575284973472694334.

Suderman, Peter. "Don't Fear the E-reader." *Reason*, 23 Mar. 2010, reason.com/archives/2010/03/23/dont-fear-the-e-reader.

19

require a
brief critical
response

Position Papers

A course instructor may ask you to respond to an assigned reading, lecture, film, or other activity with a position paper, in which you record your reactions to the material, such as your impressions or observations. Such a paper is usually brief—often not much longer than a page or two—and due the next class session. Typically, you won't have time for more than a draft and quick revision. But take the assignment seriously.

At a glance . . .

- Review the response assignment carefully.
- Find ideas or quotations in the target texts or activities especially worthy of comment.
- Choose an appropriate genre or structure for your response.
- Edit the paper carefully.

UNDERSTANDING POSITION
PAPERS. Instructors have various reasons for assigning position or response papers: to focus attention on particular readings or class presentations; to measure how well you've understood course materials; to push you to connect course concepts or readings. You might be asked to summarize and assess the findings in a journal article, speculate about the work of a feminist theorist reviewed in class, respond to a panel discussion in class, or—like the student in the model at the end of this chapter—react to a controversial film. Instructors may mark position papers less completely than full essays and grade them by different standards because they usually want you to take intellectual risks.

Protesters Taking a Position—While some feel that security cameras ensure safety, others believe them to be an invasion of privacy.

But don't blow off these quick, often low-stakes assignments. Position or response papers give you practice in writing about a subject and thus prepare you for other papers and exams. These assignments *may* even preview the style of essay questions an instructor favors. Just as important, position papers establish your ethos in a course, marking you as a conscientious reader and thinker or, alternatively, someone just along for the ride.

Use a few simple strategies to write a strong position paper.

Read the assignment carefully. Understand exactly what your instructor expects you to read, examine, or respond to. Then look for key words in the assignment, such as *summarize, describe, classify, evaluate, compare, compare and contrast,* and *analyze,* and appreciate the differences between them.

confused? ◄

Review the assigned material. If asked to respond to written texts, consider printing or photocopying them so that you can annotate in the margins and underscore key claims and evidence. Look for conflicts, points of difference, or issues raised in class or in the public arena—what some writers call *hooks*. Then use the most provocative points to spur your thinking, using whatever brainstorming techniques work best for you. **O**

Mine the texts for evidence. Look for sentences worth quoting or ideas worth describing in detail. **O** Anchor your position paper around such strong statements or arguments. Quote a brief passage you admire for how well it explains a key concept or highlight a paragraph full of claims that you resist. Then discuss these passages in your draft.

develop a draft p. 338   get an idea p. 16   use quotations p. 463

Be sure you merge any quoted materials smoothly into your own writing, being careful to surround them with quotation marks.

Organize the paper sensibly. Unless the assignment specifically states otherwise, don't write the position paper off the top of your head. Take the time to offer a thesis or to set up a comparison, an evaluation, or another pattern of organization. Give a position paper the same structural integrity you would a longer and more consequential assignment.

Getting the details right

Although the assignment may seem minor, edit and proofread any position or response paper carefully. **O** Think of it as a trial run for a longer essay. As such, it should follow the conventions of any given field or major.

Clearly identify your subject. A surprising number of students forget to do that in response papers, assuming their instructors will know. That's simply inept. Take the time to identify a reading by its author and title, name the book, movie, or performance you have watched, describe a panel discussion—maybe even name its participants. Make sure any quotations are set up accurately, properly introduced, and documented. Offer page numbers for any direct quotations. **O**

Identify key terms and concepts and use them correctly and often. The instructor may be checking to see how diligently you read assigned material. So, in your paper, make a point of referring to the new concepts or terms you've discovered in the reading, as Heidi Rogers does with *ethos*, *pathos*, and *logos* in the model essay on page 271.

Spell names and concepts correctly. You lose credibility *very* quickly if you misspell technical terms or proper nouns, especially any that appear throughout the course readings. In literary papers especially, get characters' names and book titles right.

Respond tactfully to your classmates' work. Position papers are often posted to electronic discussion boards to encourage online conversations. So take the opportunity to reply substantively to what your classmates have written there. Don't just say "I agree" or "You're kidding!" Add good reasons and evidence to your remarks. Remember, too, that your instructor might review these comments, looking for evidence of your engagement with the course. **O**

revise and edit
p. 350

understand citation
styles p. 467

comment
p. 357

Examining a model

Here's a position paper written by Heidi Rogers as an early assignment in a lower-level course on visual rhetoric. Rogers's assignment was to offer an honest response to director Leni Riefenstahl's infamous documentary, *Triumph of the Will*, which showcases the National Socialist Party rallies in Munich in 1934. In the film, we see the German people embracing Hitler and his Nazi regime as they consolidate their power.

Rogers 1

Heidi Rogers

Professor Chappell

Writing 203

September 22, 20--

Triumph of the Lens

The 1935 film *Triumph of the Will*, directed by Leni Riefenstahl, masterfully shows how visuals can be a powerful form of rhetoric. In the documentary we see Adolf Hitler, one of the greatest mass murderers in history, portrayed as an inspirational leader who could be the savior of Germany. Watching the film, I was taken aback. I am supposed to detest Hitler for his brutal crimes against humanity, and yet I found myself liking him, even smiling as he greets his fellow Germans on the streets of Munich. How did Riefenstahl accomplish this, drawing viewers into her film and giving Germans such pride in their leader?

Riefenstahl's technique is to layer selected visuals so as to evoke the emotions she wants her audience to feel toward Hitler and his regime. Her first step is to introduce images of nature and locations that are peaceful and soothing. Next, she inserts images of the German people themselves: children playing, women blowing kisses to Hitler, men in uniform proudly

> Offers a thesis to explain how the film makes Hitler attractive.

Rogers 2

Rogers describes the patterns she sees in Riefenstahl's editing technique.

Provides an extended example to support her claim about how *Triumph of the Will* was edited.

Explores implications of her claim—that clever editing enabled Riefenstahl to reach many audiences.

united under the Nazi flag. The next step is to weave images of Hitler himself among these German people, so that even when he isn't smiling or showing any emotions, it seems as if he is conveying the happiness, pride, or strength evoked by the images edited around him. The final piece of the puzzle is always to put Hitler front and center, usually giving a rousing speech, which makes him seem larger than life.

A good example of this technique comes during the youth rally sequence. First, Riefenstahl presents peaceful images of the area around the Munich stadium, including beautiful trees with the sun streaming between the branches. We then see the vastness of the city stadium, designed by Hitler himself. Then we watch thousands of young boys and girls smiling and cheering in the stands. These masses erupt when Hitler enters the arena and Riefenstahl artfully juxtaposes images of him, usually with a cold, emotionless face, with enthusiastic youth looking up to him as if he were a god. Hitler then delivers an intoxicating speech about the future of Germany and the greatness that the people will achieve under his leadership. The crowd goes wild as he leaves the stage, and we see an audience filled with awe and purpose.

What Riefenstahl did in *Triumph of the Will* is a common technique in film editing. When you have to reach a massive audience, you want to cover all of your bases and appeal to all of

Rogers 3

them at once. Therefore, the more kinds of *ethos, pathos,* and *logos* you can layer onto a piece of film, the better your chances will be of convincing the greatest number of people of your cause. As hard as this is to admit, if I had lived in a devastated 1935 Germany and I had seen this film, I might have wanted this guy to lead my country too.

Universal History Archive/Getty Images

Triumph of the Will features numerous imposing shots of highly regimented crowds cheering for Hitler.

Writing about Writing   Many media sources and publications encourage readers to comment on their postings or products, and people can't resist the urge to critique. Practice your critical skills, by responding to prompts on several sites you are already familiar with. For example, on a news or political blog, locate a thought-provoking article to which some readers have already offered substantive responses (more than a line or two). Read the article yourself, thinking about what you might post in response. Then read through the actual comments. How does your brief response compare with what others have said? What strategies have they used that you admire? How did the best responders establish their credibility? And which responders did you take less seriously, *and why*?

Chances are you'll be disappointed in much of what you read in online commentary and social media. People may react from prejudiced positions, focus on irrelevant points, or just take potshots at the original author. From such critics, you may learn what not to do in a serious academic paper.

● **Adapting material?** Organize your presentation. See page 277.

Oral Reports

20

present
information
to a live
audience

Oral reports required in many classes make some students wonder what exactly these presentations have to do with learning course material. Arguably, preparing a report gives you expertise on a topic of your own choosing that you can share with classmates, who are doing the same for you. Just as important, a class presentation, a relatively low-stakes event, represents an opportunity to practice a skill useful throughout your life—the ability to speak confidently before audiences of all kinds. Fortunately, it *is* a skill you can acquire and refine.

At a glance . . .

● Understand what your presentation assignment requires.
● Find a subject you can make interesting, appealing, and significant.
● Develop a structure that keeps listeners informed and interested.
● Practice every element of the presentation.

UNDERSTANDING ORAL REPORTS. Oral presentations are common throughout the academic world, ranging from PowerPoint slides at orientation sessions to harangues at student government meetings to poster sessions at conferences in business and the sciences. In a psychology course, you might use presentation software to describe the results of an experiment you and several classmates designed. In a Shakespeare class, a classmate might use slides for an oral report on Elizabethan theaters that draws upon research she is doing for an end-of-semester term paper. And, some afternoon, you might use a bullhorn and a little humor to inform fellow protestors of the very serious ground rules for staging peaceful demonstrations on the grounds of the state capitol.

All these occasions require strategies for conveying information powerfully, memorably, and sometimes graphically. But oral reports can be deceptive. When watching someone give an effective five-minute talk, you might assume the speaker spent less time preparing it than he or she would a ten-page paper. You'd be wrong: Oral presentations demand the same research, analysis, strategy, and commitment as any other assignment—and then some. Here is advice for preparing effective oral reports.

Choose your subject well. For an oral report, you won't, of course, always have the luxury of choice. But when you do, begin with a topic that intrigues you, a subject you really might investigate on your own. Or follow up on interests you already have. Start off broad to be sure you have a workable topic—a report on Elizabethan theaters sounds grand. But you'll have only, let's say, ten minutes of class time, and the audience in your Shakespeare class already knows something about the Globe Theater—its picture is right on the textbook cover.

You need to focus. Fortunately, you do know something about the fashion industry today and so you wonder about actors' costumes way back in the 1590s. What were they like? Who made them? How expensive and elaborate? And how do we even know these things? Answering any one of these questions could easily fill the allotted time and keep classmates interested. So the principle is simple: Start wide and narrow a topic until it becomes novel, engaging, and manageable.

You can do the same even when subjects are assigned. An instructor will likely offer general subject areas for oral reports, depending on the course: for instance, personality disorders (psychology), professional ethics (business), therapeutic exercise (kinesiology), the French Revolution (history), executive privilege (government). Your task is to explore resources in the field to find an aspect of the subject, concept, or controversy that would intrigue both you and classmates.

Know your stuff. You need to do serious research to make a report accurate and interesting. Knowledge also brings you confidence that will ease some anxieties about public speaking. When you command a subject, audiences will find you believable and persuasive. And you'll feel more comfortable if you have to improvise or take questions. You'll even survive if equipment fails or you misplace a note card.

Knowing your stuff also means finding and using the best sources. So research an oral report the same way you would a research paper (see Part 7, Academic Research and Sources, for details). Your instructor may even request a bibliography from you after the presentation to confirm the work you did. And it won't hurt to briefly identify sources for any surprising claims or controversial positions you make in the presentation.

Highlight arresting details. Audiences always like to be surprised. So, during your research for the report, look for facts and details that are fresh to you. They'll likely strike classmates (if not your instructor) the same way. Give priority to authoritative facts and figures and important new research, and look for memorable (and brief) quotations. Keep an eye out, too, for visual items that might reinforce key points you expect to make, understanding that all such items need to have an impact at a distance. (If you find a table of statistics or mathematical formulas readers need to appreciate, photocopy them for distribution—don't throw hard-to-read or complex information up on a slide.)

Adapting ◄ material?

Organize your presentation. Since listeners, unlike readers, can't go back to find their places in an oral report, a key to organizing successful presentations is simplicity:

Tell listeners what you are going to do.

Do it.

Then tell listeners what you did and why it matters.

Of course, you can't get to this organizational stage until you've researched your subject and know what you need to cover. Once you do, list the items or points you think matter and arrange them to attract and hold listeners, choosing a pattern of organization that suits your topic and purpose: for example, *narrative, report,* or *argument.* A narrative structure simply lists points by date, time, or even procedure (*first, second, third*):

Introduction: Race to the moon

In 1957 . . . in the late 50s . . . initially

In 1963 . . . in the early sixties . . . then

In 1969 . . . at the end of the decade . . . finally

Conclusion: Race won by Apollo 11

Factual reports vary enormously in structure. But begin with a thesis and select a limited number of points to support it:

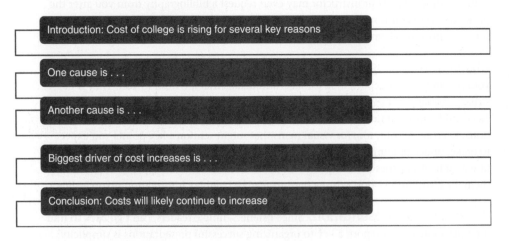

Introduction: Cost of college is rising for several key reasons

One cause is . . .

Another cause is . . .

Biggest driver of cost increases is . . .

Conclusion: Costs will likely continue to increase

Arguments can add complexities, such as objections or concessions. In written academic arguments, these objections are sometimes addressed toward the end. But if you want an oral presentation to persuade an audience, acknowledge some opposing points earlier and then conclude with an unqualified endorsement of your claim.

Introduction: I believe Congress should privatize VA hospitals

One argument is . . .

• However, some say . . .

Another argument is

• However, many believe . . .

Most compelling argument is . . .

Conclusion: Congress should privatize VA hospitals

Patterns like these are only suggestions: Use any *explicit* structure that suits your material. And don't underestimate how easy it is for listeners to get lost. You've succeeded if your audience walks away thinking about just two or three ideas. You can make the report seem spontaneous, but should plan every move.

Keep your audience on track. Obviously, transitions play important roles in reinforcing the structure of any speech and oral report. ○ Remind listeners of what you are doing with a transitional word or phrase:

Topical Press Agency/Getty Images

> *The second issue I wish to discuss . . .*
>
> *Now that we've examined the phenomenon, let's analyze its consequences . . .*
>
> *So, in conclusion let me restate my thesis . . .*

Don't be shy about making points this directly and don't worry about repetition. In an oral report, strategic repetition is a friend.

The best equipment can't save a poorly prepared report.

Stay connected to your listeners. For about thirty seconds, you'll have the spontaneous goodwill of most audiences. After that, you've got to earn every minute of their attention. Begin by introducing yourself and your subject, if no one else performs that task. For longer reports, consider easing into your material with an anecdote that connects you, your subject, and your listeners. Self-deprecating humor usually works. (Short, in-class presentations won't need much, if any, warm-up.)

Establish eye contact with individual members of the group right from the start. Watch their reactions. When it's clear you've made a point, move on. If you see puzzled looks, explain more. No speaker charms everyone, so don't let a random yawn throw you. But if the whole crowd starts to snooze, you *are* the problem. Connect or lose 'em: Pick up your pace; move on to the next point; skip to your best material. Readers won't know you've changed your strategy. ○

Just as important, be sure to speak *to* your listeners, not to your text or note cards. Arrange your materials and print them large enough so that you can read them easily from a distance and not lose your place. If you look downward too often or gaze at your own slides, you'll break eye contact and your voice will be muffled, even with a microphone.

Use your voice and body. Speak clearly and deliberately, and be sure people in the back of the room can hear you. Nervous speakers unconsciously speed up until they're racing to their conclusions. If you get skittish, calm yourself by taking a deep breath and smiling.

order ideas p. 345 | connect ideas p. 391

If the room is large and you're not confined by a fixed microphone, move around on the stage to address more of the audience. Use gestures too. They are a natural part of public speaking, especially for arguments and personal narratives. If you get stuck behind a podium, be sure to scan the entire audience (not just speak to the middle of the room) and modulate your voice. Keep your body steady too: Don't rock or sway as you speak.

Adapt your material to the time available. If you know your subject well, don't worry about running out of things to say. Most speakers have the opposite problem: They talk too much. So be realistic about how much you can cover within an assigned time limit, especially if you have to take questions at the end. Tie your key ideas to fixed points on a clock. Know where you need to be at a quarter, half, and three-quarters of the way through the available time. If you're taking questions after your presentation, simply follow up with *Any questions?* Then give listeners time to come up with some. You'll score points with an instructor if you handle a few questions well.

Practice your talk. With any oral report, you need several dry runs to increase your confidence and identify potential problems. Speak your material aloud *exactly* as you intend to deliver it and go through all the motions, especially if you will use media, such as slides or video clips. Have one or more friends or classmates observe you and offer feedback.

If your presentation is collaborative, choreograph the report with the full group in attendance, agreeing on the introductions, transitions, and interactions with the audience. Who manages the laptop? Who distributes the handouts and when? Who takes the questions? Handoffs like these seem minor until they are fumbled on game day. And let members of the group work to their strengths—understanding that an instructor may expect to hear from everyone.

Be sure to actually time your talk, too, and go through all your materials, including any audio and video clips. If you review the presentation only in your head, you'll greatly underestimate its length.

Prep for the occasion. Before the report, check out the physical location if possible, as well as any equipment you will use. Be sure your laptop will connect to the multimedia projector in the room; know how to dim the lights; be sure a screen or electrical outlets are available.

Then dress up. A little spit and polish earns the goodwill of most audiences. Your classmates may razz you about the tie or skirt, but it just proves they're paying attention. And that's a good thing.

Viorika/Getty Images

Thinking about Writing   Given the number of oral presentations and lectures you've sat through, most of them using PowerPoint, you could probably write your own chapter on this special assignment. Working with a small group, list five hallmarks of an effective oral report or seminar presentation and five characteristics of a dismal one. Annotate the list with examples that you may recall from particular reports. Then compare the features your group has come up with to those generated by other groups.

Getting the details right

There's nothing wrong with a report that relies on the spoken word alone. Still, audiences do appreciate—almost expect—supporting material, including posters, flip charts, handouts, slides, and visual or audio samplings. All such materials, clearly labeled and handsomely reproduced, should also be genuinely relevant to the report. Resist the temptation to show something just because it's cool.

Most oral reports do use presentation software of some kind, such as the dominant player in this field, PowerPoint. With presentation software, you build the report upon a sequence of slides, designing them yourself or picking them from a gallery of ready-made items. You can choose slide layouts to accommodate text-only presentations, text and photos, text and charts, images only, and so on.

Presentation software offers so many bells and whistles that novices tend to overdo it, allowing the software to dominate their reports. Here's how to make PowerPoint, Keynote, or Prezi work for you.

Be certain you need presentation software. A short talk that makes only one or two points probably works better if viewers focus on you, not on a screen. Use presentation software to keep audiences on track through more complicated material, to highlight major issues or points, or to display images viewers really need to see. A little humor or eye candy is fine once in a while, but don't expect audiences to be impressed by glitz. What matters is the content of the report. O

Use slides to introduce points, not cover them. If you find yourself reading your slides, you've put too many words on-screen. Offer the minimum that viewers need: main points, important evidence, clear charts, and essential images (see the "Presenting An Oral Report" slides on p. 285). It's fine, too, to use a slide that outlines your presentation at the beginning and summarizes key points at the end. In fact, it's quite helpful to have an item that signals your conclusion.

When your presentation focuses on an extended text that you'll need to read or analyze—a poem, lines from a treaty, a political document—be sure to reproduce it on paper and distribute it to audience members (preferably before the report starts) so they can follow the material readily. You can also annotate any such document when appropriate, using boldface, marginal comments, and so on. Make things easy for your audience.

Use a simple and consistent design. With presentation software, you can select one of its design templates or create a style of your own that fits your subject. A consistent design scheme will unify your report and minimize distractions. O

For academic presentations, choose legible fonts in a size large enough for viewers at the back of the room to read easily. For reasons of legibility, avoid elegant, playful, or eccentric fonts, including Old English styles or those that resemble handwriting. Some experts prefer sans serif fonts for headlines and serif fonts for supporting text. But don't use more than two or, more rarely, three fonts within a presentation. Use boldface very selectively for emphasis. If you have to boldface a font to make it visible at a distance, simply find a thicker font. Italics are fine for occasional use, but in some fonts they can be hard to read at a distance.

understand reports p. 38   think visually p. 417

For presentations, Prezi offers a range of design templates, as shown here.

Consider alternatives to slide-based presentations. Anything you build on a laptop can be projected on-screen. So you need not use conventional slide-based presentation software for your oral report if you can create materials on your own. For example, various interactive Web 2.0 applications, from social-network software to blogs and wikis, can be configured for oral presentations, as can mind-mapping software and PowerPoint alternatives, such as Prezi. In Prezi, sequential slides are replaced by words, images, and media presented on an unending canvas; images move, rotate, and zoom in and out to provide different perspectives on a subject.

Learn the rhetoric of poster sessions. If you are in a scientific field, you are likely familiar with poster sessions—at which a great many researchers and scholars explain their latest work to an audience moving from one presentation to another. Presenters rely on large, carefully designed and printed posters to outline the highlights of their research and get audiences to notice their ideas.

Obviously, great care must be taken in the design of these items. Everything from the title of the poster to the layout of research data must be fashioned to draw attention to a researcher's work, only a small portion of which the poster itself can present. Posters must attract general viewers, but also offer enough detail (and be readable enough) to satisfy specialists and provoke questions. That's a tough job. But there's lots of information online about creating posters. Your instructors and colleagues can help you get it all right.

But don't forget your part in the show. You need to talk about your research and do it succinctly and clearly. Invite passersby to hear your spiel, and then don't disappoint them with an unrehearsed or ineptly focused summary of your work. Get to the point and make them interested. So, once again, practice matters.

Courtesy of the University of New Hampshire, Undergraduate Research Conference

Courtesy of the University of New Hampshire, Undergraduate Research Conference

Examining a model

An instructor created the following PowerPoint presentation to improve the quality of oral reports in a history course. It worked. The slides themselves are simple: each has a heading, several bullet points, and an image or photograph to attract attention.

Presenting an Oral Report

Basics

- Introduce yourself.
- Identify your subject: *who, what, where, when.*
- Provide background information.
- Check on pronunciations.

Presenting information

- Make screens readable at a distance.
- Do not overload slides.
- Bring handouts for long texts.
- Do not read off the screen.

Watching the clock

- Keep track of your time: Do not cut into someone else's.
- Do not repeat yourself.
- Practice—using all your media.

Winning an audience

- Make eye contact.
- Smile and look confident.
- Take your time.
- Avoid "uh" and "you know."
- Remember: you are among friends!

Geraint Lewis/Alamy Stock Photo

Choosing media

- What medium works best for your subject?
- Simple lecture?
- PowerPoint/Prezi?
- Website?
- Video?

Geraint Lewis/Alamy Stock Photo

Dressing up

- Look good.
- Pay attention to posture.
- Use gestures.

Geraint Lewis/Alamy Stock Photo

Final thoughts

- Do not try to cover too much.
- Do not worry about perfection.
- Slow down!

Geraint Lewis/Alamy Stock Photo

How to start ▶

● **Want to get the reader's attention?**
Choose a sensible subject line. See page 291.

Professional Correspondence

21

communicate
electronically

E-mail is the preferred method for most business (and personal) communication today because it is quick, efficient, easy to archive, and easy to search. But occasionally items you send via e-mail will still require that a message be confirmed in classic business-letter form to underscore the seriousness of the communication. The difference between informal and formal communications is useful.

At a glance . . .

● Assess the purpose and potential audiences of the communication.

● Handle the messaging clearly and efficiently.

● Distribute or copy your message appropriately.

● Respect all conventions.

UNDERSTANDING E-MAIL. E-mail is so common and informal that writers some-times forget its multiple uses. You might casually reach out to classmates in a psychology course, looking for someone to collaborate on a Web project; or contact the coordinator of the learning center to apply for a job as a tutor, courtesy copying the message to a professor who has agreed to serve as a reference; or invite the entire College of Liberal Arts faculty to attend a student production of Chekhov's *Uncle Vanya*; or complain to your cable supplier because a premium sports channel you subscribe to has been unavailable for a week—all by e-mail and all in the course of a day. Although usually composed quickly, such e-mails have a long shelf life once they're archived. They can also spread well beyond their original audiences. So you need to take care with messages sent to organizations, businesses, professors, groups of classmates, and so on. The following strategies will help.

Assess the situation. Most professional e-mail communications are relatively informal. The opening salvo, however, typically respects e-mail conventions—a clear subject line, notice of any cc's, a semiformal salutation (*Hey, Professor* is surprisingly common), an efficient message in middle style, O a cheery closing (*Best, Cheers, Thanks!*), and detailed contact information followed by a signature, a preferred e-mail address, and cell number. Replies usually become more clipped with each exchange in a series. The salutation may disappear entirely, the writing drops to low style, O and the signature/closing may be just a first name or initials. Perfectly natural.

Although e-mail now represents the preferred vehicle for almost all professional communications, there may be times when you'll use some features of traditional business letters:

- inside addresses that include postal information: street/city/state/zip
- formal salutations and punctuation (*Dear Dean Cornell:*)
- conventional phrases in middle/high style (*I am writing to request . . . I would like to apply*)
- formulaic closings (*Yours truly, Sincerely, With gratitude*)
- some facsimile of a signature

Gasp—you might even have to resort to paper and an envelope. Occasions that require a more traditional format might include formal complaints, official notices, congratulations, some thank-you messages, and application letters for school, internships, jobs, organizational memberships, and promotions.

Explain your purpose clearly and logically. Write any professional message so that it will still make sense a year or more later. Use both the subject line and first paragraph of an e-mail to explain your reason for writing. If necessary, introduce who you are and what your relationship might be to the recipient. Be specific about names, titles, dates, places, expectations, requirements, and so on, especially when you make a request or inquiry, invite a discussion, announce an event, or explain a policy.

Tell readers what you want or expect from them. In a professional e-mail, lay out a clear agenda for accomplishing one major task: Ask for information, a document or form, a response, or even a reply by a specific date. If you're applying for a job, scholarship, or admission to a program, name the exact position or program and mention that your résumé is attached. If you have multiple requests to make of a single person or group, consider writing separate e-mails. It's easier to track short, single-purpose e-mails than to deal with complex documents requiring multiple actions.

Write for intended audiences. Quite often, you won't know the people to whom you are sending a business letter. So you have to construct a letter imagining how an executive, employer, admissions officer, or complaints manager might be best approached or persuaded. Courtesy and goodwill go a long way—although sometimes you may have to be firm and impersonal. Avoid phony emotions or tributes.

Write for unintended audiences too. The specific audience in the "To" line may be the primary audience for your message. But e-mail communications are more public than traditional surface mail, easily duplicated, and readily shared with lists of contacts with just a click. So compose your professional communications as if they *might* be read by everyone in a unit or even published in a local paper. Assume that nothing in business e-mail is private.

Keep messages brief. Lengthy blocks of prose typed without paragraph breaks irritate readers, and most communications—formal or informal—become hard to process when they extend much beyond one page. A busy administrator or employee prefers a concise message, handsomely laid out on a screen or page. Even a job-application letter should be relatively short, highlighting just your strongest credentials: Leave it to the accompanying résumé or dossier to flesh out the details.

Indeed, meandering or chatty messaging in any situation can make a writer seem disorganized and out of control. Try to limit your e-mail communications to what fits on a single screen. Remember that most people now review their e-mail on mobile devices. O

think visually
p. 417

Distribute your messages sensibly.   Send a copy of an e-mail to anyone directly involved in the message, as well as to those who might need to be informed. For example, if you were filing a grade complaint with an instructor, you might also copy the chair of his or her academic department or the dean of students. But don't let the copy (CC) and blind copy (BCC) lines in the e-mail header tempt you to send messages beyond the essential audience.

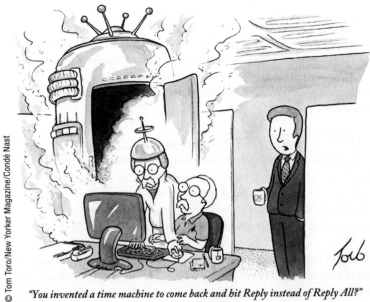

"You invented a time machine to come back and hit Reply instead of Reply All?"

Getting the details right: informal e-mails

Because people receive e-mail so frequently, make sure messages you send are easy to process.

want to get ◄ the reader's attention?

Use informative subject lines. They should clearly identify the topic and include helpful keywords that might later be searched. If your e-mail is specifically about a grading policy, your student loan, or mold in your gym locker, make sure a word you'll recall afterward—like *policy, loan,* or *mold*—gets in the subject line. In professional e-mails, subjects such as *A question, Hi!* or *Meeting* are useless.

Arrange your text sensibly. You can do almost as much visually in an e-mail as you can in a word-processing program, including choosing fonts, inserting lines, and adding color, images, and videos. But because so many people read messages on mobile devices, a simple block style with spaces between single-spaced paragraphs works best. Keep the paragraphs brief. Consider, too, that a list of incoming e-mails on a cell phone typically previews just the first few lines of a message. If you want a reader's attention, make your point immediately.

Include an appropriate signature. Professional e-mail of any kind should include a signature that identifies you and provides contact information readers need. Your e-mail address alone may not be clear enough to identify who you are, especially when you are writing to an instructor. Be sure to set up a signature for your laptop, desktop, or mobile device. But be careful: Don't provide readers with a home phone number or address since you won't know who might see your e-mail message. When you send e-mail, the recipient can reach you simply by replying.

Use standard grammar. Professional e-mails should be almost as polished as business letters: At least give readers the courtesy of a quick review to catch humiliating gaffes or misspellings in your messages. O

Check the recipient list before you hit send. Routinely double-check all the recipient fields—especially when you're replying to a message. The original writer may have copied a message widely: Do you want to send your reply to that entire group or just to the original writer?

Don't be a pain. You just add to the daily clutter if you send unnecessary replies to e-mails—a pointless *thanks* or *Yes!* or *WooHoo!* Just as bad is CCing everyone on a list when you've received a query that needs to go to one person only.

revise and edit p. 350

> **Thinking about Writing**   Take a quick look at the formatting of the
> e-mails that appear on a mobile device. Most phones now display images,
> complex page formats, or other textual features within e-mail. But note the
> limitations too. Images can clutter a message on a small screen, so place
> them after your text. And you might not want to put links you include too
> close together because they can be hard to select.

Getting the details right: formal e-mails or conventional business letters

Perhaps the most important detail in a business letter is keeping the format you use consistent and correct. Be sure to arrange your business letter appropriately on screen or print it on good-quality paper or letterhead and send it in a proper business envelope, one large enough to accommodate a page 8½ inches wide.

Use consistent margins and spacing for print documents. Generally, 1-inch margins all around work well, but you can use larger margins (up to 1½ inches) when your message is short. The top margin can also be adjusted if you want to balance the letter on the page, though the body need not be centered.

Finesse the greeting. When writing formally to a particular person at a firm or institution, address him or her as *Mr.* or *Ms.*—unless a person has a different title (*Dr., Professor*) or none at all. You may also address people by their full names: *Dear Margaret Hitchens.* When you don't have a name, you might use a person's title: *Dear Admissions Director* or *Dear Hiring Manager.* Or you can fall back on *Dear Sir or Madam* or *To Whom It May Concern*, though these forms of address (especially *madam*) are dated. When it doesn't sound absurd, you can even address the institution or entity: *Dear Exxon* or *Dear IRS*—again, this is not a preferred form.

Distribute paper copies of a letter, if necessary. Copy anyone involved in a message, as well as anyone who might have a *legitimate* interest in your action. For example, in filing a product complaint with a company, you may also want to send your formal letter to the state office of consumer affairs. Copies of paper letters are noted and listed at the bottom of the page, introduced by the abbreviation CC (for *courtesy copy*).

Spell everything right. Be scrupulous about the grammar and mechanics too—especially in a job-application letter. Until you get an interview, that piece of paper represents you to a potential client or employer. Would you hire someone who misspelled your company's name or made noticeable errors? O

Gero Breloer/dpa picture alliance archive/Alamy Stock Photo

Photocopy any paper letter as a record. An important business letter needs a paper copy, even when you have an electronic version archived: The photocopied signature may mean something.

Don't forget the promised enclosures. A résumé should routinely accompany a job-application letter. O

Fold a paper business letter correctly and send it in a suitable envelope. Business letters always go on 8½ × 11 inch paper and are sent in standard business envelopes, generally 4⅛ × 9½ inches. Fold the letter in three sections, trying to put the creases through white space in the letter so that the body of the message remains readable.

Thinking about Writing   Have you received a business letter recently on paper? If so, pull it out and take a moment to note the specific features described in this chapter. They are easy to overlook: letterhead, date, inside address, greeting, closing, attachments, spacing. Are their functions obvious and do they make sense? Now take a look at a recent e-mail you may have received from an institution or business (rather than a friend or classmate). What features does the business e-mail have in common with a business letter? In what ways are they different?

---

help with common errors
p. 536

understand résumés
p. 296

Examining models

Here's a fairly typical e-mail query from a student to a professor. The e-mail provides clear and direct information (note that the student's majors are identified in the signature) and poses one clear question. It gets to the point quickly and politely asks for a response.

To: John Ruszkiewicz

From: Kori Strickland

Sent: October 3, 2015 11:56 AM

Re: Writing Center Course Eligibility

CC: Davida Charney

Specific subject line.

Business letters use a colon after greeting, but e-mails are often less formal.

Dear Professor Ruszkiewicz,

    I'm currently a junior at the University of Texas at Austin applying for your Rhetoric 368C Writing Center Internship course in spring 2016. I have a question about my eligibility.

Opening paragraph explains point of e-mail.

    The course description online says preference is given to students who can work two or more semesters in the writing center after they take the class. Do I still stand a reasonable chance at being admitted to RHE 368C if I will be able to work only one semester because of a study-abroad opportunity my senior year?

Second paragraph poses one specific question.

Signature is simple, informative, and professional.

    Please let me know. In any case, I am attaching the required writing sample and have asked Professor Charney to write the brief recommendation requested for RHE 368C candidates.

Tone is professional and correct.

Final paragraph asks for a reply and spells out other actions the writer has taken.

Sincerely,

Kori Strickland

University of Texas Political Communication and English

Fine Arts Council Copresident

Attachment included as indicated in the letter.

Following is an application/cover letter from a student formatted as a print letter in conventional modified block form.

1001 Harold Circle #10

Austin, TX 78712

June 28, 20--

Mr. Josh Greenwood

ABC Corporate Advisers, Inc.

9034 Brae Rd., Suite 1111

Austin, TX 78731

Dear Mr. Greenwood:

Rita Weeks, a prelaw adviser at the University of Texas at Austin, e-mailed me about an internship opportunity at your firm. Working at ABC Corporate Advisers sounds like an excellent chance for me to further my interests in finance and corporate law. I would like to apply for the position.

As my attached résumé demonstrates, I have already interned at an estate-planning law firm, where I learned to serve the needs of an office of professionals and clients. I also have a record of achievement on campus: I used my skills as a writer and speaker to obtain funding for the Honors Business Association at UT-Austin, for which I serve as vice president and financial director. By contacting corporate recruiters, I raised $5,500 from Microsoft, ExxonMobil, Deloitte, and other companies.

I am ready for a job that more closely relates to my academic training and career goal: becoming a certified financial analyst and corporate lawyer. Please contact me at 210-555-0000 or NLINN @abcd.com to schedule an interview. Thank you for considering me as a potential intern. I look forward to meeting you.

Sincerely,

N. Linn

Nancy Linn

Enclosure: Résumé
CC: Rita Weeks

In modified-block form, return address, date, closing, and signature are centered.

Opening paragraph clearly states thesis of letter: Nancy Linn wants this job.

Candidate repeatedly explains how internship fits career goals.

Letter highlights key accomplishments succinctly and specifically.

Additional contact information provided.

Courtesy copy of letter sent to adviser mentioned in first paragraph; can be contacted as reference.

How to start ▶ ● **Want to get a job?** Design pages that are easy to read. See page 299.

22

record
professional
achievements

Résumés

A one-page résumé usually accompanies any letter of application you send for a position or job. The résumé gathers and organizes details about your experiences at school, on the job, and in the community. In some careers, you may recap years of work and achievements in a longer, but similarly organized, document called a CV (curriculum vitae).

At a glance . . .

- Gather materials that describe your career: education, work, community service, other.
- Categorize your accomplishments.
- Arrange your information purposefully.
- Produce a professional document.

UNDERSTANDING RÉSUMÉS. The point of a résumé is to provide a quick, easy-to-scan summary of your accomplishments to someone interested in your credentials. Currently, you might seek a part-time position at a local day-care center, membership in a service organization, an internship with a law firm, or a scholarship from a veteran's group. In the future, you might apply to graduate school, to a professional program (law, medicine, nursing), or for a full-time job. All of these are circumstances that call for a résumé.

A document you prepare to represent yourself to readers must be readable at a glance, meticulously accurate, and reasonably handsome. Think of it this way: A résumé is your one- or two-page chance to make a good first impression.

Résumés do vary enormously in design. You have to decide on everything from fonts and headings to alignments and quality of paper (if the document is printed). You can pay companies to craft your résumé or use widely available templates to format it and then post it online. But your word processor has all the power you need to create a competent résumé on your own. Here's some advice.

At a Walt Disney Company job fair for returning veterans, experts help vets polish their résumés.

Associated Press/Reed Saxon

Gather the necessary information. You'll have to collect this career data sooner or later. It's much simpler if you start in college and gradually build a full résumé. Don't guess or rely on memory for résumé information: Get the data right. Verify your job titles and your months or years of employment; give your major as it is identified in your college catalog; make an accurate list of your achievements and activities without embellishing them. Don't turn an afternoon at a sandlot into "coaching high school baseball." Focus on attainments during your college years and beyond. Grade school and high school achievements don't mean much, unless you're LeBron James.

Decide on appropriate categories. Contrary to what you may think, there's no standard form for résumés, but they do usually contain some mix of the following information:

- Basic contact data in the heading: your name, address, phone number, and e-mail address
- Educational attainments (usually college and above, once you have a BA, BS, or other postsecondary credential): degrees earned, where, and when
- Work experience: job titles, companies, and dates of employment, with a brief list of skills you used in specific jobs (such as customer service, sales, software programs, language proficiencies, and so on)
- Other accomplishments: significant internships, extracurricular activities, community service, volunteer work, honors, awards, and so on. These may be broken into subcategories

Depending on the situation, you might also include the following elements:

- A brief statement of career goals
- A list of people willing to serve as references (with their contact information)

Leave off any subjective self-descriptions or evaluative phrases, even if they are true: *great organizer, go-to manager, people person, self-starter*. Let the facts speak for themselves.

You can add categories to a résumé as your career evolves, whenever they might improve your chances for a position. For instance, your résumé may eventually include items such as administrative appointments, committee service, patents, publications, lectures, participation in business organizations, community service, honors and awards, and so on. But keep the document compact. Ordinarily, a first résumé shouldn't exceed one page—though it may have to run longer if you are expected to provide references.

Arrange the information within categories strategically. Given how easy it is now to create different versions of a résumé, you may want to tailor those you distribute for different purposes. Applying for a scholarship, you might give priority to academic accomplishments and school-related activities, listing such information first. A résumé to accompany a job application might emphasize your employment history. And if you're running for public office or seeking membership in a service organization, you might list more community activities and volunteer stints than you'd normally include.

Typically, items within categories are arranged in reverse chronological order: The most recent attainments come first in each of your categories. But if such a list threatens to bury your most significant items, you have several options: Cut the lesser achievements from the list, highlight notable accomplishments in some consistent way, or focus on them in the cover letter that usually accompanies a résumé. **O**

Design pages that are easy to read. Basic design principles aren't rocket science: Headings and key information should stand out and individual items should be clearly separated. The pages should look substantive but not cluttered. White space makes any document friendly, but too much in a résumé can suggest a lack of achievement. **O**

In general, treat the résumé as a conservative document. This is not the time to experiment with fonts and flash or curlicues. Don't include a photograph either, even a good one.

want to get ◄
a job?

Applying for a job
need not be as
dreary as it once
was—or as sexist.

Hulton Deutsch/Getty Images

understand professional
correspondence p. 287

think visually
p. 417

Getting the details right

With its fussy dates, headings, columns, and margins, a résumé is all about the details. Fortunately, it is brief enough to make a thorough going-over easy. Here are some important considerations.

Proofread every line in the résumé several times. Careful editing isn't a minor "detail" when it comes to résumés: It can be the whole ball game. When employers have more job candidates than they can handle, they may look for reasons to dismiss weak cases. Misspelled words, poor design of headings and text, and incomplete or confusing chronology are the kinds of mistakes that can terminate a job quest. O

Don't leave unexplained gaps in your education or work career. Readers will wonder about blanks in your history (Are you hiding something?) and so may dismiss your application in favor of candidates whose career paths raise no red flags. Simply account for any long periods (a year or so) you may have spent wandering the capitals of Europe or selling magazines. Do so either in the résumé or in the job-application/cover letter—especially if the experiences contributed to your skills.

Be consistent and efficient. Initially, readers will scan your document to see whether you have necessary qualifications. So be sure the language of your résumé is tight and parallel: Make it a point to edit for wordiness too. If a term is unnecessary, cut it. Because of space limitations, you should typically use phrases rather than complete sentences, trying to keep the language within groups consistent:

- Performed research for editors . . .
- Used tools such as LexisNexis . . .
- Assisted department heads . . .
- Organized discussion sessions . . .

Boldface major heads and set them in all caps if they are relatively short:

CAREER OBJECTIVE

EDUCATION

EXPERIENCE

ACCOMPLISHMENTS

REFERENCES

help with common errors
p. 536

Keep alignment of headings and columns beneath them uniform throughout the document. (To be certain that the careful alignments and design of your résumé are preserved when transmitted electronically, always send them as .pdf documents, not .doc.) Express all dates in the same form: For example, if you abbreviate months, do so everywhere. Use en-dashes between inclusive dates: July 2016–May 2017. (Check online for how to create en-dashes on your computer.)

Protect your personal data. You don't have to volunteer information about your race, gender, age, or sexual orientation on a job application or résumé. Neither should you provide financial data, Social Security or credit card numbers, nor other information you don't want in the public domain and that is not pertinent to your job search. However, you do need to be accurate and honest about the relevant job information: Any disparity between what you state on a résumé and your actual accomplishments may be a firing offense down the road.

Look for help. Check whether your campus career center or writing center offers assistance with résumés. Online sites, such as Monster or Ask A Manager, may also offer useful tips and tools for preparing and posting a résumé.

Examining a model

The following résumé by Taylor Rowane is arranged to emphasize journalism credentials. Rowane uses a simple design that aligns all items to the far left, allowing space for ample details about accomplishments and emphasizing a prestigious internship.

Contact information is centered at the top of the page for quick reference. If necessary, more information might be given.

Taylor Rowane

Austin, Texas

Phone: 750-555-1234; E-email: TR.xxx@xxxx.xxx; Twitter: @xxxxxxxxx

OBJECTIVE

Editing/copy editing position at a newspaper or magazine

Optional "objective" drives the selection of résumé credentials.

EXPERIENCE

Speechwriting Intern, Smithsonian Institution; Washington, DC, June 2017–August 2017

- Undertook background research for speechwriters for administrators and staff
- Performed fact-checking duties using LexisNexis
- Provided administrative support for speechwriters
- Organized lunch-and-learns between staff and interns

Copy Editing Intern, *The Wisconsin Bulletin*; Eau Claire, WI, June 2016–August 2016

- Edited stories from reporters on a diverse range of topics
- Fact-checked articles and collaborated with writers to remedy inconsistencies
- Drafted headlines and captions for stories and columns
- Proofread stories for grammar, spelling, and style
- Tagged articles with key terms for indexing and research

Senior Reporter, *The Daily Texan*; Austin, Texas, January 2016–May 2017

- Wrote up to five articles per week on subjects relating to higher education
- Routinely covered short-notice assignments and breaking news
- Pitched stories to editorial staff
- Awarded a key academic honor while working as senior reporter

Writing Consultant, University Writing Center; Austin, Texas, January 2015–May 2016

- Assisted undergraduates from all departments with writing projects on various topics
- Supported students' research, drafting, and revision processes
- Completed over one hundred student consultations

EDUCATION AND SKILLS

- The University of Texas at Austin, Honors Program/English, December 2018
- 3.97 GPA
- Proficient in LexisNexis, ProQuest, and InCopy

ACTIVITIES

- Texas Unions Board of Directors, September 2015–May 2106
- Big Brother Big Sisters of Central Texas, September 2015–December 2017

REFERENCES

- Available on request

Experiences are roughly sequential, but a top credential gets priority.

Ample, but not excessive whitespace, enhances readability.

How to start ● **Feeling lost?** Decide on a focus.
See page 306.

23

explain a person's experiences and goals

Personal Statements

Preparing a short personal statement has become almost a ritual among people applying for admission to college, professional school, or graduate school, or for jobs, promotions, scholarships, internships, or even elective office.

At a glance . . .

● Learn all you can about the people or institution asking for your personal statement.

● Review your credentials and make a statement about them.

● Write for your specific audience.

● Revise and edit your document carefully.

UNDERSTANDING PERSONAL STATEMENTS. Institutions that ask for personal statements are rarely interested in who you are. Rather, they want to see whether you can *represent* yourself as a person with whom they might want to be affiliated. That may seem harsh, but consider the personal statements you have already written. At best, they are a slice of your life—the verbal equivalent of you all dressed up for the prom.

If you want a sense of what a school, business, or other institution expects in the essays it requests from applicants, review whatever passes for that group's core values or mission statement, often available online. If the words sound a bit solemn, inflated, and unrealistic, you've got your answer—except that you shouldn't actually sound as pretentious as an institution. A little blood has to flow through the veins of your essay, just not so much that someone in an office gets nervous about you.

Hitting the right balance between displaying overwhelming competence and admitting human foibles in a personal statement is tough. Here's some advice for composing a successful essay.

Be realistic about your audience.

Your personal statements will be read by strangers. That's scary, but you can usually count on them to be reasonable people willing to give you a fair hearing. They will measure you against other applicants—not unreachable standards of perfection. How might you overcome any initial anxiety? Experienced writing tutor Jacob Pietsch suggests that you address the statement to real people in your life who don't know you very well: "Visualize them, and get ready to write them a letter."

Read the essay prompt carefully.

Essay topics for personal statements are often deliberately open-ended to give you some freedom in pursuing a topic. But be sure to address issues actually raised by the prompt—not ones you'd prefer to deal with. Do look for opportunities to focus on specific strengths of your work or education, especially when a question is more generic.

Review your credentials.

Don't repeat in your personal statement what's already on record in an application letter or résumé. Instead, look for items that will bring your résumé lines to life. For example, if a prompt encourages personal reminiscences (for example, *the person who influenced you the most*), think about how to connect that story (subtly) to your own credentials.

Decide on a focus or theme. Personal statements are short, so make the best use of a reader's time. Don't ramble about summer jobs or vague educational ideals. Instead, find a theme that illustrates your strengths. If you're driven by a passion for research, arrange the elements of your life to illustrate this. If your strongest work is extracurricular, show how your specific commitments to people and organizations make you a well-rounded applicant. In other words, turn your life into a thesis statement and make a clear point about yourself. ○

Above all be honest and forthright. Here's good advice from a woman who worked with high school students who were composing college admission statements:

> In my years handling applications to elite schools, from Harvard to Haverford, Davidson to Dickinson, and everything in between, I was often surprised by where students did gain acceptance. But in every case it was a student who wrote a fabulously independent essay. Not necessarily hyper-sophisticated. But true.
>
> My students always asked me, What should I write about?
>
> I'd answer: You are a student of the world. What is it that moves you? What incites you, enrages you? The first-person pronoun is a mighty tool. Use it.
>
> I have had successful students write about the virtues of napping (Middlebury), failing a course (Harvard), and having to shoot a farm dog because it couldn't work stock (Princeton). Once a student came out to me in his fifth (and best) draft. His parents probably still don't know, but they got the Ivy Leaguer they wanted (Penn).
>
> —Lacy Crawford, "Writing the Right College-Entrance Essay"

When you apply for professional programs, scholarships, and internships, your audiences will be different, but the basic principles outlined here still hold.

Organize the piece strategically. Many personal statements take a narrative form, though they may also borrow elements of reports and even proposals. Malia Hamilton, a writing center consultant, offers a structure to consider: "Whenever I read a personal statement, I look to see if the writer has told me three things: (1) who they were, (2) who they are, and (3) who they want to be. If the writer has effectively incorporated these three stages of themselves into their personal statement, it's almost always an effective one." Whatever structures you adopt for your essay, pay attention to transitions: You cannot risk readers getting confused or lost. ○

develop a statement
p. 333   connect ideas p. 391

Getting the details right

As with résumés, there's no room for errors or slips in personal statements. O They are a test of your writing skills, plain and simple, so you need to get the spelling, mechanics, and usage correct. In addition, consider the following advice.

Try a high or middle style. You don't want to be breezy or casual in an essay for law school or medical school, but a *personal* statement does invite a human voice. So a style that marries the correctness and formal vocabulary of a high style with the occasional untailored feel of the middle style might be perfect for many personal statements. O

Don't get artsy. A striking image or two may work well in the statement, as may the occasional metaphor or simile. But don't build your essay around a fussy theme, an extended analogy, or a pop-culture allusion that a reader might dismiss as hokey or simply not get. If a phrase or feature stands out too noticeably, change it, even though you may like it.

Use common sense. You probably already have the good grace not to offend gender, racial, religious, and ethnic groups in your personal statement. You should also take the time to read your essay from the point of view of people from less protected groups who may take umbrage at your dismissal of *old folks*, *fundamentalists*, or even *Republicans*. You don't know who may be reading your essay.

Compose the statement yourself. It's the ethical thing to do. If you don't and you're caught, you're toast. You might ask someone to review your essay or take a draft to a writing center for a consultation. O Any help you receive from a parent or English-major roommate should not purge your voice from the essay. Remember, too, that when you arrive at a job or internship, you'll be expected to write at the level you display in the statement that got you there.

> **Thinking about Writing**   Amused by the thought of your life as a thesis
> statement? Give it a try. Compose *three* thesis sentences that might be
> plausibly used to organize three different personal statements, emphasizing
> varying aspects of your life and career. Which statement do you think describes
> you best? Would it always be the best thesis for a personal statement? Why or
> why not?

---

define your style p. 368   help with common errors   peer review p. 357
                            p. 536

Examining a model

The Academic Service Partnership Foundation asked candidates for an internship to prepare an essay addressing a series of questions. The prompt and one response to it follow.

ASPF NATIONAL INTERNSHIP PROGRAM

Please submit a 250- to 500-word typed essay answering the following three questions:

1. Why do you want an internship with the ASPF?
2. What do you hope to accomplish in your academic and professional career goals?
3. What are your strengths and skills, and how would you use these in your internship?

> Specific questions limit reply, but also help organize it.

Michael Villaverde

April 14, 20--

> Opening sentence states the writer's thesis or intent; first two paragraphs address the first question.

The opportunity to work within a health-related government agency alongside top-notch professionals initially attracted me to the Academic Service Partnership Foundation (ASPF) National Internship Program. Participating in the ASPF's internship program would enable me to augment the health-services research skills I've gained working at the VERDICT Research Center in San Antonio and the M. D. Anderson Cancer Center in Houston. This internship could also help me gain experience in health policy and administration.

I support the ASPF's mission to foster closer relations between formal education and public service and believe that

> Essay uses first person (*I, me*) but is fairly formal in tone and vocabulary, between high and middle style.

The author sounds a personal note in expressing enthusiasm for the internship opportunity.

I could contribute to this mission. If selected as an ASPF intern, I will become an active alumnus of the program. I would love to do my part by advising younger students and recruiting future ASPF interns. Most important, I make it a point to improve the operations of programs from which I benefit. Any opportunities provided to me by the ASPF will be repaid in kind.

This statement transitions smoothly into the second issue raised in prompt.

Other strengths I bring to the ASPF's National Internship Program are my broad educational background and dedication. My undergraduate studies will culminate in two honors degrees (finance and liberal arts) with additional premed course work. Afterward, I wish to enroll in a combined MD/PhD program in health-services research. Following my formal education, I will devote my career to seeing patients in a primary-care setting, researching health-care issues as a university faculty member, teaching bioethics, and developing public policy at a health-related government agency.

Formidable and specific goals speak for themselves in straight-forward language.

Another transition introduces the third issue raised by the prompt.

The course work at my undergraduate institution has provided me with basic laboratory and computer experience, but my strengths lie in oral and written communication. Comparing digital and film-screen mammography equipment for a project at M. D. Anderson honed my technical-writing skills and comprehension of statistical analysis. The qualitative analysis methods I learned at VERDICT while evaluating strategies used by the Veterans Health Administration in implementing clinical practice guidelines will be a significant

Qualifications listed are numerous and detailed.

△

Special interest/ concern is noted and is likely to impress reviewers of statement.

resource to any prospective employer. By the end of this semester, I will also possess basic knowledge of Statistical Package for the Social Sciences (SPSS) software.

During my internship I would like to research one of the following topics: health-care finance, health policy, or ethnic disparities in access to high-quality health care. I have read much about the Patient Protection and Affordable Care Act of 2010 and anticipate studying its implications. I would learn a great deal from working with officials responsible for the operation and strategic planning of a program like Medicare (or a nonprofit hospital system). The greater the prospects for multiple responsibilities, the more excited I will be to show up at work each day.

Final sentence affirms enthusiasm for technical internship.

How to start ▶ ● **First time assembling a portfolio?** Think about what you should include. See page 312.

Writing Portfolios

24

gather
samples of
your work

Professionals in creative fields—art, architecture, photography, modeling—have long used portfolios to inventory their achievements or document their skills to potential clients or employers. The practice has spread to other fields because these careful collections of work provide an in-depth look at what people have actually accomplished over time. Not surprisingly, many schools now encourage (or require) students to assemble writing portfolios of various sorts to display what they have learned and to assist them in the job market. It is an important and sometimes complicated endeavor.

At a glance . . .

- Define the scope of your portfolio
- Assess the audience for the work you collect
- Collect the materials
- Reflect on your materials and progress

▶ first time
assembling
a portfolio?

UNDERSTANDING WRITING PORTFOLIOS. As assignments, portfolios vary enormously in what they aim to do and how they achieve their goals. They typically serve as learning tools for specific writing or humanities courses, supporting students as they develop composing skills; not incidentally, they also provide material for helpful assessments of written work. Such portfolios, which are now usually compiled online, typically include some of the following elements:

- Literacy narratives or statements of goals
- Brainstorming/prewriting activities for individual assignments
- Research logs and maps or annotated bibliographies
- Topic proposals and comments
- First drafts and revisions, with the writer's reflections
- Peer and instructor comments
- Final drafts, with the writer's reflections
- Writer's midcourse and/or final assessments of learning goals
- Additional documents or media materials selected by the writer
- A holistic assessment of the portfolio by the teacher (rather than grading of individual items)

Instructors and classmates may play a role at every stage of the composing process, especially when the portfolio is developed online.

In other situations, materials collected in a portfolio furnish evidence that a student has mastered specific proficiencies required for a job or professional advancement. Such career portfolios (for example, for prospective teachers) may stretch across a sequence of classes, whole degree programs, or college careers. Owners of the portfolio usually have some responsibility for shaping their collection, but certain elements may be recommended or mandated, such as the following:

- A personal statement or profile describing accomplishments and learning trajectory as well as career goals
- Work that illustrates mastery of a specific subject matter
- Evidence of proficiency in technical or research skills
- Written reflections on specific issues in a field, such as teaching philosophy, diversity, or professional ethics
- Various defined assessments, evaluations, and outsider comments
- Documents that illustrate skills in writing, media, technology, or other areas

This list is partial. College programs that require career or degree portfolios typically offer detailed specifications, criteria of evaluation, templates, and lots of support.

Take charge of the portfolio assignment. Many students are intimidated by the prospect of assembling a writing portfolio. But you won't have a problem if, right from the start, you study the instructions for the assignment, figure out your responsibilities, ask important questions, and get hands-on experience with the required technology. Since most writing portfolios now come together online, sit down with the platform and learn how it works. In many cases, you'll be expected not only to post your own work and reflections but also to respond regularly to your classmates' materials.

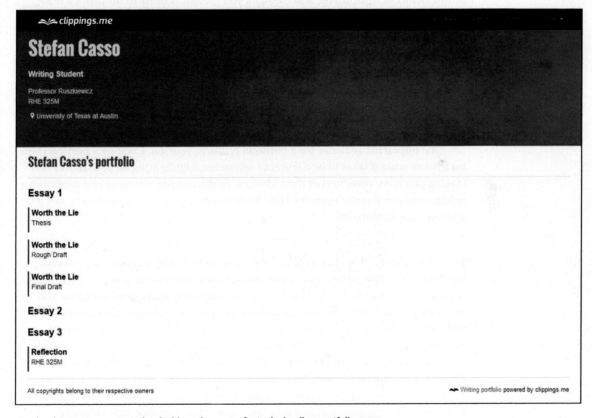

Here's where you can start: the dashboard screen of a typical online portfolio program.

If you are submitting a portfolio in paper form, study the specifications carefully. Then, right from the start, settle on a template for all your submissions: consistent margins, fonts, headings, headers, pagination, captions, and so on. (You might simply adhere to MLA or APA guidelines.) Your work will be more impressive if you give careful attention to design.

Appreciate the audiences for a portfolio.
Portfolios are usually requested by instructors or institutions, and the work you present is likely to influence a grade, certification, or even a job opportunity. Fortunately, such readers will typically offer clear-cut rubrics for measuring your performance. Study those standards carefully to find out what exactly a teacher or program expects in a portfolio.

You'll often prepare a portfolio in the company of classmates and you should be grateful when that is the case. Since they are in the same boat, they can keep you grounded and you can usually count on them for timely feedback and even encouragement. Respond in kind. In the long run, you may learn as much from these rough-and-tumble peer interactions as from your instructor.

One important audience for a portfolio remains: yourself. Creating a portfolio will underscore what it takes to be a writer or researcher, highlighting all your moves and making you more conscious of these choices. By discovering strengths and confronting weaknesses, you'll really learn the craft. So treat a portfolio as an opportunity, not just another long assignment.

Present authentic materials.
A writing portfolio demonstrates a process of learning, not a glide path to perfection. So be honest about what you post there, from topic proposals that feel reckless to first drafts that flop grandly. Your instructor will probably be more interested in your development as a writer than in any particular texts you produce: It's your overall performance that will be assessed, not a single, isolated assignment. Think of your portfolio as a video, not a snapshot.

When you are allowed to choose what to include, look for materials that tell an important or illustrative story, from topic proposal and first draft through the final version. Remember, too, that you can control this narrative (somewhat) through your reflections on these pieces. Here's how one student takes up that self-evaluative challenge in the first paragraph of an end-of-term assessment:

> Honestly, on the first day of English 109, I was not a happy student; I had failed the University of Waterloo English Proficiency Exam. Although I told everyone it was not a big deal after it happened, deep down I was bitter. So, signing up for this class to avoid retaking the proficiency exam, I decided to use the course to prove I was not illiterate. The Writing Clinic was wrong to think I was incompetent—a fifty-minute test would not define my writing abilities.

Take reflections seriously. Several times during a semester or at various stages in the writing process, an instructor may ask you to comment on your own work. Here, for example, is a brief reflective paragraph that accompanied the first draft of Susan Wilcox's "Marathons for Women," a report that appears in Chapter 8 (see p. 53):

> I focused my paper on the evolution of women in marathoning and the struggle for sporting equality with men. I had problems in deciding which incidents to include and which to ignore. Additionally, I'm expecting to hear back from some marathoners so I can possibly include their experiences in my paper; however, none of them have gotten back to me yet. When they do return the interview questions, I'll have to decide what, if anything, to remove from the paper to make room for personal anecdotes. Finally, I need some work on my introduction and conclusion. What do the current versions lack?

Like Susan, you might use the reflection to ask classmates for specific advice or for editing suggestions.

Most reflections for a portfolio will be lengthier and more evaluative. An instructor might ask for an explanatory comment after the final version of a paper is submitted. You can talk about items such as the following:

- Your goals in writing a paper and how well you have met them
- How you have defined your audience/readers and how you've adjusted your paper for them
- The strategies behind your organization or style
- How you addressed problems pointed out by your instructor or peer editors
- What you believe succeeds and what you'd like to handle better
- What specifically you learned from composing the paper

Don't try to answer all these questions. Focus your reflection on a point or two. But all comments should be candid: An instructor will want to know both what you have learned and what you intend to work on more in subsequent assignments.

If asked to compose a midcourse evaluation or a final reflection, broaden your scope and think about the trajectory of your learning across a series of activities and assignments. Again, your instructor may specify what form this comprehensive reflection should take. Some instructors will ask focused questions, others may tie your responses to a particular learning rubric, and still others may even encourage you to write a letter. Here are some questions to think about on your own:

- What were your original goals for the writing course, and how well have you met them?
- What types of audiences do you expect to address in the future, and how prepared are you now to deal with them?

- What strategies of organization and style have you mastered?
- What did you gain from the responses and advice of classmates?
- What exactly did you learn during the term?
- What goals do you have for the writing you expect to do in the future?

If space permits, illustrate your points with examples from your papers or from comments you have received from classmates. For a sample mid-semester course reflection, see "Examining a model" on page 318.

Getting the details right

Some parts of a writing portfolio may be more heavily edited than others: Midterm reflections might go through several drafts while topic proposals are often tentative and open-ended. And a writing portfolio might contain peer editing and other fairly off-the-cuff items. Yet the overall project should look competent, feel conscientious, and show attention to design.

With a career portfolio, plan on submitting nothing less than your best work—from cover to cover.

Polish your portfolio. If you complain that pop quizzes or one-shot final exams don't reflect your true abilities, what excuse can you offer when you turn in a bungled course portfolio? This is not an assignment to do at the last minute. So keep up with all prompts and activities—and that includes giving timely feedback to the work of your classmates. Online portfolio platforms may help keep you on track, but you'll still need to meet due dates and submit required documents.

Understand the portfolio activities. You may be unfamiliar with some of the specific features of a writing portfolio. If you've never done a literacy narrative or a topic proposal, ask your instructor for models (or see p. 8 and p. 432). If your instructor suggests brainstorming activities, look to Chapter 3. Other questions? Ask your instructor *and* talk with classmates.

Give honest feedback to classmates. Most students seriously underestimate the value of the comments they make on their classmates' work. Simply because you are an experienced reader, you will recognize when ideas are unclear, arguments are hard to follow, evidence seems unconvincing, sentences are confusing, and so on. You don't have to fix the problems you point to; writers just need to know where they are and how you are reacting to them. Be as clear as you can and focus on big issues: content, organization, audience, style. It's fine to point out problems in grammar and mechanics, but they shouldn't be your first priority when you are a peer editor. And don't forget to mention what in a paper strikes you as distinctive and successful. Writers need to know that as well. You'll be surprised how much you'll gain from peer editing. For more information, see Chapter 31.

Thinking about Writing Search for the term "portfolio" on the Web sites for several postsecondary schools in your area—community colleges, colleges and universities, technical schools. (You might exclude references to business and investment portfolios.) What kinds of portfolio programs or activities do you find described there? What do they have in common and how do they differ?

Examining a model

In the following brief midterm reflection, student Desiree Lopez describes her work in an internship class designed to train tutors for a campus writing center.

Describes initial course expectations.

When I first began the internship course, I was apprehensive and anxious about what was to come. To be honest, I had never been to the writing center and so I had little knowledge about the work the Undergraduate Writing Center (UWC) tutors did. My expectation was that writing tutors were people who helped polish student papers. I thought of the writing center as not so much a one-stop fix-it shop, but rather a center that anticipated what university professors were looking for in their students' papers and knew how to guide those students in the right direction.

Offers a revised point of view.

However, now that the semester is halfway completed and I have had the opportunity to observe tutors in action, my perception of the work done by campus writing centers has completely changed. I now see that, rather than polishing papers that are rough around the edges, the UWC helps students realize their potential while giving them the skills to polish their own papers.

Lists specific techniques and skills already learned.

I have learned how to help students identify what they are trying to do and organize their writing in ways appropriate to an assignment by asking simple questions such as "What are you trying to say here?" and "What do you want your readers to take from this?" I am happy to say that these tools have helped me hone my own skills as well. I have learned to ask myself those same questions while writing, and I now have a class of more than twenty peers to help me improve when I can't seem to figure out on my own what needs tweaking. Lastly, I have learned (mainly from the grammar quizzes) that my first instincts are generally right; if the sentence sounds correct, it probably is correct and I am just overthinking.

I know I still have more to learn about the writer–tutor relationship that can only be acquired through practice and hands-on experience. I am confident that I now have some of the tools I need and I know that, given the opportunity, I can tailor consultations to individual students and help them perceive their strengths and weaknesses. However, I am still nervous about the idea of conducting a consultation on my own. I worry that I have not yet perfected the art of nondirective/non-evaluative tutoring and that I will slip up—telling students I believe that their papers are interesting or really good or better than something I might have written on the subject. But I'll resist that temptation and simply ask them, "What do *you* think you've done well?"

Explains concerns that still remain.

Map your own writing process.

Where are you in your process?	Look for more help here.

Creating a Structure →

Choosing a Style and Design →

**Need more help?
Try these Visual Tutorials.**

reference

A Writer's Routines

4

part four

Need help organizing or drafting? See p. 345.

Smart Reading

There's probably no better strategy for generating ideas than reading. Reading can deepen your impression of any topic you explore, provide background information, sharpen your insights, and introduce you to alternative views. Reading also leads you to experts who know more about a subject than you do.

Unfortunately, in the abstract, critical reading can feel more like a virtue than a tool—a practice to be admired more than used. Do you have time for it, really, when you face a project due next week? In fact, critical reading, like critical thinking (see chapter 26), is hard to avoid when you intend to do respectable academic work. Here's some practical advice to hone your skills.

Recall the basics. You've certainly been schooled in basic techniques of academic reading: *Survey the table of contents* of books, *preread to get a sense of the whole, look up names and terms you don't recognize, highlight and annotate important material, summarize what you've read in notes*, and so on. Such techniques really do help, especially when you encounter challenging scholarly or professional material.

Read to deepen what you already know. Whatever your academic project might involve, you're not alone—as quick Web searches reveal these days. Others have explored similar paths and have written about them already. Reading their work should give you confidence to bring your own thoughts to public attention. Build upon their insights.

For example, if you have worked at a fast-food franchise and want to report about what goes on there, you will find a book like Eric Schlosser's classic *Fast Food Nation: The Dark Side of the All-American*

Meal engrossing. Moreover, your own experience makes you an informed critic. You can agree and disagree intelligently with Schlosser and, perhaps, figure out how to extend his arguments in your own writing. At a minimum, you'll walk away from the book knowing the titles of dozens of additional sources, should you want to learn even more.

Read above your level of knowledge. It's easy to connect with people online who share your interests, but they often don't know much more about a topic than you do. To find fresh ideas, push your reading to more demanding levels. Spend time with experts whose books and articles you can't blow right through. You'll know you're there when you find yourself looking up names, adding items to your vocabulary, and feeling humbled by what you still need to learn. That's when invention occurs and ideas germinate.

Read what makes you uncomfortable. Most of us today have access to devices that connect us to endless sources of information. But all those voices also mean that we can choose to read (or watch) only materials that confirm our existing beliefs and prejudices—as many people do. Such narrowness will be exposed, however, whenever you write on a controversial subject and find readers arguing back with facts you never considered before. Surprise! The world is more complicated than you thought. The solution is simple: Get out of the echo chamber and read more broadly, engaging with those who see the world differently.

Read against the grain. Skeptics and naysayers may be no fun at parties, but their habits are worth emulating whenever you're a reading. It makes sense to read with an open mind, giving reputable writers and their ideas a fair hearing. But you also want to raise questions about the assumptions writers make, the logic they use, the evidence they present, and the authorities and sources upon which they build their arguments—even when you agree with them.

Reading against the grain does not mean finding fault with everything, but rather letting nothing slip by without scrutiny. Treat the world around you as a text to be read and analyzed. ○ Ask questions. Why do so few men today take liberal-arts courses? What topics does your campus paper avoid and why? Can online friendships be real? Be the person who asks peculiar questions.

Read slowly. Browsing online has made many of us superficial readers. For serious texts, forget speed-reading and your own Web habits. Settle in for the duration. Find the thesis; look up unfamiliar words and names; don't jump to another article until you've finished the one in hand.

■ ■ ▬▬▬▬▬▬
If you don't have the time to read, you don't have the time or tools to write.
■ ■

—Stephen King

Moviestore collection
Ltd/Alamy Stock Photo

think critically p. 327

Annotate what you read. Find some way to record your reactions to whatever you read. If you own the text and don't mind marking it, use highlighting pens to flag key ideas. Then converse with them and leave a record. Electronic media and e-readers offer a range of built-in commenting tools. Even Post-it notes work in some circumstances. For much more on annotating texts, see Chapter 48, "Annotating Sources."

Thinking about Writing   Working with a small group, make a list of the newspapers, Web sites, magazines, TV shows or networks, or other resources that you use to gather news and information about politics, society, and culture. Then try to locate these media resources along a ribbon that moves from the political far left to the political far right. Be prepared for considerable disagreement. When you are done, compare your placements with those of other groups working on the same project. What may account for your differences?

Far left _____ Left _____ Center _____ Right _____ Far right _____

Critical Thinking 26

We all get edgy when our written work is criticized (or even edited) because the ideas we put on a page emerge from our own thinking—writing is *us*. Granted, our words rarely express *exactly* who we are or what we've been imagining, but such distinctions get lost when someone points to our work and says, "That's stupid" or "What crap!" The criticism cuts deep; it feels personal.

Fortunately, there's a way to avoid embarrassing gaffes in your work: *critical thinking*, a term that describes mental habits that reinforce logical reasoning and analysis. There are lots of ways to develop good habits of thought, from following the strategies of smart reading described in Chapter 25 to using the rhetorical tactics presented throughout the "Guide" section of this book.

Here we focus on specific dimensions of critical thinking that you will find useful in college writing.

Think in terms of claims and reasons. Whenever you read reports, arguments, or analyses, chances are you begin by identifying the claims writers make and assessing the evidence that supports them. Logically, then, when you write in these genres, you should expect the same scrutiny.

Claims are the passages in a text where you make an assertion, offer an argument, or present a hypothesis for which you intend to provide evidence.

Using a cell phone while driving is dangerous.

Playing video games can improve intelligence.

Worrying about childhood obesity is futile.

Claims may occur almost anywhere in a paper: in a thesis statement, in the topic sentences of paragraphs, in transitional passages, or in summaries or conclusions. (An exception may be formal scientific writing, in which the hypothesis, results, and discussion will occur in specific sections of an article.)

Make sure that all your major claims in a paper are accompanied by plausible supporting *reasons* either in the same sentence or in adjoining material. Such reasons are usually introduced by expressions as straightforward as *because*, *if*, *to*, and *so*. Once you attach reasons to a claim, you have made a deeper commitment to it. You must then do the hard work of providing readers with convincing evidence, logic, or conditions for accepting your claim. Seeing your ideas fully stated on paper early in a project may even persuade you to abandon an implausible claim—one you cannot or do not want to defend.

> Using a cell phone while driving is dangerous *since* distractions are a proven cause of auto accidents.
>
> Playing video games can improve intelligence *if* they teach young gamers to make logical decisions quickly.
>
> ~~Worrying about childhood obesity is futile because there's nothing we can do about it.~~

Think in terms of premises and assumptions. Probe beneath the surface of key claims and reasons that writers offer, and you will discover their core principles, usually only implied but sometimes stated directly: These are called *premises* or *assumptions*. In oral arguments, when people say *I get where you're coming from*, they signal that they understand your assumptions. You want to achieve similar clarity, especially whenever the claims you make in a report or argument are likely to be controversial or argumentative. Your premises can be general or specific, conventional or highly controversial, as in the following examples.

> Improving human safety and well-being is a desirable goal. [general]
>
> We should discourage behaviors that contribute to traffic accidents. [specific]
>
> Improving intelligence is desirable. [conventional]
>
> Play should train children to defy authority. [controversial]

When writing for readers who mostly share your values, you usually don't have to explain where you're coming from. But be prepared to explain your values to more general or hostile readers: *This is what I believe and why*. Naturally—and here's where the critical thinking comes in—you yourself need to understand the assumptions upon which your claims rest. Are they logical? Are they consistent? Are you prepared to stand by them? Or is it time to rethink some of your core beliefs?

Think in terms of evidence. A claim without evidence attached is just that—a barefaced assertion no better than a child's "Oh, yeah?" So you should choose supporting material carefully, always weighing whether it is sufficient, complete, reliable, and unbiased. **O** Has an author you want to cite done solid research? Or does the evidence provided seem flimsy or anecdotal? Can you offer enough evidence yourself to make a convincing case—or are you cherry-picking only those facts that support your point of view? Do you even have the expertise to evaluate the evidence you present? These are questions to ask routinely and persistently.

Anticipate objections. Critical thinkers understand that serious issues have many dimensions—and rarely just two sides. That's because they have done their homework, which means trying to understand even those positions with which they strongly disagree. When you start writing with this kind of inclusive perspective, you'll hear voices of the loyal opposition in your head, and you'll be able to address objections even before potential readers make them. At a minimum, you will enhance your credibility. But more important, you'll have done the kind of thinking that makes you smarter.

Avoid logical fallacies. Honest, fair-minded writers have nothing to hide. They name names, identify sources, and generate appropriate emotions. They acknowledge weaknesses in their arguments and concede graciously when the opposition scores a point. These are qualities you want to display in your serious academic and professional work.

One way to enhance your reputation as a writer and critical thinker is to avoid logical fallacies. *Fallacies* are rhetorical moves that corrupt solid reasoning—the verbal equivalent of sleight of hand. The following classic, but all too common, fallacies can undermine the integrity of your writing.

- **Appeals to false authority.** Be sure that any experts or authorities you cite on a topic have real credentials in the field and that their claims can be verified. Be willing to do a careful Web search to find out—and understand how difficult that can be in an era of "fake news." Similarly, don't claim or imply knowledge, authority, or credentials yourself that you don't have. Be frank about your level of expertise. Framing yourself as an honest, if amateur, broker on a subject can even raise your credibility.

- *Ad hominem* **attacks.** In arguments of all kinds, you may be tempted to bolster your position by attacking the personal integrity of your opponents when character really isn't an issue. It's easy to resort to name-calling (*socialist, racist, traitor, sexist*) or character assassination, but it usually signals that your own case is weak.

- **Dogmatism.** Writers fall back on dogmatism whenever they want to give the impression, usually false, that they control the party line on an issue and have all the right answers. You are probably indulging in dogmatism when you begin a paragraph *No serious person would disagree* or *How can anyone argue . . .*

- **Either/or choices.** A shortcut to winning arguments, which even Socrates abused, is to reduce complex situations to simplistic choices: good/bad, right/wrong, liberty/tyranny, smart/dumb, and so on. If you find yourself inclined to use some version of the *either/or* strategy, think again. Capable readers see right through this tactic and demolish it simply by pointing to alternatives that haven't been considered.

- **Scare tactics.** Avoid them. Arguments that make their appeals by preying on the fears of audiences are automatically suspect. Targets may be as vague as "unfore-seen consequences" or as specific as particular organizations or groups of people who supposedly pose threats. Whenever such fears may be legitimate, make sure to provide evidence for the danger and don't overstate it.

- **Sentimental or emotional appeals.** Maybe it's fine for the Humane Society to decorate its pleas for cash with pictures of sad puppies, but you can see how the tactic might be abused. In your own work, be wary of using language that pushes buttons the same way, *oohing* and *aahing* readers out of their best judgment.

- **Hasty or sweeping generalizations.** Drawing conclusions from too little evi-dence or too few examples is a *hasty generalization* (*Climate change must be a fraud because we sure froze last winter*); making a claim apply too broadly is a *sweeping generalization* (*All Texans love pickups*). Competent writers avoid the temptation to draw conclusions that fit their preconceived notions—or pander to the prejudices of an intended audience. But the temptation is powerful, so you might find exam-ples, even in college reading assignments.

- **Faulty causality.** Just because two events or phenomena occur close together in time doesn't mean that one caused the other. (The Astros didn't start winning *because* you put on the lucky boxers.) People are fond of leaping to such easy conclusions, and many pundits and politicians routinely exploit this weakness, particularly in situations involving economics, science, health, crime, and culture. Causal relationships are almost always complicated, and you will get credit for dealing with them honestly. **O**

- **Evasions, misstatements, and equivocations.** Evasions are utteranc-es that avoid the truth, misstatements are untruths excused as mistakes, and

understand causal
analyses p. 65

equivocations are lies made to seem like truths. Skilled readers know when a writer is using these slippery devices, so avoid them.

- **Straw men.** *Straw men* are easy or habitual targets that writers aim at to win an argument. Often the issue in such an attack has long been defused or discredited: for example, middle-class families abusing food stamps, immigrants taking jobs from hardworking citizens, the rich not paying a fair share of taxes. When you resort to straw-man arguments, you signal to your readers that you may not have much else in your arsenal.

- **Slippery-slope arguments.** Take one wrong step off the righteous path and you'll slide all the way down the hill: That's the warning that slippery-slope arguments make. They aren't always inaccurate, but they are easy to overstate. Will using plastic bags really doom the planet? Will permitting assisted suicide lead the sick and aged to think they have an obligation to die? Does the debut of autonomous cars portend the end of driving? Maybe or maybe not. If you create a causal chain, be sure that you offer adequate support for every step and don't push beyond what's plausible.

- **Bandwagon appeals.** You haven't made an argument when you tell people it's time to stop debating a issue and get with popular opinion. Too many bad decisions and policies get enacted that way. If you order readers to jump aboard a bandwagon, expect them to resist.

- **Faulty analogies.** Similes and analogies are worth applauding when they illuminate ideas or make them comprehensible or memorable. But analyze the implications of any analogies you use. Calling a military action either "another Vietnam" or a "crusade" might raise serious issues, as does routinely comparing one's opponents to Nazis. Readers have a right to be skeptical of writers who rely on such ploys.

Ariel Molvig/The New Yorker Collection/The Cartoon Bank

> **Thinking about Writing**   Working in a group, find an example of a short argument that impresses most of you. (Your instructor might suggest a particular article.) Carefully locate the claims within the piece that all of you regard as its most important, impressive, or controversial statements. Then see if you can formulate the premises or values upon which these claims rest. Try to state these premises as clearly as you can in a complete, declarative sentence. Are the assumptions you uncovered statements that you agree with? If the assumptions are controversial, does the piece explain or defend them? Be prepared to present your group's analysis and conclusions in class.

Shaping a Thesis

Offering a thesis is a move as necessary and, eventually, as instinctive to writers as stepping on a clutch before shifting used to be to drivers. No thesis, no forward motion.

A *thesis* is a statement in which a writer identifies or suggests the specific idea that will give focus to a paper. Typically, the thesis appears in an opening paragraph or section of an academic paper, but it may also emerge as the paper unfolds. In some cases, it may not be stated in explicit form until the very conclusion. A thesis can be complex enough to require several sentences to explain, or a single sentence might suffice. But a thesis idea will be in the writing somewhere.

How do you write and frame a thesis? Consider the following advice.

Compose a complete sentence. Simple phrases might identify topic areas, even intriguing ones, but they don't make specific claims that provoke thinking and then require support. Sentences do. ⭘ Neither of the following phrases comes close to providing direction for a paper.

> Human trafficking in the United States
>
> Reasons for global warming

Make a significant claim or assertion. *Significant* here means that the statement stimulates discussion or inquiry. You want to give an audience a reason to spend time with your writing by making a point or raising an issue worth exploring.

> Until communities recognize that human trafficking persists in parts of the United States, immigrant communities will be exploited by the practice.

> Global warming won't stop until industrial nations either lower their standards of living or admit the need for more nuclear power.

Write a declarative sentence, not a question. Questions do focus attention, but they are often too broad to give direction to a paper. A humdrum question acting as a thesis can invite superficial or even sarcastic responses. So, while you might use a question to introduce a topic (or to launch your own research), don't rely on it to carry a well-developed and complex claim in a paper. There are exceptions to this guideline: For example, provocative questions energize personal or exploratory essays—for more on the essay genre, see Chapter 15.

Expect your thesis to mature. Your initial thesis will usually expand and grow more complicated as you learn more about a subject. That's natural. But don't believe the myth that a satisfactory thesis *must* be a statement that breaks a subject into three parts. Theses that follow this pattern—common in so-called five-paragraph essays—often read like shopping lists, with only vague connections between the ideas presented. (See Chapter 6 for more about five-paragraph essays.)

ORIGINAL THESIS

Crime in the United States has declined because more people are in prison, the population is growing older, and DNA testing has made it harder to get away with murder.

When you slip into an easy pattern like this, look for connections between the points you have identified and then explore the subject. The result can sometimes be a far more compelling thesis.

REVISED THESIS

It is much more likely that crime in the United States has declined not because the population is growing older or DNA testing has made it harder to get away with murder, but because more people are in prison.

Introduce a thesis early in a project. This sound guideline applies especially to academic projects and term papers. Instructors usually want to know up front what the point of a report or argument will be. Whether phrased as a single sentence or several, a thesis typically needs one or more paragraphs of development to provide background and contexts for its claim. Here's the thesis (highlighted in yellow) of Andrew Kleinfeld and Judith Kleinfeld's essay "Go Ahead, Call Us Cowboys," following several sentences that offer the necessary lead-in.

> Everywhere, Americans are called *cowboys*. On foreign tongues, the reference to America's Western rural laborers is an insult. Cowboys, we are told, plundered the earth, arrogantly rode roughshod over neighbors, and were addicted to mindless violence. So some of us hang our heads in shame. We shouldn't. The cowboy is in fact our Homeric hero, an archetype that sticks because there's truth in it.

Or state a thesis late in a project.

You may have learned that the thesis statement is *always* the last sentence in the first paragraph. That may be so in conventional high school, five-paragraph essays, but you'll rarely be asked to follow so predictable a pattern in college or elsewhere.

In fact, it is not unusual, especially in some arguments, for a paper to build toward a thesis—and that statement may not appear until the final paragraph or sentence. **O** Such a strategy makes sense when a claim might not be convincing or rhetorically effective if stated baldly at the opening of the piece. Bret Stephens uses this strategy in an essay titled "Just Like Stalingrad" to debunk frequent comparisons between former President George W. Bush and either Hitler or Stalin. Stephens's real concern turns out to be not these exaggerated comparisons themselves but rather what happens to language when it is abused by sloppy writers. The final two paragraphs of his essay summarize this case and, arguably, lead up to a thesis in the very last sentence of the piece—more rhetorically convincing there because it comes as something of a surprise.

> Care for language is more than a concern for purity. When one describes President Bush as a fascist, what words remain for real fascists? When one describes Fallujah as Stalingrad-like, how can we express, in the words that remain to the language, what Stalingrad was like?
>
> George Orwell wrote that the English language "becomes ugly and inaccurate because our thoughts are foolish, but the slovenliness of our language makes it easier for us to have foolish thoughts." In taking care with language, we take care of ourselves.
>
> —*Wall Street Journal*, June 23, 2004

Write a thesis to fit your audience and purpose.

Almost everything you write will have a purpose and a point (see the following table), but not every piece will have a formal thesis. In professional and scientific writing, readers want to know your claim immediately. For persuasive and exploratory writing, you might prefer to keep readers intrigued or have them track the path of your thinking and delay the thesis until later.

understand argument p. 89

Type of Assignment	Thesis or Point
Reports	Thesis usually previews material or explains its purpose. (See thesis example on p. 41.)
Explanations	Thesis asserts or denies an explanatory or causal relationship based on an analysis of evidence. (See thesis example on p. 77.)
Arguments	Thesis makes an explicit and arguable claim. (See thesis example on p. 105.)
Evaluations	Thesis makes an explicit claim of value based on criteria of evaluation. (See thesis example on p. 141.)
Proposals	Thesis offers a proposal for action. (See thesis example on p. 159.)
Literary Analyses	Thesis explains the point of the analysis. (See thesis example on p. 190.)
Rhetorical Analysis	Thesis explains the point of the analysis. (See thesis example on p. 214.)
Essays	Thesis can be either stated or implied. (See thesis example on p. 237.)
Essay Examinations	Thesis previews the entire answer, like a mini-outline. (See thesis example on p. 249.)
Synthesis and Response Papers	Thesis summarizes and paraphrases different sources on a specific topic. (See thesis example on p. 265.)
Position Papers	Thesis makes specific assertion about reading or issue raised in class. (See thesis example on p. 271.)
Oral Reports	Introduction or a preview slide may describe the purpose. (See thesis example on p. 285.)
Professional Communications	In e-mail, subject line may function as a thesis or title. (See thesis example on p. 294.) In a business letter, a thesis offers the reason for writing. (See thesis example on p. 295.)
Résumés	"Career objective" may function as a thesis. (See thesis example on p. 302.)
Personal Statements	May either state an explicit thesis or lead readers to inferences about qualifications. (See thesis example on p. 308.)
Portfolios	Various items may include a thesis, especially any summary reflections on work presented or done. (See thesis example on p. 317.)

Writing about Writing   Transform two or three of the following political slogans, past and present, into full-blown thesis statements that might be suitable in an academic paper or a serious newspaper op-ed piece. Expand the slogan into a full statement with good reasons attached and update the language, as needed.

"A fair day's wage for a fair day's pay"

"Power to the people"

"Don't mess with Texas"

"Drill, baby, drill"

"Yes, we can"

"Give me liberty, or give me death"

"No taxation without representation"

"Think globally, act locally"

"Make America great again"

"Stronger together"

28

**develop
a draft**

Strategies of Development

This chapter looks at some essential patterns of writing—such as description, division, classification, definition, and comparison/contrast—that function more like strategies than actual genres. While you may sometimes write "descriptions" for their own sake or you may "compare and contrast" movies, smartphones, or college majors just for the heck of it, mostly you will use these patterns for some larger purpose: to tell a story, clarify a point, evaluate things, or move an argument forward.

Use description to set a scene. Descriptions, which use language to re-create physical scenes and impressions, can be impressive enough to stand on their own. But you'll often employ them to support other kinds of writing—perhaps you'll write a descriptive sentence to set the context for an essay or develop a cluster of paragraphs in a term paper to conjure up an historical event. Writers adapt descriptions to particular situations. Your depiction of an apparatus in a lab report might be cold and technical, while a novelist might describe a scene just as factually yet suggest a whole lot more, as in the following paragraph.

> *Malpais*, translated literally from the Spanish, means "bad country." In New Mexico, it signifies specifically those great expanses of lava flow which make black patches on the map of the state. The malpais of the Checkerboard country lies just below Mount Taylor, having been produced by the same volcanic fault that, a millennium earlier, had thrust the mountain fifteen thousand feet into the sky. Now the mountain has worn down to a less spectacular eleven thousand feet and relatively modern eruptions from cracks

at its base have sent successive floods of melted basalt flowing southward for forty miles to fill the long valley between Cebolleta Mesa and the Zuni Mountains.

—Tony Hillerman, *People of Darkness*

Passages like this always involve selection. Just as a photographer carefully frames a subject, you have to decide which elements (visual, aural, tactile, and so on) in a scene will convey a situation most accurately, efficiently, or memorably and then turn them into words. Think nouns first, and only then modifiers: Adjectives and adverbs are essential, but it's easy to ruin a description by overdressing it. Be specific, tangible, and honest. ⭘

A smart procedure is to write down everything you want to include in a descriptive passage and then cut out any words or phrases not pulling their weight. Be sure to sketch a scene that a reader can imagine easily, providing directions for the eyes and mind. The following descriptive paragraphs are from the opening of a student's account of a trip she made to South Africa: Notice how lean and specific her sentences are, full of details that tell a story all on their own.

> In Soweto, I am seventeen, curious, and in the largest shantytown in the world, so many thousands of miles away from my home. Streets are dusty, houses are made of cinderblock, and their yards are pressed-flat dirt. If there is grass, there is no way to see the trails of a snake.
>
> Doors to homes are rare and inside I can see tired grandmothers with babies on their curved backs making spicy *potjieko* over smoky, single-burner stoves. Skinny cats stretch out in the sunshine. Every few homes has a flat-screen TV, shockingly out of place, wearing a veil of dust. They were stolen.
>
> Soweto spreads over forty miles and nearly one million people call it home. It is a striking sight to see so close to the upscale suburbs of Johannesburg. There are row upon row of homemade houses, punctuated by schools and churches with fresh coats of paint from well-meaning Westerners. Lean-to shacks on the corner sell cucumbers and *naartjes*. The ground is flat for as far as I can see.

—Lily Parish, "Sala Kahle, South Africa"

Use division to divide a subject. This strategy of writing is so common you might not notice it. A division involves no more than breaking a subject into its major components or enumerating its parts. In a report for an art history class, you might present a famous cathedral by listing and then describing its chief architectural features, one by one: facade, nave, towers, windows, and so on. Or in a sports column on the Big Ten's NCAA football championship prospects, you could just run through its roster of twelve teams. That's a reasonable structure for a review, given the topic.

⭘
improve your
sentences p. 375

Division also puts ideas into coherent relationships that make them easier for readers to understand and use. The challenge comes when a subject doesn't break apart as neatly as a tangerine. Then you have to decide which parts are essential and which are subordinate. Divisions of this sort are more than mechanical exercises: They require your clear understanding of a subject. For example, in organizing a Web site for your school or student organization, you'd probably start by deciding which aspects of the institution merit top-tier placement on the home page. ○ Such a decision will then shape the entire project.

Use classification to sort objects or ideas by consistent principles.

Classification divides subjects up not by separating their parts but by clustering their elements according to meaningful or consistent principles. Just think of all the ways by which people can be classified:

Body type: endomorph, ectomorph, mesomorph

Hair color: black, brown, blond, red, gray, other

Weight: underweight, normal, overweight, obese

Sexual orientation: asexual, homosexual, heterosexual, bisexual, other

Religion: Hindu, Buddhist, Muslim, Christian, Jew, other, no religion

Ideally, a principle of classification should apply to every member of the general class studied (in this case, people), and there would be no overlap among the resulting groups. But almost all useful efforts to classify complex phenomena—whether people,

learn media
conventions p. 404

things, or ideas—have holes, gaps, overlaps, and inconsistencies. Classifying people by religious beliefs, for instance, usually means mentioning the major groups and then lumping tens of millions of other people in a convenient category called "other."

Even scientists who organize everything from natural elements to species of birds run into problems with creatures that cross boundaries (plant or animal?) or discoveries that upset familiar categories. You'll wrestle with such problems routinely these days when, for instance, you argue about social policy.

Use definition to clarify meaning. Definitions don't appear only in dictionaries. Like other strategies in this chapter, they occur in many genres. A definition might become the subject of a scientific report (*What is a planet?*), the bone of contention in a legal argument (*How does the statute define* life?), or the framework for a cultural analysis (*Can a comic book be a serious literary work?*). In all such cases, writers need to know how to construct valid definitions.

Although definitions come in various forms, the classic dictionary definition is based on principles of classification discussed in the previous section. Typically a term is defined first by placing it in a general class. Then its distinguishing features or characteristics are enumerated, separating it from other members of the larger class. You can see the principle operating in this satirical paragraph, which first places "dorks" into the general class of "somebody," that is to say, a *person*, and then claims two distinguishing characteristics.

> It's important to define what I truly mean by "dork," just so he or she doesn't get casually lumped in with "losers," "burnouts," and "lone psychopath bullies." To me, the dork is somebody **who didn't fit in at school** and who **therefore sought consolation in a particular field**—computers, *Star Trek*, theater, heavy metal, medieval war reenactments, fantasy, sports trivia, even isolation sports like cross-country and ice skating.
>
> —Ian R. Williams, "Twilight of the Dorks?" *Salon.com*, October 23, 2003

In much writing, definitions become crucial when a question is raised about whether a particular object does or does not fit into a particular group. You engage in this kind of debate when you argue about what is or isn't a sport, a hate crime, an act of terrorism, and so on. In outline form, the structure of such a discussion looks like this:

Defined group:

—General class

—Distinguishing characteristic 1

—Distinguishing characteristic 2 . . .

Controversial term

—Is/is not in the general class

—Does/does not share characteristic 1

—Does/does not share characteristic 2 . . .

Controversial term is/is not in the defined group

Use comparison and contrast to show similarity and difference. We seem to think better when we place ideas or objects side by side. So it's not surprising that comparisons and contrasts play a role in all sorts of writing, especially reports, arguments, and analyses. Paragraphs are routinely organized to show how things are alike or different.

Adam Zyglis, *The Buffalo News*
(blogs.buffalonews/adam-zyglis)

The late 1960s and early 1970s were a time of cultural conflict, a battle between what I have called the beautiful people and the dutiful people. While Manhattan glitterati thronged Leonard Bernstein's apartment to celebrate the murderous Black Panthers, ordinary people in the outer boroughs and the far-flung suburbs of New Jersey like Hamilton Township were going to work, raising their families, and teaching their children to obey lawful authority and work their way up in the world.

—Michael Barone, "The Beautiful People vs. the Dutiful People," *U.S. News & World Report*, January 16, 2006

Much larger projects can be built on similar structures of comparison and/or contrast.

To keep extended comparisons on track, the simplest structure is to evaluate one subject at a time, running through its features completely before moving on to the next.

Let's say you decided to contrast economic conditions in France and Germany. Here's how such a paper might look in a scratch outline if you focused on the countries one at a time. **O**

France and Germany: An Economic Report Card

I.   France

   A. Rate of growth

   B. Unemployment rate

   C. Productivity

II. Germany

   A. Rate of growth

   B. Unemployment rate

   C. Productivity

The disadvantage of evaluating subjects one at a time is that actual comparisons, for example, of rates of employment in the outline above, might appear pages apart. So in some cases, you might prefer a comparison/contrast structure that looks at features point by point. **O**

France and Germany: An Economic Report Card

I.   Rate of growth

   A. France

   B. Germany

II. Unemployment rate

   A. France

   B. Germany

III. Productivity

   A. France

   B. Germany

order ideas p. 345

understand
evaluations p. 120

Thinking about Writing   In a paper you have recently written (or an article you've been asked to read), point out all the examples you can find of the strategies described in this chapter: description, division, classification, definition, and comparison/contrast. Does the strategy dominate the piece—as comparison/contrast might in an essay evaluating different smartphones or describing law schools? Or is the use of the strategy incidental, for example, just a line or two of description or a quick definition offered to clarify a point?

<h1>Outlining **29**</h1>

shape your
work

To describe the structure of their projects, writers often use metaphors or other figures of speech, visualizing their work in terms of links, frames, templates, maps, or even skeletons. Such images help writers keep emerging ideas on track and moving forward. One of the most useful ways of imagining writing projects is a very traditional one: outlining. The technique works well for many writers, whether they work mainly with simple scratch outlines or move on to full outlines. If you have problems organizing projects, you may find this chapter both familiar and helpful. (See Chapter 6 for more general information on organization).

Begin with a scratch outline. Think of a scratch outline as the verbal equivalent of the clever mechanical idea hastily drawn on a cocktail napkin. Good ideas do often emerge from simple, sometimes crude, notions that suddenly make sense when seen on paper. Both the Internet and the structure of the DNA molecule can be traced to such visualizations.

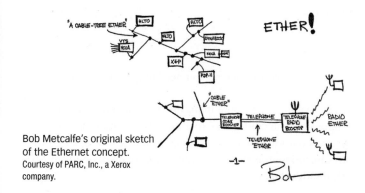

Bob Metcalfe's original sketch
of the Ethernet concept.
Courtesy of PARC, Inc., a Xerox
company.

Scratch outlines usually begin with ragged lists of ideas related to your topic idea. Simply write down your preliminary thoughts and claims so you can see exactly how they relate, merging any that obviously overlap. Keep these notes brief but specific—using words and phrases rather than complete sentences. At this stage, you might find yourself posing questions too. In fact, your initial scratch outline might resemble a mildly edited brainstorming list (see Chapter 6). Here's the first stage of a scratch outline addressing a simple topic sometimes discussed around the dinner table: new pet—cat or dog?

- Cats are independent, need little care.
- Dogs are trainable.
- Cats kill birds—and mice.
- Dog breeds are more diverse than cats.
- Dogs like their owners.
- Cats don't bark.
- Dogs protect homes and property.
- Cats can live indoors.
- Cats use litter boxes.
- Dogs do their business outside.
- Dogs are better with small children.
- Cats eat less.
- Dogs demand attention.
- Cats don't need to be walked.
- Dogs are outgoing and friendly.
- Dogs bite.
- Cats don't need yards.
- Cats don't need to be trained.
- Cats cough up hairballs.
- Dog activities keep owners healthy.

A sprawling list like this could grow even longer, so you need to get it under control.

Look for relationships. Examine the initial items on your list and try grouping *like* with *like*—or look for opposites and contrasts. Experiment with various arrangements or clusters. In the scratch outline above, for example, you might decide that the items fall into four obvious categories of relationship: advantages of dogs; disadvantages of dogs; advantages of cats; disadvantages of cats.

ADVANTAGES OF DOGS

- Dogs are trainable.
- Dog breeds are more diverse than cats.
- Dogs like their owners.
- Dogs protect homes and property.
- Dogs do their business outside.
- Dogs are outgoing and friendly.
- Dog activities keep owners healthy.

DISADVANTAGES OF DOGS

- Dogs demand attention.
- Dogs bite.

ADVANTAGES OF CATS

- Cats are independent, need little care.
- Cats don't bark.
- Cats don't need yards.
- Cats eat less.
- Cats can live indoors.
- Cats use litter boxes.
- Cats don't need to be walked.
- Cats don't need yards.
- Cats don't need to be trained.

DISADVANTAGES OF CATS

- Cats kill birds—and mice.
- Cats cough up hairballs.

You could, of course, now present an argument between cats and dogs by simply offering a report discussing the relative advantages of each pet—perhaps dismissing the disadvantages as trivial. You'd likely rank the items for each animal from least to most important and let readers decide. But considering what you have, you might also do more.

Subordinate ideas. In moving from scratch outlines to more formal ones, you'll find yourself arranging subjects into topics and subtopics. This means that some ideas belong not only grouped with others but also grouped *under* them—which is to say, they become a subset within a larger group. As you sort through your initial ideas this way, more complex relationships may emerge.

For instance, looking at the initial groupings of cat/dog advantages above, you might notice a richer idea lurking *above* the mundane notion that cats and dogs differ. These pets may, in fact, be suited for different kinds of owners or households. So you might tinker with the subpoints now to decide whether they might support more specific (and interesting) claims:

DOGS: BEST FOR ACTIVE, ENGAGED HOUSEHOLDS

- Rambunctious and like their owners.
- Protect homes and property.
- Are trainable.
- Keep owners healthy.
- Demand attention.

CATS: BEST FOR SEDATE AND ORDERLY HOUSEHOLDS

- Quiet and need little care.
- Don't need yards and can live indoors.
- Don't need to be trained.
- Don't need walks.
- Are independent.

After fleshing out the categories above, it's now easy to image a third section—possibly the opening of the paper—acknowledging the familiar downsides of each animal.

DOGS AND CATS EACH COME WITH PROBLEMS

- Dogs occasionally bite and often bark.
- Cats cough up hairballs and scratch.

Prepare a complete outline if required. At this stage, you are probably ready for a full outline: What began as a random list is emerging as an engaging, possibly amusing, report. You can now convert all your observations into complete sentences, parallel in structure, and flesh out your ideas, as needed. Here, presented in conventional, full-outline form is a possible report on the topic developed in this chapter:

Thesis: <u>Although both have problems, dogs and cats can be perfect pets for the right households.</u>

I. Dogs and cats each come with problems.

   A. Dogs occasionally bite and often bark.

   B. Cats cough up hairballs and scratch.

II. Dogs make better pets for active, engaged, family-oriented households.

   A. They are outgoing and rambunctious.

   B. They demand attention.

      1. They are trainable and protective.

      2. Their activities keep owners healthy.

III. Cats make better pets for sedate, even single-person, households.

   A. Cats need comparatively little care.

      1. They can live indoors.

      2. They don't need walks.

   B. Cats don't need to (and mostly can't) be trained.

   C. Cats are content to be solitary and independent.

Formatting a Formal Outline

Carefully align the headings at every level (see example above).

Have at least two items at every heading level (I, A, and 1). If you can't find a second item to match the first in a new level of heads, perhaps the new level isn't needed.

Express all items (except the thesis) as complete and parallel statements (not questions), properly punctuated.

Position your thesis sentence above the outline, either underlined or italicized.

For more on organizing papers, including reverse outlining and transitional words and phrases, see Chapter 6.

30

Revising, Editing, and Proofreading

How much time should you spend revising a draft? That depends on the importance of the document and the time available to complete it. A job-application letter, résumé, or term paper had better be impressive and mechanically correct. But you shouldn't send even an e-mail without a quick review, if only to make certain you're directing it to the right people and that your tone is spot-on. Errors might not bother you, but don't assume that other readers are just as easygoing. A well-edited piece always trumps sloppy work.

How you revise your work is a different matter. Some people edit line by line, perfecting every sentence before moving on to the next. Others write whole drafts quickly and then revise, and others combine these methods.

In most cases, it makes sense to draft a project fairly quickly and then edit it. Why? Because revising is hierarchical: Some issues matter more to your success than others. You might spend hours on a draft, getting each comma right and deleting every unneeded word. But then you read the whole thing and get that sinking feeling: The paper doesn't meet the assignment or is aimed at the wrong audience. So you trash paragraph after carefully edited paragraph and reorganize many of your ideas. Maybe you even begin from scratch.

Wouldn't it have been better to discover those big problems early on, before you put in so many hours polishing the punctuation? So for major projects at least, think of *revising* as making sweeping changes to top-tier issues like content and organization, *editing* as fine-tuning the supporting details, and *proofreading* as fixing mechanical mistakes.

Revise to see the big picture. Be willing to overhaul a whole project, if necessary, when you revise. Of course, you'll need a draft first and it should be a real one with actual words on the page, not just good intentions. Revisions at this global level may require heavy-duty rewrites of the paper, even starting over. Whatever it takes.

- **Does the project meet the assignment?** You really can get so wrapped up in a paper that you forget the original assignment. If you received an assignment sheet, go back and measure your first draft against its specifications. If it asks for a report and you have offered an argument, prepare for a major overhaul. Review, too, any requirements set for length, format, or use of sources.

- **Does the project reach its intended audience?** Who will read your paper? Are its tone and level of vocabulary right for these people? Have you used the types of sources readers expect: scholarly books and articles for an academic audience? Adjustments to satisfy the assigned audience may ripple throughout the piece.

- **Does the project do justice to its subject?** This is a tough question and you may want to get another reader's input. It might also help to review successful models of the assignment before you revise your paper. Look for such work in magazines, newspapers, and textbooks. How well does your piece compare?

Edit to make the paper flow.   There are different opinions as to exactly what *flow* means when applied to writing, but everyone agrees that it's a good thing. With the major requirements of an assignment met, check how well you have put the piece together.

- **Does the organization work for the reader?** You may understand the paper, but will its structure be obvious to readers? Is a thesis statement, when one is required, clearly in place? Do your paragraphs develop coherent points? Pay particular attention to the opening sentences in those paragraphs: They must both connect to what you just wrote and preview the upcoming material.

- **Does the paper have smooth and frequent transitions?** Transitional words and phrases are road signs to help keep readers on track. Make sure they appear not only at the beginning of paragraphs but also throughout the project. To test your transitions, try reading your paper aloud. If you stumble, readers will too. Review Chapter 37 for much more on transitions.

- **Is the paper readable?** Tinker to your heart's content with the language, varying sentence structures, choosing words to match the level of style you want, and paring away clumsy verbiage (which almost rhymes with *garbage*). Review Part 5 on style and apply those suggestions to the paper at this stage.

Proofread to get the details right. When proofreading a paper, nothing clears your mind as much as putting a draft aside for a few days and then looking at it with fresh eyes. You will be amazed at all the changes you will want to make. But you have to plan ahead to take advantage of this unsurpassed proofreading technique. Wait until the last minute to complete a project and you lose that opportunity.

- **Is the format correct right down to the details?** Many academic and professional projects follow templates from which you cannot vary. In fact, you may be expected to learn these requirements as a condition for entering a profession or major. So if you are asked to prepare a paper in Modern Language Association (MLA) or American Psychological Association (APA) style, for instance, invest the few minutes it takes to get the titles, margins, headings, and page numbers right. ○ Give similar attention to the formats for lab reports, e-mails, Web sites, and so on. You'll look like a pro if you do.

- **Are the grammar and mechanics right?** Word-processing programs offer a surprising amount of help in these areas. But use this assistance only as a first line of defense, not as a replacement for carefully rereading every word yourself. Even then, you still have to pay close attention to errors you make habitually. You know what they are. ○

- **Is the spelling correct?** Spell-checkers pick up some obvious gaffes but may not be any help with proper nouns or other special items—such as your professor's last name. They also don't catch correctly spelled words that simply aren't the ones you meant to use: *the* instead of *then*, *rein* instead of *reign*, and so on.

understand citation
styles p. 463

help with common
errors p. 550

Thinking about Writing Advice about revising can sound dreary, but the process is an important one you engage in regularly—or should. In a discussion with your classmates (or in a paragraph or two), describe your habits of revision. Explore questions such as the following:

- Do you revise as you write, or do you prefer to wait until you have a full draft?

- How willing are you to make big changes in a draft?

- Have you ever been embarrassed or hurt by what seemed like minor errors?

- Do you know your specific areas of weakness, and how do you address them?

- Do you allow yourself enough time to give your projects a close second look? Should you?

- Have you ever had a surprising success with a paper you wrote at the last minute and turned in almost unrevised? How does that happen?

1

Put the paper aside for a few days
(or at least a few hours) before
revising.

2 Print out the paper, clear space on your desk, and read with fresh eyes. Does the paper respond to the assignment? Will it make sense to readers?

3 Read your paper aloud to yourself, your roommate, your goldfish—anyone who will listen. Mark the parts that confuse you or your audience.

Proofread these items carefully in college papers . . .

Title page: Your name; instructor/course; date; title of paper

Format: Correct margins; double-spacing; page numbers; running head, if required; paragraph indention

Punctuation: No run-ons; no comma splices; semicolons, dashes/hyphens used correctly

Quotations: Quotation marks correctly placed; quotations introduced or framed

Spelling: Check especially names, proper nouns, errors you make routinely: it's/its, to/too, affect/effect, lose/loose, etc.

Documentation: Check format of quotations, in-text citations; all bibliography items.

Peer Editing

"Will you read this for me?" Many people get nervous when they hear the question. Perhaps they don't want to offend a friend or classmate with potential criticisms or they doubt their own writing abilities. These are predictable reactions, but you need to get beyond them if you are asked to serve as a peer editor.

Your job in peer editing drafts is not to criticize other writers but to help them. And you will accomplish that best by approaching a project honestly, from the perspective of a typical reader. You may not grasp all the finer points of grammar, but you will know if a paper is boring, confusing, or unconvincing. Writers (including you) need this feedback.

And yet most peer editors in college or professional situations focus on tiny matters, such as misspellings or commas, and ignore arguments that completely lack evidence or paragraphs dull enough to make accountants yawn. Of course, spelling and punctuation errors are easy to catch. It's much tougher to suggest that whole pages need to be reconsidered or that a colleague should do more thorough research. But there's nothing charitable about ignoring these deeper issues when a writer's grade or career may be on the line. So what should you do?

First, before you edit any project, agree on ground rules for making comments. It is painless to annotate electronic drafts since you don't have to touch or change the original file. But writers may be more protective of paper copies of their work. Always ask whether you may write comments on a paper and then make sure that your handwriting is legible and your remarks are identified, perhaps by your initials.

Peer edit the same way you revise your own work. As suggested in Chapter 30, pay attention to global issues first. ○ Examine the purpose, audience, and subject matter of the project before dealing with its sentence structure, grammar, or mechanics—if that's what the writer allows. Deal with these major issues in a thoughtful

revise and edit p. 350

357

and supportive written comment at the end of the paper. Use marginal comments and proofreading symbols (see p. 359) to highlight mechanical problems. But don't correct these items. Leave it to the writer to figure out what is wrong. Or fix one error that appears frequently in the draft and let the writer correct other occurrences.

Be specific in identifying problems or opportunities.
For instance, it doesn't help a writer to read "organization is confusing." Instead, point to places where the draft went off track. If one sentence or paragraph exemplifies a particular problem—or strength—highlight it in some fashion and mention it in the final comment. Nothing helps a writer less than vague complaints or cheerleading:

> *You did a real good job, though I'm not sure you supported your thesis.*

It's far better to write something like the following:

> *Your thesis on the opening page is clear and challenging, but by the second page, you have forgotten what you are trying to prove. The paragraphs there don't seem connected to the original claim, and I don't find strong evidence to support the points you do make. Restructure these opening pages?*

Too tough? Not at all. This editor takes a colleague's paper seriously enough to explain why it's not working.

Offer suggestions for improvement.
You soften criticism when you follow it up with reasonable suggestions or strategies for revision. It's fine, too, to direct writers to resources they might use, from better sources to more effective software to an appointment at the local writing center (see p. 433). Avoid the tendency, however, to revise the paper for your classmate or to recast it to suit your own opinions.

Praise what is genuinely good in the paper.
An editor can easily overlook what's working well in a paper, yet a writer needs that information as much as any apt criticism. Find something good to say, too, even about a paper that mostly doesn't work. You'll encourage the writer, who may be facing some lengthy revisions. But don't make an issue of it. Writers will know immediately if you are scraping bottom to find something to praise. Here's a detailed comment at the end of a first draft that makes many helpful moves in a supportive tone, from encouraging a writer to making quite specific criticisms.

> Whit,
>   *I liked your draft and the direction your paper is going. Your use of imagery throughout was spot-on. I've never seen the movie* Mad Max, *but I can see the post-apocalyptic setting in my head.*
>   *Your thesis is clear and concise, but as we discussed, perhaps you can do away with the low-budget innovation portion? That way you can focus on the film's themes and social impact, both of which relate more to why* Mad Max *should be treated as a film classic.... Also, focus more of your energy on the movie's influence because I think that is the best argument to support your claim.*

"No passion in the world is equal to the passion to alter someone else's draft."

—H. G. Wells

Library of Congress, Prints and Photographs Division, LC-DIG-ggbain-21320

I do think your paper could benefit from more personal ethos: Say you are an avid film watcher and a humble fan of the movie so that the reader can trust your opinion easily.

In terms of style, I found some of your sentences to be long and overbearing. Switch up short and long sentences so the reader can move through the paper easily.

I think that's it. I can't wait to read the final draft of this paper, because I know it's going to be good. Good luck.

—*Stefan*

Use proofreading symbols. Proofreading marks may seem fussy or impersonal, but they can be a useful way of quickly highlighting some basic errors or omissions. Here are some you might want to remember and use when editing a paper draft.

Symbol	Meaning
sp	Word misspelled (not a standard mark, but useful)
✗	Check for error here (not a standard mark)
ℐ	Delete marked item
⌒	Close up space
∧	Insert word or phrase
⌄	Insert comma
⌄ ⌄	Insert quotation marks
≡	Capitalize
⊙	Insert period
⌒⌄	Transpose or reverse the items marked
¶	Begin new paragraph
#	Insert or open up space
(ital)	Italicize word or phrase

Keep comments tactful and confidential. Treat another writer's work the way you'd like to have your own efforts treated. Slips in writing can be embarrassing enough without an editor tweeting about them.

> **Writing about Writing**   Anderson Cooper of CNN reported on a teacher in North Carolina suspended without pay for two weeks for writing "Loser" on a sixth-grader's papers. Apparently the student wasn't offended because the teacher was known to be a "jokester," but administrators were. Did they overreact with the suspension (without pay), or should teachers and editors show discretion when commenting on something as personal as writing? Is there any room for sarcasm when peer editing? Make the case, one way or the other, in an exploratory paragraph.

Insert a comment in a Word document

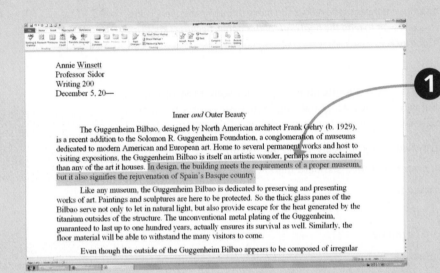

1 Highlight the section on which you would like to comment.

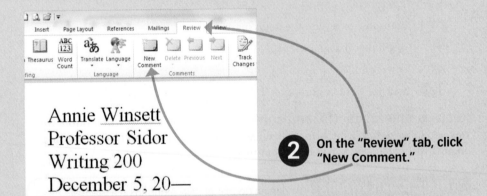

2 On the "Review" tab, click "New Comment."

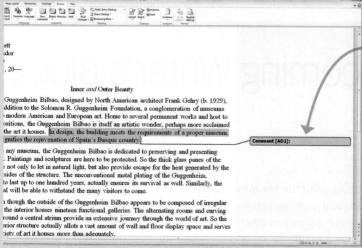

3 Type your comment.

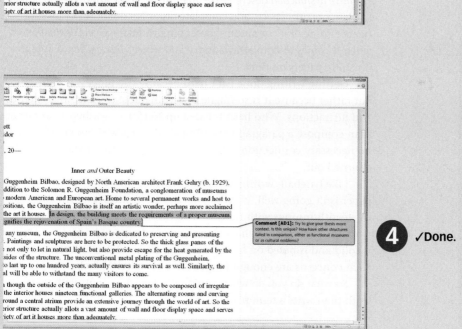

4 ✓Done.

32

Overcoming Writer's Block

Waiting until the last minute to write a paper hasn't been defined as a medical problem yet. But give it time. Already a condition called *executive dysfunction* describes the inability of some children and adults to plan, organize, pace, and complete tasks. No doubt we've all experienced some of its symptoms, describing the state as *procrastination* when it comes to doing the laundry and *writer's block* when it applies to finishing papers on time.

Getting writing done isn't hard because the process is painful, but rather because it is so fragile and vulnerable to ridiculous excuses and distractions. Who hasn't dialed up Netflix or washed a car rather than compose a paragraph? Writing also comes with no guarantees, no necessary connection between labor put in and satisfactory pages churned out.

Like baseball, writing is a game without time limits. When a paper isn't going well, you can stretch into fruitless twelfth and thirteenth innings with no end in sight. And if you do finish, readers may not like what you have done—even when you know your work is solid and is based on honest reading, observation, and research. Such concerns are enough to give anyone writer's block.

So what do you do when you'd rather crack walnuts with your teeth than write a term paper?

Break the project into parts. Getting started is usually the hard part for writers simply because the project taken as a whole seems overwhelming. Even a simple one-page position paper can ruin a whole weekend, and a term paper—with its multiple drafts, abstract, notes, bibliography, tables, and graphs—stretches beyond the pale.

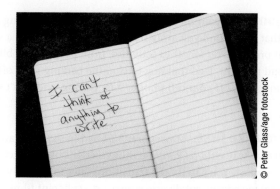

© Peter Glass/age fotostock

But what if, instead of stewing over how much time and energy the whole project will absorb, you divide it into manageable stages? Then you can do the work in chunks and enjoy the success that comes from completing each part. That position paper might be broken down into two, maybe three, less daunting steps: doing the assigned reading; brainstorming the paper; writing the page required. The same procedure makes a research paper less intimidating: You have more elements to manage, but you also have a strategy to finish them.

Set manageable goals.
Unless you are very disciplined, writing projects expand to fill the time available for them. Worse, you'll probably expend more energy fretting than working. To gain control, set levelheaded goals for completing the project and stick to them. In other words, don't dedicate a whole Saturday to preparing your résumé or working up a lab report; instead, commit yourself to the full and uninterrupted two hours the task will really take if you sit down and concentrate.

If you have trouble estimating how much time a project may require, consider that it is better to set a goal than to face an open-ended commitment. That's one good reason both instructors and publishers set deadlines.

Create a calendar.
For complicated assignments that extend over weeks or even months, create a calendar or timeline and stick with it. ○ First, break the task into parts and estimate how much time each stage of the paper or other project will take. Knowing your own work habits, you can draw on past experiences with similar assignments to construct a feasible plan. You'll feel better once you've got a road map that leads to completion.

Don't draw up a schedule so elaborate that you build in failure by trying to manage too many events. Assume that some stages, especially research or drafting, may take more time than you originally expect. But do stick to your schedule, even if it means starting a draft with research still remaining or cutting off the drafting process to allow time for necessary revisions.

■ ■

Inspiration is wonderful when it happens, but the writer must develop an approach for the rest of the time. . . . The wait is simply too long.

■ ■

—Leonard Bernstein

Photo by Marion S. Trikusko, *U.S. News & World Report* Magazine Photograph Collection/Library of Congress, Prints and Photographs Division, LC-U9-24858-17 (P & P).

plan a project p. 428

Limit distractions. Put yourself in a place that encourages writing and minimizes any temptations that might pull you away from your work. Schedule a specific time for writing and give it priority over all other activities, from paying your bills to feeding the dog. (On second thought, feed that dog to stop the barking.) Log off your Facebook and Twitter accounts, turn off your cell phone, start writing, and don't stop for an hour. Really.

Do the parts you like first. Movies aren't filmed in sequence and papers don't have to be written that way either. Compose those sections of a project that feel ready to go or interest you most. You can fix the transitions later to make the paper feel seamless, the way movie editors cut diverse scenes into coherent films. Once you have whole pages in hand, you'll be more inclined to keep working on a paper: The project suddenly seems manageable.

Write a zero draft. When you are *really* blocked, try a zero draft—that is, a version of the paper composed in one sitting, virtually nonstop. The process may resemble freewriting (see p. 226), but this time you aren't trawling for topic ideas. You've already done the necessary background reading and research, and so you're primed to write. You might even have a thesis and an outline. All you lack is the gumption to turn all this preparation into coherent sentences. Repress your inhibitions by writing relentlessly, without pausing to reread and review your stuff. Keep at it for several *hours* if need be. You can do it—just imagine you're writing a timed exam. **O**

The draft you produce won't be elegant (though you might surprise yourself), and some spots will be rough indeed. But keep pushing until you've finished a full text, from introduction to conclusion. Set this version aside, delaying any revision for a few hours or even days. Then, instead of facing an empty tablet or screen, you will have full pages of prose to work with.

Peter Dazeley/Getty Images

Reward yourself. People respond remarkably well to incentives, so promise yourself some prize correlated to

understand essay exams
p. 245

the writing task you face. Finishing a position paper is probably worth a pizza. A term paper might earn you dinner and a movie. A dissertation is worth a used Honda Civic.

Writing about Writing   Do you have a good writer's block story to share? You might describe an odd thing you have done rather than start a paper— especially one that might seem far more arduous than putting words down on a page. Or maybe you have figured out an infallible method for overcoming procrastination. Or you have endured a roommate's endless excuses for failing to complete *anything*. Tell your story in a paragraph or two, which you will start writing *now*.

Style

5

part five

Need help revising and editing? See p. 350. / Need help with common errors? See p. 550.

33

define your style/refine your tone

Levels of Style

We all have an ear for the way words work in sentences and paragraphs, for the distinctive melding of voice, tone, rhythm, and texture some call *style*. You might not be able to explain exactly why one paragraph sparkles and another is as flat as day-old soda, but you know when writing feels energetic, precise, and clear or stodgy, lifeless, and plodding. Choices you make about sentence type, sentence length, vocabulary, pronouns, and punctuation *do* create distinctive verbal styles—which may or may not fit particular types of writing. ○

In fact, there are as many styles of writing as of dress. In most cases, language that is clear, active, and economical will do the job. But even such a bedrock style has variations. Since the time of the ancient Greeks, writers have imagined a "high" or formal style at one end of a scale and a "low" or colloquial style at the other, bracketing a just-right porridge in the middle. Style is more complex than that, but keeping the full range in mind reveals some of your options.

Even dining has distinct levels of style and formality you grasp immediately.
Left: anouchka/Getty Images.
Center: Steve Debenport/Getty Images. *Right:* Mary Altaffer/ AP Images.

improve your sentences
p. 375

Use high style for formal, scientific, and scholarly writing. You will find high style in professional journals, scholarly books, legal briefs, formal addresses, many newspaper editorials, some types of technical writing, and even traditional wedding invitations. Use it yourself when a lot is at stake—in a scholarship application, for example, or a job letter, term paper, or thesis. High style is signaled by some combination of the following features—all of which can vary.

John Cole/Cagle Cartoons

- Serious or professional subjects
- Knowledgeable or professional audiences
- Impersonal point of view signaled by dominant, though not exclusive, third-person (*he, she, it, they*) pronouns
- Relatively complex and self-consciously patterned sentences (that display *parallelism, balance, repetition*)
- Sophisticated or professional vocabulary, often abstract and technical
- Few or no contractions or colloquial expressions
- Conventional grammar and punctuation; standard document design
- Formal documentation, when required, often with notes and a bibliography

The following example is from a scholarly journal. The article uses a formal scientific style, appropriate when an expert in a field is writing for an audience of his or her peers.

> Temperament is a construct closely related to personality. In human research, temperament has been defined by some researchers as the inherited, early appearing tendencies that continue throughout life and serve as the foundation for personality (A. H. Buss, 1995; Goldsmith et al., 1987). Although this definition is not adopted uniformly by human researchers (McCrae et al., 2000), animal researchers agree even less about how to define temperament (Budaev, 2000). In some cases, the word *temperament* appears to be used purely to avoid using the word *personality*, which some animal researchers associate with anthropomorphism. Thus, to ensure that my review captured all potentially relevant reports, I searched for studies that examined either personality or temperament.
>
> —Sam D. Gosling, "From Mice to Men: What Can We Learn about Personality from Animal Research?" *Psychological Bulletin*

Technical terms introduced and defined.

Sources documented.

Perspective generally impersonal—though *I* is used.

The following excerpt from a 2013 presidential proclamation marking National Arts and Humanities Month also uses a formal style. The occasion calls for an expressive reflection on a consequential subject.

Opening is general and serious—with carefully balanced sentences.

Throughout our history, America has advanced not only because of our people's will or our leaders' vision, but also because of paintings and poems, stories and songs, dramas and dances. These works open our minds and nourish our souls, helping us understand what it means to be human and what it means to be American. . . .

Our history is a testament to the boundless capacity of the arts and

Vocabulary is learned and dignified.

humanities to shape our views of democracy, freedom, and tolerance. Each of us knows what it is like to have our beliefs changed by a writer's perspective, our understanding deepened by a historian's insight, or our waning spirit lifted by a singer's voice. These are some of the most striking and memorable moments in

Ideas expressed are abstract and uplifting.

our lives, and they reflect lasting truths—that the arts and humanities speak to everyone and that in the great arsenal of progress, the human imagination is our most powerful tool.

Ensuring our children and our grandchildren can share these same experiences and hone their own talents is essential to our Nation's future. Somewhere in America, the next great author is wrestling with a sentence in her first short story, and the next great artist is doodling in the pages of his notebook.

Voice is "presidential," speaking for the nation.

We need these young people to succeed as much as we need our next generation of engineers and scientists to succeed. And that is why my administration remains dedicated to strengthening initiatives that not only provide young people with the nurturing that will help their talents grow, but also the skills to think critically and creatively throughout their lives.

Final paragraph evokes well-calibrated emotions.

This month, we pay tribute to the indelible ways the arts and humanities have shaped our Union. Let us encourage future generations to carry this tradition forward. And as we do so, let us celebrate the power of artistic expression to bridge our differences and reveal our common heritage.

— Presidential Proclamation, National Arts and Humanities Month, September 20, 2013

Use middle style for personal, argumentative, and some academic writing.

This style, perhaps the most common, falls between the extremes and, like the other styles, varies enormously. It is the language of journalism, popular books and magazines, professional memos and nonscientific reports, instructional guides and manuals, and most commercial Web sites. Use this style in position papers, letters to the editor, personal statements, and business e-mails and memos—even in some business and professional work, once you are comfortable with the people to whom you are writing. Middle style doesn't so much claim features of its own as it walks a path between formal and everyday language. It may combine some of the following characteristics:

- Full range of topics, from serious to humorous
- General audiences
- Range of perspectives, including first-person (*I*) and second-person (*you*) points of view
- Typically, a personal rather than an institutional voice
- Sentences in active voice that vary in complexity and length
- General vocabulary, more specific than abstract, with concrete nouns and action verbs and with unfamiliar terms or concepts defined
- Informal expressions, occasional dialogue, slang, and contractions, when appropriate to the subject or audience
- Conventional grammar and reasonably correct formats
- Informal documentation, usually without notes

In the following excerpt from an article that appeared in the popular magazine *Psychology Today*, Ellen McGrath uses a conversational but serious middle style to present scientific information to a general audience.

Families often inherit a negative thinking style that carries the germ of depression. Typically it is a legacy passed from one generation to the next, a pattern of pessimism invoked to protect loved ones from disappointment or stress. But in fact, negative thinking patterns do just the opposite, eroding the mental health of all exposed.

> Vocabulary is sophisticated but not technical.

When Dad consistently expresses his disappointment in Josh for bringing home a B minus in chemistry although all the other grades are A's, he is exhibiting a kind of cognitive distortion that children learn to deploy on themselves—a mental filtering that screens out positive experience from consideration.

> Familiar example (fictional son is even named) illustrates technical term: *cognitive distortion*.

Or perhaps the father envisions catastrophe, seeing such grades as foreclosing the possibility of a top college, thus dooming his son's future. It is their repetition over time that gives these events power to shape a person's belief system.

> Phrase following dash offers further clarification helpful to educated, but nonexpert, readers.

—"Is Depression Contagious?," July 1, 2003

The middle style works especially well for speakers addressing actual audiences. Compare the informal and personal style of Michelle Obama, then in her role as first lady, advocating for arts education at an awards luncheon to the more stately language her husband used in his presidential proclamation, also on the subject of the arts (p. 370).

Style is personal, with feelings close to the surface.

So for every Janelle Monae [an artist recognized at the luncheon], there are so many young people with so much promise [that] they never have the chance to develop. And think about how that must feel for a kid to have so much talent, so much that they want to express, but it's all bottled up inside because no one ever puts a paintbrush or an instrument or a script into their hand.

Sentences and clauses are parallel, rhythmic, and evocatively short.

Think about what that means for our communities, that frustration bottled up. Think about the neighborhoods where so many of our kids live—neighborhoods torn apart by poverty and violence. Those kids have no good outlets or opportunities, so for them everything that's bottled up—all that despair and anger and fear—it comes out in all the wrong places. It comes out through guns and gangs and drugs, and the cycle just continues.

Vocabulary choices are crisp and varied. Note the use of "kids" throughout.

But the arts are a way to channel that pain and frustration into something meaningful and productive and beautiful. And every human being needs that, particularly our kids. And when they don't have that outlet, that is such a tremendous loss, not just for our kids, but for our nation. And that's why the work you all are doing is so important.

— Remarks by the First Lady at the Grammy Museum's Jane Ortner Education Award Luncheon, July 14, 2014

Use a low style for personal, informal, and even playful writing.

Don't think of "low" here in a negative sense: A colloquial or informal style is perfect when you want or need to sound more open and at ease. Low style can be right for your personal e-mails and instant messaging, of course, as well as in advertisements, magazines trying to be hip, personal narratives, humor writing, and many blogs. Low style has many of the following features:

- Everyday or off-the-wall subjects, often humorous or parodic
- In-group or specialized readers
- Highly personal and idiosyncratic points of view; lots of *I, me, you, us,* and dialogue
- Shorter sentences and irregular constructions, especially fragments
- Vocabulary from pop culture and the street—idiomatic, allusive, and obscure to outsiders
- Colloquial expressions resembling speech
- Unconventional grammar and mechanics and alternative formats
- No systematic acknowledgment of sources

Here's the opening of a satire in comic "low style" published online by *McSweeney's Internet Tendency* (May 2, 2016) by Robin Lee Mozer—who you might guess teaches writing. It is entitled "I Would Rather Do Anything Than Grade Your Final Papers."

Dear Students Who Have Just Completed My Class,

I would rather do anything else than grade your Final Papers.

I would rather base jump off of the parking garage next to the student activity center or eat that entire sketchy tray of taco meat left over from last week's student achievement luncheon that's sitting in the department refrigerator or walk all the way from my house to the airport on my hands than grade your Final Papers.

I would rather have a sustained conversation with my grandfather about politics and government-supported healthcare and what's wrong with the system today and why he doesn't believe in homeowner's insurance because it's all a scam than grade your Final Papers.

Rather than grade your Final Papers, I would stand in the aisle at Lowe's and listen patiently to All the Men mansplain the process of buying lumber and how essential it is to sight down the board before you buy it to ensure that it's not bowed or cupped or crooked because if you buy lumber with defects like that you're just wasting your money even as I am standing there, sighting down a 2 × 4 the way my father taught me fifteen years ago.

I would rather go to Costco on the Friday afternoon before a three-day weekend. With my preschooler. After preschool.

I would rather go through natural childbirth with twins. . . .

> Opening lines create the vehicle for the satire, a letter to students.

> Windy, inelegant sentences full of mundane details and deliberate repetition (*I would rather*) underscore the horrors of grading.

> The hyperbolic prose perhaps mimics student speech?

> Deliberate fragments for emphasis.

As the expression goes, you should read the whole thing. Mozer's piece is available online.

Thinking about Writing Over the next day, look for three pieces of writing that seem to you to represent examples of high, middle, and low style. Then study several paragraphs or a section of each in detail, paying attention to the features listed in the checklists for the three styles. How well do the pieces actually conform to the descriptions of high, middle, and low style? Where would you place your three examples on a continuum that moves from high to low? Do the pieces share some stylistic features? Do you find any variations of style within the individual passages you examined?

Panels combine verbal and visual elements to tell a story.

Political figures become characters in a real-life drama.

Sounds (*Shoom!*) are represented visually—as in superhero tales.

Real images (the photograph on the left) are sometimes juxtaposed with cartoon panels as part of the collage.

The very serious story told in the 9/11 Commission Report was retold in *The 9/11 Report: A Graphic Adaptation*. Creators Sid Jacobson and Ernie Colón use the colloquial visual style of a comic book to make the formidable data and conclusions of a government report accessible to a wider audience. For more on choosing a genre, see Chapter 2.

Clear and Vigorous Writing

Ordinarily, tips and tricks don't do much to enhance your skills as a writer. But a few guidelines, applied sensibly, can improve your sentences and paragraphs noticeably—and upgrade your credibility as a writer. You sound more professional and confident when every word and phrase pulls its weight.

Always consider the big picture in applying the following tips: Work with whole pages and paragraphs, not just individual sentences. Remember, too, that these are guidelines, not rules. Ignore them when your good sense suggests a better alternative.

Build sentences around specific and tangible subjects and objects.

Scholar Richard Lanham famously advised writers troubled by tangled sentences to ask, "Who is kicking who?" This question expresses the principle that readers shouldn't have to puzzle over what they read. They are less likely to be confused when they can identify the people or things in a sentence that act upon other people and things. Answering Professor Lanham's question often leads to stronger verbs and tighter sentences too.

CONFUSING	Current tax policies necessitate congressional reform if the reoccurrence of a recession is to be avoided.
BETTER	Congress needs to reform current tax policies to avoid future recessions.

CONFUSING   In the prohibition era, tuning cars enabled the bootleggers to turn ordinary automobiles into speed machines for the transportation of illegal alcohol by simply altering certain components of the cars.

BETTER   In the prohibition era, bootleggers modified their cars to turn them into speed machines for transporting illegal alcohol.

Both of the confusing sentences here work better with subjects capable of action: *Congress* and *bootleggers*. Once identified, these subjects make it easy to simplify the sentences, giving them more power.

Look for opportunities to use specific nouns and noun phrases rather than general ones. This advice depends very much on context. Academic reports and arguments often require broad statements and general terms. But don't ignore the power and energy of specific words and phrases; they create more memorable images for readers, so they may have more impact.

GENERAL	SPECIFIC
bird	roadrunner
cactus	prickly pear
lawbreaker	drug dealer
business	pizzeria
jeans	501s

Many writers incline toward generic terms and the impenetrable phrases they inspire because they sound serious and sophisticated. But such language can be hard to figure out or may even suggest a cover-up. What better way to hide an inconvenient truth than to bury it in words? So revise those ugly, unreadable, inhuman sentences:

ABSTRACT   All of the separate constituencies at this academic institution must be invited to participate in the decision-making process under the current fiscal pressures we face.

BETTER   Faculty, students, and staff at this school must all have a say during this current budget crunch.

■ ■
Don't use words too big for the subject. Don't say "infinitely" when you mean "very"; otherwise you'll have no word left when you want to talk about something really infinite.
■ ■

Wolf Suschitzky/Getty Images

—C. S. Lewis

Avoid sprawling phrases. These constructions give readers fits, especially when they thicken, sentence after sentence, like pond sludge. Be alert whenever your prose shows any combination of the following features:

- Strings of prepositional phrases
- Verbs turned into nouns via endings such as *-ation* (*implement* becomes *implementation*)
- Lots of articles (*the, a*)
- Lots of heavily modified verbals

Such expressions are not inaccurate or wrong, just tedious. They make readers work hard for no good reason. Fortunately, they are also easy to clean up once you notice the accumulation.

WORDY	members of the student body at Arizona State
BETTER	students at Arizona State
WORDY	the producing of products made up of steel
BETTER	steel production
WORDY	the prioritization of decisions for policies of the student government
BETTER	the student government's priorities

Avoid sentences with long windups. The more stuff you pile up ahead of the main verb, the more readers have to remember. Very skillful writers can pull off complex sentences of this kind because they know how to build interest and manage clauses. But a safer strategy in academic and professional writing is to get to the point of your sentences quickly. Here's a sentence from the Internal Revenue Service Web site that keeps readers waiting far too long for a verb. Yet it's simple to fix once its problem is diagnosed:

ORIGINAL	A new scam e-mail that appears to be a solicitation from the IRS and the U.S. government for charitable contributions to victims of the recent Southern California wildfires has been making the rounds.
REVISED	A new scam e-mail making the rounds asks for charitable contributions to victims of the recent Southern California wildfires. Although it appears to be from the IRS and the U.S. government, it is a fake.

Favor simple, active verbs. When a sentence, even a short one, goes off track, consider whether the problem might be a nebulous, strung-out, or unimaginative verb. Replace it with a verb that does something:

WORDY VERB PHRASE	We must make a decision soon.
BETTER	We must decide soon.
WORDY VERB PHRASE	Students are absolutely reliant on federal loans.
BETTER	Students need federal loans.
WORDY VERB PHRASE	Engineers proceeded to reinforce the levee.
BETTER	Engineers reinforced the levee.

You'll write better whenever you apply this guideline.

Avoid strings of prepositional phrases. Prepositional phrases are simple structures, consisting of prepositions and their objects and an occasional modifier: *from the beginning; under the spreading chestnut tree; between you and me; in the line of duty; over the rainbow.* You can't write much without prepositional phrases. But use more than two or, rarely, three in a row and they drain the energy from a sentence. When that's the case, try turning the prepositions into more compact modifiers or moving them into different positions within the sentence. Sometimes you may need to revise the sentence even more substantially.

TOO MANY PHRASES	We stood in line at the observatory on the top of a hill in the mountains to look in a huge telescope at the moons of Saturn.
BETTER	We lined up at the mountaintop observatory to view Saturn's moons through a huge telescope.
TOO MANY PHRASES	To help first-year students in their adjustment to the rigors of college life, the Faculty Council voted for the creation of a new midterm break during the third week of October.
BETTER	To help first-year students adjust to college life, the Faculty Council endorsed a new break in mid-October.

Don't repeat key words close together. You can often improve the style of a passage just by making sure you haven't used a particular word or phrase too often—unless you repeat it deliberately for effect (*government of the people, by the people, for the people*). Your sentences will sound fresher after you have eliminated pointless repetition; they may also end up shorter.

REPETITIVE	Students in writing courses are often assigned common readings that they are expected to read to prepare for various student writing projects.
BETTER	Students in writing courses are often assigned common readings to prepare them for projects.

This is a guideline to apply sensibly: Sometimes for clarity, you must repeat key expressions over and over—especially in technical writing.

> The *New Horizons* payload is incredibly power efficient, with the instruments collectively drawing only about 28 watts. The payload consists of three optical instruments, two plasma instruments, a dust sensor, and a radio science receiver/radiometer.
>
> —NASA, "*New Horizons* Spacecraft Ready for Flight"

Avoid doublings.

In speech, we tend to repeat ourselves or say things two or three different ways to be sure listeners get the point. Such repetitions are natural, even appreciated. But in writing, the habit of doubling may irritate readers. And it is very much a habit, backed by a long literary tradition comfortable with pairings such as *home and hearth, friend and colleague, tried and true, clean and sober, neat and tidy*, and so on. Need we add *dull and boring*?

Sometimes, writers will add an extra noun or two to be sure they have covered the bases: *colleges and universities, books and articles, ideas and opinions*. There may be good reasons for a second (or third) item. But the doubling is often just extra baggage that slows down the train. Leave it at the station.

The same goes for redundant expressions. For the most part, they go unnoticed, except by readers who crawl up walls when someone writes *young **in age**, bold **in character**, **totally** dead, **basically** unhappy, **current** fashion, **empty** hole, **extremely** outraged, later **in time**, mix **together**, reply **back**,* and so on. (In each case, the boldfaced words restate what is already obvious.) People precise enough to care about such details deserve consideration.

Turn clauses into more direct modifiers.

If you are fond of *that, which,* and *who* clauses, be sure you need them. You can sometimes save a word or two by pulling the modifiers out of the clause and moving them directly ahead of the words they explain. Or you may be able to tighten a sentence just by cutting *that, which,* or *who*.

WORDY	Our football coach, who is nationally renowned, expected a raise.
BETTER	Our nationally renowned football coach expected a raise.
WORDY	Our football coach, who is nationally renowned and already rich, still expected a raise.
BETTER	Our football coach, nationally renowned and already rich, still expected a raise.

Cut introductory expressions such as *it is* and *there is/are* when you can. These slow-moving expressions, called *expletives*, are fine when they are conventional, as in the following sentences, which would be difficult to rephrase.

> *It's* going to rain today.
> *It was* her first Oscar.
> *There is* a tide in the affairs of men.

But don't default to easy expletives at the beginning of every other sentence. Your prose will suffer. Fortunately, revision is easy.

WORDY	It is necessary that we reform the housing policies.
BETTER	We need to reform the housing policies.
WORDY	There were many incentives offered by the company to its sales force.
BETTER	The company offered its sales force many incentives.

Expletives in a sentence often attract other wordy and vague expressions. Then the language swells like a blister. Imagine having to read paragraph after paragraph of prose like the following sentence.

SLOW	It is quite evident that an argument sociologist Annette Lareau supports is that it is important to find the balance between authoritarian and indulgent styles of parenting because it contributes to successful child development.
BETTER	Clearly, sociologist Annette Lareau believes that balancing authoritarian and indulgent styles of parenting contributes to successful child development.

Vary your sentence lengths and structures. Sentences, like music, have rhythm. If all your sentences run about the same length or rarely vary from a predictable subject-verb-object pattern, readers will grow bored without knowing why. Every so often, surprise them with a really short statement. Or begin with a longer-than-usual introductory phrase. Or try compound subjects or verbs, or attach a series of parallel modifiers to the verb or object. Or let a sentence roll toward a grand conclusion, as in the following example.

> [Carl] Newman is a singing encyclopedia of pop power. He has identified, cultured, and cloned the most buoyant elements of his favorite Squeeze, Raspberries, Supertramp, and Sparks records, and he's pretty pathological about making sure there's something unpredictable and catchy happening in a New Pornographers song every couple of seconds—a stereo flurry of *ooohs*, an extra beat or two bubbling up unexpectedly.
>
> —Douglas Wolk, "Something to Talk About," *Spin*, August 2005

Read aloud what you have written. Then fix any words or phrases that cause you to pause or stumble, and rethink sentences that feel *awkward*—a notoriously vague reaction that should still be taken seriously. Reading drafts aloud is a great way to find problems. After all, if you can't move smoothly through your own writing, a reader won't be able to either. Better yet, persuade a friend or roommate to read your draft to you. Take notes.

Understand, though, that prose never sounds quite like spoken language—and thank goodness for that. Accurate transcripts of dialogue are almost unreadable, full of gaps, disconnected phrases, pauses, repetitions, and the occasional obscenity. And yet written language, especially in the middle style, should resemble the human voice, with all its cadences and rhythms pulling readers along, making them want to read more.

Cut a first draft by 25 percent—or more. If you tend to be wordy, try to cut your first drafts by at least one-quarter. Put all your thoughts down on the page when drafting a paper. But when editing, cut every unnecessary expression. Think of it as a competition. However, don't eliminate any important ideas and facts. If possible, ask an honest friend to read your work and point out where you might tighten your language.

If you ~~are aware that you~~ tend to ^*be wordy,* ~~say more than you need to in your writing,~~

~~then get in the habit of~~ trying to cut ~~the~~ ^*your* first drafts ~~that you have written~~ by

at least one-quarter. ~~There may be good reasons for you to~~ ^*P* put all your

thoughts ~~and ideas~~ down on the page when ~~you are in the process of~~

I believe more in the scissors than I do in the pencil.

—Truman Capote

Roger Higgins/New York World-Telegram and the Sun Newspapers Photograph Collection/Library of Congress, Prints and Photographs Division, LC-USZ62-119336.

drafting a paper ~~or project~~. But when ~~you are in the process of~~ editing, ~~you should be sure to~~ cut every unnecessary word ~~that is not needed or necessary. You may find it advantageous to~~ *expression.* think of it as a competition ~~or a game. In making your cuts, it is important that you~~ *However,* don't eliminate any important ideas ~~that may be essential or~~ facts ~~that may be important.~~ *and* If ~~you~~ find it possible, ~~you might consider~~ asking an honest friend ~~whom you trust~~ to read your ~~writing~~ *work* and ~~ask them to~~ point out ~~those places in your writing~~ where you might ~~make~~ your language *tighten* ~~tighter.~~

Thinking about Writing   Think your prose is as tight as Scrooge? Take a first draft you have written and try the 25 percent challenge. Count the words in your original (or let software do it for you) and then pare down until you come in under quota. And, while you are at it, turn abstract nouns and strung-out verbs into livelier expressions and eliminate long windups and boring chains of prepositional phrases. When done, read the revised version aloud—then revise one more time.

Inclusive Writing

Remember Polish jokes? Let's hope not, and that's a good thing. Slowly, we're all learning to avoid offensive racial, ethnic, and gender stereotypes in our public lives and the bigoted language that propagated them. Thanks to electronic media, the world is smaller and more diverse today: When you compose any document electronically, it may sail quickly around the Web, conveying not only ideas but also your attitudes and prejudices. You can't please every reader in this vast potential audience, but you can at least write respectfully, accurately, and, yes, honestly. Language that is both inclusive and culturally sensitive can and should have the qualities described in the following guidelines.

Avoid expressions that stereotype genders or sexual orientation.

Largely purged from contemporary English usage are job titles that suggest they are occupied exclusively by men or women. Gone are *stewardess* and *poetess, policeman* and *chairman, male nurse* and *woman scientist*. When referring to professions, even those still dominated by one gender or another, avoid using a gendered pronoun.

Don't strain sense to be politically correct. *Nun* and *NFL quarterback* are still gendered, as are *witch* and *warlock*—and *surrogate mother*. Here are some easy solutions.

STEREOTYPED	The postman came up the walk.
INCLUSIVE	The letter carrier came up the walk.
STEREOTYPED	Among all her other tasks, a nurse must also stay up-to-date on her medical education.
INCLUSIVE	Among all their other tasks, nurses must also stay up-to-date on their medical education.

Outdated Terms	Alternatives
fireman	firefighter
mankind	humankind, people, humans
congressman	congressional representative
gunman	shooter
policewoman	police officer
stewardess	flight attendant
actress, poetess	actor, poet

Avoid expressions that stereotype races, ethnic groups, or religious groups.

Deliberate racial slurs these days tend to be rare in professional writing. But it is still not unusual to find clueless writers (and politicians) noting how "hardworking," "articulate," "athletic," "well-groomed," or "ambitious" members of minority and religious groups are. The praise rings hollow because it draws on old and brutal stereotypes. You have an obligation to learn the history and nature of such ethnic caricatures and grow beyond them. It's part of your education, no matter what group or groups you belong to.

Refer to people and groups by the expressions used in serious publications, understanding that almost all racial and ethnic terms are contested: *African American, black* (or *Black*), *Negro, people of color, Asian American, Hispanic, Mexican American, Cuban American, Native American, Indian, Inuit, Anglo, white* (or *White*). Even the ancient group of American Indians once called Anasazi now goes by the more culturally and historically accurate Native Puebloans. While shifts of this sort may seem fussy or politically correct to some, it costs little to address people as they prefer, acknowledging both their humanity and our differences.

Be aware, too, that being part of an ethnic or racial group usually gives you license to say things about the group not open to outsiders. Anjelah Johnson and Hari Kondabolu can joke about topics that Jimmy Fallon can't touch, using epithets that would cost the

Tonight Show host his job. In academic and professional settings, show similar discretion in your language — though not in your treatment of serious subjects. Sensitivities of language should not become an excuse for avoiding open debate nor a weapon to chill it. In the following table are suggestions for inclusive, culturally sensitive terms.

Outdated Terms	Alternatives
Eskimo	Inuit
Oriental	Asian (better to specify country of origin)
Hispanic	Specify: Mexican, Cuban, Nicaraguan, and so on
Negro (acceptable to some)	African American, black
colored	people of color
a gay, the gays	gay, lesbian, gays and lesbians, the LGBT community
cancer victim	cancer survivor
boys, girls (to refer to adults)	men, women

Handle pronouns appropriately. Singular pronouns in English have gender markers: he, his, him; she, hers, her. It is of course appropriate to use masculine pronouns to refer to men and feminine pronouns to refer to women when the people you are writing about are comfortable with those terms. But you should also respect the identity of transgender people, referring to them by pronouns of their choice—whether it is a "he" or "his," "she" or "hers," or increasingly a plural "they" or "their," but never "he/she" or "his/her."

> I spoke with Taylor and he claimed that the book was his.
> I spoke with Taylor and she claimed that the book was hers.
> I spoke with Taylor and they claimed that the book was theirs.

Treat all people with respect. This policy makes sense in all writing. Some slights may not be intended—against the elderly, for example. But writing that someone drives *like an old woman* manages to offend two groups. In other cases—such as when you are describing members of campus groups, religious groups, the military, transgender colleagues, athletes, and so on—you might crudely use language that implies most readers share your own prejudices or narrow vision. You know the derogatory terms and references well enough, and you should avoid them if for no other reason than the Golden Rule. Everyone is a member of some group that has at one time or another been mocked or stereotyped. So writing that is respectful will itself be treated with respect.

Avoid sensational language. It happens every semester. One or more students ask the instructor whether it's okay to use four-letter words in their papers. Some instructors tolerate expletives in personal narratives, but it is difficult to make a case for them in academic reports, research papers, or position papers unless they are part of quoted material—as they may be in writing about contemporary literature or song lyrics.

Writing about Writing   Write a paragraph or two about any pet peeve you may have with language use. Your problem may address a serious issue like insensitivities in naming your ethnicity, community, or beliefs. Or you may just be tired of a friend insisting that you describe Sweetie Pie as your "animal companion" rather than use that demeaning and hegemonic term "pet." You'll want to share your paragraph and also read what others have written.

Purposeful Paragraphs

Paragraphs are a practical invention, created to make long blocks of prose easier to read by dividing them up. Here are some helpful ways to think about them.

Make sure paragraphs lead somewhere. Typically, you'll place a topic sentence at or near the beginning of a paragraph to introduce a claim that the rest of the paragraph will develop. Notice how the topic sentences highlighted in the passage below give structure to individual paragraphs and also move an argument forward. The author is explaining the use American patriots made of Magna Carta, a document that lords and bishops forced King John of England to sign in 1215, establishing a fundamental rule of law. **O**

> The American Revolutionaries weren't rejecting their identity as Englishmen; they were asserting it. As they saw it, George III was violating the "ancient constitution" just as King John and the Stuarts had done. It was therefore not just their right but their duty to resist, in the words of the delegates to the first Continental Congress in 1774, "as Englishmen our ancestors in like cases have usually done."
>
> Nowhere, at this stage, do we find the slightest hint that the patriots were fighting for universal rights. On the contrary, they were very clear that they were fighting for the privileges bestowed on them by Magna Carta. The concept of "no taxation without representation" was not an abstract principle. It could be found, rather, in Article 12 of the Great Charter: "No scutage or aid is to be levied in our realm except by the

develop a
statement p. 333

common counsel of our realm." In 1775, Massachusetts duly adopted as its state seal a patriot with a sword in one hand and a copy of Magna Carta in the other.

—Daniel Hannan, "Magna Carta: Eight Centuries of Liberty," *Wall Street Journal*, May 29, 2015

But paragraphs make claims in many different ways. You may weave a key idea throughout the fabric of an entire paragraph, restating it in various ways. Or, as in many introductory paragraphs, you may build to a point divulged in a concluding sentence. Gustavo Arellano uses that strategy in the first paragraph in an op-ed on Mexican superstar singer Juan Gabriel:

It's 1992, and I'm hating on my mom's newest CD: a synth-heavy recording by Mexican girl group Pandora called ". . . Con Amor Eterno" ("With Eternal Love"). She plays it every Saturday morning while doing morning chores, blasting it from Kenwood speakers and making my teenage life miserable. I don't mind the tight harmonies of the trio, or even the overwrought music and lyrics of love and lament. What I can't stand is the man who wrote their tunes: Juan Gabriel.

—Gustavo Arellano, "As a Boy, I Was Taught to Ridicule Juan Gabriel. As an Adult, I Revered Him"

Whatever your plan, all paragraphs should do serious work: introduce a subject, move a narrative forward, offer a new argument or claim, provide support for a claim already made, contradict another point, amplify an idea, furnish more examples, even bring discussion to an end. In short, a paragraph has to do something that readers recognize as purposeful and connected to what comes before and after.

Develop ideas adequately.
Instructors who insist that paragraphs run a minimum number of sentences (say 6–10) are usually just tired of students who don't back up claims with enough evidence. **O** In fact, experienced writers don't count sentences when they build paragraphs. Instead, they develop a sense for paragraph length, matching the swell of their ideas to the habits of their intended readers.

Consider the following paragraph that describes the last moments of the final Apollo moon mission in December 1972. The paragraph might be reduced to a single sentence: *All that remained of the 363-foot Apollo 17 launch vehicle was a 9-foot capsule recovered in the ocean.* But what would be lost? The pleasure of the full paragraph resides in the details the writer musters to support the final sentence, which reveals his point.

A powerful Sikorsky Sea King helicopter, already hovering nearby as they [the *Apollo 17* crew] hit the water, retrieved the astronauts and brought them to the carrier, where the spacecraft was recovered shortly later. The recovery crew saw

understand arguments
p. 89

not a gleaming instrument of exotic perfection, but a blasted, torn, and ragged survivor, its titanic strength utterly exhausted, a husk now, a shell. The capsule they hauled out of the ocean was all that remained of the *Apollo 17* Saturn V. The journey had spent, incinerated, smashed, or blistered into atoms every other part of the colossal, 363-foot white rocket, leaving only this burnt and brutalized 9-foot capsule. A great shining army had set out over the horizon, and a lone squadron had returned, savaged beyond recognition, collapsing into the arms of its rescuers, dead. Such was the price of reaching for another world.

—David West Reynolds, *Apollo: The Epic Journey to the Moon*

Organize paragraphs logically. It would be surprising if paragraphs didn't use the same structures found in many essays: thesis and support, division, classification, narrative. But it's ideas that drive the shape of paragraphs, not patterns of organization. Writers don't puzzle over whether their next paragraph should follow a comparison/contrast or cause/effect plan. They just write it, making sure it makes a point and appeals to readers.

In fact, individual paragraphs in any longer piece can be organized many different ways. And because paragraphs are relatively short, you usually see their patterns unfold right before your eyes. The following two passages are from an essay by Jon Katz titled "Do Dogs Think?" The paragraphs within them follow structures Katz needs at that given moment.

Blue, Heather's normally affectionate and obedient Rottweiler, began tearing up the house shortly after Heather went back to work as an accountant after several years at home. The contents of the trash cans were strewn all over the house. A favorite comforter was destroyed. Then Blue began peeing all over Heather's expensive new living-room carpet and systematically ripped through cables and electrical wires.

> Narrative paragraph describes changes in Blue's behavior.

Lots of dogs get nervous when they don't know what's expected of them, and when they get anxious, they can also grow restless. Blue hadn't had to occupy time alone before. Dogs can get unnerved by this. They bark, chew, scratch, destroy. Getting yelled at and punished later doesn't help: The dog probably knows it's doing something wrong, but it has no idea what. Since there's nobody around to correct behaviors when the dog is alone, how could the dog know which behavior is the problem? Which action was wrong?

> Katz uses causal pattern to explore Blue's behavioral problem.

I don't believe that dogs act out of spite or that they can plot retribution, though countless dog owners swear otherwise. To punish or deceive requires the perpetrator to understand that his victim or object has a particular point of view and to consciously work to manipulate or thwart it. That requires mental processes dogs don't have.

> A simple statement/proof structure organizes this paragraph.

Taken together, the two paragraphs in this second passage follow a problem/solution structure common in proposal arguments.

Why will Clementine come instantly if she's looking at me, but not if she's sniffing deer droppings? Is it because she's being stubborn or, as many people tell me, going through "adolescence"? Or because, when following her keen predatory instincts, she simply doesn't hear me? Should my response be to tug at her leash or yell? Maybe I should be sure we've established eye contact before I give her a command, or better yet, offer a liver treat as an alternative to whatever's distracting her. But how do I establish eye contact when her nose is buried? Can I cluck or bark? Use a whistle or hoot like an owl?

I've found that coughing, of all things, fascinates her, catches her attention, and makes her head swivel, after which she responds. If you walk with us, you will hear me clearing my throat repeatedly. What can I say? It works. She looks at me, comes to me, gets rewarded.

—*Slate.com*, October 6, 2005

Use paragraphs to manage transitions. Paragraphs often give direction to a paper. An opening paragraph, for example, can outline the content of a report or set the scene for a narrative. ○ In lengthy projects, you might need full paragraphs at critical junctures to summarize what has been covered and then send readers off in new directions.

You might even use very brief paragraphs—sometimes just a sentence or two long—to punctuate a piece by drawing attention to a turn in your thinking or offering a strong judgment. You've probably seen paragraphs that consist of nothing more than an indignant "Nonsense!" or a sarcastic "Go figure." There's a risk in penning paragraphs with so much attitude, but it's an option when the subject calls for it.

Design paragraphs for readability. It's common sense: Paragraph breaks work best when they coincide with shifts of thought within the writing itself. When they meet a new paragraph, readers assume that your ideas have moved in some (sometimes small) way. But paragraphs are often at the mercy of a text's physical environment as well. When you read news items on the Web, the short paragraphs used in those single-column stories look fine. But hit the "print this article" button and the text suddenly sprawls across the screen, becoming difficult to read.

The point? You should adjust the length and shape of paragraphs to the space where your words will appear.

shape a beginning p. 395

Strategic Transitions

What exactly makes words, sentences, and ideas flow from paragraph to paragraph as fluidly as Michael Phelps slipping through the water? *Transitional words and phrases*, many writers would reply—thinking of words such as *and, but, however, neither . . . nor, first . . . second . . . third*, and so on. Placed where readers need them, these connecting words make a paper read smoothly. But they are only part of the story.

Almost any successful piece of writing is held together by more devices than most writers can consciously juggle. A few of the ties—such as connections between pronouns and their referents—are almost invisible and seem to take care of themselves. Here are some guidelines for making smooth transitions between ideas in paragraphs and sections of your writing.

Steve Terrill/Getty Images

Common Transitions

Connection or Consequence	Contrast	Correlation	Sequence or Time	Indication
and	but	if . . . then	first . . . second	this
or	yet	either . . . or	and then	that
so	however	from . . . to	initially	there
because	nevertheless		subsequently	for instance
moreover	on the contrary		before	for example
consequently	despite		after	in this case
hence	still		until	
therefore	although		next	
			in conclusion	

Use appropriate transitional words and phrases. There's nothing complicated or arcane about them: You'll recognize every word in any list of transitions. But be aware that they have different functions and uses, with subtle distinctions even between words as close in meaning as *but* and *yet*.

Transitional words are often found at the beginnings of sentences and paragraphs simply because that's the place where readers expect a little guidance. There are no rules, per se, for positioning transitions—though they can be set off from the rest of the sentence with commas.

Use the right word or phrase to show time or sequence. Readers often need specific words or phrases to help keep events in order. Such expressions can simply mark off stages: *first, second, third*. Or they might help readers keep track of more complicated passages of time. Consider the subtle time signals in this paragraph from an essay about a writer's coffee obsession:

> For a time, coffee wasn't just my passion, it was my livelihood. In my 20s, I managed a coffee shop in a tony Cincinnati neighborhood where we played Yo La Tengo on the stereo in the morning and Miles Davis at night. When Starbucks came to town in the mid '90s, I signed on as an assistant manager and remained in that position until I was 28 years old. I watched with little shame as my friends became lawyers and business owners, journalists and chemists. I was proud of the fact that I knew my ginger-bready Ethiopian Sidamos from my rummy Ethiopian Harrars. I knew that it took 19 seconds to pull the perfect espresso shot. For a while, I considered entering a Starbucks training program that would

allow me to open a location of my own. I wanted coffee—really good coffee—to be my life.

—Keith Pandolfi, "The Case for Bad Coffee"

Use sentence structure to connect ideas. When you build sentences with similar structures, readers will infer that the ideas in them are related. Devices you can use to make this kind of linkage include parallelism O and repetition.

In the following example, the first three paragraphs of James P. Gannon's "America's Quiet Anger," you can see both strategies at work, setting up an emotional argument that continues in this pattern for another three paragraphs. Parallel items are highlighted.

> There is a quiet anger boiling in America.
>
> It is the anger of millions of hardworking citizens who pay their bills, send in their income taxes, maintain their homes, and repay their mortgage loans—and see their government reward those who do not.
>
> It is the anger of small town and Middle American folks who have never been to Manhattan, who put their savings in a community bank and borrow from a local credit union, who watch Washington lawmakers and presidents of both parties hand billions in taxpayer bailouts to the reckless Wall Street titans who brought down the economy in 2008.
>
> —*American Spectator*, March 20, 2010

Pay attention to nouns and pronouns. Understated transitions in a piece can occur between pronouns and their antecedents, but make sure the relationships between the nouns and pronouns are clear. O And, fortunately, readers usually don't mind encountering a pronoun over and over—except maybe *I*. Note how effortlessly Adam Nicolson moves between *George Abbot, he,* and *man* in the following paragraph from *God's Secretaries* (2003), in which he describes one of the men responsible for the King James translation of the Bible:

> George Abbot was perhaps the ugliest of them all, a morose, intemperate man, whose portraits exude a sullen rage. Even in death, he was portrayed on his tomb in Holy Trinity, Guilford, as a man of immense weight, with heavy, wrinkled brow and coldly open, staring eyes. He looks like a bruiser, a man of such conviction and seriousness that anyone would think twice about crossing him. What was it that made George Abbot so angry?

Use synonyms. Simply by repeating a noun from sentence to sentence, you make an obvious and logical connection within a paper—whether you are naming an object, an idea, or a person. To avoid monotony, vary terms you have to use frequently. But don't strain with archaic or inappropriate synonyms that will distract the reader.

Note the sensible variants on the word *trailer* in the following paragraph.

parallelism p. 571   help with common errors
                      p. 543

Hype and hysteria have always been a part of movie advertising, but the frenzy of film trailers today follows a visual style first introduced by music videos in the 1980s. The quick cut is everything, accompanied by a deafening soundtrack. Next time you go to a film, study the three or four previews that precede the main feature. How are these teasers constructed? What are their common features? What emotions or reactions do they raise in you? What might trailers say about the expectations of audiences today?

Use physical devices for transitions. You know all the ways movies manage transitions between scenes, from quick cuts to various kinds of dissolves. Writing has fewer visual techniques to mark transitions, but they are important. Titles and headings in lab reports, for instance, let your reader know precisely when you are moving from "Methods" to "Results" to "Discussion." In books, you'll encounter chapter breaks as well as divisions within chapters, sometimes marked by asterisks or perhaps a blank space. Seeing these markers, readers expect that the narration is changing in some way. Even the numbers in a list or shaded boxes in a magazine can be effective transitional devices, moving readers from one place to another.

Read a draft aloud to locate weak transitions. The best way to test your transitions in a paper or project may be to listen to yourself. As you read, mark every point in the paper where you pause, stumble, or find yourself adding a transitional word or phrase not in the original text. Record even the smallest bobble because tiny slips have a way of cascading into bigger problems.

Simone End/Getty Images

Memorable Openings and Closings

shape a
beginning
and an
ending

Introductions and conclusions are among the most important parts of a project. An introduction has to grab and hold a reader's attention while identifying topic and purpose and setting a context. A conclusion has to bring all the parts of a paper together and seal the deal with readers. None of these tasks—which vary according to genre—are easy.

Shape an introduction. The opening of some projects must follow a template. Writing a story for a newspaper, you begin by providing essential facts, identifying *who*, *what*, *where*, and *when*. You'll also follow conventions with technical materials (lab reports, research articles, scholarly essays). To get such introductions right, study models of these genres and then imitate their structures.

When not constrained by a template, you have many options for an introduction, the most straightforward being simply to announce your project. This blunt approach is common in academic papers where it makes sense to identify a subject and preview your plan for developing it. Quite often, the introductory material leads directly into a thesis or a hypothesis, as in the following student paper:

Paper opens by identifying its general topic or theme.

In her novel *Wuthering Heights* (1847), Emily Brontë presents the story of the families of Wuthering Heights and Thrushcross Grange through the seemingly impartial perspective of Nelly Dean, a servant who grows up with the families. Upon closer inspection, however, it becomes apparent that Nelly acts as much more than a bystander in the tragic events taking place around her. In her status as an outsider with influence over the families, Nelly strikingly resembles the Byronic hero Heathcliff and competes with him for power. Although the author depicts Heathcliff as the more overt gothic hero, Brontë allows the reader to infer from

Detailed thesis states what paper will prove.

Nelly's story her true character and role in the family. The author draws a parallel between Nelly Dean and Heathcliff in their relationships to the Earnshaw family, in their similar roles as tortured heroes, and in their competition for power within their adoptive families.

—Manasi Deshpande, "Servant and Stranger: Nelly and Heathcliff in *Wuthering Heights*"

Reports and arguments may open more slowly, using an introductory section that helps readers appreciate why an issue deserves attention. You might, for example, present an anecdote, describe a trend, or point to some phenomenon readers may not have noticed. Then you can thrash out its significance or implications.

Opening paragraphs can also deliver necessary background information. The trick is always to decide what exactly readers need to know about a subject. Provide too little background information on a subject and readers may find the project confusing. Supply too much context and you lose fans quickly.

Even towns sometimes need introductions. Yee haw!

And yet, even when readers know a subject well, be sure to supply basic facts about the project. Name names in your introduction, provide accurate titles for works you are discussing, furnish dates, and explain what exactly your subject is. Imagine readers from just slightly outside your target audience who might not instantly recall, for instance, that it was Shakespeare who wrote a play titled *Henry V* or that Edwin "Buzz" Aldrin was the *second* person to walk on the surface of the moon. Don't leave readers guessing. But it's fair game to intrigue them.

So give them reasons to enter your text. Invite them with a compelling incident or provocative story, with a recitation of surprising or intriguing facts, with a dramatic question, with a memorable description or quotation. Naturally, any opening has to be in sync with the material that follows—not outrageously emotional if the argument is sober, not lighthearted and comic if the paper has a serious theme.

Typically, readers use an introduction to determine whether they belong to the audience of the piece. A paper that opens with highly technical language says "specialists only," while a more personal or colloquial style welcomes a broader group. Readers are also making judgments about you in those opening lines, so you can't afford errors of fact or even grammar and usage there. Such slips-ups cloud their impression of all that follows.

One last bit of advice: Don't write an introduction until you're ready. The opening of a project can be notoriously difficult to frame because it does so much work. If you are blocked at the beginning of a project, plunge directly into the body of the paper and see what happens. You can even write the opening section last, after you know precisely where the paper goes. No one will know.

Draw a conclusion. Like introductions, conclusions serve different purposes and audiences. An e-mail to a professor may need no more of a sign-off than a signature, while a senior thesis could require a whole chapter to wrap things up. In reports and arguments, you typically use the concluding section to summarize what you've covered and draw out the implications. The following is the no-nonsense conclusion of a college report on a childhood developmental disorder, cri du chat syndrome (CDCS). Note that this summary paragraph also leads where many other scientific and scholarly articles do: to a call for additional research.

Major point

Major point

Conclusion ties
together main points
made in the paper,
using transitional
words and phrases.

Though research on CDCS remains far from abundant, existing studies prescribe early and ongoing intervention by a team of specialists, including speech-language pathologists, physical and occupational therapists, various medical and educational professionals, and parents. Such intervention has been shown to allow individuals with CDCS to live happy, long, and full lives. Their search, however, indicates that the syndrome affects all aspects of a child's development and should therefore be taken quite seriously. Most children require numerous medical interventions, including surgery (especially to correct heart defects), feeding tubes, body braces, and repeated treatment of infections. Currently, the best attempts are being made to help young children with CDCS reach developmental milestones earlier, communicate effectively, and function as independently as possible. However, as the authors of the aforementioned studies suggest, much more research is needed to clarify the causes of varying degrees of disability, to identify effective and innovative treatments/interventions (especially in the area of education), and to individualize intervention plans.

—Marissa Dahlstrom, "Developmental Disorders: Cri du Chat Syndrome"

On other occasions, you will want to finish dramatically and memorably, especially in arguments and personal narratives that seek to influence readers or change opinions. Since final paragraphs are what readers remember, it makes sense to use powerful language or memorable images. Here's the conclusion of a lengthy essay exploring the concept of adulthood:

Opening sentences
reflect on the complexity
of the discussion.

Social norms change.

Final sentences
offer a metaphor for
adulthood.

What adulthood means in a society is an ocean fed by too many rivers to count. . . . Science can advance understanding of maturity, but it can't get us all the way there. Social norms change, people opt out of traditional roles, or are forced to take them on way too soon. . . . Adulthood altogether is an Impressionist painting—if you stand far enough away, you can see a blurry picture, but if you press your nose to it, it's millions of tiny strokes. Imperfect, irregular, but indubitably part of a greater whole.

—Julie Beck, "When Are You Really an Adult?"

Informative Titles

Titles may not strike you as an important aspect of writing, but they can be. Sometimes the struggle to find a good title helps a writer shape a piece or define its main point. Of course, a proper title tells readers what a paper is about and makes searching for the document easier.

Use titles to focus documents. A title that is too broad early on in a project is a sure sign that you have yet to find a manageable topic. If all you have is "Sea Battles in World War II" or "Children in America," you need to do more reading and research. If no title comes to mind at all, it means you don't have a subject. ○ You're still brainstorming.

For academic papers, titles need to be descriptive. Consider these items culled at random from one issue of the *Stanford Undergraduate Research Journal*. As you might guess, scientific papers aimed at knowledgeable specialists have highly technical titles. Titles in the social sciences and humanities are less intimidating but just as focused on providing information about their subjects.

> "Molecular and Morphological Characterization of Two Species of Sea Cucumber, *Parastichopus parvimensis* and *Parastichopus californicus*, in Monterey, CA"
>
> — Christine O'Connell, Alison J. Haupt, Stephen R. Palumbi

> "Justifiers of the British Opium Trade: Arguments by Parliament, Traders, and the *Times* Leading Up to the Opium War"
>
> — Christine Su

> "The Incongruence of the Schopenhauerian Ending in Wagner's *Götterdämmerung*"
>
> — James Locus

develop a statement
p. 387

Create searchable titles. For academic or professional papers, a thoughtful title makes sense standing on its own and out of context. It should also include keywords by which it might be searched for in a database or online. For example, an essay titled "Smile!" wouldn't offer many clues about its content or purpose; far more useful is the title of a real journal article by Christina Kotchemidova, "From Good Cheer to 'Drive-By Smiling': A Social History of Cheerfulness." When Professor Kotchemidova's paper winds up in someone's bibliography or in an online database, readers know what its subject is.

If you must be clever or allusive, follow the cute title with a colon and an explanatory subtitle.

"Out, Damn'd Spot!: Images of Conscience and Remorse in Shakespeare's *Macbeth*"
"Out, Damn'd Spot!: Housebreaking Your Puppy"

Gerard Whyman/CartoonStock

"Out damn Spot!"

CartoonStock.com

Avoid whimsical or suggestive titles. A bad title will haunt you. At this point, you may not worry about publication, but documents take on a life of their own when uploaded to the Web or listed on a résumé. Any document posted where the public can search for it online needs a levelheaded title, especially when you enter the job market.

Capitalize and punctuate titles carefully. The guidelines for capitalizing titles vary between disciplines. See Chapters 53 and 54 for the MLA and APA guidelines, or consult the style manual for your discipline.

Your titles should avoid all caps, boldface, underscoring, and, with some exceptions, italics (titles within titles and foreign terms may be italicized; see examples above). For Web sites, newsletters, PowerPoint presentations, and so on, you can be bolder graphically. **O**

think visually p. 417

Design and Digital Media

part six

Understanding Digital Media

Media changes so fast that it's hard to keep up or predict anything. Who would have imagined, prior to the 2016 election season, that free Twitter messaging might have more impact on politics than costly television advertising. Surely, old-style political rallies wouldn't matter in such an era, and yet this time-honored medium roared back Don't assume it's secure to life too. Email?

Eric Fischer, using data from the Twitter streaming API and the Flickr Search API

Plotting Flickr and Twitter locations in Europe in 2011 produced this luminous map of the continent, suggesting the sweep of new media activity. Imagine how bright the map would be today.

Electronic media have indelibly altered the way we communicate *and* think. Predictably, schools, businesses, and professional organizations continue to find new uses for the tools and services we now take for granted—blogs, wikis, digital video, Web-mapping software, social networks, and more. And just as predictably, electronic media of all kinds play a role in many classrooms today, with multi-modal writing assignments increasingly common. Writing is no longer just about words on paper.

Choose a media format based on what you hope to accomplish.

You are employing new media if you contribute to a college service project hosted on a blog, schedule study sessions with classmates via Facebook, use slide software to spiff up a report to the student government, create an infographic to explain a concept in sociology, or even just find yourself enrolled in online courses.

Of course, a decision to compose with digital tools or to work in environments such as Facebook, Twitter, or Instagram should be based on what these media offer you. An electronic tool may support your project in ways that conventional printed texts simply cannot—and that's the reason to select it. Various media writing, reading, and composing options are described in the following table.

Format	Elements	Purpose	Software Technology/Tools
Social networks, group messaging, blogs	Online discussion postings; interactive; text; images; video; links	Create communities (fan, political, academic); distribute news and information	Facebook; Twitter; Snapchat; Reddit; Instagram; Tumblr; GroupMe; Medium; Blogger; WordPress
Web sites	Web-based information site; text; images; video; links; interactive posts	Compile and distribute information; establish presence on Web; sell merchandise, etc.	Dreamweaver; Drupal; WordPress; Google Sites
Wikis	Collaboratively authored linked texts and posts; Web-based; information; text; images; data	Create and edit collaborative documents based on community expertise; distribute and share information	DokuWiki; MediaWiki; Tiki Wiki; Wiki.com (search)
Podcasts, music, audio books	Digital file-based audio or (sometimes) video recording; downloadable; voice; music; episodic	Distribute mainly audio texts; document or archive audio texts and performances	Audacity; GarageBand; Librivox

(continued)

Format	Elements	Purpose	Software Technology/Tools
Maps, data visualization, infographics	Interactive image maps; text; data; images; mind maps	Give spatial or geographical dimension to data, texts, ideas; help users locate or visualize information	iMapBuilder; Google Earth; Google Maps; Infogram; MindMup, NovaMind, Photoshop; Piktochart, RawGraphs, Tableau, TimeMapper, Venngage, Voyant
Video	Recorded images; live-action images; enhanced slides; animation; sound; music	Record events; provide visual documentation; create presentations; furnish instructions, etc.	Animoto; Camtasia; iMovie; Movie Maker; Blender; Soundslides, YouTube
Research & databases	Texts; videos; audio files; images; .pdfs	Collect data; index sources; search sources; create bibliographies; share data	EasyBib, Endnote, Mendeley, Qiqqa, Zotero

Use social networks and blogs to create communities. You know, of course, that Facebook, Twitter, Instagram, Tumblr, and the like have transformed the way people share their lives and ideas. Social networks such as these are vastly more interactive versions of the online exchanges hosted by groups or individuals on blogs—which typically focus on topics such as politics, news, sports, technology, and entertainment. Social networks and blogs integrate comments, images, videos, and links in various ways; they are constantly updated, most are searchable, and some are archived.

College courses might use social networks and blogs to spur discussion of class materials, to distribute information, and to document research activities. Students in courses often set up their own social media groups. When networking or blogging is part of a course assignment, understand the ground rules. Instructors often require a defined number of postings/comments of a specific length. Participate regularly by reading and commenting on other students' posts; by making substantive comments of your own on the assigned topic; and by contributing relevant images, videos, and links.

Keep your academic postings focused, title them descriptively, and make sure they reflect the style of the course—most likely informal, but not quite as colloquial as public online groups. Pay attention to grammar and mechanics too. Avoid the vitriol you may encounter on national sites: Remember that anyone—from your mother to a future employer—might read your remarks.

Create Web sites to share information. Not long ago, building Web sites was at the leading edge of technological savvy in the classroom. Today, social networks, blogs, and wikis are far more efficient vehicles for academic communication. Still, Web sites remain useful because of their capacity to organize large amounts of text and information online. A Web site you create for a course might report research findings or provide a portal to information on a complex topic.

When creating a site with multiple pages, plan early on how to organize that information; the structure will depend on your purpose and audience. A simple site with sequential information (e.g., a photo-essay) might lead readers through items one by one. More complicated sites may require a complex, hierarchical structure, with materials organized around careful topic divisions. The more comprehensive the site, the more deliberately you will need to map out its structure, allowing for easy navigation and growth.

Use wikis to collaborate with others.

If you have ever looked at Wikipedia, you know what a wiki does: It enables a group to collaborate on the development of an ongoing online project—from a comprehensive encyclopedia to focused databases on just about any imaginable topic. Such an effort combines the knowledge of all its contributors, ideally making the whole greater than its parts.

In academic courses, instructors may ask class members to publish articles on an existing wiki—in which case you should read the site guidelines, examine its current entries and templates, and then post your item. More likely, though, you will use wiki software to develop a collaborative project for the course itself—bringing together research on a specific academic topic. A wiki might even be used for a service project in which participants gather useful information about nutrition, jobs, or arts opportunities for specific communities.

As always with electronic projects, you need to learn the software—which will involve not only uploading material to the wiki but also editing and developing texts that classmates have already placed there.

Make videos and podcasts to share information.

With most cell phones now equipped with cameras, digital video has become the go-to medium for recording just about any event or for sharing ideas and information. In a sociology or government course, you might want to record important interviews; in a biology or engineering course, a video could be the best way to demonstrate a complex procedure. Software such as Movie Maker or iMovie can help you tell a story or make an argument; you can edit and mix digital scenes, refine the sound, add special effects and captions, and so on. If your subject is better served by animation, software such as Blender gives you different choices. You can construct nonnarrative kinds of video writing by combining text, film clips, still photos, and music using software such as Animoto, Soundslides, or Camtasia.

Podcasts remain a viable option for sharing downloadable audio or video files. Playable on various portable devices from MP3 players to phones, podcasts are often published in series. Academic podcasts usually need to be scripted and edited. Producing a podcast is a two-step process. First you must record the podcast; then you need to upload it to a Web site for distribution. Software such as GarageBand can do both.

Use maps to position ideas.
You use mapping services such as Google Maps whenever you search online for a restaurant, store, or hotel. The service quickly provides maps and directions to available facilities, often embellished with links, information, and images. Not surprisingly, Google Maps, the related Google Earth, and other mapping software are finding classroom applications.

Multimedia maps also make it possible to display information such as economic trends, movements of people, climate data, and other variables graphically and dynamically, using color, text, images, and video/audio clips to emphasize movement and change across space and time. Even literary texts can be mapped so that scholars or readers may track events or characters as they move in real or imaginary landscapes. Mapping thus becomes a vehicle for reporting and sharing information, telling personal stories, revealing trends, exploring causal relationships, or making arguments.

Use appropriate digital formats.
Digital documents come in many forms, but you will use familiar word-processing, presentation, or spreadsheet software for most of your academic work. Compatibility is rarely an issue today when you move materials across computer platforms (PC to Mac) or download a presentation in a classroom for an oral report. Still, it never hurts to check ahead of time if, for example, you use Keynote or Prezi for a report rather than the more common PowerPoint.

Occasionally you need to save digital files in special formats. Sharing a file with someone using an older version of Word or Office may require saving a document in compatibility mode (.doc) rather than the now-standard .docx mode. Or moving across different applications may be easier if you use a plain text (.txt) or rich text format (.rtf)—in which case your document will lose some features, though the text will be preserved. When you want to share a document exactly as you wrote it and send it successfully across platforms, choose the .pdf mode. Files in .pdf form arrive just as you sent them, without any shifts in headings, alignments, or image locations—important, for example, when you send a résumé. Just as important, a .pdf file you create cannot be easily altered.

Even if you have only a limited knowledge of differing image file formats (such as JPG, GIF, or TIFF), you probably understand that digital files come in varying sizes. The size of a digital-image file is directly related to the quality, or resolution, of the image. Attach a few high-resolution 26-megapixel photos to an e-mail and you'll clog the recipient's mailbox (or the e-mail will bounce back).

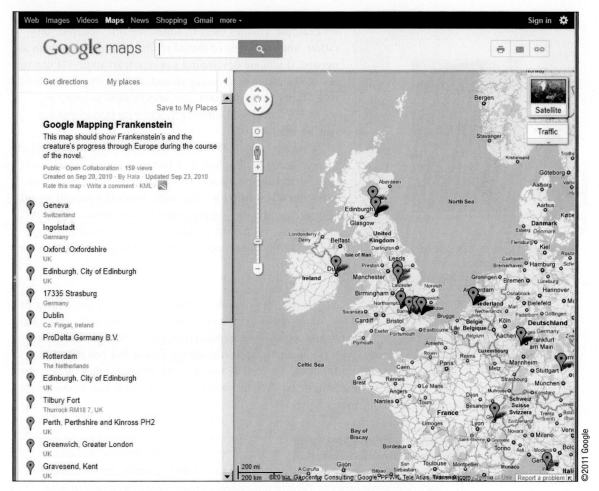

English instructor Hala Herbly asked students to map the movements across Europe of the monster from Mary Shelley's novel *Frankenstein*.

For most Web pages and online documents, compressed or lower-resolution images will be acceptable. On the other hand, if you intend to print an image—in a paper or brochure, for example—use the highest-resolution image (the greatest number of pixels) available to assure maximum sharpness and quality.

Edit and save digital elements. Nonprint media texts often require as much revising and editing as traditional written ones. In fact, the tools for manipulating video, audio, and still-image files are among the most remarkable accomplishments

John J. Ruszkiewicz

Image-editing software offers numerous options for enhancing picture files. Look for these options on format tabs, palettes, or dropdown menus.

of the digital age. Even the simplest image-editing software, for example, enables users to adjust the tint, contrast, saturation, and sharpness of digital photographs or crop them as needed. If you are developing a podcast, an audio file can be tweaked a dozen ways using an audio editor like GarageBand or Audacity; such programs can also be used to create or refine musical clips. Comparable software is available for editing video clips.

Do keep careful tabs on any electronic content you collect for a project. Create a dedicated folder on your desktop, hard drive, or online storage and save each item with a name that will remind you where it came from. Keeping a printed record of images, with more detailed information about copyrights and sources, will pay dividends later, when you are putting your project or paper together and need to give proper credit to contributors.

Respect copyrights. The images you find, whether online or in print, belong to someone. You cannot use someone else's property—photographs, Web sites, brochures, posters, magazine articles, and so on—for commercial purposes without permission. You may use a reasonable number of images in academic papers, but you must be careful not to go beyond "fair use," especially for any work you put online. Search the term "academic fair use" online for detailed guidelines. Be prepared, too, to document images in academic research papers.

Thinking about Writing   Most of the software programs mentioned in this chapter have Web sites that describe their features, and some sites even include sample projects. Explore one or two of these programs online to learn about their capabilities. Then describe a new media project you would like to create using the software.

Tables, Graphs, and Infographics

Just as images and photographs are often the media of choice for conveying visual information, tables, graphs, and other "infographics" are essential tools for displaying numerical and statistical data. They take raw data and transform it into a story or picture readers can interpret.

Most such items are created in spreadsheet programs such as Excel that format charts and graphs and offer numerous design templates—although you will find basic graphics tools in Word and PowerPoint, as well. Charts and graphs can be drawn with software such as Adobe Illustrator, Infogram, Venngage, and others.

Creating effective tables and graphs is an art in itself, driven as always by your purpose and audience. A table in a printed report that a reader will study can be rich in detail; a bar graph on screen for only a few moments must make its point quickly and memorably. Function always trumps appearance. Yet there's no question that handsome visual texts appeal to audiences. So spend the time necessary to design effective items. Use color to emphasize and clarify graphs, not just to decorate them. Label items clearly (avoiding symbols or keys that are hard to interpret), and don't add more detail than necessary.

In academic projects, be sure to label (*Fig.*, *Table*), number, and caption your important graphic items, especially any that you mention in your text. Both MLA and APA style offer guidelines for handling labels; the APA rules are particularly detailed and specific.

Use tables to present statistical data. Tables can do all kinds of work. They are essential for organizing and recording information as it comes in, for example, daily weather events: temperature,

Figure 1 Data from College Board, *Education Pays, 2016: The Benefits of Higher Education for Individuals and Society* by Jennifer Ma, Mateo Pender, and Meredith Welch, p. 24.

	Median Earnings of Full-Time Year-Round Workers, 2010–2014							
Age	Less than a High School Diploma	High School Diploma	Some College, No Degree	Associate Degree	Bachelor's Degree	Master's Degree	Doctoral Degree	Professional Degree
25 to 29	$22,600	$28,600	$31,200	$35,200	$44,100	$50,600	$61,900	$57,200
50 to 54	$29,000	$39,500	$47,200	$51,500	$71,800	$83,500	$106,900	$127,400
60 to 64	$29,100	$37,400	$45,900	$50,700	$65,500	$77,600	$105,400	$123,600

Sources: U.S. Census Bureau, American Community Survey, 2010–2014 Five-Year Public Use Microdata Sample; calculations by the authors.

> **Often the most effective way to describe, explore, and summarize a set of numbers— even a very large set—is to look at pictures of those numbers.**

—Edward R. Tufte

Inge Druckrey

precipitation, wind velocities, and so on. A table may also show trends or emphasize contrasts. In such cases, tables may make an argument (in a print ad, for example) or readers may be left to interpret complex data on their own—one of the pleasures of studying such material.

Tables typically consist of horizontal rows and vertical columns into which you drop data. The axes of the chart provide different and significant ways of presenting data, relating *x* to *y*: for example, in Table 1, the annual incomes of workers with different educational attainments are plotted against age, showing that people with more education earn more all their lives.

In designing a table, determine how many horizontal rows and vertical columns are needed, how to label them, and whether to use color or shading to enhance the readability of the data. Software templates will provide options. Good tables can be very plain. In fact, many of the tables on federal government Web sites, although packed with information, are dirt simple and yet quite clear.

Use line graphs to display changes or trends. Line graphs are dynamic images, visually plotting and connecting variables on horizontal *x*- and vertical *y*-axes so that readers can see how relationships change or trends emerge, usually over time. As such, line graphs often contribute to political or social arguments by tracking fluctuations in income, unemployment, educational attainment, stock prices, and so on.

Properly designed, line graphs are easy to read and informative, especially when just a single variable is presented. But it is possible to display several items on

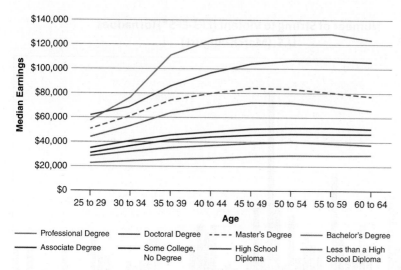

Figure 2 Median Earnings (in 2014 Dollars) of Full-Time Year-Round Workers by Age and Education Level, 2010–2014. Data from College Board.

an axis, complicating the line graph but increasing the amount of information it offers. Figure 2, also from *Education Pays 2016* and using the same data in Figure 1, visually highlights the steep rise in income that comes from greater educational attainment.

Use bar and column graphs to plot relationships within sets of data.
Column and bar graphs use rectangles to represent information either horizontally (bar graph) or vertically (column graph). In either form, these graphs emphasize differences and can show changes over time; they enable readers to grasp relationships that would otherwise take many words to explain. Bar and column graphs present data precisely, if their *x*- and *y*-axes are carefully drawn to scale. In Figure 3, for example, a reader can determine the number of major tornadoes in any of more than fifty years and also note a slight trend toward fewer severe storms.

But it is easy to ask a single graphic image to do too much. For example, many readers probably find Figure 4 hard to interpret. Is this chart about the number of storms, their growing frequency, or their actual and adjusted costs? Storm effects in the background of the graphic just add to the clutter.

Figure 3 Number of Strong to Violent (EF3–EF5) Tornadoes. Source: From NOAA Satellite and Information Service. National Oceanic and Atmospheric Administration and the Department of Commerce.

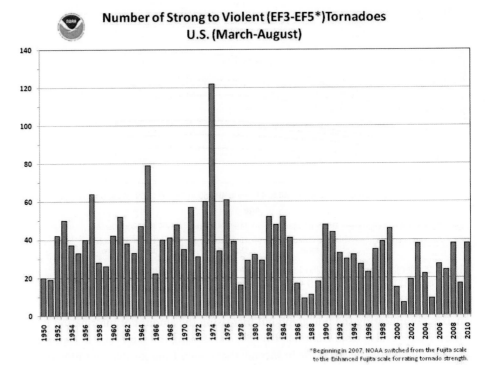

Number of Strong to Violent (EF3-EF5*)Tornadoes U.S. (March-August)

*Beginning in 2007, NOAA switched from the Fujita scale to the Enhanced Fujita scale for rating tornado strength.

Figure 4 Billion Dollar U.S. Weather Disasters 1980–2011. From NOAA Satellite and Information Service. National Oceanic and Atmospheric Administration, National Environmental Satellite, Data and Information Service, and the National Climatic Data Center. Source: NOAA Satellite and Information Service.

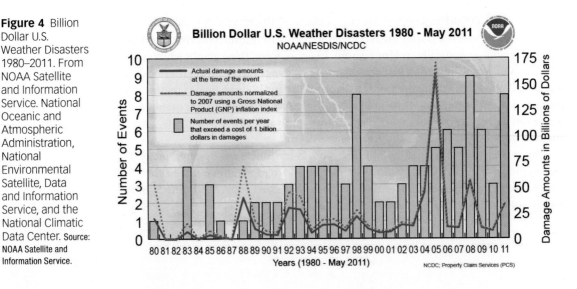

Billion Dollar U.S. Weather Disasters 1980 - May 2011
NOAA/NESDIS/NCDC

Actual damage amounts at the time of the event

Damage amounts normalized to 2007 using a Gross National Product (GNP) inflation index

Number of events per year that exceed a cost of 1 billion dollars in damages

Number of Events

Damage Amounts in Billions of Dollars

Years (1980 - May 2011)

NCDC; Property Claim Services (PCS)

Use pie charts to display proportions. A typical pie chart is a circle broken into segments that represent some proportion of a whole. Such charts illustrate which parts of that whole have greater or lesser significance, but they do not display precise numbers well. Note, for example, that while Figure 5 makes it immediately clear that people spend most of their leisure time watching TV, the actual amounts of time involved in each leisure activity have to be added outside the chart. And since the segments in a typical pie chart need to total 100 percent, you sometimes have to include—as the Bureau of Labor Statistics chart does—a segment called "Others / Don't know" to account for items not actually present in the major categories.

Pie-chart sections can be cut only so thin before they begin to lose clarity. If you wanted to use a pie chart to depict dozens of items—say the payrolls of all thirty major league baseball teams—you'd find yourself with slivers readers couldn't interpret confidently. Better to transfer the data to a bar graph that could incorporate more detailed information.

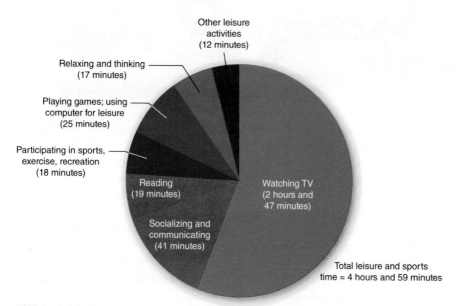

NOTE: Data include all persons age 15 and over. Data include all days of the week and are annual averages for 2015.

Figure 5 Leisure time on the average day. Source: Bureau of Labor Statistics, American Time Use Survey.

Figure 6 "Making a Persuasive Infographic" was designed by Beck Wise for students in her own writing course. To watch its embedded videos, go to magic .piktochart.com /output/15053202 -rhe306-fographic -tutorial. Beck Wise.

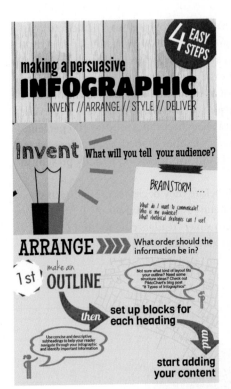

Explore the possibilities of infographics. Under the rubric of "infographics," many organizations and information specialists create data-driven visual texts about subjects from climate change to trends in music. Such presentations part ways with traditional academic conventions to tell lively but information-rich stories. One writer calls these focused presentations—freely combining charts, tables, timelines, maps, and other design elements—"visual essays." But many infographics are, in fact, "visual arguments" that use the medium to support particular claims or points of view: They combine images and data to dramatize an issue.

Various tools are available online to support the creation of infographics, including Infogram, Piktochart, StatPlanet, and Wordle. For more about infographics and many examples, search the term online.

Thinking about Writing   Visual texts such as the one Beck Wise designed may not be accessible to all readers. So she also created a "plain text version" that could be machine-readable (not reprinted here).

Designing Print and Online Documents

Much advice about good visual design is common sense: *Of course*, academic and professional documents should look uncluttered, consistent, and harmonious. But it is not always easy to translate principles into practice. Nor are any visual guidelines absolute. A balanced and consistent design is exactly what you want for research reports and government documents, but brochures or infographics may need more snap.

Understand the power of images. Most of us realize how powerful images can be, particularly when they perfectly capture a moment or make an argument that words alone struggle to express. The famous "Blue Marble" shot of the Earth taken by *Apollo 17* in 1972 is one such image—conveying both the wonder and fragility of our planet hanging in space.

Visual texts can be important elements in your own work. Use photographs to tell arresting stories or use videos to underscore important points in an argument. In fact, you can craft the style of any page or screen—its colors, shapes, headings, type fonts, and so on—to make a text more visually appealing, focused, and accessible.

Be sure, though, to identify or caption any photos, videos, or audio files in your project. Captions, in particular, help readers appreciate the significance of the specific texts you have included. If you also number these items in longer papers (e.g., *Fig. 1; Table 4*), you can direct readers to them unambiguously.

NASA Photo/Alamy Stock Photo

417

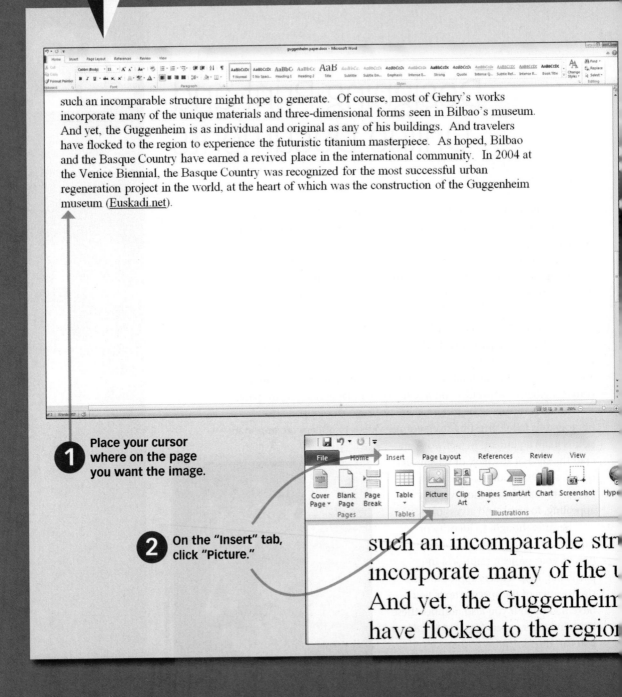

1 Place your cursor where on the page you want the image.

2 On the "Insert" tab, click "Picture."

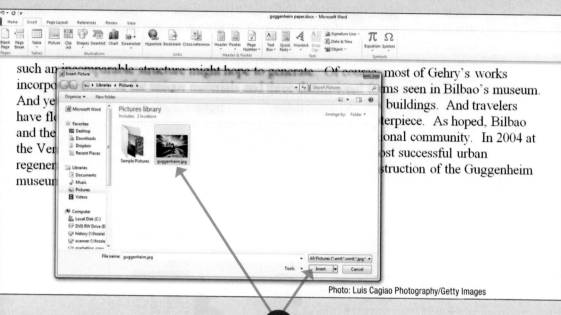

such an incomparable structure might hope to generate. Of course, most of Gehry's works incorpo... ...ms seen in Bilbao's museum. And ye... ...buildings. And travelers have fl... ...terpiece. As hoped, Bilbao and the... ...onal community. In 2004 at the Ven... ...ost successful urban regener... ...struction of the Guggenheim museum...

Photo: Luis Cagiao Photography/Getty Images

3 **Select an image from your folder, then click "Insert."**

4 **✓Done.**

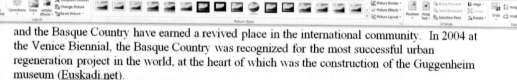

and the Basque Country have earned a revived place in the international community. In 2004 at the Venice Biennial, the Basque Country was recognized for the most successful urban regeneration project in the world, at the heart of which was the construction of the Guggenheim museum (Euskadi.net).

Luis Cagiao Photography/Getty Images

Keep page designs simple and uncluttered. Simple doesn't mean a design should be simplistic, only that you shouldn't try to do more on a page than it (or your design skills) can handle. You want readers to find information they need, navigate your document without missteps, and grasp the structure of your project. Key information should stand out. If you make the basic design intuitive, you can present lots of information without a page feeling cluttered.

Consider, for example, how cleverly Anthro Technology Furniture uses design cues as simple as *Step 1, Step 2,* and *Step 3* to guide consumers on a Web page through the complex process of configuring a workstation. Readers simply move left to right across a page, making specific choices. They don't feel overwhelmed by the options, even though the material is detailed.

Horizontal header guides reader across page.

Configuring the piece of furniture is broken into four easy steps.

Thumbnail images depict wide range of possible accessories.

Special box keeps track of consumer's decisions.

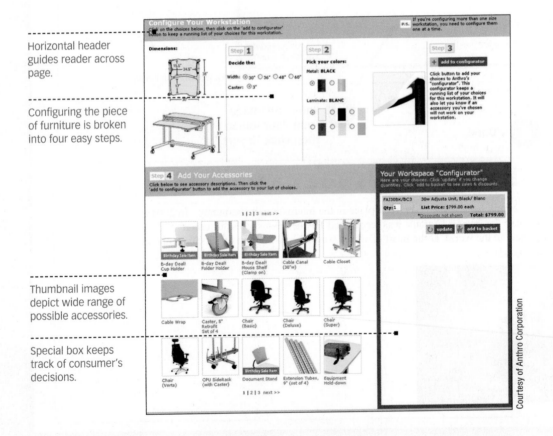

Courtesy of Anthro Corporation

Keep the design logical and consistent. Readers should grasp the logic of a design quickly and then understand how its elements operate throughout a document—especially on Web sites, in PowerPoint presentations, and in long papers. It might be noted, though, that infographics sometimes cultivate a deliberate clutter, often using complex visuals to move you through a series of related texts, images, videos, and more.

Look to successful Web sites for models of logical, consistent, and yet complex design. Many sites build their pages around distinct horizontal and vertical columns that help readers find information. A main menu generally appears near the top of the page, more detailed navigational links are usually located in a narrow side column, and featured stories often appear in wide columns in the center. To separate columns as well as individual items, the site designers use headlines, horizontal rules, images, or some combination of these devices. Handled well, pages are easy to navigate and thick with information, yet somehow they seem uncluttered.

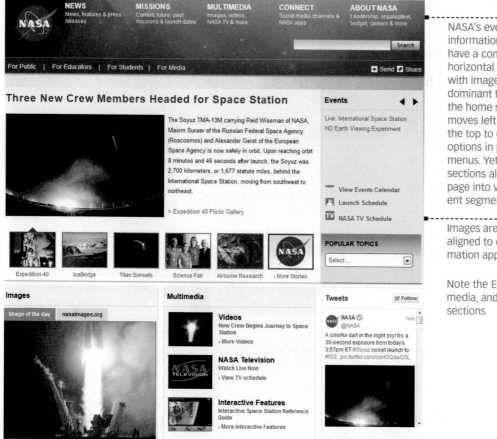

NASA's ever-evolving, information-rich pages have a consistent horizontal orientation with images now more dominant than ever. On the home screen, the eye moves left to right across the top to explore major options in pull-down menus. Yet distinct boxed sections also break the page into visually coherent segments.

Images are carefully aligned to convey information appealingly.

Note the Events, Multimedia, and Tweets sections

NASA

To attract readers, interior section previews top the simple masthead.

Bold headline gives impact to this national story.

Pittsburgh Post-Gazette

ONE OF AMERICA'S GREAT NEWSPAPERS

STEELERS FANS IN MIDSEASON FORM

Trump replaces Priebus

Local sports story dominates the news, importance signaled by placement and upbeat, eye-catching photo.

No clear path for GOP after latest repeal effort fails

Inmate beaten; family wants answers

Pa. loosens Highmark restrictions

Dental clinic gives hundreds reason to smile

Below the fold, another photo emphasizes a human-interest story.

North Korea's second ICBM test puts much of U.S. within range

Keep the design balanced. Think of balance as an operative term—what you hope to achieve *overall* in a design. You probably don't want many pages that, if split down the middle, would show mirror images. Strive instead for dynamic designs that keep the eye moving—in which, for example, a large photograph on one side of a document is offset on the other by blocks of print and maybe several smaller images. The overall effect achieved is rough symmetry, even though various page elements may all differ in size and shape.

You can see conventional design principles at work on the front pages of most newspapers (print or online), where editors try to come up with a look that gives impact to the news. They have many elements to work with, including their paper's masthead, headlines of varying size, photographs and images, columns of copy, screened boxes, and much more. The pages of a newspaper can teach you a lot about design.

But you can learn, too, from the boundaries being pushed by designers of Web infographics, who use elaborate media effects to present information efficiently yet imaginatively (see an example in Chapter 41). Unlike newspapers, magazines, or full Web sites, which must follow consistent specifications for page after page, a typical infographic focuses on a single theme or subject, and its creator chooses the media tools best suited to the topic, whether graphs, flowcharts, maps, images, diagrams, cutaways—or all the above.

Use templates sensibly. If you have the time and talent to design all your own documents, that's terrific. But for many projects, you could do worse than to begin with the templates offered by many software products. The templates in Microsoft Office, for example, help you create business letters, brochures, newsletters, signs, and much more. It sets up a generic document, placing the document's margins, aligning key elements and graphics, and offering an array of customizations. No two projects based on the same template need look alike.

If you resist borrowing such materials from software, not wanting yet another part of your life packaged by corporate types, know that it is tough to design documents from scratch. Even when you do intend to create an item yourself, consider studying a template to figure out what parts it must have and how to assemble a complex document. Take what you learn from the model and then strike out on your own.

Coordinate your colors. Your mother was right: Pay attention to shades and patterns when you dress and when you design color documents. To learn elementary principles of color coordination, try searching "color wheel" on the Web, but recognize that the subject is both complicated and more art than science. As an amateur, keep your design palettes relatively conventional and model your work on documents that you find attractive.

For academic papers, the text is always black and the background is white. Color is fine in graphs and illustrations if the paper will be reviewed onscreen or printed in color. But be sure that no important elements are lost if the document is printed in black and white: A bar graph that relies on subtle shades of color to display differences might become unreadable. For Web sites and other projects, keep background shades light, if you use them at all, and maintain adequate contrast between text and background. Avoid either bright or pale fonts for passages of text.

Use headings if needed. Readers appreciate headings as pathways through a text. In academic work, they should be descriptive rather than clever. If you have prepared a good scratch or topic outline, the major points may provide you with almost ready-made headings. O Just like items in an outline, headings at the same level in your project should be roughly parallel in phrasing. O

A short paper (three to five pages) doesn't require much more than a title. For longer papers (ten to twenty pages), it's possible to use top-level items from your outline as headings. For some projects, especially in the sciences, you should use the headings you're given. This is especially true for lab reports and scientific articles, and you shouldn't vary from the template: for example, *Authors, Title, Abstract, Results, Discussion, Conclusion, References, Acknowledgments.*

Choose appropriate fonts. There are probably dozens or even hundreds of fonts to work with on your computer, but simple is generally best. Here is some basic information to help you choose an appropriate font for your needs.

Serif fonts, such as Times New Roman or Garamond, show thin flares and embellishments (called serifs; circled in the illustration on p. 425) at the tops and bottoms of their letters and characters. These fonts have a traditional look. In contrast, *sans serif* fonts, such as Arial or Helvetica, lack the decorations of serif fonts. They are smoother and more contemporary. On the sample newspaper front page (see p. 422), serif fonts dominate, but sans serif fonts are used for several minor items.

Serif fonts are more readable than sans serif for extended passages of writing, such as papers. Headings in a sans serif font can offer welcome contrast in a document that uses a serif font for its text. Some designers prefer sans serif fonts for Web sites and PowerPoint presentations, especially for headings.

For typical academic projects, all text, headings, and other elements—including the title—are set in one font size, either 10 or 12 point. The standard font is Times New Roman. In professional or business projects, however, such as résumés, newsletters, or PowerPoint slides, you may want to vary fonts and type sizes in order to set off headings, captions, and headlines from other elements.

order ideas p. 377   help with common errors p. 550

You can boldface words and phrases selectively to make them stand out clearly on a page. But boldfaced items or headings close together can make a page look heavy and cluttered. Such items should be rare. Never use boldface as the regular text throughout a project. If you want an emphatic font, find one that looks that way in its regular form.

Fonts described as *display* and *decorative* are designed to attract attention (see, for example the masthead of the *Pittsburgh Post-Gazette* on p. 422). You should avoid them for academic and professional writing, but you may want to explore their use when creating posters, brochures, or special PowerPoint presentations. Never use them for extended passages of writing.

Times New Roman

Times New Roman, a serif font.

Helvetica

Helvetica, a sans serif font.

Academic Research and Sources

7

part seven

43

plan a project

Beginning Research

Research can be part of any writing project. When doing research, you examine what is already known about a topic and then, sometimes, push the boundaries of knowledge forward. For humanities courses, this typically involves examining a wide range of books, articles, and Web sources. In the social and natural sciences, you might perform experiments or do field research and then share new data you have collected on a topic. For more on choosing a genre, see Chapter 3, "Claiming Topics."

So where do you begin your research project, and how do you keep from being swamped by the sheer quantity of information available? You need smart research strategies.

Know your assignment. When one is provided, review the assignment sheet for any project to establish exactly the kinds of research the paper requires. You may need to use only the reference section of the

John J. Ruszkiewicz

library for a one-page position paper related to a class discussion. An argument about current events will usually send you to newspapers, magazines, Web sites, and social media, while a full-length term paper will need references drawn from academic books and journals. (For details and advice on a wide variety of assignments, refer to Parts 2 and 3.)

Come up with a plan. Research takes time because you have to find sources, read them, record your findings, and then write about them. Most research projects also require full documentation and some type of formal presentation, either as a research paper or, perhaps, an oral report, poster presentation, or Ted Talk. This stuff cannot be thrown together the night before. One way to avoid mayhem is to prepare a project calendar that ties specific tasks to specific dates. Simply creating the schedule (and you should keep it *simple*) might even jump-start your actual research. At a minimum, record important due dates in your phone or day planner. Here's a full schedule for a serious research paper with three key deadlines.

Schedule: Research Paper

February 20: Topic proposal due
____ Explore and select a topic
____ Do preliminary library/Web research
____ Define a thesis or hypothesis
____ Prepare an annotated bibliography

March 26: First draft due
____ Read, summarize, paraphrase, and synthesize sources
____ Organize the paper
____ Draft the paper

April 16: Final draft due
____ Get peer feedback on draft
____ Revise the project
____ Check documentation
____ Edit the project

Find a manageable topic. For a research project, this often means defining a problem you can solve with available resources. (For advice on finding and developing topics, see Part 4, especially Chapter 27, "Shaping a Thesis.") Look for a question within the scope of the assignment that you can answer in the time available.

When asked to submit a ten- or twenty-page term paper, some writers panic, thinking they need a massive, general topic to fill up all those blank pages. But the opposite is true. You will have more success finding useful sources if you break off small but intriguing parts of much larger subjects.

not Military Aircraft, *but* The Development of Jet Fighters in World War II

not The History of Punk Rock, *but* The Influence of 1970s Punk Rock on Nirvana

not Developmental Disorders in Children, *but* Cri du Chat Syndrome

It's fine to read widely at first to find a general subject. But you have to narrow the project to a specific topic so that you can explore focused questions in your preliminary research. At this early stage in the research process, your goal is to turn a topic idea into a claim at least one full sentence long. ○

In the natural and social sciences, topics sometimes evolve from research problems already on the table in various fields. Presented with such a research agenda, do a "review of the literature" to find out what represents state-of-the-art thinking on the topic. You do this by reading what others have published on this subject in major journals. Then create an experiment in which your specific research question—offered as a claim called a *hypothesis*—either confirms the direction of ongoing work in the field or advances or changes it. In basic science courses, get plenty of advice from your instructor about formulating workable research questions and hypotheses.

❚❚ Research is formalized curiosity. It is poking and prying with a purpose. **❚❚**

—Zora Neale Hurston

Carl Van Vechten/ Library of Congress, Prints and Photographs Division, LC-USZ62-79898.

Ask for help. During preliminary research, you'll quickly learn that not all sources are equal. ○ They differ in purpose, method, media, audience, and authority. Until you get your legs as a researcher, never hesitate to ask questions about research tools and strategies: Get recommendations about the best available journals, books, and authors from instructors and reference librarians. Ask them which publishers, institutions, and experts carry the most intellectual weight in their fields. If your topic is highly specialized, expect to spend additional time tracking down sources from outside your own library.

Distinguish between primary and secondary sources. A *primary source* is a document that provides an eyewitness account of an event or phenomenon; a *secondary source* is a step or two removed, an article or book that interprets or reports on events and phenomena described in primary sources. The famous Zapruder film of the John F. Kennedy assassination in Dallas (November 22, 1963) is a memorable primary historical document; the many books or articles that draw on the film to comment on the assassination are secondary sources. Both types of sources are useful to you as a researcher.

Use primary sources when doing research that breaks new ground. Primary sources represent raw data—letters, journals, newspaper accounts, official documents, laws, court opinions, statistics, research reports, audio and video recordings, and so on. Working with primary materials, you generate your own ideas about a subject, free of anyone else's opinions or explanations. Or you can review the actual evidence others

develop a statement
p. 362

find reliable sources
p. 448

have used to make their claims and arguments, perhaps reinterpreting their findings, correcting them, or bringing a new perspective to the subject.

Use secondary sources to learn what others have discovered or claimed about a subject. In many fields, you spend most of your time reviewing secondary materials, especially when a subject is new to you. Secondary sources include scholarly books and articles, encyclopedias, magazine pieces, and many Web sites. In academic assignments, you may find yourself moving between different kinds of materials, first reading a primary text like *Hamlet* and then reading various commentaries on it.

Record every source you examine. Whether you examine sources in libraries or look at them online, *you must* accurately list, right from the start, every research item you encounter, gathering the following information:

- Authors, editors, translators, sponsors (of Web sites), or other major contributors
- Titles, subtitles, edition numbers, and volumes
- Container/publication information—that is, within what is the source found: book, periodical, movie, TV series, website, etc. Record places of publication and publishers (for books); titles of magazines and journals, as well as volume and page numbers; dates of publication and access (the latter for online materials)
- Page numbers, URLs, electronic pathways, keywords, DOIs (digital object identifiers), or other locators

You'll need this information later to document your sources.

It might seem obsessive to collect so much data on books and articles you may not even use. But when you spend weeks or months on an assignment, you don't want to have to backtrack, wondering at some point, "Did I read this source?" A log tells you whether you have.

Prepare a topic proposal. Your instructor may request a topic proposal. Typically, this includes a topic idea, a draft thesis or hypothesis, potential sources, your intended approach, and a list of potential problems. It may also include an annotated bibliography of the books, articles, and other materials you anticipate using in your project—see Chapter 17 for more on annotated bibliographies.

Remember that such proposals are written to get feedback about your project's feasibility and that even a good idea raises questions. The following sample proposal for a short project is directed chiefly at classmates, who must respond via electronic discussion board as part of the assignment.

Eades 1

Micah Eades

Professor Kurtz

English 201

March 20, 20--

Causal Analysis Proposal: Awkward Atmospheres

People don't like going to the doctor's office. You wait in an office room decorated from the 1980s reading *Highlights* or last year's *Field & Stream* and listen to patients in the next room talking about the details of their proctology exam. Since I am planning a future as a primary care physician, I don't want people to dread coming to see me.

My paper will propose that patient dissatisfaction with visits to their physicians may be due not entirely to fear of upcoming medical examinations but rather to the unwelcoming atmosphere of most waiting and treatment rooms. More specifically, I will examine the negative effect that noise, poor interior design, and unsympathetic staff attitudes may have on patient comfort. I will propose that these factors have a much larger impact on patient well-being than previously expected. Additionally, I will propose possible remedies and ways to change these negative perceptions.

My biggest problem may be finding concrete evidence for my claims. For evidence, I do intend to cite the relatively few clinical studies that have been conducted on patient satisfaction and atmosphere. My audience will be a tough crowd: doctors who have neither an awareness of the problems I describe nor much desire to improve the ambience of their offices.

Title indicates that proposal responds to a specific assignment.

Opening paragraph offers a rationale for subject choice.

Describes planned content and structure of paper.

Has done enough research to know that literature on subject is not extensive.

Paper will be directed to a specific audience.

Consulting Experts

44

ask for help

Forget about *expert* as an intimidating word. When you need help with your research and writing, seek advice from authorities who either know more about your subject than you do or have more experience developing such a project. Advice may come from different sources, but that's not a problem: The more people you talk to, the better.

Talk with your instructor. Don't be timid. Instructors hold office hours to answer your questions, especially about research assignments. Save yourself time and, perhaps, much grief by getting early feedback on your ideas and topic. It's better to learn that your thesis is unworkable before you compose a first draft.

Just as important, your instructor might help you see aspects of a topic you hadn't noticed or direct you to essential sources. Don't write a paper just to please instructors, but you'd be foolish to ignore their counsel.

Take your ideas to the writing center. Many student writers think the only time to use a campus writing center is when their instructor returns a draft on life support. Most writing-center tutors prefer not to be seen as EMTs. So they are eager to help at the start of a project, when you're still developing ideas. Tutors may not be experts on your subject, but they have reviewed enough papers to offer sensible advice for focusing a topic, shaping a thesis, or adapting a subject to an audience. ○ They also recognize when you're so clueless that you need to talk with your instructor pronto. For more about using a writing center, see Chapter 1 "Academic Goals and Expectations."

develop a statement
p. 333

Find local experts. Don't trouble an expert for information you could find easily yourself in the library or online: Save human contacts for when you need serious help on a major project—a research paper or senior thesis, an important story for a campus periodical, a public presentation on a controversial subject. But, then, do take advantage of the human resources around you. Campuses are teeming with knowledgeable people and that doesn't just include faculty in their various disciplines. Staff and administrative personnel at your school can advise you on everything from trends in college admissions to local crime statistics.

Look to the local community for expertise and advice as well. Is there a paper to be written about declining audiences for Hollywood blockbusters? You couldn't call J. J. Abrams and get through, but you could chat with a few local theater owners or managers to learn what they think about the business. Their insights might change the direction of your project.

Check with librarians. Campus librarians have lots of experience helping writers find information, steering them toward feasible projects and away from ideas that may not have much intellectual standing. Librarians can't be as specific or directive as, for example, your instructor, but they know what sorts of topics the library's resources will and will not support.

Chat with peers. Peers aren't really experts, but an honest classroom conversation with fellow students can be an eye-opening experience. You'll probably see a wide spectrum of opinions (if the discussion is frank) and even be surprised by objections you hadn't anticipated to your topic idea or first draft. Peers often have a surprising range of knowledge and, if the group is diverse, your classmates might bring enlightening life experiences to the conversation.

Universities are usually happy to offer the service of its campus experts. Following, for example the help page at the University of Texas at Austin, is especially aimed at serving the community. But you could browse a comparable list to see who is knowledgeable about a subject that interest you—especially when you are thinking about a major research project or senior thesis.

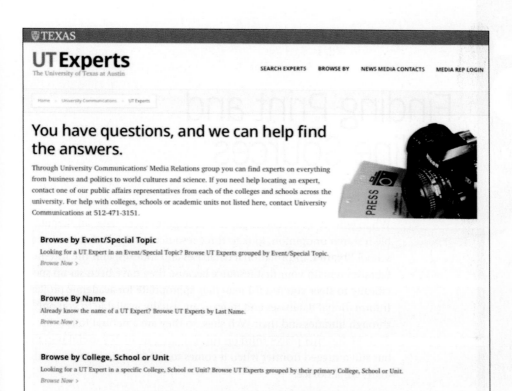

UT Experts
The University of Texas at Austin

SEARCH EXPERTS   BROWSE BY   NEWS MEDIA CONTACTS   MEDIA REP LOGIN

Home · University Communications · UT Experts

You have questions, and we can help find the answers.

Through University Communications' Media Relations group you can find experts on everything from business and politics to world cultures and science. If you need help locating an expert, contact one of our public affairs representatives from each of the colleges and schools across the university. For help with colleges, schools or academic units not listed here, contact University Communications at 512-471-3151.

Browse by Event/Special Topic

Looking for a UT Expert in an Event/Special Topic? Browse UT Experts grouped by Event/Special Topic.
Browse Now >

Browse By Name

Already know the name of a UT Expert? Browse UT Experts by Last Name.
Browse Now >

Browse by College, School or Unit

Looking for a UT Expert in a specific College, School or Unit? Browse UT Experts grouped by their primary College, School or Unit.
Browse Now >

Thinking about Writing   If you were asked to identify yourself as an expert on a subject, what would it be? Don't consider academic subjects only. Think about any areas or activities about which you could confidently offer reliable advice. Make a list and share it with your classmates. Do their lists give you additional ideas about the kinds of expertise you may possess?

Finding Print and Online Sources

When writing an academic paper that requires facts, data, and reputable research or opinion, look to three resources in this order: local and school libraries, informational databases and indexes, and the Internet. Libraries remain your first resource because they have been set up specifically to steer you toward materials appropriate for academic projects. Informational databases and indexes are usually available to you only through libraries and their Web sites, so they are a natural follow-up. And the Internet places third on this list, an undeniably useful resource but still a rugged frontier when it comes to reliable information, particularly for a novice.

Search libraries strategically. At the library you'll find books, journals, newspapers, and other materials, both print and electronic, in a collection expertly overseen by librarians and information specialists, who are, perhaps, the most valuable resources in the building. They are specifically trained to help you find what you need. Get to know them.

Of course, the key to navigating a library is its catalog. All but the smallest or most specialized libraries now organize their collections electronically (rather than with printed cards), but there's still a learning curve. The temptation will be to plunge in and start searching. After all, you can locate most items by author, title, subject, keywords, and even call number. But spend a few minutes reading the available Help screens to discover the features and protocols of the catalog. Most searches tell you immediately if the library has a book or journal you need, where it is on the shelves or in data collections, and whether it is available.

Do not ignore, either, the advanced features of a catalog (such as searches by language, by date, by type of content); these options help you find just the items you need or can use. And since you will often use a library not to find specific materials but to choose and develop topics, pay attention to the keywords or search terms the catalog uses to index the subject you're exploring: You can use index terms for sources you find to look for other similar materials—an important way of generating leads on a subject.

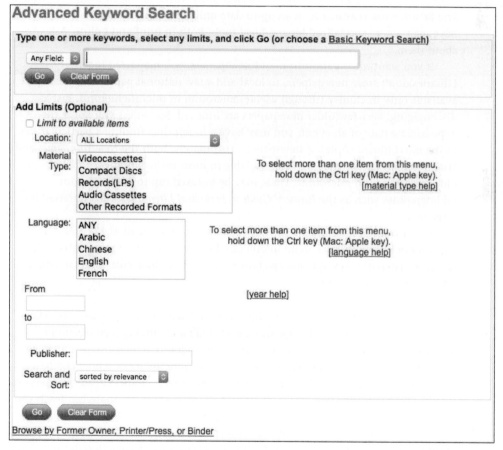

A library search screen for materials by location, type, language, date, and relevance (title or date). The University of Texas Libraries.

Explore library reference tools. In the age of Wikipedia, it's easy to forget that libraries still offer truly authoritative source materials in their reference rooms or online reference collections. Such standard works include encyclopedias, almanacs, historical records, maps, archived newspapers, and so on.

Quite often, for instance, you will need reliable biographical facts about important people—dates of birth, countries of origin, schools attended, career paths, and so on. You *might* find enough data from a Web search or a Wikipedia entry for people currently in the news. But to get accurate and substantial materials on historical figures, consult library tools such as the *Oxford Dictionary of National Biography* (focusing on the United Kingdom) or the *Dictionary of American Biography*. The British work is available in an up-to-date online version. Libraries also have many more specialized biographical tools, both in print and online. Ask about them.

If you want information from old newspapers, you may need ingenuity. Libraries don't store newspapers, so local and a few national papers will be available only in clumsy (though usable) microfilm or microfiche form. Just as discouraging, very few older newspapers are indexed. So, unless you know the approximate date of an event, you may have a tough time finding a particular story in the microfilmed copies of newspapers. Fortunately, both the *New York Times* and *Wall Street Journal* are indexed and available in most major libraries. You'll also find older magazines on microfilm. These may be indexed (up to 1982) in print bibliographies such as the *Readers' Guide to Periodical Literature*. Ask a librarian for assistance.

When your local library doesn't have resources you need, ask the people at the checkout or reference desks about interlibrary loan. If cooperating libraries have the books or materials you want, you can borrow them at minimal cost. But plan ahead. The loan process takes time.

Use professional databases. Information databases and indexes—our second category of research materials—are also found at libraries, among their electronic resources. These tools give you access to professional journals, magazines, and newspaper archives, in either summary or full-text form. Your library or school purchases licenses to make these valuable, often password-protected, resources available—services such as *EBSCOhost*, *InfoTrac*, and *Lexis-Nexis*. And, once again, librarians can teach you how to navigate such complex databases efficiently.

Many academic research projects, for instance, begin with a search of multidisciplinary databases such as *LexisNexis Academic, Academic OneFile,* or *Academic Search Premier*. These über-indexes cover a wide range of materials, including newspapers, reputable magazines, and many academic periodicals. Most libraries subscribe to one or more of these information services, which you can search online much like library catalogs, using basic and advanced search features.

For even more in-depth research, you need to learn to use databases within your specific field or major, tools such as *Ei* in engineering or the *MLA International Bibliography* in language and literature studies. There are, in fact, hundreds of such databases, far too many to list here, and some of them may be too specialized or technical for projects early in a college career. Librarians or instructors can direct you to the ones you can handle and, when necessary, explain how to use them. Such databases are sometimes less accessible than they seem at first glance.

Explore the Internet. As you well know, you can find information simply by exploring the Web from your laptop or tablet, using search engines such as Google and Bing to locate data and generate ideas. Or you can explore the resources available via Internet Archive at Archive.org. Online territory may seem familiar because you spend so much time there, but don't overestimate your ability to find what you need online. Browsing the Web daily to check sports scores and favorite blogs is completely different from using the Web for academic work.

Research suggests that many students begin their projects by simply typing obvious terms into Web browsers, ignoring the advanced capabilities of search engines. To take more control of searches, follow the links on search engine screens that you now probably ignore: Learn to use the tools such as Advanced Search; Search Help; Help; Fix a Problem; Tips & Tricks; Useful Features; and More. You'll be amazed what you discover.

Keep current with Web developments too (and make sure any sites you use are themselves current). Web companies such as Google are making more books and journal articles both searchable and available through their sites. Examine these resources as they come online. For instance, a tool such as Google Scholar will direct you to academic studies and scholarly papers on a given topic—exactly the kind of material you want to use in term papers or reports. O

As an experiment, you might compare the hits you get on a topic with a regular Google search with those that turn up when you select the Scholar option. You'll quickly notice that the Scholar items are more serious and technical—and also more difficult to access. In some cases, you may see only an abstract of a journal article or the first page of the item. Yet the materials that you locate may be worth a trip to the library to retrieve in their entirety.

find reliable sources
p. 433

Google Scholar

About   **Search**   Citations   Inclusion   Metrics   Publishers   Libraries   Search Scholar

Overview

Searching

Alerts

Library

Export

Coverage

Corrections

Questions

Search Tips

Get the most out of Google Scholar with some helpful tips on searches, email alerts, citation export, and more.

Finding recent papers

Your search results are normally sorted by relevance, not by date. To find newer articles, try the following options in the left sidebar:

1. click "Since Year" to show only recently published papers, sorted by relevance;
2. click "Sort by date" to show just the new additions, sorted by date;
3. click the envelope icon to have new results periodically delivered by email.

Locating the full text of an article

Abstracts are freely available for most of the articles. Alas, reading the entire article may require a subscription. Here're a few things to try:

1. click a library link, e.g., "FindIt@Harvard", to the right of the search result;
2. click a link labeled [PDF] to the right of the search result;
3. click "All versions" under the search result and check out the alternative sources;
4. click "Related articles" or "Cited by" under the search result to explore similar articles.

If you're affiliated with a university, but don't see links such as "FindIt@Harvard", please check with your local library about the best way to access their online subscriptions. You may need to do search from a computer on campus, or to configure your browser to use a library proxy.

Getting better answers

- If you're new to the subject, it may be helpful to pick up the terminology from secondary sources. E.g., a Wikipedia article for "overweight" might suggest a Scholar search for "pediatric hyperalimentation".

- If the search results are too specific for your needs, check out what they're citing in their "References" sections. Referenced works are often more general in nature.

- Similarly, if the search results are too basic for you, click "Cited by" to see newer papers that referenced them. These newer papers will often be more specific.

- Explore! There's rarely a single answer to a research question. Click "Related articles" or "Cited by" to see closely related work, or search for author's name and see what else they have written.

Be sure to study any guides to resources such as Google Scholar.

Resources to Consult When Conducting Academic Research

Source	What It Provides	Usefulness in Academic Research	Where to Find It
Scholarly Books	Fully documented and detailed primary research and analyses by scholars	Highly useful if not too high-level or technical	Library, Google Scholar
Scholarly Journals	Carefully documented primary research by scientists and scholars	Highly useful if not too high-level or technical	Library, databases
Newspapers	Accounts of current events	Useful as starting point	Library, microfilm, databases (*LexisNexis*), Internet
Magazines	Wide topic range, usually based on secondary research; written for popular audience	Useful if magazine has serious reputation	Libraries, newsstands, databases (*EBSCOhost*, *InfoTrac*), Internet
Encyclopedias (General or Discipline-Specific)	Brief articles	Useful as starting point	Libraries, Internet
Wikipedia	Open-source encyclopedia: entries written/edited by online contributors	Not considered reliable for academic projects, but can be a useful starting point.	Internet: www.wikipedia.org
Special Collections	Materials such as maps, paintings, artifacts, etc.	Highly useful for technical projects	Libraries, museums; images available via Internet
Government, Academic, or Organization Web Sites	Vast data compilations of varying quality, some of it reviewed	Highly useful	Internet sites with URLs ending in *.gov*, *.edu*, or *.org*
Commercial Web Sites	Information on many subjects; quality varies	Useful when possible interests/biases are known	Internet sites
Blogs, social media	Controlled, often highly partisan discussions of specialized topics	Useful when affiliated with reputable sources such as newspapers	Internet
Personal Web Sites	Often idiosyncratic information	Rarely useful; content varies widely	Internet

46

Evaluating Sources

In Chapter 45, you were directed to the best possible print and online sources for your research. But the fact is, all sources, no matter how prestigious, have strengths and weaknesses, biases and limitations. And these days, you might encounter sources online that have no credibility at all. So evaluating all the sources you've either found or been directed to is a necessary part of the research process. Here are some strategies for making those judgments.

Preview source materials for their key features and strategies. Give any source a quick once-over, looking for clues to its aim, content, and structure. Begin with the title and subtitle, taking seriously its key terms and qualifiers. A good title tells what a piece is—and is not—about. For many scholarly articles, the subtitle (which typically follows a colon) describes the substance of the argument.

Then scan the introduction (in a book) or abstract (in an article). From these items, you should be able to quickly grasp what the source covers, what its methods are, and what the author hopes to prove or accomplish.

Inspect the table of contents in a book or the headings in an article methodically, using them to figure out the overall structure of the work or to find specific information. Briefly review charts, tables, and illustrations, too, to discover what they offer. If a book has an index—and a serious book should—look for the key terms or subjects you are researching to see how well they are covered.

If the work appears promising, read its final section or chapter. Knowing how the material concludes gives insight into its value for your research. Look over the bibliography. The list of sources indicates how thorough the author has been and, not incidentally, points you to other materials you might want to examine. If the material seems up to snuff, look for professional reviews—if available—and browse them.

Check who published or produced the source.

In general, books published by presses associated with colleges and universities (Harvard, Oxford, Stanford, etc.) are reputable sources for college papers. So are articles from professional journals described as *refereed* or *peer-reviewed*. These terms are used for journals in which the articles have been impartially evaluated by panels of experts prior to publication. Instructors and librarians can help you grasp these distinctions.

You can also usually rely on material from reputable commercial publishers and from established institutions and agencies. The *New York Times;* the *Wall Street Journal;* Random House; Farrar, Straus & Giroux; Simon & Schuster; and the U.S. Government Printing Office make their ample share of mistakes, of course, but are generally considered to be far more reliable than Web sites, blogs, or social media. But you always need to be cautious.

Check who wrote the work.

Ordinarily, you should cite recognized authorities on your topic. Look for authors who are mentioned frequently and favorably within a field or whose works appear regularly in notes or bibliographies. Get familiar with them.

The Web does makes it possible to examine the careers of other authors whom you might not recognize. Search for their names online to confirm that they are reputable journalists or recognized experts in their field. Avoid citing authors working too far beyond their areas of professional expertise. Celebrities especially like to cross boundaries, sometimes mistaking their passion for an issue (environmentalism, diet, public health) for genuine mastery of a subject.

Consider the audience for a source.

What passes for adequate information in the general marketplace of ideas may not cut it when you're doing academic research. Many widely read books and articles that popularize a subject—such as climate change or problems with education—may, in fact, be based on more technical scholarly books and articles. For academic projects, rely primarily on those scholarly works themselves, even if you were inspired to choose a subject by reading respectable nonfiction. Glossy magazines shouldn't play a role in your research either, though the lines can get blurry. *People, O, Rolling Stone,* or *Spin* might be important if you are writing about popular culture or music. Similarly, Wikipedia is invaluable for a quick introduction to a subject, but don't cite it as an authority in an academic paper. Finally, be sure to recognize when political or cultural pieces are directed at audiences who already agree with a writer's positions or ideas. That doesn't disqualify a potential source, but places it within a context you should mention to your readers if you use the material.

Establish how current a source is. Scholarly work doesn't come with an expiration date, but you should base your research on the latest information. For fields in which research builds on previous work, the date of publication may even be highlighted within its system of documentation. For books, you'll find the date of publication on the copyright page, which is the reverse side of the title page (see p. 484).

Check the source's documentation. All serious scholarly and scientific research is documented. Claims are based on solid evidence backed up by formal notes, data are packed into charts and tables, and there is a bibliography at the end. All of this is done so that readers can verify the claims an author makes.

In a news story, journalists may establish the credibility of their information by simply naming their sources or, at a minimum, attributing their findings to reliable unnamed sources—and usually more than one. The authors of serious magazine pieces don't use footnotes and bibliographies either, but they, too, credit their major sources somewhere in the work. No serious claim should be left hanging. **O**

For your own academic projects, avoid authors and sources with undocumented assertions. Sometimes you have to trust authors when they are writing about personal experiences or working as field reporters, but let readers know when your claims are based on uncorroborated personal accounts.

Entertainer Jenny McCarthy has disturbed many public health officials by her claims of a connection between childhood vaccination and autism. She has a personal connection to the issue but no medical or scientific credentials.

WENN Ltd/Alamy Stock Photo

Avoid the echo chamber and fake news. Exercise extreme caution with web sources, social media, and, indeed, all news sources these days as sources for academic papers. Always be sure you know who is responsible for the material you are reading (for instance, a government agency, a congressional office, a news service, a corporation), who is posting it, who is the author of the material or sponsor of the Web site, what the date of publication is, and so on. **O** A site's information may be skewed by those who run it, pay its bills, have uses for it beyond reporting facts and transmitting information; it can also be outdated if no one regularly updates the resource.

Of course, all news sources—from NPR to Fox News—have biases in how they cover stories and in what they decide to emphasize or ignore. Yet these

think critically p. 327   find reliable sources
p. 433

Evaluation Checklist

- Quick overview to establish usefulness/legitimacy of the source: check reviews

- Examine publisher, publication or container for legitimacy, standing in field, reliability

- Investigate the author(s): credentials, previous work, publishing in-field, reputation

- Consider the audience for the source: in-field scholars or scientists; other professionals or experts, knowledgeable readers; general public; true believers

- Consider the date of the source: does currency matter to your research? Is the research cited a classic worth knowing?

- Assess the source's use of other sources. Does the piece need to be professionally documented? Does it handle its own sources professionally so you could trace them if necessary?

major players have professionals on their staffs, show at least some accountability for their work, and will typically acknowledge errors in their reporting. You likely know by now that many online sources, especially those with heavy "sponsored" presence in social media, offer little more than click-bait headlines designed to attract readers to dubious political or cultural stories that are, at best, misleading and often just hoaxes. These items are often unattributed (no author you can search), have no credible news affiliations or connections, do not cite reputable sources, and leave no trail you could trace. Obviously you can't use such stuff in an academic paper.

Adam Zyglis, The Buffalo News

You can learn a lot about a
source by previewing a few
basic elements.

Available online at www.sciencedirect.com

SCIENCE $\overline{d}$ DIRECT®

ACADEMIC
PRESS   Journal of Research in Personality 36 (2002) 607–614

JOURNAL OF
RESEARCH IN
PERSONALITY

www.academicpress.com

Brief report

Are we barking up the right tree?
Evaluating a comparative approach
to personality

Samuel D. Gosling * and Simine Vazire

Department of Psychology, University of Texas, Austin, TX, USA

Playful title none-
theless fits: Article is
about animals.

Abstract

Animal studies can enrich the field of human personality psychology by addressing questions that are difficult or impossible to address with human studies
alone. However, the benefits of a comparative approach to personality cannot be
reaped until the tenability of the personality construct has been established in animals. Using criteria established in the wake of the person–situation debate (Kenrick & Funder, 1988), the authors evaluate the status of personality traits in
animals. The animal literature provides strong evidence that personality does exist
in animals. That is, personality ratings of animals: (a) show strong levels of inte-
robserver agreement, (b) show evidence of validity in terms of predicting behaviors and real-world outcomes, and (c) do not merely reflect the implicit theories of
observers projected onto animals. Although much work remains to be done, the
preliminary groundwork has been laid for a comparative approach to personality.
© 2002 Elsevier Science (USA). All rights reserved.

Abstract previews
entire article.

Introduction

Personality characteristics have been examined in a broad range of nonhuman species including chimpanzees, rhesus monkeys, ferrets, hyenas, rats,

Headings through-
out signal this is a
research article.

* Corresponding author. Fax: 1-512- 471-5935.
  E-mail address: gosling@psy.utexas.edu (S.D. Gosling).

0092-6566/02/$ - see front matter © 2002 Elsevier Science (USA). All rights reserved.
PII: S0092-6566(02)00511-1

608   *Brief report / Journal of Research in Personality 36 (2002) 607 614*

sheep, rhinoceros, hedgehogs, zebra finches, garter snakes, guppies, and octopuses (for a full review, see Gosling, 2001). Such research is important because animal studies can be used to tackle questions that are difficult or impossible to address with human studies alone. By reaping the benefits of animal research, a comparative approach to personality can enrich the field of human personality psychology, providing unique opportunities to examine the biological, genetic, and environmental bases of personality, and to study personality development, personality-health links, and personality perception. However, all of these benefits hinge on the tenability of the personality construct in non-human animals. Thus, the purpose of the present paper is to address a key question in the animal domain: is personality real? That is, do personality traits reflect real properties of individuals or are they fictions in the minds of perceivers?

Thirty years ago, the question of the reality of personality occupied the attention of human-personality researchers, so our evaluation of the comparative approach to personality draws on the lessons learned in the human domain. Mischel's (1968) influential critique of research on human personality was the first of a series of direct challenges to the assumptions that personality exists and predicts meaningful real-world behaviors. Based on a review of the personality literature, Mischel (1968) pointed to the lack of evidence that individuals' behaviors are consistent across situations (Mischel & Peake, 1982). Over the next two decades, personality researchers garnered substantial empirical evidence to counter the critiques of personality. In an important article, Kenrick and Funder (1988) carefully analyzed the various arguments that had been leveled against personality and summarized the theoretical and empirical work refuting these arguments.

The recent appearance of studies of animal personality has elicited renewed debate about the status of personality traits. Gosling, Lilienfeld, and Marino (in press) proposed that the conditions put forward by Kenrick and Funder (1988) to evaluate the idea of human personality can be mobilized in the service of evaluating the idea of animal personality. Gosling et al. (in press) used these criteria to evaluate research on personality in nonhuman primates. In the present paper, we extend their analysis to the broader field of comparative psychology, considering research on nonhuman animals from several species and taxa. Kenrick and Funder's paper delineates three major criteria that must be met to establish the existence of personality traits: (1) assessments by independent observers must agree with one another; (2) these assessments must predict behaviors and real-world outcomes; and (3) observer ratings must be shown to reflect genuine attributes of the individuals rated, not merely the observers' implicit theories about how personality traits covary. Drawing on evidence from the animal-behavior literature, we evaluate whether these three criteria have been met with respect to animal personality.

■- -

Point of this brief study is defined at end of opening paragraph.

■- -

This page reviews literature on studies of animal personality. ◯

47

interview and observe

Doing Field Research

While most writing you do will be built on the work of others—that is, their books, articles, and fact-finding—you can do research of your own in many situations. For instance, you might interview people with experiences or information related to the subject you're exploring. ○ Or you could support a claim for a psychology or marketing paper by carefully observing and recording how people actually think or behave.

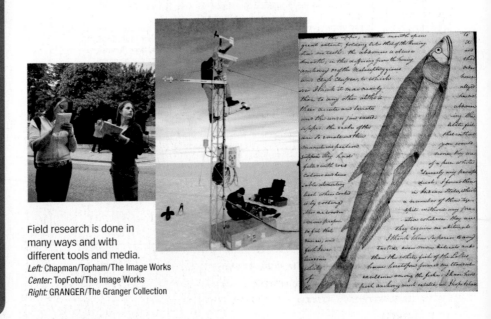

Field research is done in many ways and with different tools and media.
Left: Chapman/Topham/The Image Works
Center: TopFoto/The Image Works
Right: GRANGER/The Granger Collection

ask for help p. 433

Interview people with unique knowledge of your subject. When considering whether an interview makes sense for your project, ask yourself this important question: "What do I expect to learn from the interviewee?" If the information you seek is easily available online or in print, don't waste everyone's time with an interview. If, on the other hand, this person offers a fresh perspective on your topic, a personal interview could advance your research.

Interviews can be written or spoken. Written interviews, whether by e-mail or letter, instant messaging or online chat, allow you to keep questions and answers focused and provide a written record of the interviewee's responses. But spoken interviews, both in person or via Skype, allow in-depth discussion of a topic and may lead to more memorable reactions and deeper insights. Be flexible in setting up the type of interview most convenient for your subject. For oral interviews, keep the following suggestions in mind:

- Request an interview formally by phone, confirming it with a follow-up message.

- Give your subjects a compelling reason for meeting or corresponding with you; briefly explain your research project and why their knowledge or experience is important to your work.

- Let potential interviewees know how you chose them as subjects. If possible, identify a personal reference—that is, a professor or administrator who can vouch for you.

- Prepare a set of purposeful interview questions. Don't wing it.

- Think about how to phrase questions to open the interview. Avoid queries that can be answered in one word. Don't ask, *Did you enjoy your years in Asia?* Instead, lead with, *What did you enjoy most about the decade you spent in Tokyo?*

- Start interviews by thanking interviewees for their time and providing a very brief description of your research project.

- Keep a written record of material you intend to quote. If necessary, confirm the exact wording with your interviewee.

- End the interview by again expressing your thanks.

- Follow up with a thank-you note or e-mail and, if the contributions of interviewees were substantial, send them a copy of the final research paper.

- In your paper, give credit to any people interviewed by documenting the information they provided.

For an interview conducted in person, arrive at the predetermined meeting place on time and dressed professionally. If you wish to record the interview, be sure to ask permission first.

If you conduct your interview in writing, request a response by a certain date—one or two weeks is reasonable for ten questions. Refer to Chapter 21 for guidelines on professional communications.

For telephone interviews, call from a place with good reception, where you will not be interrupted. Your cell phone should be fully charged or plugged in.

Writing about Writing   Prepare a full set of questions you would use to interview a classmate about some *academic* issue—for example, study habits, methods for writing papers, or career objectives. Think about how to sequence your questions, how to avoid one-word responses, and how to follow up on possible replies (if the interview is oral). Write your questions down and then pair up with a classmate for a set of mutual interviews.

When you are done, write a one-page report based on what you learn and share the results with classmates.

Make careful research observations. The point of systematic observation is to provide a reliable way of studying a narrowly defined activity or phenomenon. But in preparing reports or arguments that focus on small groups or local communities, you might find yourself without enough data to move your claims beyond mere opinion.

For example, an anecdote or two won't persuade administrators that community rooms in the student union are being scheduled inefficiently. But you could conduct a simple study of these facilities, showing exactly how many student groups use them and for what purposes, over a given period of time.

This kind of evidence usually carries more weight with readers, who can decide whether to accept or challenge your numbers.

Some situations can't be counted or measured as readily as the one described above. If you wanted, let's say, to compare the various community rooms to determine whether those with windows encouraged more productive discussions than rooms without, your observations would be "softer" and more qualitative. You might have to describe the tone of speakers' voices or the general mood of the room. But numbers might play a part; you could, for instance, track how many people participated in the discussion or the number of tasks accomplished during the meeting.

To avoid bias in their observations, many researchers use double-column notebooks. In the first column, they record the physical details of their observations as objectively as possible—descriptions, sounds, countable data, weather, time, circumstances, activity, and so on. In the second column, they record their interpretations and commentaries on the data.

In addition to careful and objective note-taking techniques, devices such as cameras, video recorders, and tape recorders provide reliable backup evidence about an event. Also, having more than one witness observe a situation can help verify your findings.

Learn more about fieldwork. In those disciplines or college majors that use fieldwork, you will find guides or manuals to explain the details of such research procedures. You will also discover that fieldwork comes in many varieties, from naturalist observations and case studies to time studies and market research.

OBSERVABLE DATA	COMMENTARY
9/12/18	
2 P.M.	
Meeting of Entertainment Committee	
Room MUB210 (no windows)	
91 degrees outside	*Heat and lack of a/c probably making*
Air conditioning broken	*everyone miserable.*
People appear quiet, tired, hot	

A double-column notebook entry.

48

analyze claims and evidence/ take notes

Annotating Sources

Once you locate trustworthy sources, review them to zero in on the best ideas and most convincing evidence for your project. During this process of critical reading, you annotate, summarize, O synthesize, O and paraphrase O your sources—in effect creating the notes you need to compose your own work.

Annotate sources to understand them. "To annotate" simply means to add notes, comments, remarks, observations, criticism, or even corrections to a source you are reviewing—using whatever tools are available to record such reactions. Close or critical reading indicates active engagement with ideas, so it's natural to leave traces. With their wide paper margins, books in print—when you own them—are almost hard *not* to mark. Online works, including Kindle books, often have tools that enable you to share highlights and comments with other readers.

In a research project, you want to examine important sources closely enough to figure out both what they say and also how authors reached their conclusions or gathered their data. Think of critical reading as becoming an expert on the materials you read and eventually cite. To preserve your insights, mark up key texts with whatever tools work for you—notes in the margins, Post-it notes, electronic

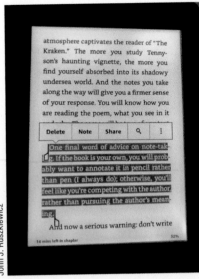

John J. Ruszkiewicz

David Mikics comments on note-taking in his book *Slow Reading in a Hurried Age*

sum up ideas p. 457 | understand synthesis p. 258 | restate ideas p. 460

452

comments, and so forth. Simply composing these comments will draw you deeper into source materials and make you think more about them.

Read sources to identify claims.

Begin by highlighting any specific claims, themes, or thesis statements a writer offers early in a text. Then pay attention to the way these key ideas recur throughout the work, especially near the conclusion. At a minimum, decide whether a writer has made reasonable claims, developed them consistently, and delivered on promised evidence. In the example on pages 454–56, claims and reasons are highlighted in yellow.

Read sources to understand assumptions.

Finding and annotating the assumptions in a source can be *much* trickier than locating claims. Highlight any assumptions stated outright in the source; they may be rare. More often, you have to infer a writer's assumptions, put them into your own words, and perhaps record them in marginal notes.

Identifying controversial or debatable assumptions is particularly important. For instance, if a writer makes the claim that *America needs tighter border security to prevent terrorist attacks*, you draw the inference that the writer believes that terrorism is caused by people crossing inadequately patrolled borders. Is that assumption accurate? Should the writer explain or defend it? Raise such questions. The one key assumption in the example that follows is highlighted in gray.

Read sources to find evidence.

Look for evidence that an author uses to support both the claims and assumptions in a text. Evidence can come in the form of data, examples, illustrations, or logical inferences. Since most academic materials you read will be thick with evidence, highlight only key items—especially any facts or materials you might cite in your own project. Make sure no crucial point goes unsupported; if you find one, make a note of it. In the following example, key evidence is highlighted in blue.

Record your personal reactions to source material.

When reading multiple sources, you'll want a record of what you favored or objected to in them. To be certain you don't later mistake your personal comments for observations *from* the source, use first person or pose questions as you respond. Use personal annotations, as well, to draw connections to other source materials you have read. In the following example, an opinion piece published in *Time*, possible reactions appear in annotations in the margins. Claims and reasons are highlighted in yellow; evidence is highlighted in blue; a key assumption is marked in gray.

CAMPUS FREE SPEECH IS NOT UP FOR DEBATE
HEATHER GERKEN • DEAN OF YALE LAW SCHOOL
JULY 13, 2017

In this, the summer of our discontent, many college presidents are breathing a sigh of relief that they made it through a politically fraught spring without their campuses erupting. Nobody wants to be the next Middlebury or Claremont McKenna, where demonstrations disrupted controversial speakers.

CLAIM
College campuses were troubled in 2017.

Law deans, in sharp contrast, have reason to be cheery. Their campuses have been largely exempt from ugly free-speech incidents like these. Charles Murray, the controversial scholar whose speech drew violent reaction at Middlebury, has spoken at Yale Law School twice during the past few years. Students and faculty engaged with him, and students held a separate event to protest and discuss the implications of his work. But he spoke without interruption. That's exactly how a university is supposed to work.

CLAIM / REASON
Law schools are doing better than other campuses.

EVIDENCE
Law schools tolerate controversial scholars.

CLAIM
Universities should allow controversial scholars to speak.

There may be a reason why law students haven't resorted to the extreme tactics we've seen on college campuses: their training. Law school conditions you to know the difference between righteousness and self-righteousness. That's why lawyers know how to go to war without turning the other side into an enemy. People love to tell lawyer jokes, but maybe it's time for the rest of the country to take a lesson from the profession they love to hate.

CLAIM

READER'S REACTION
Why are lawyers held in low regard?

In law schools we don't just teach our students to know the weaknesses in their own arguments. We demand that they imaginatively and sympathetically reconstruct the best argument on the other side. From the first day in class, students must defend an argument they don't believe or pretend to be a judge whose values they dislike. Every professor I know assigns cases that vindicate the side she favors—then

CLAIM

EVIDENCE
Tolerance of free speech is part of law school culture and education.

brutally dismantles their reasoning. Lawyers learn to see the world as their opponents do, and nothing is more humbling than that. We teach students that even the grandest principles have limits. The day you really become a lawyer is the day you realize that the law doesn't—and shouldn't—match everything you believe. The litigation system is premised on the hope that truth will emerge if we ensure that everyone has a chance to have her say.

> **ASSUMPTION**
> Legal system cannot function without free speech.

The rituals of respect shown inside and outside the courtroom come from this training. Those rituals are so powerful that they can trump even the deepest divides. As Kenneth Mack recounts in his book Representing the Race: The Creation of the Civil Rights Lawyer, Thurgood Marshall was able to do things in court that a black man could never do in any other forum, like subjecting a white woman to cross-examination. Marshall was able to practice even in small, segregated towns in rural Maryland during the early days of the civil rights movement. The reason was simple: despite their bigotry, members of the Maryland bar had decided to treat Marshall as a lawyer, first and foremost.

> **CLAIM**

> **EVIDENCE**

The values in which my profession is steeped were once values in politics as well. In 2008, I was one of the lawyers in the Obama campaign's "boiler room." Buses delivered the staff to Grant Park to watch Barack Obama accept the win. We arrived just as Senator John McCain was giving his concession speech on the Jumbotrons. The election was hard fought, and there was no love lost between the two campaigns. But even as the crowd around us jeered, the Obama staff practically stood at attention. It was like watching an army surrender—one of the most moving experiences I remember from that extraordinary campaign.

> **CLAIM**

> **EVIDENCE**
> Political rivals used to show more respect for opponents.

We need to return to what were once core values in politics and what remain core values in my profession. Make no mistake, we are in the midst of a war over values. We should fight, and fight hard, for what we believe. But even as we do battle, it's crucial to recognize the best in the other side and the worst in your own.

—Heather Gerken, Dean of Yale Law School

READER'S REACTION
Why has politics become more hostile? Who is responsible for violence protests on campus

CLAIM
This final claim is, arguably, the thesis of this opinion piece.

Thinking about Writing   How do you react to the claims, reasons, and evidence in Dean Gerken's "Campus Free Speech Is Not Up for Debate?" Read the essay and the annotations carefully and consider how you might have marked the piece differently.

Writing about Writing   Exchange a draft of a paper you are developing with that of a classmate. Then read your colleague's paper closely, as outlined in this chapter, imagining how you might use it as a source. First highlight its major claims and reasons; then identify any key assumptions in the paper. Bracket the sections of the project that primarily offer evidence. Finally, offer your personal reactions to various parts of the paper.

You might use highlighting pens of different colors to separate claims/reasons from assumptions and evidence, as in the sample essay.

Summarizing Sources

49

sum up
ideas

Once you determine which materials deserve closer attention and you have read these articles, books, and other texts critically—with an eye toward using their insights and data in your research project (see Chapter 48)—you're ready to summarize the individual items, putting ideas you've found into your own words. These brief summaries or fuller paraphrases (see Chapter 50) can become the springboard to composing your paper. **O**

Prepare a summary for every item you examine in a project. This advice seems self-evident, but it is not. A quick look may tell you that an article or book has no bearing on your paper. Even so, describe it very briefly on a note card or in an electronic file (with complete bibliographic data). Such a record reminds you that you have, in fact, seen and reviewed that item—which can be no small comfort when working on projects, such as a senior thesis— that take several weeks or months to complete. After you've examined dozens and dozens of sources, it's easy to forget what exactly you've read.

Use a summary to recap what a writer has said. When a source is clearly relevant to your project, look carefully for its main point and build your summary on it, making sure that this statement *does* reflect the actual content of the source, not your opinion of it. Be certain that the summary is *entirely* in your own words. Include the author and title of the work, too, so you can easily cite it later. The following is a basic summary of the *Time* opinion piece reprinted on pages 454–56, with all the required citation information:

restate ideas p. 460

In "Campus Free Speech Is Not Up for Debate" (July 13, 2017), Heather Gerken, the Dean of Yale Law School, argues that law schools have avoided violent protests against controversial speakers because legal training insists on the ability to understand alternative points of view.

Source: Gerken, Heather. "Campus Free Speech Is Not Up for Debate." Opinion. *Time*, 19 Jan. 2006, http://time.com/4856225/law-school-free-speech/.

Be sure your summary is accurate and complete. Even when a source makes several points, moves in contradictory directions, or offers a complex conclusion, your job is simply to describe what the material does. Don't embellish the material or blur the distinction between the source's words and yours. Include all bibliographical information (title, author, and date) from the source. The following summary of "Campus Free Speech Is Not Up for Debate" shows what can go wrong if you are not careful.

Omits title and attributes the opinion to *Time*, not the actual author.

Writer inserts a personal opinion.

According to *Time* magazine, law schools are fed up with violent protesters on college campuses opposing free speech. And they should be. Students need to be taught the same way lawyers are so that everyone has a chance to have their say. That way we will understand the best in the other side and the worst in our own.

Opening claim is not in the editorial.

Summary improperly uses source's exact words. Might lead to inadvertent plagiarism later on.

Use a summary to record your take on a source. In addition to reporting the contents of the material accurately, note also how the source might (or might not) contribute to your paper. But make certain that your comments won't be confused with claims made in the summarized article itself. The following are two acceptable sample summaries for "Campus Free Speech Is Not Up for Debate" that include information a writer might want to recall later:

In "Campus Free Speech Is Not Up for Debate," *Time* (July 13, 2017), the Dean of Yale Law School Heather Gerken suggests that law schools have largely avoided disruptive protests against controversial speakers because their teaching stresses the need to hear and understand opposing arguments. The culture of respect flourishing in law schools needs to return to the realm of politics. The article is recent, but it might be useful to check to see if law schools really have retained the open-mindedness toward speakers that Gerken describes.

In an opinion piece in *Time* (July 13, 2017) entitled "Campus Free Speech Is Not Up for Debate," Heather Gerken, Dean of Yale Law School, argues that politics needs to recover the principles that still operate in law schools—where students are taught to respect a system in which conflicting opinions are valued as a way to find the truth. In her piece, Gerken does not consider what factors might be driving undergraduate students today to silence speakers they regard as offensive or hurtful, especially to disadvantaged groups.

Use summaries to prepare an annotated bibliography. In an annotated bibliography, brief summaries are provided for every item in an alphabetical list of sources. These summaries help readers understand the content and scope of materials. For more about annotated bibliographies, see Chapter 17. **O**

Writing about Writing   Practice writing summaries by pairing up with a classmate and finding (probably online) a newspaper or blog page with a variety of opinion-oriented articles. For instance, check out the "Opinion" page in the *New York Times* or the home page of *Arts & Letters Daily* or the *Huffington Post*.

Agree on one or two pieces that both of you will recap separately. Then write the paired summaries, being careful to identify the items, describe them accurately, and separate your recaps from any comments you make about the material you have read. When you are done, compare your summaries. Discuss their accuracy, and make certain that neither of you has inadvertently borrowed language from the original articles.

---

understand annotated
bibliographies p. 251

50

restate ideas

Paraphrasing Sources

Paraphrases provide more complete records of the research materials you examine than do the summaries described in Chapter 49. **O** Like a summary, a paraphrase records a book or article's main point, but it also recaps the reasons and key evidence supporting that conclusion. Paraphrase any materials you later expect to use extensively in a project. Then consider how the research materials you have gathered stand in relationship to each other.

Identify the major claims and the structure of the source. Determine the main points made by the article, chapter, or text you are paraphrasing, and examine how the work organizes information to support its claims. **O** Then follow the same structure when you paraphrase the source. For example, your paraphrase will probably be arranged sequentially when a work has a story to tell, be arranged topic by topic when you're dealing with reported information, or be structured logically—by claims and evidence—when you take notes from arguments or editorials.

Track the source faithfully. A paraphrase should move through an article, chapter, or book succinctly while remaining faithful to its purpose, organization, tone, and, to some extent, style. In effect, you are preparing an abstract of the material, complete and readable on its own. Take concise and practical notes, adapting the paraphrase to your needs—understanding that materials especially valuable to your project will need to be described thoroughly. **O**

sum up ideas p. 457   think critically p. 327   take notes p. 452

Record key pieces of evidence. Thanks to photocopies and downloaded files, you don't usually have to copy data laboriously into your notes—and you probably shouldn't. (Chances of error greatly multiply whenever you transcribe information by hand.) Be certain, though, that your paraphrase sets down supporting reasons for all major claims in the source, as well as key evidence and facts. Key evidence is whatever proves a point or makes an argument notable or convincing. For print documents, keep track of page numbers for all the important data so you can later cite this material in your paper without having to return to the original source.

Be certain your notes are entirely in your own words. If you copy the language of sources as you paraphrase them, you risk plagiarism. Deliberately or not, you could transfer big chunks of someone else's writing into your project. But if you have paraphrased by the rules—carefully setting any borrowed phrases or sentences between quotation marks—it's safe to import those notes directly into your project, so long as you give the original writers due credit for their ideas. When you write competent paraphrases, you have material to use when you compose your own paper. There is no lost motion.

The following is a possible paraphrase of "Campus Free Speech Is Not Up for Debate," the complete, fully annotated text of which appears in Chapter 48 (pp. 454–56).

> In "Campus Free Speech Is Not Up for Debate" (*Time*, July 13, 2017), Heather Gerken, Dean of Yale Law School, notes that law schools like hers have largely avoided problems encountered on other campuses where demonstrators have disrupted controversial speakers, such as Charles Murray. She attributes the greater tolerance of law students to training they receive in appreciating "the difference between righteousness and self-righteousness." Law students, she points out, learn to appreciate opponents' arguments and to criticize their own, since the legal system requires that all sides be heard. She emphasizes the importance of "rituals of respect" within the legal profession, pointing out how that principle made it possible for Thurgood Marshall to argue cases even in racist times. She laments the fact that civility has declined markedly among political foes and urges that they return to values still in place within the legal community.

Avoid misleading or inaccurate paraphrasing. Your notes won't be worth much if your paraphrases of sources distort the content of what you read. Don't rearrange the information, give it a spin you might prefer, or offer your own opinions on a subject. Whenever your comments focus just on particular sections or chapters of a source, rather than on the entire piece, identify those parts in your paraphrase: *only in the first part of the essay; throughout chapter 3.* That way, you won't misread your notes days later and give readers a misleading description of a complex article or book. The following is a paraphrase of "Campus Free Speech Is Not Up for Debate" that gets almost *everything* wrong.

Opening wrongly attributes the opinion to *Time*.

Introduces personal opinion.

Misreads the argument of the piece entirely.

In "Campus Free Speech" (2017), *Time* notes that college campuses wouldn't have problems with controversial speakers if they listened to lawyers who are trained to be ritually respectful. In 2008, Obama supporters didn't boo defeated Republican candidate John McCain the night he lost to their candidate. But today no one wants to listen to what others say. All students should be trained to think like lawyers who brutally dismantle each other's reasoning. So big changes are needed so law schools don't become places where demonstrations disrupt controversial speakers.

Doesn't follow the structure of the essay being paraphrased.

Exaggerates a point made in the essay.

Use your paraphrases to synthesize sources. If you are asked to prepare a literature review or synthesis paper on a subject, begin that work by carefully summarizing and paraphrasing a range of reputable sources. For more about synthesis and response papers, see Chapter 18. **O**

Writing about Writing   Practice writing paraphrases by pairing up with a classmate and choosing a full essay to paraphrase from Part 2 of this book.

Write your paraphrases of the agreed-upon essay separately, just as if you intended to cite the piece later in a report, research paper, or argument yourself. When both of you are done, compare your paraphrases. What did you identify as the main point(s) or thesis of the piece? What kind of structure did the article follow: for example, narrative, report, comparison/contrast, argument, and so on? What evidence or details from the article did you include in your paraphrases? How do your paraphrases compare in length?

Discuss the differences. How might you account for them?

---

understand synthesis papers
p. 258

Incorporating Sources into Your Work

When you introduce sources into your research projects cogently, you give readers information they need to appraise the thinking you've done. They discover what you've read and learned and how much grasp you have on ideas. Yet incorporating borrowed ideas and quoted passages into papers is far from easy. You need to acknowledge and identify all paraphrased or quoted materials, clearly highlight any edits you made to quotations for accuracy or clarity, and keep the prose flowing smoothly.

Cue the reader in some way whenever you introduce borrowed materials. In reviewing your work, readers *always* need to know what words and ideas are yours and what you have culled from other authors and sources. So give them a verbal signal whenever you summarize, paraphrase, or quote directly from sources. That signal is typically a word or phrase that identifies authors or sources and inserts their ideas into the context of your own writing. Think of the process as *framing* either borrowed ideas or direct quotations to help readers appreciate their relevance or importance. Such frames can be simple or quite complex:

EXACT WORDS

Nancy Pelosi argued on *The View* that "... [quotation]."
"[Quotation] ...," says Jack Welch, former CEO of General Electric, pointing out that "... [more quotation]."

MLA and APA Style

The examples in this section follow MLA (Modern Language Association) style, covered in Chapter 53. For information on APA (American Psychological Association) style, see Chapter 54.

SUMMARIZED FACTS

According to a report in *Scientific American* (December 2016), the Mars rover *Curiosity* discovered . . . [your own words].

PARAPHRASED IDEA

Can a person talk intelligently about books even without reading them? Pierre Bayard, for one, suggests that . . . [your own words].

YOUR SUMMARY WITH QUOTATION

In *Encounters with the Archdruid*, author John McPhee introduces readers to conservationist David Brower, whom he credits with [your own words], calling him ". . . [quotation]."

As you see, a frame can introduce, interrupt, follow, or even surround the words or ideas taken from sources, but be sure that your signal phrases are grammatical and lead smoothly into the material.

Select an appropriate "verb of attribution" to frame borrowed material. These "signal verbs" influence what readers think of borrowed ideas or quoted material. Use neutral verbs of attribution in reports; save descriptive or highly connotative terms for arguments. Note that, by MLA convention, verbs of attribution are usually in the present tense when talking about current work or ideas. (In APA, these verbs are generally in the past or present perfect tense.)

Verbs of Attribution

Neutral	Descriptive	Connotative
adds	acknowledges	admits
explains	argues	charges
finds	asserts	confesses
notes	believes	confuses
offers	claims	derides
observes	confirms	disputes
says	disagrees	evades
shows	responds	impugns
states	reveals	pretends
writes	suggests	smears

Use ellipsis marks [. . .] to shorten a lengthy quotation. When quoting a source in your paper, it's not necessary to use every word or sentence, as long as the cuts you make don't distort the meaning of the original material. An ellipsis mark, formed from three spaced periods, shows where words, phrases, full sentences, or more have been removed from a quotation. The mark doesn't replace punctuation within a sentence. Thus, you might see a period or a comma immediately followed by an ellipsis mark.

ORIGINAL PASSAGE

Although gift giving has been a pillar of Hopi society, trade has also flourished in Hopi towns since prehistory, with a network that extended from the Great Plains to the Pacific Coast, and from the Great Basin, centered on present-day Nevada and Utah, to the Valley of Mexico. Manufactured goods, raw materials, and gems drove the trade, supplemented by exotic items such as parrots. The Hopis were producers as well, manufacturing large quantities of cotton cloth and ceramics for the trade. To this day, interhousehold trade and barter, especially for items of traditional manufacture for ceremonial use (such as basketry, bows, cloth, moccasins, pottery, and rattles), remain vigorous.

Highlighting shows words to be deleted when passage is quoted.

—Peter M. Whiteley, "Ties That Bind: Hopi Gift Culture and Its First Encounter with the United States," *Natural History*, November 2004, p. 26

PASSAGE WITH ELLIPSES

Whiteley has characterized the practice this way:

Although gift giving has been a pillar of Hopi society, trade has also flourished in Hopi towns since prehistory. . . . Manufactured goods, raw materials, and gems drove the trade, supplemented by exotic items such as parrots. The Hopis were producers as well, manufacturing large quantities of cotton cloth and ceramics for the trade. To this day, interhousehold trade and barter, especially for items of traditional manufacture for ceremonial use, . . . remain vigorous. (26)

Ellipses show where words have been deleted.

Use brackets [ ] to insert explanatory material into a quotation. By convention, readers understand that the bracketed words are not part of the original material.

Writing in the *London Review of Books* (January 26, 2006), John Lancaster describes the fears of publishers: "At the moment Google says they have no intention of providing access to this content [scanned books still under copyright]; but why should anybody believe them?"

Use ellipsis marks, brackets, and other devices to make quoted materials fit the grammar of your sentences. Sometimes, the structure of sentences you want to quote doesn't quite suit the grammar, tense, or perspectives of your own surrounding prose. If necessary, cut up a quoted passage to slip appropriate sections into your own sentences, adding bracketed changes or explanations to smooth the transition.

ORIGINAL PASSAGE

Words to be quoted are highlighted.

Among Chandler's most charming sights are the business-casual dads joining their wives and kids for lunch in the mall food court. The food isn't the point, let alone whether it's from Subway or Dairy Queen. The restaurants merely provide the props and setting for the family time. When those kids grow up, they'll remember the food court as happily as an older generation recalls the diners and motels of Route 66—not because of the businesses' innate appeal but because of the memories they evoke.

—Virginia Postrel, "In Defense of Chain Stores," *The Atlantic*, December 2006

MATERIAL AS QUOTED

Words quoted from source are highlighted.

People who dislike chain stores should ponder the small-town America that cultural critic Virginia Postrel describes, one where "business-casual dads [join] their wives and kids for lunch in the mall food court," a place that future generations of kids will remember "as happily as an older generation recalls the diners and motels of Route 66."

Use [sic] to signal an obvious error in quoted material. You don't want readers to blame a mistake on you, and yet you are obligated to reproduce a quotation exactly—including blunders in the original. You can highlight an error by putting *sic* (the Latin word for "thus") in brackets immediately following the mistake. The device says, in effect, that this is the way you found it.

The late Senator Edward Kennedy once took Supreme Court nominee Samuel Alito to task for his record: "In an era when America is still too divided by race and riches, Judge Alioto [sic] has not written one single opinion on the merits in favor of a person of color alleging race discrimination on the job."

Documenting Sources

Required to document a research paper or other academic assignment?
It seems simple in theory: List your sources and note where and how
you use them. But the practice can be intimidating. For one thing, you
have to follow rules for everything from capitalizing titles to caption-
ing images. For another, documentation systems differ between fields.
What worked for a Shakespeare paper won't transfer to your psychology research project. Bummer. What do you need to do?

Understand the point of documentation. Documentation
systems differ to serve the writers and researchers who use them. Modern Language Association (MLA) documentation, which you probably know from composition and literature classes, highlights author
names and the titles of works and assumes that writers will be quoting
a lot—as literature scholars do. American Psychological Association
(APA) documentation, gospel in psychology and social sciences, focuses
on publication dates because scholars in these fields value the latest
research. Council of Science Editors (CSE) documentation, used in the
hard sciences, provides detailed advice for handling formulas and numbers. So systems of documentation aren't arbitrary. Their rules reflect
the specialized needs of writers in various fields.

In Part 8, "Handbook", you will find thorough coverage of MLA
documentation in Chapter 53 and of APA documentation in Chapter 54.

**Understand what you accomplish through
documentation.** First, you clearly identify the sources you have
used. In a world awash with data, readers really do need to have reliable
information about titles, authors, data, medium of publication, and so on.

In addition, by citing your sources, you certify the quality of your research and, in turn, receive credit for your labor. You also offer evidence for your claims. An appreciative reader or instructor can tell a lot from your bibliography alone.

Finally, when you document a paper, you encourage readers to follow up on your work. When you've done a good job, serious readers will want to know more about your subject. Both your citations and your bibliography enable them to take the next step in their research.

Style Guides Used in Various Disciplines

Anthropology	*AAA Style Guide* (2009, online) *Chicago Manual of Style* • 17th edition Kate L. Turabian, *Manual for Writers of Research Papers, Theses, and Dissertations* • 8th edition
Art	Chicago • Turabian
Biology	*Scientific Style and Format: The CSE Manual for Authors, Editors, and Publishers* • 8th edition
Business	*The Business Style Handbook* (2nd ed., 2012) Chicago • Turabian
Chemistry	*The ACS Style Guide: Effective Communication of Scientific Information* • 3rd edition • ACS style
Communications	*MLA Handbook* • 8th edition
Computer Science	Chicago • Turabian
Earth Science	*Geowriting: A Guide to Writing, Editing, and Printing in Earth Science* • 5th edition
Education	*Publication Manual of the American Psychological Association* • 6th edition
Engineering	Varies by area; *IEEE Standards Manual* (online)
History	Chicago • Turabian
Humanities	*MLA Handbook*
Journalism	*The Associated Press Stylebook* • Updated annually • AP style
Language & Literature	*MLA Handbook*
Law	*Uniform System of Citations: The Bluebook* • 20th edition
Mathematics	*American Mathematical Society Handbook* • AMS style
Music	*Writing About Music: An Introductory Guide* • 4th edition Chicago • Turabian
Nursing	*Writing for Publication in Nursing* • 3rd edition
Political Science	*Style Manual for Political Science* • 2nd edition • APSA style

(Continued)

Psychology	*Publication Manual of the American Psychological Association* • 6th edition • APA style
Religion	Chicago • Turabian *MLA Handbook*
Rhetoric	*MLA Handbook* *Publication Manual of the American Psychological Association* • 6th edition
Sciences	*Scientific Style and Format: The CSE Manual for Authors, Editors, and Publishers* • 8th edition • CSE style
Sociology	*American Sociological Association Style Guide* • 4th edition
Theater	*MLA Handbook* Chicago • Turabian
U.S. Government	*United States Government Publishing Office Style Manual* • 31st edition • GPO style

Handbook

part eight

53

MLA Documentation and Format

The style of the Modern Language Association (MLA) is used in many humanities disciplines. For complete details about MLA style, consult the *MLA Handbook*, 8th ed. (2016). The basic details for documenting sources and formatting research papers in MLA style are presented below.

Document sources according to convention. When you use sources in a research paper, you are required to cite them, letting readers know that the information has been borrowed from somewhere else and showing them how to find the original material if they would like to study it further. An MLA-style citation includes two parts: a brief in-text citation and a more detailed works cited entry to be included in a list at the end of your paper.

In-text citations must include the author's name as well as the number of the page where the borrowed material can be found. The author's name (shaded in orange) is generally included in the signal phrase that introduces the passage, and the page number (shaded in yellow) is included in parentheses after the borrowed text.

> Frazier points out that the Wetherill-sponsored expedition to explore Chaco Canyon was roundly criticized (43).

Alternatively, the author's name can be included in parentheses along with the page number.

> The Wetherill-sponsored expedition to explore Chaco Canyon was roundly criticized (Frazier 43).

At the end of the paper, in the works cited list, a more detailed citation includes the author's name as well as the title (shaded in green) and publication information about the source (shaded in blue).

Frazier, Kendrick. *People of Chaco: A Canyon and Its Culture.* Revised ed., W. W. Norton, 1999.

Both in-text citations and works cited entries can vary greatly depending on the type of source cited (book, periodical, Web site, etc.). The following pages give specific examples of how to cite a wide range of sources in MLA style.

Directory of MLA In-Text Citations

1. Author named in signal phrase 474
2. Author named in parentheses 474
3. With block quotations 474
4. Two authors 475
5. Three or more authors 475
6. Group, corporate, or government author 475
7. Two or more works by the same author 475
8. Authors with same last name 475
9. Unidentified author 476
10. Multivolume work 476
11. Work in an anthology or a collection 476
12. Entry in a reference book 476
13. Literary work 477
14. Sacred work 477
15. Entire work 477
16. Secondary source 477
17. No page numbers 478
18. Multiple sources in the same citation 478

MLA in-text citation

1. Author Named in Signal Phrase

Include the author's name in the signal phrase that introduces the borrowed material. Follow the borrowed material with the page number of the source in parentheses. Note that the period comes after the parentheses. For a source without an author, see item 9; for a source without a page number, see item 17.

> According to Seabrook, "astronomy was a vital and practical form of knowledge" for the ancient Greeks (98).

2. Author Named in Parentheses

Follow the borrowed material with the author and page number of the source in parentheses and end with a period. For a source without an author, see item 9; for a source without a page number, see item 17.

> For the ancient Greeks, "astronomy was a vital and practical form of knowledge" (Seabrook 98).

Note: Most of the examples below follow the style of item 1, but naming the author in parentheses (as shown in item 2) is also acceptable.

3. With Block Quotations

For quotations of four or more lines, MLA requires that you set off the borrowed material indented one-half inch from the left-hand margin. Include the author's name in the introductory text (or in the parentheses at the end). End the block quotation with the page number(s) in parentheses, *after* the end punctuation of the quoted material.

> Jake Page, writing in *American History*, underscores the significance of the well-organized Pueblo revolt:
>
> > Although their victory proved temporary, in the history of Indian–white relations in North America the Pueblo Indians were the only Native Americans to successfully oust European invaders from their territory. . . . Apart from the Pueblos, only the Seminoles were able to retain some of their homeland for any length of time, by waging war from the swamps of the Florida Everglades. (36)

4. Two Authors

If your source has two authors, include both their names in either the signal phrase or parentheses.

> Muhlheim and Heusser assert that the story "analyzes how crucially our actions are shaped by the society . . . in which we live" (29).

5. Three or More Authors

If your source has three or more authors, list the first author's name followed by "et al." (meaning "and others") in the signal phrase or parentheses.

> Hansen et al. estimate that the amount of fish caught and sold illegally worldwide is between 10 and 30 percent (974).

> According to some experts, "Children fear adult attempts to fix their social lives" (Thompson et al. 8).

6. Group, Corporate, or Government Author

Treat the name of the group, corporation, or government agency just as you would any other author, including the name in either the signal phrase or the parentheses.

> The United States Environmental Protection Agency states that if a public water supply contains dangerous amounts of lead, the municipality is required to educate the public about the problems associated with lead in drinking water (3).

7. Two or More Works by the Same Author

If your paper includes two or more works by the same author, add a brief version of the works' titles (shaded in green) in parentheses to help readers locate the right source.

> Mills suggests that new assessments of older archaeological work, not new discoveries in the field, are revising the history of Chaco Canyon ("Recent Research" 66). She argues, for example, that new analysis of public spaces can teach us about the ritual of feasting in the Puebloan Southwest (Mills, "Performing the Feast" 211).

8. Authors with Same Last Name

If your paper includes two or more sources whose authors have the same last name, include a first initial with the last name in either the signal phrase or the parentheses.

> According to T. Smith, "[A]s much as 60 percent of the computers sold in India are unbranded and made by local assemblers at about a third of the price of overseas brands" (12).

9. Unidentified Author

If the author of your work is unknown, include a brief title of the work in parentheses.

> Though a single language, Spanish varies considerably, a fact that "befuddles advertisers who would aim to sell to the entire Spanish-speaking world, like the shampoo-maker who discovered that *cabello chino* ("Chinese hair") means curly hair in almost all Latin America save Ecuador, where it means straight hair" ("Rise of Spanish" 1).

10. Multivolume Work

If you cite material from more than one volume of a multivolume work, include in the parentheses the volume number followed by a colon before the page number. (See also item 11, on p. 483, for including multivolume works in your works cited list.)

> Odekon defines *access-to-enterprise zones* as "geographic areas in which taxes and government regulations are lowered or eliminated as a way to stimulate business activity and create jobs" (1: 2).

11. Work in an Anthology or a Collection

Include the author of the work in the signal phrase or parentheses. There is no need to refer to the editor of the anthology in the in-text citation; this and other details will be included in the works cited list at the end of your paper.

> Vonnegut suggests that *Hamlet* is considered such a masterpiece because "Shakespeare told us the truth, and [writers] so rarely tell us the truth" (354).

12. Entry in a Reference Book

In the signal phrase, include the author of the entry you are referring to, if there is an author. In the parentheses following the in-text citation, include the title of the entry and the page number(s) on which the entry appears.

> Willis points out that the Empire State Building, 1,250 feet tall and built in just over one year, was a record-breaking feat of engineering ("Empire State Building" 375–76).

For reference entries with no author (such as dictionaries), simply include the name of the article or entry in quotation marks along with the page reference in parentheses.

> Supersize—one of the newest pop culture terms added to the dictionary—is a verb meaning "to increase considerably the size, amount, or extent of" ("Supersize" 714).

13. Literary Work

Include as much information as possible to help readers locate your borrowed material. For classic novels, which are available in many editions, include the page number, followed by a semicolon, and additional information such as book ("book"), volume ("vol."), or chapter ("ch.") numbers.

> At the climax of Brontë's *Jane Eyre*, Jane fears that her wedding is doomed, and her description of the chestnut tree that has been struck by lightning is ominous: "it stood up, black and riven: the trunk, split down the center, gaped ghastly" (274; vol. 2, ch. 25).

For classic poems and plays, include division numbers such as act, scene, and line numbers; do not include page numbers. Separate all numbers with periods. Use Arabic (1, 2, 3, etc.) numerals instead of Roman (I, II, III, etc.) unless your instructor prefers otherwise.

> In Homer's epic poem *The Iliad*, Agamemnon admits that he has been wrong to fight with Achilles, but he blames Zeus, whom he says "has given me bitterness, who drives me into unprofitable abuse and quarrels" (2.375–76).

14. Sacred Work

Instead of page numbers, include book, chapter, and verse numbers when citing material from sacred texts.

> Jesus's association with the sun is undeniable in this familiar passage from the Bible: "I am the light of the world. Whoever follows me will not walk in darkness, but will have the light of life" (John 8.12).

15. Entire Work

When referring to an entire work, there is no need to include page numbers in parentheses; simply include the author's name(s) in the signal phrase.

> Dobelli claims that cognitive errors tend to be ingrained in us, making it likely we'll stumble over the same mistakes again and again unless we alter our way of thinking.

16. Secondary Source

To cite a source you found within another source, include the name of the original author in the signal phrase. In the parentheses, include the term "qtd. in" and give the author of the source where you found the quote, along with the page number. Note that your works cited entry for this material will be listed under the secondary source name (Pollan) rather than the original writer (Howard).

Writing in 1943, Howard asserted that "artificial manures lead inevitably to artificial nutrition, artificial food, artificial animals, and finally to artificial men and women" (qtd. in Pollan148).

17. No Page Numbers

If the work you are citing has no page numbers, include only the author's name (or the brief title, if there is no author) for your in-text citation.

> According to Broder, the Federal Trade Commission has begun to police and crack down on false company claims of producing "environmentally friendly" or "green" merchandise.

18. Multiple Sources in the Same Citation

If one statement in your paper can be attributed to multiple sources, alphabetically list all the authors with page numbers, separated by semicolons.

> Two distinct Harlems coexisted in the late 1920s: one a cultural and artistic force—the birthplace of a renaissance of literature, music, and dance—and the other, a slum and profit center for organized crime (Giddins and DeVeaux 132; Gioia 89).

Directory of MLA Works Cited Entries

(Continued)

Directory of MLA Works Cited Entries (*Continued*)

General Guidelines for MLA Works Cited Entries

AUTHOR NAMES

- Authors listed at the start of an entry should be listed last name first and should end with a period.
- Subsequent author names, or the names of authors or editors listed in the middle of an entry, should be listed first name first.

(*Continued*)

General Guidelines for MLA Works Cited Entries (*Continued*)

DATES

- Format dates as day month year: 27 May 2018.
- Use abbreviations for all months except for May, June, and July, which are short enough to spell out: Jan., Feb., Mar., Apr., Aug., Sept., Oct., Nov., Dec. (Months should always be spelled out in the text of your paper.)
- If the source has no date, give your date of access at the end: Accessed 24 Feb. 2016.

TITLES

- Italicize the titles of long works—such as books, plays, periodicals, entire Web sites, and films. (Underlining is an acceptable alternative to italics, but note that whichever format you choose, you should be consistent throughout your paper.)
- Titles of short works—such as essays, articles, poems, and songs—should be placed in quotation marks.

PUBLICATION INFORMATION

- Provide the publisher's full name as listed on the title page, leaving out business terms such as "Inc." and "Corp." If no publisher is given on the title page, look at the copyright page.
- Do not abbreviate words in the publisher's name, except for "University" ("U") and "Press" ("P") in the case of academic publishers.
- Use the abbreviations "vol." ("volume") and "no." ("number") for issues of periodicals, and precede page numbers with "pp." ("pages").

MLA works cited entries

AUTHOR INFORMATION

1. Single Author

Author's Last Name, First Name. *Book Title*. Publisher, Year of Publication.

Bazelon, Emily. *Sticks and Stones: Defeating the Culture of Bullying and Rediscovering the Power of Character and Empathy*. Random House, 2013.

2. Two Authors

List the authors in the order shown on the title page.

> First Author's Last Name, First Name, and Second Author's First Name Last
> Name. *Book Title*. Publisher, Year of Publication.

> Power, Michael L., and Jay Schulkin. *The Evolution of Obesity*. Johns Hopkins
> UP, 2009.

3. Three or More Authors

When a source has four or more authors, list only the name of the first author (last
name first) followed by a comma and the Latin term "et al." (meaning "and others").

> First Author's Last Name, First Name, et al. *Book Title*. Publisher, Year of
> Publication.

> Michaels, Ed, et al. *The War for Talent*. Harvard Business School, 2001.

> Roark, James L., et al. *The American Promise: A History of the United States*.
> 5th ed., Bedford/St. Martin's, 2012.

4. Corporate Author

If a group or corporation rather than a person appears to be the author, include that
name as the work's author in your list of works cited. (If the organization is also the
author, omit the author name.)

> Name of Corporation. *Book Title*. Publisher, Year of Publication.

> United States, Department of Commerce. *Statistical Abstract of the United
> States 2012–2013: The National Data Book*. Skyhorse Publishing, 2012.

> *Technical Report of the TDR Thematic Reference Group on Environment,
> Agriculture, and Infectious Diseases of Poverty*. World Health
> Organization, 2013.

5. Unidentified Author

If the author of a work is unknown, begin the works cited entry with the title of the work.
Note that in the example given, "The New Yorker" is not italicized because it is a
title within a title (see item 19).

> *Book Title*. Publisher, Year of Publication.

> The New Yorker *Top 100 Cartoons*. Cartoon Bank, 2004.

6. Multiple Works by the Same Author

To cite two or more works by the same author in your list of works cited, organize the works alphabetically by title (ignoring introductory articles such as The and A). Include the author's name only for the first entry; for subsequent entries by this same author, type three hyphens followed by a period in place of the author's name.

Author's Last Name, First Name. *Title of Work*. Publisher, Year of Publication.

---. *Title of Work*. Publisher, Year of Publication.

---. *Three Cups of Deceit: How Greg Mortenson, Humanitarian Hero, Lost His Way*. Anchor Books, 2011.

Krakauer, Jon. *Under the Banner of Heaven: A Story of Violent Faith*. Anchor Books, 2004.

BOOKS

7. Book: Basic Format

The example here is the basic format for a book with one author. For author variations, see items 1–6. For more information on the treatment of authors, dates, titles, and publication information, see the box on page 478. After listing the author's name, include the title (and subtitle, if any) of the book, italicized. Next give the publisher's name and year of publication.

Author's Last Name, First Name. *Book Title: Book Subtitle*. Publisher, Publication Year.

Seeling, Charlotte. *Fashion: 150 Years of Couturiers, Designers, Labels*. H. F. Ullmann Publishing, 2012.

8. Author and Editor

Include the author's name first if you are referring to the text itself. If, however, you are citing material written by the editor, include the editor's name first, followed by a comma and "editor."

Author's Last Name, First Name. *Book Title*. *Year of Original Publication*. Edited by Editor's First Name Last Name. Publisher, Year of Publication.

Editor's Last Name, First Name, editor. *Book Title*. *Year of Original Publication*. By Author's First Name Last Name. Publisher, Year of Publication.

Dickens, Charles. *Great Expectations*. 1861. Edited by Janice Carlisle, Bedford/St. Martin's, 1996.

Carlisle, Janice, editor. *Great Expectations*. 1861. By Charles Dickens, Bedford/St. Martin's, 1996.

9. Edited Collection

> Editor's Last Name, First Name, editor. *Book Title.* Publisher, Year of
> Publication.

> Abbott, Megan, editor. *A Hell of a Woman: An Anthology of Female Noir.*
> Busted Flush Press, 2007.

10. Work in an Anthology or a Collection

> Author's Last Name, First Name. "Title of Work." *Book Title,* edited by
> Editor's First Name Last Name, Publisher, Year of Publication, Page
> Numbers of Work.

> Okpewho, Isidore. "The Cousins of Uncle Remus." *The Black Columbiad:
> Defining Moments in African American Literature and Culture,* edited by
> Werner Sollors and Maria Diedrich, Harvard UP, 1994, pp. 15–27.

11. Multivolume Work

To cite one volume of a multivolume work, include the volume number after the title.
Including the volume number in your list of works cited means that you do not need
to list it in your in-text citation. To cite two or more volumes, include the number of
volumes at the end of the entry. In this case, you would need to include the specific
volume number in each of your in-text citations for this source.

> Author or Editor's Last Name, First Name. *Title of Work. Vol. Number,*
> Publisher, Year of Publication.

> Odekon, Mehmet, editor. *Encyclopedia of World Poverty.* Vol. 2, Sage
> Publishing, 2006.

> Author or Editor's Last Name, First Name. *Title of Work.* Publisher, Year of
> Publication. Number of vols.

> Odekon, Mehmet, editor. *Encyclopedia of World Poverty.* Sage Publishing,
> 2006. 3 vols.

12. Part of a Series

After the publication information, include the series title and number (if any) from the
title page.

> Author or Editor's Last Name, First Name. *Title of Work.* Publisher, Year of
> Publication. *Title of Series,* Number in series.

> Andersen, Jack, editor. *Genre Theory in Information Studies.* Emerald Group
> Publishing, 2015. Studies in Information, no. 11.

Cite from a book (MLA)

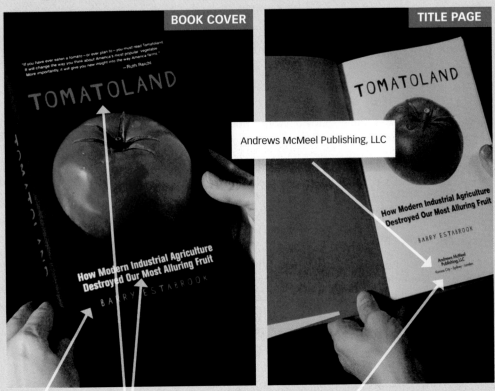

BOOK COVER

TITLE PAGE

Andrews McMeel Publishing, LLC

Art on pages 486–87: Abridged from *Tomatoland: How Modern Industrial Agriculture Destroyed Our Most Alluring Fruit*, by Barry Estabrook (published by Andrews McMeel, 2011). © 2011 by Barry Estabrook. Used by permission of the Author.

1 author

2 book title and subtitle

3 publisher

If a publisher's name includes business terms like "LLC," leave them out.

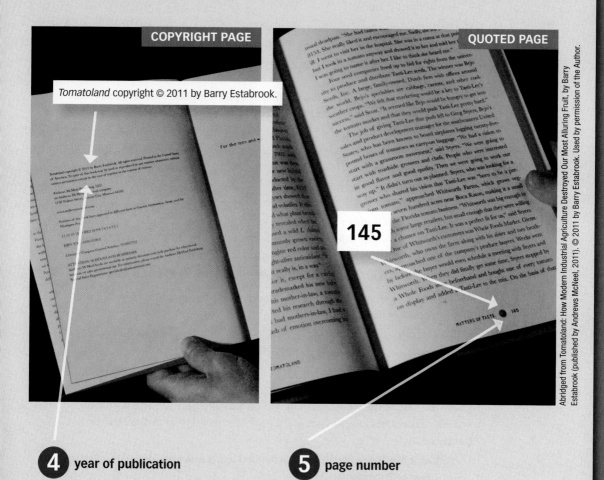

COPYRIGHT PAGE

Tomatoland copyright © 2011 by Barry Estabrook.

QUOTED PAGE

145

4 year of publication   **5** page number

MLA in-text citation

Describing his vision for the new tomato breed, the seed company owner explained, "We were going to start with roadside growers and chefs. People who were interested in good flavor and good quality" (Estabrook 145).

1   **5**

MLA works cited entry

1   **2**

Estabrook, Barry. *Tomatoland: How Modern Industrial Agriculture Destroyed*

3   **4**

Our Most Alluring Fruit. Andrews McMeel Publishing, 2011.

13. Republished Book

If the book you are citing was previously published, include the original publication date after the title. If the new publication includes additional text, such as an introduction, include that, along with the name of its author, before the current publication information.

> Author's Last Name, First Name. *Title of Work.* Original Year of Publication. New Material Author's First Name Last Name, Publisher, Year of Publication.

> Davidson, Bruce. *Subway.* 1986. Introduction by Fred Brathwaite, Aperture Foundation, 2011.

14. Later Edition

Include the edition number as a numeral with letters ("2nd," "3rd," "4th," etc.) followed by "ed." after the book's title. If the edition is listed on the title page as "Revised" or similar without a number, use the word with "ed." after the title of the book.

> Author(s). *Title of Work.* Number ed., Publisher, Year of Publication.

> Bodley, John H. *Anthropology and Contemporary Human Problems.* 6th ed., AltaMira Press, 2012.

> Holt, Hamilton. *The Life Stories of Distinguished Americans as Told by Themselves.* Expanded ed., Routledge, 2000.

15. Sacred Work

Include the title of the work as it is shown on the title page. If there is an editor or a translator listed, include the name after the title with either "Edited by" or "Translated by."

> *Title of Work.* Edited by or Translated by First Name Last Name, Publisher, Year of Publication.

> *The King James Bible: 400th Anniversary Edition.* Oxford UP, 2010.

> *The Qur'an.* Translated by M. A. S. Abdel Haleem, Oxford UP, 2008.

16. Translation

> Original Author's Last Name, First Name. *Title of Work.* Translated by Translator's First Name Last Name, Publisher, Year of Publication.

> Alighieri, Dante. *Inferno: A New Translation.* Translated by Mary Jo Bang, Graywolf Press, 2012.

17. Article in a Reference Book

If there is no article author, begin with the title of the article.

> Article Author's Last Name, First Name. "Title of Article." *Book Title*,
>   Publisher, Year of Publication.

> Dirr, Michael A. "Brunfelsia." *Dirr's Encyclopedia of Trees and Shrubs*, Timber
>   Press, 2011.

> "Supreme Court Decisions." *The World Almanac and Book of Facts 2013*.
>   World Almanac, 2013.

18. Introduction, Preface, Foreword, or Afterword

> Book Part Author's Last Name, First Name. Description of Book Part. *Book
>   Title*, by Book Author's First Name Last Name, Publisher, Year of
>   Publication, Page Numbers.

> Gladwell, Malcolm. Foreword. *The Book of Basketball: The NBA According to
>   The Sports Guy*, by Bill Simmons, Ballantine Books, 2009, pp. xi–xiii.

19. Title within a Title

If a book's title includes the title of another long work (play, book, or periodical) within it, do not italicize the internal title.

> Author's Last Name, First Name. *Book Title* Title within Title. Publisher, Year
>   of Publication.

> Mayhew, Robert, editor. *Essays on Ayn Rand's* Atlas Shrugged. Lexington
>   Books, 2009.

PERIODICALS

20. Article in a Scholarly Journal

List the author(s) first, and then include the article title, the journal title (in italics), the volume number, the issue number, the publication date, and the page numbers.

> Author's Last Name, First Name. "Title of Article." *Title of Journal*, Volume
>   Number, Issue Number, Date of Publication, Page Numbers.

> Dorson, James. "Demystifying the Judge: Law and Mythical Violence in
>   Cormac McCarthy's *Blood Meridian*." *Journal of Modern Literature*,
>   vol. 36, no. 2, Winter 2013, pp. 105–21.

21. Article in a Scholarly Journal with No Volume Number

Follow the format for scholarly journals (as shown in item 20), but list only the issue number before the date of publication.

> Author's Last Name, First Name. "Title of Article." *Title of Journal*, Issue Number, Date of Publication, Page Numbers.

> Leow, Joanne. "Mis-mappings and Mis-duplications: Interdiscursivity and the Poetry of Wayde Compton." *Canadian Literature*, no. 214, 2012, pp. 47–66.

22. Magazine Article

Include the date of publication rather than volume and issue numbers. If page numbers are not consecutive, add "+" after the initial page.

> Author's Last Name, First Name. "Title of Article." *Title of Magazine*, Date of Publication, Page Numbers.

> Wasik, Bill. "Welcome to the Programmable World." *Wired*, June 2013, pp. 202–9.

23. Newspaper Article

If a specific edition is listed on the newspaper's masthead, such as "Late Edition" or "National Edition," include this edition before the date. If page numbers are not consecutive, add "+" after the initial page.

> Author's Last Name, First Name. "Title of Article." *Title of Newspaper*, Date of Publication, Page Numbers.

> Birnbaum, Michael. "Autobahn Speed Limit Proposal Revs Up Debate in Germany." *Washington Post*, 20 May 2013, pp. A1+.

> Author's Last Name, First Name. "Title of Article." *Title of Newspaper*, Specific ed., Date of Publication, Page Numbers.

> Kaminer, Ariel. "On a College Waiting List? Sending Cookies Isn't Going to Help." *New York Times*, National ed.,11 May 2013, p. 2.

If a newspaper numbers each section individually, without attaching letters to the page numbers, include the section number in your citation.

> Author's Last Name, First Name. "Title of Article." *Title of Newspaper*, Date of Publication, sec. Section Number, Page Numbers.

> Bowley, Graham. "Keeping Up with the Windsors." *New York Times*, 15 July 2007, sec. 3, pp. 1+.

24. Editorial

For a newspaper editorial, do not include an author, but do include the label "Editorial," followed by a period, at the end of the entry.

"Title of Article." *Title of Newspaper,* Date of Publication, Page Number(s). Editorial.

"Do Teachers Really Discriminate against Boys?" *Time,* 6 Feb. 2013, p. 37. Editorial.

25. Letter to the Editor

Letter Writer's Last Name, First Name. Letter. *Title of Newspaper,* Date of Publication, Page Number.

Le Tellier, Alexandra. Letter. *Los Angeles Times,* 18 Apr. 2013, p. 12.

26. Unsigned Article

"Title of Article." *Title of Newspaper,* Date of Publication, Page Number.

"An Ounce of Prevention." *The Economist,* 20 Apr. 2013, p. 27.

MAGAZINE COVER

March 2010

ARTICLE

By Marcus E. Raichle

1 magazine title

2 publication date

3 author

4 article title

48

44   **49**

5 page number of quoted passage

6 first and last page numbers of article

MLA in-text citation

As early as 1929, Hans Berger proposed that "we have to assume that the central nervous system is always, and not only during wakefulness, in a state of considerable activity" (Raichle 48).

3 **5**

MLA works cited entry

3 **4** **1** **2**

Raichle, Marcus E. "The Brain's Dark Energy." *Scientific American,* Mar.

6

2010, pp. 44–49.

27. Review

Add "Review of" before the title of the work being reviewed.

> Review Author's Last Name, First Name. Review of *Title of Work Being Reviewed*, by Author of Work Being Reviewed First Name Last Name. *Title of Publication in Which Review Appears*, Date of Publication, Page Numbers.

> Gogolak, Emily. Review of *The Unchangeable Spots of Leopards*, by Kristopher Jansma. *The Village Voice*, 20 Mar. 2013, p. 9.

ELECTRONIC SOURCES

28. Short Work from a Web Site

> Short Work Author's Last Name, First Name. "Title of Short Work." *Title of Web Site*, Publisher or Sponsor of Web site (if Different from Title), Date of Publication, URL.

> Frick, Kit. "On Heroism and The Oregon Trail." *Booth*, Butler University, 8 Feb. 2013, booth. butler. edu/2013/02/08/on-heroism-the-oregon-trail/.

> Myers, Alex. "Switching Gender, Breaking from the Family Line." *Newsweek*, 11 Oct. 2015, www.newsweek.com/switching-gender-breaking-family-line-381443.

29. Entire Web Site

> Web Site Author's Last Name, First Name. *Title of Web Site*. Publisher of Web Site (if Different from Name or Title), Date Range of Production, URL.

> Zaretsky, Staci. *Above the Law*. Breaking Media, 2011–14, abovethelaw.com/author/stacizaretsky/.

30. Entire Blog (Weblog)

Treat an entire blog as you would an entire Web site, including any of the following elements that are available.

> Blog Author's Last Name, First Name. *Title of Blog*. Publisher/Sponsor of Blog (if Different from Name or Title), Date of Most Recent Post, URL.

> Asher, Levi. *Literary Kicks*, 18 May 2013, www.litkicks.com/.

31. Entry in a Blog (Weblog)

Entry Author's Last Name, First Name. "Title of Blog Entry." *Title of Blog*, Publisher/Sponsor of Blog (if Different from Name or Title), Date of Entry, URL.

Kemmerly, John. "Confessions of a Texas Book Dealer." *Literary Kicks*, created by Levi Ascher, 15 Jan. 2013, www.litkicks.com/ TexasBookDealer.

32. Online Book

Book Author's Last Name, First Name. *Title of Book*. Book Publisher, Book Publication Year. *Title of Web Site*, URL.

Wells, H. G. *A Short History of the World*. MacMillan, 1922. *Bartleby.com: Great Books Online*, www.bartleby.com/86/.

33. Work from a Library Subscription Service (such as InfoTrac or FirstSearch)

Follow the format for periodical articles as shown in items 20–27, above. End the citation with the database name (in italics) followed by the DOI (if available) or the URL assigned to the article.

Article Author(s). "Title of Article." *Title of Periodical*, Volume Number, Issue Number, Date of Publication, Page Numbers. *Name of Database*, DOI or URL.

Chou, Shin-Yi et al. "Fast-Food Advertising on Television and Its Influence on Childhood Obesity." *Journal of Law and Economics*, vol. 51, no. 4, Nov. 2008, pp. 599–618. *JSTOR*, www.jstor.org/stable/10.1086/590132.

Waters, Mary C., et al., editors. "Coming of Age in America: The Transition to Adulthood in the Twenty-First Century." *American Journal of Sociology*, vol. 118, no. 2, Sept. 2012, pp. 517–19. *InfoTrac*, doi:10.1086/666372.

Cite from a Web site (MLA)

1 Web site title   **2** article title

TOP OF WEB PAGE

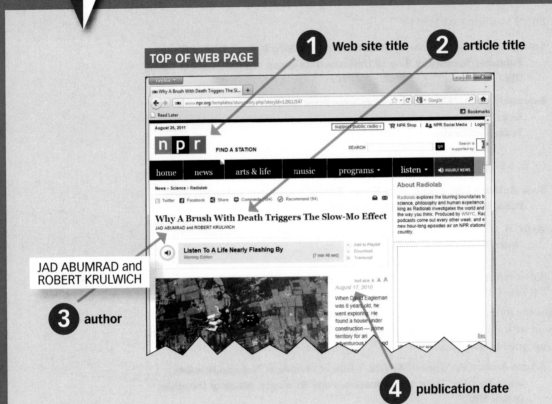

JAD ABUMRAD and
ROBERT KRULWICH

3 author

4 publication date

BOTTOM OF WEB PAGE

Copyright 2011 NPR

7 URL

www.npr.org/
templates/story/
story.php?
storyId=129112147.

5 Web site publisher (in this case same as Web site title)

6 date of access (include only if a date of publication or last update is not available)

MLA in-text citation

Dr. Eagleman suggests that near-death panic prompts the brain to form memories of otherwise-ignored stimuli, making "the experience feels like it must have taken a very long time" (Abumrad and Krulwich).

3

MLA works cited entry

3   **2**

Abumrad, Jad, and Robert Krulwich. "Why a Brush with Death Triggers the

1   **4**   **7**

Slow-Mo Effect." *NPR*, 17 Aug. 2010, www.npr.org/templates/story/story.
php?storyId=129112147.

Cite from a database (MLA)

DATABASE SCREEN

5 volume and issue number

6 publication date

7 name of database

1 journal title

2 article title

3 author

4 pagenumbers

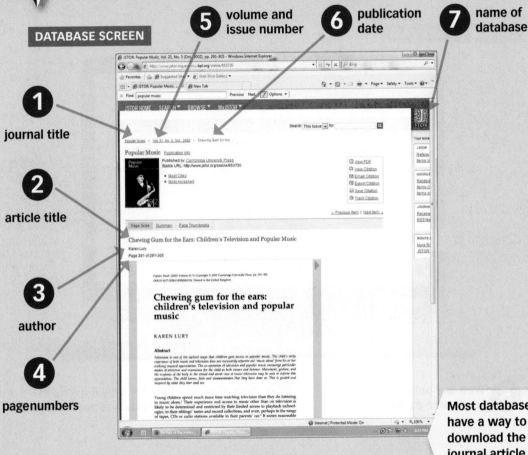

Most databases have a way to download the journal article, often as a PDF.

PDF VIEW

> Use the PDF to double-check your citation elements. If the article has a DOI, use it instead of the URL.

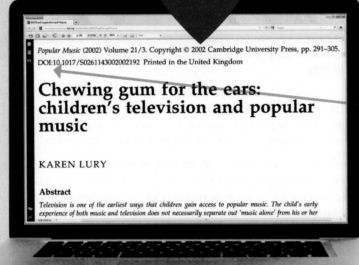

Popular Music (2002) Volume 21/3. Copyright © 2002 Cambridge University Press, pp. 291–305.
DOI:10.1017/S0261143002002192 Printed in the United Kingdom

Chewing gum for the ears: children's television and popular music

KAREN LURY

Abstract

Television is one of the earliest ways that children gain access to popular music. The child's early experience of both music and television does not necessarily separate out 'music alone' from his or her

8 DOI

MLA in-text citation

Children accept even nonsensical lyrics as legitimate musical expression, and one researcher calls their tolerance "a mode of engagement carried productively into the adult's experience of popular songs" (Lury 300).

3 **4**

MLA works cited entry

3   **2**
Lury, Karen. "Chewing Gum for the Ears: Children's Television and

1   **5**   **6**   **4**
Popular Music." *Popular Music*, vol. 21, no. 3, Oct. 2002, pp. 291–305.

7   **8**
JSTOR, doi:10.1017/SO261143002002192.

34. Work from an Online Periodical

Follow the format for periodical articles as shown in items 20–27, above, listing the Web site name, in italics, as the periodical title. For articles in scholarly journals, include page numbers if page numbers are available). End the citation with the DOI (or the URL if a DOI is not provided).

> Journal Article Author(s). "Title of Article." *Title of Online Journal,* Volume
> Number, Issue Number, Date Year of Publication, Page Numbers, DOI
> or URL.

> Clarke, Laura Hurd, and Erica Bennett. "'You Learn to Live with All the
> Things That Are Wrong with You': Gender and the Experience of
> Multiple Chronic Conditions in Later Life." *Ageing and Society*, vol. 33,
> no. 2, Feb. 2013, pp. 342, doi:10.1017/S0144686X11001127.

For articles appearing in online magazines and newspapers, you may list the publisher's name after the online periodical title if the publisher and title are different, but listing the publisher is not necessary. Page numbers are not required for nonscholarly articles published online.

> Magazine or Newspaper Article Author(s). "Title of Article." *Title of Online
> Periodical,* Periodical Publisher, Publication Date, URL.

> Gogoi, Pallavi. "The Trouble with Business Ethics." *BusinessWeek*,
> Bloomberg, 25 June 2007, www.bloomberg.com/news/
> articles/2007-06-22/the-trouble-with-business-ethicsbusinessweek-
> business-news-stock-market-and-financial-advice.

35. Online Posting

> Post Author's Last Name, First Name. "Title (or Subject) of Post." *Title of
> Message Board or Site Name,* Date of Post, URL.

> Cravens, Jayne. "Can a 6 Second Video Make a Difference?" *TechSoup
> Forum*, 5 May 2013, forums.techsoup.org/cs/community/f/32/t/37146.
> aspx.

36. E-mail

> E-mail Author's Last Name, First Name. "Subject of E-mail." Received by
> Name of Recipient, Date Sent.

> Jobs, Steve. "HarperCollins." Received by James Murdoch, 22 Jan. 2010.

37. CD-ROM

CD-ROM Author's (if any) Last Name, First Name. *Title of CD-ROM,* Names
and Function of Pertinent Individual(s), Publisher, Publication Year.

Car Talk: 25 Years of Lousy Car Advice. Performances by Ray Magliozzi and
Tom Magliozzi, HighBridge, 2013.

38. Podcast

Author's Last Name, First Name. "Title of Podcast." *Title of Web Site,* Name
of Publisher or Sponsoring Organization, Date of Publication, URL.

Valsler, Ben, and Meera Senthilingam. "Are Humans Meant for Monogamy?"
The Naked Scientists, Cambridge University, 14 Feb. 2013, www.
thenakedscientists.com/HTML/podcasts/qotw/show/20130214-2/.

39. Entry in a Wiki

Wiki content is continually edited by its users, so there is no author to cite.

"Title of Entry." *Title of Wiki,* Name of Publisher or Sponsoring Organization
(if Different from Title of Wiki), Date of Publication or Most Recent
Update, URL.

"Selfie." *Wikipedia,* Wikimedia Foundation, 24 May 2013, en.wikipedia.org/
wiki/Selfie.

OTHER

40. Dissertation and Master's Thesis

MLA no longer distinguishes between unpublished and published dissertations. Always
provide a date of completion. You may also name the school granting the degree and
the appropriate description: PhD dissertation or MA/MS thesis.

Author's Last Name, First Name. *Dissertation Title.* Year. Name of University,
Description of work.

Yadav, Lekha. *The Effect of Ozone on the Growth and Development of
Selected Food Spoilage Fungi.* 2009. Newcastle U, PhD dissertation.

41. Published Conference Proceedings

List the name(s) of the editor(s), followed by "editor" or "editors," and italicize the title of the proceedings. Before the conference information, add "Proceedings of" and follow with the conference title, date, and location.

> Editor(s), editor(s). *Title of Proceedings.* Proceedings of Conference Title, Conference Date, Conference Location. Publisher, Year.

> Frischer, Bernard et al., editors. *Making History Interactive: Computer Applications and Quantitative Methods in Archaeology.* Proceedings of the Conference of Computer Applications and Quantitative Methods in Archaeology, March 2010, Williamsburg, VA. Archaeopress, 2010.

42. Government Document

List the government (usually a country or state) that issued the document, and then list the department or agency as the author.

> Government, Department or Agency. *Title of Document.* Publisher, Date of Publication.

> United States, National Cancer Institute. *Clear Pathways: Winning the Fight against Tobacco.* National Institutes of Health, Jan. 2013.

43. Pamphlet

> *Pamphlet Title.* Publisher, Year of Publication.

> *Weathering the Storm: Financial Education Resources for Hurricane Recovery. Gulf Coast Edition: Alabama, Florida, Louisiana, Mississippi, Texas.* U.S. Department of the Treasury, 2012.

44. Letter (Personal and Published)

For personal letters that you received, give the name of the letter writer, followed by the description "Letter to the author" (with no italics or quotation marks). For e-mail, see item 36.

> Letter Writer's Last Name, First Name. Letter to the author, Date of Letter.

> Warren, Elizabeth. Letter to the author, 10 Feb. 2018.

For published letters, list the letter writer as well as the recipient.

> Letter Writer's Last Name, First Name. Letter to First Name Last Name,
> Date of Letter. *Title of Book*, edited by Editor's First Name Last Name,
> Publisher, Year.

> Lincoln, Abraham. Letter to T. J. Pickett, 16 Apr. 1859. *Wit & Wisdom of
> Abraham Lincoln: As Reflected in His Letters and Speeches*, edited by
> H. Jack Lang, Stackpole, 2006.

45. Legal Source

List the names of laws or acts (with no underlining or quotation marks), followed by the Public Law number and the date when the law was enacted. Also give the Statutes at Large cataloging number. For other legal sources, refer to *The Bluebook: A Uniform System of Citation*, 19th ed. (Cambridge: Harvard Law Review Assn., 2010).

> Title of Law. Pub. L. number. Stat. number. Date of Enactment.

> Violence against Women Reauthorization Act. Pub. L. 113–114. Stat. 47. 7
> Mar. 2013.

46. Lecture or Public Address

End the citation with a label that describes the type of speech ("Reading," "Address," "Lecture," etc.).

> Speaker's Last Name, First Name. "Title of Speech." Name of Sponsoring
> Institution, Location of Speech, Date of Speech. Type of speech.

> Brooks, David. "What Not to Worry About." Indiana University, Bloomington,
> IN, 3 May 2013. Address.

47. Interview

For published or broadcast interviews, give the title (if any), followed by the publication or broadcast information for the source that aired or published the interview. If there is no title, use "Interview by," followed by the interviewer's name and a period.

> Interviewee's Last Name, First Name. "Title of Interview." Interview by
> Interviewer's First Name Last Name, *Book, Periodical, Web Site, or
> Program Title*, Publication or Broadcast Information (see specific entry for
> guidance).

Biden, Joe. "Joe Biden: The *Rolling Stone* Interview." Interview by Douglas
    Brinkley, *Rolling Stone*, 9 May 2013, pp. 33–36.

Brooks, Mel. Interview by Terry Gross, *Fresh Air*, National Public Radio,
    20 May 2013.

For interviews that you conduct yourself, include the name of the interviewee,
interview type ("Personal interview," "E-mail interview," "Telephone interview," etc.),
and date.

Clarke, Evette Diane. E-mail interview, 3 May 2016.

48. Television or Radio Program

If you access an archived show online, include the source and the URL.

"Episode Title." *Program Title or Series Title*, season number, episode
    number, Production Company or Network, Air Date. Source of
    Access, URL.

"War and Weft & Sins of the Father." *Victoria*, season 2, episode 5,
    PBS, 11 Feb. 2018. KLRU, www.pbs.org/video/warp-and-
    weft-the-sins-of-the-father-dcdg2i/.

"The Future of Marriage." *On Being American*, Public Media,
    4 Apr. 2013. NPR, www.onbeing.org/program/future-
    marriage-david-blankenhorn-and-jonathan-rauch/4883/audio.

49. Film or Video Recording

If you accessed the film via videocassette , DVD, or Blu-ray, include the distributor
name and release date.

Film Title. Function and Name of Pertinent Individual(s), Original Distributor
    and Release Date. Distributor of Recording, Release Date of Recording.

3:10 to Yuma. Directed by Delmer Daves, Columbia Pictures, 1957. Criterion,
    2013.

To highlight a particular individual's performance or contribution, begin with that
person's name, followed by a descriptive label (for example, "performer" or
"choreographer").

Ford, Glenn, performer. *3:10 to Yuma.* Directed by Delmer Daves, Columbia
    Pictures, 1957. Criterion, 2013.

50. Sound Recording

Performer's Last Name, First Name or Band's Name. "Title of Song." *Title of Album*, Record Label, Year.

Benson, George. "Unforgettable." *Inspiration: A Tribute to Nat King Cole*, Concord Jazz, 2013.

51. Musical Composition

Long works such as operas, ballets, and named symphonies should be italicized. Additional information, such as key or movement, may be added at the end.

Composer's Last Name, First Name. *Title of Long Work*. Artists' names, conducted by Conductor's Name, Orchestra, Manufacturer, Date.

Bellini, Vincenzo. *I Capuleti e i Montecchi*. Performances by Beverly Sills, Janet Baker, Nicolai Gedda, Raimund Herincx, and Robert Lloyd, conducted by Giuseppe Patanè, New Philharmonia Orchestra, EMI Classics, 2005.

Mozart, Wolfgang Amadeus. *Sonata for 2 Pianos in D Major, K. 448*. Performances by RaduLupu and Murray Perahia, Sony, 2003.

52. Live Performance

Performance Title. By Author Name, directed by Director Name, performances by Performer Name(s), Date of Performance, Theater or Venue Name, City.

Lucky Guy. By Nora Ephron, directed by George C. Wolfe, performances by Tom Hanks and Peter Scolari, 3 July 2013, Broadhurst Theatre, New York.

53. Work of Art

Artist's Last Name, First Name. *Title of Artwork*. Date, Institution, City.

Picasso, Pablo. *Les Demoiselles d'Avignon*. 1907, Museum of Modern Art, New York City.

A publication medium is required only for reproduced works, such as in books or online. For works accessed on the Web, include the source and the URL.

Opie, Catherine. *Untitled #1 (Michigan Womyn's Music Festival)*. 2010, Institute of Contemporary Art, Boston. *ICA Online*, www.icaboston.org/art/catherine-opie/untitled-1-michigan-womyns-music-festival.

54. Map or Chart

Title of Map. Publisher Name, Year. Map.

West Coast Trail and Carmanah Valley. International Travel Maps, 2010. Map.

If you accessed the map online, include the URL and the label "Map" if the title does not identify it as such.

Cambodia. Google Maps, 2014. www.google.com/maps/place/Cambodia/. Map.

55. Cartoon or Comic Strip

Artist's Last Name, First Name. "Cartoon Title" (if given). *Title of Periodical,* Date, Page Number. Cartoon.

Crawford, Michael. "Effective Catcalls." *The New Yorker,* 11 Feb. 2013, p. 109. Cartoon.

56. Advertisement

Product Name. *Title of Periodical,* Date, Page Number(s). Advertisement.

Pictionary. *Reader's Digest,* 23 Nov. 2011, pp. 12–13. Advertisement.

If you accessed the advertisement online, include the URL.

iPhone X. *YouTube,* 11 Feb. 2018, www.youtube.com/watch?v= dQez2uPP2G8. Advertisement.

Format an MLA paper correctly. You can now find software to format your academic papers in MLA style, but the key alignments for such documents are usually simple enough for you to manage on your own.

- Set up a header on the right-hand side of each page, one-half inch from the top. The header should include your last name and the page number.
- In the upper left on the first—or title—page, include your name, the instructor's name, the course title and/or number, and the date.
- Center the title above the first line of text.
- Use one-inch margins on all sides of the paper.
- Double-space the entire paper (including your name and course information, the title, and any block quotations).
- Indent paragraphs one-half inch.

- Use block quotations for quoted material of four or more lines. Indent block quotations one-half inch from the left margin.

- Do not include a separate title page unless your instructor requires one.

- When you document using MLA style, you'll need to create an alphabetically arranged works cited page at the end of the paper so that readers have a convenient list of all the books, articles, and other data you have used.

Wilcox 1

Susan Wilcox

Professor Longmire

Rhetoric 325M

March 7, 20--

Marathons for Women

     Today in America, five women are running. Two of them live in Minnesota, one in Virginia, and two in Texas. Their careers are different, their political views are divergent, and their other hobbies are irrelevant, for it is running that draws these women together. They are marathoners. Between them, they are eighteen-time veterans of the 26.2-mile march of exhaustion and exhilaration.

     These five women are not alone; over 205,000 women in the United States alone ran a marathon in 2010 ("Annual Marathon Report"). They sacrifice sleeping late, watching TV, and sometimes even toenails (lost toenails are a common malady among marathon runners) for the sake of their sport. Why do these women do this to themselves? Karin Warren explains, "It started out being about losing weight and getting fit again. But I enjoyed running so much—not just how physically fit I felt afterward, but the actual act of running and how it cleared my mind and made me feel better about myself in all aspects of my life—that it became a part of who I am." The other women agree, using words like "conquer," "powerful," and "confident" to describe how running makes them feel.

Annotations (margin notes):

- Student's name, instructor's name, course title, and date appear in upper-left corner.
- One-inch margin on all sides of page.
- Half-inch indent for new paragraph.
- Center the title.
- Double-space all elements on title page.
- Source information appears in parentheses.

Wilcox 2

However, these women know that only a generation ago, marathons weren't considered suitable for women. Tammy Moriearty and Wendy Anderson remember hearing that running could make a woman's uterus fall out; Tammy adds, "It floors me that medical professionals used to believe that." Michelle Gibson says that her friends cautioned her against running when she was pregnant (she ran anyway; it's safe). Naomi Olson has never heard a specific caution, but "lots of people think I am crazy," she says. Female runners, like their male counterparts, do have to maintain adequate nutrition during training (Matheson), but "there are no inherent health risks involved with marathon preparation and participation" (Dilworth). Unfortunately, scientists were not researching running health for women when the marathon was born, and most people thought women were too fragile to run that far. The myth that marathoning is dangerous for women was allowed to fester in the minds of race organizers around the world.

Legend holds that the original marathon runner, Pheidippides, ran from the Battle of Marathon to Athens to bring news of the Athenian victory over Persia. Pheidippides died of exhaustion after giving the news, and the marathon race today is held in honor of his final journey (Lovett x). Historians doubt all the details of this legend, including that a professional runner in Greece would die after what would have been a relatively short distance for him (x–xi). Nevertheless, the myth

Wilcox 8

Works Cited

Anderson, Wendy. Facebook interview, 25 Feb. 2012.

"Annual Marathon Report." *Running USA*, 16 Mar. 2011,
　　www.runningusa.org/index.cfm?fuseaction=news
　　.details&ArticleId=332.

Associated Press. "Paula Radcliffe to Keep Marathon
　　Record." *ESPN Olympic Sports*, 9 Nov. 2011, espn.go.com/
　　olympics/trackandfield/story/_/id/7212726/paula-radcliffe
　　-keep-women-marathon-record-iaaf-reverses-decision.

Brown, Gwilym S. "A Game Girl in a Man's Game." *Sports
　　Illustrated Vault*, 2 May 1966, www.si.com/vault/
　　1966/05/02/609229/a-game-girl-in-a-mans-game.

Dilworth, Mark. "Women Running Marathons: Health Risks."
　　EmpowHER, 23 Apr. 2010, www.empowher.com/fitness/
　　content/women-running-marathons-health-risks.

Gibb, Roberta. "A Run of One's Own." *Running Past*, 2011,
　　www.runningpast.com/gibb_story.htm.

Gibson, Michelle. Facebook interview, 20 Feb. 2012.

"History of Women's Distance Running." *Run Like a Girl*,
　　runlikeagirlfilm.com/history.php. Accessed 20 Feb. 2012.

Longman, Jeré. "Still Playing Catch-Up." *New York Times*, 5 Nov.
　　2011, www.nytimes.com/2011/11/06/sports/radcliffes
　　-womens-record-for-marathon-looks-unbreakable.html.

Lovett, Charles C. *Olympic Marathon: A Centennial History of
　　the Games' Most Storied Race*. Praeger Publishers, 1997.

"Works Cited" centered at top of page.

Entire page is double-spaced: no extra spaces between entries.

Entries arranged alphabetically.

Second and subsequent lines of entries indent five spaces or one-half inch.

Wilcox 9

Matheson, Christie. "Women Running Marathons: Do Benefits

Outweigh Risks?" *Lifescript*, 2012, www.lifescript.com/

diet-fitness/articles/w/women_running_marathons_do_

benefits_outweigh_risks.aspx.

Moriearty, Tammy. Facebook interview, 21 Feb. 2012.

Olson, Naomi. Facebook interview, 21 Feb. 2012.

Switzer, Kathrine. *Marathon Woman: Running the Race to

Revolutionize Women's Sports*. Da Capo Press, 2007.

Warren, Karin. Facebook interview, 21 Feb. 2012.

54

cite in APA

APA Documentation and Format

APA (American Psychological Association) style is used in many social science disciplines. For full details about APA style and documentation, consult the *Publication Manual of the American Psychological Association*, 6th ed. (2010). The basic details for documenting sources and formatting research papers in APA style are presented below.

Document sources according to convention. When you use sources in a research paper, you are required to cite the source, letting readers know that the information has been borrowed from somewhere else and showing them how to find the original material if they would like to study it further. Like MLA style, APA includes two parts: a brief in-text citation and a more detailed reference entry.

In-text citations should include the author's name, the year the material was published, and the page number(s) that the borrowed material can be found on. The author's name and year of publication are generally included in a signal phrase that introduces the passage, and the page number is included in parentheses after the borrowed text. Note that for APA style, the verb in the signal phrase should be in the past tense (*reported,* as in the following example) or present perfect tense (*has reported*).

> Millman (2007) reported that college students around the country are participating in Harry Potter discussion groups, sports activities, and even courses for college credit (p. A4).

Alternatively, the author's name and year can be included in parentheses with the page number.

> College students around the country are participating in Harry Potter discussion groups, sports activities, and even courses for college credit (Millman, 2007, p. A4).

The list of references at the end of the paper contains a more detailed citation that repeats the author's name and publication year and includes the title and additional publication information about the source. Inclusive page numbers are included for periodical articles and parts of books.

> Millman, S. (2007). Generation hex. *Chronicle of Higher Education*, 53(46), A4.

Both in-text citations and reference entries can vary greatly depending on the type of source cited (book, periodical, Web site, etc.). The following pages give specific examples of how to cite a wide range of sources in APA style.

Directory of APA In-Text Citations

General Guidelines for In-Text Citations in APA Style

AUTHOR NAMES

- Give last names only, unless two authors have the same last name (see item 9 on p. 515) or the source is a personal communication (see item 11 on p. 515). In these cases, include the first initial before the last name ("J. Smith").

DATES

- Give only the year in the in-text citation. The one exception to this rule is personal communications, which should include a full date (see item 11 on p. 515).
- Months and days for periodical publications should not be given with the year in in-text citations; this information will be provided as needed in the reference entry at the end of your paper.
- Add a small letter to the common date to differentiate between the items. See item 8 on page 514.
- If you can't locate a date for your source, include the abbreviation "n.d." (for "no date") in place of the date in parentheses.

TITLES

- Titles of works generally do not need to be given in in-text citations. Exceptions include two or more works by the same author and works with no author. See items 8 and 10 on pages 515-16 for details.

PAGE NUMBERS

- Include page numbers whenever possible in parentheses after borrowed material. Put "p." (or "pp.") before the page number(s).
- When you have a range of pages, list the full first and last page numbers (for example, "311–320"). If the borrowed material isn't printed on consecutive pages, list all the pages it appears on (for example, "A1, A4–A6").
- If page numbers are not available, use section names and/or paragraph (written as "para.") numbers when available to help a reader locate a specific quotation. See items 7 and 12 on pages 514 and 516 for examples.

APA in-text citation

1. Author Named in Signal Phrase

While McWilliams (2010) acknowledged not only the growing popularity but also the ecological and cultural benefits of the locavore diet, he still maintained that "eating local is not, in and of itself, a viable answer to sustainable food production on a global level" (p. 2).

2. Author Named in Parentheses

For a source without an author, see item 10; for an electronic source without a page number, see item 12.

"Eating local is not, in and of itself, a viable answer to sustainable food production on a global level" (McWilliams, 2010, p. 2).

3. With Block Quotations

For excerpts of forty or more words, indent the quoted material one-half inch and include the page number at the end of the quotation after the end punctuation.

Pollan (2006) suggested that the prized marbled meat that results from feeding corn to cattle (ruminants) may not be good for us:

> Yet this corn-fed meat is demonstrably less healthy for us, since it contains more saturated fat and less omega-3 fatty acids than the meat of animals fed grass. A growing body of research suggests that many of the health problems associated with eating beef are really problems with corn-fed beef. . . . In the same way ruminants are ill adapted to eating corn, humans in turn may be poorly adapted to eating ruminants that eat corn. (p. 75)

4. Two Authors

Note that if you name the authors in the parentheses, connect them with an ampersand (&).

Sharpe and Young (2005) reported that new understandings about tooth development, along with advances in stem cell technology, have brought researchers closer to the possibility of producing replacement teeth from human tissue (p. 36).

New understandings about tooth development, along with advances in stem cell technology, have brought researchers closer to the possibility of producing replacement teeth from human tissue (Sharpe & Young, 2005, p. 36).

5. Three to Five Authors

The first time you cite a source with three to five authors, list all their names in either the signal phrase or parentheses. If you cite the same source again in your paper, use just the first author's name followed by "et al."

> Frueh, Anouk, Elhai, and Ford (2010) identified the homecoming of Vietnam veterans as the advent for PTSD's eventual inclusion in the DSM, pointing out that "in the immediate, post-Vietnam era, compensation for significant functional impairment was difficult to obtain other than for observable physical injuries, and access to Veterans Administration (VA) medical services were possible only via a 'war-related' disorder" (p. 3).

> Frueh et al. (2010) presented data to combat the assumption that although most people who endure a trauma will develop PTSD, "only a small minority of people will develop distress and functional impairment that rises to the level of a psychiatric disorder. Instead, long-term resilience is actually the norm rather than the exception for people after trauma" (p. 7).

6. Six or More Authors

List the first author's name only, followed by "et al."

> While supportive parenting has not been found to decrease the incidence of depression in bullied adolescents, Bilsky et al. (2013) have insisted that parental support can still offset or counterbalance the negative effects of peer victimization (p. 417).

7. Group, Corporate, or Government Author

Treat the name just as you would any other author, and include the name in either the signal phrase or the parentheses.

> The resolution called on the United States to ban all forms of torture in interrogation procedures (American Psychological Association [APA], 2007, para. 1). It also reasserted "the organization's absolute opposition to all forms of torture and abuse, regardless of circumstance" (APA, 2007, para. 5).

8. Two or More Works by the Same Author

Two or more works by the same author will be differentiated by the publication year of the work being referenced, unless you're citing two works by the same author that were published in the same year. In this case, add a lowercase letter after the year to indicate which entry in the reference list is being cited.

To see reference list entries for these sources, see item 6 on page 520.

Shermer (2005a) has reported that false acupuncture (in placebo experiments) is as effective as true acupuncture (p. 30).

Shermer (2005b) has observed that psychics rely on vague and flattering statements, such as "You are wise in the ways of the world, a wisdom gained through hard experience rather than book learning," to earn the trust of their clients (p. 6).

9. Authors with the Same Last Name

Distinguish the authors in your in-text citations by including initials of their first names.

S. Harris (2012) argued that free will is actually an illusion—a by-product of our past experiences, over which we believe we have more control than we actually do (p. 64).

10. Unknown Author

Identify the item by its title. However, if the author is actually listed as "Anonymous," treat this term as the author in your citation.

Tilapia provides more protein when eaten than it consumes when alive, making it a sustainable fish ("Dream Fish," 2007, p. 26).

The book *Go Ask Alice* (Anonymous, 1971) portrayed the fictional life of a teenager who was destroyed by her addiction to drugs.

11. Personal Communication

If you cite personal letters or e-mails or your own interviews for your research paper, cite these as personal communication in your in-text citation, including the author of the material (with first initial), the term "personal communication," and the date. Personal communications should not be included in your reference list.

One instructor has argued that it is important to "make peer review a lot more than a proofreading/grammar/mechanics exercise" (J. Bone, personal communication, July 27, 2017).

To include the author of a personal communication in the signal phrase, use the following format:

C. Garcia (personal communication, December 11, 2016) has argued that "while it's important to accept criticism of your writing, you should be able to distinguish between a valid suggestion and an opinion that your target audience does not share."

12. Electronic Source

If page numbers are not given, use section names or paragraph numbers to help your readers track down the source.

> Our natural feelings of disgust—for example, at the sight of rotten food or squirming maggots—are "evolutionary messages telling us to get as far away as possible from the source of our discomfort" ("How Our Brains Separate Empathy from Disgust," 2013, para. 15).

13. Musical Recording

A musical piece is identified by its composer and date.

> In an ironic twist, Mick Jagger sang backup on the song "You're So Vain" (Simon, 1972, track 3).

14. Secondary Source

Include the name of the original author in the signal phrase. In the parentheses, add "as cited in," and give the author of the quoted material along with the date and page number. Note that your end-of-paper reference entry for this material will be listed under the secondary source name (Pollan) rather than the original writer (Howard).

> Writing in 1943, Howard asserted that "artificial manures lead inevitably to artificial nutrition, artificial food, artificial animals, and finally to artificial men and women" (as cited in Pollan, 2006, p. 148).

15. Multiple Sources in Same Citation

If one statement in your paper can be attributed to multiple sources, alphabetically list all the authors with dates, separated by semicolons.

> Black Sabbath, considered the originators of heavy metal music, used their bleak upbringing in the failing industrial town of Birmingham, England, to power the darkness and passion in a sound that wowed the masses and disgusted the critics (Christe, 2004; Widerhorn & Turman, 2013).

Directory of APA Reference Entries

General Guidelines for Reference Entries in APA Style

AUTHOR NAMES

- When an author's name appears *before* the title of the work, list it by last name followed by a comma and first initial followed by a period. (Middle initials may also be included.)
- If an author, editor, or other name is listed *after* the title, then the initial(s) precede the last name (see examples on pp. 520, 521-22, and 523).
- When multiple authors are listed, their names should be separated by commas, and an ampersand (&) should precede the final author.

DATES

- For scholarly journals, include only the year (2018).
- For monthly magazines, include the year followed by a comma and the month (2018, May).
- For newspapers and weekly magazines, include the year followed by a comma and the month and the day (2018, May 27).
- Access dates for electronic documents using the month-day-year format: "Retrieved May 27, 2018."
- Months should not be abbreviated.
- If a date is not available, use "n.d." (for "no date") in parentheses.

TITLES

- Titles of periodicals should be italicized, and all major words capitalized (*Psychology Today; Journal of Archaeological Research*).
- Titles of books, Web sites, and other non-periodical long works should be italicized. Capitalize the first word of the title (and subtitle, if any) and proper nouns only (*Legacy of ashes: The history of the CIA*).
- For short works such as essays, articles, and chapters, capitalize the first word of the title (and subtitle, if any) and proper nouns only (The black sites: A rare look inside the CIA's secret interrogation program).

PAGE NUMBERS

- Reference entries for periodical articles and sections of books should include the range of pages: "245–257." For material in parentheses, include the abbreviation "p." or "pp." before the page numbers ("pp. A4–A5").
- If the pages are not continuous, list all the pages separated by commas: "245, 249, 301–306."

APA reference entries

AUTHOR INFORMATION

1. One Author

Senna, D. (2017). *New people*. New York, NY: Riverhead.

2. Two Authors

Cox, B., & Cohen, A. (2011). *Wonders of the universe*. New York, NY: HarperCollins.

3. Three or More Authors

List every author up to and including seven; for a work with eight or more authors, give the first six names followed by three ellipsis dots and the last author's name.

Holstein, M. B., Parks, J., & Waymack, M. (2010). *Ethics, aging, and society: The critical turn*. New York, NY: Springer.

Barry, A. E., Stellefson, M. L., Piazza-Gardner, A. K., Chaney, B. H., & Dodd, V. (2013). The impact of pre-gaming on subsequent blood alcohol concentrations: An event-level analysis. *Addictive Behaviors, 38*(8), 2374–2377.

4. Group, Corporate, or Government Author

In many cases, the group name is the same as the publisher. Instead of repeating the group name, use the term "Author" for the publisher's name.

Scientific American Editors. (2012). *Storm warnings: Climate change and extreme weather*. New York, NY: Author.

5. Unidentified Author

If the author is listed on the work as "Anonymous," list that in your reference entry, alphabetizing accordingly. Otherwise, start with and alphabetize by title.

Anonymous. (1996). *Primary colors: A novel of politics*. New York, NY: Random House.

Quantum computing: Faster, slower—or both at once? (2013, May). *The Economist*, 57–58.

6. Multiple Works by the Same Author

Note in the examples below that both the title of a journal and its volume number are italicized.

> Shermer, M. (2003). I knew you would say that [Review of the book *Intuition: Its powers and perils*]. *Skeptic, 10*(1), 92–94.

> Shermer, M. (2005a, August). Full of holes: The curious case of acupuncture. *Scientific American, 293*(2), 30.

> Shermer, M. (2005b). *Science friction*. New York, NY: Henry Holt, 6.

BOOKS

7. Book: Basic Format

> Author. (Publication Year). Book title: Book subtitle. Publication City, State (abbreviated) or Country of Publication: Publisher.

> O'Neil, S. K. (2013). *Two nations indivisible: Mexico, the United States, and the road ahead*. New York, NY: Oxford University Press.

8. Author and Editor

> Author. (Publication Year). Book title: Book subtitle (Editor's Initial(s). Editor's Last Name, Ed.). Publication City, State (abbreviated) or Country of Publication: Publisher.

> Faulkner, W. (2004). *Essays, speeches, and public letters* (J. B. Meriwether, Ed.). New York, NY: Modern Library.

9. Work in an Anthology or a Collection

Begin with the author and date of the short work and include the title as you would a periodical title (no quotations and minimal capitalization). Then list "In" and the editor's first initial and last name followed by "Ed." in parentheses. Next give the anthology title and page numbers in parentheses. End with the publication information. If an anthology has two editors, connect them with an ampersand (&) and use "Eds."

> Author. (Publication Year). Title of short work. In Editor's initials. Editor's Last Name (Ed.), Title of anthology (pp. Page Numbers). Publication City, State (abbreviated) or Country of Publication: Publisher.

> Keller, H. (2008). I go adventuring. In P. Lopate (Ed.), *Writing New York: A literary anthology* (pp. 505–508). New York, NY: Library of America.

For more than two editors, connect them with commas and an ampersand. For large editorial boards, give the name of the lead editor followed by "et al."

> J. Smith, L. Hoey, & R. Burns (Eds.)

> N. Mallen et al. (Eds.)

10. Edited Collection

> Editor. (Ed.). (Publication Year). *Book title: Book subtitle.* Publication City, State (abbreviated) or Country of Publication: Publisher.

> Glenn, C., & Mountford, R. (Eds.). (2017). *Rhetoric and writing studies in the new century: Historiography, pedagogy, and politics.* Carbondale, IL: Southern Illinois University Press.

11. Multivolume Work

> Author(s) or Editor(s) (Eds.). (Publication Year). Book title: Book subtitle (Vols. volume numbers). Publication City, State (abbreviated) or Country of Publication: Publisher.

> Wright, W., Gardner, S., Graves, J., & Ruffin, P. (Eds.). (2011). *The southern poetry anthology* (Vols. 1–5). Huntsville, TX: Texas Review Press.

12. Later Edition

In parentheses include the edition type (such as "Rev." for "Revised" or "Abr." for "Abridged") or number ("2nd," "3rd," "4th," etc.) as shown on the title page, along with the abbreviation "ed." after the book title.

> Author(s). (Publication Year). Book title (Edition Type or Number ed.). Publication City, State (abbreviated) or Country of Publication: Publisher.

> Akmajian, A., Demers, R. A., Farmer, A. K., & Harnish, R. M. (2010). *Linguistics: An introduction to language and communication* (6th ed.). Cambridge, MA: MIT Press.

13. Translation

List the translator's initial, last name, and "Trans." in parentheses after the title. After the publication information, list "Original work published" and year in parentheses. Note that the period is omitted after the final parenthesis.

> Author. (Publication Year of Translation). Book title (Translator Initial(s). Last Name, Trans.). Publication City, State (abbreviated) or Country of Publication: Publisher. (Original work published Year)

> Camus, A. (1988). *The stranger* (M. Ward, Trans.). New York, NY: Knopf. (Original work published 1942)

14. Article in a Reference Book

Article Author. (Publication Year). Article title. In Initial(s). Last Name of
Editor (Ed.), Reference book title (pp. Page Numbers). Publication City,
State (abbreviated) or Country of Publication: Publisher.

Stroud, S. (2013). Value theory. In H. LaFollette (Ed.), *The international encyclopedia of ethics* (pp. 789–790). Malden, MA: John Wiley & Sons.

If a reference book entry has no author, begin with the title of the article.

Article title. (Publication Year). In Book title. Publication City, State
(abbreviated) or Country of Publication: Publisher.

Top 10 news topics of 2012. (2012). In *The world almanac and book of facts
2013*. New York, NY: World Almanac Books.

PERIODICALS

15. Article in a Journal Paginated by Volume

Article Author. (Publication Year). Title of article. *Title of Journal, Volume
Number,* Page Numbers.

Mace, B. L., Corser, G. C., Zitting, L., & Denison, J. (2013). Effects of over
flights on the national park experience. *Journal of Environmental
Psychology, 35,* 30–39.

16. Article in a Journal Paginated by Issue

Article Author. (Publication Year). Title of article. *Title of Journal, Volume
Number* (Issue Number), Page Numbers.

Clancy, S., & Simpson, L. (2002). Literacy learning for indigenous students:
Setting a research agenda. *Australian Journal of Language and Literacy,
25*(2), 47–64.

17. Magazine Article

Article Author. (Publication Year, Month). Title of article. *Title of Magazine,
Volume Number*(Issue Number), Page Number(s).

Doll, J. (2013, June). The evolution of hand gestures: Why do some die out
and others endure? *The Atlantic, 200*(1167): 58–60.

18. Newspaper Article

Article Author. (Publication Year, Month Day). Title of article. *Title of Newspaper,* p. Page Number.

Tobar, H. (2013, May 28). Tech-savvy parents prefer print over e-books for kids, PEW reports. *Los Angeles Times,* p. 24.

19. Letter to the Editor

Include "Letter to the editor" in brackets after the letter title (if any) and before the period.

Author. (Publication Year, Month Day). Title of letter [Letter to the editor]. *Title of Newspaper,* p. Page Number.

Murray, M. (2013, April 24). Giving cash to panhandlers is the wrong way to help [Letter to the editor]. *Denver Post,* p. A17.

20. Review

After the review title (if any), include in brackets "Review of the" and the medium of the work being reviewed ("book," "film," "CD," etc.), followed by the title of the work in italics. If the reviewed work is a book, include the author's name after a comma; if it's a film or other media, include the year of release.

Author Name. (Publication Year, Month Day). Title of review [Review of the book *Book title*, by Author Name]. *Title of Periodical, Volume Number,* Page Number.

Abramson, J. (2012, November 11). Grand bargainer [Review of the book *Thomas Jefferson: The art of power*, by J. Meacham]. *New York Times Book Review, 3,* 1.

ELECTRONIC SOURCES

21. Article with a DOI

A DOI (digital object identifier) is a unique number assigned to specific content, such as a journal article. Include the DOI but not the database name or URL. Note that there is no period after the DOI.

DiGangi, J., Jason, L. A., Mendoza, L., Miller, S. A., & Contreras, R. (2013). The relationship between wisdom and abstinence behaviors in women in recovery from substance abuse. *American Journal of Drug and Alcohol Abuse, 39*(1), 33–37. doi: 10.3109/00952990.2012.702172

22. Article without a DOI

Give the exact URL or the URL for the journal's home page if access requires a subscription. Do not give the database name. Note that there is no period after the URL.

> McDermott, L. A., & Pettijohn, T. F., II (2011). The influence of clothing
>   fashion and race on the perceived socioeconomic status and person
>   perception of college students. *Psychology & Society, 4*(2), 64–75.
>   Retrieved from http://www.psychologyandsociety.org/__assets/
>   __original/2012/01/McDermott_Pettijohn.pdf

23. Article in Internet-Only Periodical

An article published exclusively online is unlikely to have page numbers.

> Palmer, B. (2013, May 24). How accurate are AAA's travel forecasts? *Slate.*
>   *com.* Retrieved from http://www.slate.com/articles/health_and_science/
>   explainer/2013/05/aaa_memorial_day_travel_forecast_are_holiday_
>   driving_predictions_accurate.html

24. Multipage Web Site

Include a retrieval date before the URL if the material is likely to be changed or updated or if it lacks a set publication date. Do not add a period at the end of the entry.

> Web Site Author or Sponsor. (Date of Most Recent Update). *Title of Web site.*
>   Retrieved date, from URL

> Department of Homeland Security. (2013). *Disasters.* Retrieved January 14,
>   2014, from http://www.dhs.gov/topic/disasters

> Linder, D. O. (2013). *Famous trials.* Retrieved March 2, 2014, from http://law2.
>   umkc.edu/faculty/projects/ftrials/ftrials.htm

25. Part of a Web Site

> Short Work Author. (Date of Most Recent Update). Title of short work. *Title of*
>   *Web site.* Retrieved date, from URL

> Slate, M., & Sestan, N. (2012, September 18). The emerging biology of autism
>   spectrum disorders. *Autism speaks.* Retrieved from http://www.
>   autismspeaks.org/blog/2012/09/18/emerging-biology-autism-spectrum-
>   disorders

26. Online Posting

For detailed advice on citing social media, see http://blog.apastyle.org/apastyle/social-media.

> Post Author. (Year, Month Day of post). Title of post [Description of post].
>   Retrieved from URL

Parkin, G. (2011, December 5). Mobile learning platforms and tools [Online forum comment]. Retrieved from http://community.astd.org/eve/forums/a/tpc/f/6401041/m/142107851

27. Computer Software or App

If the software or app has an author or editor listed, the reference begins with that.

Title of software [Computer software]. (Publication Year). Publication City, State (abbreviated) or Country of Publication: Publisher.

History: The French revolution [Computer software]. (2009). San Jose, CA: Innovative Knowledge.

When citing an app, look at the most recent update for the publication date.

Title of app. (Publication Year). Creator (Version number) [Mobile application software]. Retrieval information.

Medscape. (2014). WebMD Health (Version 4.4.1) [Mobile application software]. Retrieved from http://itunes.apple.com

28. Entry in a Blog (Weblog)

Hasselbrink, K. (2013, February 5). Chai [Web log post]. Retrieved from http://theyearinfood.com/2013/02/chai.html

29. Podcast

Fogarty, M. (Producer). (2013, May 10). How texting is changing English. [Audio podcast]. *Grammar Girl*. Retrieved from http://grammar.quickanddirtytips.com/how-texting-is-changingenglish.aspx

30. Entry in a Wiki

Article title. Posting date (if any). Retrieved date, from URL

Selfie. (n.d.). Retrieved July 27, 2013, from http://en.wikipedia.org/wiki/Selfie

2 publisher of report
(if not named as author)

1 publication
date

3 report
number

4 title of
online
report

5 author

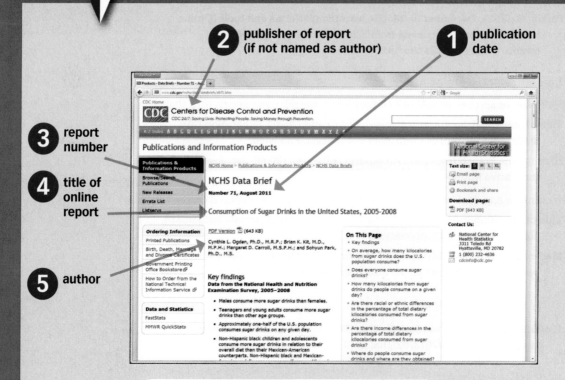

If you cite a source with three or more
authors more than once in text, only list all of
the authors the first time. Subsequent times
only need the first author's last name, like
this: (Ogden et al.).

SECTION BEING CITED

7 section title

6 URL of section

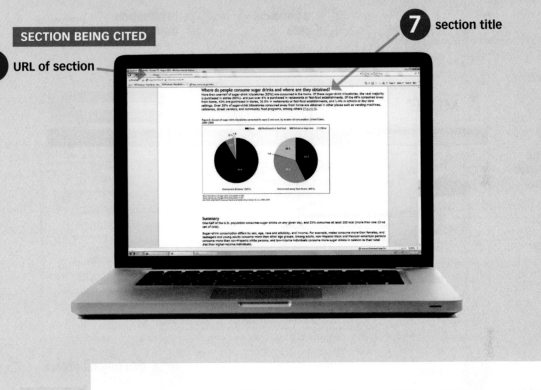

APA in-text citation

A nutrition survey of U.S. behavior between 2005 and 2008 found that an overwhelming 92 percent of sugar-drink kilocalories consumed outside the home were from drinks purchased in stores, not restaurants (Ogden, Kit, Carroll,& Park, 2011).

1 **5** **7**

APA references list entry

Ogden, C. L., Kit, B. K., Carroll, M. D., & Park S. (2011, August). Where do

4

people consume sugar drinks and where are they obtained? In Consumption

3

of sugar drinks in the United States, 2005–2008 (NCHS Data Brief No. 71).

2

Retrieved from Centers for Disease Control and Prevention web site:

6

http://www.cdc.gov/nchs/data/databriefs/db71.htm#people

Cite from a database (APA)

DATABASE SCREEN

2 periodical title

3 publication date

PDF Version

1 volume and issue number

6 article title

5 author

4 DOI (digital object identifier)

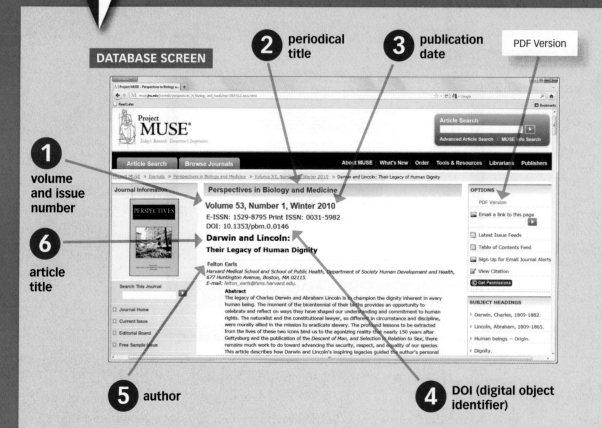

PDF VIEW (FIRST PAGE)

If you're reading an article in an Internet browser and aren't sure where to find the information you need, try viewing the article as a PDF, which usually shows what originally appeared in the print journal.

I T IS WITH A SENSE of intellectual excitement that this year we celebrate the bicentennial of two extraordinary men who just happened to be born on the same day, February 12, 1809. Charles Darwin was born into a learned and landed family in Shropshire, England. Quite a different social and economic setting prevailed in Abraham Lincoln's home in Kentucky. His father was a poor and une-

Harvard Medical School and School of Public Health , Department of Society Human Development and Health, 677 Huntington Avenue, Boston, MA 02115.
E-mail: felton_earls@hms.harvard.edu.

*Max Perutz Memorial Lecture, Ninth Biennial Meeting, International Human Rights Network of Academies and Scholarly Societies, Rabat, Morocco, May 21, 2009.

Perspectives in Biology and Medicine, volume 53, number 1 (winter 2010):3–15
© 2010 by The Johns Hopkins University Press

3

7 page range

APA in-text citation

It's important to note the contributions of Darwin and Lincoln to modern conceptions of human rights, particularly the beliefs that scientists are free to pursue knowledge, no matter how different from or risky to the prevailing wisdom, and that one of the responsibilities of modern governments is to protect this right to rationality and critical inquiry" (Earls, 2011, 4).

5 **3** **7**

5 **3** **6**

APA references list entry

Earls, F. (2011, Winter). Darwin and Lincoln: Their legacy of human dignity.

2 **1** **7** **4**

Perspectives in Biology and Medicine, 53(1), 3–15. doi:10.1353/pbm.0.0146

OTHER

31. Group, Corporate, or Government Document

List the group or agency as the author, and include any identifying numbers. Many federal agencies' works are published by the U.S. Government Printing Office. If the group is also the publisher, use the word "Author" rather than repeating the group name at the end of the entry.

> Name of Group, Corporation, or Government Agency. (Publication Year). *Title of document* (Identifying number, if any). Publication City, State (abbreviated) or Country of Publication: Publisher.

> National Equal Pay Task Force. (2013). *Fifty years after the Equal Pay Act: Assessing the past, taking stock of the future* (PREX 1.2:EQ 2). Washington, DC: U.S. Government Printing Office.

> Maine Department of Health and Human Services. (2011). *Connections: A guide for family caregivers in Maine.* Augusta, ME: Author.

32. Published Conference Proceedings

> Editor(s). (Eds.). (Publication Year). *Proceedings of the Conference Name: Book title.* Publication City, State (abbreviated) or Country of Publication: Publisher.

> Contreras, F., Farjas, M., & Melero, F. J. (Eds.). (2013). *Proceedings of the 38th annual Conference on Computer Applications and Quantitative Methods in Archaeology: Fusion of cultures.* Oxford, United Kingdom: Archaeopress.

33. Dissertation Abstract

For dissertations abstracted in Dissertation Abstracts International, include the author's name, date, and dissertation title. Then include the volume, issue, and page number. If you access the dissertation from an electronic database, identify the type of work ("Doctoral dissertation") before giving the database name and any identifying number. If you retrieve the abstract from the Web, include the name of the institution in the parentheses, and then give the URL.

> Author. (Year of Publication). *Title of dissertation. Dissertation Abstracts International, Volume Number* (Issue Number), Page Number.

> Hand, J. A. (2011). *Making sense of change: Sexuality transformation at midlife. Dissertation Abstracts International, 72*(9), 8745B.

> Hand, J. A. (2011). *Making sense of change: Sexuality transformation at midlife* (Doctoral dissertation). Available from ProQuest Dissertations and Theses database. (9347727101).

Hand, J. A. (2011). *Making sense of change: Sexuality transformation at midlife* (Doctoral dissertation. Temple University). Retrieved from http://cdm16002.contentdm.oclc.org/cdm/compoundobject/collection/p245801coll10/id/108810/rec/14

34. Film

Writer(s), & Producer(s), & Director(s). (Release year). *Film title* [Motion picture]. Country of Origin: Movie Studio.

Peele, J. (Writer/Director) & Blum, J. (Producer). (2017). *Get Out* [Motion picture]. United States: Universal Pictures.

35. Television Program

Writer(s), & Producer(s), & Director(s). (Year of Release). Title of episode [Television series episode]. In Producer Initials. Last Name (Producer), *Title of series*. City, State (abbreviated) or Country of Publication: Broadcast Company.

Zwonitzer, M. (Writer/Producer/Director). (2013). Jesse James [Television series episode]. In M. Samels (Producer), *American Experience*. Boston, MA: WGBH.

36. Musical Recording

Writer. (Copyright Year). Title of song [Recorded by Artist Name]. On *Album title* [Recording medium]. City of Recording, State (abbreviated) or Country of Publication: Record Label. (Recording Year).

Lennon, J., & McCartney, P. (1967). With a little help from my friends [Recorded by The Beatles]. On *Sgt. Pepper's Lonely Hearts Club Band: Remastered* [CD]. Los Angeles, CA: Capitol. (2009).

Format an APA paper correctly. The following guidelines will help you prepare a manuscript using APA style.

- Set up a header on each page, one-half inch from the top. The header should include a brief title (shortened to no more than fifty characters) in all capital letters and should align left. Page numbers should appear in the upper right corner.

- Margins should be set at one inch on all sides of the paper.

- Check with your instructor to see if a title page is preferred. If so, at the top of the page, you need the short title you'll use in your header, in all capital letters, preceded by the words "Running head" and a colon. The page number appears on the far right. Next, the full title of your paper, your name, and your affiliation (or school) appear in the middle of the page, centered.

- If you include an abstract for your paper, put it on a separate page, immediately following the title page.
- All lines of text (including the title page, abstract, block quotations, and the list of references) should be double-spaced.
- Indent the first lines of paragraphs one-half inch or five spaces.
- Use block quotations for quoted material of four or more lines. Indent block quotations one inch from the left margin.
- When you document a paper using APA style, you'll need to create alphabetically arranged reference page(s) at the end of the project so that readers have a convenient list of all the books, articles, and other data you have used in the paper or project.

Sample APA Pages

Short title in all capitals is aligned left. Arabic numerals are used for page numbers.

Developmental Disorders:

Cri du Chat Syndrome

Marissa Dahlstrom

University of Texas at Austin

Full title, writer's name, and affiliation are all centered in middle of page.

CRI DU CHAT SYNDROME   2

Developmental Disorders: Cri du Chat Syndrome

Developmental disorders pose a serious threat to young
children. However, early detection, treatment, and intervention
often allow a child to lead a fulfilling life. To detect a problem at
the beginning of life, medical professionals and caregivers must
recognize normal development as well as potential warning
signs. Research provides this knowledge. In most cases, research
also allows for accurate diagnosis and effective intervention. Such
is the case with cri du chat syndrome (CDCS), also commonly
known as cat cry syndrome and 5p– (5p minus) syndrome.

Cri du chat syndrome, a fairly rare genetic disorder first
identified in 1963 by Dr. Jerome Lejeune, affects between 1 in
15,000 to 1 in 50,000 live births (Campbell, Carlin, Justen, &
Baird, 2004).The syndrome is caused by partial deletion of
chromosome number 5, specifically the portion labeled as 5p;
hence the alternative name for the disorder (5P– Society). While
the exact cause of the deletion is unknown, it is likely that "the
majority of cases are due to spontaneous loss . . . during
development of an egg or sperm. A minority of cases result from
one parent carrying a rearrangement of chromosome 5 called a
translocation" (Sondheimer, 2005). The deletion leads to many
different symptoms and outcomes. Perhaps the most noted
characteristic of children affected by this syndrome — a high-
pitched cry resembling the mewing of a cat — explains
Lejeune's choice of the name cri du chat. Pediatric nurse Mary
Kugler writes that the cry is caused by "problems with the

CRI DU CHAT SYNDROME   6

References

Campbell, D., Carlin M., Justen, J., III, & Baird, S. (2004).

    Cri-du-chat syndrome: A topical overview. *5P– Society*

    Retrieved from http://www.fivepminus.org/online.htm

Denny, M., Marchand-Martella, N., Martella, R., Reilly, J. R., &

    Reilly, J. F. (2000). Using parent-delivered graduated

    guidance to teach functional living skills to a child with

    cri du chat syndrome. *Education & Treatment of Children,*

    23(4), 441.

5P– Society. (n.d.). About 5P–syndrome. *5P– Society Web site.*

    Retrieved from http://www.fivepminus.org/about.htm

Kugler, M. (2006). Cri-du-chat syndrome: Distinctive kitten

    like cry in infancy. *About.com Rare Diseases.* Retrieved

    from http://rarediseases.about.com/cs/criduchatsynd/

    a/010704.htm

McClean, P. (1997). Genomic analysis: *In situ* hybridization.

    Retrieved from http://www.ndsu.nodak.edu/instruct/

    mcclean/plsc431/genomic/genomic2.htm

Sarimski, K. (2003). Early play behavior in children with

    5p–syndrome. *Journal of Intellectual Disability Research,*

    47(2), 113-120. doi: 10.1046/j.1365-2788.2003.00448.x

Sondheimer, N. (2005). Cri du chat syndrome. In *MedlinePlus*

    medical encyclopedia. Retrieved from http://www.nlm

    .nih.gov/medlineplus/ency/article/001593.htm

Grammar

This brief chapter addresses specific grammar issues that bedevil college writers—problems that show up often in academic papers. Such trouble spots become less worrisome once you can recognize them—whether you're a native speaker or have learned English in school as a second (or third) language.

55a Verb Tense and Voice

Verbs pose difficulties for writers because they change form frequently and serve many roles. Following is a refresher on some of their complications.

Verbs express time. That aspect is called *tense*. The basic verb tenses are simple past, present, and future tenses.

PAST	I *worked*.
PRESENT	I *work*.
FUTURE	I *will work*.

But relationships of time are more complicated, and so English verbs take various helpers to express those nuances. Here are some of them:

PAST PERFECT	I *had worked* there once.
PRESENT PERFECT	I *have worked* there all my life.
FUTURE PERFECT	I *will have worked* there for a year soon.
PAST PROGRESSIVE	I *was working* all morning.

PRESENT PROGRESSIVE	I *am working* now.
FUTURE PROGRESSIVE	I *will be working* throughout the weekend.
PAST PERFECT PROGRESSIVE	I *had been working* for many hours when you arrived.
PRESENT PERFECT PROGRESSIVE	I *have been working* all my life.
FUTURE PERFECT PROGRESSIVE	I *will have been working* for a year on the project soon.

The distinctions seem subtle, but there are times when you will need them.

Verbs have voice.
Writers are commonly advised to "favor active rather than passive voice" (see p. 378). Verbs are in active voice when the subject of a sentence performs the action the verb describes.

| ACTIVE VOICE | I *added* chlorine to the solution. |
| ACTIVE VOICE | Jaylen Smith *filed* the student government's free speech protest. |

Verbs are passive when the action of the sentence is done to the subject:

| PASSIVE VOICE | Chlorine *was added* to the solution. |
| PASSIVE VOICE | The student government's free speech protest *was filed* by Jaylen Smith. |

In general, sentences in the active voice are tauter than those in passive voice. That's why many writing instructors favor the active voice and may circle passive verb forms when they see them.

But the passive voice—common in most scientific papers and lab reports—enables writers to step out of the picture whenever their presence isn't important: *Chlorine was added to the solution.* Just as important, the choice between active and passive voice determines the focal point of a sentence. So deciding to use an active or passive verb is a rhetorical or stylistic choice, not a matter of right or wrong.

Verbs have mood.
English has three major moods—*indicative, imperative,* and *subjunctive.* The first two cause few problems. You use the indicative whenever you are making direct statements of fact—which is most of the time. You shift to the imperative mood when you make a request or give a command.

| INDICATIVE | There *was* salt on the table. |
| IMPERATIVE | *Pass* the salt, please. |

The subjunctive mood, increasingly rare, expresses possibility or desire rather than actual fact. That's a tough situation to describe, but you'll recognize the subjunctive voice in the following examples.

Come what may, we'll be ready.
God *save* the Queen!

Please *be* on time for the meal.
Would that there *were* salt on the table!
If I *were* in charge, there would be salt on the table.

Understand *verbals*.

Verbals closely resemble verbs but function like other parts of speech. These items include *infinitives*, *participles*, and *gerunds*.

You'll recognize infinitives as the base forms of verbs preceded by *to*: *to find, to understand, to appreciate*. Infinitives and infinitive phrases can function as nouns, adverbs, or adjectives:

INFINITIVE AS NOUN PHRASE	*To pass this course* is my primary goal.
INFINITIVE AS ADJECTIVE	I still have a paper *to finish* for the class.
INFINITIVE AS ADVERB	I read three books *to complete* that paper.

In some situations, infinitives can stand alone to modify whole sentences:

To be frank, we hired the wrong people to fix our software problem.

Of course, you don't need to identify the grammatical function of an infinitive to use one.

Participles are verbs that function as modifiers. Present participles add an *–ing* ending to the base form of a verb:

    bursting bubbles   *freezing* weather   *ringing* bells

Past participles add an *–ed ending* for regular verbs or use the equivalent form for an irregular verb.

    advertised price   *forgotten* man   *stolen* goods

Like verbs, participles can express time and even take objects and modifiers.

Aiming the telescope precisely, the astronomer photographed the dim star.

The movie *being filmed on the mall* was the director's first.

Having been fed, the dog fell asleep, *dreaming of yet more bones*.

Gerunds, which typically end in *-ing* can look exactly like present participles, but they function as nouns rather than as modifiers.

GERUND	*Running* is good exercise.
PARTICIPLE	Never leave an engine *running* in a closed garage.
GERUND	I admired the design in Mrs. Begay's *weaving*.
PARTICIPLE	I was in awe of Mrs. Begay *weaving* at the show.

Is it wrong to split an infinitive? Likely, you've heard that it is grammatically wrong to place a modifier between the "to" and the verb in an infinitive phrase:

> To **really** appreciate Inception, you need to see the movie more than once.
> I don't expect to **ever** change his mind about Trump or Clinton.

In fact, split infinitives are the fake news of English grammar: The construction is acceptable so long as it doesn't create ambiguity or break up the flow of a sentence—as might be the case in the following examples.

> Professor Todd resolved to **only** ignore students arriving late.
> She didn't want to, **so far as it was possible**, allow them to disrupt her lecture.

55b Subject/Verb Agreement

You know that regular verbs routinely change form in the present tense to reflect whether their subjects are either singular or plural:

> Jayla prefers coffee, while Cameron and Kiara prefer tea.
> She goes to Los Angeles whenever we go to Detroit.

But agreement gets troublesome if the actual subject of the verb is hard to identify.

Be sure a verb agrees with its real subject.
It's tempting to link a verb to the noun(s) closest to it (in purple below) instead of the real subject, but that can be a mistake when that noun isn't actually the subject.

WRONG	Cameras and professional lenses that cost as much as a small **car** makes photography an expensive hobby.
CORRECTED	Cameras and professional lenses that cost as much as a small car make photography an expensive hobby.
WRONG	Bottled water from **groceries** or convenience **stores** usually cost far more per ounce than gasoline.
CORRECTED	Bottled water from groceries or convenience stores usually costs far more per ounce than gasoline.

Some of the indefinite pronouns described as variable (see chart on p. 541) are exceptions to the rule. Whether they are singular or plural depends on the nouns that follow them (see the following sections).

In most cases, treat multiple subjects joined by *and* as plural. But when a subject with *and* clearly expresses a single notion, that subject is singular.

Hip-hop, rock, and country are dominant forms of popular music today. [subject is plural]

Blues and folk have their fans too. [subject is plural]

Rock and roll often strikes a political chord. [subject is singular]

Peanut butter and jelly is the sandwich of choice in our house. [subject is singular]

When singular subjects are followed by expressions such as *along with*, *together with*, or *as well as*, the subjects may feel plural, but technically they remain singular.

> **WRONG**   Chance the Rapper, as well as Kelsea Ballerini, Maren Morris, Anderson .Paak, and The Chainsmokers, were competing for Best New Artist at the 2017 Grammys.

> **CORRECTED**   Chance the Rapper, as well as Kelsea Ballerini, Maren Morris, Anderson . Paak, and The Chainsmokers, was competing for Best New Artist at the 2017 Grammys.

If the corrected version sounds awkward, try revising the sentence.

> **CORRECTED**   Chance the Rapper, Kelsea Ballerini, Maren Morris, Anderson .Paak, and The Chainsmokers were all competing for Best New Artist at the 2017 Grammys.

When compound subjects are linked by *either . . . or* or *neither . . . nor,* make the verb agree with the nearer part of the subject. (Knowing this rule will make you one person among a thousand.)

Neither my sisters nor my mother is a fan of Kanye West.

When possible, put the plural part of the subject closer to the verb to make it sound less awkward.

Neither my mother nor my sisters are fans of Kanye West.

Indefinite Pronouns

Singular	Plural	Variable
anybody	both	all
anyone	few	any
anything	many	more
each	others	most
everybody	several	none
everyone		some
everything		
nobody		
no one		
nothing		
one		
somebody		
someone		
something		

When an indefinite pronoun is your subject, confirm whether it is singular, plural, or variable. Most indefinite pronouns are singular, but consult the chart above to double-check.

> Everybody complains about politics, but nobody does much about it.
> Each of the women expects a promotion.
> Something needs to be done about the budget crisis.

A few indefinite pronouns are obviously plural: *both, few, many, others, several.*

> Many complain about politics, but few do much about it.

And some indefinite pronouns shift in number, depending on the prepositional phrases that modify them.

> All of the votes are in the ballot box.
> All of the fruit is spoiled.
> Most of the rules are less complicated.
> Most of the globe is covered by oceans.
> None of the rules make sense.
> On the Security Council, none but the Russians favor the resolution.

Be consistent with collective nouns. Many of these words describing a group can be treated as either singular or plural subjects: *band, class, jury, choir, group, committee.*

> The **jury seems** to resent the lawyer's playing to **its** emotions.
> The **jury seem** to resent the lawyer's playing to **their** emotions.
> The **band was** unhappy with **its** latest release.
> The **band were** unhappy with **their** latest release.

A basic principle is to be consistent throughout a passage. If *the band* is singular the first time you mention it, keep it that way for the remainder of the project. Be sensible too. If a sentence sounds odd to your ear, modify it:

> **AWKWARD**   The **band were** unhappy with their latest release.
>
> **BETTER**   The **members** of the band **were** unhappy with their latest release.

55c Irregular Verbs

Verbs are considered regular if the past and past participle—which you use to construct various tenses—are formed by simply adding -d or -ed to the base of the verb. Below are several regular verbs.

Base Form	Past Tense	Past Participle
smile	smiled	smiled
accept	accepted	accepted
manage	managed	managed

Unfortunately, the most common verbs in English are irregular. The chart below lists some of them. When in doubt about the proper form of a verb, check a dictionary.

Base Form	Past Tense	Past Participle
be	was, were	been
become	became	become
break	broke	broken
buy	bought	bought
choose	chose	chosen
come	came	come
dive	dived, dove	dived

(Continued)

Base Form	Past Tense	Past Participle
do	did	done
drink	drank	drunk
drive	drove	driven
eat	ate	eaten
get	got	gotten
give	gave	given
go	went	gone
have	had	had
lay (to put or place)	laid	laid
lie (to recline)	lay	lain
ride	rode	ridden
ring	rang, rung	rung
rise	rose	risen
see	saw	seen
set	set	set
shine	shone, shined	shone, shined
sing	sang, sung	sung
sink	sank, sunk	sunk
speak	spoke	spoken
swear	swore	sworn
throw	threw	thrown
wake	woke, waked	woken, waked
write	wrote	written

55d Pronoun/Antecedent Agreement

Pronouns take the place of nouns; antecedents are the words pronouns refer to. So pronouns share the markers of the words they replace, such as gender and number.

SINGULAR/FEMININE   The nun merely smiled because she had taken a vow of silence.

SINGULAR/MASCULINE   The NFL quarterback complained that he got too little media attention.

SINGULAR/NEUTER	The chess team took **itself** too seriously.
PLURAL	Members of the chess team took **themselves** too seriously.
PLURAL	**They** seemed awfully subdued for pro athletes.
PLURAL	The bridal couple wrote **their** own marriage vows.
PLURAL	Many in the terminal resented searches of **their** luggage.

In general, make sure pronouns you select have the same number and gender as the words they stand for.

| DRAFT | When a student spends too much time on sorority activities, **they** may suffer academically. |
| CORRECTED | When a student spends too much time on sorority activities, **she** may suffer academically. |

As always, though, there are trouble spots and numerous exceptions. The following guidelines can help you avoid common problems.

Check the number of indefinite pronouns.
Some of the most common singular indefinite pronouns—especially *anybody, everybody, everyone*—may seem plural, but they have been treated as singular in academic or formal writing. However, in common usage, you will routinely see *their* preferred. (For the complete list of indefinite pronouns, see the chart on p. 541.)

| COMMON USAGE | Has everybody completed **their** assignment by now? |
| ACADEMIC USAGE | Has everybody completed **his or her** assignment by now? |

If using *his or her* sounds awkward (and it almost always does), you can always revise the sentence.

Have all students completed **their** assignments by now?

Acknowledge gender preferences.
Using either *his* or *her* alone (instead of *his or her*) to refer to an indefinite pronoun has been considered sexist usage for some time—unless the pronoun clearly refers only to males or females. The principle also applies to *he* and *she* when the pronouns are similarly exclusionary. ◯ Here are some options for avoiding sexist usage.

ORIGINAL	Don't trust a driver using her cell phone on the freeway.
PREFERRED	Don't trust a driver using **his or her** cell phone on the freeway.
PREFERRED	Don't trust drivers using **their** cell phones on the freeway.

respect your readers
p. 383

To expand gender possibilities, so-called singular "they/their" has become increasingly accepted in these situations. It is a usage justified by common usage and endorsed by linguistics and the *Washington Post* stylebook.

COMMON   Don't believe a student who claims **they** never use Wikipedia for papers. Each of the researchers has submitted **their** results.

Treat collective nouns consistently. Collective nouns—such as *team, herd, congregation, mob,* and so on—can be treated as either singular or plural.

The Roman **legion** marched until **it** reached **its** camp in Gaul.
The Roman **legion** marched until **they** reached **their** camp in Gaul.

But be consistent and sensible in your usage. Treat a collective noun the same way, as either singular or plural, throughout a paper or project. And don't hesitate to modify a sentence when even a correct usage sounds awkward.

AWKWARD   The **team** smiled as **it** received **its** championship jerseys.

BETTER   Members of the **team** smiled as **they** received **their** championship jerseys.

© MARK ANDERSON, WWW.ANDERTOONS.COM

Mark Anderson, www.Andertoons.com

"Pronouns?! We haven't even done amateur nouns yet!"

55e Pronoun Reference

A pronoun should refer back clearly to a noun or pronoun (its *antecedent*), usually the one nearest to it that matches it in number and, when necessary, gender.

> **Consumers** will buy a **Rolex** because they covet **its** snob appeal.
> **Nancy Pelosi** spoke at the news conference instead of **Chuck Schumer**.
> because she had more interest in the legislation than **he** did.

Problems arise when readers can't tell who is connected to what.

Clarify confusing pronoun antecedents.
Revise sentences in which readers might wonder who is doing what to whom. Multiple revisions are usually possible, depending on how the confusing sentence could be interpreted.

CONFUSING	The batter collided with the first baseman, but he wasn't injured.
BETTER	The batter collided with the first baseman, who wasn't injured.
BETTER	The batter wasn't injured by his collision with the first baseman.

Make sure a pronoun has a plausible antecedent.
Sometimes the antecedent is only implied. In such cases, either reconsider the antecedent/pronoun relationship or replace the pronoun with a noun.

CONFUSING	Grandmother had cardiac surgery two months ago, and it is already fully healed.

In the above sentence, the implied antecedent for *it* is *heart*, but that word isn't in the sentence.

BETTER	Grandmother had cardiac surgery two months ago, and her heart is already fully healed.

Be certain that the antecedent of *this, that,* or *which* isn't vague.
In the following example, a vague *this* is asked to shoulder the burden of a writer who hasn't quite figured out how to pull together all the ideas raised in the preceding sentences. What exactly might the antecedent for *this* be? It doesn't exist. To fix the problem, the writer needs to replace *this* with a more thoughtful analysis.

FINAL SENTENCE VAGUE

The university staff is underpaid, the labs are short on equipment, and campus maintenance is neglected. Moreover, we need two or three new parking garages to make up for the lots lost because of recent construction projects. Yet students cannot be expected to shoulder additional costs because tuition and fees are high already. This is a problem that must be solved.

FINAL SENTENCE CLARIFIED

The problem to be solved is how to fund both academic departments and infrastructure needs without increasing students' financial burdens.

55f Pronoun Case

Like nouns, pronouns can act as subjects, objects, or possessives in sentences, so their forms vary to show which case they express.

Subjective Pronouns	Objective Pronouns	Possessive Pronouns
I	me	my, mine
you	you	your, yours
he, she, it	him, her, it	his, her, hers, its
we	us	our, ours
they	them	their, theirs
who	whom	whose

Unfortunately, determining case isn't always easy. Here are strategies for dealing with these common situations.

Use the subjective case for pronouns that are subjects. When a pronoun is the lone subject in a clause, it rarely causes a problem. But double the subject and there's potential trouble.

> Sara and *me* ..., or is it Sara and *I*? ... wrote the report.

To make the correct choice, phrase the sentence for each subject alone, one at a time.

> Sara wrote the report.
> I wrote the report.

The revision becomes obvious:

> *Sara and I* wrote the report.

Use the objective case for pronouns that are objects. Again, choosing one objective pronoun is generally easy, but with two objects, the choice becomes less clear.

> The corporate attorney will represent both Geoff and *I* ... Geoff and *me*?

Again, deal with one object at a time.

> The corporate attorney will represent *Geoff*.
> The corporate attorney will represent *me*.
> The corporate attorney will represent *Geoff and me*.

Or, to be more concise:

> The corporate attorney will represent *us*.

Note that *us* is also an objective form of the pronoun. The subjective form *we* would not work here.

Use *whom* when appropriate.

One pronoun choice brings many writers to their knees: *who* or *whom*. The rule, however, is the same as for other pronouns: Use the subjective case (*who*) for subjects and the objective case (*whom*) for objects.

DRAFT	*Whom* wrote the report?
CORRECTED	*Who* wrote the report?
DRAFT	By *who* was the report written?
CORRECTED	By *whom* was the report written?

This usage becomes tricky when you're dealing with subordinate clauses.

WRONG	The shelter needs help from *whomever* can volunteer three hours per week.

The previous example may sound right because *whomever* immediately follows the preposition *from*. But, because the pronoun is the subject of a subordinate clause, it needs to be in the subjective case.

CORRECTED	The shelter needs help from *whoever* can volunteer three hours per week.

When in doubt, prefer *who* to *whom*. Even when you err, you won't sound ridiculous.

Finish comparisons to determine the right case.

When writers make comparisons, they sometimes omit some information they believe is understood.

> I've always thought John was more talented than Paul.
> (I've always thought John was more talented than Paul *was*.)

But leaving this information out can lead to confusion when it comes to choosing the correct pronoun case. Try the sentence, adding *him*.

WRONG	I've always thought John was more talented than *him*.
	I've always thought John was more talented than *him was*.
CORRECTED	I've always thought John was more talented than *he*.

Don't be misled by an appositive.
An *appositive* is a word or phrase that amplifies or renames a noun or pronoun. In the example below, *Americans* is the appositive. First, try reading the sentence without it.

WRONG	*Us* Americans must defend our civil rights.
APPOSITIVE CUT	*Us* must defend our civil rights. [*Us* can't be a subject.]
CORRECTED	*We* Americans must defend our civil rights.

Note that when the pronoun is contained within the appositive, as in the examples that follow, the pronoun uses the case of the word or words it stands in for. This rule makes more sense when seen in an example.

SUBJECTIVE	*The runners* leading the marathon, Matt, Luci, and I, all had trained at Central High School.
OBJECTIVE	The race was won *by the runners* from Central High, Matt, Luci, and *me*.

In the first example, *runners* is the subject of the sentence. Since *Matt, Luci,* and *I* merely rename that subject, they share its subjective case. In the second example, *the runners* have become the object of a preposition: *by the runners*. So the threesome now moves into the objective case as well: *Matt, Luci, and me*.

56

get details
right

Mechanics

If grammar is about the basic structures and principles of a language (see Chapter 55), mechanics is a word used to describe all the guidelines and conventions that give its written form clarity and consistency. The sentences you speak don't indicate what's capitalized or italicized, nor do you need to worry about where commas, quotation marks, exclamation points, or other punctuation might go. But when you write, such details matter, particularly in college and thereafter. If these norms seem fussy, think about the rules you observe in the sports or games you enjoy. They irritate you sometimes, but they make the game possible.

56a Capitalization

You know to capitalize most proper nouns (and the proper adjectives formed from them), the first words of sentences, book and movie titles, and so on. But you need to make judgment calls too when capitalizing, some of which may require a dictionary or online search. Here are a few of the special cases.

Capitalize the names of ethnic, religious, and political groups. The names of these groups are considered proper nouns. Nonspecific groups, however, are lowercase.

South Korean	Native Americans	native peoples
Buddhists	Muslims	true believers
Black Lives Matter	Republicans	political junkies
the Miami City Council	NRA	the city council

Capitalize Internet and Web?

The terms were usually capitalized when the Internet and Web were new. But time and popular usage alters usage and, given how widespread the technologies have become, it is common now to see the words in lowercase: *internet* and *web*. *AP Stylebook*, widely used by journalists, officially endorses the use of lower case, MLA urges consistency without specifying which option to choose, while APA and Chicago style still mandate capitalization.

Capitalize modifiers formed from proper nouns. In a few cases, such as *French* (in *french fries* or *french toast*), the expressions have become so common that the adjective is not routinely capitalized. When in doubt, consult a dictionary.

PROPER NOUN	PROPER NOUN USED AS MODIFIER
French	French music
Navajo	Navajo rug
Jew	Jewish lore
American	American history

Capitalize all words in titles except prepositions, articles, or conjunctions. This is the basic rule for the titles of books, movies, long poems, and so on.

Dickens and the Dream of Cinema

In the Company of Cheerful Ladies

Variations and exceptions to this general rule, however, are numerous. MLA style specifies that the first and last words in titles always be capitalized, including any articles or prepositions.

The Guide to National Parks of the Southwest

To the Lighthouse

Such Stuff as Dreams Are Made Of

APA style doesn't make that qualification, but does specify that words longer than four letters be capitalized in titles—even prepositions. (This rule applies to titles mentioned within articles and essays themselves, not to titles in APA-style documentation, discussed below.)

A Walk Among the Tombstones

Sleeping Through the Night and Other Lies

In all major styles, any word following a colon or dash in a title is capitalized, even an article or preposition:

True Blood: All Together Now

The Exile: An Outlander Graphic Novel

Finally, note that in APA style —that is, within the in-text citations and on the references page, titles are capitalized differently. Only the first word in most titles, any proper nouns or adjectives, and any word following a colon are capitalized. All other words are lowercase:

Bat predation and the evolution of frog vocalizations in the neotropics

Human aging: Usual and successful

Take care with compass points, directions, and specific geographical areas Points of the compass and simple directions are not capitalized when referring to general locations.

north	southwest
northern Ohio	eastern Canada

But these same terms *are* capitalized when they refer to specific regions that are geographically, culturally, or politically significant. Such terms are often preceded by the definite article, *the*.

the West	the Third Coast
Middle Eastern politics	Southern California

Understand academic conventions. Academic degrees are not capitalized, except when abbreviated.

bachelor of arts	doctor of medicine
MA	PhD

Specific course titles are capitalized, but they are lowercase when used as general subjects. Exception: Languages are always capitalized when referring to academic subjects.

Organic Chemistry 101	Contemporary British Poetry
an organic chemistry course	an English literature paper

Capitalize months, days, holidays, and historical periods. But don't capitalize the seasons.

January	the Enlightenment
a Monday in spring	Halloween

56b Apostrophes

Apostrophes have two major functions: to signal that a noun is possessive and to indicate where letters have been left out in contractions. They are tricky in a few situations and everyone sometimes confuses *it's/its*.

GRAMMARIANS IN THERAPY

PARTIES HAVE BECOME IMPOSSIBLE -- SHE'S MORE POSSESSIVE THAN AN APOSTROPHE.

rhymeswithorange.com

Rhymes With Orange ©Hilary Price. Distributed by King Features Syndicate

Use apostrophes to form the possessive. For singular nouns, add 's to the end of the word:

the wolf's lair

the photographer's portfolio

IBM's profits

Some possessives, while correct, look or sound awkward. In these cases, try an alternative:

ORIGINAL	REVISED
the class's photo	the class photo; the photo of the class
Alicia Keys's latest hit	the latest hit by Alicia Keys

For plural nouns that do not end in *s*, also add 's to the end of the word:

men's shoes   the mice's tails   the geese's nemesis

For plural nouns that do end in *s*, add an apostrophe after that terminal *s*:

the wolves' pups

the Bushes' foreign policies

three senators' votes

Use apostrophes in contractions. An apostrophe in a contraction takes the place of missing letters. Edit carefully.

WRONG	Its a shame that its come to this.
CORRECTED	It's (It is) a shame that it's (it has) come to this.
WRONG	Whose got the list of whose going on the trip?
CORRECTED	Who's (Who has) got the list of who's (who is) going on the trip?

Don't use apostrophes with possessive pronouns. The following possessives do not take apostrophes: *its, whose, his, hers, ours, yours,* and *theirs.*

WRONG	We photographed the tower at it's best angle.
CORRECTED	We photographed the tower at its best angle.
WRONG	Their's may be an Oscar-winning film, but our's is still better.
CORRECTED	Theirs may be an Oscar-winning film, but ours is still better.

There is, inevitably, an exception. Indefinite pronouns such as *everybody, anybody, nobody,* and so on do show possession via *'s.*

Stranger Things was everybody's favorite series.

Why it was so popular is anybody's guess.

56c Commas

▶ need to connect ideas?

The comma (,) has more uses than any other punctuation mark. The following guidelines will help you handle commas appropriately in academic writing.

Use a comma and a coordinating conjunction to join two independent clauses.
An independent clause can stand on its own as a sentence. To join two of them, you need both a coordinating conjunction *and* a comma. A comma alone is not enough.

Fiona's car broke down. She had to walk two miles to the train station.

Fiona's car broke down, so she had to walk two miles to the train station.

Omitting the coordinating conjunction creates an error known as a comma splice (see pp. 567-68).

Use a comma after an introductory word group.
Introductory word groups are descriptive phrases or clauses that open a sentence. Separate these introductions from the main part of the sentence with a comma.

Within two years of getting a degree in journalism, Ishan was writing for the *Wall Street Journal.*

For very brief introductory phrases, the comma may be omitted, but it is not wrong to leave it in.

> Before college I served in the Marines.

> Before college, I served in the Marines.

Use commas with common connective words and phrases. These

would include items such as *however; therefore; consequently; finally; furthermore; nonetheless; specifically; as a result; in addition; for instance; in fact; on the other hand; that is.* A connective word or phrase that opens a sentence is usually followed by a comma:

> Furthermore, medical reports suggest that trans fats lower the amount of good cholesterol found in the body.

Used within a sentence, such expressions should be set off by a pair of commas.

> Big payrolls mean success in professional sports. In baseball, for example, teams from New York and Boston are almost always competitive. There are, however, notable exceptions.

Be especially careful with punctuation around *however* and *therefore*. A common error is to place commas around these connective words to link a pair of related sentences. This move produces an error called a comma splice (see pp. 567-68 for more details). Here's what that error looks like:

> **COMMA SPLICE**   Pro baseball teams with big payrolls are usually competitive, however, there are exceptions.

To correct this type of comma splice, place a semicolon before *however* or *therefore*. Or create two separate sentences:

> Pro baseball teams with big payrolls are usually competitive; however, there are exceptions.

> Pro baseball teams with big payrolls are usually competitive. However, there are exceptions.

Put commas around nonrestrictive (that is, nonessential) elements.

You'll know that a word or phrase is functioning as a nonrestrictive modifier if you can remove it from the sentence without obscuring the overall meaning of the sentence.

> Cicero, ancient Rome's greatest orator and lawyer, was a self-made man.

> Cicero was a self-made man.

The second sentence is less informative but still makes sense. See also the guideline on page 557, "Do not use commas to set off restrictive elements."

Use commas to separate items in a series. Commas are necessary when you have three or more items in a series.

Americans still love muscle cars such as Mustangs, Camaros, and Challengers.

The Oxford Comma Debate

When you have items in a series, some writers and professional stylebooks insist that no comma is needed before the *and* that terminates it.

Americans still love muscle cars such as Mustangs, Camaros and Challengers.

But other writers, following the practice of Oxford University Press and other academic publishers, insist that a comma is required for clarity.

Americans still love muscle cars such as Mustangs, Camaros, and Challengers.

That additional mark is known as the **Oxford** or **serial** comma. The choice is yours to make, but be consistent and check your stylebook. If you are a journalist following AP style, for example, you go without the final comma.

Do not use commas to separate compound verbs. It's easy to confuse a true compound sentence (which has two independent clauses) with a sentence like the following that simply has two verbs.

DRAFT	They rumbled through city streets, and smoked down drag strips.
CORRECTED	They rumbled through city streets and smoked down drag strips.

And is all you need to join two verbs that share a common subject (in this case, *they*). When a sentence has three or more verbs, however, treat them as items in a series and separate them with commas. Compare the following examples:

TWO VERBS	Muscle cars guzzled gasoline and burned rubber.
THREE VERBS	Muscle cars guzzled gasoline, burned rubber, and drove parents crazy.

Do not use a comma between subject and verb. The error is obvious in a short sentence.

DRAFT	Keeping focused, can be difficult.
CORRECTED	Keeping focused can be difficult.

But you might be more tempted to insert the comma when a sentence is longer. The commas in the following two sentences should be omitted.

UNNECESSARY COMMAS	Keeping focused on driving while simultaneously trying to operate a cell phone, can be difficult.
	The excuses that some people come up with to defend their bad habits on the road, sound pathetic.

Do not use commas to set off restrictive or essential elements.

These are phrases you could not remove from a sentence without altering its meaning.

Only nations that recognize a right to free speech and free press should be eligible for seats on international human rights commissions.

Students who have a perfect attendance record will earn three points for class participation.

Putting commas around such phrases creates the false impression that they could be removed.

56d End punctuation

Compared to commas, the punctuation marks that terminate sentences—periods, question marks, and exclamation points—pose few problems.

Periods (.) mark the end of statements, indirect questions, and moderate commands. Most sentences end in periods.

STATEMENT	Water, taken in moderation, cannot hurt anybody. —Mark Twain
INDIRECT QUESTION	Pundits ask whether the current American two-party system can long survive.
MODERATE COMMAND	Submit this form online by the end of the week.

In American English, a closing quotation mark typically follows a final period.

. BEFORE "	Mark Twain believed that "Water, taken in moderation, cannot hurt anybody."

Question marks (?) conclude sentences that make inquiries of various kinds.

INQUIRY	Who wrote the novel *The Godfather*?
	How could you say that to me?
	The new iPhone looks great, but who will pay its lofty price?

Question marks can also follow questions that are embedded within statements.

EMBEDDED ?	Making perfect morning coffee—is any drink more important?—takes the right beans and brewing techniques.

In American English, a closing quotation mark follows a question mark when the whole sentence poses a question. But if a question itself is quoted in the sentence, the punctuation marks are reversed.

? AFTER "	Did Mark Twain really believe that "Water, taken in moderation, cannot hurt anybody"?
" AFTER ?	The lecturer asked, "Does anyone want coffee?"

Exclamation points (!) conclude very strong statements or commands. They should be used rarely in academic prose and never doubled or tripled.

We lost again!

Shape up or I'll fire you!

With closing quotation marks, exclamations are handled the same way as questions.

56e Semicolons and colons

Both semicolons (;) and colons (:) link elements within sentences, but their functions are slightly different. Semicolons emphasize the connections between comparable items, while colons function like pointers or arrows.

Use semicolons to link equivalent units within a sentence. This means that you may use semicolons to join independent clauses *or* related phrases *or* items within a list.

BETWEEN CLAUSES	In 1957, <u>the USSR launched Sputnik 1</u>, the first earth satellite; in 1969, <u>American astronauts landed</u> on the Moon.
	Napoleon <u>captured</u> Moscow; however, his invasion of Russia <u>failed</u>.
BETWEEN COMPLEX PHRASES	Presidential candidates need many talents, including <u>a knack for</u> defining key issues, especially in difficult times; <u>ease in</u> speaking with voters from all regions, whether urban, suburban, or rural; and <u>confidence in</u> facing hostile questions.
IN COMPLEX LISTS	The application said we needed to include an up-to-date <u>résumé</u>; three <u>letters</u> from current or former instructors, with full contact information; <u>.pdf files</u> of recent written work; and <u>a video</u>—no more than three minutes—in which we explained why we wanted to join the honors society.

Don't use a colon between different types of sentence elements. In most cases, such items should be linked (or separated) by commas or, more rarely, dashes.

WRONG	Presidential candidates need many talents; especially confidence.
RIGHT	Presidential candidates need many talents, especially confidence.

Use colons in sentences to give emphasis or draw attention to items that follow the mark. Colons can link independent clauses or introduce phrases, quotations, examples, and lists. Think of colons as a signal for readers to pay attention.

BETWEEN CLAUSES	Sputnik 1 changed American attitudes: its sense of technological leadership suddenly vanished.
INTRODUCE QUOTATIONS	In a 1962 speech, President Kennedy challenged Americans: "We choose to go to the Moon in this decade and do the other things, not because they are easy, but because they are hard."
INTRODUCE LISTS	In the 1960's American scientists design three manned space vehicles: Mercury, Gemini, and Apollo.

In sentences, colons replace introductory words and phrases: *said, such as, for example.* Using a colon after them is usually unnecessary, although usage varies.

© MARK ANDERSON, WWW.ANDERTOONS.COM

Mark Anderson, www.Andertoons.com

"Can anyone, *anyone*, tell me how a semicolon is used
other than in emoticons?!"

56f Hyphens, Dashes, Ellipses, Parenthesis, and Brackets

Academic readers will appreciate your accurate handling of the specialty marks
available to writers.

Hyphens (-) connect prefixes to words. They also link words to each other
as modifiers or compound phrases. The following examples show how the mark is used.

WITH PREFIXES	Ex-president Obama
	pre-existing conditions
	anti-American sentiment
WITH SIMPLE MODIFIERS	twenty-dollar sandwich
	well-spoken student
	front-row seats
WITH COMPOUNDS	mother-in-law
	over-the-counter drugs
	choice of four-, six-, or eight-cylinder engines

Check a dictionary if you are uncertain whether a term with a prefix requires a hyphen. Some like *nonstop, antislavery,* or *preteen* do not. Modifiers that end in *–ly* are not hyphenated: *rarely seen animals; carefully phrased words.* And while compound modifiers placed before a word ordinarily need hyphens, the hyphens disappear when the same modifiers appear after the word: *a well-spoken student/a student who is well spoken; a well-drilled regiment/a regiment that is well drilled.*

Use em dashes (—) to insert information within or at the end of sentences.
Em dashes, the wider and more familiar of the two sizes of dash, are the width of a capital M. The following examples show the mark used in sentences.

TO BRACKET INFORMATION	NASA—the National Aeronautics and Space Administration—sponsors scientific projects in many fields.
	The Empire State Building—the tallest skyscraper in the world for forty years—was constructed in just over a year.
TO CONNECT INFORMATION	Sociology, anthropology, psychology—these social sciences focus on the human condition.
	Many generals have gone on to serve as president of the United States—including George Washington, Andrew Jackson, Ulysses S. Grant, and Dwight D. Eisenhower.

To form em dashes correctly, use the appropriate keystroke on your keyboard or type two hyphens without any spacing. Some writers do use spaced hyphens to form dashes: -- . Don't use more than one pair of dashes per sentence.

Use en dashes (–) to insert information within or at the end of sentences.
En dashes, narrower than em dashes, are the width of a capital "N." Use en dashes between words and numbers as a substitute for *to* (but not after *from* or *between*).

Pete Seeger (1919–2014) and Bob Dylan (1941–) were successful folk artists.

The Albuquerque–Jackson Hole flight is delayed.

The meeting is today, 2–3:30 p.m.

Search online to learn the appropriate keystroke on your computer to form an "en" dash.

Use ellipses (…) to mark omissions or deletions in a sentence or quotation or to suggest a pause or an unfinished remark.
When you shorten a passage with ellipsis, make sure the cuts don't affect the sense or grammar of the passage. Following is a paragraph from a speech by then-Senator Barack Obama,

followed by a version shortened by ellipses. When an ellipses is added after a complete sentence, the period at the end of the sentence is retained, followed by the ellipsis mark.

Original The pundits, the pundits like to slice-and-dice our country into red states and blue states; red states for Republicans, blue states for Democrats. But I've got news for them, too. We worship an awesome God in the blue states, and we don't like federal agents poking around in our libraries in the red states. We coach Little League in the blue states and yes, we've got some gay friends in the red states. There are patriots who opposed the war in Iraq and there are patriots who supported the war in Iraq. We are one people, all of us pledging allegiance to the stars and stripes, all of us defending the United States of America. —2004 Democratic National Convention Keynote Address

With ellipses The pundits . . . like to slice-and-dice our country into red states and blue states . . . But I've got news for them . . . We worship an awesome God in the blue states, and we don't like federal agents poking around in our libraries in the red states. We coach Little League in the blue states and yes, we've got some gay friends in the red states. . . . We are one people . . . all of us defending the United States of America.

Note that you don't ordinarily need ellipses to show that you've cut something when you quote from the middle of a sentence. The small letter that begins such quotations signals to readers that other words or phrases precede that material.

In his speech to Democrats, Senator Obama notes that, "yes, we've got some gay friends in the red states."

If Obama's full sentence were cited, the quotation would begin with a capital letter.

In his speech to Democrats, Senator Obama notes that, "We coach Little League in the blue states and yes, we've got some gay friends in the red states."

You can type an ellipsis mark as three spaced periods or find a keyboard command for the three periods.

Understand differences between parenthesis ( ) and brackets [ ].

Parentheses are so common that they need little explanation. Always used in pairs, parentheses are used to insert information, data, comments, explanations, or asides into sentences. They may enclose everything from complete sentences and phrases to parenthetical documentation required in research papers.

I missed your call. (My cell service was down.) Sorry.

She considered the Ivy League, but quickly narrowed her choices to one of the Big Ten schools (likely either Michigan or Ohio State).

Activists are demanding rights for people whose cells are used in scientific experiments (Skloot 319).

In the examples above, note that closing punctuation falls inside the parentheses only when an entire sentence is enclosed.

Brackets have highly specialized uses. One is to insert information within direct quotations. Readers understand that what's between the brackets is not part of the quotation itself.

> The president rejected the German chancellor's proposal: "Her [Merkel's] idea just preserves the status quo."

Brackets surrounding the Latin word *sic* (meaning "thus") can also be inserted wherever you find an obvious error in quoted material. The [sic] tells readers the mistake is not yours.

> A poster declared the protestors willingness "to meat [sic] administrators in good faith" to discuss their demands.

56g Quotations Marks and Quotations

Quotation marks have special uses—such as marking dialogue, setting off titles, and emphasizing particular words. But in academic work, you typically use quotation marks to signal when you are using someone else's words. And quoting is a serious and sometimes difficult matter.

Use quotation marks to set off dialogue. Whether composing dialogue for a short story or quoting characters from a novel or play, surround the words spoken by characters with quotation marks, and indicate in some way who is speaking to whom. It is a convention—sometimes ignored—to start a new paragraph with each change of speaker.

> The radio speaker made an uncertain noise, then produced the voice of Officer Delbert Nez. " . . . running on fumes. I'm going to have to buy some of that high-cost Red Rock gasoline or walk home."
>
> "If you do, I advise you pay for it out of your pocket," Chee said. "Better than explaining to the captain why you forgot to fill it up."
>
> "I think . . ." Nez said and then the voice faded out.
>
> —Tony Hillerman, *Coyote Waits*

Use quotation marks to highlight titles or emphasize words in a sentence. In academic writing, the titles of newspaper, magazine, and journal articles, as well as songs, short stories, and most poems are set in quotation marks.

"Birds Beware: The Preying Mantis Wants Your Brain"

—NYT

"Kill 'em With Kindness"

—Selena Gomez

"Stopping by Woods on a Snowy Evening"

—Robert Frost

You can also use quotation marks to emphasize or focus on particular words or phrases, but don't overdo it.

Our speaker evidently misinterpreted the meaning of "brief remarks."

Use quotation marks whenever you quote directly from sources.

Quotations generally need to be introduced or framed in some way and the surrounding punctuation must follow conventions. Some marks, such as commas, periods, and exclamation points, generally fall inside quotation marks, while colons and semicolons are placed outside. In these examples, notice how the quotations are framed (in boldface) and the punctuation around and within the quotation marks as well.

"If you think healthcare is expensive now," humorist P. J. O'Rourke once warned, "wait until you see what it costs when it's free."

"How glorious a greeting the sun gives the mountains!" John Muir wrote.

In 1992, Bill Clinton won "the bubba vote": working-class Americans embraced his message.

Jimmy Carter observed that, "unless both sides win, no agreement can be permanent"; it's a lesson more statesmen could take to heart.

In *The Immortal Life of Henrietta Lacks*, Rebecca Skloot claims that activists are now demanding "regulations that would grant people the right to control their [bodily] tissues" (319).

Punctuating quotations at the end of sentences can be especially tricky. Periods always fall within the quotation mark in American usage. However, question marks and explanation points go within the quotation marks when they are part of a quotation; they fall outside the quotation marks when they apply to the entire sentence.

Who can disagree with Jefferson that people "are endowed by their Creator with certain inalienable rights"?

From *Taxi Driver* (1976), one of cinema's most famous lines has to be "You talkin' to me?"

You will note that other languages mark quotations differently and even American and British usage can be at odds.

56h Italics and Boldface

Technology has given just about every writer typographical options formerly available only to printers. Two you might use often are italics and boldface.

Use italics to highlight foreign words and expressions. This is a simple and useful convention.

> The phrase I used most often in Paris was *je ne comprends pas.*
>
> "*In vino veritas*," the professor said, raising her glass.

Foreign words and expressions used commonly in English and some Latin abbreviations are not italicized.

adobe	à la mode	doppelgänger
etc.	viz.	Q.E.D.

As always, such terms are problematic. You may have to use a single dictionary consistently in a project or check a specific style book to determine whether to italicize some items. For example, while "ad hoc" is never italicized, "in absentia" may be.

Use italics for the titles or names of books, newspapers, magazines, films, plays, TV/radio shows, works of art, and albums. Titles of articles, book chapters, songs, and other shorter works should be set in italics. Sacred works such as the Bible or the Qur'an and important legal documents such as the Bill of Rights are not highlighted in either way.

> *The Color Purple* (book)
>
> *Wall Street Journal* (newspaper)
>
> *Latina* (magazine)
>
> *Star Wars: The Force Awakens* (movie)
>
> *Hamilton* (play)
>
> *MacGyver* (media program)
>
> *Look, It Flies* (artwork)
>
> *More Life* (album)

Use italics to highlight words or phrases you want to set off or emphasize. Quite often, you would also have the option of using quotation marks in these situations.

> Could you explain exactly what you mean by *boys will be boys*?
>
> Many British words that end in *–our* are simplified to *–or* in American usage, for example, *humour/humor* or *neighbour/neighbor*.

57

fix sentence problems

Sentence Issues

Successful writing arises from phrases and clauses working together coherently and strategically. So you'll find general advice about style in Chapter 33, "Levels of Style," and detailed discussion of sentence-level issues in Chapter 34, "Clear and Vigorous Writing." Moreover, every chapter in Part 2, "Key Academic Genres," includes a discussion of style. Below, you'll find advice about sentence trouble spots that cross all genres of academic and professional writing.

© MARK ANDERSON, WWW.ANDERTOONS.COM

"You're just messing with me, aren't you."

55 a Comma Splices and Run-Ons

The sentence errors marked most often in college writing are comma splices and run-ons.

Identify comma splices and run-ons. A *comma splice* occurs when only a comma is used to join two independent clauses (an independent clause contains a complete subject and verb). Identify a comma splice simply by reading the clauses on either side of a doubtful comma. If *both* clauses stand on their own as sentences (with their own subjects and verbs), it's a comma splice.

COMMA SPLICES

> Officials at many elementary schools are trying to reduce childhood obesity on their campuses, research suggests that few of their strategies will work.

> Some schools emphasize a need for more exercise, others have even gone so far as to reinstate recess.

A *run-on* sentence resembles a comma splice, but this somewhat rarer mistake doesn't even include the comma to mark a break between independent clauses. The clauses just slam together, confusing readers.

RUN-ON SENTENCES

> Officials at many elementary schools are trying to reduce childhood obesity on their campuses research suggests that few of their strategies will work.

> Some schools emphasize a need for more exercise others have even gone so far as to reinstate recess.

Common Coordinating Conjunctions	
and	or
but	so
for	yet
nor	

Fix comma splices and run-ons. To repair comma splices and run-ons, you have many options. The first is to connect the two independent clauses by inserting *both* a comma and a coordinating conjunction between them.

> Officials at many elementary schools are trying to reduce childhood obesity on their campuses, **but** research suggests that few of their strategies will work.

> Some schools emphasize a need for more exercise, **and** others have even gone so far as to reinstate recess.

A second fix is to use a semicolon alone to join the two clauses.

> Officials at many elementary schools are trying to reduce childhood obesity on their campuses; research suggests that few of their strategies will work.

> Some schools emphasize a need for more exercise; others have even gone so far as to reinstate recess.

Less frequently, colons or dashes may be used as connecting punctuation when the second clause summarizes or illustrates the main point of the first clause.

> Some schools have taken extreme measures: They have banned cookies, snacks, and other high-calorie foods from their vending machines.

Along with the semicolon (or colon or dash), you may wish to add a transitional word or phrase (such as *however* or *in fact*). If you do, set off the transitional word or phrase with commas. **O**

> Officials at many elementary schools are trying to reduce childhood obesity on their campuses; research, however, suggests that few of their strategies will work.

> Some schools emphasize a need for more exercise—in fact, some have even gone so far as to reinstate recess.

Alternatively, you can rewrite the sentence to make one of the clauses clearly subordinate to the other. To do that, introduce one of the clauses with a subordinating conjunction so that it can no longer stand as a sentence on its own. Compare the two corrected versions to see your options:

DRAFT	Officials at many elementary schools are trying to reduce childhood obesity on their campuses, research suggests that few of their strategies will work.
CORRECTED	Although officials at many elementary schools are trying to reduce childhood obesity on their campuses, research suggests that few of their strategies will work.
CORRECTED	Officials at many elementary schools are trying to reduce childhood obesity on their campuses, even though research suggests that few of their strategies will work.

Finally, you can simply use end punctuation to create two independent sentences. Here, a period between the clauses eliminates either a comma splice or a run-on.

> Officials at many elementary schools are trying to reduce childhood obesity on their campuses. Research suggests that few of their strategies will work.

Common Subordinating Conjunctions

after	once
although	since
as	that
because	though
before	unless
except	until
if	when

connect ideas p. 391

57b Sentence Fragments

Sentence fragments can be a challenge because, while they are natural in many kinds of writing, you must be careful about employing them in academic assignments. To use them well, you've got to know what they are and do.

Identify sentence fragments. A sentence fragment is a word group that lacks a subject, verb, or possibly both. As such, it is not a complete sentence and is usually not appropriate for much academic and professional work. (You will find fragments routinely in fiction and popular writing.)

> **FRAGMENT** Climatologists see much physical evidence of climate change. Especially in the receding of glaciers around the world.

Fix sentence fragments in your work. You have two options for fixing sentence fragments. Attach the fragment to a nearby sentence with appropriate punctuation, often a comma:

> **COMPLETE SENTENCE** Climatologists see much physical evidence of climate change, especially in the receding of glaciers around the world.

> **COMPLETE SENTENCE** Climatologists see much physical evidence of climate change. They are especially concerned by the receding of glaciers around the world.

Watch for fragments in the following situations. Often a fragment will follow a complete sentence and start with a subordinating conjunction.

> **FRAGMENT** Climate change seems to be the product of human activity. Though some scientists believe sun cycles may explain the changing climate.

> **COMPLETE SENTENCE** Climate change seems to be the product of human activity, though some scientists believe sun cycles may explain the changing climate.

Participles (such as *breaking, seeking, finding*) and infinitives (such as *to break, to seek, to find*) can also lead you into fragments.

> **FRAGMENT** Of course, many people welcome the warmer weather. Upsetting scientists who fear governments will not act until global warming becomes irreversible.

> **COMPLETE SENTENCE** Of course, many people welcome the warmer weather. Their attitude upsets scientists who fear governments will not act until global warming becomes irreversible.

Use deliberate fragments only in appropriate situations. You'll find that fragments are common in advertising, fiction, and informal writing. In personal e-mail or on social networking sites, for example, expressions or clichés such as the following would probably be acceptable to your audience.

In your dreams.   Excellent!

Not on your life.   When pigs fly.

57c Misplaced and Dangling Modifiers

▶ are your descriptions clear?

In general, modifiers need to be close and obviously connected to the words they modify. When they aren't, readers may become confused—or amused.

Position modifiers close to the words they modify.

MISPLACED   Layered like a wedding cake, Mrs. DeLeon unveiled her model for the parade float.

Mrs. DeLeon is not layered like a wedding cake; the model for the parade float is.

REVISED   Mrs. DeLeon unveiled her model for the parade float, which was layered like a wedding cake.

Place adverbs such as *only, almost, especially*, and *even* carefully.

If these modifiers are placed improperly, their purpose can be vague or ambiguous.

VAGUE   The speaker almost angered everyone in the room.

CLEARER   The speaker angered almost everyone in the room.

AMBIGUOUS   Joan only drove a pickup.

CLEARER   Only Joan drove a pickup.

CLEARER   Joan drove only a pickup.

Don't allow a modifier to dangle. A modifying word or phrase at the beginning of a sentence should usually be followed by a subject to which it connects clearly. When it doesn't, the modifier is said to dangle, especially when there is no other word in the sentence it can logically describe.

DANGLING   Arriving at sunset, the Grand Canyon was awash in golden light.

Nothing in the sentence is actually modified by the opening phrase. Revision is necessary.

REVISED   Arriving at sunset, we beheld the Grand Canyon awash in golden light.

Don't, however, confuse dangling modifiers with *absolutes,* which are phrases that can, in fact, modify entire sentences without connecting to particular words or subjects. Here are some examples:

All things considered, the vacation was a success.

To be honest, our hotel room at the park left much to be desired.

Rhymes With Orange ©Hillary Price.
Distributed by King Features Syndicate

57d Maintaining Parallelism

When items in sentences follow similar patterns of language, they are described as parallel. Parallel structure makes your writing easier to read and understand.

When possible, make compound items parallel. Don't confuse your readers by requiring them to untangle subjects, verbs, modifiers, or other items that could easily be parallel.

NOT PARALLEL	Becoming a lawyer and to write a novel are Casey's goals.
PARALLEL	Becoming a lawyer and writing a novel are Casey's goals.
NOT PARALLEL	The college will demolish its aging stadium and bricks from it are being sold.
PARALLEL	The college will demolish its aging stadium and sell the bricks.

| NOT PARALLEL | The TV anchor reported the story thoroughly and with compassion. |
| PARALLEL | The TV anchor reported the story thoroughly and compassionately. |

Keep items in a series parallel. This means that once you start a series, all the items in it should share the same form or structure. You might have a series of adjectives (*tough, smart,* and *aggressive*), adverbs (*slowly* and *carefully*), participles (*kicking, screaming,* and *giggling*), infinitives (*to break the siege* and *to free the hostages*), and so on.

NOT PARALLEL	She was a fine rookie teacher—eager, very patient, and gets her work done.
PARALLEL	She was a fine rookie teacher—eager, very patient, and conscientious.
NOT PARALLEL	We expected to rehabilitate the historic property, breaking even on the investment, and earn the goodwill of the community.
PARALLEL	We expected to rehabilitate the historic property, break even on the investment, and earn the goodwill of the community.

Keep headings and lists parallel, especially in documents. If you use headings to break up the text of a document, use a similar language pattern and design for all of them. It may help to type the headings out separately from the text to make sure you are keeping them parallel. Items in a printed list should be parallel as well. Parallelism is especially important in a professional document such as a résumé, which a reader is likely to scan quickly (see p. 296).

Similarly, when creating slides for a PowerPoint presentation, consider whether the individual slides should share at least some parallel structures in headings and page design. Viewers should not have to adjust to a new visual structure with each item you display (see an example on pp. 285–86).

Troublesome Pairs 58

respect subtle differences

Many terms in English give writers pause—which is the right word to use? *It's* or *its*? *Can* or *may*? *Imply* or *infer*? You can always check a dictionary. Or spend a few minutes reviewing the items on this list.

advice *or* advise? Think noun and verb. You give someone *advice* (n.), while you might *advise* (vb.) someone to do something: *Given your recent bankruptcy, I would **advise** you to stop offering financial **advice**.*

affect *or* effect? This pair is complicated. *Affect* is usually a verb meaning "to influence," though it can also mean "to pretend": *The booing audience **affected** the actors, but they **affected** not to notice. Effect* is usually a noun meaning "result" or "outcome": *We could not guess what the **effect** of the treatment would be.* Yet both *affect* and *effect* have alternative meanings. As a noun, "affect" is a specialized term in psychology meaning "emotion." And as verb, "effect" means "to bring about": *The 2016 election **effected** a shift in political attitudes.*

aggravate *or* irritate? *Aggravate* means "to make worse"; *irritate* means to vex or anger: *It **irritated** some voters that all the new spending would only **aggravate** the national debt.*

allude *or* elude? *Allude* means "to refer to something indirectly"; *elude* means "to avoid" or "to escape." The words aren't interchangeable. In a review of the musical, Ellah *alluded* to Mike's off-key singing, but her sarcasm *eluded* him.

a lot *or* alot? *Alot* is a misspelling so common that most readers don't notice it or care. But use only "a lot" in academic and professional writing.

among *or* between? *Among* refers to three or more objects, *between* to just two: *Just **between** you and me, I wouldn't want to be popular **among** that crowd.*

bad *or* badly? *Bad* is an adjective and *badly* is an adverb. The trouble occurs with the verb *to feel*. Sensing that *I feel bad* sounds ungrammatical, writers default to *I feel badly*—which technically means that their sense of touch is poor, the adverb *badly* modifying the verb *feel* rather than the subject *I*. *I feel bad* is fine—if you are ill.

can *or* may? *Can* describes an "ability" while "may" indicates possibility or permission: *If you **can** fly the plane, you **may**.*

conscience *or* conscious? Confusion of these terms is usually a gaffe in editing. The words mean different things: *Can sociopaths be **conscious** of their lack of **conscience**?*

discreet *or* discrete? Easy to confuse these terms—look them up when necessary. *Discreet* means "careful" or tactful": *A **discreet** inquiry revealed many gaps in the employee's timesheets.* *Discrete* means "distinct" or "separate": *The worker offered three **discrete** explanations for the omissions, none of them plausible.*

disinterested *or* uninterested? The distinction here is an important one to recognize in academic writing. *Disinterested* means to be "above the fray," "neutral," or "unprejudiced": *The dispute was submitted to a panel of **disinterested** experts.* *Uninterested* means to be "bored" or "disengaged": *We were simply **uninterested** in the gossip.*

eminent *or* imminent? *Eminent* means "famous or prominent"; *imminent* describes something about to occur: *The departure of our **eminent** speaker was **imminent**.*

fewer *or* less? *Fewer* is correctly used with items that can be counted and *less* with those that cannot: *The speaker hoped for **less** booing and **fewer** hard questions.* Many speakers and writers ignore this fine point.

hanged *or* hung? Let's hope you have few occasions to make this distinction. Only people have the misfortune to be ***hanged***. All other things are ***hung***, sometimes on the chimney with care.

imply *or* infer? The difference between the terms is important in academic writing. Think of the terms as complements: what someone *implies* (that is, suggests or hints at), someone else might *infer* (that is, figure out or deduce): *Whenever reporters **implied** that the president had lied, he **inferred** that their motives were political.*

its *or* it's? Typically an oversight in editing. You likely know the difference between *its* (a possessive form) and *it's* (the contraction for *it is*).

judgement *or* judgment? The British spell the word with two *e*'s, Americans need just one.

majority *or* plurality? A *majority* represents more than half of any group; a *plurality* is the largest group within a population when no group can claim a majority.

persecute *or* prosecute? *To persecute* means "to abuse" and "to harass"; *to prosecute* means "to bring legal charges": *Critics of the proposed legislation worried that legal **prosecution** might soon become a tool for **persecuting** specific individuals or groups.*

medium *or* media? When defined as a channel of communication, medium is singular: *The **medium** of television remains powerful.* And while many people think of "the media" as a singular entity, the word remains the plural of *medium*. So *media* usually takes a plural verb form: *The Washington **media** are powerful advocates for government growth.*

principal *or* principle? *Principal* has various meanings: as a noun, "head of a school" or "sum of money lent"; as an adjective, "chief" or "most important." A *principle*, however, is a "guideline" or "fundamental belief": *The sophomores discovered that their **principal** had no **principles**.*

reign *or* rein? *Very* commonly confused. You need to learn the not-so-subtle difference: Kings and queens ***reign***; horses, on the other hand, wear ***reins***—by which they are ***reined in***. Keep the difference in mind when using these terms in other contexts: *The Patriots long reign as NFL favorites will end when other teams rein in their once-dominant offense.*

stationary *or* stationery? The words mean different things entirely. *Stationary* is an adjective that describes a lack of change or motion: *a **stationary** bike*. *Stationery* is a noun that means paper for writing and even matching letterhead and envelopes: *I purchased **stationery**.*

that *or* which? Traditionally, *that* is used to introduce essential information or specifications—and it does so without commas surrounding the clause. Removing a "that clause" alters or even undermines the meaning of a sentence: *The films **that the director made prior to World War II** are better than those **that came after***. *Which* is used to introduce related and additional but not essential information; such clauses are surrounded by commas: *The director's films, **which spanned several decades**, vary enormously in critical reputation.* Writers do frequently use *which* in place of *that*.

weather *or* whether?   The words mean different things. *Weather* describes the climate: a **weather** advisory. *Whether* presents a choice: "***Whether** 'tis nobler in the mind to suffer the slings and arrows of outrageous fortune."*

your *or* you're?   Yet another gaffe made by writers in a hurry. *Your* is a possessive form: ***your** coat*. *You're* is the contraction for "you are": ***You're** going to forget **your** coat*.

reader

Readings

part nine

Need help with critical reading? See page 324. / Need help analyzing claims and evidence?
See page 452.

59

Reports: Readings

GENRE MOVES Descriptive Report

N. SCOTT MOMADAY

From *The Way to Rainy Mountain*

A single knoll rises out of the plain in Oklahoma, north and west of the Wichita Range. For my people, the Kiowas, it is an old landmark, and they gave it the name Rainy Mountain. The hardest weather in the world is there. Winter brings blizzards, hot tornadic winds arise in the spring, and in summer the prairie is an anvil's edge. The grass turns brittle and brown, and it cracks beneath your feet. There are green belts along the rivers and creeks, linear groves of hickory and pecan, willow and witch hazel. At a distance in July or August the steaming foliage seems almost to writhe in fire. Great green and yellow grasshoppers are everywhere in the tall grass, popping up like corn to sting the flesh, and tortoises crawl about on the red earth, going nowhere in the plenty of time. Loneliness is an aspect of the land. All things in the plain are isolate; there is no confusion of objects in the eye, but one hill or one tree or one man.

Give life to scenes and settings.

For many descriptive reports, it is important for authors to *show* their readers vivid scenes and settings, so readers can fully understand where the report takes place and can thus better imagine the action. But creating an authentic experience of the scene or setting requires more than just observing a few details. If N. Scott Momaday had simply described the size and color of the knoll, this passage might not have been very successful. What makes the knoll vivid is Momaday's description of the life of this scene over the course of a year. He describes the weather, the vegetation, and the creatures that populate the space, using metaphors to bring these details alive. The result is that the reader receives not just a view of this landscape but a feel for this world.

    If you are writing a report in which location matters (such as a report on a local school), consider not only giving your reader a thorough description of the place, but describing it over the course of time. Momaday offers a view of one specific knoll, but he describes what happens to this space over the course of the seasons. Consider not just the objects and static details of the place you are reporting on—but also how that space has been filled with life. Describe the place by taking on Momaday's perspective: Imagine that you are standing or sitting still in front of it at the time when you first encountered it, and describe what you see. But then imagine the days and months streaming past, as though in fast-forward. Write about how that space is animated by the people who inhabit it and the actions and changes that occur there.

INFORMATIONAL REPORT   Lewis Dartnell is a researcher and astrobiology professor who focuses on how scientists can better communicate with the public. He practices what he teaches as the author of several popular science books and essays including a book called "The Knowledge" that explores how we could rebuild the earth from scratch after a cataclysmic event. While humans argue over what we might have to gain from further space exploration, in this report, Dartnell asks why aliens might want to come to us.

LEWIS DARTNELL

Why Would Aliens Even Bother with Earth? The Pros and Cons of a Trip to the Planet We Call Home

As an astrobiologist I spend a lot of my time working in the lab with samples from some of the most extreme places on Earth, investigating how life might survive on other worlds in our solar system and what signs of their existence we could detect. If there is biology beyond the Earth, the vast majority of life in the Galaxy will be microbial—hardy single-celled life forms that tolerate a much greater range of conditions than more complex organisms can. To be honest, my own point of view is pretty pessimistic. Don't get me wrong—if the Earth received an alien tweet tomorrow, or some other text message beamed at us by radio or laser pulse, then I'd be absolutely thrilled. So far, though, we've seen no convincing evidence of other civilizations among the stars in our skies.

But let's say, just for the sake of argument, that there are one or more star-faring alien civilizations in the Milky Way. We're all familiar with Hollywood's darker depictions of what aliens might do when they come to the Earth: zapping the White

House, harvesting humanity for food like a herd of cattle, or sucking our oceans dry. These scenarios make great films, but don't really stand up to rational scrutiny. So let's run through a thought experiment on what reasons aliens might possibly have to visit the Earth, not because I reckon we need to ready our defenses or assemble a welcoming party, but because I think considering these possibilities is a great way of exploring many of the core themes of the science of astrobiology.

> **"We're all familiar with Hollywood's darker descriptions of what aliens might do when they come to the Earth: zapping the White House, harvesting humanity for food like a herd of cattle, or sucking our oceans dry."**

I. Aliens come to Earth to enslave humanity or for breeding partners

Alien races enslaving each other is a common trope of many science fiction universes. While enslavement of defeated enemies or other vulnerable populations has regrettably been a common feature of our history on Earth, it's hard to see why a species with the capability of voyaging between the stars, and therefore having already demonstrated the mastery of a highly advanced level of machinery and of marshaling energy resources, would have any need for slaves. Constructing robots, or other forms of automation or mechanization, would be a far more effective solution for labor—people are feeble in comparison, harder to fix, and need to be fed.

Likewise, the idea of an alien species needing humans for breeding doesn't really stand up to scrutiny. The act of sexual reproduction, on a genetic level, involves the combination of DNA from two individuals. So on the most fundamental level, for an alien race to be compatible with us, they would need not only to use the same polymer, deoxyribonucleic acid, as the storage molecule for their genetic information, but also to use the same four "letters" for their genetic alphabet (and not other purine and pyrimidine bases that exist in chemistry), and the same coding system for translating those sequences of genetic letters into proteins, and the same organizational structure of the DNA strands into chromosomes, and so on. There is a lot of ongoing research on whether extraterrestrial life is likely to use DNA, or what molecular alternatives there might be, but it is a huge stretch to expect alien life to be that similar to human genetics. Humans cant even interbreed with our closest evolutionary relatives on Earth, the chimpanzees (indeed, this is the basis of the definition for different species—two organisms which are not able to reproduce fertile offspring), and so it is overwhelmingly improbable that an alien life form from a completely different evolutionary lineage would be compatible.

II. Aliens come to Earth to harvest us for food

If aliens wouldn't be bothered about enslaving or breeding with us, might they simply be coming to Earth for a drive-by meal? The question of whether an alien biochemistry would be able to digest us as food actually comes down to some very fundamental features of the molecules of life. Our cells are made up of various organic molecules: proteins (polymers of amino acids), nucleic acids DNA and RNA (polymers of bases and sugars), and membranes of phospholipids. And so for making more cells for reproduction, growth and repair of our bodies we need a source of these simple building blocks. We eat other animals or plants and our digestive system breaks them down into their component amino acids, sugars, and fatty acids, which we then use as the building blocks for ourselves. So in order to derive any useful nutrition from eating a human, an alien monster would need to be based on very similar biochemistry, and thus have the enzymes needed for processing the molecules we are built from.

A whole variety of amino acids, sugars and fatty molecules are actually found in certain meteorites, having been produced by astrochemistry in outer space, and so maybe extraterrestrial life would be based on the same basic building blocks as us. But there's another, very interesting subtlety here. Simple organic molecules like amino acids and sugars can exist in two different forms, mirror images of each other (in the same way your two hands are similar shapes but cant be placed exactly one on top of the other). These two versions are known as enantiomers, and it turns out that all life on Earth uses only left-handed amino acids and right-handed sugars, whereas non-living chemistry produces even mixtures of both kinds.

So if we do find traces of amino acids on Mars, one very good way of telling whether these organic molecules are the relics of ancient Martian life or are just the product of astrochemistry would be to check if they are mostly left- or right-handed forms, or just an even mixture. The most exciting discovery would be to detect traces of ancient bacteria on Mars and to find that they employ the opposite forms of organic molecules to us: right-handed amino acids or left-handed sugars, because then we would know for sure that this life was definitely extraterrestrial and not merely contamination from Earth. So here's a fascinating thought: alien invaders could be based on exactly the same organic molecules (amino acids, sugars, etc.), but they still wouldn't gain any nutrition from eating us as the origins of life on their own planet settled on the opposite enantiomers. We'd be mirror images of each other, on a molecular level.

III. Aliens come to Earth to suck our oceans dry

If alien marauders would need to have an essentially identical biochemistry to bother culling us for food, maybe they come to Earth to harvest some other vital substance. All life on Earth is water-based; H_2O is astonishingly versatile as a solvent and participant in biochemistry and so it seems likely that extraterrestrial life would also be based on this compound. Perhaps, then, aliens may be drawn to the Earth for our wonderfully wet oceans and seas and rivers and lakes—to siphon off our hydrological cycle.

The problem with this supposition is that there are loads of far better sources of water in space. In fact, we think that when Earth first formed from the swirling disc of gas and dust around the proto-Sun it was actually a pretty dry planet; the water to fill our oceans was delivered later by a barrage of comets and asteroids from the colder, outer regions of the solar system. In fact, Europa, one of the moons orbiting Jupiter, contains more liquid water in the global ocean beneath its frozen surface than our entire planet—Europa, and not Earth, is the Waterworld of our solar system. So if you were an alien voyaging between star systems in need of a drink, youd have access to a far greater amount of water in the icy moons and cometary halo of the outer solar system. Youd also find it much more practical to operate in deep space, rather than trying to suck up the oceans against the gravitational pull of the planet Earth.

IV. Aliens come to Earth for some other raw material

If not water, then maybe there's some other natural resource that aliens might invade the Earth to exploit. Perhaps they intend to wipe away our cities and begin strip-mining the crust of the planet for ores to extract metals and build more vast spaceships. But in fact, because the Earth formed from a molten state with iron sinking down to the core, our planet's crust is actually pretty depleted of useful metals like iron, nickel, platinum, tungsten and gold. And as with the water, it's hard to see why aliens would bother extracting material against the gravity of the Earth when the asteroids are composed of the same basic rocky stuff. In fact, some asteroids are believed to be essentially pure lumps of metal—they were once the cores of proto-planets that were smashed apart again by the colossal collisions in the early history of the solar system. Several companies are already proposing to launch asteroid mining operations to exploit these exceedingly valuable resources.

Perhaps, though, there might be a reason that our hypothetical aliens would come to mine the Earth. While it's true that the asteroids and Earth, and other terrestrial planets, are made up of essentially the same rocky material, the Earth isn't simply an inert lump; it s a very active, dynamic place. In particular, the thin crust of the Earth is fractured into separate shards that are continually sliding around on top of the hot gooey mantle, rubbing alongside each other, crunching head-on, subducting one beneath another, or pulling apart to create fresh crust. This is the churning process of plate tectonics.

So far, astronomers have already found over four and a half thousand extrasolar planets—worlds orbiting other stars—and the expectation now is that there are billions of rocky planets in our Galaxy. But here's a thought right on the forefront of current planetary science and astrobiology. Perhaps terrestrial planets are common, but terrestrial planets *with plate tectonics* are rare. Plate tectonics is thought to be vital for keeping the Earths climate stable over billions of years to allow complex life like ours to evolve, and it also acts to concentrate certain metals into rich ores. It seems likely that only a small proportion of terrestrial planets undergo plate tectonics (neither Mars nor Venus does). So perhaps an alien civilization would come to the Earth for our exceptional plate tectonics and concentration of particular metals, and the fact that the same tectonics had also enabled a rich biosphere to develop would be merely an inconvenience.

V. Aliens come to Earth looking for a new home

There is a considerable amount of rocky real estate in the galaxy for aliens to consider moving home to, but a terrestrial planet might need to offer more than just a habitable zone locale to be able to support complex life. Communities of hardy microbial cells thriving off inorganic energy deep underground might be able to survive pretty much anywhere, but complex life requires much narrower environmental conditions on the surface. Various features of the Earth beyond our warm oceans are thought to be crucial to maintaining a stable surface environment for geological time periods. These include plate tectonics acting to regulate the climate, a large moon preventing the spin axis of the planet from wobbling too much, and a global magnetic field for deflecting aside the solar wind and preventing the atmosphere being blown away into space. For these reasons, maybe planets like the Earth are something of a rarity, and so present particularly desirable targets for alien colonization.

But while it's true that such worlds may well be required for complex life to evolve in the first place, once an intelligent species becomes technologically advanced enough to travel between the stars it's also likely to be able to artificially manage a planet s environment. For example, many people are already starting to talk seriously about "mega-engineering" or "geoengineering" projects to avoid the worst effects of global warming on Earth, and we've worked out, at least in broad terms so far, how further in the future we could "terraform" Mars to create a habitable environment for humans to live on the surface without needing spacesuits. Indeed, the very fact that Earth is already teeming with its own life (most of which is tenacious microbes that affect the chemistry of the atmosphere and oceans) may well be a hindrance to an alien species, with its own quirky biochemistry, looking for somewhere to colonize. It may well be easier to find a terrestrial world that hasn't already developed life of its own, and install its own biosphere on an empty planet.

VI. Aliens come to the Earth for the Earthlings

To my mind, then, the enormous amounts of time and energy that are likely to be necessary for traveling between the stars in a galaxy, and the fact that raw materials can be sought elsewhere more practically, would rule out aliens coming to the Earth simply to take something we have. I think we can safely rest assured that even if intelligent alien species do exist in our galaxy, they are not about to appear in our skies with an invasion fleet to subjugate humanity and begin stripping our world. Perhaps the thing that may attract only extraterrestrials to Earth is us. I suspect that if aliens did come to Earth, it would be as researchers: biologists, anthropologists, linguists, keen to understand the peculiar workings of life on Earth, to meet humanity and learn of our art, music, culture, languages, philosophies and religions.

If aliens do come to pay us a visit, there's one final way that the movies have probably got it all wrong. The laws of physics (at least as we currently understand them—after all, in 100 years we may have worked out how to build a practical warp drive or stretch stable wormholes through the fabric of space-time) strongly constrain movement across the vast gulfs between stars. To make the journey time from one star system to the next anything less than scores of millennia, you need to accelerate your spaceship to a fair fraction of the speed of light. The greater the mass you need to accelerate, the greater the energy required, so you really want to keep your starships as small and light as possible.

Intelligent life forms like humans are inherently bulky things, particularly when you want to send a team of them along with all the life support machinery and re-generation systems for keeping them alive in space. But a much more plausible alternative presents itself. Perhaps it's unrealistic to expect ET to go through all the discomfort and bother of actually voyaging in person across the oceans of inter-stellar space to far-flung worlds, but instead to travel by proxy. To cross the galaxy not by encasing wet, vulnerable biological organisms *within* complex life-support technology, but *as* the hardened, durable technology itself. With a more complete understanding of how the human brain works—the neuronal wiring diagram and other interactions that give rise to intelligence and consciousness—it stands to reason that we could not only simulate this perfectly within hardware to construct an AI (artificial intelligence), but also potentially upload the consciousness of a living person into a computer.

Contained within a capsule of miniaturized electronics and systems for self-repair you'd not only be essentially immortal, but also incredibly compact and light and much better suited for inter- stellar travel. In this sense, perhaps most life in the galaxy isn't carbon-based (organic), but silicon-based. I don't mean this in the sense of silicoid monsters imagined living inside volcanoes in *The X-Files* or *Star Trek,* but as the hardware supporting complex sentient computer programs. Silicon life would be second generation, existing only because it has been designed and created by a precursor organic species, which itself evolved naturally on a habitable world.

For these reasons, it strikes me that if there is intelligent alien life out there in our galaxy, they almost certainly wouldn't pay us a visit in person in huge city-sized motherships, but by sending their sentient robots as emissaries. But how would they know we're here in the first place? Humanity has been leaking (or deliberately transmitting) radio waves out into space for roughly a century.

So an alien civilization running a SETI program with sensitive radio telescopes could detect us. But this radio bubble announcing our technological emergence, centered on the Earth and expanding out into space at light speed, is only around 200 light years across. That is a minuscule region of space in the galaxy as a whole, a disc 100,000 light years in diameter, and so even if the galaxy does contain other intelligent life forms, they would likely still be oblivious to our recent appearance. But although humanity has only been detectably civilized for a century, the Earth itself has been conspicuously alive for many hundreds of millions of years, and this links to one of the hottest topics in current astrobiology. Life on Earth, and specifically photosynthetic life such as plants and cyanobacteria that grow by absorbing the energy of sunlight and splitting water, has been releasing oxygen as a waste gas at such a high rate that it has built up in the atmosphere, first to just a few per cent, and today constituting a fifth of the Earth's air. Oxygen is a very reactive gas, and the only reason it has been able to accumulate in the atmosphere is that it is constantly being replenished by living organisms. In fact, the presence of oxygen in the atmosphere is thought to be so unusual to the geochemistry of a planet that astrobiologists consider it to be a biosignature of life (specifically if oxygen and a reduced gas like methane are both present).

We are currently on the verge of building space-based telescopes that use spectroscopy to read the composition of the atmospheres of terrestrial exoplanets, and so survey the night sky for signs of life. And we're only relative newcomers on the galactic scene. There's nothing special about this exact moment in galactic history, and life on another planet could have evolved intelligence millions of years ago and used their own telescopes to look out for planets displaying the telltale sign of an oxygen-rich atmosphere. But apparently, as far as we can tell the fact that the Earth is obviously sporting biology has not prompted anyone to say hello.

This is a very curious observation, and to my mind could be down to two equally intriguing possibilities. The fact that Earth's oxygen-rich atmosphere has apparently attracted no one's attention may simply be because life is so rare that there is not a single other civilization in the galaxy with us to have their attention drawn. Or perhaps planets with an oxygen-rich atmosphere are so staggeringly common that the Earth just doesn't stand out among the masses. In the first possibility we are solitary and lonely intelligent beings in the galaxy; in the second, life is absolutely rife in the cosmos. Both, to me, are equally profound realizations. And the most exciting aspect is that within your and my lifetime we will have launched our atmosphere-reading space telescopes and the science of astrobiology will have been able to tell which one is right.

What a time to be an intelligent life form on Earth!

"Speculating about what aliens look like has kept children, film producers, and scientists amused for decades. If they exist, will extraterrestrials turn out to look similar to us or might they take a form beyond our wildest imaginings? The answer to this question really depends on how we think evolution works at the deepest level."

Reading the Genre

1. How is this report organized? What are the benefits and the drawbacks of the unique organization of this essay? Does this organization work better for a report than it would for an argument or a narrative? What would happen if you took one of your own essays and reorganized it in this way? (For more on organizing reports, see p. 38.)

2. Dartnell creates a sense of tension in this report. How does he describe aliens and what do these descriptions lend to the report? What strategies does he use to structure the writing toward a climax? How does the tone of his writing encourage the reader to share his interest in astronomy? Can you find specific words, phrases, or constructions that seem to convey this interest and seem likely to inspire readers?

3. How does Dartnell describe complicated ideas in simple language? Are there some concepts that could be better or more carefully described? Identify two such concepts and try revising the description. (For more on using language strategically, see Part 5, "Style," p. 366.)

4. WRITING: Dartnell's essay feels only half-serious. Not all readers will believe that aliens even exist. Nevertheless, focusing on the reasons why aliens might want to visit our planet creates a terrific thought experiment, forcing us to consider what we should value and protect here on earth. In a similar experiment, imagine that our telescopes recognize an alien vehicle approaching earth. It will arrive in one month. What are the most important things humans should do to prepare for this visit? Structure this writing as a report, in a style similar to Dartnell's.

5. MULTIMODALITY—EMOJI STORIES: To create visual images to accompany each of the six possible scenarios that Dartnell describes for alien visitation, use a series of emojis. Putting emojis in order can create a sentence or story made up of images, and it is okay to use some words as well. The master list of emojis can be found at *unicode.org*—and you can find alien emojis there, of course. This work could be done in small groups, with each group taking on one scenario.

Further Reading

Wills, Matthew. "What do aliens look like? The clue is in evolution." TheConversation.com (2016).

DEFINITIONAL REPORT   Steve Silberman writes about science for *Wired* magazine. Silberman hosts several "conferences" on the online community site The Well, and his Twitter account has made *Time*'s list of best feeds. His book *Neurotribes: The Legacy of Autism and the Future of Neurodiversity* won dozens of awards and has even been optioned by Hollywood to be made into a movie.

Wired

Posted: April 16, 2013, at 6:30 AM
From: Steve Silberman

Neurodiversity Rewires Conventional Thinking about Brains

"Despite the rise in work by autistic people, "autism" remains, in both the popular and academic press, not a question of individuals or of social disability, but an Othered impairment, an affliction that is imposing on, and trying the patience of, non-autistic society."

In the late 1990s, a sociologist named Judy Singer—who is on the autism spectrum herself—invented a new word to describe conditions like autism, dyslexia, and ADHD: *neurodiversity*. In a radical stroke, she hoped to shift the focus of discourse about atypical ways of thinking and learning away from the usual litany of deficits, disorders, and impairments. Echoing positive terms like *biodiversity* and *cultural diversity*, her neologism called attention to the fact that many atypical forms of brain wiring also convey unusual skills and aptitudes.

Autistic people, for instance, have prodigious memories for facts, are often highly intelligent in ways that don't register on verbal IQ tests, and are capable of focusing for long periods on tasks that take advantage of their natural gift for detecting flaws in visual patterns. By autistic standards, the "normal" human brain is easily distractible, is obsessively social, and suffers from a deficit of attention to detail. "I was interested in the liberatory, activist aspects of it," Singer explained to journalist Andrew Solomon in 2008, "to do for neurologically different people what feminism and gay rights had done for their constituencies."

The new word first appeared in print in a 1998 *Atlantic* article about *Wired* magazine's Web site, HotWired, by journalist Harvey Blume. "Neurodiversity may be every bit as crucial for the human race as biodiversity is for life in general," he declared. "Who can say what form of wiring will prove best at any given moment? Cybernetics and computer culture, for example, may favor a somewhat autistic cast of mind."

Thinking this way is no mere exercise in postmodern relativism. One reason that the vast majority of autistic adults are chronically unemployed or underemployed, consigned to make-work jobs like assembling keychains in sheltered workshops, is because HR departments are hesitant to hire workers who look, act, or communicate in non-neurotypical ways—say, by using a keyboard and text-to-speech software to express themselves, rather than by chattering around the water cooler.

One way to understand neurodiversity is to remember that just because a PC is not running Windows doesn't mean that it's broken. Not all the features of atypical human operating systems are bugs. We owe many of the wonders of modern life to innovators who were brilliant in non-neurotypical ways. Herman Hollerith, who helped launch the age of computing by inventing a machine to tabulate and sort punch cards, once leaped out of a school window to escape his spelling lessons because he was dyslexic. So were Carver Mead, the father of very large-scale integrated circuits, and William Dreyer, who designed one of the first protein sequencers.

Singer's subversive meme has also become the rallying cry of the first new civil rights movement to take off in the twenty-first century. Empowered by the Internet, autistic self-advocates, proud dyslexics, unapologetic Touretters, and others who think differently are raising the rainbow banner of neurodiversity to encourage society to appreciate and celebrate cognitive differences, while demanding reasonable accommodations in schools, housing, and the workplace.

A nonprofit group called the Autistic Self Advocacy Network is working with the U.S. Department of Labor to develop better employment opportunities for all people on the spectrum, including those who rely on screen-based devices to communicate (and who doesn't these days?). "Trying to make someone 'normal' isn't always the best way to improve their life," says ASAN cofounder Ari Ne'eman, the first openly autistic White House appointee.

Neurodiversity is also gaining traction in special education, where experts are learning that helping students make the most of their native strengths and special interests, rather than focusing on trying to correct their deficits or normalize their behavior, is a more effective method of educating young people with atypical minds so they can make meaningful contributions to society. "We don't pathologize a calla lily by saying it has a 'petal deficit disorder'," writes Thomas Armstrong, author of a new book called *Neurodiversity in the Classroom*. "Similarly, we ought not to pathologize children who have different kinds of brains and different ways of thinking and learning."

In forests and tide pools, the value of biological diversity is resilience: the ability to withstand shifting conditions and resist attacks from predators. In a world changing faster than ever, honoring and nurturing neurodiversity is civilization's best chance to thrive in an uncertain future.

Reading the Genre

1. What key terms does Silberman define in this short report? Read through the text, and when he defines a key term or theory, underline it. How important are these definitions to Silberman's report?

2. This short report might also be seen as a long definition of "neurodiversity." How does the report center on the term, and how does the focus on one term help the reader to understand a larger issue like autism in new ways? (For more on organizing reports by definition, see p. 38.)

3. It is notable that Silberman does not just reference doctors or scientists in this report, though those are the people who most often define autism in our culture. Discuss the significance of the sources that Silberman *does* cite in this report, and comment on how he establishes the authority of each source. Why do you think he focuses on the sources he does? (For more on where and how to find sources, see pp. 436, 442, and 448.)

4. WRITING: Neurodiversity is a neologism, an invented word. Every year, the *Washington Post* publishes a list of the best neologisms of the year. Search through some of these lists and find a word that intrigues you. Then write a report about where exactly this word came from and the cultural impact it has had.

Further Reading

Ryskamp, Dani Alexis. "Stories of Autism: What the Rise of Books on Autism Tells Us About, Well, Autism." *Disability Studies Quarterly* 37.1 (2017).

LEGAL REPORT   Philip Deloria, a descendant of the famous Sioux (Dakota) leader Tipi Sapa, is a well-known and highly regarded scholar. He teaches history, American culture, and Native American studies at Harvard University. Both of his books, *Playing Indian* (1998) and *Indians in Unexpected Places* (2004), were awarded prizes for academic excellence. The following essay appears in the book *A New Literary History of America*, by Greil Marcus and Werner Sollors (2009).

PHILIP DELORIA

The *Cherokee Nation* Decision

"**T**his gathering of nations is unprecedented in Native American history. There is a sense of history in the making. No one at the camp really wants to think about the possibility of the pipeline crossing the river. But there is definitely a sense that something bigger is happening."

This is a story about the law. For me, however, it begins elsewhere, with a cryptic little book, measuring three by five inches and covered with a crumbling leather binding. Open it to the title page—*A History of the Black Hawk War* by "An Old Resident of the Military Tract" (1832)—and you will think it a historical memoir, published locally at Fort Armstrong, Iowa. The Black Hawk War, which "opened up" the Mississippi Midwest to white settlement, did indeed take place in 1832. Continue reading, however, and you will find not history, but sixty-three pages of ciphered and mnemonic figures:

Indian

1. (I) g t t e a g o * w c t chief o # # t o o a t p
2. (I) # I I - -
3. (I) a a p Indians- - (II) I w a a r * - -# VI- -%
4. (II) y w s y t a p a Indians

And so it continues, through four tantalizing sections (Indian, Squaw, Warrior, and Braves). The book feels a bit like Poe, dark, desperate, and strange. Each section represents a role in the rituals of a white fraternal group that pretended, in its secret ceremonies, to be the Indian people so recently dispossessed in the war. Holding it I *feel* the 1830s, furtive and confused, a time of dark lanterns and sinister killings, treasure hunting and magic, secret ciphers, and houses (full of dead people and greasy playing cards) floating intact on the cresting Mississippi, with plenty of sorry to go around.

A fulcrum moment, these 1830s, of precarious cultural shifts, when the generative American contradiction between *killing Indians* and *becoming them* still lay close to the surface. That contradiction, long embodied in captivity narratives, frontier folk mythologies, and performances of Indian "American" identities, erupted in the 1830s into the realm of law. The eruption came in response to the crisis of an American nation that fully believed in its imperial destiny, yet spoke of its dominations only haltingly. It structures the lives, literatures, and politics of American Indian people—and thus *all* Americans—to the present day.

One phrase—"domestic dependent nations"—reordered the world of the 1830s. Authored by John Marshall, the chief justice of the U.S. Supreme Court, the three words translated the older cultural contradictions into new law and politics. If killing the Indian had allowed settlers to claim land and proclaim independence, "becoming" the Indian had let those same settlers incorporate themselves *into* the land and lodge the ancient memory of Indian aboriginality in American souls. The new words applied (in reverse) the same contradictory structure of logic to Indian people themselves: Somehow, they could be distinct nations—and yet be simultaneously incorporated within the American body politic. As nations, they might claim to be independent—and yet they were in fact dependent on the federal government.

John Marshall named Indian people as "domestic dependent nations" in the second of three closely linked legal cases involving the Cherokees. In the first case, *Johnson v. M'Intosh* (1823), Marshall wrote an unnecessarily elaborate opinion in which he codified the "discovery doctrine." He argued that, in the wake of contact between New World and Old, title to Indian lands no longer resided with Indian people but accrued instead to the European nation claiming first discovery. Indian people could sell the "claim" to their land, but only to the discovering sovereign—or a rightful successor, in most cases (conveniently) the United States. Marshall used this "discovery" argument carelessly, to prop up the land claims of Virginia militiamen, former comrades during the War for Independence. This set the legal terms for the second case, *Cherokee Nation v. Georgia*.

In 1828, the discovery of gold on Cherokee lands led the state of Georgia to try to eliminate the Cherokees. Earlier, Georgians had forsworn territorial claims in return for a federal promise to remove the Cherokees as soon as was practical. The passage in 1830 of the Indian Removal Act—which encouraged tribes to exchange their eastern land for territory west of the Mississippi—suggested that the time for Cherokee removal was at hand. President Andrew Jackson was more than sympathetic.

Before the violent dispossessions of Removal, however, Cherokees, Georgians, and the federal government fought over their respective sovereignties. The federal government claimed power over the individual states—which meant the continued validity of federally negotiated Indian treaties (with the Cherokees, for example). South Carolina and other states in the South claimed primacy for themselves, insisting that they could "nullify" federal laws they deemed unconstitutional. And within their state borders, Georgians confronted the Cherokee Nation, an independent society replete with a constitution, representative government, educational institutions, written language, and other appurtenances of "civilization," including chattel slavery.

Asserting its own state sovereignty, Georgia could hardly embrace the rising sovereign nation of the Cherokees. In 1828 the Georgia legislature passed an act to make Cherokee territory part of and subject to the laws of Georgia. The following year, a second act added a provision "to annul all laws and ordinances made by the Cherokee nation of Indians." In 1830 Georgia seized and sentenced to death George Tassells, a Cherokee man who had killed another Cherokee within the bounds of the Cherokee Nation—a case in which the Cherokee justice system had clear jurisdiction. After a failed appeal at the state level (Georgians used the "doctrine of discovery" to insist on their own jurisdiction), the Cherokees sought help from the U.S. Supreme Court, and John Marshall ordered a stay of execution. Georgia defied the Court (and suddenly, a dry legal narrative turns sinister: emergency sessions of the legislature, a rushed message on horseback from the governor—probably a dark lantern involved somewhere—and a hasty Christmas Eve hanging from a tree in a lonely field).

The Supreme Court said little about the legalized murder of Tassells, however, preferring to concentrate on *Cherokee Nation v. Georgia*, filed only days before by Cherokee chief John Ross in an effort to overturn Georgia's assertions of sovereignty. In the debate over the Indian Removal Act, many advocates insisted that Indian people *did* hold title to their lands—and thus national and territorial sovereignty, recognized through treaties and land purchases. The basis for this understanding, however, had been effectively undermined by the discovery doctrine. Brandishing a Supreme Court decision, Removal advocates argued that Indians had no title to their land and could be evicted at the pleasure of the United States, inheritor of the European rights of discovery.

Marshall ignored both the discovery doctrine and the defiance of Georgia (which refused to appear before the court), focusing instead on the question of jurisdiction. He framed the case around a grand historical narrative and situated the Cherokees at a decisive turning point, one that required political recalibration. "If courts were permitted to indulge their sympathies," he wrote,

> a case better calculated to excite them can scarcely be imagined. A people once numerous, powerful, and truly independent, found by our ancestors in the quiet and uncontrolled possession of an ample domain, gradually sinking beneath our superior policy, our arts and our arms, have yielded their lands by successive treaties, each of which contains a solemn guarantee of the residue, until they retain no more of their formerly extensive territory than is deemed necessary to their comfortable subsistence. To preserve this remnant, the present application is made.

The key words—"independent," "powerful," "uncontrolled possession"—make the beginnings of his narrative clear. Indians were distinct, autonomous peoples ("nations" in a European sense). They formed alliances and negotiated treaties. The proper executive-branch office for Indian affairs was the War Department and the proper political relation was diplomacy or formal conflict. In the 1830s, however, Americans began saying out loud that after decades of conflicts, land cessions, removals, and dislocations, those relations had changed. Witness the key terms that seemed to shift the ground: "sinking beneath," "yielded their lands," "preserve this remnant."

The first rhetoric reflects a distinct form of colonial practice, characterized by warfare, treaties, a nation-to-nation relationship, and a cultural imagination that played with Indian otherness. The second calls into being a new and different kind of colonialism. Indian people were consolidated and segregated in regional spaces—the so-called Indian territory—the better to manage, reeducate, and incorporate them. This segregation enabled the development of American imperial governance based on the demographic shift from Indian to white and the political transitions from mixed territory to white state and from Indian "nation" to Indian "tribe." The militiamen hunting down Black Hawk in 1832 engaged in exactly this process of containment. The results were clear: the states of Iowa, Illinois, and Wisconsin, the removal of many Indians from the Midwest, and a secret fraternal order with a book of coded rituals.

In this new form of colonialism, Indian nations could be viewed as something like states, though vastly inferior. The proper executive branch office for their oversight was now the Department of the Interior (the shift from the War Department was made in 1849) and the proper relationship would be that of a paternalistic guardian to its immature ward. Marshall's historical narrative—and American cultural production in general—repositioned 1830s Indians; once a foreign affairs problem, they were now a domestic issue.

And that is how it played out. The third article of the Constitution gives the Supreme Court jurisdiction over "controversies between a state or the citizens thereof, and foreign states, citizens, or subjects." Were the Cherokees a foreign state? If they were, then the Court would have jurisdiction and Marshall might indulge his sympathies and perhaps undo the damage he had caused. And yet, as foreign states, Indian nations would also be able to sign treaties with other nations, establish trade alliances with American enemies, and subject U.S. citizens to Indian laws, all acts the United States would construe as hostile. Despite any sympathies, the Court proved unwilling to see the Cherokees as a foreign nation.

So what were they? Indian tribes were distinct nations—but they existed in relation to the United States and within the borders it claimed. And so Marshall wrote: "It may well be doubted whether those tribes that reside within the acknowledged boundaries of the United States can, with strict accuracy, be denominated foreign nations. They may, more correctly, perhaps, be denominated domestic dependent nations. . . . Their relation to the United States resembles that of a ward to his guardian." Lacking jurisdiction, John Marshall could not use the case to recall the unanticipated consequences of the discovery doctrine. But when the last of the three Cherokee cases came to the Court the following year, he reversed himself, ruling in *Worcester v. Georgia* that American Indian tribes were in fact sovereign nations and that they retained all sovereign rights not given up by treaty or lost in a just war. Cherokee claims to Cherokee homelands were guaranteed by those solemn federal treaties, and Georgia's claims to jurisdiction over those homelands were invalid.

It was too late. Southern courts responded to Marshall's decisions with their own cases—*Georgia v. Tassells* (1830), *Caldwell v. Alabama* (1831), and *Tennessee v. Forman* (1835)—each of which denied not only Marshall's belated assertion of tribal sovereignty but also the power of the Supreme Court itself. These Southern cases gave the doctrine of discovery new form, primarily around stark assertions of Indian racial inferiority. And, since Andrew Jackson's executive branch refused to enforce the Supreme Court's decision in *Worcester*, calling it "stillborn," it was the Southern decisions that structured Indian removal and the new colonialism of consolidation and reservation rule. They became the de facto legal precedents, even if *Worcester* theoretically dictated the rule of law.

The decision paved the way for the Trail of Tears, a forced migration to Indian territory in 1838 during which more than four thousand Cherokees died. Similar removals and consolidations of Indians would become central to American policy over the next six decades. The federal government stopped making treaties in 1871, began reeducating Indian children in boarding schools, chopped up reservation land, and restricted tribes' religious practices. In law and politics, the paternalist language of guardians and wards was everywhere; indeed, it seemed to take precedence over "domestic dependent nations"—not to mention the idea that a tribe might have sovereignty.

These displacements existed in complex relation to the omnipresent cultural trope of the "vanishing" Indian. James Fenimore Cooper's *Last of the Mohicans* (1826) ends with noble Chingachgook alone, with no legacy or future. John Augustus Stone's *Metamora* (1829)—one of the most popular plays of the nineteenth century— finishes with tragic Indian death and a promising white future. John Mix Stanley's evocative painting *Last of the Race* (1857) shows a sad remnant of different tribes at sunset on the shores of the Pacific. And white fraternal orders in Iowa and elsewhere gathered at night, pretending to be now-departed Indians in order to perpetuate their memory.

And yet, Indian people did not vanish but began slowly reworking John Marshall's words. Some emphasized "domestic" and "dependent," focusing on American treaty obligations and using the language of "guardian" and "ward" to press the federal government for support for education, health, economic development, and other forms of assistance enshrined in treaty agreements. Others went in a different direction, skipping over "domestic" and "dependent" to argue for Indian nationhood and autonomy. In 1972, for example, following the Trail of Broken Treaties march on Washington, D.C., Indian activists demanded that all Indian people be governed by treaty relations, that the government restore a nation-to-nation relationship, ratify unapproved treaties, and establish a commission to review violations of treaty rights. Contemporary movements have pushed for Indian sovereignty, and they emphasize the word with a range of adjectives: political, legal, economic, intellectual, cultural.

When you hear about Indian casino gaming or tribal taxing authority or license plates, you are hearing—through the word "sovereignty"—the echoes of the *Cherokee Nation* decision. That decision has come full circle with the efforts of some Cherokees to dis-enroll Cherokee freedmen, the descendants of Cherokee-owned slaves guaranteed tribal citizenship under a treaty signed in 1866. The issue plays out on the grounds of Cherokee sovereignty (in the tribe's Supreme Court cases and electoral processes), nation-to-nation relations (in the Treaty of 1866), and guardianship oversight (in federal membership lists, a federal Indian blood quantum card, and a congressional effort to strip the Cherokees of federal recognition and funding). The complications of the 1830s—and sometimes their mood and tone—have continuously erupted into a series of presents.

Bibliography

Tim Alan Garrison, *The Legal Ideology of Removal: The Southern Judiciary and the Sovereignty of Native American Nations* (Athens, GA, 2002).

Lindsay G. Robertson, *Conquest by Law: How the Discovery of America Dispossessed Indigenous Peoples of Their Lands* (New York, 2005).

David E. Wilkins, *American Indian Sovereignty and the U.S. Supreme Court: The Masking of Justice* (Austin, TX, 1997).

Robert A. Williams, *The American Indian in Western Legal Thought: The Discourses of Conquest* (New York, 1990).

Reading the Genre

1. Deloria identifies several key terms in this report. What are they? How does Deloria explain them and their importance?

2. What strategy does Deloria use to organize information? (Hint: Take another look at the key terms from question 1.) How does the structure of the report make it accessible and easy to read? How does Deloria's organization help readers follow his argument?

3. In his conclusion, Deloria asks readers to consider how this legal history reaches into "a series of presents." What are some of the ways this happens? Where can we see the impact of the *Cherokee Nation* decision today?

4. Deloria quotes several historical figures and summarizes the work of four legal researchers in this report. How does he manage to include so much information efficiently, and how does he use it to support his thesis or main idea? See "Find reliable sources" (p. 40), "Finding and developing materials" (p. 46), "Base reports on the best available sources" (p. 46), and Chapter 46, "Evaluating Sources," p. 442.

5. WRITING: Deloria begins his report by stating, "This is a story about the law." The same is true, in a way, of any legal report. Choose a brief legal report from the Pew Research Web site (pewtrusts.org) and rewrite it as a short story. Try to follow the simplest narrative structure you can: Once upon a time there was a legal problem; it affected this group of characters; they decided to do some things about it; there was a struggle and a series of compromises and resolutions; this was the conclusion.

Further Reading

Whittle, Joe. "'We opened eyes': at Standing Rock, my fellow Native Americans make history." *The Guardian*, 30 Nov. 2016, www.theguardian.com/us-news/2016/nov/30/standing-rock-indigenous-people-history-north-dakota-access-pipeline-protest. Accessed 20 Sept. 2017.

MULTIMODAL REPORT   CyeKeia Lee is the Director of Higher Education Initiatives for the National Association for the Education of Homeless Children and Youth. She was a low-income student herself, and now brings that experience into her work empowering young people, educating teachers, and arguing for more resources to support homeless students, especially college students. Sara Goldrick-Rabb is a Professor at Temple University who has had significant influence over federal education policy, specifically with regards to college affordability and debt.

CYEKEIA LEE AND SARA GOLDRICK-RABB

Navigating College: Resource Guide for Homeless and Low Income Students *from* MoneyGeek

College poses unique challenges, but for low-income or homeless students, making it through can require Herculean effort. The relative wealth of college students' families remains a strong predictor of matriculation, and though college completion rates have increased across the board in recent decades, the rate for students from low income households is lower than that of high income students.

For homeless youth, there are many barriers to academic success and degree completion. In addition to family homelessness, 1.6 to 1.7 million youth experience homelessness on their own each year, without being accompanied by a parent (called UHY or Unaccompanied Homeless Youth). The highly stressful experience of poverty often accompanying homelessness frequently hinders academic focus and achievement. Homeless youth are also less likely to have educational role models and mentors in their lives who help to encourage their academic interests and life aspirations.

According to a 2015 study from the Wisconsin HOPE Lab, half of all community college students struggle with food or housing insecurity. 20 percent of these students deal with acute hunger and 13 percent with homelessness.

The study found that a huge number of the students most in need of basic resources are not asking for them. This resource guide addresses that very issue: where to find assistance, on and off campus, and how to ask for it.

Navigating the Essential Costs

Tuition is often a major obstacle to low-income students, but it is not the only significant cost. Housing, meals, transportation, textbooks and school supplies, and health care also must be managed. Fortunately, there are myriad resources available to defray costs for low-income students.

Tuition

Tuition remains the college cost that can most deter low-income students from applying and remaining enrolled. Since 2000, average tuition has increased by almost 50 percent at four-year private institutions and two-year public institutions, while almost doubling at four-year public institutions. Tuition at private four-year institutions now averages $34,483 per year, while public four-year institutions average $15,022 per year. Financing this costs is onerous for any prospective college student, but presents a difficult challenge to homeless and low-income students.

The major resources available for coping with these costs include scholarships, federal aid and federal student loans.

Scholarships

Many types of institutions grant scholarships based on a variety of criteria. Most scholarships are merit-based, in recognition of outstanding achievements, or need-based, on the basis of financial need if certain minimum criteria of academic achievement are met.

The types of institutions awarding scholarships include the following:

▸ **Individual academic institutions**
Most four-year schools offer merit-based and need-based financial aid. The types of scholarships available are typically listed on the institution's admissions page, which may also link to third-party resources. This page on Affordability and Financial Aid at the University of California Los Angeles, for instance, describes the scholarships offered by the university and provides links to other scholarship databases.

▸ **Organizations and Nonprofits**
Some organizations offer scholarships to students based on specific criteria, including demographics: socio-economic status, gender, race, academic achievements, extracurricular activities, and prospective fields of study.

Finding the Right Scholarship

A partial list of scholarship programs that serve low-income and homeless youth includes:

Dell Scholars Program

The Dell Scholars Program provides $20,000 to winners over the course of six years, in addition to tutoring, networking and technology resources. The scholarships are awarded based on financial need and at-risk status.

Gates Millennium Scholars

GMS provides scholarships for low-income, minority students. The 1000 annual scholarships may be awarded to African American, Hispanic, Native American, native Alaskans and Pacific Islanders and offer a full ride.

Horatio Alger Association

This provides up to $22,000 in scholarship funds to students who demonstrate critical financial need and who have "faced and overcome great obstacles in their young lives."

National Association for the Education of Homeless Children and Youth (NAEHCY)
A minimum of two $2,000 scholarships are awarded annually to students who are currently struggling with or have experienced homelessness in the past. Scholarships may be put toward tuition, fees, books and prep courses.

More Scholarship Resources:

Moneygeek's Scholarship database

Affordable College Scholarships for At-Risk Studens

College Board Scholarship Search

Scholarship America Dreamkeepers

Federal Aid

The federal government provides financial aid via grants and loans. Grants do not have to be repaid, but typically don't cover the entire cost of college attendance. Federal loans, on the other hand, must be repaid, but have low-interest rates. A comprehensive source for information is the Federal Student Aid website.

Applications for both federal grants and federal loans are made through the Free Application for Federal Student Aid (FAFSA). The information on your FAFSA is transmitted to schools you choose, who use the information to assess your need for student aid. MoneyGeek provides an extensive FAFSA Guide to help students understand the requirements of the application process. College Goal Sunday is an organization that hosts FAFSA completion events.

UHY and the FAFSA

If you are a UHY student, the College Cost Reduction and Access Act allows your financial aid to be calculated on your own income, not your parents' and you don't need a parent signature on your FAFSA.

TO BE DESIGNATED UHY (UNACCOMPANIED HOMELESS YOUTH), YOU NEED VERIFICATION FROM ADVOCATES WHO HAVE WORKED WITH THE YOU AND WITNESSED YOUR CIRCUMSTANCES INCLUDING:

- School district or high school McKinney-Vento liaison (ask your guidance counselor for help)
- Director or designee of an emergency shelter or transitional housing program
- Director or designee of a runaway or homeless youth basic center or transitional living program
- Financial aid administrators

Details are outlined in this NAEHCY pdf.

WHEN YOU FILL OUT THE FAFSA AS A UHY:

- Mark on the form that you belong to the "special circumstances" category and cannot provide your parents' information.
- For the number of members in household on the FAFSA, include only yourself (Household = 1)
- Follow up with schools' financial aid offices to determine if any additional documentation or information is needed.

SOME ADDITIONAL DOCUMENTATION COULD INCLUDE:

- Personal statement describing the situation
- Applicable court or legal documentation
- Letters from teachers, social workers, counselors or clergy members

UHY under age 22 are considered independent and may fill out the forms without parental information. It is important to note that students are not considered automatically independent until they reach the age of 24, and a dependency status appeal must be made each year until that time. Both UHY and low-income students need to be aware that FAFSA money comes in 10 days before the semester starts at the earliest, and it could be weeks into the semester, depending on how late in the process they filed.

Federal Grants

Pell Grants

- A Federal Pell Grant, unlike a loan, does not have to be repaid.
- The maximum Pell Grant for the 2016–17 award year (July 1, 2016, to June 30, 2017) is $5,815.
- The amount depends on your financial need, costs to attend school, status as a full-time or part-time student, and plans to attend school for a full academic year or less.
- If you're eligible for a Federal Pell Grant, you'll receive the full amount you qualify for.
- The amount of other student aid you receive does not affect the amount of your Pell Grant.
- Your school can apply Pell Grant funds to your school costs, pay you directly, or combine these methods.

Extensive information on Pell Grants can be found at on this Department of Education webpage.

Federal Supplemental Educational Opportunity Grants (FSEOG):

These grants provide supplemental aid, administered directly by participating schools, in addition to Pell Grants awards made by the federal government. They range from $100 to $4000 but schools receive limited funds and not every qualifying student will receive an FSEOG. Not every school participates. Students receiving Pell Grants are first in line.

Because of the limited FSEOG funds available at any school, apply for federal student aid as early as you can. A school's deadline can be found on its website or by asking someone in its financial aid office.

Federal Student Loans

The federal government offers two classes of low-interest loans for students: Direct Loans (also known as Stafford Loans) and Perkins Loans.

Direct Loans

Direct Loans are generally awarded as part of a larger award packages provided by the schools, which also include federal grants and institutional scholarships.

The Direct Loan Program offers the following types of loans:

▶ **Subsidized**

for students with demonstrated financial need, as determined by federal regulations. No interest is charged while a student is in school at least half-time, during the grace period, and during deferment periods.

▶ **Unsubsidized**

not based on financial need; interest is charged during all periods, even during the time a student is in school and during grace and deferment periods.

▶ **PLUS**

unsubsidized loans for the parents of dependent students and for graduate/professional students. PLUS loans help pay for education expenses up to the cost of attendance minus all other financial assistance. Interest is charged during all periods.

▶ **Consolidation**

Eligible federal student loans can be combined into one Direct Consolidation Loan.

Your school will tell you how much you may borrow and the types of loans you are eligible to receive. The school will notify you of the loan amounts that it is offering, usually in an award letter that lists all of your proposed financial aid awards (your award package).

Evaluate the aid offer carefully. For loans, keep in mind that whatever amount you borrow must be paid back with interest. You can decline the loan or request a lower loan amount. The award letter will tell you how to do this.

Perkins Loans

The Federal Perkins Loan Program provides low-interest loans of up to $5,500 per undergraduate year through a revolving Perkins loan fund at each of the 1,700 participating institutions. The school is the lender for this loan, not the government, so you will repay them. In addition to completing the FAFSA, students also will need to complete a Perkins promissory note.

Housing

Residential Life Offices

When looking for housing options on-campus or off, talk with your school's Residential Life Office. The counselors are there to help you and are familiar with school and community resources. Some schools, such as Kennesaw State University, have year-round housing (including over holidays when dorms are normally closed) for homeless and at-risk students. This university also has a center that provides emergency housing, toiletries, food, and clothing. Even if your school does not have an established program, talk with the staff to find out how they can help you.

Off-Campus Housing Resources

Cheap Apartments for College Students – Sublet.com
Search for apartments by state, region and city.

StudentHousing.com
American Campus Communities operates this list of student apartments, search-able by college location, state or community.

Questions Low-Income Students and UHY Should Ask About Housing:

What are the options outside traditional on-campus or off-campus housing?
The Residential Life Office at your school is most likely to know what economical options are actually available in the local community.

What are trade-offs between cost, comfort, convenience, and safety?
Evaluate how much proximity to campus, comfort of the living space, and your feeling of safety in the neighborhood matter to you in comparison to the cost of rent. Consider that the most stable, quiet home environment may be the best platform for your education.

What are popular neighborhoods/apartment complexes/areas for students to live?
There are often well-established off-campus areas where students cluster. Land-lords there are used to dealing with students and often have multiple properties available, so if one type of living arrangement is too expensive, they can often show you other options.

What should I do if I have no credit or limited credit?
Ask your Residential Life office about how to handle landlords who give you guff about this: being a student with no credit or limited credit is not unusual. There may be opportunities to prove your reliability without a credit score or co-signer, otherwise subletting can be a good option.

What services am I generally responsible for providing, and what do these typically cost?
These will likely include utilities like gas, electricity, water, and internet service. Residential Life offices can estimate what students pay for these services.

Local Shelters

Many cities offer resource centers where homeless youth can make reservations for a one-night or seven-night stay. In most cases, these services are offered on a first-come-first-serve basis, but are available with no questions asked.

UHY can also take advantage of full-service youth shelters specifically for young adults. Services will vary, but may include computer labs, kitchen and dining areas, laundry facilities, bathrooms, and assistive programs to help young adults build a more stable life.

Resources

Although your school's Residential Life Office can likely provide the most relevant shelter recommendations, other online resources include:

ShelterListings
A comprehensive, state-by-state masterlist of shelters and supportive housing.

The TeenProject Shelter Finder
This organization aids teenagers aging out of the foster system by providing opportunities for higher education and independent living.

Resources for Homeless Youth – HUD Exchange
The U.S. Department of Housing & Urban Development offers resources, pertinent links and publications as part of its Special Needs Assistance Programs (SNAP).

Public Housing

You may have heard the term "public housing" used to describe housing with rents partially subsidized by government. There are two types of subsidized housing: Section 8 housing, and the more formally defined Public Housing. Students enrolled at institutions of higher education, however, are not eligible for Section 8 housing.

▸ **Call your Local Housing Authority**
Public housing is available to low-income individuals and families and students are allowed. Information on eligibility and the housing application process can be found on HUD's website and applications are issued through your local housing authority.

▸ **Qualify for a Federal Foster Program**
Through the Fostering Connection to Success and Increasing Adoptions Act, various federal programs offer financial support and foster care to young adults, including the John H. Chafee Foster Care Independence Program, which serves young adults ages 18-21 who have aged out of the foster care system. Though not necessarily targeted to college students in need of housing, this can still be a helpful option.

▸ **Sign up for School-Sponsored Community Service Trips and Study Abroad**
During winter and summer breaks, many schools offer enrichment opportunities for students, including service trips and study abroad grants that include housing. Some trips may be free, while others will have a fee. These opportunities also allow you to give back and gain valuable skills through meaningful community work. Contact the Student Life and Study Abroad offices at your school.

▸ **Apply for a Resident Assistant Position**
Many schools run summer programs for children, prospective students, and alumni, all of whom require housing on-campus. Schools employ current

students as Resident Assistants as resources for these guests, providing them housing as a part of the RA employment package.

▸ **Check out Greek Housing**

Many colleges allow Greek housing to remain open to students during summer break (but are usually closed during winter). Homeless students who are part of a fraternity or sorority should find out if their house will be open during summer, if there are any restrictions, and if there is a fee to stay.

▸ **Stay With Friends**

Some homeless students opt to stay with friends who do not go home during the break. If a student has multiple friends who will be staying in the area, he or she can set up a plan with friends to rotate visits, if staying with one friend the whole break is not feasible. It may also be possible to go home with a friend over break.

Meals

Dining Services

Contact campus dining services about options for free and low-cost meals at school. Dining services may maintain a list of local food banks and programs offering living essentials, including daily meals. Dining services can also inform you about on-campus food assistance programs, such as Campus Kitchens, student food banks, and meal plan voucher programs.

Campus Kitchens Project

The Campus Kitchens Project provides access to meals from surplus on-campus and community food sources, in exchange for volunteering. Website resources help students develop campus kitchens in their neighborhoods–so if your school is not one of the 49 current locations of a Campus Kitchen, you can take the initiative in creating one.

Student Food Banks

Student food banks are similar to the Campus Kitchens project, but focus specifically on providing for university students facing food insecurity. Student food banks collect donations locally and provide information about other

"College conjures up images of all-you-can-eat dining halls, midnight runs for pizza, tubs of ice cream in the dorm-room fridge, and ethnically sensitive burritos [but] recent research on hunger at colleges opens serious questions about those assumptions."

options for free or discounted local food, and organize events to raise funds for the food bank. Examples include the Michigan State University Food Bank and the Associated Students Food Bank at the University of California Santa Barbara. Their websites provide a wealth of information about their conception and operation, providing models for students who are considering starting food banks at their own schools.

The College and University Food Bank Alliance (CUFBA), founded by the Oregon State University Food Pantry and Michigan State Student Food Bank, provides support for new and existing college food banks across the country.

Voucher Programs

Students who purchased meal plans may not use their entire quota of meals. Instead of letting these funds and food to go waste, some schools have implemented programs that allow students in need to use unused swipes for a meal. Ask your Dining Services office about this.

Community-Based Options

▸ **Supplemental Nutrition Assistance Program (SNAP, formerly known as Food Stamps)**

For UHY who have recognized independent status, SNAP may be an option. The largest program in the domestic hunger safety net, SNAP offers nutrition assistance to millions of eligible, low-income individuals and families and provides economic benefits to communities.

Millions of potentially eligible Americans forgo application to SNAP, either out of difficulty in navigating the application process, or due to a perceived stigma associated federal aid.

It is not necessary to have a permanent address, or to be single, to be eligible for SNAP. To see if you might be eligible, visit the SNAP pre-screening tool. To apply for benefits, or for information about the Supplemental Nutrition Assistance Program, contact your local SNAP office.

▸ **Food Banks, Pantries and Shelters**

Many cities and communities have food bank/pantries and shelters that offer meals for free or low cost. Two online resources are especially helpful in finding them:

Feeding America

This network of 200 food banks across the country distributes more than 3 million meals a year to needy Americans. The site includes a search tool for locating food banks by community or zip code.

FoodPantries.org

Visitors to the site can learn about non-profit organizations, food banks and soup kitchens across the U.S. Participating organizations include ministries and fellowships, community food banks and housing organizations. Search for food pantries by state or zip code.

5 No-Prep Meal Hacks for a (Very) Limited Budget

Apple or Banana with Peanut Butter/Almond Butter/Cashew Butter

Almond and Cashew butter can be expensive per jar, but, like peanut butter, are extremely filling and can last a long time with careful rationing.

Rolled Oats with Cinnamon, Maple Syrup, Fruit

A hot pot or electric kettle can be a major (and manageably small) investment. Sunbeam has a hot pot for 14.99 at Target. Check the home appliance section of local thrift stores—you may get lucky. Buy a value pack of oats rather than buying store-made flavored brands. Plus, you might like the flavor more if you make it yourself.

Bean and Cheese Burritos

If a microwave isn't in the budget, gas stations usually have these and will let you use them for free or if you are a paying customer. Your gas station might also sell cheese (or beans or tortillas), which you'll need to come equipped with to make these simple burritos.

High Fiber Cereal with Fruit, Milk

A box of healthy, high fiber cereal may run you $3.50-5.50 per box, but a serving of high fiber will also fill you up faster than sugary cereals with less nutritional value. If you don't have (or don't have a place for) a refrigerator or mini-fridge, you might ask the dining staff at your university if you can make arrangements to either use space in their refrigerator storage or to pay a small fee for a cup of milk every day. If not, soft fruit like banana can help soften the texture of cereal.

Veggies & Rolls

Ask a local Italian restaurant if you can give them $1-2 dollars for a bag of rolls. Restaurants have to make fresh rolls, so offer to come by at the end of the day when they might even give you their extras for free. Buying frozen vegetables is often the cheaper option, but be sure to thaw before cooking to speed up the process. To steam, you will need to invest in tinfoil and some kind of pot or container with makeshift top. Boil water in your hot pot and transfer to the container, but not to the top. Put the vegetables in tinfoil and wrap the tinfoil around the edges of the container, above the water. Place a lid on the container and wait for steam to rise to cook your vegetables.

Transportation

Public Transit Discounts

Many public transit systems offer discounts for students and/or low-income earners. You can typically access these discounts through the transit authority's website. The U-Pass offered through the Chicago Transit Authority (CTA) is a great example: over 50 schools in the Chicago area participate in the discounted student rate program. Some programs even allow students to ride for free, such as the South Bend Transpo student pass option at the University of Notre Dame, Saint Mary's College, and other area institutions.

Carpool

Carpooling with classmates who own cars is a terrific option–convenient, reliable, and generally cheap (you only have to pitch in gas money! And friends may even let you ride for free). We caution against owning your own car, which can quickly bring unexpected maintenance costs, require insurance payments, and become a hassle when parking is scarce.

Carpooling needn't only be with classmates. Craigslist has a dedicated section for ridesharing, making it possible to find non-student residents in your community interested in sharing rides. Through companies like Zipcar, you can gain access to cars for low monthly fees.

Textbooks and School Supplies

The cost of textbooks and school supplies has ballooned in recent years and now represents significant hurdles for low-income students. Textbooks can cost upwards of $200-$400 each. According to a Student PIRGS report on textbook costs, nearly one-third of all students reported using financial aid to purchase textbooks, and their costs averaged more than $300 per semester; over the course of a four-year degree, that amounts to over $2,400 on average.

5 Hacks for Saving on Textbooks

Library (university or local)

Libraries may have multiple copies of textbooks available for borrowing. There will always be a limited supply and a limited number of renewals. This may be a good option if several of your classmates want to establish a renewal cycle share the textbook.

Campus Book Swap

Your school may arrange for swaps at the end and beginning of semesters to allow students to directly exchange used textbooks and other supplies.

Online Options

There are many used bookstores online, some of which specialize in used textbooks. Options include Alibris, Skyo, Better World Books, and Half.com If affording internet in an off-campus location is an issue, AT&T has an Access Program that provides low-cost internet services to qualifying SNAP participants in a 21-state service area (barring any outstanding debt to AT&T).

Campus Bookstore

While prices here may be higher, they have a good supply of the exact textbooks used in recent years and sold back to the bookstore. There's less guesswork about whether you're getting the right version of a textbook, and you generally have a guaranteed buy-back option at the end of the semester (at a reduced price, of course).

Textbook Rentals

Many sites, including Amazon.com allow you to rent a textbook for a semester at a fraction of the cover price.

E-book Versions

Often cheaper than their hardcover cousins, they are typically accessible through portable e-readers and online portals.

Medical Care

Campus Health Center

Today, most colleges and universities offer extensive physical and mental health services to students, often in on-campus settings with full-time staff and on-campus pharmacies. Fees for these services will vary, but are generally available to students at much lower costs than they would pay elsewhere.

Local clinics

There may be a free clinic in your community. These facilities may also be called sliding scale clinics or low-cost clinics; their purpose is to serve low-income individuals for free or at a nominal cost, based on income levels relative to the poverty line. Free clinics do not provide emergency care.

Homelessness and Medical Care

Accessing adequate health care can be especially challenging for those experiencing homelessness. The two organizations linked below focus specifically on advocating for and providing health care access to the homeless.

National Health Care for the Homeless Council

More than 10,000 physicians, patients, nurses, social workers and other healthcare professionals provide support to more than 200 public health centers and Health Care for the Homeless programs in all 50 states.

Health Care for the Homeless

HCH provides comprehensive health care services and supportive services to people experiencing homelessness.

Mental Health Care

College life can be very demanding and stressful. When stresses become acute, it's important to seek help. Depression and anxiety are on the rise among college students, with 87 percent of students reporting feeling overwhelmed and 33 percent reporting "feeling so depressed it was difficult to function" in a 2014 survey by the American College Health Association. Another survey conducted by the National Alliance on Mental Illness (NAMI) reveals that 50 percent of students who stopped attending college due to a mental illness had not accessed any on-campus mental health care services.

50 PERCENT of students who stopped attending college due to mental illness HAD NOT ACCESSED any of the on-campus mental health care services.

▸ **On-Campus Mental Health Services**

Contact your Health Services office for assistance with mental health issues. Most schools have counselors available.

▸ **On-Campus Advocates**

If you live on campus, RAs are an excellent place to turn. You will likely have established a personal connection with them and they tend to be sensitive to the multi-faceted nature of students' issues. They can provide a trusting environment in which you can open up without fear of judgment–and they know what other campus and community resources to recommend.

At most colleges, you will have an academic advisor. While their primary role is to guide you in achieving academic goals, they can also act as confidantes, especially because so much anxiety in college stems from academics. Advisors are familiar with these stresses and may have valuable insights about coping in very concrete ways–for instance, how to better structure your study habits to reduce last-minute cramming for a test.

▸ **Student-Run Helplines**

Some colleges maintain 24-hour telephone helplines where students can talk through their feelings with sympathetic and supportive staff. While professional staff almost always compose part of the team, students often play major roles. The helpline at Texas A&M University is an example of how one of these helplines typically operates.

▸ **National Suicide Prevention Lifeline: 1 (800) 273-8255**

At this number, you'll be connected to a skilled, trained counselor at a crisis center in your area (whether you are at school or away), 24/7, all year round.

▸ **Joining the National Conversation**

One repeated finding in studies on mental illness among students is the perceived stigma of admitting to mental and emotional distress. Student advocacy organizations encourage a more open, national dialogue about the issues of mental and emotional health among college students. These organizations provide education, training, and student-run chapters creating safe spaces for talking through these issues.

Activeminds.org

Active Minds supports a network of campus-based chapters that provide their campuses with a wide range of programming that educates peers about mental health, connects students to resources, and aims to change negative perceptions about mental health disorders.

Jed Foundation

The Jed Foundation's mission is to promote emotional health and prevent suicide among college and university students. The foundation has several student-centered educational initiatives, including ULifeline, a free online screening tool to help students better understand if their mental health could benefit from professional help, and Half of Us, to broadcast the stories of students and high-profile artists seeking help for their mental health challenges.

Collegiate Events and Opportunities

▸ **Free On-Campus Events**

Schools host and sponsor free events to enrich students' educational and social experiences. These range from lectures by renowned scholars to movie screenings, concerts and dances, career fairs, intramural sports leagues, retreats and university-funded clubs.

▸ **Alumni Network**

All of the former students of your school compose its informal alumni network. Many alumni wish to extend a helping hand to current students. Schools maintain alumni databases, cataloguing their occupations and contact information. Your school's alumni center also may coordinate a network of alumni clubs, providing support and resources for regional chapters that provide opportunities for alumni to gather.

Perhaps the most important function of the alumni network for current students is the opportunity to contact alumni regarding their fields of interest and potential job opportunities. Even if the alumni themselves don't currently know of any job opportunities in your field, they often have an extensive network of contacts, and are more than willing to make introductions on behalf of students.

▸ **Use the Campus as a Playground**

Taking care of your physical health goes a very long way towards taking care of your mental health–and consistent physical activity enhances your cognitive abilities. Grassy quads and athletic fields are perfect places to play pick-up games and relax in a vibrant setting. Athletic facilities are often available to all students, not just athletes.

▸ **Community Discounts**

The benefits of being a student in college often extend into the surrounding community, where you can find student discounts at museums, restaurants, movie theaters, bookstores, gyms, and a host of other establishments.

The Balancing Act: School and Work

Although it's important to attend classes and complete coursework, you will probably be attempting to balance college with the demands of a job.

▸ **Inform Your Employer**
  Tell your supervisors and your employer's Human Resources (HR) department about your educational pursuits. Your employer may be able to adjust your schedule and work tasks to better accommodate your needs. Some businesses offer support for continuing education, including scholarships, part-time work arrangements, or discounts on classes.

▸ **Make a (Realistic) Weekly Goal Chart**
  Accomplishing realistic goals in well-defined blocks of time is a life skill useful beyond the classroom.

▸ **Listen to Your Inner Rhythm**
  You will optimize your study time. Notice when you tend to feel most energetic and focused: schedule study sessions during these times.

▸ **Prioritize**
  Don't try to do everything. Make a list of potential activities and assess how each would help you towards your ultimate goals, then prioritize those that seem the most beneficial.

▸ **Schedule Downtime**
  Relaxation and rest are essential for recharging your energy and motivation.

Many aspects of higher education's value are ultimately unquantifiable–the close friendships, the shaping of the mind, the development of values. But higher education also remains one of the most important economic investments you can make in your future. According to the Georgetown Public Policy Institute, by 2020 more than 65% of jobs will demand training and education beyond high school. And there will be no shortage of demand: 55 million job opportunities will present through 2020 from a combination of baby boomer retirement and new job creation. There will be a shortage of supply, however: the report projects that there will be a shortfall of 5 million workers for available jobs requiring college-level education and skills. This means that a college education will only continue to increase in value. For low-income and homeless students, college presents numerous hurdles, but clearing them presents remarkable opportunity.

How widespread is the problem of homelessness when it comes to college students?

Currently there is no one way to capture the number of homeless students on college campuses. The number of homeless students within the K-12 system has continued to rise and we know that many homeless students are able to access higher education, often their housing status does not change. Additionally, there is an increasing number of students that become homeless once enrolled in college due to many different factors . . . Some of [the reasons students become homeless] include but are not limited to: poverty, loss of income, lack of affordable housing, abuse or neglect in the home, domestic violence in the home, family conflict, parental incarnation, mental illness, or death.

What unique problems do these students face and how are they able to overcome them? Are they less likely to complete their degrees?

Many homeless students struggle to have the most basic needs while attending college and struggle to find stable housing, food, clothing and hygiene products. Aside from basic needs students may also suffer from trauma and stress. Financial Aid, and financial stability are also barriers for these students as they are difficult to obtain without parental support. Many college campuses have implemented our Single Point of Contact (SPOC) model to have a supportive campus administrator to assist homeless students with on an off campus supports. Students can also tap into campus resources such as housing, food and clothing banks, financial aid, and mental health supports to overcome these barriers. There have not been any studies on degree completion for homeless students at this time.

Is there any public or private help available for these students? Are the colleges stepping in to provide assistance?

Many campuses are appointing a SPOC on campus to assist homeless students, or they are opening food banks, allowing residents halls to stay open year round, and some campuses are also awarding specific scholarships for homeless students. Resources vary from state to state and at each higher education institution. NAEHCY has a scholarship program from homeless college students in addition to our national toll-free helpline where we connect students to many resources.

What advice would you give a person who is homeless that wants to go to college and earn a degree?

I would say that your homeless status alone does not have to hinder you from earning a degree. Students should check with their campus to see what resources and supports are available to assist them with their academic goals.

How widespread is the problem of homelessness when it comes to college students?

It's hard to know the truth because nobody is systematically measuring that. It's not like there is some nationwide survey of college students. The Free Application for Federal Student Aid has questions that ask if you are homeless. If you want to check that box you have to prove you are homeless by getting paperwork, which is very difficult to do. It usually means going to a shelter and staying there overnight to get the proper documentation. There's a severe undercount, but the latest estimate is that 58,000 students around the country were able to prove their homelessness on FAFSA. My guess is that [represents] less than one-quarter of homeless students.

What are the main causes of it?

There are a couple of things . . . There is a genuine housing crisis in many cities that's creating homelessness in general. There's a shortage of affordable housing . . . and an overall rising cost of living. The other part is, in the past people going through such circumstance didn't go to college. We have gone through a period of time where we pushed more people toward college because there's no other way out of poverty. They feel trapped. They grew up poor and they don't want to stay poor so they go to college. And while they might get more financial aid it doesn't make it affordable. It doesn't cover that much at all and it doesn't cover their living costs. They end up paying the price in a pretty big way. I've met students that say the only way to stay in school and afford books is to forgo having a roof over their head. UCLA is about to open its first homeless shelter this fall showcasing how things have gotten so bad.

What unique problems do these students face and how are they able to overcome them? Are they less likely to complete their degrees?

They do appear less likely to graduate. It's hard enough for some students [who are] first in their families to go to college and fit in and it's really hard for a homeless student to feel like they belong . . . They try really hard to not look homeless. Then there's the big issue of supplies for school because there's no safe place to put them in a shelter. Where are they supposed to study? It's hard enough to be homeless but it is really hard to be homeless and trying to do this college thing.

Is there any public or private help available for these students? Are the colleges stepping in to provide assistance?

At the college level the hard part is many colleges and universities either don't see themselves as an appropriate provider of those services or have the resources to help. Funding at places where the homeless go to school is incredibly short. And while there are community services for homeless people, students don't want to go to those places. They are separating themselves in their heads from other homeless people and feel a lot of shame and stigma when they are treated likely any other homeless person. There's not a lot of systematic help. There's a lot of small programs like Single Stop based in New York, which operates in about two dozen colleges around the country to help students get access to government programs. I estimate fewer than 200 colleges out of more than 4,000 are doing much of anything. There's also no Federal funding stream for it. In K-12 there are all these federal polices about serving homeless children but the minute they turn 18 all bets are off.

What advice would you give a person who is homeless that wants to go to college and earn a degree?

I think the hardest thing for them to do to make sure the college knows the situation, but it's important. Students have to find someone at the college that they can try to trust. They need to find somebody who can become an advocate because the chances are pretty good they will run in to some real challenges and somebody has got to be able to explain that. They need to know they are not alone by any stretch . . .

Reading the Genre

1. The authors have carefully created a report that gathers together essential information for homeless and low income college students. But there is a *lot* of information here. How do they organize the report so that all of this information doesn't overwhelm the reader?

2. This is a report, and it is designed for a specific group of students. But do you think that the report also has an argument or thesis that might apply to a wider audience? How do the authors want this broader audience to act on their report, and what do they want this broader audience to learn? (See Chapter 8, "Reports," p. 38.)

3. So many of the key suggestions in this report are framed by an uncomfortable reality: too many students fail to access resources that are free and that are designed for them to use. Clearly, there is a problem with communication or implementation. How do the authors frame their report for an audience who the authors know might not listen to their advice? What techniques are used to reach these people? Could the authors do more?

4. WRITING: Explore some of the key resources available for low-income students at your own school or in your own community. Or, consider some of the "hacks" that you or your friends use to stay on budget. Create a report that presents some of these resources and shares your knowledge. What other key information might the authors of this report have missed?

5. MULTIMODALITY—DATA VISUALIZATION: There are some key, relatively shocking, statistics in this report. Create a larger visualization for one of these key statistics (For more on data visualization, see Chapter 41, "Tables, Graphs, and Infographics," p. 411.)

Further Reading

McKenna, Laura. "The hidden hunger on college campuses." *The Atlantic* (2016).

Explanations: Readings

GENRE MOVES Causal Analysis

JAMES BALDWIN

From *If Black English Isn't a Language, Then Tell Me, What Is?*

I say that the present skirmish is rooted in American history, and it is. Black English is the creation of the black diaspora. Blacks came to the United States chained to each other, but from different tribes: Neither could speak the other's language. If two black people, at that bitter hour of the world's history, had been able to speak to each other, the institution of chattel slavery could never have lasted as long as it did. Subsequently, the slave was given, under the eye, and the gun, of his master, Congo Square, and the Bible—or in other words, and under these conditions, the slave began the formation of the black church, and it is within this unprecedented tabernacle that black English began to be formed. This was not, merely, as in the European example, the adoption of a foreign tongue, but an alchemy that transformed ancient elements into a new language: *A language comes into existence by means of brutal necessity, and the rules of the language are dictated by what the language must convey.*

There was a moment, in time, and in this place, when my brother, or my mother, or my father, or my sister, had to convey to me, for example, the danger in which I was standing from the white man standing just behind me, and to convey this with a speed, and in a language, that the white man could not possibly understand, and that, indeed, he cannot understand, until today. He cannot afford to understand it. This understanding would reveal to him too much about himself, and smash that mirror before which he has been frozen for so long.

Now, if this passion, this skill, this (to quote Toni Morrison) "sheer intelligence," this incredible music, the mighty achievement of having brought a people utterly unknown to, or despised by "history"—to have brought this people to their present, troubled, troubling, and unassailable and unanswerable place—if this absolutely unprecedented journey does not indicate that black English is a language, I am curious to know what definition of language is to be trusted.

Offer a causal narrative.

One of the most effective ways to illustrate probable causes and effects is to tell a story. Here, to oppose claims that Black English isn't a language, James Baldwin focuses on how Black American English most likely came into being. For a causal analysis, you might not be able to *prove* cause and effect beyond a doubt, but if you can present a realistic and convincing chain of events supported by evidence, you will give your reader a compelling picture.

Baldwin could have focused on linguistic evidence to argue for the sophistication of Black English, but instead he focuses on social and cultural conditions that made the creation of a unique language inevitable. He also manages to very effectively show that the language cannot be separated from a history of oppression by explaining the exact nature of the situation and the dire necessity that created Black English. Creating a narrative, then, also allows Baldwin to avoid oversimplification, which is a common pitfall of causal analysis essays. Rather than reduce the analysis to its bare facts, Baldwin brings it to life.

In your own causal analysis research, look for the stories and the rich contexts that accompany causes and effects. For instance, if you are looking at how tuition costs have risen over time, why young people have stopped voting, or the effect of increased screen time on children, look for specific stories and examples that will help you illustrate probable causal relationships. While those stories won't make up the total of your evidence, they can provide a much-needed perspective.

CAUSAL ANALYSIS   Rita J. King is the executive vice president of Science House, a creative consultancy that connects science and business and funds science and math education projects for kids. King previously worked as a futurist at the National Institute of Aerospace and speaks internationally about creative collaboration. In this essay, King reflects on her own uses of Twitter and highlights the innovative ways others have used the platform.

Co.Exist

Posted: May 22, 2013, at 8:30 AM
From: Rita J. King

How Twitter Is Reshaping the Future of Storytelling

We might have fewer characters to work with, but we still hunger for narrative. New mediums aren't destroying fiction; they're allowing us to innovate even more in how we create and consume our stories.

Editor's Note: This post is part of *Co.Exist's* "Futurist Forum," a series of articles by some of the world's leading futurists about what the world will look like in the near and distant future, and how you can improve how you navigate future scenarios through better forecasting.

Every five days, a billion tiny stories are generated by people around the world. Those messages aren't just being lost in the ether, like the imaginary output of monkeys randomly attempting to produce the works of Shakespeare. Instead, the tweets are being archived by the Library of Congress as part of the organization's mission to tell the story of America. The archive now includes 170 billion posts and counting.

The patterns of human life will be stored in this Twitter archive like a form of digital sediment. Every meme and revelation will leave an imprint in the record constructed of posts by half a billion Twitter users around the world (and over 150,000 more signing up every day).

How has the future of storytelling been influenced by Twitter?

Sparking the Imagination

Writer and actor John Hodgman recalls how derisive many people were about Twitter when it first entered the public consciousness. "Many jokes were made," he said, "about 'why would I ever want to hear about what sandwich someone ate today?'"

"The early detractors failed to note that Twitter, while faddish, was not only a fad: It is a tool, one with almost as many unique uses as there are humans to take it up," Hodgman says. "Twitter offered a very restrictive set of protocols that awaken the imagination: What can I do with 140 characters that will be meaningful to others? The solution has proven to be pretty much endless. And do you know what? If the right person is telling the story, I'll read a tweet stream of sandwiches all day long."

We've gotten to know new characters through Twitter, Hodgman says, from Bigfoot to God, and their tweet streams are "more than just jokes, which themselves are the shortest stories of all." Instead, tweets are "a new kind of epistolary—postcards from a sensibility that over time, describe whole worlds."

"It is true," Hodgman says, "that this kind of storytelling is quick, even ephemeral, and largely improvised. It's really more like broadcasting than writing, and one of the things that makes Twitter so intimate, even in its rowdy, buzzing, crowd-y-ness, is that you are reading someone's work in real time."

A Future Biography

Prolific novelist Joyce Carol Oates recently tweeted:

"Creating a Twitter-self is like constructing with tweezers & toothpicks. Much patience required, some sense of purpose, & a sense of humor."

While many people struggle to make sense of what identity looks like as the lines between personal and professional, private and public continue to blur, some just rely on straightforward candor.

Twitter has produced several celebrities, including Kelly Oxford, thirty-five, who transformed from a stay-at-home mother of three to the best-selling author of *Everything Is Perfect When You're a Liar*. Nicole Sperling of the *L.A. Times* noted: "Oxford's writing is marked by the same wry voice that's made her a social media sensation." "I always felt like the child actor playing myself in the biography from the future," Oxford told Sperling.

Twitter forces us to learn how to play compelling characters in a shared biography, a snapshot of this moment we are living and sharing right now, but I can't help thinking about a comment made by Noam Chomsky in *Manufacturing Consent*. He talks about context in the mainstream media, and the need for more space to explain ideas that go against the grain of the status quo. Twitter also has a context problem: When you come late to a conversation, for example, and only see a couple of previous tweets.

In the nearly six years since I've been using Twitter, I've generated over fourteen thousand tweets. How can these be used in the social mapping of a shared story that goes well beyond, but still includes, me?

Future Forms of Snippet Storytelling

Twitter itself is exploring ways to harness the power of future storytelling forms. The addition of Vine to the mix could be powerful—think of the difference between a "wheels up" tweet about a flight and a six-second video of floating above clouds. The Tribeca Film Festival just included Vine as a platform for a competition, posted through the #6secfilms hashtag.

Andrew Fitzgerald works for Twitter, driving experimentation in storytelling and looking for people doing it inventively. So many people post their favorite Taylor Swift lyrics, he said, that the singer could retweet an entire song based on found tweets, like W. W. Norton did for Hamlet's famous soliloquy.

The Twitter Fiction Festival was a successful experiment that featured authors from around the world in multiple languages. New forms of storytelling include Jennifer Egan's experimental "Black Box," tweeted out in blocks of 140 characters or less by the *New Yorker*. Fitzgerald, who loved the experiment, acknowledged that some criticized the serialized sentences because, they say, "that's not how you do fiction."

For people who love compelling writing, there's something tantalizing about lines being shared one at a time. A line on its own changes a reader's relationship to the very texture of the syllables and ideas. Twitter story experiments aren't shackled by the linear requirements of paper.

Elliott Holt's Twitter experiment grabbed readers and lured them into a heavily hashtagged mystery story, the first of its kind:

"On November 28 at 10:13 pm EST a woman identified as Miranda Brown, 44, of Brooklyn, fell to her death from the roof of a Manhattan hotel."

So began Holt's story, followed by a second tweet:

"Investigators are trying to determine whether Ms. Brown's death was an accident or if, as some speculate, she was pushed off that roof."

From there, Holt built a narrative through threaded Twitter feeds with distinct voices from each of three characters to reconstruct the party at which the character died.

"Holt embraces Twitter for what it is," Slate wrote, "rather than trying to bend it into some tool that it isn't. With its simultaneous narrators and fractured storyline, this is not the kind of tale that could march steadily across a continuous expanse of white space. It's actually made for the medium."

The medium is also remaking us.

Reading the Genre

1. Look for Twitter feeds that you think use Twitter as a "tool" in an innovative way, and discuss these examples in relation to King's essay. For instance, does the feed use Twitter's limitations to its advantage, or does it find a way to work around them?

2. Is the medium of Twitter actually "remaking us"? Are there ways that you think or interact differently because of Twitter? How will social media sites like Twitter change the shape of your future relationships and your future career?

3. WRITING: Consider turning your answer to question 2 into a full causal analysis essay. How has Twitter changed politics? Personal relationships? Marketing and advertising? Celebrity culture? For an example of causal analysis, you can look online for several articles showing how Twitter has allowed people to make specific stock market predictions.

4. MULTIMODALITY—TWITTER REWRITE: How would you write King's essay over Twitter? Limit yourself to writing just ten to fifteen key 140-character tweets to summarize the essay. Consider using @s, hashtags, links, and images not only to add information to your summaries but also to engage others and encourage them to recirculate the essay and respond to it.

CAUSAL ANALYSIS   Robert W. Gehl is an assistant professor of New Media at the University of Utah, where he teaches critical studies of communication design and technology. His research centers on issues of technology and culture, and he is the author of *Reverse Engineering Social Media* (2014). In this essay, Gehl offers a genealogy and a critique of "liking" online.

The New Inquiry

Posted: March 27, 2013
From: Robert W. Gehl

A History of Like

"The marketing field has long been obsessed with likability, but Facebook may be inadvertently revealing how shallow our liking goes."

If you blog, run a university home page, do e-commerce, write news articles for a local paper, have a local government site, or do nearly anything with the Internet, you're pretty much required to have users "like" your pages. Otherwise, you're going to be left out of the new economy of quantified affect. We live in what Carolin Gerlitz and Anne Helmond call a Like Economy, a distributed centralized Web of binary switches allowing us to signal if we like something or not, all powered by the now ubiquitous Facebook "Like" button.

But why "Like"? Why not "Love," or "I agree," or "This is awesome"? At first it seems like one of those accidents of popular culture, where an arbitrary boardroom decision eventually dictates our everyday language. In fact, one history of Facebook's Like button presents it in these very terms: Facebook engineer Adam Bosworth noted that the button began as an Awesome button but was later changed to Like because *like* is more universal. If it had stayed Awesome, perhaps we'd be talking about an economy of Awesomes binding together the social Web and we would sound more like Teenage Mutant Ninja Turtles than Valley Girls.

There's a deeper history to "like," though, that is far older than Facebook. The marketing subfield of Liking Studies, which began before Internet use became mainstream, is key to understanding how this somewhat bland, reductive signal of affect became central to the larger consumer economy we live in. It also explains why Facebook will never install a Dislike button.

What's the best way to predict whether an advertisement increases sales or not? The marketing field has searched for the answer to this question for decades. (If I knew, I would be the head of some unctuous marketing firm instead of a state employee.)In the early 1990s, the Advertising Research Foundation's (ARF) "Copy Research Validity Project" proposed a simple answer: The advertisement is "likable." The massive study compared pairs of television ads in various settings and methods, against a wide range of accepted marketing measures: persuasive elements, how well the advertisement is recalled afterword, the clarity of the message, and (seemingly as an afterthought) how well the ad was "liked."

Of all the measures, "likability" was the surprise winner. "The average impression of the commercial, derived from a five-point liking scale, picked sales winners directionally 87 percent of the time and had an index of 300 (i.e., picked winners and was significant 60 percent of the time)." In other words, you like, you buy.

As the authors of the report, Russell Haley and Allan Baldinger, explain, "It appears probable that 'liking' is what Gordon Brown has called a 'creative magnifier' for both persuasive messages and for messages that are recalled." Likable ads, they conclude, are more persuasive and memorable than others. This triggered the development of Liking Studies, as academic and practicing marketers set out to further refine the contours of liking as an ad-copy-test measure.

Liking studies further decomposed likability into cognitive and affective elements. On the cognitive side, researchers theorized that viewers who like an ad pay attention and thus recall its message better. In terms of affect, a 1994 study by David Walker and Tony M. Dubinsky in the *Journal of Advertising Research* explores a "theory of 'affect transfer'," which "asserts that if viewers experience positive feelings towards the advertising, they will associate those feelings with the advertiser or the advertised brand." A likable ad thus promises to encode brands into our bodies as precognitive desire.

Of course, affect and cognition are complex phenomena. To be fair to academic marketers, there are repeated calls in the advertising research literature to resist reducing this complexity to liking and, at the very least, to continue to use other copy-testing measures in addition to likability to predict an ad's success. However, the underlying complexity of cognition and affect actually reinforces the value of likability as a measurable aspect of ads. The value of like is that it abstracts and condenses the complex thoughts and emotions it contains and, like any good abstraction, provides a simple and commensurable quantification of complexity. If a test subject says, "I like this ad!" it seems to stand in for the less cut-and-dried aspects of recall and emotion.

For a largely empirical, positivist field such as marketing—which has pretensions of being a science, not an art—independent variables such as likability have value because of their perceived universal predictive power. With globalization, marketing is in greater need of just such a universal measure capable of predicting the success of global branding campaigns across cultural contexts. Cultural variations might change how marketers go about getting us to like brands, but the goal is always likability.

One vertigo-inducing marketing moment illustrates this well. Since 1989, *USA Today* has published metrics on the most well-liked Super Bowl ads. These metrics partly inspired the makers of FedEx's 2005 "Perfect" Super Bowl ad, which combined the top ten likable elements of previous Super Bowl ads. (It featured Burt Reynolds getting kicked in the nuts by a dancing bear while a cute kid and sexy cheerleaders looked on. The bear talked to Reynolds about *Smokey and the Bandit* after Journey's "Don't Stop Believing" played. Oh, and somewhere in there is a message about how effective FedEx is at delivering things.) After this ad proved quite likable, the academic authors of a 2013 study of Super Bowl ad likability used many of its elements to measure the likability of other Super Bowl ads in the 2000s. Their discovery: Animals, cute kids, and humor are all elements of a likable ad. Their study also used data from, where else, *USA Today*'s Ad Meter likability measures. This self-referential loop will likely sentence us to ads featuring animals, cute kids, and bad humor for the rest of our Super Bowl watching lives.

Or maybe not. We are now allowed, even expected, to like other things than what's sold in Super Bowl ads. If you read even only the first two sentences of any given marketing paper today, you invariably learn that we are living in a new age where the user is in control. Social media in general, and Facebook in particular, are supposedly driving a brand-new world where marketers, editors, and other gatekeepers are marginalized and mass culture is dissolving into niche cultures and individual expression.

But if we keep the history of marketing in mind, including the development of Liking Studies, we see how Facebook is caught up in longer histories, specifically the history of the desire to dissect, study, and recompose a particular subject, the sovereign consumer.

Facebook's Like button has been lauded as a radically democratic tool allowing users to finally make their opinions heard, but the marketing field has always regarded the sovereign consumer's opinions the most important element in the circuit of production. After all, sovereign consumers realize the value locked away in commodities: When they buy, the corporation gets paid. In order to have us be better value-realization machines, marketers know they need to know what we like. The Like button is a logical extension of the studies and practices developed by marketing since the 1990 ARF study and the *USA Today* Ad Meter system which, after all, have asked us to tell them what we like for decades.

Of course, the Facebook Like button does provide increased data about which ads are likable. With the Like button, marketers can constantly experiment with variations on ads with test audiences, seeing what works and then scaling up small experiments quickly. With a universal measure provided by Like, marketers can test ads across different segments, greatly aiding the globalization of marketing campaigns.

But this only begins to describe the continual monitoring of users who have clicked Like in Facebook. The choice to like an ad or brand in Facebook is seen as an affirmative interaction with that brand—and an agreement to have one's profile image associated with that brand and to have that approval follow you across the Web. If you like a brand, you must like to be a target for marketing messages, both from that brand and from others similar to it. You're providing just a bit more information to help Facebook build a profile of your tastes and desires, all of which is for sale.

But again, these things are not really all that new. Since even before the advent of Liking Studies, marketers have experimented with advertising messages and tracked users to determine ad effectiveness. Whether the branding happens on TV, in a magazine, or online, we like, we buy. We like, they know. The science of marketing has always been the science of placing us in taxonomies based on what we like.

So what is new about Facebook and the Like button? Oddly enough, it reveals too much. The great sin of Facebook is that it made "like" far too important and too obvious. Marketing is in part the practice of eliding the underlying complexity, messiness, and wastefulness of capitalist production with neat abstractions. Every ad, every customer service interaction, every display, and every package contributes to the commodity fetish, covering up the conditions of production with desire and fantasy. As such, Facebook may reveal too much of the underlying architecture of emotional capitalism. The Like button tears aside this veil to reveal the cloying, pathetic, Willy Lomanesque need of marketers to have their brands be well-liked. Keep liking, keep buying. Like us! Like us! Like us!

Liking in marketing was always meant to be a metonym for many other complex processes—persuasion, affect, cognition, recall—but it wasn't meant to be exposed to the public as such. In Facebook, however, the "Like" button further reduces this reduction and makes it visible, making the whole process somewhat cartoonish and tiresome. The consequences can be seen in "Like us on Facebook to enter to win!" promotions and the obsession with Like counts among businesses large and small (not to mention the would-be "personal branded").

Because likability is now so visible, so prevalent as the preferred emotional response to brands and ideas, users have predictably called for the expansion of the emotional repertoire. They call for a Dislike button. At first glance, we might think this binary-emotional expansion would be welcome to marketers: It would add to their collected data on our desires. However, marketing's subfield of Liking Studies has already revealed that disliked ads poison everything they touch. Negative sentiment—disliking—is asymmetrical in its power to shape consumer's opinions of a brand: for every ten likes, one dislike could tear a brand apart. Such negative emotion requires much brand damage control. One thing Facebook will never do, then, is install a Dislike button.

This is not to say that Facebook won't introduce other binary-emotional switches. Facebook's flirtation with a Want button indicates their potential willingness to expand our binary-emotional repertoire. One could imagine users getting a Love button. But we are not allowed to dislike. And herein lies a way out of the Like Economy. Dissent, dissensus, refusal are not easily afforded in Facebook. Dissenters have to work for it: They have to write out comments, start up a blog, seek out other dislikers. They are not lulled into slackivism or "clickivism," replacing the work of activism with clicking "like" on a cause as if the sheer aggregate of sentiment will make someone somewhere change something.

Instead, frustrated dislikers must think through their negative affect and find ways to articulate it into networks of dislike. If dislike scares off brands, so be it. Brands aren't going to fix the world's problems—but the dislikers might.

Reading the Genre

1. This causal analysis examines the way that marketing has shaped the landscape of media, including social media. As a class, explore the ways that marketing has become a science and discuss what this will mean for the future of commercials. How will marketing also change our communication on social media?

2. Whenever you are writing a causal analysis, it is important to consider a wide range of possible causes and causal relationships. What other factors do you think might have led to our current "like" economy and "like" culture? (See "Appreciate your limits," p. 66.)

3. Investigate Gerlitz and Helmond's "Like Economy," which Gehl discusses at the opening of his essay, and the connected concepts of the "hit economy" and the "link economy." What do you think might come next in this progression?

4. How have companies like Cambridge Analytica accessed "likes" for specific political purposes? How do privacy concerns impact how we currently view people's likes, dislikes, and other habits on social media?

5. WRITING: Gehl's essay examines the history of the "like" button, analyzing how it has both reflected and shaped our attitudes toward culture, especially our consumer habits. Choose another element of social media—such as the hashtag, the share, the humblebrag, the vaguebook comment, the favorite, or the subtweet—and explore how it both reflects and shapes attitudes.

6. MULTIMODALITY—LIKABLE ADVERTISEMENT: Gehl recounts the story of a Super Bowl ad that was designed to incorporate all the elements of previously "liked" Super Bowl ads. As a class, develop a way to determine which four features of print advertisements the entire group "likes" most. Then, individually, create print advertisements that incorporate all four elements to advertise a product of your choice. The ad that the class finally "likes" the most, "wins."

VISUAL EXPLANATION   Matt Daniels is one of the creators, and a frequent contributor for *The Pudding*, a self-described "journal of visual essays" where "code, data, and animation replace dense prose to construct a different sort of story." You can see all kinds of interesting visualizations by following him on Twitter @matt_daniels.

MATT DANIELS

Where New Slang Comes From

In 2014, I researched the musical origin of the word "shorty." Turns out that Too $hort was the first to rap it and Lil Jon coined the southern-drawled "shawty."

Shorty wasn't pervasive, however, until 50 Cent intro'd In Da Club with "Go shorty. It's your birthday."

50 Cent, arguably, made "shorty" mainstream slang.

Identifying these moments is fascinating: the tipping point for when slang reaches the masses. If 2015 was the year of "Netflix and chill" and 2014 was "on fleek," what slang tipped in 2016?

Using Google searches for words' definitions, I examined slang that was once rarely searched but is now relatively popular. Here's what blew up last year:

How the Kids Speak

Emerging* slang, by the year it rose into popularity

2016	2015	2014	2013
1. Triggered	1. Blase	1. Fleek	1. Selfie
2. Shook	2. Netflix and	2. Fam	2. Bae
3. Juju	Chill	3. Felicia	3. Turn Up
4. Broccoli	3. Glock	4. Anaconda	4. Red Nose
5. Woke	4. Lowkey	5. Slay	5. Emoji
6. Holosexual	5. Pleb	6. Yeet	6. Turnt
7. Shill	6. Quan	7. Silt	7. Sapiosexual
8. Gaslighting	7. Pepe	8. Calvary	8. Sus
9. Bigly	8. Stoop	9. Becky	
10. SJW	9. Burnt	10. Hawking	
11. Dank Memes	10. Simmer		
12. Vexing			
13. Bough			
14. Boolin			
15. Wavy			

By "searches for a word's definition" I mean a search for [word] + "define", "dictionary", or "definition." This list excludes proper nouns and acronyms. . . . To remove words attached to the news cycle, I filtered for terms that consistently rose in popularity throughout the year (which excludes terms such as "electoral college," which spiked suddenly in November).

If you're over 25 years old, these words still might seem foreign. While they've "tipped," they're still in an early stage of their lifecycle. Since I can decipher most of the slang from 2013–2015, perhaps 2016's words need a few more months to bake before reaching elder Millennials and Gen X'rs.

*Passing a search interest (number of searches per capita) that is typical for a common, pervasive word in English. Proper nouns and acronyms are removed. All words are required to exhibit weekly positive, linear growth throughout the course of the year.

Why did these words have an "In Da Club" moment and surge in popularity? I did some digging on 2016's slang; here are three obvious catalysts:

Catalyst 1: Hip hop with slang as the title

Three of 2016's top words are rooted in hip hop. There's a long history of hip hop and slang: pre-Internet, it was arguably one of the richest transcriptions of African American Vernacular English (the source for copious English slang). Let's examine the songs responsible for each word.

Broccoli (noun) - weed

Props to rapper D.R.A.M.: he single-handedly transformed "broccoli" into popular slang (#4 on 2016's list). Ever since D.R.A.M. released the song "Broccoli" in April 2016, searches for the word's definition have climbed to about 75% of where "Netflix and chill" peaked in 2015.

Check out the growth for "Broccoli" in the red line below.

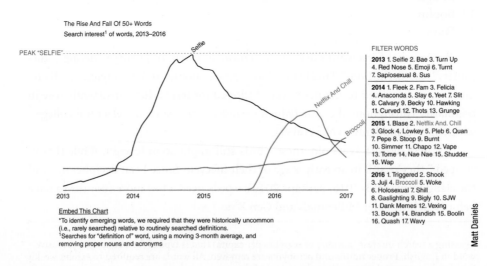

The Rise And Fall Of 50+ Words
Search interest[1] of words, 2013–2016

PEAK "SELFIE"

Selfie

Netflix And Chill

Broccoli

2013   2014   2015   2016   2017

Embed This Chart

*To identify emerging words, we required that they were historically uncommon (i.e., rarely searched) relative to routinely searched definitions.
[1]Searches for "definition of" word, using a moving 3-month average, and removing proper nouns and acronyms

FILTER WORDS

2013 1. Selfie 2. Bae 3. Turn Up 4. Red Nose 5. Emoji 6. Turnt 7. Sapiosexual 8. Sus

2014 1. Fleek 2. Fam 3. Felicia 4. Anaconda 5. Slay 6. Yeet 7. Slit 8. Calvary 9. Becky 10. Hawking 11. Curved 12. Thots 13. Grunge

2015 1. Blase 2. Netflix And. Chill 3. Glock 4. Lowkey 5. Pleb 6. Quan 7. Pepe 8. Stoop 9. Burnt 10. Simmer 11. Chapo 12. Vape 13. Torne 14. Nae Nae 15. Shudder 16. Wap

2016 1. Triggered 2. Shook 3. Juji 4. Broccoli 5. Woke 6. Holosexual 7. Shill 8. Gaslighting 9. Bigly 10. SJW 11. Dank Memes 12. Vexing 13. Bough 14. Brandish 15. Boolin 16. Quash 17. Wavy

Matt Daniels

It's worth noting that D.R.A.M. did not coin "broccoli" as slang; E-40 used it at least 10 years prior (as did Raekwon in '97). But as with 50 Cent and "shorty," D.R.A.M. pushed the word into mainstream English.

Juju (noun) - a dance

"Juju On That Beat" by Zay Hilfigerrr has over 100 million streams on Spotify.

"Juju" refers to a dance, so linguists could argue that it's a proper noun and not slang (but then what is "twerk"?). That said, it's #3 on 2016's list, a testament to hip hop's effect on language.

Wavy (adj.) - progressive, cool, swag, well-dressed

"Wavy" has been around for many years, but only recently surged in popularity. All signals suggest that Ty Dolla $ign's track "Wavy" was the cause, which dropped in early 2016, coinciding with the subsequent growth of the word (though it had been locally popular in Virginia well beforehand).

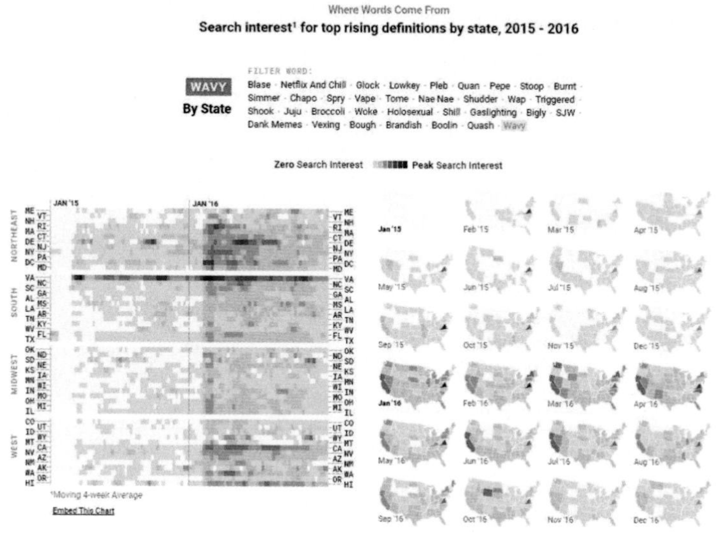
Where Words Come From
Search interest¹ for top rising definitions by state, 2015 - 2016
WAVY
By State
FILTER WORD:
Blase · Netflix And Chill · Glock · Lowkey · Pleb · Quan · Pepe · Stoop · Burnt · Simmer · Chapo · Spry · Vape · Tome · Nae Nae · Shudder · Wap · Triggered · Shook · Juju · Broccoli · Woke · Holosexual · Shill · Gaslighting · Bigly · SJW · Dank Memes · Vexing · Bough · Brandish · Boolin · Quash · Wavy
Zero Search Interest
Peak Search Interest
JAN '15
JAN '16
NORTHEAST
SOUTH
MIDWEST
WEST
¹Moving 4-week Average
Embed This Chart

Matt Daniels

Ty Dolla $ign's "Wavy" was never that popular (it didn't even chart), and searches for wavy's definition continue to grow. So unlike "In Da Club," I think of Ty's track as an initial spark rather than *the cause*. For all the kids using "wavy," few probably know its roots (Max B. coined it) or that Ty Dolla $ign had any role in its recent popularity.

Catalyst 2: Politics

In the US, last year's political circus tipped five of 2016's top slang into the mainstream.

Woke (noun) - *aware of (racial) social injustice*

"Woke" is the one term on 2016's list that's been growing organically for at least a decade. There was no major event that propelled it into the spotlight–it just finally crossed the threshold of mainstream use.

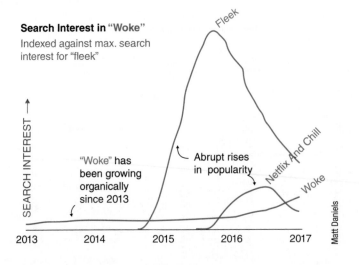

Search Interest in "Woke"
Indexed against max. search interest for "fleek"

SEARCH INTEREST →

"Woke" has been growing organically since 2013

Abrupt rises in popularity

Fleek

Netflix And Chill

Woke

2013   2014   2015   2016   2017

Matt Daniels

There were some unique events in 2016 for "woke." In terms of semantics, there's the notion that 2016's U.S. election cycle whitewashed the term. Today, I see it used broadly as "political awareness," beyond its historic racial connotations. Childish Gambino's "Redbone" helped too (~50M streams on Spotify), which dropped in November 2016. The song's hook repeats the phrase "stay woke," helping to normalize the phrase.

Geographically, you'll find early signs of "woke" in liberal-leaning blue states, such as Vermont, Massachusetts, Rhode Island, New York, and California. Relative to other states, folks in the south (specifically South Carolina and Arkansas) are falling behind on the "woke" trend.

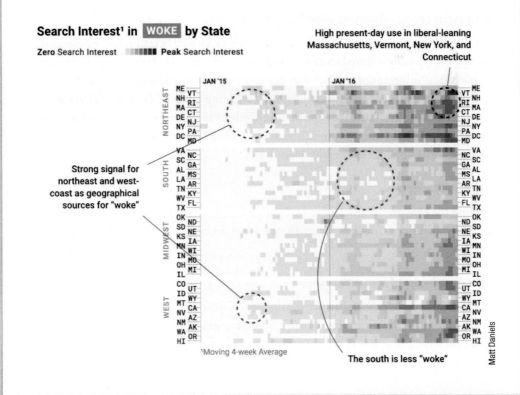

Search Interest[1] in **WOKE** **by State**

Zero Search Interest ▮▮▮▮▮▮ Peak Search Interest

High present-day use in liberal-leaning Massachusetts, Vermont, New York, and Connecticut

JAN '15   JAN '16

Strong signal for northeast and west-coast as geographical sources for "woke"

[1]Moving 4-week Average

The south is less "woke"

Matt Daniels

Triggered (verb) - "getting filled with hate after seeing, hearing, or experiencing something you can't stand" (via Urban Dictionary)

The word "triggered" has existed for years in psychology, short for "trauma triggers" (e.g., gunshots for a veteran who suffers from PTSD). Recently, this evolved into the politically divisive "trigger warnings" for books, films, and discussions that may trigger similar distress. "Triggered" has now evolved into a quasi liberal-directed insult, effectively meaning "emotional meltdown." For example, this Breitbart headline following Trump's election victory, "Triggered Students Across Country Melt Down in Response to Trump Victory."

Gaslighting (verb) - distorting/disputing facts and events

The etymology of "gaslighting" begins with the 1938 play "Gas Light." For several decades, it typically referred to a form of domestic emotional abuse where the victim is given false information so that they question their own memory and reality.

The word's recent prominence is due to Trump's use of facts (i.e., alternative facts, fake news, post-truth) or conflicting versions of events (e.g., the inauguration crowd size). "Gaslighting" is now a liberal critique of Trump's disagreement with the media over what happened versus what didn't.

Bigly (adj.) - big time

During the U.S. presidential debates, Donald Trump's use of "big league" was heard as "bigly," thus creating a meme and a new word for both anti- and pro-Trump supporters.

SJW (noun) - Social Justice Warrior

SJW is an acronym for social justice warrior. It is now a derogatory term, often wielded against liberals. Here's a great Urban Dictionary entry, "someone who repeatedly and vehemently engages in arguments on social justice on the Internet, often in a shallow or not well-thought-out way, for the purpose of raising their own personal reputation." Similar to "woke," it's been slowly growing organically, and the 2016 election cycle likely tipped it over the threshold for mainstream use.

Among political words, it's also one of the youngest terms on 2016's list.

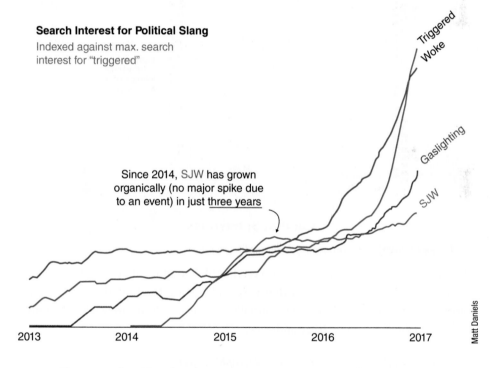

Search Interest for Political Slang
Indexed against max. search interest for "triggered"

Since 2014, SJW has grown organically (no major spike due to an event) in just three years

Triggered
Woke
Gaslighting
SJW

2013   2014   2015   2016   2017

Matt Daniels

And because of its liberal nature, we can see it growing in left-leaning states such as Oregon and Vermont.

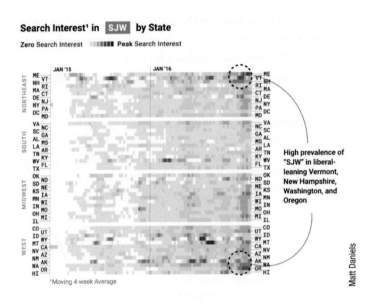

Search Interest¹ in `SJW` **by State**

Zero Search Interest ▓▓▓▓ Peak Search Interest

High prevalence of "SJW" in liberal-leaning Vermont, New Hampshire, Washington, and Oregon

Matt Daniels

¹Moving 4-week Average

Catalyst 3: Internets

Dank meme (noun) - an (ironically) high-quality meme

The etymology of "dank meme" is complex, though Reddit is where it initially found momentum. What's important is that it spread beyond the underbelly of Reddit sometime last year. While "dank" was initially used ironically, it's now taken literally as "high-quality" by a more basic audience.

Holosexual (noun) - strong attraction to holographic objects

"Holo" and "Holosexual" took off last year, largely due to YouTuber Simply Nailogical's obsession with holographic nail art.

Unknown (help needed!)

Sadly, I'm unable to find the causes for the popularity of three words.

Boolin (verb) - chilling

The origin of "boolin" is the Bloods' habit of replacing c's with b's (cool becomes bool). It is at least four years old – I found use of "boolin" by rapper YG in 2012. What's interesting is that the word's recent growth is firmly rooted in the south.

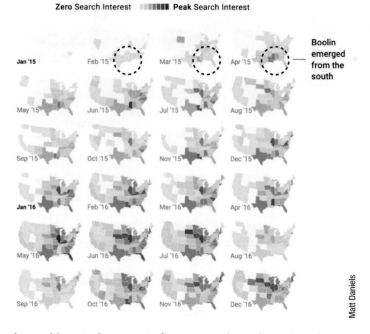

Search Interest¹ in BOOLIN by State

Zero Search Interest ▦▦▦ Peak Search Interest

Jan '15   Feb '15   Mar '15   Apr '15   Boolin emerged from the south

May '15   Jun '15   Jul '15   Aug '15

Sep '15   Oct '15   Nov '15   Dec '15

Jan '16   Feb '16   Mar '16   Apr '16

May '16   Jun '16   Jul '16   Aug '16

Sep '16   Oct '16   Nov '16   Dec '16

Matt Daniels

The problem is that I can't figure out why. Atlanta-based rapper Young Thug uses "boolin" quite often in his music, but I can't reason that this is the cause for its growth (and subsequent national spread).

Shook (adj.) - scared

Shook has been around for decades. Yet for some reason, the word blew up in California this summer.

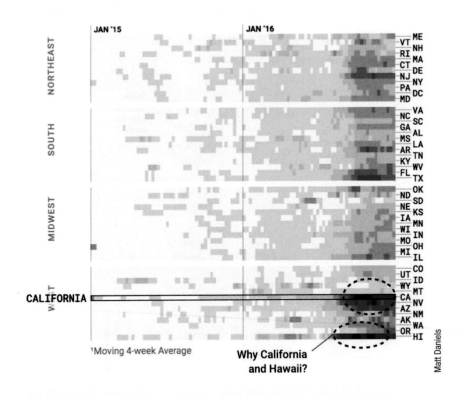

Search Interest[1] in SHOOK by State

Zero Search Interest   ▨▨▨▨▨   Peak Search Interest

[1]Moving 4-week Average

Why California and Hawaii?

Matt Daniels

Bough (?)

I have no idea what this means and why it grew in popularity. It's a thing in Mississippi though.

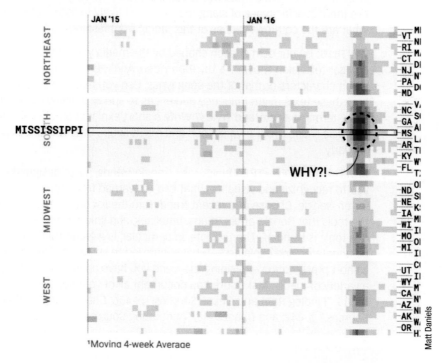

Search Interest¹ in BOUGH by State

Zero Search Interest ▫▫▫▪▪▪ Peak Search Interest

¹Moving 4-week Average

Matt Daniels

If you have any leads on boolin, shook, or bough, hit me up: matt@pudding.cool or tweet at @puddingviz

Reading the Genre

1. The tone of this article is not always exactly serious. But the research Daniels has done certainly is. His graphs are also highly sophisticated. How does this mixture of high and low style suit this topic? What type of audience does this mixture of styles work for? (See Chapter 26, "Critical Thinking," p. 327, and Chapter 33, "Levels of Style," p. 368.)

2. Daniels's explanation relies on the definition of when and how a word has "tipped." What does "tipped" mean for Daniels, and how does he go about defining it? What other definitions are important to this explanation?

3. In response to Daniels's article, consider researching the opposite trend: Look for slang words and terms that used to be popular, but now definitely are not. What are some terms that have faded from fashion? Why have they faded? Are there specific types of slang that are most likely to fade, to be overused? What are the common causes of this fading from fashion?

4. WRITING: Is your own speech shaped by the media you consume? Watch a popular television show or a YouTube video. Analyze the language of the television characters or that of the song lyrics. Can you make inferences about how these texts might influence audiences to speak similarly—using the same terms, dialects, and styles? Write a short explanation of how television or music shapes your own speech and might shape other people's speech similarly.

5. MULTIMODALITY—TRENDING: Visit Google Trends, a site designed to help you to recognize and visualize what can be learned from what people search for on Google. Choose one recent trend from the list on the site, and using the tools that Google offers (maps, timelines, and links to stories), explain why this topic is trending. The timeline, in particular, is a graph that could easily be annotated and explained—what events led to spikes on the graph? Create a short presentation explaining the trend you have chosen to explore, using a variety of media. Make sure you document all of your sources. (See Chapter 45, "Finding Print and Online Sources," p. 436; Chapter 46, "Evaluating Sources," p. 442; and Chapter 48, "Annotating Sources," p. 452.)

Further Reading

Matsa, Katerina Eva, et al. "Searching for News: The Flint Water Crisis." *Pew Research Center's Journalism Project*, 27 Apr. 2017, www.journalism.org/essay/searching-for-news/. Accessed 25 Aug. 2017.

CULTURAL EXPLANATION Eddo Stern is a game developer and artist, specializing in the overlaps between art and experimental game design. He is a professor of Design and Media Arts at UCLA. He also directs the UCLA Game Lab. World of Warcraft has been around for longer than most college students have been alive, but continues to be one of the most popular video game franchises in the world.

EDDO STERN

Warcrack for the Hordes:
Why Warcraft Owns the World

"First there are the utopias. Utopias are sites with no real place. They are sites that have a general relation of direct or inverted analogy with the real space of Society. They present society itself in a perfected form, or else society turned upside down, but in any case these utopias are fundamentally unreal spaces. There are also, probably in every culture, in every civilization, real places—places that do exist and that are formed in the very founding of society—which are something like counter-sites, a kind of effectively enacted utopia in which the real sites, all the other real sites that can be found within the culture, are simultaneously represented, contested, and inverted. Places of this kind are outside of all places, even though it may be possible to indicate their location in reality. Because these places are absolutely different from all the sites that they reflect and speak about, I shall call them, by way of contrast to utopias, heterotopias."[1]

Fantasy-themed, text-based, Multi-User Dungeons (MUDs) have been around since the late 1970s, but in 1997, the addition of real-time graphics and the mainstreaming of the Internet allowed Ultima Online to become the first major commercial success of the Massively Multiplayer Online Role Playing Game (MMORPG, MMOG, MMO) genre.

World of Warcraft, released in November 2004, was preceded by a litany of 3-D sword and sorcery MMOs dating back to 1996, including Meridian 59, Everquest, Asheron's Call, Shadowbane, Dark Age of Camelot, Phantasy Star Online, Final Fantasy XI, Asheron's Call II, Ragnarok Online, and Everquest II. More recently a series of big budget online fantasy games have been released to great fanfare, including Vanguard, Hellgate London, Age of Conan, and most recently Warhammer Online.

But none of these "post WoW" games has been able to hit the mainstream nerve the way WoW has with its 11 million-plus player base and pop-cultural prominence. The common wisdom you will often hear about WoW's massive appeal is that Blizzard simply just "got it right." "A fundamentally well designed and executed game at the base level. WoW just feels right when you play it, something that we didn't really have in the MMOG genre prior." Or, "Why is it so popular? It's easy. That's about as simple as it gets.'[2]

Truedat . . . but is there something more about World of Warcraft that has made it the best selling MMO ever and allowed it to redefine the position of online role-playing games in the cultural landscape, from what was previously a gamer geek subculture to a mainstream cultural phenomenon? Maybe.

World of Warcraft is a Heterotopia.

The term was coined by Michael Foucault in his 1967 lecture titled "Of Other Spaces," and fits World of Warcraft like a Furious Gladiator's Mooncloth Glove. Foucault writes: "The heterotopia is capable of juxtaposing in a single real place several spaces, several sites that are in themselves incompatible."[3] WoW allows for a multitude of permutations and paradoxical combinations in its gameplay and narrative structures that do exactly this to manifest it as a unique game in its genre.

The most significant change that WoW brought to the fantasy MMO genre was the Alliance/Horde player faction division. Warring factions are not new to MMOs. Neither is the division of the world into "good" and "evil" races. Yet what WoW has done with its faction-centered dichotomy is fundamentally different. Playing the

Alliance faction "races" in WoW—Humans, Elves, Dwarves, and their friends—affords the player not only an identification with the heroic archetypes belonging to the traditional high-fantasy genre, but an advertent alignment as a stereotypical member of the fantasy role-playing game community, what some might call a "classic geek gamer." By introducing the Horde as a gang of playable races that includes the thuggish Ores, the Rastafarian Trolls, and the cannibalistic Forsaken, WoW has transformed the familiar offering of "evil" into something much more radical—the Horde are the "other."

Earlier MMOs such as Everquest offered a small selection of playable "evil" races such as Dark Elves or Trolls. Choosing these races allowed players to play against the common "heroic" grain, but as Everquest was a collaborative game, players of these races routinely blended in and teamed up with the good races, nullifying any non-cosmetic difference between the races. WoW's Horde, who cannot communicate with the Alliance, exist on the periphery of the fantasy world's diegesis. Their inclusion as active agents feels alien to the genre. WoW offers players an opportunity to participate in the fantasy of World of Warcraft without buying into its narrative core. Horde play as interlopers, outsiders who are here to crash the party, who seemingly play the same game but do so in a subversive and ironic way. The Horde defines the unique culture of World of Warcraft while simultaneously occupying its counterculture. By allowing players the choice of experiencing the game sincerely as members of the Alliance or ironically as the Horde, WoW lets us have our cake and eat it too.

In his often-cited 1996 essay "Hearts, Clubs, Diamonds, Spades: Players Who Suit MUDs," Richard Bartle presents a taxonomy of player motivations in multi-user games. Bartle divides players into the following categories: Achievers, who "regard points gathering and rising in levels as their main goal," Explorers, who "delight in having the game expose its internal machinations to them," Socialises, who "are interested in people, and what they have to say," and Killers, who "get their kicks from imposing themselves on others."[4] In general, MMO designers have been wise to try to accommodate all four player archetypes and their various permutations.

At first, as was the case with Ultima Online, game designers tried to create a "realistic" simulation of society—allowing for the coexistence of players who wish to kill other playera for fun with players who had no such motivations. The experiment proved to be too big a challenge, as killers ruined the experience of non-killers and Ultima Online became a utopia for killers and a dystopia for the rest of the population. The eventual solution, introduced in Everquest and epitomized in World of Warcraft, is to divide the player population into separate versions of the game played on different servers: Player vs. Player servers for the Killers and Player vs. Environment servers for the rest. By offering a selection of parallel game worlds identical in all ways except for their social rules of engagement tailored to accommodate opposing worldviews, WoW offers players the choice between one utopia and another.

Most gamers who strongly identify with the more aggressive and competitive First Person Shooter (FPS) and Real Time Strategy (RTS) genres—hardcore Counterstrike or Starcraft players—avoid and stigmatize the congenial fantasy Role Playing Game (RPG) genre. World of Warcraft provides an opening for such players through the kind of counterplay offered by Player vs. Player servers and by identifying with the Horde and keeps them playing by offering game experiences that mimic the FPS and RTS genres' core game mechanics.

WoW is structured as a multi-genre game—a game that contains within its framework a diverse variety of game experiences. Players looking for standard RPG experiences—such as detailed game-lore, a narrative back story, monster slaying, dungeon crawling, character development, and loot collecting—may spend their time completing quests on their own or with real-life friends or family, random strangers, long-term in-game acquaintances, or fellow guild members. Players can scratch their RTS and FPS itches by engaging in strategically complex Player vs. Player group battles, both in staged arenas or in open-ended planned encounters. Ranked Arena PVP seasons offer an even more acutely competitive context for the same sorts of gameplay dynamics offered by RTS and FPS tournaments. This wide range of gameplay experiences allows WoW to function more like a closed circuit television network with its own selection of internal channels to choose from.

Tom Shippey, in his writing on J.R.R Tolkien's work, points to the variety of main characters in *The Lord of the Rings* as a key contributing factor to the book's unprecedented mass appeal. For his analysis, Shippey uses Northrop Frye's framework of literary modes. In summary, Frye's model divides narrative into five hierarchical categories with myth at the top, followed by romance, high mimesis (tragedy or epic narratives), low mimesis (the classical novel), and finally, irony. Shippey identifies *The Lord of the Rings* as belonging to all five categories at once. He maps the main characters from the book as follows: Samwise as irony, Frodo and the other hobbits as low mimesis, humans as high mimesis, the Elves and Dwarves as figures of romance, and finally Gandalf, Bombadil, and Sauron as belonging to the realm of myth. He also points to the way Tolkien navigates these modes: "The flexibility with which Tolkien moves between the modes is a major cause for the success of *The Lord of the Rings*. It is at once ambitious (much more so than novels are allowed to be) and insidious (getting under the guard of the modem reader, trained to reject or to ironize, the assumptions of tragedy or epic)."[5]

A similar process is at work in World of Warcraft. Looking again at the choices of race that players can choose from in WoW, and considering that even within the countercultural frame of the Horde there are modes of engagement that develop beyond an initial irony in relation to the high-fantasy genre, I would categorize the choices in the following way: Forsaken, Gnomes and female Dwarves as irony, Taurens, Ores, Draenai, Dark Elves, Trolls, and Dwarves as low mimesis, Humans, Elves, and Forsaken (again) as high mimesis or romance. The specific placement of playable races using this model is subjective to each player, but WoW offers players a choice of how they prefer to identify their relationship to the narrative experience of the game world through the choice of character. The stratification of WoW's literary modes as a consequence of character race is brought to the foreground when players have more than one character they can play. The race of the active character often mirrors the player's current mood. Want to create an earnest alter ego? Likely you will not choose a female dwarf for the task, but when creating an alternative character used for casually chit-chatting in town, picking a female dwarf character for your roster does come in handy.

Even the more concrete design elements serve WoW's appeal to a wide range of players and player emotions. The art styling is extremely bold, even expressionistic, all the while hedging the ironic against the sublime. The overall effect is uncanny. The blocky, low-polygon character models and colorful pixelated textures are comically exaggerated. The animations are smooth, yet childishly cartoonish or grotesque. The outdoor environments are vividly colorized and ever flowing. The game is littered with in-jokes and pop cultural references to books, movies, celebrities, games, and other real-world paraphernalia. The dialogue is overtly goofy and self-deprecating. The sound effects are deft. The music goes hand in hand with the environments to mesmerize the player, the score is epic, and while the compositions may be high-fantasy cliches, they do not engage the player cerebrally the way the character models, animations, and dialogue do. It is as if WoW's world craft is calibrated to swallow you up in its synthetic world and just as you are on the brink of total immersion, it spits you out. And then sucks you back in again.

World of Warcraft exists within a nexus of game-related contexts, sometimes referred to as the Meta-game, the extra-diegetic game world, or simply the WoW community. This context includes personal fan sites and blogs, guild home pages, official and nonofficial discussion forums, game databases, strategy guides, encyclopedias, player ranking lists, sites that offer game add-ons and modifications, portals of fan-made films, and game-related news sites. The cultural artifacts generated in the Meta-game—guides, tricks, rants, treasure maps, walkthroughs, helper applications as well as fan-created stories, comics, and films—are openly fed back to the in-game experience. Nick Yee, who uses polling and statistical analysis to examine MMO player behavior, reports, "the average player spends about 10.8 hours each week performing game-related tasks outside of the game. . . . players spent on average

23.4 hours each week in the game. Thus, on average, the majority of players spend about an additional 50 percent of their game-playing time outside of the game performing game-related activities."[6]

WoW is perhaps the first online role-playing game to truly function in tune with the Internet generation, where a more hermetic idea of "fantasy" as a cordoned-off reality of hardcore role playing has been consciously replaced by a porous pseudo-fantasy game. The illusion has been shattered long ago, bearded paladins are swapping Chuck Norris jokes, Dark Elves are doing the Napoleon Dynamite, and Undead Warlocks are talking Pakistan in Orgrimmar, while everyone else is doing their best Leeroy Jenkins impersonation. WoW coolly embraces the Meta-game and paradoxically, by letting its guard down and allowing bits of reality to slip in and out of its fantasy world, has become the most compelling and immersive game ever.

"In the mirror, I see myself there where I am not, in an unreal, virtual space that opens up behind the surface; I am over there, there where I am not, a sort of shadow that gives my own visibility to myself, that enables me to see myself there where I am absent: such is the utopia of the mirror. But it is also a heterotopia in so far as the mirror does exist in reality, where it exerts a sort of counteraction on the position that I occupy.[7]

Notes

1. Michel Foucault, "Of Other Spaces (1967), Heterotopias," http://www.foucault.info/documents/heteroTonia/foucault.heteroTonia.en.html
2. http://hgamer.blogsnot.com/2007/09/whv-is-world-of-warcraft-so-nonular.html
3. Foucault.
4. Richard Bartle, "Hearts, Clubs, Diamonds, Spades: Players Who Suit MUDs", 1986, http://www.mud.co.uk/richard/hcds.htm
5. Tom Shippey, *J.R.R. Tolkien, Author of the Century*, Princeton 2000, p. 223.
6. Nick Yee, "Time Spent in the Meta-Game," from "The Daedalus Project," http://www.nickvee.com/daedalus/archives/001535.php
7. Foucault.

Reading the Genre

1. Stern develops a very complex explanation for the success of World of Warcraft (WoW), relying heavily on the French theorist Michel Foucault. What would happen if you took Foucault out of this essay altogether? Does he need to use Foucault to explain WoW? What does this theory add to the essay, and what might it take away?

2. Stern cites other scholars—in addition to Foucault—to both ground and extend this analysis. To what effect? Find examples of his use of secondary sources, and consider what the use of each of these sources allows Stern to do as a writer. (See Chapter 46, "Evaluating Sources," p. 442.)

3. Find passages where it is obvious that Stern is speaking directly to other WoW players and might be excluding readers who don't know the game. How important is it for Stern to show that he is an "insider" who really understands the game? How does he balance this against the need to connect with readers who may have never played the game? (See Chapter 35, "Inclusive Writing," p. 383.)

4. What does Stern mean when he calls WoW a "meta-game"? Can you think of other games, television shows, music, or other texts that are "meta" like WoW? What characteristics of these texts make them "meta"? What does this meta-content do for the text and for its audience?

5. This essay explains how a video game has become popular, but it does so through the use of the tools of literary analysis. How is a video game like a literary text, and how is it unlike a novel, play, or poem? How, then, do these literary analysis tools work for Stern, and how do they fail to capture the unique character of the video game? (See Chapter 13, "Literary Analyses," p. 196.)

6. WRITING: There are dozens of journals that publish research on video games. Find one of these journals through your library databases and explore some recent articles. Write a summary of a single article or summarize a series of articles about the same game. Try to identify some of the strategies that are used in this field to evaluate the impact and importance of games. (See Chapter 45, "Finding Print and Online Sources," p. 436; Chapter 46, "Evaluating Sources," p. 442; and Chapter 48, "Annotating Sources," p. 452.)

7. MULTIMODALITY—EXPLAINING GAMES: In the original version of this article, Stern includes three screen-captures from WoW, but doesn't directly explain what is happening in any of the images. For non-players, the images are confusing. As a means of exploring how one of your own favorite games works, create a screen-capture that you can offer a detailed explanation of. In explaining the screen, speak directly to an audience who has never played the game, and seek to convince them of the virtues and values of this game.

Further Reading

Schaap, Julian, and Stef Aupers. "'Gods in World of Warcraft Exist': Religious Reflexivity and the Quest for Meaning in Online Computer Games." *new media & society* (2016).

61

Arguments: Readings

GENRE MOVES Argumentative Speech

SOJOURNER TRUTH

From "Ain't I a Woman?"

Well, children, where there is so much racket there must be something out of kilter. I think that 'twixt the negroes of the South and the women at the North, all talking about rights, the white men will be in a fix pretty soon. But what's all this here talking about?

Frame the problem.

This famous speech from 1851 begins when Sojourner Truth recognizes a "racket": disenfranchised groups talking about rights and advocating for themselves in a way that's perceived as disruptive by those in power. She then goes on to argue powerfully for women's rights. The "racket" provides framing for the argument. We know there is an issue, problem, or current event that requires our attention, giving Truth occasion to address the issue, and telling the audience how important it is to pay attention.

To generate ideas for your own arguments, think about what "racket" can be heard around rights issues in our current society. What, as Truth would put it, is "out of kilter" in the world around us? Or, more simply, what are people making a racket about in news media, or on Twitter, or on the street? By starting with a question that lots of people are asking, you lend your argument immediacy and importance, allowing you to easily draw your readers in.

Once you've found a topic and explored the arguments others have made about it, begin your own essay by identifying the problem, as Truth does. Frame the problem in a way that showcases its urgency and importance. Then, in your argument, show what can be done to respond to this racket—or what might be at stake if we ignore it.

ANALYSIS OF CULTURAL VALUES Paul Argenti is a professor of Corporate Communication, an area that he might suggest modern corporations should care more about. Argenti was recently named one of the 100 most influential people in business ethics.

PAUL ARGENTI

Corporate Ethics in the Era of Millennials

Corporate social responsibility has been added to the growing list of demands that investors, customers, and employees present to companies.

In 2015, 81 percent of Fortune 500 companies published sustainability reports, up from 20 percent in 2011, according to a report released by the Governance & Accountability Institute in June. Companies are publicizing their ethical standards and responsibility efforts, and consumers are punishing companies that appear to fall short. Even as headlines proclaim "greed is back," companies are investing time and resources into instituting more ethical practices.

Why is there such dissonance?

As is so often the case these days, businesses are taking cues from millennials. This generation (currently 18-35 years old) represents more than a quarter of the U.S. workforce—and this amount is expected to grow to over 50 percent by 2020. They will account for a third of retail sales in the same year. Businesses *not* thinking about how to interact with this generation are in serious trouble.

So how do millennials think about corporate social responsibility—or CSR?

A 2014 Nielsen survey showed that millennials are significantly more responsive to CSR in both consumption as well as employment decisions. Of those surveyed who would pay a premium for sustainable products, verify packaging, and choose a company with a higher CSR reputation as employer, about half were millennials. These millennials are choosing to spend their resources—be it time or money—on organizations that appear to represent a set of values.

With their significant buying power, millennials are placing huge demands on companies to respond with genuine CSR strategies.

Where can companies start in building out this strategy?

As millennials look for companies that focus on a triple bottom line (people, planet, profit), companies are looking to millennials for guidance. CSR actions should align with a company's values, brand proposition, and business model but, at the same time, the company must listen and respond to its constituents.

A key element for any successful CSR strategy is corporate communication. In the early days of CSR, corporations relied heavily on traditional media, delivering their message through advertising. Many did not institutionalize CSR as a separate business activity, relying on the marketing and public relations functions instead. Millennials, however, are far less responsive to press and television ads and must be engaged differently. In scientific terms, their "BS meters" are very finely tuned. As so-called digital natives, this generation looks to social media to both consume and influence information and opinions. Peers are a trusted source; the official company flack is not.

What's more, as opposed to traditional advertising, which is unidirectional, social media is a more delicate instrument where companies receive real-time feedback from their audience. Millennials expect to have their opinions listened and responded to, meaning that companies need to engage in more two-way conversations with their constituents. Establishing a communication strategy that is both consistent and practically nuanced to respond to changes in the environment is a difficult but necessary process for companies to go through.

Overall, millennials are more demanding, more in touch, and more skeptical. Brushing these off as cynicism is too simplistic. It puts the onus on organizations to show that they are not simply paying lip service to CSR, as consumers will sniff out and publicize anything that smells of hypocrisy. What's more, it has resulted in companies adapting to—or at least learning valuable lessons about—being more responsible entities.

A recent example is Perdue Farms, one of America's largest poultry companies. In response to the growing demand, particularly from millennials, for cruelty-free meat, Perdue is changing its chicken breeding operations. Working alongside the Humane Society, Perdue has made massive changes to its farming processes, including reducing the use of antibiotics, providing more natural light, and changing the way animals are slaughtered. Jim Perdue, chairman of Perdue Farms, has said that increased sales should compensate for the increased costs. He is confident that by going along with what Perdue's customers want, the company will be successful. This way of conducting CSR is a direct response to what consumers saw as a problem.

A proactive approach involves building CSR into the culture of a company, something that many millennials look for as both employees and consumers. This approach can and should also add to the bottom line. Scott Moorehead, CEO of TCC, one of Verizon's largest retailers, said: "The commoditization of wireless retail stores meant we needed to do more to differentiate ourselves in order to grow a loyal customer and employee base." With millennials accounting for 85 percent of its workforce, TCC started the Culture of Good program to engage its employees. Among other things, employees are allowed 16 hours per year of paid time off to devote to volunteer efforts. In 2015, the company donated $1.2 million to employee-led charity efforts. Such a policy fits well with two of the major requests from millennials: empowerment and the ability to affect local communities. The company says the result has been higher employee retention and satisfaction, as well as an increase in customers.

TCC and Perdue were successful in different ways in responding to millennials' need for CSR efforts. Both as consumers and as employees, millennials want more from companies. On the company's side, CSR efforts should not be undertaken simply to be the good guys. In keeping faith with investors and creditors, these efforts should be genuinely beneficial to the organization. Not all efforts to implement CSR strategies have been successful in this. American Apparel learned that even the best of intentions in the realm of CSR could be derailed by simple economics.

CSR is arguably at the very core of American Apparel's business model. The company produces its products in the United States and offers competitive pay and benefits. Studies of millennials' preference for buying local indicate that such a "sweatshop-free" model should be attractive and successful in commanding a premium. Faced with the reality of the world after the Great Recession and stuck with its ethical sourcing strategy, though, American Apparel wasn't able to cut costs as aggressively as competitors did and has failed to make a profit since 2009. The company has also heavily relied on a "sex sells" approach to marketing, something that often overshadowed any ethical positioning the company tried to assume.

Other companies have stumbled into unfortunate CSR debacles. Starbucks began a well-intentioned but badly executed social media conversation about race, privilege, and gentrification with its #RaceTogether campaign. Volkswagen is reeling from a 40 percent loss in share price and $15 billion in regulatory fines after its public commitment to sustainability was shown to be a cover for some truly bad behavior. The list of companies goes on. But we still argue that attempts at quality CSR are a vital component of a successful business strategy.

Organizations need to appreciate the degree to which the latest generation joining the workforce is making employment and consumption decisions based on CSR efforts. For a CSR strategy to be successful it needs to be authentic, in line with the brand image, and attentive to what the public demands.

In the 1970s, Milton Friedman argued strongly—even convincingly—against CSR, considering it a form of taxation exercised on shareholders, consumers, or employees by managers who had no legitimacy to do so. This argument relies on the premise that CSR initiatives imply negative net contributions to the bottom line. If we consider, instead, that well-executed CSR strategies lead to customer acquisition, increased sales, employee satisfaction, better teamwork, higher productivity, while lack of CSR can lead to disaster, Friedman's argument fails miserably today. The rise of the millennials as a powerful economic force increasingly exposes the fallacy of Friedman's argument.

The think pieces about the millennials have been written, dissected, and rewritten. Although each generation bemoans the faults of the following ones, perhaps it's time we give millennials credit where credit is due: They are forcing business to do good while doing well. Companies need to rise to this challenge quickly or risk becoming an anachronism.

Reading the Genre

1. Argenti suggests that "the think pieces about millennials have been written and rewritten." He knows that any article that mentions this generation generally falls into specific patterns and stereotypes. How does he craft this article to fit into this established subgenre, but also to react against it?

2. Argenti uses a series of questions in this report to pivot directions and to add complexity. How does this strategy differ from, for instance, using headings? What tone do these questions establish, and what other rhetorical strategies does Argenti use to engage his audience? (See Part 5, "Style," p. 366.)

3. Is this essay written for millennials or for people older than this generation? What cues exist in the essay that allow us to understand who the audience is? See "Understanding your audience" (p. 144) and Chapter 35, "Inclusive Writing" (p. 383).

4. This essay originally appeared as an "Opinion" piece for *National Public Radio*. Opinion pieces are generally short arguments, like this one, about current issues. How do you think the length restriction shapes the style, tone, and form of argumentation in this essay?

5. WRITING: Write a letter to the CEO of a corporation that you believe shows a lack of corporate responsibility. Building from Argenti's research, make an argument for why this company needs to shape up; show the CEO what the negative impact will be if they do not. Offer tangible suggestions for how this company can change their path and become more responsive and responsible.

6. MULTIMODALITY—SUBVERTISING: Look for an advertising or promotional campaign that you believe has backfired or showed a lack of corporate responsibility. How can you rewrite this campaign to highlight what is wrong with it? Using the tools of irony and satire, create a tagline, images, or even a physical artifact (like a coffee cup) that pokes fun at, and critiques, the original campaign.

Further Reading

Stein, Joel. "Millennials: The Me Me Me generation." *Time Magazine* (2013): 1–8.

ARGUMENTATIVE REPORT   Jeff Wise is a contributing editor at *Popular Mechanics* and the author of *Extreme Fear: The Science of Your Mind in Danger*, as well as a contributor to magazines such as *Psychology Today*, where this article first appeared. He writes on the subjects of psychology, fear, aviation, and technology. Perhaps not surprisingly, Wise is also an airplane and glider pilot. From a quick Google Image search of his name, he doesn't appear to be a hipster.

Extreme Fear

Posted: September 8, 2010
From: Jeff Wise

The Sad Science of Hipsterism: The Psychology of Indie Bands, PBR, and Weird Facial Hair

"This article explores the contemporary jogger pant by looking back to the mid-twentieth-century coding of hipness through material consumption, racial mastery, and urbanity."

Behold the hipster, the stylishly disaffected breed of twentysomethings whose fog of twee whimsy envelops Williamsburg and the East Village. Most who encounter the hipster in its natural habitat respond in one of two ways: derision or ridicule.

But science does not cast judgment. Its goal is to explore and explain dispassionately whether the object of study be the noble eagle or the lowly nematode. So what does science have to tell us about this fascinatingly misunderstood breed, the indigenous North American hipster?

Tetra Images/Alamy

Surprisingly much.

In a paper in an upcoming issue of the *Journal of Consumer Research* entitled "Demythologizing Consumption Practices: How Consumers Protect Their Field-Dependent Identity Investments from Devaluing Marketplace Myths," authors Zeynep Arsel and Craig J. Thompson delve deep into the phenomenon of hipsterism, and in particular its most abiding mystery: If everyone hates hipsters, why would anyone want to be one?

The long and short of it is that they don't.

In general, psychologists who study consumers understand that people are largely motivated to spend money not just on things that they materially need, but that bolster their sense of identity. They purchase not just goods and services, but mythologies. Imagining themselves as rugged, rebellious patriots, they buy a Harley-Davidson. Imagining themselves as respected and well-heeled, they buy a Lexus.

Hipsters, though, follow a different paradigm. Their problem is that their purchases tend to place them within a category whose mythology they despise. That's right: Nobody likes hipsters, not even hipsters.

As Arsel and Thompson put it, the beats of the '50s and hippies of the '60s and '70s, both of which had an admirable authenticity about them even if you didn't care for the particulars, eventually gave rise to "the millennial hipster," which "came to be represented as an über-consumer of trends and as a new, and rather gullible, target market that consumes cool rather than creating it." As examples of the dorkification, they cite online parodies of the iconic Mac v. PC ads and this viral YouTube video.[1]

The upshot being that any people who legitimately enjoy all the trappings of hipsterhood—the authors mention Pabst Blue Ribbon, Puma, and the trucker hat— must psychologically distance themselves from the demographic group of which they are so clearly a part. And so their subconscious brains have to work double time so that they can convince themselves that the things they buy do not reflect on their true character.

Arsel and Thompson interviewed hipsters and asked them how they dealt with the problem of being identified as such. The answer, they found, was to "demythologize" the hipster experience, that is, to psychologically reclassify their own behavior as

---

[1] http://youtu.be/0tBH0E7A8BA

being separate from the aggregate activity that the rest of the world lumps together as "hipster." They interviewed one consumer, identified as Scarlet, who told them:

> I'm not gonna lie, I shop at Urban [Outfitters] sometimes, only when it's on sale of course. . . . I like doing a lot of the things that are the hipster thing to do, but I do them because I like to do them, not because they're the cool thing to do. And because I am immersed in the social scene where there are a lot of hipsters, people mistake me for being one of them.

The deeper irony is that those who try to assert their independence from the commodification of identity wind up tapping into another marketplace myth, what the authors call "the myth of consumer sovereignty." This is the idea that by assiduously selecting from all the identity markers available for purchase, a person can assemble one that authentically reflects their true self-independence of the marketplace. Some of the hipsters that Arsel and Thompson talked to are well aware of the futility of this project. Said one, identified as "Tom":

> I don't necessarily know every single weird obscure band. I don't necessarily want to. But I mean, yeah, who do I hang out with? I hang out with like a bunch of tattooed indie dorks. So, yeah, I guess I am but I wouldn't self-identify, I think. I'd listen to stuff that's outside the mainstream or it's like I dress weird compared to the majority of the population. I just try not to think about it too much. The minute you start identifying with a subculture . . . you kind of lose individuality, surrender part of your identity, and we don't wanna do that.

This, then, is the essence of being a hipster. Pretending you aren't one.

Reading the Genre

1. This essay starts out with an anthropological mission, to study a subculture: hipsters. But the article was published in *Psychology Today*, so it also has the goal of studying the hipster mentality. Read through the essay and identify the sections that seem anthropological and the sections that seem psychological.

2. Using your library's online databases, track down the research paper that Wise summarizes in this article. Compare the full paper with Wise's short report. What does Wise miss? Did he do a responsible job of representing the larger research study?

3. Wise seems to assume that most of his readers will see hipsters as objects of ridicule. What assumptions are built into Wise's writing and the research he cites, and how do these assumptions distract us from seeing the positives associated with hipsterism? How could Wise conduct further research to determine if these assumptions are valid? (For more on finding common ground with readers, see p. 221.)

4. **WRITING:** Wise writes that "people are largely motivated to spend money not just on things that they materially need, but that bolster their sense of identity." Write an analysis of one specific product that you believe has become a specific marker of identity—a product that people buy specifically to build their "identity." Explore how this identity-building does or does not work in practice, and consider interviewing people about their reasons for making this purchase.

Further Reading

Gilson, Duane. "The revolution in our pants: Hipsters, race and American fashion." *International Journal of Fashion Studies* 4.1 (2017): 35–49.

ARGUMENT FOR CHANGE   Emily Bazelon is a former senior editor at the online magazine *Slate* *.com*, where she wrote about legal affairs. She continues to take part in a long-running weekly *Slate* podcast called "The Gabfest," talking about current political issues. Bazelon is now a staff writer for the New York Times Magazine and has also written for the *Atlantic, Mother Jones,* and the *Yale Law Journal.* In this essay from Slate, Bazelon examines an age-old domestic issue: spanking.

slate.com

Posted: Thursday, January 25, 2007, at 6:16 PM ET
From: Emily Bazelon

Hitting Bottom: Why America Should Outlaw Spanking

"The traditional feminist argument against decriminalization is that legitimizing prostitution will harm women by leading to more sexual inequality. The human rights argument for it is that it will make people's lives better, and safer. In this fight over whose voices to listen to, who speaks for whom and when to use the power of criminal law, the sex-workers' rights movement is a rebellion against punishment and shame. It demands respect for a group that has rarely received it, insisting that you can only really help people if you respect them."

Sally Lieber, the California assemblywoman who proposed a ban on spanking last week, must be sorry she ever opened her mouth. Before Lieber could introduce her bill, a poll showed that only 23 percent of respondents supported it. Some pediatricians disparaged the idea of outlawing spanking, and her fellow politicians called her crazy. Anyone with the slightest libertarian streak seems to believe that outlawing corporal punishment is silly. More government intrusion, and for what—to spare kids a few swats? Or, if you're pro-spanking, a spanking ban represents a sinister effort to take a crucial disciplinary tool out of the hands of good mothers and fathers—and to encourage the sort of permissive parenting that turns kids ratty and rotten.

Why, though, are we so eager to retain the right to hit our kids? Lieber's ban would apply only to children under the age of four. Little kids may be the most infuriating; they are also the most vulnerable. And if you think that most spanking takes place in a fit of temper—and that banning it would gradually lead more parents to restrain themselves—then the idea of a hard-and-fast rule against it starts to seem not so ridiculous.

The purpose of Lieber's proposal isn't to send parents to jail, or children to foster care, because of a firm smack. Rather, it would make it easier for prosecutors to bring charges for instances of corporal punishment that they think are tantamount to child abuse. Currently, California law (and the law of other states) allows for spanking that is reasonable, age-appropriate, and does not carry a risk of serious injury. That forces judges to referee what's reasonable and what's not. How do they tell? Often, they may resort to looking for signs of injury. If a smack leaves a bruise or causes a fracture, it's illegal. If not, bombs away. In other words, allowing for "reasonable" spanking gives parents a lot of leeway to cause pain.

Who should we worry about more: the well-intentioned parent who smacks a child's bottom and gets hauled off to court or the kid who keeps getting pounded because the cops can't find a bruise? A United Nations report on violence against children argues that "[t]he de minimis principle—that the law does not concern itself with trivial matters" will keep minor assaults on children out of court, just as it does almost all minor assaults between adults. The U.N. Committee on the Rights of the Child has been urging countries to ban corporal punishment since 1996. The idea is that by making it illegal to hit your kids, countries will make hurting them socially unacceptable.

The United Nations has a lot of converting to do in this part of the world. Its report cites a survey showing that 84 percent of Americans believe that it's "sometimes necessary to discipline a child with a good hard spanking." On this front, we are in the company of the Koreans, 90 percent of whom reported thinking that corporal punishment is "necessary." On the other side of the spanking map are nineteen countries that have banned spanking and three others that have partially banned it.

The grandmother of the bunch is Sweden, which passed a law against corporal punishment in 1979. The effects of that ban are cited by advocates on both sides of the spanking debate. Parents almost universally used corporal punishment on Swedish children born in the 1950s; the numbers dropped to 14 percent for kids born in the late 1980s, and only 8 percent of parents reported physically punishing their kids in 2000. Plus, only one child in Sweden died as the result of physical abuse by a parent between 1980 and 1996. Those statistics suggest that making spanking illegal contributes to making it less prevalent and also to making kids safer. On the other hand, reports to police of child abuse soared in the decades after the spanking ban, as did the incidence of juvenile violence. Did reports rise because frustrated, spanking-barred parents lashed out against their kids in other ways or because the law made people more aware of child abuse? The latter is what occurred in the United States when reports of abuse spiked following the enactment of child-protective laws in the 1970s. Is the rise in kids beating on each other evidence of undisciplined, unruly child mobs or the result of other unrelated forces? The data don't tell us, so take your pick.

A similar split exists in the American social-science literature. In a 2000 article in the *Clinical Child and Family Psychology Review*, Dr. Robert Larzelere (who approves of spanking if it's "conditional" and not abusive) reviewed thirty-eight studies and found that spanking posed no harm to kids under the age of seven and reduced misbehavior when deployed alongside milder punishments like scolding and time-outs. By contrast, a 2002 article in *Psychology Bulletin* by Dr. Elizabeth Gershoff (not a spanking fan) reviewed eighty-eight studies and found an association between corporal punishment and a higher level of childhood aggression and a greater risk of physical abuse.

This is the sort of research impasse that leaves advocates free to argue what they will—and parents without much guidance. But one study stands out: an effort by University of California at Berkeley psychologist Diana Baumrind to tease out the effects of occasional spanking compared to frequent spanking and no spanking at all. Baumrind tracked about one hundred white, middle-class families in the East Bay area of northern California from 1968 to 1980. The children who were hit frequently were more likely to be maladjusted. The ones who were occasionally spanked had slightly higher misbehavior scores than those who were not spanked at all. But this difference largely disappeared when Baumrind accounted for the children's poor behavior at a younger age. In other words, the kids who acted out as toddlers and preschoolers were more likely to act out later, whether they were spanked occasionally or never. Lots of spanking was bad for kids. A little didn't seem to matter.

Baumrind concluded that it is "*reliance* on physical punishment, not whether it is used at all, that is associated with harm to the child." The italics are mine. While

Baumrind's evidence undercuts the abolitionist position, it doesn't justify spanking as a regular punishment. In addition, Baumrind draws a telling distinction between "impulsive and reactive" spanking and punishments that require "some restraint and forethought." In my experience as a very occasional (once or twice) spanker, impulsivity was what hitting my kid was all about. I know that I'm supposed to spank my sons more in sorrow than in anger. But does that really describe most parents, especially occasional spankers, when they raise their hand to their children? More often, I think, we strike kids when we're mad—enraged, in fact. Baumrind's findings suggest that occasional spankers don't need to worry about this much. I hope she's right. But her numbers are small: Only three children in her study weren't spanked at all. That's a tiny control group.

Baumrind argues that if the social-science research doesn't support an outright ban on spanking, then we shouldn't fight over the occasional spank, because it diverts attention from the larger problems of serious abuse and neglect. "Professional advice that categorically rejects any and all use of a disciplinary practice favored and considered functional by parents is more likely to alienate than educate them," she argues. The extremely negative reaction to Lieber's proposed ban is her best proof.

It's always difficult and awkward—and arguably misguided—to use the law as a tool for changing attitudes. In the case of corporal punishment, though, I'm not sure we'd be crazy to try. A hard-and-fast rule like Sweden's would infuriate and frustrate some perfectly loving parents. It would also make it easier for police and prosecutors to go after the really bad ones. The state would have more power over parents. But then parents have near infinite amounts of power over their kids.

Reading the Genre

1. How does Bazelon look at the many arguments against a ban on spanking? How does she address these arguments with her own refutations and arguments for a ban? Do you think that she fairly considers counterarguments? See "Understand opposing claims and points of view" (p. 90) and "Anticipate objections" (p. 329).

2. Who are the key stakeholders in this debate—that is, whom does spanking directly affect, and who should care most about it? Make a list of people involved in this debate, and rank them in order of the impact that spanking has on their lives. How does Bazelon address these different stakeholders in the essay? Does she pay attention to the right people? How could identifying the stakeholders in an issue influence your own argumentative writing?

3. Bazelon uses hard evidence and other forms of research to support her arguments. Make an outline of her use of research: What kinds of research does she cite, what authority does it have, and how exactly does she use it to support her own claims? See "Assemble your hard evidence" (p. 99) "Creating a structure" (p. 229), Chapter 46, "Evaluating Sources" (p. 442), and Chapter 51, "Incorporating Sources into Your Work" (p. 463).

4. WRITING: Many people find it easy to criticize or second-guess parents. Write a short argument paper that makes a few suggestions to parents about how to best raise children. Keep in mind that your audience of parents might not want your advice, so write accordingly, considering possible counterarguments.

Further Reading

Bazelon, Emily. "Should Prostitution Be a Crime?" *New York Times*, 5 May 2016, www.nytimes.com/2016/05/08/magazine/should-prostitution-be-a-crime.html?rr ef=collection%2Fbyline%2Femily-bazelon&action=click&contentCollection=unde fined®ion=stream&module=stream_unit&version=latest&contentPlacement=24 &pgtype=collection. Accessed 20 Sept. 2017.

POLICY ARGUMENT   Daniel Engber writes a regular science column for *Slate.com* and has published articles in *Popular Mechanics, Popular Science, Salon.com*, and the *Chronicle of Higher Education*. A deliberately quirky writer, he has drawn on his graduate education in neuroscience to argue for distracting free-throw shooters at NBA games, for creating foolproof viral videos, and, in this article, for ending the backlash against obesity.

slate.com

Posted: Monday, October 5, 2009, at 6:02 PM ET
From: Daniel Engber

Glutton Intolerance: What If a War on Obesity Only Makes the Problem Worse?

"Current guidelines recommend that "overweight" and "obese" individuals lose weight through engaging in lifestyle modification involving diet, exercise, and other behavior change. Concern has arisen that this weight focus is not only ineffective at producing thinner, healthier bodies, but may also have unintended consequences, contributing to food and body preoccupation, repeated cycles of weight loss and regain, distraction from other personal health goals and wider health determinants, reduced self-esteem, eating disorders, other health decrement, and weight stigmatization and discrimination."

Just about every discussion of obesity and health care begins with the same purported fact: The diseases associated with excess weight are impoverishing the nation with $147 billion in unnecessary medical bills every year.

In my last column ("Give Us Your Tired, Your Poor, Your Big Fat Asses . . ."), I argued that obesity can also make us poor individually, since fat people face rampant discrimination on the job and marriage markets.

A recent paper from Yale's Rudd Center for Food Policy & Obesity hints at the scope of this anti-fat prejudice. We know, for example, that if you're fat, you make less money. Lots of studies have shown how body size plays out in the working world: According to one, women who are two standard deviations (or sixty-four pounds) overweight suffer a wage penalty of 9 percent; another found that severely obese white women lose out on one-quarter of their potential income. There's also evidence that obese women are less likely to attend college or maintain romantic relationships, even controlling for socioeconomic background. (One survey found that a few extra pounds could reduce a woman's chance of getting married by 20 percent.)

Heavy people may face discrimination in medical settings, too. The authors of the review, Rebecca Puhl and Chelsea Heuer, cite numerous surveys of anti-fat attitudes among health-care workers, who tend to see obese patients as ugly, lazy, weak-willed, and lacking in motivation to improve their health. Doctors describe treating fatties as a waste of time, and the staff at teaching hospitals appear to single them out for derogatory jokes. Unsurprisingly, many obese people avoid seeing their primary care providers altogether, and those who do are less likely to be screened for breast, cervical, and colorectal cancers. (That's true even among those with health insurance and college degrees.)

These data points suggest a rather simple approach to America's obesity problem: Stop hating. If we weren't such unrepentant body bigots, fat people might earn more money, stay in school, and receive better medical care in hospitals and doctors' offices. All that would go a long way toward mitigating the health effects of excess weight—and its putative costs. But there's an even better reason to think that America's glutton intolerance is a threat to public health and the federal budget. Recent epidemiological research implies that the shame of being obese poses its own medical risk. Mental anguish harms the body; weight stigma can break your heart.

The victims of chronic stress or depression, whatever their size, tend to maintain higher levels of certain inflammatory chemicals in their bloodstream. Under normal circumstances—and over the short term—these cytokines help to control the body's response to dangerous situations like injury or illness. The chemicals create their own problems, though, when they stick around too long. A sustained or elevated stress response seems to increase your risk of heart disease, hypertension, and diabetes. That may explain some of the relationships between health and wealth: Blood tests show unusual cytokine activity among those of low socioeconomic status as well as patients with post-traumatic stress and panic disorders.

It turns out that obese people have unusual cytokine readings, too, and these are often taken as the cause of weight-related illness. According to one theory, the presence of visceral fat cells can set off a biochemical chain reaction that leads to the inflammatory response. (Fat cells may even secrete the cytokines themselves.) As a result, someone who's fat and someone who's chronically stressed will be at risk for many of the same diseases.

It may be that obesity and stress are independent risk factors that happen to affect the body in similar ways. Or maybe chronic stress leads to weight gain, which in turn causes inflammation.

According to epidemiologist Peter Muennig, there's another pathway from excess weight to disease. In his 2008 paper "The Body Politic: The Relationship between Stigma and Obesity-Associated Disease," Muennig argues that the stress and shame of being fat causes those cytokine abnormalities. In other words, obesity makes you sick by stressing you out.

According to Muennig's theory, the health effects of obesity should vary with the intensity of anti-fat bias—the more abuse you take, the worse the disease. Women are more likely than men to have eating disorders, and they face greater weight-based discrimination in the overweight range. (According to Puhl, men get harsher treatment when they're really obese.) And, sure enough, women are seven times more likely to experience significant illness or death as a result of being overweight. (Obese women are especially vulnerable to clinical depression, which is itself a risk factor for cardiovascular disease.)

White people also appear to suffer disproportionately from weight-related illness, as compared with black people. According to Muennig, a black woman who's 5 feet 5 inches and less than sixty years old won't develop any weight-related risk of early death until she reaches 225 lbs. Meanwhile, a white woman of the same height and age group would hit the same threshold at 170 lbs. That fits with the idea that body-size norms differ among blacks and whites. (Black people also tend to be less susceptible to eating disorders and weight-based wage discrimination.)

There are some alternative explanations for these disparities. They might, for example, be an artifact of the crude way in which we measure obesity. Black people tend to have less abdominal fat (associated with cardiovascular disease) than white people given the same BMI reading, and women also tend to have more adipose tissue, and smaller waist-to-hip ratios, than men. But even the most accurate measures of fatness—like dual energy X-ray absorptiometry—don't really improve our ability to predict health outcomes across the population. It may be that the exact volume of adipose tissue in someone's body is less important than the way they look to others. (Muennig suggests that merely having "big bones" could be bad for your health.)

That's not to say obesity won't affect your body, independent of any social factors. As Muennig points out, obese lab rodents aren't likely to suffer much emotional abuse from their fellow mice, but they seem to have higher levels of pro-inflammatory cytokines nonetheless. Still, there's plenty of evidence that body-shape discrimination plays a role in human disease outcomes. Shortness, for example, is associated with an increased risk of coronary heart disease, diabetes, and early death—as well as lower wages and fewer long-term relationships. For some reason, though, the health effects of being short are worse for men than they are for women. Could it be that the social consequences of height and weight go in opposite directions?

If anti-fat bias can affect our bodies, then it's worth considering how an all-out war on obesity plays out in terms of public health. When we reach out to poor communities and educate them about the risks of being overweight, we are, in effect, exporting the weight stigma that happens to be most prevalent among rich, white people. Indeed, Rebecca Puhl says the reported prevalence of weight discrimination has increased by two-thirds since the mid-1990s, while media coverage of the "obesity epidemic" has quintupled over roughly the same interval. (Meanwhile, the U.S. diet industry has just about doubled its annual revenues—to nearly $60 billion.)

We've worked hard to frame excess weight as a major health risk and a drain on the economy. The motivation is generous enough: Anti-obesity rhetoric encourages people to eat less and exercise more. But what if it also encourages discrimination? If that's the case, a war on obesity would come at a significant cost to the fattest Americans—in terms of lower wages, less education, and more stress-related illness.

Fat activists argue that the risks of such a policy far outweigh its potential benefits. (They say that doctors should encourage healthy lifestyles instead of trying to enforce an ideal body size.)

But few mainstream public-health advocates take such claims seriously. They point out that many interventions in poor communities focus on diet and exercise rather than weight per se. If BMI is used as a measure of success in these programs, that's because it's a quick way to see whether people really are pursuing a healthy lifestyle. For Kelly Brownell, director of the Rudd Center and a leading researcher on both health policy and weight bias, the dangers of discrimination are important but relatively modest. What about the idea that targeting obesity might be counterproductive for the fattest Americans? He doesn't buy it.

The fact is, very few researchers have tried to measure the combined health effects of anti-fat prejudice. Nor have legislators spent much effort on the social consequences of weight stigma. Only a handful of cities—Washington, D.C.; San Francisco; and Santa Cruz, Calif.—have passed laws to protect the rights of obese people, and there's only one state—Michigan — that forbids employers from discriminating on the basis of body size. If you're victimized for being fat anywhere else in the United States, good luck. You can sue your employer under the Americans with Disabilities Act, but you'll have to prove that your weight condition is something like being wheelchair-bound or mentally retarded—not such a good way to reduce weight stigma overall.

Given the risks associated with weight stigma, we should at least reconsider our tendency to blame obesity for the country's health crisis. (I suggested last week that we could target poverty instead.) If obesity prevention measures do end up in the health bill, let's make sure they'll do more good than harm. The Rudd Center has called for a new federal ban on weight discrimination or an expansion of the Civil Rights Act. Both would go a long way toward protecting the two-thirds of all Americans who are classified as overweight or obese.

Reading the Genre

1. Engber opens his argument with an overview of recent scientific research on the costs of obesity and then startles readers with his thesis—"Stop hating"—in the fifth paragraph. Reread the article and locate other instances when Engber switches between academic and conversational style. How does he want his audience to respond when he makes these shifts in style? See Chapter 33, "Levels of Style" (p. 366).

2. Find Engber's restatement of his thesis in the last paragraph. How does the thesis change between Engber's introduction and his conclusion? See Chapter 27, "Shaping A Thesis" (p. 333).

3. Engber tests the logic of several theories, offers a range of possible causes for obesity, and considers the effects of being obese on individuals and on society. What do these causal analyses contribute to his argument? See Chapter 13, "Literary Analyses" (p. 169).

4. Engber's article is thoroughly researched. Choose a few of the sources he names in his text, find them online or through your library's databases, and create a list of works cited in MLA style or a references list in APA style. See Chapter 53, "MLA Documentation and Format" (p. 470) and Chapter 54, "APA Documentation and Format" (p. 536.)

5. **WRITING:** Visit the Yale Rudd Center on Food Policy's "Hot Topics" Web page (www.yaleruddcenter.org/hot_topics.aspx) and select a food policy issue that interests you. Read five to ten of the articles and studies about this issue linked on the page, and then write an argumentative essay on your topic. Be sure to have a clearly expressed thesis and to document your sources as appropriate.

Further Reading

Bacon, Linda, and Lucy Aphramor. "Weight science: evaluating the evidence for a paradigm shift." *Nutrition Journal* 10.1 (2011): 9.

62 Evaluations: Readings

GENRE MOVES Evaluation

NAOMI KLEIN
From *No Logo*

The most sophisticated culture jams are not stand-alone ad parodies but interceptions; counter-messages that hack into a corporation's own method of communication to send a message starkly at odds with the one that was intended. The process forces the company to foot the bill for its own subversion, either literally because the company is the one that paid for the billboard, or figuratively because anytime people mess with a logo, they are tapping into the vast resources spent to make that logo meaningful. Kalle Lasn, editor of Vancouver-based *Adbusters* magazine, uses the martial art of jujitsu as a precise metaphor to explain the mechanics of the jam: "In one simple deft move you slap the giant on its back. We use the momentum of the enemy." It's an image borrowed from Saul Alinsky, who, in his activist bible, *Rules for Radicals*, defines "mass political jujitsu" as "utilizing the power of one part of the power structure against another part[;] ... the superior strength of the Haves become their own undoing."

Establish your own criteria by borrowing from others.

For any evaluation, a key task is to clearly establish the criteria you will use to evaluate. What makes the act or object that you are evaluating good or bad? How can it be fairly measured against other similar acts or objects? In "Culture Jamming," a chapter from her book *No Logo*, Naomi Klein lays out her own criteria: The best culture jams "intercept" and "hack." But then she uses ideas from Lasn and Alinsky to expand on these criteria by relating the best culture jams to jujitsu in terms of their deft maneuvers against powerful enemies. Expanding her criteria allows her, later in the chapter, to evaluate other groups' culture jams with a precise, critical eye. Her criteria are clear, but they are also supported by the criteria of other experts.

As you develop criteria for evaluation in your own essay, look at how other experts have evaluated your object or objects like it. You can borrow some of their criteria and justifications to support your own. Or you can disagree with these experts, especially if their criteria show a bias or are based on unrealistic expectations. Don't be afraid to borrow and modify ideas from others, even as you develop your own unique evaluation. Just be sure to cite properly, as Klein does.

TELEVISION REVIEW   Emily Nussbaum writes about culture for *The New Yorker*. Nussbaum is quickly becoming one of the most influential voices discussing the roles and representations of gender on TV. This article, published in April 2013, focuses on subgenres of cooking shows and gives readers a glimpse of Nussbaum's critical thinking.

To Stir, with Love

The Modern Cooking Show, from Hell's Kitchen *to* Barefoot Contessa

EMILY NUSSBAUM

In 1968, Nora Ephron wrote a tart exposé of New York's backbiting food establishment; at the end, she asked its members if haute cuisine would survive. "Of course it will last," Poppy Cannon argued. "Just in the way sculpture will last." Nika Hazelton disagreed, sighing that "the old cuisine is gone for good and dying out." She predicted, "Ultimately, cooking will be like an indoor sport, just like making lace and handiwork."

The late sixties are not generally considered an age of innocence, but there you go. Neither Cannon nor Hazelton, nor Ephron herself, envisioned anything like today's gladiatorial, whirligig culinary culture, which has expanded far beyond the salons of the Upper East Side. Instead of a few competing cookbooks and restaurants, we have *Lucky Peach* and Chowhound and *Iron Chef*, not to mention Sandra Lee on YouTube making a baked potato out of ice cream, rolling it in cocoa powder, and garnishing it with "chives" (pistachios dyed deep green). Culinary taste now indicates not merely economic class but morality and environmental chic as well. Across the globe, celebrity chefs clash, like clans in *Game of Thrones*. Yet, even as whole channels of food programming have emerged, I've been a conscientious objector (or maybe a deserter). Unlike Ephron, I'm a subsistence cook at best: My specialty is a Turkish spinach-lentil soup from the cookbook *Sundays at Moosewood Restaurant* which I haven't actually prepared in three years.

Among the many options, two TV genres dominate: the traditional "stand-and-stir," popularized by Julia Child, and the reality competition, spearheaded by *Iron Chef*. They suggest opposing food philosophies. Julia Child took an occult discipline, once reserved for men in tall hats, and made it accessible to all. Her show implied that food might, in fact, be easier than you ever imagined—and that cooking itself was no big deal. The reality show begs to differ. In these chef-versus-chef contests, food is a perpetual emergency. Every single contestant might, under more ordinary circumstances, be an excellent cook, capable of hosting relaxed weekly dinner parties. But, when they are faced with a rasher of kelp plus extra-virgin honey and a ticking timer, even the production of appetizers becomes something out of *24*.

Given my own culinary ineptitude, it might have been wiser to start in the welcoming bosom of Nigella Lawson. Instead, I walked straight into the wood-fired oven: the gleeful dystopia of Gordon Ramsay's *Hell's Kitchen*. Filmed in a Los Angeles soundstage-restaurant, the show has aired for eleven seasons and spawned several spinoffs, also Inferno-themed. In this iteration (Ramsay is apparently much nicer on *MasterChef*), the chef is a Scottish-accented Heat Miser, with forehead furrows that deepen into canyons when he screams. On *Hell's Kitchen*, he screams a lot, when not delivering Schwarzeneggerian wisecracks like "Did you throw up on this plate?" One contestant gets booted each week; the grand prize this season is a job in Ramsay's employ, which seems like a mixed blessing. The drama is (as the participants point out with regularity) *intense*, with challenges such as extracting the meat from as many lobsters as possible in ten minutes. Praise is doled out in scraps, like liver pâté tossed to mongrels.

For all I know, this is actually a reasonable approximation of restaurant life, with a closer resemblance to the brutality of Orwell's *Down and Out in Paris and London* than to Bravo's likable, globe-trotting *Top Chef*, on which Padma Lakshmi might smile at your pasta. It's loud and it's ugly, but it's also refreshing to come across participants who are not telegenic Hollywood types, let alone celebrity chefs: Instead, they're fat and sweaty, male and female, line cooks and small-time chefs, from a wide range of backgrounds—ordinary mugs hoping for their big break. A few might be ringers, and it's hard not to suspect that some of the competition is rigged, but who cares? Food is pain, Princess.

Still, I learned almost nothing about cooking, other than that it's a bad idea to set asparagus on fire and that you must scream "Yes, Chef!" at your boss—a fact I already knew from *Treme*. For more depth, I checked out *Chopped*, on the Food Network. The formula here is as strict as a sonnet: Four contestants open mystery baskets, find four ingredients, and improvise dishes on deadline.

A typical basket featured rack of antelope, stinging nettles, jicama, and portwine cheese; the results included a luscious-looking Peruvian spiced antelope with polenta. Ted Allen, who made his name on *Queer Eye for the Straight Guy*, oversees the festivities. "I know the jicama wants to be a salsa," one contestant says—and then there's a knife accident. "That will definitely disqualify him," a judge observes. "If there's blood on the plates." That's as frightening as things get. Soothing in its repetitions, the show has the reliable charm of *Law & Order: Seared-Veal Unit*.

These shows—and other old reliables like *Iron Chef America*, currently in its eleventh season—are primarily about restaurant life. They concern the fantasies and fears of working in a professional kitchen, as the underling of a person with a tremendous ego, which you hope someday to replace with your own. Like much of TV drama, they glamorize workaholism and on the better shows the gimmickry is half the appeal: If you can survive this obstacle course, no regular kitchen can defeat you. In contrast, the modern stand-and-stir is more about the dream of an idyllic home kitchen, with everything in its place and nothing burning. As a result, these shows tend to be as static as network news: There's a kitchen, there's a person, there are ingredients pre-prepped in bowls, and, often, a significant amount of purring while things sizzle. (You might imagine there is nothing more wholesome than a cooking show, but in my survey there were as many double-entendres as on *Archer*.)

A few shows do try to expand the genre's visual rhetoric, including the food-science series *Good Eats*, hosted by Alton Brown, which is no longer producing new episodes but is still on the air. Unlike the preening celebrity chefs, Brown is all shop-class enthusiasm and dorky competence. His show focuses on one food per episode, and it features quick-cut editing and puns, reminding me a bit of *Blue's Clues*. In one session, Brown bought some beef, defattified it, and then butterflied it, all while juggling props. He delivered an abstruse explanation of "reticulum" and "elastin" which I didn't quite catch, although I did absorb the fact that steaks should be at room temperature when cooking begins. Also that peppercorns were used as currency in the Middle Ages. By the final sequence, when Brown tore into some steak au poivre, I found myself wishing I could join him—the sign of success for any such show.

I cannot advise you on whose cooking tips are the most reliable, but then these shows are often more about the fantasy of one's perfect life. Which would you prefer: down-home southern cooking for the in-laws or dinners for ten elderly men from the U.N.? Of the fancier options, the one that drew me in most was *Barefoot Contessa*, which is set in East Hampton, a luxurious Narnia in which guests are due for cocktails in the new library. Despite the posh milieu, the Contessa, Ina Garten, seems down-to-earth and perpetually amused. She knows just how to handle fennel and zest. After twenty minutes, I gave in—and began to follow directions. "Fresh figs I save for eating just the way they are," she confided. I got on FreshDirect and ordered figs. "I love things that you can just assemble," she cooed. Nigella Lawson may be the planet's most sensuous food celebrity (and the woman does have a way with phrases like "sticky bits of caramelized scallop juice"), but the Contessa was clearly my soul mate.

You'll have to find your own, though. After hours of flipping between the Food Network and PBS, I was forced to admit the truth: I was never going to be able to tell a cassoulet from a cassava. The shows didn't bore me, exactly: As with sports, it can be fun to look at athletes, even if you can't throw a ball. But while I'd like to announce that my brief immersion inspired me to raise my game, the truth is I mostly learned that watching food TV makes me ravenous. So I ordered in.

Reading the Genre

1. Following the two main genres of cooking shows suggested by Nussbaum, list as many "stand-and-stir" and as many "reality competition" shows as you can. Can you also come up with any other genres of cooking shows that Nussbaum has neglected? For Nussbaum's two genres, and for any genres you can identify yourself, list as many rules or conventions as you can that define these types of shows. (For more on understanding genres, see the Introduction, p. 12.)

2. Nussbaum uses vivid similes and metaphors in her evaluation. Find as many metaphors and similes as you can, and think about what they each add to this essay. What work can figurative language do for an author trying to capture a visual medium like television in a written essay?

3. Throughout the essay, Nussbaum alludes to the economics of cooking shows: Stand-and-stir shows are set in idealized kitchens; winners get jobs; the contestants are line cooks looking for a "big break." How could you respond to Nussbaum's article by further exploring the economics that food shows reveal? Consider the costs of eating out or preparing food, about the underpaid labor of those who cook, serve, and clean at restaurants, and other economic questions.

4. WRITING: Write your own evaluation of a television show, paying attention to how it fits into a popular "genre" or type of television show. How does the show follow specific genre rules, how does it break them, and what is the intended impact on the audience? Are there any genre rules that the show has created and other shows now follow?

5. MULTIMODALITY—STILL IMAGE ANALYSIS: Nussbaum writes about the "visual rhetoric" of these cooking shows—the dominant settings, camera shots, and images. Choose one cooking show to watch, and look for opportunities to pause the video (whether on television or online) in a key moment of "visual rhetoric." Choose just one still, describe it in detail, and evaluate what this one visual moment can teach us about the show. (See "Present evaluations visually," p. 135.)

EVALUATION   Mark Yakich is a creative writer and a professor of creative writing. As you'll see in this essay, Yakich is able to find poetry wherever he looks. This essay comes from a series in *The Atlantic* magazine called "Object Lessons"—short articles focused on the secret lives of ordinary things.

The Football Play

from Object Lessons

MARK YAKICH

"Put that to music," intoned NBC analyst Chris Collinsworth, after wide receiver Odell Beckham Jr.'s one-handed catch for a touchdown last November. Video of the play went viral, and soon fans young and old tried to emulate Beckham's ballet-like catch in playgrounds and backyards everywhere.

It was a beautiful feat. A dazzling one. Some called it poetic. And although it has been heralded as a one-of-a-kind catch, it joins a list of other one-of-a-kind catches and all-time great plays collected on highlight reels. But besides oohing and aahing over such moments, what more is there to say?

As a literature professor, I find myself watching football in poetic terms.

And by that, I don't mean generalized notions of "beauty" or "grace under pressure." The enjoyment I find in a poem is in the words, sounds, and structures that repeat, connect, or hang together in specific ways—its patterns—and especially in those moments that deviate and surprise—its variations. For me, football is most beautiful in the interplay of such pattern and variation.

Take the back-shoulder throw that many quarterbacks have now mastered. The quarterback throws the ball to the receiver's "back" or "outside" shoulder—usually before the receiver (and the defender) has turned around to see it. It's a modification of the in-stride, over-the-shoulder pass, and it's extremely difficult to defend. The poetry of this play is found in its timing variation, not in its elegance. In its innovation on an established pattern.

On any given Sunday, you will hear commentators allude to variation. The quarterback "reads" the defense, sets up in the "read-option," or recognizes a "hot read." These "reads" are all about identifying formations (patterns) and using options (variations) to defeat the defense's expectation. Likewise, defenses show different "looks" and make modifications often at the last second before the ball is snapped.

One hallmark of a great quarterback is his ability to audible: to modify verbally the set-play at the line. Conventional thinking says that an audible is beautiful when the variation results in a successful play. But even if the play fails, I often find beauty in the language of the audible. In Peyton Manning's "Omaha, Omaha, Omaha" or "Bags Montana Fat Man," where the "poetry" lies in strange variation where one doesn't expect it.

So back to Beckham Jr. The beauty of the play comes from its high degree of variation: to catch a 43-yard pass at the goal line, after being fouled, bent over backwards, with only two fingers and a thumb. It's unexpected and stunning. And then: it's a new pattern in your mind, for watching the next game.

Al Bello/Getty Images

Reading the Genre

1. When this essay was originally published, it was accompanied with video of Beckham's tremendous catch. But how does Yakich write this essay so that we can understand the catch *without* seeing it? How does he craft the essay for people who don't know football very well? (See "Write for novices," p. 127).

2. In this essay about football, Yakich never specifically tells us what the score was in the game, who won, any of Beckham's stats, or even who threw him the ball. These details form the standard criteria for both description and evaluation of sports. So, what criteria does Yakich create to actually evaluate the play? Does he effectively convince his readers that these plays are important? (See "Decide on your criteria," p. 128.)

3. The metaphorical connection between football and poetry is essential to Yakich's evaluation. What are some other metaphors that often get used to describe sports? Do you think Yakich's metaphor is original enough? Do you think he establishes the metaphorical connections effectively enough?

4. WRITING: Create your own "Object Lesson" by writing an evaluation of a simple, small, everyday thing—something that you could surprise your reader by evaluating, because the reader may not have ever thought to appreciate it. The key is to look for an object that you can prove has poetry, romance, intrigue, true utility, or art in it, and thus is worth a second look.

5. MULTIMODALITY—COLOR COMMENTARY: Yakich begins the essay by quoting Chris Collinsworth, who was the color commentator on the television broadcast when Beckham made his catch. Color commentary is, in fact, a sort of real-time explanation and evaluation of sporting events. Try listening to a color commentary of a sporting event, or to movie or music reviews delivered on the radio, on a station like NPR. How do the evaluators alter their tone and style to fit the time limits and other constraints of this medium? Try to compose and deliver your own evaluation following these conventions. This activity can easily be adapted for students with disabilities using ASL or text-to-voice software.

Further Reading

Elcombe, Tim L. "Sport, Aesthetic Experience, and Art as the Ideal Embodied Metaphor." *Journal of the Philosophy of Sport* 39.2 (2012): 201–217.

GAME EVALUATION   Marcel O'Gorman is an English professor at the University of Waterloo. He is the creator of his own "DIY" phone-locking case, The Resistor (resistorcase.org). But here, he reviews a series of other approaches to phone-locking, including the Yondr (overyondr.com), and places this within a long history of resisting technology.

The Case for Locking Up Your Smartphone

from **The Atlantic**

MARCEL O'GORMAN

If abstinence from alcohol originated in Protestant England, maybe abstinence from digital devices will come from Catholic France. The country has recently rolled out a new labor law called the "right to disconnect," and following a campaign promise made by President Emmanuel Macron, the French Ministry of Education plans to ban the use of smartphones in all of its public schools.* Philippe Vincent, a member of the French head teachers' union, has estimated that it would take about 3 million lockers to keep cell phones out of the hands of wired écoliers.

Lockers seem to be the smartphone prophylactic of choice for French ministers who must attend meetings sans portable, but for school students, the ensuing nomophobia—the fear of being without your smartphone—might be enough to provoke a revolution.

The policy shows how humans are struggling to adapt to the most captivating prosthesis they have ever invented. And France's plans exemplify a digital temperance movement that might yet become widespread. In fact, it is already well underway—and with promising results.

* * *

France isn't the first killjoy to quit the smartphone party. In 2015, the Canadian artist Garnet Hertz invented a cheeky device called "Phonesafe," a masochistic lockbox designed to incarcerate smartphones for

"If you attend a Guns n' Roses concert or a comedy performance by Dave Chappelle, ushers will require you to lock your device in a neoprene pouch and take it into the show in that state."

a set period of time. Hertz meant Phonesafe as a provocation, but the same idea quickly became a product. Today, you can buy similar, but mass-produced, containers on Amazon, and multi-phone lockers have become a mainstay in corporate offices and schools around the world. A McDonald's in Singapore has even installed a locker designed to promote "family togetherness" and face-to-face conversation.

The phone-locking pouch, made by a San Francisco company called Yondr, has a wide opening at the short end for inserting a smartphone. A magnetic locking mechanism, similar to those on antitheft tags in retail stores, engages to hold it closed. After the show, this clasp is swiped across a counter-magnet, which releases the lock. Yondr is a surefire way to cut down on bootleg YouTube videos.

In *Wired*, Alice Gregory recently took a tough look at the device. Gregory recounts her experience at a Chris Rock performance, where audience members waiting in the lobby had to forgo smartphone usage. The affair reduced them to "a roomful of jonesing fiends," as she puts it. Ultimately, Gregory connects Yondr to a thorny question about civil liberties: the right of the people to keep and bear smartphones.

It's an ironic conclusion, because Yondr is sold as a tool to provide freedom, rather than to take it away. To "Be Here Now," as the company's tagline puts it. It's a promise to deliver presence—a tricky calling, to say the least. Presence has a long history in religion and philosophy, from Buddhist practices to the metaphysics of the 20th-century philosopher Martin Heidegger. Today, presence is most common in the various mindfulness trends that have overtaken individual and corporate life, in Silicon Valley in particular—collectively the critic R. John Williams has called them "technê-zen."

Cutting through the history and the rhetoric, it's productive to think about presence in terms of attention. You're present where you focus your attention—and you only have so much attention to pay. In the case of Chris Rock, he wants attention directed toward him, live on stage. Rock's show might involve awkward improvisation or new material that he doesn't want circulated online. Teachers are less concerned about copyright than comedians are, but they still demand attention.

I have tested Yondr's effects on mind-wandering in classroom experiments with Dan Smilek of the University of Waterloo Vision and Attention Lab. Our research is based in part on the assumption that instructors want students to focus on the course materials, and not on Instagram, Facebook, or other distractions. Yondr can be a remarkably effective tool for enforcing digital abstinence in these contexts, thanks primarily to its portability. Rather than locking away devices inside lockers, or even inside a disused Catholic tabernacle, as I have done in a performance piece, Yondr buffers the anxiety of being isolated from your device.

Graham Dugoni, the inventor of the Yondr, holds up the device.

Given that the mere presence of one's smartphone can reduce cognitive capacity, Yondr offers a way to surf between the waves of a device's presence and absence. You can hold it, but you can't use it. This might be an especially important balance in classroom situations, where students see a teacher's "phone shoebox" as an unwelcome imposition of authority.

* * *

Needless to say, Yondr is still an imposition. And controlling attention requires more than just locking a device in a binge-breaking neoprene pouch. Joelle Renstrom has reported the results of her own Yondr experiment in a class at Boston University, where she had her 30 students lock away their devices over the course of a semester. At first, 37 percent of the students found the policy annoying, but by the end of the term that figure had dropped to 14 percent.

Those are promising, if tentative, results, but Renstrom's anecdotal comments about the experiment may be more instructive than the data she collected. Renstrom describes her students' initial experience of Yondr as "akin to caging a pet, a clear denial of freedom." Moreover, she observes that some students left their cases unlocked as a sign of rebellion, even though they didn't remove the phones from them.

Rather than becoming "active resistors to technology," as the scholars Christine Satchell and Paul Dourish call people who choose to ignore their devices, Yondr users are ultimately the victims of technological disenfranchisement. When implemented as a mandatory smartphone prophylactic, Yondr becomes a means of control, not of choice, let alone of presence.

Such top-down tactics might be enforced easily at live performances, as one of my research assistants observed firsthand at a Chris Rock show in Niagara Falls. However, as a daily ritual for high-school students, all-or-nothing digital abstinence enforced by an authority figure seems destined to backfire, possibly leading to rejection—or even worse, a legal complaint.

In an attempt to tackle this disciplinary problem, I have been offering workshops to schoolteachers that riff on and revise the design Yondr originated. In the workshops, I provide a kit that allows students to make their own digital abstinence case, but with an obnoxiously loud Velcro enclosure rather than a silent, magnetic clasp. This semipermeable design—the Resistor Case, I call it— is intended to promote self-regulation, not authoritarian control. The Velcro acts as a gateway to conscience: It provides just enough resistance and noise to make its owner think twice before opening it.

Michael I. Norton, Daniel Mochon, and Dan Ariely coined the "IKEA effect" to name the increase in value people assign to self-made products. With the Resistor Case, I'm counting on a similar effect, that students who fist construct and then choose to make use of their DIY phone-lockers might be more compelled to use them. Of course, the kit will only work if the teacher provides a context for it that includes a discussion of responsible smartphone use. (The kit provides a series of cards to prompt this conversation.)

When I teach these workshops, I introduce students to the French translation of paying attention: faire attention, or "making" attention. It suggests that attention is not something to be bought or sold, but something to craft. This is a concept that could benefit anyone who considers adjusting school, work, or entertainment plans to accommodate the supposedly shorter attention spans of digital life.

* * *

Admittedly, Resistor Case is still a type of "cell-phone straitjacket," as the writer David Sax has labeled Yondr. But other designs that promote attention-crafting digital rituals are also possible. The Sabbath Manifesto group, for example, offers a bondage-free cellphone sleeping bag that can be used during "digital Sabbaths" or on the National Day of Unplugging. One of my students designed a fashion-forward digital chastity belt that would deliver a shock to the crotch when the phone was removed from its holder. Maybe eventually Kate Spade or Hermès will offer a fashion-forward digital-abstinence clutch.

No matter the design, if the technology-addled are going to abstain from their devices, they need to think beyond cognitive behavior and toward bodies and physical actions. More than a millennium and a half ago, Saint Augustine said of the carnal urges, "No one can use them wisely, unless he or she also is able to refrain from using them." To support temperance, successful digital abstinence requires users to develop new rituals for their devices, rituals that go beyond the ones endorsed by the technology companies that provide these devices.

The effectiveness of a phone locker, portable or not, hinges on the repeated habits it can promote. It might be difficult to imagine a future where digital-abstinence products are recognized as emblems of moral fortitude (let alone as something cool) rather than as artistic provocations or as thieves of personal liberty. But I'm willing to make a case for it.

Reading the Genre

1. While this essay presents itself as a review, it contains elements of a report or even an argument. The title itself uses a pun ("the case") to show that it will both make an argumentative case and review (telephone-locking) cases. Go through the essay and highlight the sections that evaluate the technologies, the sections that report on developments in smartphone-locking more broadly, and the sections that feel argumentative. How do the sections work together? How would you classify the essay overall? See Chapter 8, "Reports" (p. 38); Chapter 10, "Arguments" (p. 119); and Chapter 11, "Evaluations" (p. 120).

2. O'Gorman comes across as incredibly knowledgeable about the scientific research around attention and smartphone use; but he also seems to understand the issue philosophically. How does he make a case for locking smartphones by citing cognitive research *and* philosophy? How do these comparisons help to establish his authority or *ethos*? (See "Compare and contrast," p. 132 and "Consider and control your ethos," p. 97.)

3. O'Gorman suggests that, in fact, smartphone locking will only really work if users have ways to control and adapt the processes themselves. What are the current rules you have for yourself around smartphone use? Do you always follow them?

4. **WRITING:** For one day, each time you use your phone, record the "feelings" and emotions that you identify with that use. This can be recorded on a chart. At the end of the day, look back on this record of use, and the emotions that you have associated with different uses of your phone, and write a short self-evaluation: How would you like to change the ways you *feel* about this technology?

Further Reading

Gregory, Alice. "This Company Wants to Neutralize Your Phone—and Un-Change the World." *Wired*.

PRODUCT REVIEW   Heather Radke creates written and audio essays on a wide variety of topics, and her work has been featured in dozens of publications. This essay was published in *The Paris Review*. The JUMPSUIT project that she highlights in this review has since been featured at the Museum of Modern Art in New York. You can buy your own jumpsuit for $199.99 from their website, or download a pattern for free and make your own.

HEATHER RADKE

The Jumpsuit That Will Replace all Clothing Forever

It's fifty degrees in January, and the air in the Garment District smells strangely of pea soup. The building I've been directed to is supposed to be an art gallery, but all I can find is an office-supply showroom. I wait outside on a street dotted with FedEx trucks, Pret A Mangers, and fabric stores selling colorful sequined silks and heavy white brocades—the expensive material of saris and wedding dresses. In the early twentieth century, when New York City was still the center of the American garment industry, this neighborhood housed sewing factories where Eastern European immigrants made the petticoats and shirtwaists sold on Fifth Avenue. Most multinational fashion brands have since moved their operations overseas, and the sewing work that is still done in the Garment District is usually completed by newly graduated FIT students working as interns, not by members of the International Ladies' Garment Workers' Union.

I'm here to meet Abigail Glaum-Lathbury, who will give me a jumpsuit she made just for me that I will wear as

Lara Kastner

my only article of clothing for the next three weeks. Abigail is one of two artists who comprise the Rational Dress Society, a collective committed to what the group calls "counter-fashion"—a critique of fashion and capitalism through political dress. Abigail and her partner in counter-fashion, Maura Brewer, have been wearing only jumpsuits for the past three years—to weddings, to job interviews, to teach their classes at art school, and to visit their families over Thanksgiving. Their closets are nearly empty: they each have three jumpsuits, a few jumpsuit-compatible sweaters, workout clothes, pajamas, and underthings—that's it. They don't have to buy new clothes or wonder how they'll look in the culottes that have recently come into fashion. They never have to choose a new outfit because they've already picked the one they'll wear forever.

My phone buzzes. It's Abigail, telling me she's running late, asking if I want a coffee, and explaining to me that the gallery is not, in fact, in the office-supply showroom but on the third floor of an adjacent building. I make my way upstairs to a room full of wires, hardware, half-installed clothes racks, and unpacked boxes. Although Maura and Abigail's primary project is JUMPSUIT, the Rational Dress Society is an art practice whose components are varied. The gallery's current show, "Omega Workshop," highlights other artists working in counter-fashion, including an LA collective who designs dayglow sparkle clothes for queer-crip bodies, an artist who deconstructed and redesigned a high-heel shoe, and the artist Frau Fiber, who will lead a DIY workshop on how to sew a Soviet hippie poncho. Abigail and Maura are also working on a project called "Make America Rational Again"—they are collecting "gently used and emphatically discarded" Ivanka Trump–label clothing to melt down into a polyester slurry, which they will transform into millennial-pink jumpsuits.

The politics of consumer choice are at the heart of the Rational Dress Society's ideology. By making a single choice and sticking to it, Maura and Abigail are attempting to draw attention to the way that democracy and choice have become conflated under capitalism. Although it may seem as if we have endless choices of what to wear, as if our ability to choose is part of what makes us free, we really only have the choices that the market makes available to us. We can wear a tube top from

Hot Topic or a baggy tunic from Eileen Fischer, but we must buy new things, and we must buy more. Abigail and Maura hope that their project will help us see the choices that have been shoved outside of our field of vision: to mend the clothes we have, to halt consumption, and perhaps to opt out of capitalism entirely.

The Rational Dress Society looks to both the future and the past. Their name is borrowed from the Victorian reform movement that, in an era of bustles and corsets, advocated for pants and other "rational dress." Yet the garment they are promoting is emblematic of science fiction. A portion of the proceeds of all their work will go toward the purchase of a full-page ad in *Vogue*. The ad isn't intended to sell more jumpsuits; Abigail and Maura don't want to replace one consumer product with another. Once the ad is paid for, the project will close up shop.

The Rational Dress Society makes jumpsuits in two hundred forty-eight sizes culled from NASA data to fit almost any body type. Anyone can print the pattern for free from their website or, for a hundred and fifty dollars, order one that will arrive ready-made out of sustainable fabric and hand sewn by well-paid seamstresses. The design was inspired by patterns for work wear, and the finished garment looks like painters' coveralls. But on the bodies of Maura and Abigail, both hip art-school grads with fashionable glasses and haircuts, the jumpsuits look simply chic, as though there is nothing more sensible or cool a person could wear.

I have never looked simply chic—for me, fashion has always been a chore. I can't quite keep up with the churn of the seasons, and if I get rid of clothes before they are threadbare, I am racked with thrifty guilt. I believe in the power of dress to communicate something to the world; it is in many ways the first thing we say about ourselves, the threshold between our private and public lives. But the messages available to me have always felt predetermined, the choices hollow. So the promise of Abigail and Maura's jumpsuit appealed. My message would be provided not by corporate America but by two artists. The message would be a rebuke to the system that had long brought me frustration and shame.

*

Abigail arrives at the gallery in a smiley flurry—she is perpetually cheerful and excited. She is wearing a white jumpsuit and black glasses with saucer-size lenses and carrying a tray of coffees. She points me toward an enormous duffel bag on the floor, full of jumpsuits, and then pulls out mine—a perfectly folded denim rectangle.

That night, I pull my jumpsuit out of my bag with excitement and slip it on. It fits oddly—too long in the crotch and too loose in the legs. My small waist, the part of me about which I am most vain, is obscured by a swath of dark-blue denim that falls straight from my shoulders to my hips. Nothing cinches my middle, and I feel fat. I will learn later that this style is called a "drop waist" and was popularized by flappers in the twenties, women whose ideal body was straight and androgynous—two adjectives that definitely do not describe my figure.

I pull the jumpsuit down so that the bodice is taut, but then the crotch is low—nearly down to my knees. I take another tack and pull the jumpsuit up so that the waistband is at my natural waist, and a poof of fabric emerges at my chest. I look in the mirror and see a figure I don't quite recognize—I look unfeminine and the wrong size, bulky and overstuffed. But this garment had been made to my exact measurements. I had imagined it fitting my body perfectly, flattering my figure and making me look magically thinner, stronger, better. Had I been given the wrong one? The problem with subverting the tyranny of choice is that you arrive at sameness, and bodies are not the same. Even with two hundred forty-eight sizes, there aren't enough for the body I have.

*

Maura and Abigail have invited me to watch a sewing workshop they are running the next day at MOMA, where they would teach fifteen strangers how to turn several yards of fabric into a sleeve and a bodice. I show up in my normal clothes, but my jumpsuit is wadded in my bag.

The museum has set up six sewing machines on large gray tables, which are arranged in a semicircle in an open space between galleries. The group is almost all youngish white women, with the exception of a man in his late twenties with a scruffy beard and curly brown hair pulled back in a ponytail. One woman is wearing a hijab; another is wearing a non–Rational Dress jumpsuit. Several older women are wandering around wearing white sashes with RATIONAL DRESS printed in bold black sans-serif type—expert seamstresses here to help the novices thread bobbins and cut out patterns. One of them, Joann, tells me that when she read the email from MOMA about the program, she called the front desk to make sure it wasn't a hoax. The notice had mentioned the Rational Dress Society's anti-Trump project, and she couldn't believe the museum would do something so overtly political.

The sound of a triangle rings, and Maura steps up to a microphone. Maura and Abigail are, of course, both wearing jumpsuits—white ones this time. Maura wears red, white, and blue Converse; Abigail, sensible black boots.

"I'm comrade Maura."

"I'm comrade Abigail. Together, we make JUMPSUIT, the open-source, ungendered monogarment to replace all clothes in perpetuity."

"All of you will be able to go home, and based on the information you receive here, combined with additional guidance from our online instructional video, you will be able to sew your own jumpsuit from beginning to end. After you have completed your monogarment, we invite you to throw away all of your clothes," Maura says.

The women go back and forth describing the rationale of their project, a speech they've clearly memorized from a script. It's a performance, but it's also a workshop. It's art, but it's also a sewing lesson. H&M, they tell us, purposefully designs their clothes to fall apart after ten washings. And in their Cambodian factories, the workers don't have sick leave. They are discriminated against for being pregnant, they are fainting en masse, and they are very often children. The politics Abigail and Maura describe are of radical consumer choice. By making a choice not to buy any clothes at all, to instead wear a long-lasting garment that can be repaired, the jumpsuit wearer is not participating in a boycott—they are rejecting the underlying system that caused the need for the boycott in the first place.

Abigail and Maura finish their speech, ring the triangle again, and the sewing begins. Maura puts on the Rational Dress Society playlist, which includes songs about worker solidarity, revolution, and jumping. Abigail walks everyone through the first stage of the process—cutting out the pattern for the sleeves. She peppers her descriptions with technical language: seam allowance, control notches, belt-loop positioning, drill holes, selvage edge. These are the words that she uses in her every-day life as a teacher in the fashion department at the School of the Art Institute of Chicago, and she delights in teaching them to the group.

"I don't like choices," the bearded man, Aaron, tells me as he waits his turn for a sewing machine. He's come with his fiancée, Lizzie, who wants to learn how to tailor clothes she buys at thrift stores. Aaron believes in the politics of the the Rational Dress Society, but part of the appeal is not having to pick out his clothes every morning.

Buthaina, who sits at the machine next to Aaron and Lizzie, grew up in Milan, where she says everyone is a shopaholic. She's been moving from one country to another for three years, and she's had to get rid of the clothes she's accumulated. "Moving makes you conscious of your life priorities," she tells me.

After the group cuts out their sleeves and they begin taking turns at the sewing machines, a woman with a Russian accent emerges from another exhibit and sheepishly asks me, "What is this?" I try to explain that these are artists who make jumpsuits and that this group has gathered in the middle of this famous museum to sew. "Yes, but why are they playing the Soviet national anthem?" she asks. I'm not quite sure how to answer. Maura and Abigail offer the aesthetic of "the worker" with unrestrained delight, but it seems suddenly tone-deaf in the presence of a woman who has presumably grown up in the shadow of Stalin. The Rational Dress Society's critique of choice is meant to be a critique of American late-stage capitalism.

But the aesthetics of that critique seem to hearken back to a time and a place ruled by a different tyranny: one of scarcity and political oppression.

Maura and Abigail have been accused of fascism before. Americans are primed to equate lack of choice with lack of freedom, and the aesthetics of the project, from the cut of the jumpsuit to the music on the playlist, look and feel decidedly Soviet. When I ask Maura about it, she tells me that people forget the project isn't about forcing people to wear the same thing; it's about encouraging them to end their participation in a harmful system. "JUMPSUIT is not a mandate," she says. "You have to choose to reject choice." Maura and Abigail are unabashedly influenced by artists of the early Soviet Union, who had aesthetics very different from the harsh socialist realism of the Stalinist era. Early Soviet artists designed clothes for ease of work and play rather than for opulent display. "The Soviet artists realized that the transformation of society would have to happen not just through direct political action but also through a transformation in lifestyle, facilitated by art and design," Maura and Abigail tell me.

At the end of the day, I go to the bathroom, step out of my shoes, and peel off my skinny jeans for the last time. The jumpsuit is a mass of fabric, a whale of a thing bulking up the bags I've been carrying around the city. I pull it on and walk out of the stall, feeling like Superman but also like a child in a costume.

When I come back to the gallery, Abigail and Maura fuss over the jumpsuit a bit but assure me that it's definitely the right size. Abigail tells me she wasn't so sure about the fit at first either but that she grew to love it after a few days. Out of earshot, I ask Joann, the expert seamstress, what she thinks. I get the feeling she's the kind of older New York lady who would tell me the brutal truth. "Do I look fat?" I whisper. I know it's the wrong question to be asking, but I can't help myself. Joann just laughs.

*

I give it a try. I want to see what changes when I wear the same garment every single day. Abigail and Maura have been doing it for three years; I can do it for three weeks.

The next morning, as I walk to work, I realize that it's the first time in years, maybe decades, that I am wearing such loose-fitting clothing in public. Sure, I'll wear a baggy sweater or a swing dress, but there is always a bit of Lycra or a constricting band in there somewhere—a pair of tights or skinny jeans, a too-tight sleeve or an uncomfortable armpit. Abigail and Maura tell me that clothing companies make everything tight and stretchy so they can make fewer sizes—it's cheaper to cut three sizes than six.

As I walk up the stairs to my office, no fabric grips my skin, and I feel unencumbered. Although I have been worried about how I look, the truth is I've never felt less fat. The garment does not constantly remind me of my girth; it does not threaten to bust at the seams if I move too quickly or eat too much. I'm not just thwarting the tyranny of capitalism—I'm thwarting the tyranny of tightness.

Several women compliment me on the first day—"I love your coveralls!" one coworker shouts casually across the room. Two others tell me that while they think I look great, the garment would never work on their body. It's a constant refrain I'll hear during my time in the jumpsuit. We all seem to think our bodies are impossible—too fat or thin, too long a torso or too thick a waist—to be accommodated.

Not choosing an outfit really does save time. But more than time, it saves a kind of emotional labor that I hadn't realized I was doing. I spent so much time wondering, What should I wear? The answer seemed to lie in discerning what other people would expect, how I could impress them, what would look cool. But after a beat of contemplation, I'd remember I already knew what I was going to wear. I was going to wear a jumpsuit. I could move on to other things. I began to sleep in a little later. I actually sat down to eat breakfast and got some reading in before heading off to work. But the real freedom came from not starting every day thinking about all the problems with my body or my wardrobe.

As the days passed and the novelty wore off, a different set of truths settled in. Two weeks in, I sat in a work meeting across from a woman with beautifully blow-dried hair, perfectly applied makeup, and a colorful pencil skirt. I felt, by comparison, like a manly baby wearing a onesie and work boots, and I was distracted by my need to prove both my femininity and my professionalism. I realized how much of my sense of self as a woman was wrapped up in how the world sees my body. There were days when I put on too much makeup to compensate for not wearing dresses and tight jeans. Other days, I wore no makeup, feeling like my plain face suited the outfit more. I realized I was afraid people wouldn't find me sexy—that if they couldn't see my waist, my curves, my ass, they wouldn't know that I was attractive. And I began to question that fear.

But then I was also grateful to be able to hide in the looseness of the garment, to feel like my worth would have to be found elsewhere. I didn't miss the choices in the morning when I picked out my clothes, but I missed the identity the clothes give me—the costume of "woman" or "professional." It was unsettling to feel that those identities came from the outside rather than the inside—that I convinced myself I was an adult by wearing a pencil skirt, that I convinced myself I was a woman by wearing high heels.

*

On that afternoon three weeks ago, when Abigail first gave me my jumpsuit, we sat on the enormous windowsill of the gallery loft. The sun was setting, and a melancholy pink light filled the room. The garment industry invented lofts like these—the high ceilings were tall enough to accommodate the enormous machinery, and the windows let in light, which cut down the owners' electricity bills, and let in air, which was supposed to reduce illness among the workers. At the turn of the twentieth century, consumers were afraid that epidemics of typhoid and tuberculosis were being spread because ill sweatshop workers were infecting the clothes.

In a loft across the street, backlit with blue light, women were sewing. I hadn't noticed them, but Abigail pointed out the oak-tag patterns—manila-paper shapes used in industrial production. There are still factories here, likely high-end manufacturers making clothes for expensive designers, she explained. "The garment industry is the birth of capitalism," Abigail reminded me. "The industrial revolution was about making cloth."

For Maura and Abigail, Utopia is a party where everyone is wearing the exact same thing. It's a place where consumers choose to reject choice because they see that choice isn't always linked to freedom, a place where laborers are paid and treated well. But like most Utopian visions, it surely will never be fully realized. Most people probably won't switch to a jumpsuit-only wardrobe. Even the culmination of the project—the purchase of an ad in the pages of *Vogue*—will almost certainly stay forever out of reach.

JUMPSUIT promises to subvert capitalism, but what it really does is make you aware of it. I felt it in the looseness of the garment, in the chafe as it rubbed against my thighs, in the compliments, and in the odd stares that seemed to say, You're wearing that again? And I felt it when the three weeks of wearing a jumpsuit were finally up. I stood in front of my closet, exhausted by the choice of what to put on. I needed to triangulate the weather conditions, the various tasks of the day, my level of bloat, and my desire to feel beautiful or cool or sexy. It was only through being momentarily freed from it that I noticed the comical constraint of tight clothing or the way that my identity had become so deeply bound up in consumption. Capitalism is so omnipresent that it can become impossible to identify. Both in a jumpsuit and out of it, I could feel something on my body that had long been rendered invisible: a set of restrictions that had once felt like freedom.

Reading the Genre

1. Radke's article takes the form of a testimonial. She grudgingly agrees to wear a jumpsuit for three weeks. This allows her to experience the changes in people's perceptions of her over time and, most importantly, how her perception of her own body changes. How does this change the evaluation from what she might deduce wearing the suit one day, or not wearing it at all? How do all writers need to prove to their readers that they have really "lived in" the texts they are analyzing? (See "Consider how well reasoned a piece is," p. 206, and Chapter 21, "Critical Thinking," p. 287)

2. In what ways does this essay take on the form of a personal narrative? Does Radke allow the reader to imagine themselves in her shoes (and in their own JUMPSUIT)? In many cases, an evaluation that is too personal can be limited in its effectiveness. Is this the case for Radke's essay? (See Chapter 7, "Narrative," p. 35.)

3. Radke's evaluation urges readers to change their minds, at least a little bit, about not just the JUMPSUIT, but about fashion in general. It is clear that Radke changed her own mind. What does this acknowledgment of the process of change do to strengthen her thesis? What does it mean at the end, then, that Radke stops wearing the JUMPSUIT? (See Chapter 24, "Thesis," p. 320 and "Expect your thesis to mature," p. 334.)

4. WRITING: Consider another group of people in North America who wear jumpsuits, but do so because they are incarcerated. Visit Roland Sherrill's "Jumpsuit Project" (www.jumpsuitproject.com) and think about the key differences between these two artistic endeavors. In what ways do Sherrill and JUMPSUIT have similar points to make, and in what ways are their experiments radically different? Then, look at the "Fashion" page on Kickstarter and choose another project that uses fashion to make a political or cultural statement. For instance, you might find sunglasses made from recycled water bottles in Flint, Michigan; or the "leave me alone sweater." Write your own evaluation of one of these projects.

Further Reading

Hess, Amanda. "'I Feel Pretty' and the Rise of Beauty-Standard Denialism." *The New York Times*, 24 Apr. 2018, mobile.nytimes.com/2018/04/23/movies/i-feel-pretty-amy-schumer-beauty.html.

63 Proposals: Readings

GENRE MOVES Proposal

RACHEL CARSON

From "The Obligation to Endure"

The history of life on earth has been a history of interaction between living things and their surroundings. To a large extent, the physical form and the habits of the earth's vegetation and its animal life have been molded by the environment. Considering the whole span of earthly time, the opposite effect, in which life actually modifies its surroundings, has been relatively slight. Only within the moment of time represented by the present century has one species—man—acquired significant power to alter the nature of his world.

During the past quarter century this power has not only increased to one of disturbing magnitude but it has changed in character. . . .

It took hundreds of millions of years to produce the life that now inhabits the earth—eons of time in which that developing and evolving and diversifying life reached a state of adjustment and balance with its surroundings. The environment, rigorously shaping and directing the life it supported, contained elements that were hostile as well as supporting. Certain rocks gave out dangerous radiation; even within the light of the sun, from which all life draws its energy, there were short-wave radiations with power to injure. Given time—time not in years but in millennia—life adjusts, and a balance has been reached. For time is the essential ingredient; but in the modern world there is no time.

The rapidity of change and the speed with which new situations are created follow the impetuous and heedless pace of man rather than the deliberate pace of nature.

Zoom out.

As Neil deGrasse Tyson does in his proposal essay (p. 732), Rachel Carson urges her readers to take a much wider, broader perspective on human life. What both authors understand is that proposals very often focus on the way a new course of action can create change. Proposal essays often ask their audience to *stop* behaving or acting in one way and instead take a different path. For Tyson, this means taking a "cosmic" perspective. For Carson, this means looking at time ecologically—"time not in years but in millennia." Both perspectives urge humans to take a more humble stance and then to act as though they *don't* own this place.

In many proposals, the trick is to convince readers to put someone else's, or something else's, interests before their own. Writers can accomplish this by showing readers the broader impact of their actions or by changing perspective—by zooming out. In your own proposal, examine what the wider impact of your proposed actions might be—or the broader implications of *not* acting. For instance, if you are proposing something like mandatory voting laws, think about how this will affect the next two or three generations, not just your own. If you are proposing higher taxes on petroleum, investigate what this will mean to nonhuman animals or the environment, or imagine how this will change the world by 2100. Such imagining might not be the central focus of an evidence-based proposal, but it could make for a compelling introduction or conclusion.

PROPOSAL FOR CHANGE　Michael Todd writes on environmental issues for the *Pacific Standard,* a publication devoted to studying "the science of society." This 2013 essay is based on a short proposal put forward by two scientific researchers in the journal *Nature*. In his essay, Todd interviews these researchers and explores their ideas, putting them into conversation with other movements to ban plastic or to regulate its disposal.

Is That Plastic in Your Trash a Hazard?

MICHAEL TODD

There are medical, chemical, and environmental issues associated with some pretty common plastic products. Is it time to label these as hazardous waste?

Plastic has taken its lumps of late. Plastic bags are being chased from store checkouts around the world. Bisphenol A, or BPA, in plastic containers has been linked to a Pandora's box of hormonal and genetic problems. And the Pacific, Atlantic, and Indian oceans each have a gigantic soupy concoction of plastic waste at their centers[1]—the Pacific and Atlantic have one such patch in both the Northern and Southern Hemispheres.

Despite this, the world's general attitude to plastic has been pretty cavalier. And since we're not sweating the advent of peak oil as much, at least not in North America, that plastics are made from petrochemicals doesn't seem so problematic. In fact, if current trends continue, the 280 million tons of plastic produced in 2012 will grow to 33 billion tons in 2050.

How cavalier would we be if plastics, always assumed to be chemically inert, were a hazardous waste?

A group of researchers led by ecologists Chelsea M. Rochman and Mark Anthony Browne, commenting in the journal *Nature*,[2] call for governments around the world to classify some plastics, such as PVC, polystyrene, polyurethane, and polycarbonate, as hazardous waste. Such a move, if undertaken by major producers like the United States, China, and the European Union, would—in the researchers' view—foster a virtuous circle of less waste, result-ing in less potentially toxic material that ends up in oceans or leaches harm-ful chemicals from landfills, and could even create new jobs as industry sought safer replacement materials.

Neither Rochman or Browne are anti-plastic. There's a time and place for the petrochemical-based product, they explained recently over hot drinks at a Star-bucks. (The toll? Two throwaway cups, one plastic and unused takeaway lid, and one battered plastic travel mug.) But the present overreliance on plastic, from food containers to fleece clothing to cheap housewares and electronics, is a concern.

Browne points to an increase in plastic milk containers in Britain as a prime example of plastic's overreach. For a century milk had been delivered in reusable glass containers, which were chemically inert, sustainable, and fostered local pro-duction. To use some jargon, it was a "closed-loop system." Then plastic swept in. It was cheap and weighed less, making it easier to move longer distances, which tended both to erase the smaller carbon footprint gains from its lightness and allow dairies to be further and further from their customers. Then, of course, once the plastic jug was empty, it either had to be broken down for recycling or just trashed.

In the United States, the EPA estimates 45 percent of plastics[3] were used as containers or for packaging, and just 12 percent of that gets recycled. In New York City, it's estimated the average citizen tosses out 107 pounds of different kinds of plastic waste each year, and only 17 pounds[4] of that was even designed for recycling,[5] much less recycled. "We create things just so we can throw them away," Browne laments.

But while recycling is a positive outcome, declaring some plastics as haz-ardous waste isn't an end run, the ecologists say, but a necessary step based on reality. Many plastics can be toxic in themselves in some contexts, or can absorb a surprising array of pollutants. "Yet," reads the commentary in *Nature*, "in the United States, Europe, Australia, and Japan, plastics are qualified as solid waste—so are treated the same way as food scraps or glass clippings." And, both Browne and Rochman aver, no way is plastic that innocent, even as they admit they're still trying to get a grip on both the size of the issue and plastic's ecological impacts.

For example, some plastics that are seen as benign in their consumer forms can have nasty attributes when they break down. Rochman has studied how dif-ferent kinds of plastic absorb pollutants in the oceans[6]—she calls plastic-filled seas "cocktails of contaminants." The kinds of plastic used in detergent bottles and shopping bags, for example, after breaking down into waterborne pellets, can continue to suck up pollutants for months and even years. The *Nature* piece points to an unpublished analysis that found that at least 71 percent of priority pollutants listed by the EPA and 61 percent listed by the European Union are associated with plastic debris.

These poisonous pellets can then bob around in the water or settle and concentrate in the sediment; or they can get eaten by animals or microorganisms and enter the food web.

Rochman's work shows that not all plastics are equal. Those used in water bottles, or PVC, used in clear-food packaging, aren't as powerful at absorbing pollutants. On the other hand, vinyl chloride, a component in polyvinyl chloride (PVC), has been identified as carcinogenic.

In fact, while many plastics in their final form are considered safe, many of the chemicals used to make them are known to be hazardous to health, or conversely, individual chemical compounds may have received a green light for safety but haven't been tested as they interact with other compounds. Plus, as plastics degrade into smaller pieces, their properties can change. The particles that come from polyester or acrylic clothing—think of that warm fleece jacket made out of recycled two-liter soda bottles—can be ingested or inhaled with malign effects at the cellular level.

Again, says Browne, a lack of research has hampered the ability to make definitive statements, but not, he hopes, from invoking the precautionary principle. He and his coauthors would like producers and packagers to have to show that their products are safe.

"Our goal is to provide information. We're not telling people what to do but allowing them to make choices. But they should know that plastic is not an inert material."

While government and industry haven't necessarily embraced the idea of declaring plastic waste as hazardous, in some cases they've supported basic research—one of Rochman's experiments had funding from the American Chemistry Council—or started phasing out the most likely serious offenders.

There are laws from the local to international level that could help. In the European Union, regulations (described as the most complex sets of rules in the EU's history[7]) are in place to test out the hazards of chemicals in everyday use,[8] although the effects of these findings aren't expected to hit industry and consumers for years. And even long-standing rules may not effectively address long-standing problems. For example, the International Convention for the Prevention of Pollution from Ships[9] has banned disposing of plastic at sea since 1988, but since then things like the so-called "Great Pacific Garbage Patch" have gotten worse.

But there are stronger efforts afoot. The Center for Biological Diversity, for example, has petitioned the U.S. Environmental Protection Agency[10] to develop rules, using the Clean Water Act, to reverse the tide of plastic pollution in the oceans.

"We hope to be able to use existing laws—which industry wants us to do—to foster closed-loop systems," Browne says. That still leaves the door open to some plastics, especially those that can easily be reused and recycled, and to other materials that are benign by design.

Notes

1. Skenazy, Matt. "Ocean Garbage Patches: A Scientific Sifting." *Pacific Standard.* April 26, 2012.

2. Rochman, Chelsea M., Mark Anthony Browne, et al. "Policy: Classify Plastic Waste as Hazardous." *Nature* 494, 169–171. February 14, 2013.

3. "Plastics." EPA.gov. http://www.epa.gov/osw/conserve/materials/plastics.htm

4. "Quantities of Different Plastics in NYC's Waste." NYC.gov. http://www.nyc.gov/html/nycwasteless/html/resources/plastics_quantities.shtml

5. "What Plastics to Recycle in NYC." NYC.gov. http://www.nyc.gov/html/nycwasteless/html/resources/plastics_nycrecycles.shtml

6. Rochman, Chelsea M., Eunha Hoh, et al. "Long-Term Field Measurement of Sorption of Organic Contaminants to Five Types of Plastic Pellets: Implications for Plastic Marine Debris." *Environmental Science & Technology* 47 (3), 1646–1654. December 27, 2012.

7. Rettman, Andrew. "EU's REACH Chemicals Law Begins Life in Helsinki." *EUObserver.* May 31, 2007.

8. "REACH." European Commission. http://ec.europa.eu/environment/chemicals/reach/reach_en.htm

9. "International Convention for the Prevention of Pollution from Ships (MARPOL)." International Maritime Organization. http://www.imo.org/About/Conventions/listofconventions/pages/international-convention-for-the-prevention-of-pollution-from-ships-%28marpol%29.aspx

10. "Petition for Water Quality Criteria for Plastic Pollution under the Clean Water Act, 33 USC § 1314." The Center for Biological Diversity. August 22, 2012. http://www.biologicaldiversity.org/campaigns/ocean_plastics/pdfs/Petition_Plastic_WQC_08-22-2012.pdf

Reading the Genre

1. Todd bases this essay around the work of Chelsea M. Rochman and Mark Anthony Browne, whose short and provocative proposal to label plastic hazardous was intended to get other scientists and commentators to explore the issue further. Do you feel that Todd does a good job exploring and researching the issue? What further evidence does Todd provide to support his proposal?

2. Look into some of the laws and regulations that Todd discusses at the very end of his proposal. What would happen if these laws or regulations were passed in your own country? Pick one of the laws and discuss how it might affect your daily life. (For more help with research, see Chapter 45, "Finding Print and Online Sources," p. 436.)

3. MULTIMODALITY—PUBLIC AWARENESS POSTER: Create a public awareness poster that might be put on garbage cans across your campus to warn students what happens when they throw plastics in the trash instead of recycling. Use words and images carefully to grab people's attention and to persuade them. (For help with thinking about design and images, see Chapter 42, "Designing Print and Online Documents," p. 417.)

4. WRITING: Create a list of products that you consider "hazardous." The products could be hazardous to health, or they could be hazardous to self-esteem, or they could pose dangers to families and relationships, or to society more broadly. Write a proposal that suggests a way to "label" one of these products so that people fully understand its danger and can either avoid it or develop ways to use it more carefully.

PROPOSAL FOR CHANGE   Jane McGonigal designs alternate reality games intended to "improve real lives or solve real problems." She is the author of the best-selling book *Reality Is Broken: Why Games Make Us Better and How They Can Change the World* (2011) and serves as creative director for the group Social Chocolate and director of game research and development at the Institute for the Future. This article first appeared in the *Huffington Post* in February 2011. In this essay, McGonigal offers a modest and perhaps counterintuitive proposal about gaming.

The Huffington Post

Posted: February 15, 2011, at 7:05 AM
From: Jane McGonigal

Video Games:
An Hour a Day Is Key to Success in Life

The single biggest misconception about games is that they're an escapist waste of time. But more than a decade's worth of scientific research shows that gaming is actually one of the most productive ways we can spend time.

No, playing games doesn't help the GDP—our traditional measure of productivity. But games help us produce something more important than economic bottom line: powerful emotions and social relationships that can change our lives—and potentially help us change the world.

Currently there are more than half a billion people worldwide playing online games at least an hour a day—and 183 million in the U.S. alone. The younger you are, the more likely you are to be a gamer—97 percent of boys under eighteen and 94 percent of girls under eighteen report playing video games regularly. And the average young person racks up ten thousand hours of gaming by the age of twenty-one. That's almost exactly as much time as they spend in a classroom during all of middle school and high school if they have perfect attendance. Most astonishingly, 5 million gamers in the U.S. are spending more than forty hours a week playing games—the same as a full-time job!

Why are we increasingly turning to games? According to my research, it's because games do a better job than ordinary life of provoking our most powerful positive emotions—like curiosity, optimism, pride, and a desire to join forces with others to achieve something extraordinary. Games also, increasingly, are a particularly effective way to bond with our friends and family—strengthening our real-life and online social networks in ways that no other kind of social interaction can.

That's what I mean when I say—in the title of my new book—that *Reality Is Broken*. The fact that so many people of all ages, all over the world, are choosing to spend so much time in game worlds is a sign of something important, a truth that we urgently need to recognize.

The truth is this: In today's society, computer and video games are fulfilling *genuine human needs* that the real world is currently unable to satisfy. Games are providing rewards that reality is not. They are teaching and inspiring and engaging us in ways that reality is not. They are bringing us together in ways that reality is not. And unless something dramatic happens to reverse the resulting exodus, we're fast on our way to becoming a society in which a substantial portion of our population devotes its greatest efforts to playing games, creates its best memories in game environments, and experiences its biggest successes in game worlds.

Fortunately, however, this temporary exodus is not a complete waste of time! When we play a good game, we get to practice being the best version of ourselves: We become more optimistic, more creative, more focused, more likely to set ambitious goals, and more resilient in the face of failure. And when we play multiplayer games, we become more collaborative and more likely to help others. In fact, we like and trust each other more after we play a game together—even if we lose! And more importantly, playing a game with someone is an incredibly effective way to get to know their strengths and weaknesses—as well as what motivates them. This is exactly the kind of social knowledge we need to be able to cooperate and collaborate with people to tackle real-world challenges.

The good news about games is that recent scientific research shows that all of these feelings and activities can trickle into our real lives.

For example: Kids who spend just thirty minutes playing a "pro-social" game like *Super Mario Sunshine* (in which you clean up pollution and graffiti around an island) are more likely to help friends, family, and neighbors in real life for a full week after playing the game.

People of all ages who play musical games like *Rock Band* and *Guitar Hero* report spending more time learning and playing real musical instruments than before they started playing the video game.

And just ninety seconds of playing a game like *World of Warcraft*—where you have a powerful avatar—can boost the confidence of college students so much that for up to twenty-four hours later, they're more likely to be successful taking a test at school and more outgoing in real-world social situations.

This "spill-over" effect of games means that young people who identify strongly as gamers have real-world talents and strengths that will undoubtedly serve them well in the future—if they understand that these are real skills and abilities, not just virtual ones. That's why I wanted to write *Reality Is Broken* to show gamers (and parents of gamers) exactly how playing games can prepare us to tackle challenges like curing cancer, ending world hunger, and stopping climate change. (Yes, it's true! There are games to help players do all of these things.)

Of course, there can always be too much of a good thing. Studies by both university researchers and the U.S. Army Mental Health Assessment Team show that playing games up to twenty-one hours a week can produce positive impacts on your health and happiness—especially if you're playing games face-to-face with friends and family, or playing cooperative games (rather than competitive games). That's why I personally recommend that parents of gamers spend as much time as they can playing, too. In fact, just this week, a new study by Brigham Young University's School of Family Life revealed that daughters who play video games with their parents report feeling much closer to their parents—and demonstrate significantly lower levels of aggression, behavior problems, and depression.

But when you hit twenty-eight hours a week of gaming or more, the time starts to distract you from real-life goals and other kinds of social interaction that are essential to leading a good life. Multiple studies have shown it's the twenty-one-hour mark that really makes the difference—more than three hours a day, and you're not going to get those positive impacts. Instead, you'll be at risk for negative impacts—like depression and social anxiety.

So what's the optimal level of gaming? For most people, an hour a day playing our favorite games will power up our ability to engage wholeheartedly with difficult challenges and strengthen our relationships with the people we care about most—while still letting us notice when it's time to stop playing in virtual worlds and bring our gamer strengths back to real life.

Reading the Genre

1. McGonigal argues for something that is counterintuitive, because many people think games are not good for us at all. How does she organize her own arguments and her research to respond to popular arguments against video games?

2. McGonigal is arguing for the positive effects of gaming for one to three hours a day, but she doesn't necessarily discuss the other things we might do with that time—things that might actually be even better for us. For instance, she cites studies that show that students perform better on tests after gaming. Yet wouldn't they be better off studying? Propose counter-arguments or qualify the arguments that McGonigal makes in this essay to account for these other possibilities.

3. Look at how McGonigal takes risks with style in this essay, using exclamation points, short sentences, and a conversational tone. How could some of these strategies help her connect with some audiences but not others?

4. WRITING: Create a short "how-to" manual for gaming in college, using the arguments in McGonigal's proposal, in addition to your own personal opinions and some secondary research on the impact of gaming on college students. How can you play video games *and* do well in school?

5. MULTIMODALITY—ADVERTISING POSTER: Look for some examples of the "pro-social" games that McGonigal references in this proposal. Create a poster advertising the benefits of one of these games, utilizing the research McGonigal mentions in this article as evidence. Aim your advertisement at both young people and their parents.

PROPOSAL   Neil deGrasse Tyson is an astrophysicist, the current director of the Hayden Planetarium in New York, and an author dedicated to communicating scientific ideas to the public. Tyson used to host a science program, *Nova Science Now*, on PBS, and he continues to be a guest on *The Daily Show*, *Jeopardy*, and other programs. Tyson has also recently appeared as the host of the new version of the show *Cosmos*. In this proposal, which appeared in *Natural History* magazine in 2007, he considers what might happen if humans felt a little less significant.

The Cosmic Perspective

NEIL DEGRASSE TYSON

Of all the sciences cultivated by mankind, Astronomy is acknowledged to be, and undoubtedly is, the most sublime, the most interesting, and the most useful. For, by knowledge derived from this science, not only the bulk of the Earth is discovered . . . ; but our very faculties are enlarged with the grandeur of the ideas it conveys, our minds exalted above [their] low contracted prejudices.

— James Ferguson, *Astronomy Explained upon Sir Isaac Newton's Principles, and Made Easy to Those Who Have Not Studied Mathematics* (1757)

Long before anyone knew that the universe had a beginning, before we knew that the nearest large galaxy lies two and a half million light-years from Earth, before we knew how stars work or whether atoms exist, James Ferguson's enthusiastic introduction to his favorite science rang true. Yet his words, apart from their eighteenth-century flourish, could have been written yesterday.

But who gets to think that way? Who gets to celebrate this cosmic view of life? Not the migrant farmworker. Not the sweatshop worker. Certainly not the homeless person rummaging through the trash for food. You need the luxury of time not spent on mere survival. You need to live in a nation whose government values the search to understand humanity's place in the universe. You need a society in which intellectual pursuit can take you to the frontiers of discovery, and in which news of your discoveries can be routinely disseminated. By those measures, most citizens of industrialized nations do quite well.

Yet the cosmic view comes with a hidden cost. When I travel thousands of miles to spend a few moments in the fast-moving shadow of the Moon during a total solar eclipse, sometimes I lose sight of Earth.

When I pause and reflect on our expanding universe, with its galaxies hurtling away from one another, embedded within the ever-stretching, four-dimensional fabric of space and time, sometimes I forget that uncounted people walk this Earth without food or shelter, and that children are disproportionately represented among them.

When I pore over the data that establish the mysterious presence of dark matter and dark energy throughout the universe, sometimes I forget that every day—every twenty-four-hour rotation of Earth—people kill and get killed in the name of someone else's conception of God, and that some people who do not kill in the name of God kill in the name of their nation's needs or wants.

When I track the orbits of asteroids, comets, and planets, each one a pirouetting dancer in a cosmic ballet choreographed by the forces of gravity, sometimes I forget that too many people act in wanton disregard for the delicate interplay of Earth's atmosphere, oceans, and land, with consequences that our children and our children's children will witness and pay for with their health and well-being.

And sometimes I forget that powerful people rarely do all they can to help those who cannot help themselves.

I occasionally forget those things because, however big the world is—in our hearts, our minds, and our outsize atlases—the universe is even bigger. A depressing thought to some, but a liberating thought to me.

Consider an adult who tends to the traumas of a child: a broken toy, a scraped knee, a schoolyard bully. Adults know that kids have no clue what constitutes a genuine problem, because inexperience greatly limits their childhood perspective.

As grown-ups, dare we admit to ourselves that we, too, have a collective immaturity of view? Dare we admit that our thoughts and behaviors spring from a belief that the world revolves around us? Apparently not. And the evidence abounds. Part the curtains of society's racial, ethnic, religious, national, and cultural conflicts, and you find the human ego turning the knobs and pulling the levers.

Now imagine a world in which everyone, but especially people with power and influence, holds an expanded view of our place in the cosmos. With that perspective, our problems would shrink—or never arise at all—and we could celebrate our earthly differences while shunning the behavior of our predecessors who slaughtered each other because of them.

Back in February 2000, the newly rebuilt Hayden Planetarium featured a space show called *Passport to the Universe*, which took visitors on a virtual zoom from New York City to the edge of the cosmos. En route the audience saw Earth, then the solar system, then the 100 billion stars of the Milky Way galaxy shrink to barely visible dots on the planetarium dome.

Within a month of opening day, I received a letter from an Ivy League professor of psychology whose expertise was things that make people feel insignificant. I never knew one could specialize in such a field. The guy wanted to administer a before-and-after questionnaire to visitors, assessing the depth of their depression after viewing the show. *Passport to the Universe*, he wrote, elicited the most dramatic feelings of smallness he had ever experienced.

How could that be? Every time I see the space show (and others we've produced), I feel alive and spirited and connected. I also feel large, knowing that the goings-on within the three-pound human brain are what enabled us to figure out our place in the universe.

Allow me to suggest that it's the professor, not I, who has misread nature. His ego was too big to begin with, inflated by delusions of significance and fed by cultural assumptions that human beings are more important than everything else in the universe.

In all fairness to the fellow, powerful forces in society leave most of us susceptible. As was I . . . until the day I learned in biology class that more bacteria live and work in one centimeter of my colon than the number of people who have ever existed in the world. That kind of information makes you think twice about who—or what—is actually in charge.

From that day on, I began to think of people not as the masters of space and time but as participants in a great cosmic chain of being, with a direct genetic link across species both living and extinct, extending back nearly 4 billion years to the earliest single-celled organisms on Earth.

I know what you're thinking: We're smarter than bacteria.

No doubt about it, we're smarter than every other living creature that ever walked, crawled, or slithered on Earth. But how smart is that? We cook our food. We compose poetry and music. We do art and science. We're good at math. Even if you're bad at math, you're probably much better at it than the smartest chimpanzee, whose genetic identity varies in only trifling ways from ours. Try as they might, primatologists will never get a chimpanzee to learn the multiplication table or do long division.

If small genetic differences between us and our fellow apes account for our vast difference in intelligence, maybe that difference in intelligence is not so vast after all.

Imagine a life-form whose brainpower is to ours as ours is to a chimpanzee's. To such a species our highest mental achievements would be trivial. Their toddlers, instead of learning their ABCs on *Sesame Street*, would learn multivariable calculus on Boolean Boulevard. Our most complex theorems, our deepest philosophies, the cherished works of our most creative artists, would be projects their schoolkids bring home for Mom and Dad to display on the refrigerator door. These creatures would study Stephen Hawking (who occupies the same endowed professorship once held by Newton at the University of Cambridge) because he's slightly more clever than other humans, owing to his ability to do theoretical astrophysics and other rudimentary calculations in his head.

If a huge genetic gap separated us from our closest relative in the animal kingdom, we could justifiably celebrate our brilliance. We might be entitled to walk around thinking we're distant and distinct from our fellow creatures. But no such gap exists. Instead, we are one with the rest of nature, fitting neither above nor below, but within.

Need more ego softeners? Simple comparisons of quantity, size, and scale do the job well.

Take water. It's simple, common, and vital. There are more molecules of water in an eight-ounce cup of the stuff than there are cups of water in all the world's oceans. Every cup that passes through a single person and eventually rejoins the world's water supply holds enough molecules to mix 1,500 of them into every other cup of water in the world. No way around it: Some of the water you just drank passed through the kidneys of Socrates, Genghis Khan, and Joan of Arc.

How about air? Also vital. A single breathful draws in more air molecules than there are breathfuls of air in Earth's entire atmosphere. That means some of the air you just breathed passed through the lungs of Napoleon, Beethoven, Lincoln, and Billy the Kid.

Time to get cosmic. There are more stars in the universe than grains of sand on any beach, more stars than seconds have passed since Earth formed, more stars than words and sounds ever uttered by all the humans who ever lived.

Want a sweeping view of the past? Our unfolding cosmic perspective takes you there. Light takes time to reach Earth's observatories from the depths of space, and so you see objects and phenomena not as they are but as they once were. That means the universe acts like a giant time machine: The farther away you look, the further back in time you see—back almost to the beginning of time itself. Within that horizon of reckoning, cosmic evolution unfolds continuously, in full view.

Want to know what we're made of? Again, the cosmic perspective offers a bigger answer than you might expect. The chemical elements of the universe are forged in the fires of high-mass stars that end their lives in stupendous explosions, enriching their host galaxies with the chemical arsenal of life as we know it. The result? The four most common chemically active elements in the universe—hydrogen, oxygen, carbon, and nitrogen—are the four most common elements of life on Earth. We are not simply in the universe. The universe is in us.

Yes, we are stardust. But we may not be of this Earth. Several separate lines of research, when considered together, have forced investigators to reassess who we think we are and where we think we came from.

First, computer simulations show that when a large asteroid strikes a planet, the surrounding areas can recoil from the impact energy, catapulting rocks into space. From there, they can travel to—and land on—other planetary surfaces. Second, microorganisms can be hardy. Some survive the extremes of temperature, pressure, and radiation inherent in space travel. If the rocky flotsam from an impact hails from a planet with life, microscopic fauna could have stowed away in the rocks' nooks and crannies. Third, recent evidence suggests that shortly after the formation of our solar system, Mars was wet, and perhaps fertile, even before Earth was.

Those findings mean it's conceivable that life began on Mars and later seeded life on Earth, a process known as panspermia. So all earthlings might—just might—be descendants of Martians.

Again and again across the centuries, cosmic discoveries have demoted our self-image. Earth was once assumed to be astronomically unique, until astronomers learned that Earth is just another planet orbiting the Sun. Then we presumed the Sun was unique, until we learned that the countless stars of the night sky are suns themselves. Then we presumed our galaxy, the Milky Way, was the entire known universe, until we established that the countless fuzzy things in the sky are other galaxies, dotting the landscape of our known universe.

Today, how easy it is to presume that one universe is all there is. Yet emerging theories of modern cosmology, as well as the continually reaffirmed improbability that anything is unique, require that we remain open to the latest assault on our plea for distinctiveness: multiple universes, otherwise known as the multiverse, in which ours is just one of countless bubbles bursting forth from the fabric of the cosmos.

The cosmic perspective flows from fundamental knowledge. But it's more than just what you know. It's also about having the wisdom and insight to apply that knowledge to assessing our place in the universe. And its attributes are clear:

- The cosmic perspective comes from the frontiers of science, yet it's not solely the province of the scientist. The cosmic perspective belongs to everyone.
- The cosmic perspective is humble.
- The cosmic perspective is spiritual—even redemptive—but not religious.
- The cosmic perspective enables us to grasp, in the same thought, the large and the small.
- The cosmic perspective opens our minds to extraordinary ideas but does not leave them so open that our brains spill out, making us susceptible to believing anything we're told.
- The cosmic perspective opens our eyes to the universe, not as a benevolent cradle designed to nurture life but as a cold, lonely, hazardous place.
- The cosmic perspective shows Earth to be a mote, but a precious mote and, for the moment, the only home we have.
- The cosmic perspective finds beauty in the images of planets, moons, stars, and nebulae but also celebrates the laws of physics that shape them.
- The cosmic perspective enables us to see beyond our circumstances, allowing us to transcend the primal search for food, shelter, and sex.
- The cosmic perspective reminds us that in space, where there is no air, a flag will not wave—an indication that perhaps flag waving and space exploration do not mix.
- The cosmic perspective not only embraces our genetic kinship with all life on Earth but also values our chemical kinship with any yet-to-be discovered life in the universe, as well as our atomic kinship with the universe itself.

At least once a week, if not once a day, we might each ponder what cosmic truths lie undiscovered before us, perhaps awaiting the arrival of a clever thinker, an ingenious experiment, or an innovative space mission to reveal them. We might further ponder how those discoveries may one day transform life on Earth.

Absent such curiosity, we are no different from the provincial farmer who expresses no need to venture beyond the county line, because his forty acres meet all his needs. Yet if all our predecessors had felt that way, the farmer would instead be a cave dweller, chasing down his dinner with a stick and a rock.

During our brief stay on planet Earth, we owe ourselves and our descendants the opportunity to explore—in part because it's fun to do. But there's a far nobler reason. The day our knowledge of the cosmos ceases to expand, we risk regressing to the childish view that the universe figuratively and literally revolves around us. In that bleak world, arms-bearing, resource-hungry people and nations would be prone to act on their low contracted prejudices. And that would be the last gasp of human enlightenment—until the rise of a visionary new culture that could once again embrace the cosmic perspective.

Reading the Genre

1. Tyson offers a series of "ego softeners" in this proposal. How important is it to the success of this proposal for Tyson to soften the audience's egos, without shattering them or making readers defensive? How effectively does he do so?

2. Does Tyson consider counterarguments in this essay? Suggest some counterarguments to his proposal. What do we lose by embracing the cosmic perspective? (For more on counterpoints, see p. 103.)

3. WRITING: Identify a current problem or crisis in your community that a "cosmic perspective" could help solve. Propose how the public could be encouraged and educated to take such a perspective and how that new perspective might lead to tangible actions to solve the problem.

4. MULTIMODALITY—COSMIC CALENDAR: Look at the "cosmic perspective" that Tyson outlines at the end of his proposal. He also suggests, "At least once a week, if not once a day, we might each ponder what cosmic truths lie undiscovered before us." Create a calendar that is at least one month long, and on every day in your calendar, add a fact or a question, a statistic or an image, that could help us to develop a more cosmic perspective.

SATIRICAL PROPOSAL   Kembrew McLeod is an activist, music critic, and documentary film producer. He focuses his work on issues of copyright and intellectual property and famously made an ironic point in 1997 by registering the phrase "Freedom of Expression" as a U.S. trademark. McLeod's books include *Freedom of Expression: Resistance and Repression in the Age of Intellectual Property* (2005), *Creative License: The Law and Culture of Digital Sampling* (2011), and *Pranksters: Making Mischief in the Modern World* (2014). He teaches communication at the University of Iowa and enjoys playing pranks.

The Huffington Post

Posted: June 29, 2010, at 12:58 PM
From: Kembrew McLeod

A Modest Free Market Proposal for Education Reform

Times are tough for public universities. Over the past quarter century, state legislatures have slashed college budgets—cuts that have only accelerated during this economic meltdown. We have been told to do more with less, make sacrifices, and be self-sufficient—and I couldn't agree more. Unlike those socialists lining up to mainline milk from the nanny state, there are many of us who favor fiscally sound solutions. We should teach our children well by following dogmatically free-market principles that reject government meddling.

My modest proposal is multipronged and forward thinking. It would hand over all aspects of academic life to private companies, creating a university system that is more efficient, profitable even. In reimagining how higher education can be rebooted, we need to ask ourselves, "What would a liberal arts education look like if McDonald's funded it?" Killing many birds with one lethal stone, we can simultaneously solve the problems created by overstuffed state budgets, overpaid professors, and—as an added, unexpected bonus—plagiarism. Let me explain.

The first part of the plan involves the sponsorship of classes, in which companies would exchange cash and services for the prominent placement of their logos on syllabi and in teaching spaces. This is a no-brainer, especially because on-campus branding has expanded in recent years. Under this plan, rational economic decisions would play a greater role in determining course offerings; less popular, unprofitable classes would necessarily fall by the wayside.

My second proposal will be more controversial, for it involves radically rethinking the way undergraduate students approach their course work. These days, professors fret over undergrads using the services of "research assistance" companies—businesses that sell finished papers on every imaginable subject. Rather than siding with these fuddy-duddies, we should instead embrace this shift in student work habits. After all, the free market is influencing the decisions our students make, and it would be disastrous to regulate an emerging marketplace during these uncertain times.

It also seems morally wrong to force undergrads to waste their time on reading, researching, writing, and revising when their labor could be better spent working service jobs and other entry-level positions. This will allow them to buy prepackaged papers and still have spending money left over to inject into the economy—a win-win.

Only lazy students who are not gainfully employed would lose out. Additionally, those who carefully manage their money (or whose families have already done so) can purchase higher-quality papers that will earn them better grades: a one-dollar, one-vote approach to learning. While it is true that this shift in pedagogy will hurt some businesses—such as companies that produce plagiarism-detecting software such as TurnItIn.com—the overall fiscal impact for society will be positive.

The third and final part of my plan takes the economic potential of education to the next level, offering great rewards with virtually no risk. Still, I anticipate that some old-school professors will be alarmed by my suggestion that we should use this new education/business model to train future faculty. It's only fair that if we allow undergraduates to use research-assistance companies, grad students should be allowed to do so as well. One such business, PhD-Dissertations.com, is leading the charge on this front. (When I first came across this Web site, I thought, Why hasn't anyone thought of this before? Talk about an untapped market!)

By no longer having to conduct original research themselves, graduate students will have more hours to spend in the classroom as adjunct instructors. Let's do the math. PhD-Dissertations.com charges $17.00 per page, which adds up to $3,400 for a 200-page dissertation (plus, their Web site states, "A discount of 10% applies to orders of 75+ pages!"). Although this might seem like a lot of money, consider the fact that most colleges pay adjuncts roughly the same, between $3,000 and $4,000, for each course taught per semester. Therefore, by just adding one extra course to his or her roster, a graduate student can pay for an entire dissertation in less than one academic year—while at the same time serving the university's undergraduate teaching needs. Once this new generation of scholar/project managers enters the profession, there will be no more need for traditional professors.

Following this course of action, universities can be transformed into a well-oiled machine that will generate more credit hours and, therefore, more tuition dollars. For years, college deans have argued that we need to find cheaper ways to process more students through the system. Predictably, many tenured radicals derisively use the phrase "credit factory" to describe this approach, but I think the industrial process is an apt metaphor for how universities should conduct their business. Fast food is another good model to follow, a point that is underscored on PhD-Dissertations. com's "Frequently Asked Questions" page:

> Will the material be one-of-a-kind and unique? Yes, of course. As they say at Jack in the Box, "We don't make it until you order it." We write all custom research materials from scratch, based on the specifications provided to us. Unlike other services with no sense of academic integrity, we do not copy-and-paste from writings that are freely available on the Internet.

Some will surely complain about this approach's "intellectually corrosive" effects, but these people—who have a practically medieval, pre-capitalist concept of what universities should do—are wrong. In fact, a legitimized research-assistance industry will most definitely improve the quality of scholarly research and writing. Because these companies exist in the private sector, they naturally do a more efficient job than researchers in bloated college bureaucracies, which have extensive, wasteful workforce redundancies. In today's universities, some scholars examine similar topics, but using different perspectives. In other words, they hire multiple people to do a job fit for one!

Corporate research factories, on the other hand, can maximize the resources needed to produce top-notch scholarship better than any state-funded school. This is because research-assistance companies have a streamlined division of labor: One specialized staff researcher writes, another proofreads, a different employee fact-checks, and another administrator can manage the whole project. As is noted on the home page for Student Network Resources, which owns PhD-Dissertations.com, "We created a highly advanced project management system for clients and writers to connect on a large scale"; only in the private sector can you achieve this level of efficiency.

Hard times call for tough choices and new ideas, which my plan will deliver. By creating synergistic links between universities and corporate sponsors—and by privatizing the work done by undergraduate student/workers and professors-in-training—we can create a lighter, leaner educational system that can better adapt to the realities of a changing world. More importantly, this approach will foster economic growth by turning the process of learning into a frictionless series of commodity exchanges. After all, what could go wrong?

Reading the Genre

1. This proposal essay is actually made up of three connected proposals. What are they, and how seriously does McLeod expect readers to take them?

2. Satire—the use of wit and irony to make a serious point—is a form of social commentary. What is McLeod criticizing with his use of satire?

3. Look up the meaning of *hyperbole* and consider how McLeod uses over-statement as a persuasive tool. How might this strategy work in a proposal that is not a satire? (See "Defend the proposal," p. 154).

4. WRITING: Because this is a satirical proposal, McLeod doesn't expect readers to follow through on his suggestions. Try to imagine real solutions to the problems McLeod addresses, and write a serious proposal for change.

5. WRITING: Using McLeod's satirical approach for inspiration, propose an outlandish change to another aspect of university life.

64

Literary Analyses: Readings

ZADIE SMITH
From *"What Does* Soulful *Mean?"*

White readers often believe they are colorblind.[1] I always thought I was a colorblind reader—until I read this *Their Eyes Were Watching God*, and that ultimate cliché of black life that is inscribed in the word *soulful* took on new weight and sense for me. But what does *soulful* even mean? The dictionary has it this way: "expressing or appearing to express deep and often sorrowful feeling." The culturally black meaning adds several more shades of color. First shade: *soulfulness* is sorrowful feeling transformed into something beautiful, creative and self-renewing, and—as it reaches a pitch—ecstatic. It is an alchemy of pain. In *Their Eyes Were Watching God*, when the townsfolk sing for the death of the mule, this is an example of *soulfulness*. Another shade: To be soulful is to follow and *fall in line* with a feeling, to go where it takes you and not to go against its grain.[2] When young Janie takes her lead from the blossoming tree and sits on her gatepost to kiss a passing boy, this is an example of *soulfulness* A final shade: The word *soulful*, like its Jewish cousin, *schmaltz*,[3] has its roots in the digestive tract. "Soul food" is simple, flavorsome, hearty, unfussy, with spice. When Janie puts on her overalls and joyfully goes to work in the muck with Tea Cake, this is an example of *soulfulness*.[4] This is a beautiful novel about soulfulness. That it should be so is a tribute to Hurston's skill. She makes "culture"—that slow and particular[5] and artificial accretion of habit and circumstance—seem as natural and organic and beautiful as the sunrise. She allows me to indulge in what Philip Roth once called "the romance of oneself," a literary value I dislike and yet, confronted with this beguiling book, cannot resist. She makes "black woman-ness" appear a real, tangible quality, an essence I can almost believe I share, however improbably, with millions of complex individuals across centuries and continents and languages and religions. . . .

Almost—but not quite. Better to say, when I'm reading this book, I believe it, with my whole soul. It allows me to say things I wouldn't normally. Things like "*She is my sister and I love her.*"

Notes

1. Until they read books featuring nonwhite characters. I once overheard a young white man at a book festival say to his friend, "Have you read the new Kureishi? Same old thing—loads of Indian people." To which you want to reply, "Have you read the new Franzen? Same old thing—loads of white people."
2. At its most common and banal: catching a beat, following a rhythm.
3. In the *Oxford English Dictionary*: "*Schmaltz* n. informal. excessive sentimentality, esp. in music or movies. ORIGIN 1930s: from Yiddish *schmaltz*, from German *Schmalz* 'dripping, lard.'"
4. Is there anything less soulful than attempting to define soulfulness?
5. In literary terms, we know that there is a tipping point at which the cultural particular—while becoming no less culturally particular—is accepted by readers as the neutral universal. The previously "Jewish fiction" of Philip Roth is now "fiction."

Consider multiple meanings.

In this section of her essay, Zadie Smith is drilling down and seeking to define "soulful"—something that the very title of her essay has promised us she will do. But instead of confidence, she offers ambivalence. Smith offers "shades," rather than one definition. Interestingly, she uses her footnotes to add layers of complexity to her own analysis. The footnotes aren't used to fortify her argument—instead, she uses the footnotes to digress and wander. The overall effect is that Smith reveals her own uncertainty, her discomfort with embracing sentiments that she usually dislikes.

In your own writing, it is okay to feel ambivalently about a character, an author, or a plot. Smith's essay is first focused on how she changed her own mind about Hurston, and then Smith shifts to an effort to change the minds of other readers. In the end, excellent literary works *have to* change minds, causing us to encounter new ideas and new feelings. So, consider using footnotes to second-guess yourself, to digress, and to wander, exploring the feelings and reactions you have to a literary work and how your mind changes.

TEXTUAL ANALYSIS   Roxane Gay writes award-winning fiction, memoir, and cultural commentary. She also teaches at Purdue University. Her most recent book is the memoir *Hunger*. Along with Ta-Nehisi Coates (also featured in this book), Gay wrote for the *Black Panther* comic book series, where she was able to create her own strong, female characters.

ROXANE GAY

Not Here to Make Friends

> My memory of men is never lit up and illuminated like my memory of women.
>
> — Marguerite Duras, The Lover

In my high school yearbook there is a note from a girl who wrote, "I like you even though you are very mean." I do not remember the girl who wrote this note. I do not remember being mean to her, or anyone for that matter. I do remember I was feral in high school, socially awkward, emotionally closed off, completely lost.

Or maybe I don't want to remember being mean because I've changed in the 20 years between now and then. Around my junior year, I went from being quiet and withdrawn to being mean where mean was saying exactly what I thought and making sarcastic comments, relentlessly. Sincerity was dead to me.

I had so few friends it didn't really matter how I behaved. I had nothing to lose. I had no idea what it meant to be likable though I was surrounded by generally likable people, or I suppose, I was surrounded by people who were very invested in projecting a likable façade, people who were willing to play by the rules. I had likable parents and brothers. I was the anomaly as a social outcast, but even from a young age, I understood that when a girl is unlikable, a girl is a problem. I also understood that I wasn't being intentionally mean. I was being honest (admittedly, without tact), and I was being human. It is either a blessing or a curse that those are rarely likable qualities in a woman.

* * *

Inevitably on every reality-television program, someone will boldly declare, "I'm not here to make friends." They do so to establish that they are on a given program to win the nebulous prize or the bachelor's heart or get the exposure they need to begin their unsteady rise to a modicum of fame. These people make this declaration by way of explaining their unlikability or the inevitably unkind edit they're going to receive from the show's producers. It isn't that they are terrible, you see. It's simply that they are not participating in the show to make friends. They are freeing themselves from the burden of likability or they are, perhaps, freeing us from the burden of guilt for the dislike and eventual contempt we might hold for them.

In the movie *Young Adult*, Charlize Theron stars as Mavis Gary. Nearly every review of the movie raises her character's unlikability, painting her with a bright scarlet U. Based on this character's critical reception, an unlikable woman embodies any number of unpleasing but entirely human characteristics. Mavis is beautiful, cold, calculating, self-absorbed, full of odd tics, insensitive, and largely dysfunctional in nearly every aspect of her life. These are, apparently, unacceptable traits for a woman, particularly given the sheer number working in concert. Some reviews go so far as to suggest that Mavis is mentally ill because there's nothing more reliable than armchair diagnosis by disapproving critics. In his review, Roger Ebert lauds Young Adult screenwriter Diablo Cody for making Mavis an alcoholic because, "without such a context, Mavis would simply be insane." Ebert, and many others, require an explanation for Mavis' behavior. They require a diagnosis for her unlikability in order to tolerate her. The simplest explanation, of Mavis as human, will not suffice.

* * *

In many ways, likability is a very elaborate lie, a performance, a code of conduct dictating the proper way to be. Characters who don't follow this code become unlikable. Critics who fault a character's unlikability cannot necessarily be faulted. They are merely expressing a wider cultural malaise with all things unpleasant, all things that dare to breach the norm of social acceptability.

***

Why is likability even a question? Why are we so concerned with, whether in fact or fiction, someone is likable? Unlikable is a fluid designation that can be applied to any character who doesn't behave in a way the reader finds palatable. Lionel Shriver notes in

"As a writer and a person who has struggled with likability—being likable, wanting to be liked, wanting to belong— I have spent a great deal of time thinking about likability in the stories I read and those I write."

an essay for *The Financial Times,* "This 'liking' business has two components: moral approval and affection." We need characters to be lovable while doing right.

Some might suggest this likability question is a byproduct of an online culture where we reflexively like or favorite every status update and bit of personal trivia shared on social networks. Certainly, online there is a culture of relentless affirmation, but it would be shortsighted to believe that this desire to be liked, this desire to express what or whom we like, begins or ends with the Internet. I have no doubt that Abraham Maslow has some ideas on this persistent desire, in so many of us, to be liked and, in turn, to belong, to have our deftness at following the proper code of conduct affirmed.

I am often drawn to unlikable characters, to those who behave in socially unacceptable ways and say whatever is on their mind and do what they want with varying levels of regard for the consequences. I want characters to do bad things and get away with their misdeeds. I want characters to think ugly thoughts and make ugly decisions. I want characters to make mistakes and put themselves first without apologizing for it.

I don't even mind unlikable characters whose behavior is psychopathic or sociopathic. This is not to say I condone, for example, murder, but American Psycho's Patrick Bateman is a very interesting man. There is a psychiatric diagnosis for his unlikability, a deviant pathology, but he has his charms, particularly in his scathing self-awareness. Serial killers are people too, and sometimes they are funny. My conscience, Bateman thinks in the novel, my pity, my hopes disappeared a long time ago (probably at Harvard) if they ever did exist.

I want characters to do the things I am afraid to do for fear of making myself more unlikable than I may already be. I want characters to be the most honest of all things—human.

* * *

That the question of likability even exists in literary conversations is odd. It implies we are engaging in a courtship. When characters are unlikable, they don't meet our mutable, varying standards. Certainly, we can find kinship in fiction, but literary merit shouldn't be dictated by whether or not we want to be friends or lovers with those about whom we read.

Frankly, I find "good," purportedly likable characters, rather unbearable. Take May Welland in Edith Wharton's *Age of Innocence.* May's likability is, to be fair, deliberate, a choice Wharton has made so Newland Archer's passion for Countess Olenska is ever more fraught and bittersweet. Still, May is the kind of woman who always does everything right, everything that is expected of her. She is a perfect society lady. She knows how to keep up appearances. Meanwhile, everyone looks down on May's unspoken rival and cousin, the Countess Olenska, a woman who dares to defy social conventions, who dares to not tolerate a terrible marriage, who dares to want real passion in her life even if that passion is found with an unsuitable man.

We're not supposed to like her, but Countess Olenska intrigues me because she is interesting. She stands apart from the blur of social conformity. We're supposed to like, or at least respect, May for being the proper and sweet innocent she carries herself as, but in Wharton's skilled hands, we eventually see that May Welland is as human, and therefore unlikable, as anyone else. This question of likability would be far more tolerable if all writers were as talented as Edith Wharton, but alas.

Far more pernicious than the characters whose likability serves a greater purpose within a narrative are the characters who are flatly likable. It's a bit silly, but I spend a great deal of time, even now, lamenting the perfection of one Elizabeth Wakefield, one of the two golden twins prominently featured in the popular Sweet Valley High young adult series. Elizabeth is the good girl who always makes the right choices, even when she has to sacrifice her own happiness. She gets good grades. She's a good daughter, sister, and girlfriend. It's boring. Elizabeth's likability is downright loathsome. I am Team Jessica. I prefer Nellie Olsen to Laura Ingalls Wilder.

This matter of likability is largely a futile one. Oftentimes, a likable character is simply designed as such to show that he or she is one who knows how to play by the rules and cares to be seen as playing by the rules. The likable character, like the unlikable character, is generally used to make some grater [sic] narrative point.

* * *

Writers are often told a character isn't likable as literary criticism, as if a character's likability is directly proportional to the quality of a novel's writing. This is particularly true for women in fiction. In literature as in life, the rules are all too often different for girls. There are many instances where an unlikable man is billed as an anti-hero, earning a special term to explain those ways in which he deviates from the norm, the traditionally likable. Beginning with Holden Caulfield in *Catcher in the Rye,* the list is long. An unlikable man is inscrutably interesting, dark, or tormented but ultimately compelling even when he might behave in distasteful ways. This is the only explanation I can come up with for the popularity of, say, the novels of Philip Roth who is one hell of a writer, but also a writer who practically revels in the unlikability of his men, their neuroses and self-loathing (and, of course humanity) boldly on display from one page to the next.

When women are unlikable, it becomes a point of obsession in critical con-versations by professional and amateur critics alike. Why are these women daring to flaunt convention? Why aren't they making themselves likable (and therefore acceptable) to polite society? In a *Publisher's Weekly* interview with Claire Messud about her recent novel *The Woman Upstairs,* which features a rather "unlikable" pro-tagonist named Nora who is bitter, bereft, and downright angry about what her life has become, the interviewer said, "I wouldn't want to be friends with Nora, would you? Her outlook is almost unbearably grim." And there we have it. A reader was here to make friends with the characters in a book and she didn't like what she found.

Messud, for her part, had a sharp response for her interviewer. "For heaven's sake, what kind of question is that? Would you want to be friends with Humbert Humbert? Would you want to be friends with Mickey Sabbath? Saleem Sinai? Ham-let? Krapp? Oedipus? Oscar Wao? Antigone? Raskolnikov? Any of the characters in *The Corrections*? Any of the characters in *Infinite Jest*? Any of the characters in anything Pynchon has ever written? Or Martin Amis? Or Orhan Pamuk? Or Alice Munro, for that matter? If you're reading to find friends, you're in deep trouble. We read to find life, in all its possibilities. The relevant question isn't 'Is this a potential friend for me?' but 'Is this character alive?'"

Perhaps, then, unlikable characters, the ones who are the most human, are also the ones who are the most alive. Perhaps this intimacy makes us uncomfortable because we don't dare be so alive.

***

In *How Fiction Works,* James Wood says, "A great deal of nonsense is written every day about characters in fiction —f rom the side of those who believe too much in character and from the side of those who believe too little. Those who believe too much have an iron set of prejudices about what characters are: We should get to 'know' them; they should 'grow' and 'develop'; and they should be nice. So they should be pretty much like us." Wood is correct, in part, but the ongoing question of character likability leaves the impression that what we're looking for in fiction is an ideal world where people behave in ideal ways. The question suggests that characters should be reflections not of us, but of our better selves.

Wood also says, "There is nothing harder than the creation of fictional character." I can attest to this difficulty though with, perhaps, less hyperbole. I have, indeed, found several other tasks harder over the years. Regardless, characters are hard to create because we need to develop people who are interesting enough to hold a reader's attention. We need to ensure that they are some measure of credible. We need to make them distinct from ourselves (and in the best of all words, [sic] from those in our lives, unless of course, there is a need to settle scores). Somehow they need to be well developed enough to carry a plot or carry a narrative without a plot or endure the tribulations we writers tend to throw at them with alacrity. It's no wonder so many characters are unlikable given what they have to put up with.

It is a seductive position a writer puts the reader in when they create an interesting, unlikable character—they make you complicit, in ways that are both uncomfortable and intriguing.

* * *

If people with messy lives are the point of certain narratives, if unlikable women are the point of certain narratives, novels like *Gone Girl*, *Treasure Island!!!*, *Dare Me*, *Magnificence*, and many others exhibit a delightful excess of purpose with stories filled with women who are deemed unlikable because they make so-called bad choices, describe the world exactly as they see it, and are, ultimately, honest and breathtakingly alive.

These novels depict women who are clearly not participating in their narratives to make friends and whose characters are the better for it. Freed from the constraints of likability, they are able to exist on and beyond the page as fully realized, interesting, and realistic characters. There is the saying that the truth hurts, and perhaps this is what lies at the heart of worrying over likability or the lack thereof: how much of the truth we're willing to subject ourselves to, how much we are willing to hurt, when we immerse ourselves in the safety of a fictional world.

Sara Levine's *Treasure Island!!!* features a narrator who is unlikable in curious ways. She is utterly self-obsessed, acts without considering consequences, and always makes choices that will benefit herself over others. She is intensely preoccupied with the book *Treasure Island*, and sets out to live her life by the book's core values: BOLD-NESS, RESOLUTION, INDEPENDENCE, and HORN-BLOWING. As she careens from one self-created disaster to another, the narrator is unrepentant. There is no redemption or lesson learned from misdeeds. There is no apology or moral to the story, and that makes an already incisive and intelligent novel even more compelling.

When you think about it, these core values the narrator in *Treasure Island!!!!* seeks to live by—BOLDNESS, RESOLUTION, INDEPENDENCE, and HORN-BLOWING— are characteristics that define how many unlikable women lead their fictional lives.

In Pamela Ribon's *You Take It From Here*, a woman, Smidge, is dying of lung cancer and wants her best friend Danielle to essentially finish the job of raising her daughter and being her husband's companion in grief. The book's premise is an interesting one, but what really stands out is how deeply unlikable Smidge is. She is the kind of person who, it might seem, shouldn't have any friends. She's bossy, intense, controlling, unrepentant, and manipulative. And yet. She has a best friend, a daughter, a husband, and a community of people who will deeply mourn her when she is gone. Ribon's steadfastness in this character's lack of likability is admirable. She never panders by making Smidge somehow have some kind of epiphany of character simply because she is dying. Ribon is unwavering in what she shows us of Smidge and the novel is the better for it.

A customer review of *You Take It From Here* on Amazon from Danae Savitri states, "I never warmed up to Smidge as a character, thought she suffered from borderline personality disorder, common among people who are charismatic narcissists, who alternately bully, manipulate, and charm others around them." Instead of judging the book, it is a woman's likability that comes into question. Again, there is an armchair diagnosis of mental disease. It is an almost Pavlovian response to pathologize the unlikable in fictional characters.

Dare Me by Megan Abbott is a book about high school cheerleaders, but it's nothing like what you might expect. Populated by women who act with boldness, resolve, independence, and a prioritizing of the self—these mighty principles from Treasure Island!!!—*Dare Me* is both engaging and terrifying because it reveals the fraught intimacy between girls. It's a novel about bodies and striving for perfection and ambition and desire so naked, so palpable, you cannot help but want the deeply flawed women in the book to get what they want no matter how terribly they go about getting it. The young women at the center of the novel, Beth and Addy, are friends as much as they are enemies. They betray each other and they betray themselves. They commit wrongs, and still, they are each other's gravitational center.

On the phone, after a drunken night, Beth asks Addy if she remembers "how we used to hang on the monkey bars, hooking our legs around each other, and how strong we got and how no one could ever beat us, and we could never beat each other, but we'd agree to each release our hands at the count of three, and that she always cheated, and I always let her, standing beneath, looking up at her and grinning my gap-toothed pre-orthodontic grin." It is a moment that shows us how Addy has always seen Beth plainly and understood her and loved her nonetheless. Throughout the novel, Beth and Addy remain unlikable, remain flawed to an extent, but there is no explanation for it, no clear trajectory between cause and effect. Traditional parameters of likability are deftly avoided throughout the novel in moments as honest and no less poignant as these.

Susan Lindley, a widow, has to move on after her husband's tragic death in Lydia Millet's *Magnificence.* From the outset we know she was unfaithful to her husband.

She inherits her uncle's mansion, filled with a rotting taxidermy collection, and sets about making some kind of order, both in the mansion and in her own life. She has a daughter involved with her boss and a boyfriend who is married to another woman. She feels responsible for her husband's death but is matter of fact in reconciling this. "Was she relieved, slut that she was?" Susan thinks to herself. "Was there something in her that was relieved by any of this? If anyone could admit such a thing, she should be able to. She was not only a slut but a killer." Susan does go on to acknowledge she feels a profound absence in the loss of her husband, a "freedom of nothing," and throughout the novel, she indulges in this freedom; she embraces it.

So much of *Magnificence* is grounded solely in Susan's experiences, her awkward perceptions of the world she has created and continues to create for herself. We also have the pleasure of seeing a woman in her late forties as a deeply sexual being who is equally unashamed in her want for material things as she becomes more and more attached to the mansion she has inherited. Though the prose often gives over to lush excess and meditation, what remains compelling is this woman who reveals little remorse for her infidelities and the ways she tends to fail the people in her life. In a lesser novel, such remorse would be the primary narrative thrust, but in *Magnificence*, we see how a woman, one deemed unlikable by many, is able to exist and be part of a story that expands far beyond remorse and the kinds of entrapments that could hold likable characters back. We are able to see just what the freedom of nothing looks like.

The short story collection *Battleborn* by Claire Vaye Watkins contains many stories with seemingly unlikable women. As much as the stories are about place, all set, in some form, in the desert of the American West, several stories are about women and their strength, where their strength comes from and how that strength can fail in unbearably human ways. The phrase "battle born" is, in fact, Nevada's state motto—meant to represent the state's strength, forged from struggle. In perhaps the most powerful story "Rondine Al Nido," there is an epigraph at the beginning. Normally,

I do not care for epigraphs. I don't want my reading of a story to be framed by the writer in such an overt way. This story's epigraph, though, is from the *Bhagavad Vita* and reads, "Now I am become Death, the destroyer of worlds." From the outset, we know only ruin lies ahead and the story becomes a matter of learning just how that ruin comes about. We learn of a woman who "walks out on a man who in the end, she'll decide, didn't love her enough, though he in fact did love her, but his love wrenched something inside him, and this caused him to hurt her." Really, though, this is a story about when the woman was a girl, 16, with a friend, Lena, the kind who would follow the narrator, "our girl," wherever she went. There is an evening in Las Vegas, and an incident in a hotel room with some boys the girls meet, one that will irrevocably change the friendship, one that could be avoided if a flawed young woman didn't make the wrong choice, the choice that makes the story everything.

Perhaps the most unlikable woman in recent fictional memory is Amy in Gillian Flynn's *Gone Girl*, a woman who goes to extraordinary lengths—faking her own murder and framing her husband Nick, to punish his infidelity—and keep him within her grasp. Amy was so excessively unlikable, so unrepentant, so shameless, that at times, this book is intensely uncomfortable. Flynn engages in a clever manipulation where we learn more and more about both Nick and Amy, in small moments so that we never quite know how to feel about them. We never quite know if they are likable or unlikable and then we do know that they are both flawed, both terrible, and stuck together in many ways and it is exhilarating to see a writer who doesn't blink, who doesn't pull back.

There is a line of anger that runs throughout *Gone Girl*, and for Amy, that anger is borne of the unreasonable burdens women are so often forced to bear. The novel is a psychological thriller but it is also an exquisite character study. Amy is, by all accounts, a woman people should like. She's "a smart, pretty, nice girl, with so many interests and enthusiasms, a cool job, a loving family. And let's say it: money." Even with all these assets, Amy finds herself single at 32, and then she finds Nick.

The most uncomfortable aspect of *Gone Girl* is the book's honesty and how desperately similar many of us likely are to Nick and Amy the ways they love and hate each other. The truth hurts. It hurts, it hurts, it hurts. When we finally begin to see the truth of Amy, she says, of the night she met Nick, "That night at the Brooklyn party, I was playing the girl who was in style, the girl a man like Nick wants: the Cool Girl. Men always say that as the defining compliment, don't they? She's a cool girl. Being the Cool Girl means I am a hot, brilliant, funny woman who adores football, poker, dirty jokes, and burping, who plays video games, drinks cheap beer, loves threesomes and anal sex, and jams hotdogs into her mouth like she's hosting the world's biggest culinary gang bang while somehow maintaining a size 2, because Cool Girls are above all hot. Hot and understanding... Men actually think this girl exists. Maybe they're fooled because so many women are willing to pretend to be this girl."

This is what is so rarely said about unlikable women in fiction—that they aren't pretending, that they won't or can't pretend to be someone they are not. They have neither the energy for it, nor the desire. They don't have the willingness of a May Welland to play the part demanded of her. In *Gone Girl*, Amy talks about the temptation of being the woman a man wants but ultimately she doesn't give in to that temptation to be "the girl who likes every fucking thing he likes and doesn't ever complain." Unlikable women refuse to give in to that temptation. They are, instead, themselves. They accept the consequences of their choices and those consequences become stories worth reading.

Reading the Genre

1. Gay's essay makes useful distinctions between criticism and critique, suggesting that we can't appreciate a literary work if we only want to make friends with the characters. How can we tell the difference between literary critique and the much more simple, and less useful, act of criticizing?

2. This is a literary analysis of a novel, but it is also an essay about the conventions of literary analysis itself. What rules does Gay set for her own critical analysis? In academic writing, how are you expected to emulate the "high style" traditionally adopted by literary critics, and in what ways do you want to respond more personally in your own analytical writing? (See "High, Middle, and Low Style," p. 366.)

3. In your own reading, what characters have you encountered that are truly unlikable? Does their unlikeability serve a greater function within the story? Are unlikeable characters more memorable than likeable ones?

4. WRITING: Write your own personal narrative about a book that you disliked, but wherein this dislike clearly served a greater purpose. This needs to be a book that you can critique without just criticizing. This could be a novel, or it could be a children's book you read when you were much younger. (To jog your memory, visit the children's section of your local library.) In this essay, reflect on your own feelings about the book and its characters, and what you might be able to learn from your emotional response to the book.

5. MULTIMODALITY—LITERARY FRIENDS: Gay makes it clear that she doesn't read novels to "make friends." But can you imagine what would happen if two characters from two different books, movies, television shows, or comics were stuck in an elevator together or on a desert island? Would Voldemort from *Harry Potter* and The Joker from *Batman* have much to say to one another? What about Anne of Green Gables and Hermione? In small groups, act out or write out dialogues between these characters to explore their personalities.

Further Reading

Cadena, Anna Teresa. *Who Needs A Hero? An Analysis of the Antiheroine on Television, 2013–2015*. Chapman University, 2016.

FILM ANALYSIS   Hunter Harris wrote this essay when she was still a student at Emerson College. She is currently an associate editor at the arts and entertainment magazine *Vulture* and a contributing writer for *New York* magazine. Beyoncé needs no introduction.

Beyoncé's 'Lemonade' Is a Celebration of Black Identity (Analysis)

HUNTER HARRIS

"Lemonade" opens with its artist under duress—not for marital or legal reasons, but historic: One of this visual album's first images shows a chain stretched from a tall structure, and many moments pass before we're allowed to look away. There's plenty of kinky hair and cornrows to come—this album, like its first single "Formation," worships being blackity black—but Beyoncé in 2016 wants us to see the iron she's inherited from her ancestors. In 2013, Beyoncé's first (official) visual album saw her smashing trophies, deconstructing every accomplishment. Those videos were all stunning, but cinematically distinct. She sipped Hennessey on a Miami beach with Jay Z for "Drunk in Love" and then rode Coney Island roller coasters for "XO." We'd seen this scattered approach many times before: individual productions that didn't exactly work together as a whole.

"Lemonade" isn't like that; it's a series of prayers, profound and profane, stitched together, with Beyoncé allowing us to see her seams. When one watches the album on Tidal, there are not any cuts or breaks between songs. The narrative experience is a requirement—you can't skip forward or backward between songs or interludes. Title cards show words like "Intuition" and "Reformation" that don't match the song names. The songs themselves are secondary; in some cases the listening album's final mix isn't entirely featured. With "Lemonade," Beyoncé plays with the boundary of what a music video really is, and who it's for.

The hour-long running time is part interpretation and part feature film. Despite the tradition of visual albums it calls to mind, this is really a coronation.

It recalls Toni Morrison's eulogy for James Baldwin, in which she quoted her longtime friend: "Our crown has already been bought and paid for. All we have to do is wear it." And so that's what "Lemonade" does: its camera glides above and around so many placid black faces, of black women both famous (Quven-zhané Wallis, Serena Williams, Amandla Stenberg) and not. These moment-long profiles have the same reverberations of Kehinde Wiley's portraits, elevating a struggle and considering it divine.

The trailer for "Lemonade" teased this divinity. With its whispery voice-overs and dreamlike pace, it calls to mind Terrence Malick more than any-thing else in Beyoncé's wheelhouse. But black faces are so rarely at the center of Malick's oeuvre, and Beyoncé has a more immediate message to deliver. The video for "Formation" highlighted graffiti asking America to stop shooting us. "Lemonade" ups the challenge, asking America to see our every face: Beyoncé as scorned wife, yes, but also Beyoncé as a black woman engaging with the rhetoric of Black Lives Matter, and Beyoncé as a product of her black mother's prayers. And so the chains return.

Beyond the speculation surrounding Jay Z's infidelity, "Lemonade" links its chains to generational trauma. Its Southern Gothic aesthetic casts black women in clothes and roles we were never permitted to assume—dressed in lace gowns and white gloves, allowed to scowl and weep and cackle and grin. When Jay Z makes an appearance, it's deeply intimate but brief—he's a supporting character in a larger exorcism of what was once the Master's house. "The past and the future merge to meet us here," Beyoncé says in the album's first monologue. Hurt has gathered us, but our crowns hint healing. It's only after the fire and the prayer circles that the sweetness of the sugar that is "Lemonade" can be tasted. That holy place of black women convening—away from the world, without the husbands or side chicks or pain—is a temporary retreat that recharges. Inevita-bly, we'll assemble again—but black men need their crowns too, and a montage of black love make the interim easier.

Reading the Genre

1. Harris uses a series of powerful metaphors to describe "Lemonade," just as she identifies the visual metaphors that Beyoncé uses to make meaning in the videos. Identify these metaphors and investigate what they allow Harris to say about the videos, and what they allow Beyoncé and the filmmakers to say within the videos. (See "Pay attention to audiences," p. 199.)

2. "Lemonade" has created a new genre, pulling together videos that usually stand alone to create a seamless film. How can this new genre be rhetorically analyzed? What conditions allow for this new form to be created? What does this new form do that traditional music videos cannot? How has the form reshaped how the music itself is received? (For more on genre, see the Introduction, p. 12.)

3. Since Harris wrote this article, there have been a series of academic analyses of Beyoncé and of "Lemonade"—the album is now taught in graduate and undergraduate courses at many North American universities. If you were creating a "Lemonade" syllabus, what music, videos, novels, and other texts would you include on the syllabus? What would you name the class?

4. WRITING: Choose another music video that you can analyze for its social and historical significance. Model your analysis on Harris' essay. Pay attention to visual symbolism and metaphors. Pay attention to the form of the video itself—how it was created and how it has been shared and received. Keep your analysis short, but aim to utilize the same artful and creative language that Harris uses.

Further Reading

Rutledge, Emerald, "Black Women's Bodies and the Restoration of Glory: Understanding Beyoncé's Lemonade as Political Resistance" (2017). *Senior Independent Study Theses.* College of Wooster, Massachusetts. http://openworks.wooster.edu/independentstudy/7868

FILM ANALYSIS   Anna Peppard teaches at York University in Toronto. She has published articles on the A-Team television series and her dissertation was on "reading the superhuman" in Marvel Comics. The 2017 film version of *Wonder Woman* was directed by a woman, Patty Jenkins—the first time a big studio superhero movie was directed by a woman.

On Marvel's First Female Superhero Written by a Woman: Comic Book Feminism 45 Years before Wonder Woman

BY ANNA F. PEPPARD

The Claws of the Cat was one of three ongoing series starring female characters that Marvel debuted in 1972, all of which were written by women; the others were *Night Nurse* (an action-romance written by Jean Thomas) and *Shanna the She-Devil* (a throwback to the *Jungle Girl* comics of the 1940s and 1950s written by Carole Seuling). The "Marvel Bullpen Bulletin" from November of that year foregrounds the female writers of these series as a potential selling point while also emphasizing the titles' wide appeal: "That's right, effendi—three great new comic mags, all written by gals—yet aimed neither at girls nor at guys, but at true lovers of comix literature everywhere!" Nonetheless, The Cat, the only superhero title of the three, can and should be viewed as Marvel's first attempt to appeal to female readers by adapting superhero conventions to the context of second-wave feminism.

In issue no. 1, The Cat, aka Greer Nelson, begins her heroic journey after her policeman husband Bill, in a clear reference to the origin story of Batman, is shot and killed by a mugger while the couple are leaving a movie theater. The feminist twist on this familiar tale is that Bill's death does not motivate Greer to vengeance so much as liberate her. Before his death, Bill actively limited Greer's independence, refusing to allow her to finish her college degree or drive a car. On their wedding day, Bill had told Greer, "You're my little girl now—and that's the way it's gonna be forever!" The narration also states that after the wedding,

"Bill cherished and protected her—and she felt more helpless than ever before, because he seemed to like that in a woman."

In this comic, Bill is an exaggerated patriarchal lover/father, treating his wife/daughter as an object of exchange rather than a fully fledged individual. The Cat's first villainous opponent, Mal Donalbain, is also an exaggerated patriarch; Donalbain is a health-club owner whose evil scheme involves creating an army of superwomen whom he plans to control. He will do this by using a "will-nullifier" that "renders the wearer helpless against the superior wishes of [his] superior mind." In the final pages of the issue, The Cat provokes Donalbain's death in a scene redolent with rape imagery. Knowing that the maniacal Donalbain has an intense phobia of being touched, Greer corners him in a dark room and slowly advances on him while uttering suggestive threats. This scene can be read as both a connotatively female revenge fantasy and an implied critique of patriarchal masculinity; because Donalbain prefers death to being touched by the active (or phallic) woman, his masculine need for dominance and control proves literally self-destructive.

In its very first issue, The Cat revises several key tropes related to female action heroes. One of the most significant revisions involves the introduction of a female mentor. After being turned down for all of the jobs she applies for after Bill's death—a state of affairs that causes "women's lib . . . to have new meaning"—Greer is finally hired as a lab assistant by Dr. Tumolo, a kindly, gray-haired female scientist who nurtures Greer's intellectual talents, and whose experiments are the source of Greer's superheroic transformation. As Jennifer Stuller has elaborated, female action heroes, mirroring the motherless Athena, generally have male mentors, sending the message that such characters "can only be as independent as they are because they lack a mother's womanly—almost always implied as passive— influence" (Ink-Stained Amazons 107).

Yet Greer's enriching relationship with Dr. Tumolo, especially when contrasted with her destructive relationship with Bill, situates The Cat's superheroism outside of, and even in opposition to, male authority and/or the quest for male approval. Many of Marvel's female superheroes of the 1960s, including the Invisible Girl, the Wasp, and Marvel Girl, become and remain superheroes primarily to stay close to their male love interests; Greer's heroism is instead inspired by a surrogate mother figure. Thinks Greer: "Dr. Tumolo really makes me proud to be a woman. I can't let her—or myself—down" (The Cat no. 1).

The Cat also revises tropes related to the physicality of female superheroes. As Trina Robbins observes, almost all of Marvel's female superheroes from the 1960s have "hands off" powers, exemplified by the force fields of the Invisible Girl (later the Invisible Woman) and the telekinesis of Marvel Girl (later Phoenix) (The Great Women Super Heroes, 113). Mike Madrid similarly notes that female superheroes commonly possess "'strike a pose and point' powers," which allow them to "keep their looks intact in the heat of battle" (292). In contrast, The Cat is an explicitly physical superhero, using her razor-sharp claws and advanced acrobatic skills to scale buildings and engage in hand-to-hand combat.

However, the way the Cat comes by her physicality is, at best, problematic. She is empowered via a scientific experiment whose reputed goal, as Dr. Tumolo states in issue no. 1, is to "someday make it possible for any woman to totally fulfill her physical and mental potential—despite the handicaps that society places on her." As Stuller observes, "While the message resonates with consciousness-raising politics of Women's Liberation in the 1970s . . . [u]sing a machine to amplify women's abilities excuses them from the responsibilities of empowering themselves" (Ink-Stained Amazons, 40).

It is worth noting, too, that aspects of The Cat's power-set essentialize her femininity. In issue no. 1, the narration states that "[Greer's] intensified perceptions were like an embodiment of that mythical quality known as woman's intuition." Greer's "superpowered intuition" allows her to both instinctively solve mechanical problems and feel the pain in the paw of an injured squirrel; as such, her power-set heightens stereotypically feminine qualities of empathy and emotionality alongside, or perhaps in compensation for, more stereotypically masculine capabilities related to engineering and problem solving.

After several convoluted plots that often strayed from the feminist purpose of its first issue, The Cat was abruptly canceled at issue no. 4. Yet despite its short existence, The Cat established a paradigm for adapting superhero narratives to female experiences and desires. This series crystallized, but left unresolved, the major contradiction that the next several decades of female superheroes would be compelled to negotiate. The Cat invokes this contradiction in the last panel of issue no. 1, after the death of Donalbain and the near-death of Dr. Tumolo: "All our plans for the betterment of womankind-! I did what I set out to do, and I did it well—but have I misused my powers? Did I become a stronger woman—only to become a poorer human being?"

Since The Cat, designing female superheroes that can appeal to female readers without alienating the traditionally male fan base has meant negotiating the meaning and consequences of female strength; in general, female superheroes created during and after second-wave feminism represent attempts to devise ways of empowering female lives and bodies that seem liberating to girls and women, while not being threatening to boys and men (or, more broadly, patriarchal gender norms). To repurpose a timeworn antiperspirant ad: during and since the era of The Cat, the commercially perfect female superhero has needed to be strong enough for a woman, while still being made (primarily) for a man.

Reading the Genre

1. Much of comics scholarship has focused on deep, close readings of individual texts. It is understood that if you want to make an argument about a comic, you need to be able to use direct evidence, citing specific cells (the individual frames in which comics unfold). How does Peppard manage these forms of citation?

2. Peppard, like many comics scholars, pays careful attention to the needs, demands, and reactions of readers. It becomes clear that comics are deeply shaped by their audiences. How does this approach allow Peppard to paint a picture of this comic's readers? Is Peppard able to critically comment on the readership? (See "Focus on social connections," p. 181.)

3. WRITING: Peppard's analysis anticipates a day when many more comics will be written with strong female characters and for a female audience. Has this happened? Write an analysis of a comic book or a superhero movie or a television show, focusing on the ways that gender roles are defined. What are the "tropes" that condition how men and women act in these texts?

4. MULTIMODALITY—COMPOSING VISUALLY: Write and illustrate a short superhero comic starring yourself as the superhero. In the comic, your job is to challenge some of the tropes and conventions of the genre—how can you comment on some of the rules of this genre by having your characters break them? If you need help generating ideas, there are lists and explanations of common comic book tropes all over the Internet, including Wikipedia.

Further Reading

Gibbons, Sarah. "'I Don't Exactly Have Quiet, Pretty Powers': Flexibility and Alterity in Ms. Marvel." *Journal of Graphic Novels and Comics* (2017): 1–14.

Rhetorical Analyses: Readings

GENRE MOVES Rhetorical Analysis

SUSAN SONTAG

From "Notes on 'Camp'"

Many things in the world have not been named; and many things, even if they have been named, have never been described. One of these is the sensibility—unmistakably modern, a variant of sophistication but hardly identical with it—that goes by the cult name of "Camp." . . .

1. To start very generally: Camp is a certain mode of aestheticism. It is one way of seeing the world as an aesthetic phenomenon. That way, the way of Camp, is not in terms of beauty, but in terms of the degree of artifice, of stylization.

2. To emphasize style is to slight content, or to introduce an attitude which is neutral with respect to content. It goes without saying that the Camp sensibility is disengaged, depoliticized—or at least apolitical.

3. Not only is there a Camp vision, a Camp way of looking at things. Camp is as well a quality discoverable in objects and the behavior of persons. There are "campy" movies, clothes, furniture, popular songs, novels, people, buildings. . . . This distinction is important. True, the Camp eye has the power to transform experience. But not everything can be seen as Camp. It's not all in the eye of the beholder.

4. Random examples of items which are part of the canon of Camp:

    Zuleika Dobson

    Tiffany lamps

    Scopitone films

    the Brown Derby restaurant on Sunset Boulevard in L.A.

    the *Enquirer*, headlines and stories

    Aubrey Beardsley drawings

Swan Lake

Bellini's operas

Visconti's direction of *Salome* and *'Tis Pity She's a Whore*

certain turn-of-the-century picture postcards

Schoedsack's *King Kong*

the Cuban pop singer La Lupe

Lynd Ward's novel in woodcuts, *Gods' Man*

the old *Flash Gordon* comics

women's clothes of the twenties (feather boas, fringed and beaded dresses, etc.)

the novels of Ronald Firbank and Ivy Compton-Burnett

Make your notes into an essay.

In this famous essay written in 1964, Susan Sontag actually lists fifty-eight "notes" about "camp" sensibility. She seems to create this long list because she simply has too much to say about "camp" to narrow her focus effectively. When assembled, though, Sontag's list of notes and "random examples" gives the reader a distinct impression of her topic and provides specifics that begin to support her generalizations about a slippery subject.

Likewise, some of the texts or performances or phenomena that you might want to analyze will feel as though they are too complicated and multifaceted for you to choose just one thesis, or even to choose just four to five supporting ideas. Or you may be the sort of writer who prefers to think in lists—and you would rather gather lots of different ideas than focus on just one to begin with.

In your own rhetorical analysis, you might create such a list as a form of prewriting. Consider simply creating a list of responses, ideas, evaluations, and arguments about the thing you are analyzing. For instance, if you are evaluating an advertisement, you'd want to watch it multiple times and record as many impressions and observations as you can about the ad. Then reorder your list to make it more organized. You might see ways that certain thoughts build on or respond to other thoughts. Then you can choose one major idea and seek some other ideas that work to support your larger thesis; the rest can probably be discarded. But you might also consider shaping your notes into an unconventional essay, as Sontag does so successfully here.

CULTURAL ANALYSIS   Christine Martorana is a writing and rhetoric professor at Florida Atlantic University.

CHRISTINE MARTORANA

Death: The End We All Have to Face(book)

When my friend Aaron unexpectedly died several years ago, I gained firsthand experience with a growing online phenomenon: mourners turning to online spaces following the death of a loved one. In what follows, I present details from Aaron's Facebook page in order to illustrate two specific observations: 1) Digital technologies are reconfiguring the permanence of death, inviting the living to recreate the deceased as a heavenly intermediary, and 2) this continued virtual existence of the deceased alongside the constant accessibility of digital technologies is opening a space for death-related egocentrism.

As I have observed Aaron's wall over the past several years, I have at times admittedly felt like a voyeur observing the unaware. Although Aaron had, by becoming my Facebook friend, granted me permission to see his wall, I am aware that I am observing sensitive and Intimate expressions I would not otherwise see. I strive to remain cognizant of the fact that Aaron is not just a Facebook profile; he is someone's son, brother, and friend. He was my friend. I hope the measures I have taken to respect Aaron's memory, identity, and those of his family and friends communicate this awareness.

Aaron has 616 Facebook friends. His profile picture is a close-up of his face, eyebrows slightly furrowed, sunglasses resting atop his head. A quick scroll through his Facebook photos reveals his active social life and love for the outdoors. His Facebook wall contains countless posts from friends and family featuring message, photos, and videos. Aaron's Facebook page appears typical; however, a closer look reveals that although Aaron's friends continue to post messages to him, Aaron has not responded to these messages in more than five years. This is because Aaron unexpectedly passed away in 2008—and yet, his Facebook page remains active.[1]

Contemporary mourners are turning to online spaces for comfort and contact.

Aaron's Facebook page is an example of a growing phenomenon: mourners turning to online spaces following the death of a loved one.[2] In the face of death, everything from blogs to YouTube series, Instagram feeds, and Tumblr pages are emerging, "bringing the conversation about bereavement and the deceased into a very public forum. [Users] seem eager for spaces to express not just the good stuff that litters everyone's Facebook newsfeed, but also the painful" (Seligson). After Aaron's passing, I became one of these online users.

Aaron and I met three years prior to his death. We'd grown up in the same area and worked together at a part-time job. Although I was about three years his senior, we were part of the first generation of high school students to join Facebook.[3] Accordingly, Aaron and I were both co-workers and Facebook friends. When I heard of Aaron's death, I was, like everyone else, shocked.

Several days later, I looked up Aaron's Facebook page. Although I never posted there myself, I became engulfed in the flood of posts after his death. As his Facebook friend, I was privy to read these posts and witness the ways in which his close family and friends were using his wall to grapple with their sudden loss. I continued to periodically look in on Aaron's page, and as time progressed, I was struck by both the heavy, ongoing volume of posts as well as some trends in their content.

Dying in a Digital Age

Digital technologies have seeped into practically every aspect of our lives: eating, sleeping, exercising, driving, shopping, dating, entertainment—and now, dying.

As *USA Today* writer Laura Petrecca notes, we are living in the age of "Mourning 2.0," where digital technology is inseparable from grieving, forever changing the ways in which we cope with lost loved ones. Grieving, which used to be "private and personal" (Farber 6), now regularly occurs online. Aaron's Facebook page provides evidence that this is indeed true: "Mourning 2.0" is in full swing.

Social media has changed the way we grieve—Mourning 2.0 has arrived.

His page not only demonstrates our "ability to instantly congregate, at least virtually, and commiserate" (Brondou), it also supports two valuable claims regarding this age of digital mourning. First, digital technologies are reconfiguring the permanence of death, inviting the living to recreate the deceased as a heavenly intermediary—a being with access to both our physical world and a heavenly world beyond. Second, this continued virtual existence of the deceased alongside the constant accessibility of digital technologies is opening a space for death-related egocentrism—a self-serving attitude that shifts responses to death from mourning loss to requesting help.

Not Physically Here, But Still Present

The vast majority of us—73 percent according to Pew Internet Research—lead both physical and virtual lives. This impacts not only how we live from day to day[4] but also our experiences with death. For although we might stand graveside and bid farewell to a loved one, we can later stand with our digital technologies and access that person's social media profile. From this perspective, death is a force with the power to remove our physical bodies yet unable to eliminate our virtual ones.

My experiences with Aaron and his Facebook page testify to this. Although I have not seen Aaron's physical body in more than five years, I see his face on a regular basis. With just a few keystrokes, I can pull up his profile picture, the same picture that has been there since the day he passed away. This photo, with its static, fixed quality, seems to freeze time, maintaining a visual representation of Aaron as he was while physically alive. When I look at his Facebook page, I see the same teenage boy I remember; as he looks back at me from the computer screen, it is as if he continues to exist virtually despite his physical passing.

The deceased remain frozen in online spaces; the presence of their virtual profiles, pictures, and status updates belie their physical absence.

This is not to say that others or I fail to recognize that Aaron has physically died. However, because Aaron's photo has remained unaffected by his physical death, it does suggest that physical death did not lead to a complete and total end to his existence. Instead, Aaron retains a presence on his Facebook page, an observation that echoes Susan Sontag's claim that, after an "event has ended, the picture will still exist, conferring on the event a kind of immortality" (11). Although Sontag wrote these words in 1973, long before Facebook entered our lives, the concept still rings true: photographs capture and preserve what might otherwise be lost with the passage of time.

What Sontag may have not been able to predict was the impact of the *digital* photograph. Through digital photos, we can not only capture and preserve moments, but we can also widely distribute and circulate them. Thus, whereas a print photo of Aaron might have previously remained only among close family and friends, today, the digital image circulates among a much larger public of family, friends, and acquaintances connected to one another by Aaron's Facebook page, unconstrained by the limitations of time and space.

My Digital Guardian Angel

The digital platform not only changes the reach and longevity of the photograph, but it also impacts our grieving process. According to Dr. April Hames, there are six stages of healthy grief: acknowledgment of loss, reaction to loss, recollection of the departed, relinquishing attachments, readjusting, and reinvesting. My observations of Aaron's page suggest the fourth stage, relinquishing attachments, is complicated by Facebook. That is, since we can often access Facebook pages even after Facebook users have passed away, this digital platform offers a new method of grieving, one that does not require relinquishment.

Specifically, the Facebook users I observed, rather than *relinquishing* attachments to Aaron, have *evolved* their attachments to Aaron so that they come to view him as an intercessor between this physical world and another cosmic, divine space. This is evidenced in posts like these:[5]

· "I GOT INTO MICHIGAN YESTERDAY! omg Im still soo excited . . . tell God I said thanks for getting me in cuz I know he had his hand in that."

· "so it was snowing this mornign and i definately think it had something to do with you becuase you would have been BOUNCING off teh walls at the first snow. haha. so it made me smile. ps. you think you could work out a snow day sometime soon??"

· "please watch over us all during this holiday season & maybe you talk the Big man into some snow? because this rain simply will not do."

· "Lots of people need prayers and watching over . . . I know you're the invisible hero in action . . . the angel of our prayers . . . thanks."

Through these posts, we can see how Aaron's virtual presence continues as well as how living Facebook users communicate directly with Aaron in the same way they might offer a prayer to a divine being. That is, instead of *letting go of their attachments* to Aaron, they have *evolved these attachments* so that Aaron moves from a lost loved one to an available intermediary, one who can communicate with God, control the weather, and hear prayers.

I am not the first to consider the impact of the digital on grieving. Robert Dobler offers a related discussion of grief as it manifests on the social networking site MySpace. According to Dobler's analysis of MySpace pages of the departed, MySpace users post "personal expressions of grief' [in an] attempt to mitigate the permanence of the loss by keeping up a direct correspondence with the departed" (176). I have found similar practices on Facebook; both social media sites offer a space in which users can construct new relationships with the deceased, evolving their attachments instead of relinquishing them.

Aaron has become a digital guardian angel, a comforting and helpful online connection to another realm.

However, whereas Dobler's analysis leads him to characterize the deceased as a "ghost" (185), my observations suggest otherwise. A ghost implies a haunting, restless spirit; however, the posts on Aaron's wall do not cast Aaron as either haunting or restless. Rather, a more appropriate image might be that of a guardian angel, what one of Aaron's friends calls "the invisible hero in action"—a comforting intercessor watching over the living, providing services and guidance as needed and requested.

Regardless of whether we think of the departed as ghosts or guarding angels, one thing is clear: the Internet offers multiple avenues for continued interactions with the deceased and their communities. These available avenues take several forms, including online memorials such as Virtual Memorial Garden, a site where mourners create digital photo memorials for lost loved ones, and the World Wide Cemetery, an online cemetery that invites mourners to create virtual monuments in memory of those lost. However, what I have observed on Aaron's Facebook page offers a slightly different conception of death in this digital age.

These Facebook interactions are taking place at an online site previously inhabited by the deceased, the Facebook page, not at one created in response to the death. We might think of this as a practice similar to "memorials erected at homes of suddenly dead celebrities" (Doss 66). Considered in this light, these Facebook posts reveal our conception of Facebook as a site of lived experience, an online home for users, a space where virtual life is contained and lived, even after physical death.

It's All About Me

Recognizing the ways in which Facebook reconfigures the permanence of death brings us to my second observation regarding this age of digital mourning: death-related egocentrism. That is, instead of explicitly mourning—or even mentioning—Aaron's death, Facebook users view his continued virtual existence as an outlet for them to share concerns and needs *about their own lives,* positing Aaron as an ever-available heavenly intermediary. The posts I have observed express candid requests for help from Aaron, explicitly describing the ways in which he can positively intervene in the lives of the living:

- "please help me finish up my last year of school. give me the strength to get through this so i can finally be a RVT!"
- "hey [aaron]. help me with my princeton app please, only you can. i love you."
- "thanks for getting me through my surgery well, now please help my dad get through his!"
- "some advice would be appreciated, you always come through for me"
- "Thank you for helping me out with my Mirco exam on thursday means alot . . . .Plz help me out this week for finals!! Miss you"

As evidenced by the above posts, the living Facebook users seem to view Aaron as a heavenly intermediary through an egocentric focus, casting Aaron as an intercessor present and available to *meet their needs.*

The constant accessibility of digital technologies undoubtedly feeds into this online egocentrism. We spend countless hours uploading pictures, videos, and details about ourselves to multiple social media platforms. Why? Because we can.

More specifically, we can no matter where we are: work, school, the grocery store, the bathroom. The omnipresence of social media, the fact that we can post from anywhere at any time, promotes an attitude of "individualism [and] self-gratification"

(Taylor). Every thought, no matter how inconsequential or fleeting, can be and often is digitally documented, uploaded, and shared.

In the context of Aaron's Facebook page, then, we can consider the ways in which our ability to access Facebook via any number of digital devices invites these egocentric posts. Not only do we have constant access to Aaron's page, but also we have constant access to a page where the Facebook user is physically unable to participate. The only activity on Aaron's page, therefore, is what living users post, turning his page into a breeding ground for egocentriclty, a space that gradually becomes *all about the living users*. A quick look at some numbers illustrates this point:

Months since Aaron's passing	Percent of posts that are egocentric
2	1 percent
6	30 percent
24	77 percent

Today, more than five years after his death, an egocentric focus dominates, suggesting that the longer Aaron is physically absent, the more likely living Facebook users are to conceptualize his continued virtual existence from a selfserving perspective.

Death and iCulture

Most teenagers today (at least in mainstream contexts) cannot recall a time without the Internet. Constituting what has been called the "iCulture" generation, teens occupy a narcissistic sphere dominated by "'ME'-centered profiles [and] the rise of technologies like cell phones that allow individuals to continually wonder, 'Who's called Me? Or texted Me?'" ("The Rise of iCulture"). Perhaps it should not be surprising, then, that egocentrism characterizes the majority of the posts on Aaron's wall. Aaron was, after all, a teenager when he died as were the majority of his friends.

Considering this specific iCulture demographic leads us to intriguing questions ripe for future discussion:

- In an online culture that values its actions based on the number of likes, favorites, and digital thumbs-up, are Aaron's Facebook friends continually posting to his wall solely because they believe *he* can read their posts, or do they also want *their peers* to see their posts?
- Does Facebook offer a valuable and necessary outlet for teenagers who require and seek out their own forms of memorialization and mourning within a community of their peers? Or, alternatively, does the intense and intimate existence of Facebook within this generation invite the emergence of egocentric memorialization behaviors that would not otherwise exist?
- Does Facebook make public the egocentric behaviors and practices that would otherwise be done in the privacy of one's own head, home, and/or place of worship?
- Just as many of us today cannot imagine relationships without the existence of Facebook and other social media venues, will we also soon be unable to imagine death without such platforms?

We are already experiencing what might be considered the next move of "Mourning 2.0" in such things as "Living Headstones"—which have, interestingly, been described as "similar to a personal Facebook page" (*Living Headstones*)—and funeral webcasting, the live-streaming and digital recording of funeral services.

There's also the "If I Die" app, an app that tells Facebook users, "You probably don't remember scheduling an appointment with death anytime soon. And you're right, but so is death—right. around. the. corner." The goal of this app is to encourage (or frighten?) Facebook users into recording a post-death video message that will be published after three chosen "trustees" confirm that the Facebook user has, in fact, died.

It seems that the patterns and behaviors I have observed on Aaron's Facebook page are just one part of a larger shift in the mourning and memorialization practices of this iCulture generation.

Shaping Our Post-Death Identities

The longer Facebook is a central part of our lives, the more pages that will continue to remain active following death and the greater awareness we will have of this future for our own pages and identities. Implicit in this recognition is an acknowledgment of the fragility of our current existence and the understanding that any Facebook profile can, without notice, turn from a "normal" profile to one of a deceased user.

As Aaron's page reveals, the virtual choices we make today, although perhaps seemingly inconsequential in the present moment, have the potential for indefinite impact. These choices include . . .

- *The profile pictures we post:* When Aaron posted his current profile picture, he was unknowingly posting his final profile picture, the one that would greet me each time I access his page, forever positing this image as the face of his post-death virtual identity.
- *The messages we type:* The messages Aaron posted to his own wall prior to his death, the information he shared in his "About Me" section, and his list of favorite quotes are permanently and publicly displayed on his Facebook page, indefinitely connected to his post-death virtual identity.
- *The Facebook friends we accept:* Throughout my observation of Aaron's page, I discovered that only those users who were Facebook friends with Aaron *before* he died can interact with his page *after* his death. This means that, in selecting his Facebook friends, Aaron was unknowingly and simultaneously selecting who would help construct his post-death virtual identity.

Ultimately, my hope is that this discussion of Aaron's page adds to our understanding of online spaces such as Facebook and will lead to more conscious and thoughtful interactions with others, both those who are still physically with us and those who are not.

Christine Martorana is a Ph.D. candidate in Rhetoric and Composition at Florida State University. She is currently finishing her dissertation on feminist agency and activism, a project she loves because it has allowed her to learn from and talk to some very smart, creative, and courageous women. She also enjoys practicing yoga, reading books by Margaret Atwood, and drinking warm lattes.

Notes

1. Aaron is not the individual's actual name. I have changed his name to respect his privacy and that of his friends and family. For the same reason, I purposefully feature Facebook posts throughout this discussion that do not include identifying information about Aaron or other Facebook users. Additionally, based on the visual heuristic of research variables provided in *The Ethics of Internet Research* (McKee and Porter 88), I decided informed consent was not necessary for this discussion.

2. This phenomenon is occurring so regularly that both Google and Facebook are responding: In April of 2013, Google piloted an "Inactive Account Manager" that offers Facebook users the opportunity to suspend their account after a designated period of inactivity. This feature is "targeted at people who want to create an automated digital will" (Gates). Additionally, Facebook offers the option to memorialize a Facebook user's page. While the Facebook page remains active after it is memorialized, no new friend requests can be accepted and no one can log into the memorialized account.

3. In September of 2005, Facebook registration opened to all high school students rather than being limited to only Harvard students, as it originally was. Aaron joined Facebook in 2006 as a high school freshman; at the time, more than 25,000 high schools were represented on Facebook (Zeevi), and Facebook quickly became one of the top means of socializing for Aaron's generation.

4. Jeff Bullas reports that a quarter of Facebook users admit to checking Facebook at least five times a day.

5. It is not possible to include every available example here; thus, select examples have been chosen for this discussion. Additionally, I quote the Facebook posts exactly as they appear on Aaron's Facebook wall; the exact spelling and syntax of every post has been preserved.

References

Brondou, Colleen. "Grieving 2.0: As Students Turn to Facebook to Mourn. How Should Parents, Teachers and Counselors React?" *Finding Dulcinea*. 28 Sept. 2010. Web. 7 Aug. 2014.

Bullas, Jeff. "22 Social Media Facts and Statistics You Should Know." *jeffbullas.com* n.d. Web. 8 Dec. 2014.

Dobler, Robert. "Ghosts in the Machine: Mourning the MySpace Dead." *Folklore and the Internet: Vernacular Expression in a Digital World*. Ed. Trevor Blank. Utah: Utah State University Press, 2009. 175–193. Web.

Farber, Lauren. "American Vernacular Memorial Art: The Politics of Mourning and Remembrance." Major Research Project. (2003) London: The London Institute, Camberwell College of Arts.

Gates, Sara. "Google 'Inactive Account Manager': New Feature Helps Users Plan for Death." *The Huffington Post*. 11 April 2013. Web. 10 May 2013.

Living Headstones. *Quiring Monuments*. 2013. Web. 09 Aug. 2014.

Petrecca, Laura. "Mourning Becomes Electric: Tech Changes the Way We Grieve." *USA Today*. 30 May 2012. Web. 30 July 2014.

Seligson, Hannah. "An Online Generation Redefines Mourning." *The New York Times*. 21 March 2014. Web. 29 July 2014.

Sontag, Susan. *On Photography*. New York: Doubleday Dell Publishing Group, Inc., 1973. Print.

Taylor, Jim. "Narcissism: On the Rise in America?" *The Huffington Post*. 28 May 2011. Web. 29 July 2014.

"The Rise of iCulture." *The New York Times*. 24 Sept. 2007. Web. 29 July 2014. *The World Wide Cemetery*. 2014. Web. 08 Aug. 2014.

Zeevl, Daniel. "The Ultimate History of Facebook." *Social Media Today*. 21 Feb. 2013. Web. 29 Aug. 2013.

Table of Contents Image credit: "Drowning in Social Media" by mkhmarketing on flickr

Reading the Genre

1. This article has two clearly-stated goals. How does the author provide evidence to support these two lines of analysis? How do the two lines of analysis come together or diverge?

2. In addition to rhetorical analysis, this essay offers a discourse analysis—a study of language use. How does Martorana present the evidence (the specific discourse) that she will analyze? How do you think she chose this evidence—these examples of discourse? (See Chapter 26, "Critical Thinking," p. 327 and Chapter 48, "Annotating Sources," p. 452; "Distinguish between primary and secondary sources," p. 430.)

3. This essay has many quotes. Closely review how Martorana handles these quotations. What kinds of signal words does she use to introduce and summarize quotes? How does her language add meaning to the quotes? (See Chapter 51, "Incorporating Sources into Your Work," p. 463.)

4. WRITING: Do some fieldwork. Sit at a busy table in a cafeteria, restaurant, or food court, and observe what is said and how. Take detailed notes, keeping your subjects anonymous or—if you're in doubt of your ability to do that—get permission from everyone you observe. Using your notes, make observations about how the people you observed interacted, based on what they said and how they said it. Then, do the same type of research through a social network like Instagram or Facebook. What are the differences and similarities in how people speak to one another, and speak about themselves, in these two different settings? (See Chapter 47, "Doing Field Research," p. 448.)

Further Reading

McCallig, Damien. "Facebook After Death: An Evolving Policy in a Social Network." *International Journal of Law and Information Technology*. 22.2 (2013): 107–140.

ANALYSIS OF AN ADVERTISEMENT   Jake Romm is a contributing editor for *The Forward*. His writing and photography have appeared in *Reading the Pictures, Phroom, Across the Margin, Humble Arts Foundation, Roads & Kingdoms, The New Inquiry*, and other outlets. The Pepsi ad that Romm analyzes in this essay has been widely acclaimed as the worst advertisement ever.

Why That Catastrophic Pepsi Ad Was Actually a Resounding Success

Pepsi recently announced that it has pulled their Kendall Jenner advertisement (it was just as much an advertisement for her as it was for Pepsi) and have issued an apology, stating "Pepsi was trying to project a global message of unity, peace and understanding. Clearly we missed the mark, and we apologize. We did not intend to make light of any serious issue. We are removing the content and halting any further rollout." But, as we well know, nothing ever gets truly erased from the Internet, and, in any event, the advertisement has already been seen (or at the very least, mocked) by millions. The damage is done, and the whole story is instructive (not least because it feeds the Think Piece Industrial Complex—second only to Big Soda in terms of power and size). You can watch the ad below, but in the event that it is successfully scrubbed from YouTube, here is a quick synopsis: a protest for "unity" and "peace" breaks out on the streets. A meticulously diverse cast of attractive, young, creative types join the march. As they proceed down the street, the marchers pass Kendall Jenner, who in a moment of spirited independence, interrupts a fashion shoot to join the "protest." As the shiniest of the group, she immediately becomes their de facto leader, and the march proceeds until it is met by a wall of policemen. Jenner, brave and bold, walks up to one of the cops (the shiniest, handsomest one, of course) and gives him a Pepsi. The crowd cheers and a new understanding and mutual goodwill is formed between the police and protestors.

So what do we have here? The ad has already been dissected on an aesthetic level elsewhere—with commentators pointing out the vapidity of the signs (which read like the wet dream of a junior advertising manager in charge of hashtags), the appropriation of imagery from the Black Lives Matter movement, the overt and ridiculous symbolism (the blonde wig is FAKE, but Pepsi, Pepsi is REAL), the tone-deafness of positioning a fabulously wealthy white woman at the head of a vague, multi-ethnic, protest movement, the insanity of the ending in which Jenner gives the policeman a Pepsi to enormous cheers . . . The list goes on—at least we can say that Pepsi created a text richly imbued with occasions for deconstruction.

But aesthetic concerns are not the primary reason behind this article, rather, let's take a broader approach. We know why Pepsi would make this ad—they want to capitalize on the energy of the growing protest movements around the country. And in this regard, it is also quite obvious how the advertisement and its reception play into the larger political landscape (though it does, interestingly, put the hyper-partisan consumer in an odd position. The ad, had it been positively received, would likely have been decried as "anti-Trump." Now that the ad been widely lambasted however, with the loudest voices coming from an anti-Trump perspective, the right is thrust into a position in which Pepsi can become an anti-left symbol. The enemy of my enemy . . .).

Before delving deeper, we must acknowledge that Pepsi is not the first offender in terms of co-opting the aesthetics of protest, nor will it be the last. And it is the fact that Pepsi is so unoriginal in this regard that makes the advertisement, and its backlash, so important. This commonplace problem should prompt us to consider the ad not within the context of the present political moment, but rather within the larger context of capitalism itself. Specifically, we might turn to Mark Fisher's seminal text "Capitalist Realism." which proves particularly prescient in this situation. The book, like the title implies, examines the ways in which capitalism colors all facets of daily life, and the ways in which capitalist realism is supplanting reality as such. To start, let's examine the advertisement in light of the following two passages:

> "What we are dealing with now is not the incorporation of materials that previously seemed to possess subversive potentials, but instead, their precorporation: the pre-emptive formatting and shaping of desires, aspirations and hopes by capitalist culture."

> "Here, even success meant failure, since to succeed would only mean that you were the new meat on which the system could feed."

One of the main problems of late capitalism, as predicted by theorists much older than Fisher, Theodor Adorno for example, is the process of incorporation, whereby things that once existed outside of the capitalist system are eventually brought into the fold. For a recent, and morbidly humorous example—we must now pay to visit Marx's grave, turning the author of the Communist Manifesto into a site of tourism and capital. Marx himself has thus been incorporated into the system. Before turning to Fisher's neologism, "precorporation," let's divert briefly to the second passage. The "Here" in question is referring to Kurt Cobain and Nirvana, but could just as easily, to bring things back to the Pepsi ad, refer to the Black Lives Matter protests. Success here is not defined as effecting change, but rather in terms of achieving visibility, and the protests have certainly succeeded in this regard—Black Lives Matter having become a national movement with widely recognized aesthetic markers and artifacts. The problem identified by Fisher is that it is precisely because of the movement's success that it has been co-opted, and thus mocked and sterilized (to an extent), by Pepsi. Capitalism compounds success with more, similar, material until the original is sucked dry—then onto the next big thing.

This all seems obvious enough, but it is with the idea of "precorporation" that Fisher makes an advance. If we look at how contemporary protest movements become successful in the first place, we can see that they are "precorporated" into the capitalist system, that is, they are necessarily constituted in such a way as to perfectly lend themselves to incorporation. In order to spread, in order to be successful on a national scale, protests must use social media, they must make use of hashtags, of merchandise, of spectacle—essentially, protests take the form of advertisements, and vice versa. Protest has its own cottage industry of commodities and codes that both feed the success of a movement and ultimately, once the process of incorporation reaches its summit, become the raison d'etre for the movement—incorporation being both a repurposing and a neutering.

In "The Demagogue Takes The Stage." a superb and important article in Places Journal, Reinhold Martin writes that in order for power, specifically political power, to properly function it "must stand on ground that has been made sacred as a stage" and this ground "is always already there, ahead of the performers, preparing the ground, laying things out, positioning speakers and addressees and establishing the basis for the reality that they will enact together." Martin uses, by way of example, "the political rally before the speech, the executive office awaiting an occupant, the pulpit awaiting a preacher," but we might also add the protest awaiting a cause. The very presence of the aesthetics of protest in the advertising world imbues the advertisement with an urgency, an abstract notion of duty that can be disassociated to fit any ideology, a readymade system of cliches that ease the "creative process" and the viewing process alike.

But with the Pepsi ad, we've seen through all that, haven't we? In general, when an advertisement faces this kind of backlash, we tend to stop at the assertion that

Pepsi has only revealed itself as yet another vapid corporation, lazily incorporating protest to sell soda, unconcerned with any political issues. Some anti-corporate rhetoric here, perhaps a boycott there,—all with afundamental belief in the vapidity of the corporate space. But underneath this abstract simulacrum of a protest is a very real ideology cleverly masked as vapidity. When corporations like Pepsi incorporate the aesthetics of protest, it does not matter what the original, incorporated protest was for; it is the act of sterilization and incorporation that's important.

This is why "unity" is the perfect buzzword. A protest, in a certain sense, is a demand for unity insofar as the ultimate goal is to persuade people to adopt a unified viewpoint on an issue. But a protest for "Unity" is incoherent—unless of course we have something to unify behind. It may seem as if the unifying "cause" is Pepsi, but "Unity" is not just oriented towards a single product—there is more at stake here than soda. The desire for "Unity" is the inherent ideology behind capitalism itself. "Unity" is the stifling of dissent, the homogenization of desires—insofar as we are "unified," our consumptive potential can go unhindered by political or even libidinal concerns. In the world of the commercial, the "unity" between protestor and state under the auspices of the Pepsi Corporation is the ultimate satisfaction of capitalist realism—finally the contradictions between capital and labor, state and individual, are erased in the single homogenous pursuit of capital.

One might argue that, despite all this, the advertisement failed—it did not unify us behind consumption but rather prompted a renewed outrage at consumption itself. But here is the tricky thing about "Unity" and capitalist realism— even in failure, even when it ostensibly undermines itself, it is enhanced by this process of undermining. As Fisher writes, "capitalist realism is very far from precluding a certain anticapitalism." The advertisement itself has incorporated some anticapitalist elements (consider Jenner removing her wig and lipstick to join the protest or the focus on performers and artists as symbols of the "real" as opposed to the "fake," that is, the commodified). According to Fisher, performative anticapitalism, like the kind we have in the Pepsi ad, creates a kind of "'interpassivity' . . . [the commercial] performs our anticapitalism for us, allowing us to continue to consume with impunity." "The Lego Movie," (the performative anti-capitalist film *par excellence* for instance, positions "big business" as the villain, thus allowing us to pat ourselves on the back for having recognized the evils of corporations while simultaneously consuming those corporations' products.

The Pepsi ad, however, operates on meta level. The ad is so nakedly performative, so nakedly and ambitiously corporate, that it is the outrage, rather than the ad itself, that inspires this inter passivity. The response to the ad is obvious to the point that it is essentially programmed into the ad itself. "We believe," Fisher writes, "that money is only a meaningless token of no intrinsic worth, yet we act as if it has a holy value. Moreover, this behavior precisely depends upon the prior disavowal—we are able to fetishize money in our actions only because we have already taken an ironic distance towards money in our heads." "The Lego Movie" achieves this effect byway of positioning business as the villain, the Pepsi ad achieves this effect by positioning *itself as* the villain. We can continue to operate as consumers, exactly as before, only because we have completed our castigation of the ad. The Pepsi ad is the sacrificial lamb on the altar of capital—it dies so that we, as consumers, might live.

Pepsi, far from pulling a gaffe, has achieved a wild success. The product might suffer in the short term, some helpless advertisement workers might lose their jobs, but the systems and ideologies that enable Pepsi to exist in the first place have been bolstered and buttressed by the "failure" of the advertisement. This is the state of our world, of capitalist realism: failure is success, success is failure, and Pepsi knows you better than you know yourself.

The Advertising Archives/Alamy Stock Photo

Reading the Genre

1. Romm offers a blow-by-blow account of this commercial, ostensibly because he believes that the ad might eventually be "scrubbed" from the Internet. But this kind of description can also be vitally important in a rhetorical analysis. What does Romm's description of the ad predict about his analysis of the ad? (See "Make the text accessible to readers," p. 210.)

2. What major rhetorical appeals are evident in the commercial? (See "Consider how well reasoned a piece is," p. 206.)

3. The purpose of a television advertisement is to sell something, not necessarily to be artistic—or intelligent. With this in mind, how is conducting a rhetorical analysis of a television commercial different from doing so with a political speech, a Web site, or an op-ed in the newspaper?

4. WRITING: If this ad is actually "brilliant," and the media actually does "know you better than you know yourself," what can we possibly do to criticize and reshape the commercial messages we are given? Can you contrast this ad with one that you truly believe does make a successful and valuable statement? List ten commercials you have recently seen, and choose one that seems deserving of study. Describe it in detail, and then jot down any inferences your description lets you make about the commercial. If the commercial still seems worthy of close examination, write a rhetorical analysis. If not, choose another commercial and start over. Repeat the process until you find a commercial worth writing about. (See "Choose a text with handles," p. 203; "Make a difference," p. 203.)

Further Reading

Schauster, Erin E., Patrick Ferrucci, and Marlene S. Neill. "Native Advertising is the New Journalism: How Deception Affects Social Responsibility." *American Behavioral Scientist* 60.12 (2016): 1408–1424.

CULTURAL ANALYSIS   Teju Cole is a Nigerian-American photographer and the photography critic at the *New York Times Magazine,* where he writes a monthly column. He teaches at Bard College. This essay comes from the collection *Known and Strange Things*, which was named a book of the year by *Time*. You can see his daily photographic experiments by following him on Instagram at _tejucole.

Finders Keepers *from* Known and Strange Things

TEJU COLE

When he visited the Plumbe National Daguerrian Gallery in Manhattan in 1846, Walt Whitman was astonished. "What a spectacle!" he wrote. "In whichever direction you turn your peering gaze, you see nought but human faces! There they stretch, from floor to ceiling—hundreds of them." In the seven years between the invention of the daguerreotype and Whitman's visit to Plumbe's, the medium had become popular enough to generate an impressive, and even hectic, stream of images. Now, toward the end of photography's second century, that stream has become torrential.

"Take lots of pictures!" is how our friends wish us a good trip, and we oblige them. Nearly one trillion photographs are taken each year, of everything at which a camera might be pointed: families, meals, landscapes, cars, toes, cats, toothpaste tubes, skies, traffic lights, atrocities, doorknobs, waterfalls, an unrestrained gallimaufry that not only indexes the world of visible things but also adds to its plenty. We are surrounded by just as many depictions of things as by things themselves.

The consequences are numerous and complicated: more instantaneous pleasure, more information, and a more cosmopolitan experience of life for huge numbers of people, but also constant exposure to illusion and an intimate knowledge of fakery. There is a photograph coming at you every few seconds, and hype is the lingua franca. It has become hard to stand still, wrapped in the glory of a single image, as the original viewers of old paintings used to do. The flood of images has increased our access to wonders and at the same time lessened our sense of wonder. We live in inescapable surfeit.

A number of artists are using this abundance as their starting point, setting their own cameras aside and turning to the horde—collecting and arranging photographs that they have found online. These artist-collectors, in placing one thing next to another, create a third thing—and this third thing, like a subatomic particle produced by a collision of two other particles, carries a charge.

A decent photograph of the sun looks similar to any other decent photograph of the sun: a pale circle with a livid red or blue sky around it. There are hundreds of thousands of such photographs online, and in the daily contest for "likes" they are close to a sure thing: easy to shoot, fun to look at, a reliable dose of awe. The American artist Penelope Umbrico downloads such photos of the sun from Flickr—she favors sunsets in particular—and then crops and prints them, assembling them into an enormous array. A typical installation may contain 2,500 photographs, organized into a rectangular mural. It is the same sun, photographed repeatedly in the same way, by a large cast of photographers, few of whom are individually remarkable as artists and none of whom are credited. But, with Umbrico's intervention, the cumulative effect of their images literally dazzles: the sun, the sun, the sun, the sun, in row upon brilliant row.

Optical brilliance is also the key to the American artist Eric Oglander's *Craigslist Mirrors* project, which is also based on found photographs. His biographical statement is deadpan: "I search Craigslist for compelling photos of mirrors." Oglander posts these pictures to his website, to Instagram, and to Tumblr. A surprising number of them are surreal or enjoyably weird, because of the crazy way a mirror interrupts the logic of whichever visual field it is placed in, and because of the unexpected things the reflection might include. Photographic work of this kind—radically dependent on context—can be unsettling for those who take "photograph" to have a straightforward meaning: an image made with a camera by a single author with a particular intention. This is where collector-artists come in: to confirm that curation and juxtaposition are basic artistic gestures.

The German artist Joachim Schmid, with a gleeful and indefatigable eye, gathers other people's photographs and organizes them into photo books. For his trouble, he has been called a thief and a fraud. Schmid initially used photographs found on the street and at sales, but more recently he has depended on digital images. His typological projects, like those in the ninety-six-book series *Other People's Photographs* (2008–2011), are alert to the mystery in artlessness. They are a mutant form, somewhere between the omnivorous vernacular of Stephen Shore's *American Surfaces* and the hypnotic minimalism of Bernd and

Hilla Becher's water towers. Schmid brings the photographs out of one kind of flow, their image-life as part of one person's Flickr account, and into another, at rest among their visual cognates.

Each book in *Other People's Photographs* is a document of how amateur digital photography nudges us toward a common but unpremeditated language of appearances. Photography is easy now, and cheap, but this does not mean that everything is documented with the same frequency or that all possibilities are equally explored. As is true of every set of expressive tools, digital photography creates its own forms of emphasis and registers of style. Cellphone cameras are great in low light, and so we have many more nocturnal photos. Most of our tiny cameras are not easy to set on a tripod, and so there is a correspondingly smaller percentage of soberly symmetrical photographs of monuments; the dominant aesthetic of the age is handheld. A camera focused at waist level, as old Rolleiflexes were, is different from one held between the eyes and the chin, the optimal placement for a live digital display.

All selfies are alike as all daguerreotype portraits were alike: an image can be more conventionally an example of its genre than a memorable depiction of its subject. A plate of food, with its four or five items of varying texture corralled into a circle, is similar to countless other plates of food. But a book full of photographed meals, meals long consumed and forgotten, is not only poking gentle fun at our obsessive documentation of the quotidian. It is also marveling at how inexpensive photography has become. Things that would not have merited a second glance are now unquestioningly, almost automatically, recorded. The doors of our fridges, glimpses of cleavage, images of our birthday cakes, the setting sun: cheap photography makes visible the ways in which we are similar, and have for a long time been similar. Now we have proof, again, and again, and again.

The sheer mass of digital imagery was itself the subject of *24 Hrs of Photos,* a project by the Dutch artist Erik Kessels (first in 2011, and other times since). Kessels downloaded every photograph uploaded to Flickr in the course of a single day, about a million in all. He printed a fraction of them, around 350,000, which he then piled up in massive wavelike heaps in a gallery. Asked to explain the project, Kessels said: "I visualize the feeling of drowning in representations of other people's experiences. But that s not art! And yet the emotions that accompany such an installation—the exasperation, the sense of wonder or inundation, the glimpses of beauty—are true of art. The shoe fits, maddening as it is.

What are the rights of the original photographers, the "non-artists" whose works have been so unceremoniously reconfigured? And how can what is found be ordered, or put into a new disorder, and presented again to give it new resonance? And how long will that resonance itself last? The real trouble is rarely about whether something counts as art—if the question comes up, the answer is almost always yes—but whether the art in question is startling, moving, or productively discomfiting. Meeting those criteria is just as difficult for straight photography as it is for appropriation-based work. After all, images made of found images are images, too. They join the never-ending cataract of images, what Whitman called the "immense Phantom concourse," and they are vulnerable, as all images are, to the dual threats of banality and oblivion—until someone shows up, says "Finders keepers," rethinks them, and, by that rethinking, brings them back to life.

Penelope Umbrico, 2,303,057 Suns from Flickr (Partial) 9/25/07, 20017, Instillation, Brisbane Gallery of Modern Art (photo credit: Huw Porter)

2,303,057 Suns from Sunsets from Flickr, as seen at the Gallery of Modern Art in Brisbane, Australia (2007)

Reading the Genre

1. Cole includes several terms and phrases that even an English professor likely can't define. Look up a few of these terms to find their definitions, but also to discover what words might have been substituted without confusing the reader. This is an essay about art, but it also uses the elevated style of the art critic. What would happen if you had the chance to rewrite Cole's essay in a "lower," clearer, plainer style? Would the analysis suffer?

2. Look for a video advertisement showcasing the qualities of a smartphone's camera. How is photography depicted in the ad—technically, artistically, romantically? What can we deduce about contemporary photography and photographers from these ads?

3. Cole argues that pictures are ubiquitous and disposable at the same time. He also argues that this ubiquity makes photos profound, collectively. On social media, what images are you most likely to ignore, and which are you most likely to stop and look at carefully? Record the characteristics of your least favorite types of images, and record the characteristics of your favorite types. Can you find anything profound in either set of characteristics? (See "Take words and images seriously," p. 199.)

4. MULTIMODALITY—PHOTO COLLAGE: Based on the lists of characteristics above (analyzing photos that you do and do not like, that you ignore or spend time examining), perform a Google Image search using these characteristics as keywords. Create collages of both types of images, using as many different pictures as you can, and present this collage, in combination with some reflections on your own visual tastes.

5. WRITING: Cole's essay is organized around a series of examples of artistic re-uses of photographs. Find three to four examples of your own—examples in which artists or individuals use photography platforms (like Instagram) to reuse, to recirculate, or simply to critique and comment on our obsession with images. Once you know what it is you'd like to say about each of these examples, and how you can connect them to one another, use the examples to create a sequence for a short rhetorical analysis essay (See "Creating a structure," p. 197).

Further Reading

Hartung, Catherine. "Selfies for/of Nepal: Acts of Global Citizenship and Bearing Witness." *Selfie Citizenship*. Springer International Publishing, 2017. 39–47.

66

Essays:
Readings

AMY TAN

From "Mother Tongue"

I later decided I should envision a reader for the stories I would write. And the reader I decided upon was my mother, because these were stories about mothers. So with this reader in mind—and in fact she did read my early drafts—I began to write stories using all the Englishes I grew up with: the English I spoke to my mother, which for lack of a better term might be described as "simple"; the English she used with me, which for lack of a better term might be described as "broken"; my translation of her Chinese, which could certainly be described as "watered down"; and what I imagined to be her translation of her Chinese if she could speak in perfect English, her internal language, and for that I sought to preserve the essence, but neither an English nor a Chinese structure. I wanted to capture what language ability tests can never reveal: her intent, her passion, her imagery, the rhythms of her speech and the nature of her thoughts.

Use lists.

Although we might think that lists should only be included in genres like reports or proposals, lists in narrative essays can be very powerful. Lists allow writers to create a sense of rhythm and momentum; they allow us to acknowledge many possibilities within a story, even if we can't explore all of them; they can mirror the stream of our thoughts. In the passage above, Amy Tan concludes her essay with two lists, one divided by semicolons, one divided by commas. Importantly, because this is a literacy narrative about "Englishes," the lists allow her to catalog and honor the diversity of the language as she knows it. By ending the essay with these lists, she offers more than one conclusion or lesson.

Try ending your own narrative with a list of things you learned from experiencing your story or a list of things you hope your readers learned from reading it. Experiment with long lists, short lists, and different styles of punctuation. Reread your list and look back to make sure your narrative has effectively communicated all the things you have listed—this is a good test to see if your narrative is as complete as you'd intended. Then you may choose to use this list as part of your conclusion, or you might cut it. Regardless, developing the ability to effectively write lists can help you write in nearly any genre.

NARRATIVE   Actor and comedian Patton Oswalt is perhaps best known as the voice of Remy, the lead character in the animated Pixar film *Ratatouille*. This short essay comes from his book of the same name: *Zombie Spaceship Wasteland* (2011), which, as in his standup comedy, mixes personal history with pop culture. In addition to standup, Oswalt has written essays for publications such as *The Believer* and *The Huffington Post*, and stories for comics. His 2015 book, *Silver Screen Fiend*, is a memoir that also chronicles his obsession with classic movies.

PATTON OSWALT

Zombie Spaceship Wasteland

Are you a Zombie, a Spaceship, or a Wasteland?

For my group of friends, after seeing *Star Wars* in 1977, around age eight, and then *Night of the Living Dead* and all the eighties slasher films once VCRs sprouted on top of our TVs, and *The Road Warrior* in 1981, the answer to that question decided our destinies.

I know there have been a thousand parsings of the pop subculture—comic books, video games, horror movies, heavy metal, science fiction, Dungeons and Dragons. There are hundreds more categories. They can be laid out in overlapping Venn diagrams—a tub full of lonely bubbles. Burnouts who are into heavy metal got there through Dungeons and Dragons, maybe some glam rock, probably horror movies. Hard-core comic book readers often became film snobs later in life (they spent their adolescence reading, essentially, storyboards). Even sports freaks[1]—with their endless, exotic game stats—overlapped into metal and, yeah, maybe comic books.

But for me, and my circle of high school friends, it came down to *Zombies, Spaceships*, or *Wastelands*. These were the three doors out of the Vestibule of Adolescence, and each opened onto a dark, echoing hallway. The corridors twisted and intertwined, like a DNA helix. Maybe those paths were a rough reflection of the DNA we were born with, which made us more likely to cherish and pursue one corridor over another.

I'm going to try to explain each of these categories (and will probably fail). And then I'll figure out where I came out, on the other end, once the cards were played. I think this essay is more for me than for you.

Each of these categories represents different aspects of a shared teen experience—not fully understanding how the world works, socially or economically. The early outcasts—like me—were late to sex and careers. If we did find a vocation, it usually involved drawing or writing or *something* creative—work that's done in the home, and usually alone. The real-world experience we're going to need, as writers or artists or filmmakers, will come later, when we actually have to get a real job to support whatever creative thing we're hoping to do.

So until then, anything we create has to involve *simplifying*, *leaving*, or *destroying* the world we're living in.

Zombies simplify. They don't understand the world any better than Spaceships or Wastelands, but they sure like the houses and highways. Every zombie story is fundamentally about a breakdown of order, with the infrastructure intact. That infrastructure might be on fire, yes. And it's great fun to crash a bus through a department store window as the driver finds himself torn to shreds by the suddenly zombified passengers. But the world, appearance-wise, survives. It might eventually become a wasteland (more advanced Zombies begin their stories far in the future, where the world is already a wasteland), but for now, it's a microcosm of archetypes, fighting for survival against the undead hordes. Usually this small group is made up of the archetypes that the teen has met thus far into his short existence—the Hero, the Unattainable Hottie, the Loudmouth Douchebag, and the Brainiac Who Knows What's Going On. Consistent with an awkward teen's roiling sense of vengeance and self-hatred, it's usually only the Loudmouth Douchebag and the Brainiac who get killed.

Usually, but not often. Since Zombies follow their path into horror, Goth, slasher films, some punk rock, and most metal, Zombies tend to be the most nihilistic of the three. Thus, most zombie movies—including the classic *Night of the Living Dead*—end with every single character dead.

A friend of mine from high school—more of a passing acquaintance, now that I think of it—was a hard-core zombie before he even knew it. He had an unshakable love for the awkward and outcast and a quiet, final disgust with the slick and false. And he divided everyone into one of these two categories, with maybe three subsets for each (Physically Awkward, Mentally Awkward, Sports Slick, Republican Slick— you get the idea).

Years later, when I'd moved to L.A., he sent me a zombie script he'd written. Not a bad effort. Not a great one.

At one point in the script, one of the characters knocks a zombie off of a boat. The zombie struggles for a moment, trying to stay afloat, and then sinks.

I asked him, innocently, "It never occurred to me—would a zombie care if it were underwater or not? They don't breathe. Would they even know?"

This was his terse answer: "For your information, zombies can live underwater, *they just don't like it.*"

He was a Zombie who'd long ago taken a zombie-eyed view of the world. You see them everywhere—rolling their eyes outside a rock club at how lame the band was, shaking their heads over a newspaper in a coffee shop, resentful under office lighting. Zombies can't believe the energy we waste on nonfood pursuits.

Night of the Living Dead (and most zombie films) is about *Zombies* who are in the process of turning the world into a *Wasteland*, and who've been brought back to life by radiation on a crashed *Spaceship*.

Spaceships leave. No surviving infrastructure for them. No Earth, period. *That* would still involve people.

Better to not only leave the world, but to create a new one and decide how the creatures (or human-looking aliens) act. Often, the alien planet they populate is a glorified wasteland. But even in that wasteland, Spaceships figure it's easier for them to build a world and know its history or, better yet, choose the limited customs and rituals that fit the story. Every Spaceship kid I knew growing up now works in computers. They got there through New Wave, post-punk, video games, and science fiction. Why bother reading subtle facial cues and emotional signals when there's a vast (yet finite) map of a motherboard to tinker with?

But, being Spaceships, they describe in the most loving detail the spaceships that zoom between worlds. "Laser cannons" take the place of conversation, "deflector shields" are emotional nuance, and "warp drive" is story exposition. The opening shot of *Star Wars*, with the sleek rebel ship and then the massive Imperial Star Destroyer, barreling across the screen like the pan across a party in an Altman film, permanently doomed a generation of Spaceships to their insular, slightly muted lives. Spaceships have the hallway with the most gravity, firmly pulling its victims down a cool tunnel of romantic vacuum. In their bodies, skulls, and spirits, a chunk of my peers became Spaceships, skimming over the surface of the world, maneuvering through their own lives. Deflector shields up.

Spaceships are the ones most likely to get married and have kids. They treat their houses like spaceships that have landed on earth, and their spouses and kids like crew members. Which makes them pretty good parents—they've always got emergency kits, lists of most-used numbers, backup supplies of ointment, painkillers, and bottled water. The two guys I spent my youth building Lego spaceships with are two of the greatest dads I've ever known—a good captain knows how to treat his crew.

Darth Vader is, essentially, a *Zombie*, born in a *Wasteland*, who works on a *Spaceship*.

Wastelands destroy. They're confused but fascinated by the world. So the idea of zooming off in a self-contained spaceship, no matter how lovingly described or sensually evoked,[2] smacks of retreat. But the blandness of the world we've built—a lot of Wastelands come from the suburbs—frustrates and frightens them as much as the coldness of space. Aliens would bring wonder, and zombies bring the surviving humans together—Wastelands aren't comfortable with either of those ideas.

The solution? Wasteland. Post-nuke, post–meteor strike, or simply a million years into the future—that's the perfect environment for the Wasteland's imagination to gallop through. The wasteland is inhabited by people or, for variety, mutants. At least mutants are outgrowths of humans. Mutants—the main inhabitants of post-apocalyptic environments—are more familiar. Variations of the human species grown amok—isn't that how some teenage outcasts already feel? Mutants bring comfort. You don't have to figure out alien biology or exotic, inhuman cultures or religions. At the most, mutants will have weird mental powers or practice cannibalism. The heroes are unmutated humans, wandering across deserts (always, weirdly, wearing leather or tattered overcoats—suburban teens are accustomed to air-conditioning, so it's not until they're older that they learn the importance of fabrics that breathe) and carrying what they need. Wastelands are great at stocking belt pouches, backpacks, and pockets. At any time, Wastelands suspect they're going to need to grab whatever's at hand and head for the horizon.

Wastelands are almost always swallowed up by punk rock and science fiction. They're also the most likely to keep journals and usually the first to get menial jobs. The Wasteland tarot card should come with a pay stub.

Weirdly, Wastelands are the most hopeful and sentimental of the bunch. Because even though they've destroyed the world as we know it, they conceive of stories in which a core of humanity—either in actual numbers of survivors or in the conscience of a lone hero—survives and endures. Wastelands, in college, love Beckett.

The monster in *Alien* was discovered on a *Spaceship* that had crashed in a *Wasteland*, and reproduced by temporarily turning its victims into alien-incubating *Zombies*.

Leatherface, Michael Myers, Jason Voorhees, Pinhead, and Freddy Krueger are, essentially, *Zombies* who want to turn our world into a *Wasteland*. Jason and Pinhead each, at one point, end up on a *Spaceship*.

The *Matrix* films are about a hero, Neo, who doesn't realize he's a *Zombie*, and also doesn't realize he's living in a *Wasteland*, until he's awoken by Morpheus, who dezombifies Neo by bringing him on board a *Spaceship*.

Every teen outcast who pursues a creative career has, at its outset, either a Zombie, Spaceship, or Wasteland work of art in them.

Looking back on it now, I realize I'm a Wasteland. A lot of comedians are Wastelands—what is stand-up comedy except isolating specific parts of culture or humanity and holding them up against a stark, vast background to approach at an oblique angle and get laughs? Or, in a broader sense, pointing out how so much of what we perceive as culture and society is disposable waste? Plus, comedians have to work the Road. We wander the country, seeking outposts full of cheap booze, nachos, and audiences in order to ply our trade. I'm amazed we all don't wear sawed-off shotguns on our hips.

The Zombie, Spaceship, or Wasteland "work" is conceived of during the nadir of puberty—a grim, low-budget film about the undead; a vast space opera; or a final battle for civilization in a blasted wasteland, where the fate of mankind is decided by a shotgun blast or a crossbow.

Turns out I had two Wasteland works in me, and I wrote them both freshman year of high school. The first was called *The Shadow Dogs*, which I figured I'd publish in paperback, like a Stephen King novel.[3] It involved—I'm not kidding—a future where mutant dogs had taken over. They were basically tall people with dog heads. The hero—I can't even remember his name—wandered the wasteland with a cool wrist gun and another sidearm that I basically swiped from *Blade Runner*, which I still think has one of the coolest movie guns.

Hey—why do the heroes always "wander" the wasteland? Wouldn't you at least have a plan to get somewhere with water or food before you started hoofing it? Even desert nomads don't "wander" around pell-mell, assuming they'll hit an oasis just before dropping dead of thirst. Is it the alliteration of it? "Wander the wasteland"? I guess "Take a well-thought-out, purposeful trek through the wasteland" lacks that movie-trailer punch.

Anyway, *The Shadow Dogs*. I spent the first eighty pages of the novel equipping my main character. I'm not kidding—he started with a bolt-action rifle and a knife, and then he killed some people and took enough canned food and other trinkets from them to trade for the wrist gun and *Blade Runner* gun. Once I realized I couldn't think of any cooler guns for him to acquire, I lost interest in the book.

The other one was called *Cholly Victor and the Wasteland Blues*, which I wrote in installments and planned to do as a massive graphic novel. Cholly Victor was a near-plotless library of everything I was obsessed with at the time—*The Road Warrior*, *El Topo*, *Eraserhead*, Richard Corben, nuclear fears, and spaghetti westerns. Holy God, was it a piece of crap. But I got it out of my system. It ends with my hero, Cholly, a shotgun-wielding wasteland scavenger, defeating a mutant, flayed-lamb robot warlord, and then continuing on down a piece of broken highway to the mythical "Westcoast."[4]

My own life didn't even come close to my defeating a robot warlord and setting out for Westcoast. In reality, I got sick of doing jokes in front of the zombies at the local comedy clubs. I moved to San Francisco. In a used Jetta, not a spaceship. And driving cross-country wasn't "wandering the wasteland," but Utah came close enough.

Notes

1. Not to be confused with jocks or athletes—a distinction beautifully laid out by Sarah Vowell in *Take the Cannoli*, a book very much worth your time.
2. The spaceship in *Battle beyond the Stars* has huge breasts and a woman's voice!
3. Stephen King, who was the first person I ever read who could meld perfectly felt, mundane life with cosmic horror, later published the *Dark Tower* series, a huge Wasteland epic that tied together most of his novels, which take place in our "real" world. And I'm pretty sure he got the idea in high school. If he didn't, I would like him to lie about it to support my thesis. Thanks, Steve!
4. Cormac McCarthy won the Pulitzer for *The Road*, about a father and son making their way for a mythical coast after an unnamed global cataclysm. But Cormac's hero didn't have a four-armed, bandolier-wearing mutant Kodiak bear sidekick, did he?

Reading the Genre

1. Think about the categories Oswalt sets up. Are you a zombie, a spaceship, or a wasteland? Or are you some parts of each? Explain why you do or don't fit into these categories. Don't be afraid to make up your own category if none of these works for you.

2. This is a narrative essay, but it also lays out its own taxonomy (a taxonomy is a way to sort or classify things). How does this classification system help Oswalt tell stories? What does this taxonomy do for his structure, organization, and characterization, and how does it help him to reflect on past experiences?

3. An anthropologist might suggest that what Oswalt is doing in this narrative is also ethnography (a way to describe groups of people through close observation and writing). Some of the goals of ethnography are that the text should help the reader better understand social life, that its authors must be sufficiently conscious of their own role in the society they study, and that the account should feel true and revealing. How does Oswalt's essay measure up to these standards?

4. WRITING: Develop your own classification system for you and your friends. As Oswalt does, use stories to illustrate why you and those you know fit in these invented categories. If it helps, you could choose one of your favorite books, films, or television shows and then show how you and your friends align with the characters from that text.

5. COMPOSING VISUALLY: Using YouTube, find examples of a zombie, spaceship, or wasteland character from a movie or television show (or from other media). Write about how the character fits this category and embed relevant video or images in your Word document or blog. Then think about how this character also reflects aspects of your own personality or the personality of someone you know. How does this fictional character (and his or her zombie-ness, spaceship-ness, or wasteland-ness) help you to better understand yourself or people you know?

GRAPHIC NARRATIVE (EXCERPT)   Lynda Barry writes the weekly comic strip *Ernie Pook's Comeek*, which can be found in many alternative weekly newspapers. Barry's work is often funny but serious, sad but optimistic. When she writes about herself, as she does in this excerpt from the book *One! Hundred! Demons!* (2002), she is very honest about her own past. She currently teaches a popular writing workshop called Writing the Unthinkable. Barry has written seventeen books; her most recent is the collection *Blabber Blabber Blabber: Volume 1 of Everything* (2011).

Lost and Found

Lynda Barry

"Lost and Found" from *One! Hundred@ Demons!* by Lynda Barry (Sasquatch Books, 2002). © 2002 by Lynda Barry. Courtesy of Drawn & Quarterly.

AFTER I LEARNED TO READ, I LOVED GETTING HOME FROM SCHOOL AND WAITING FOR THE AFTERNOON PAPER. WE DIDN'T HAVE BOOKS IN THE HOUSE, BUT THE PAPER GAVE ME PLENTY TO WORK WITH.

THE FIRST SECTION I TURNED TO WAS THE CLASSIFIEDS. I ALWAYS READ THE "LOST AND FOUND" ADS, TRYING TO MEMORIZE DESCRIPTIONS OF DOGS AND CATS WHO WERE OUT THERE ALONE AND SCARED.

EACH QUARTER-INCH AD WAS LIKE A CHAPTER IN A BOOK. I'D IMAGINE THE WHOLE STORY: THE FREAKED-OUT PEOPLE, THE FREAKED-OUT ANIMALS, AND ME, ALWAYS COMING TO THE RESCUE AND NEVER ACCEPTING THE REWARD.

NO, KEEP THE FIVE HUNDRED DOLLARS, SIR. ALL I CARE ABOUT IS THAT HENRY IS HOME.

PLEASE, MA'AM, WHAT MY NAME IS DOESN'T MATTER. AND NEITHER DOES THE TEN THOUSAND DOLLARS. ALL THAT MATTERS IS JINGLES.

LIKE MOST WRITERS, I LOVED TO READ WHEN I WAS LITTLE, BUT UNTIL RECENTLY, I NEVER REALLY THOUGHT ABOUT SOME OF THE THINGS I ENJOYED READING MOST. THE CLASSIFIED ADS FASCINATED ME.

CRYPT IN MAUSOLEUM. PRIME LOC. EYE-LEVEL. BEST OFFER. EVENINGS.

SZ. 12 WEDDING DRESS. NEVER WORN. MUST SACRIFICE.

FILL DIRT, VERY CLEAN.

PARTY PIANIST. MY PIANO OR YOURS.

THEY GAVE ME SO MANY WEIRD BLANKS TO FILL IN. LIKE WHO WAS SELLING THEIR CRYPT? I ONLY KNEW THE WORD FROM HORROR MOVIES. ZOMBIES AND VAMPIRES CAME OUT OF THEM. THE AD SAID "EVENINGS." IT SEEMED LIKE SUCH AN OBVIOUS TRICK.

DING DONG

WHO IS IT?

UH, I'M HERE ABOUT THE CRYPT?

AAHHHH!!

SAME WITH THE WEDDING DRESS AD. WHO ELSE WAS GOING TO CALL ABOUT IT EXCEPT A MAIDEN? IT SAID "MUST SACRIFICE." WHO ELSE GOT SACRIFICED BUT MAIDENS? THE POLICE WOULD BE BAFFLED BY HOW MAIDENS KEPT DISAPPEARING.

HELLO?

YES?

YOU'VE GOT TO BE KIDDING.

OK.

NOT ANOTHER MAIDEN!

I'M AFRAID SO.

DANG!

WHEN I CAME FORWARD WITH THE SOLUTION TO THESE CRIMES, AT FIRST NO ONE WOULD BELIEVE ME. I EXPECTED THAT. I WATCHED A LOT OF MOVIES. NO ONE EVER BELIEVES KIDS AT FIRST. YOU HAVE TO WAIT UNTIL ALMOST THE END. YOU HAVE TO WAIT 'TIL YOUR LIFE IS IN DANGER.

> CALLING ALL CARS! THAT KID WAS RIGHT ABOUT THE WANT ADS!

> BUT NOW THE CRYPT-VAMPIRE AND THE WEDDING DRESS-ZOMBIE HAVE HER IN THEIR CLUTCHES! WE WERE SO STUPID! REPEAT! VERY STUPID!

MOSTLY I DIED IN MY CLAS-SIFIED STORIES. EVEN THEN I LOVED TRAGIC ENDINGS. PEO-PLE WOULD BE CRYING SO HARD. THEY'D COVER MY COFFIN WITH FILL DIRT, VERY CLEAN. THE PARTY PIANIST WOULD PLAY.

> ♪ CHERISH IS THE WORD I USE TO DIS-CRI-IBE.. ♪

WHEN I READ ABOUT WRITER'S LIVES, THERE ARE USUALLY STORIES ABOUT WRITING FROM THE TIME THEY WERE LITTLE. I NEVER WROTE ANYTHING UN-TIL I WAS A TEENAGER, AND THEN IT WAS ONLY A DIARY THAT SAID THE SAME THING OVER AND OVER.

> I thought Bill liked me but turns out he doesn't. I'm so depressed about Bill. He didn't call me. I can't stop thinking about Bill.

WRITERS TALK ABOUT ALL THE BOOKS THEY LOVED WHEN THEY WERE CHILDREN. CLASSIC STORIES I NEVER READ, BUT I LIED ABOUT BECAUSE I WAS SCARED IT WAS PROOF I WASN'T REALLY A WRITER.

> AND WIND IN THE WILLOWS?

> AH, YES.

> AMAZING.

> "THE LION, THE WITCH AND THE WARDROBE?"

> INCREDIBLE. SAME WITH "WATERHEAD DOWN"

> YOU MEAN "WATERSHIP"?

> UH, YEAH.

SUPER DRAMATICALLY EDUCATED. KNOWS ABOUT "STORY STRUC-TURE" AND "ARC" AND "PLOT POINTS"

JIVE-ASS FAKER WHO CAN'T SPELL AND HAS NO IDEA WHAT "STORY STRUCTURE" EVEN MEANS

BUT ONLY CERTAIN PEOPLE WERE "ADVANCED" ENOUGH FOR WRITING AND LITERATURE. IN COLLEGE IT GOT EVEN WORSE. I LOVED THE WRONG KIND OF WRITING AND I NEVER COULD BREAK A STORY DOWN TO FIND THE SYMBOLIC MEANING, ALTHOUGH I SURE TRIED TO FAKE IT.

(3:30 AM)

In "the Bell Jar," Plath profounds her enumerated existential parthenogenesis using subvertible intra-mural insight on the dissimulation of her classic bummer of the 20th century.

MY TROUBLE ENDED WHEN I STARTED MAKING COMIC-STRIPS. IT'S NOT SOMETHING A PERSON HAS TO BE VERY "ADVANCED" TO DO. AT LEAST NOT IN THE MINDS OF LITERARY TYPES.

SO YOU'RE A CARTOONIST! HOW ADORABLE!

POLITICAL? NO. HUMOROUS? KINDA. WE'RE BOTH WRITERS.

SAY, MAYBE WE COULD COLLABORATE! WE WRITE IT AND YOU DRAW IT! HOW FUN!

NOBODY FEELS THE NEED TO PROVIDE DEEP CRITICAL IN-SIGHT TO SOMETHING WRITTEN BY HAND. MOSTLY THEY KEEP IT AS SHORT AS A WANT AD. THE WORST I GET IS, "TOO MANY WORDS. NOT FUNNY. DON'T GET THE JOKE." I CAN LIVE WITH THAT.

GALS, EVER FELT SO intimidated by the IDEA OF WRITING THAT you've never even given it a try? Think writing is only FOR "writers"? Sure is common!

ESPECIALLY BECAUSE I'M SURE THAT THE NINE-YEAR-OLD VERSION OF ME WHO MADE UP ALL THOSE "CLASSI-FIED STORIES" WOULD THINK THAT THIS ONE HAD A VERY HAPPY ENDING.

(and YES, Gals- the first thing I read in the paper is still the "lost and found")

LOST. SOMEWHERE AROUND PUBERTY. ABILITY TO MAKE UP STORIES. HAPPINESS DEPENDS ON IT. PLEASE WRITE.

Reading the Genre

1. Even though this essay is in comic form, it also addresses literacy directly, discussing the author's early reading experiences. As a literacy narrative, what does "Lost and Found" teach us about the author's approach to reading and writing? (For another example of a literacy narrative, see Laura Grisham's work on page 8.)

2. Unlike many other comic authors, Lynda Barry provides descriptions for some of her pictures. Why do you think she does this, and how do these descriptions contribute to the essay?

3. If Barry had presented her story without images, do you think your response to it would be different? How do comics present information, and why might a writer or artist choose this medium? (See Chapter 33, "Levels of Style," p. 366.)

4. WRITING: Craigslist might be the online equivalent of the newspaper's classified section. Go to craigslist.org and find an advertised item that suggests a story to you. (Hint: Try looking at the lost-and-found section or the ads for free items.) Draw a picture of this item and write a short imaginative narrative about it.

5. COMPOSING VISUALLY: This essay comes from the book *One! Hundred! Demons!* The concept for the book comes from an ancient Japanese painting exercise in which artists painted about things that worried or challenged them. As she began painting and writing about her demons, Barry explains that "at first the demons freaked me, but then I started to love watching them come out of my paintbrush." Try drawing or writing about memories from your own past as a student. What have you struggled with? In writing about these memories, have you also come to better understand them?

REFLECTION Poet and novelist Naomi Shihab Nye has written or edited more than twenty books and has won dozens of awards for her writing. Nye's mother is American and her father is Palestinian, and much of her writing is focused on helping people understand the similarities and differences between Middle Eastern and American cultures, and specifically on dispelling stereotypes about the Middle East. This piece appeared in Nye's 2001 collection *Mint Snowball*.

NAOMI SHIHAB NYE

Mint Snowball

My great-grandfather on my mother's side ran a drugstore in a small town in central Illinois. He sold pills and rubbing alcohol from behind the big cash register and creamy ice cream from the soda fountain. My mother remembers the counter's long polished sweep, its shining face. She twirled on the stools. Dreamy fans. Wide summer afternoons. Clink of nickels in anybody's hand. He sold milkshakes, cherry Cokes, old-fashioned sandwiches. What did an old-fashioned sandwich look like? Dark wooden shelves. Silver spigots on chocolate dispensers.

My great-grandfather had one specialty: a Mint Snowball which he invented. Some people drove all the way in from Decatur just to taste it. First he stirred fresh mint leaves with sugar and secret ingredients in a small pot on the stove for a very long time. He concocted a flamboyant elixir of mint. Its scent clung to his fingers even after he washed his hands. Then he shaved ice into tiny particles and served it mounded in a glass dish. Permeated with mint syrup. Scoops of rich vanilla ice cream to each side. My mother took a bite of minty ice and ice cream mixed together. The Mint Snowball tasted like winter. She closed her eyes to see the Swiss village my great-grandfather's parents came from. Snow frosting the roofs. Glistening, dangling spokes of ice.

Before my great-grandfather died, he sold the recipe for the mint syrup to someone in town for one hundred dollars. This hurt my grandfather's feelings. My grandfather thought he should have inherited it to carry on the tradition. As far as the family knew, the person who bought the recipe never used it. At least not in public. My mother had watched my grandfather make the syrup so often she thought she could replicate it. But what did he have in those little unmarked bottles? She experimented. Once she came close. She wrote down what she did. Now she has lost the paper.

Perhaps the clue to my entire personality connects to the lost Mint Snowball. I have always felt out-of-step with my environment, disjointed in the modern world. The crisp flush of cities makes me weep. Strip centers, poodle grooming, and take-out Thai. I am angry over lost department stores, wistful for something I have never tasted or seen.

Although I know how to do everything one needs to know—change airplanes, find my exit off the interstate, charge gas, send a fax—there is something missing. Perhaps the stoop of my great-grandfather over the pan, the slow patient swish of his spoon. The spin of my mother on the high stool with her whole life in front of her, something fine and fragrant still to happen. When I breathe a handful of mint, even pathetic sprigs from my sunbaked Texas earth, I close my eyes. Little chips of ice on the tongue, their cool slide down. Can we follow the long river of the word "refreshment" back to its spring? Is there another land for me? Can I find any lasting solace in the color green?

Reading the Genre

1. Nye uses sentence fragments in this essay. Examine these incomplete sentences, particularly in the first two paragraphs of the essay. How is the content of each of these shorter sentences similar, and how does this work within the essay? (See Chapter 33, "Levels of Style," p. 368 and Part 8, "Handbook," p. 470.)

2. This narrative is divided into two parts. The perspective in the second part of the story radically shifts. How would you describe the perspective, or point of view, in the first half and in the second? What can the author do in the second half that she can't in the first? Why? (See Chapter 38, "Memorable Openings and Closings," p. 395, and Chapter 39, "Informative Titles," p. 399.)

3. WRITING: Consider the work history of your own family: What kind of work do your parents do, and what kind of work did their parents do? What kind of work does your extended family do? Are there specific skills or lessons, or even ways of looking at the world, that have been passed down in your family because of the sort of work your family has done? Write a short personal reflection on this topic.

4. WRITING: Visit a local business and interview the owner about the history of this business. Then write a short narrative that tells the story of the business—how it began, what it specializes in, what makes it unique, how it has changed over the years, and so on.

LITERACY NARRATIVE   Ta-Nehisi Coates is a journalist, author, and teacher. His memoir *Between the World and Me* won the National Book Award. He is also the coauthor of the *Black Panther* comic book series with Roxane Gay, whose work also appears in this book. Coates was given a MacArthur "Genius" grant in 2015. But this essay is about Coates' struggles as a learner. He is even brave enough to share his French tests.

TA-NEHISI COATES

Acting French

I spent the majority of this summer at Middlebury College, studying at l'École Française. I had never been to Vermont. I have not been many places at all. I did not have an adult passport until I was 37 years old. Sometimes I regret this. And then sometimes not. Learning to travel when you're older allows you to be young again, to touch the childlike amazement that is so often dulled away by adult things. In the past year, I have seen more of the world than at any point before, and thus, I have been filled with that juvenile feeling more times then I can count—at a train station in Strasbourg, in an old Parisian bookstore, on a wide avenue in Lawndale. It was no different in Vermont where the green mountains loomed like giants. I would stare at these mountains out of the back window of the Davis Family Library. I would watch the clouds, which, before the rain, drooped over the mountains like lampshades, and I would wonder what, precisely, I had been doing with my life.

I was there to improve my French. My study consisted of four hours of class work and four hours of homework. I was forbidden from reading, writing, speaking, or hearing English. I watched films in French, tried to read a story in *Le Monde* each day, listened to RFI and a lot of Barbara and Karim Oeullet. At every meal I spoke French, and over the course of the seven weeks I felt myself gradually losing touch with the broader world. This was not a wholly unpleasant feeling. In the moments

I had to speak English (calling my wife, interacting with folks in town or at the book store), my mouth felt alien and my ear slightly off.

And there were the latest developments, the likes of which I perceived faintly through the French media. I had some vague sense that King James had done something grand, that the police were killing black men over cigarette sales, that a passenger plane had been shot out of the sky, and that powerful people in the world still believed that great problems could be ultimately solved with great armaments. In sum, I knew that very little had changed. And I knew this even with my feeble French eyes, which turned the news of the world into an exercise in impressionism. Everything felt distorted. I understood that things were happening out there, but their size and scope mostly eluded me.

Acquiring a second language is hard. I have been told that it is easier for children, but I am not so sure if this is for reasons of biology or because adults have so much more to learn. Still, it remains true that the vast majority of students at Middlebury were younger than me, and not just younger, but fiercer. My classmates were, in the main, the kind of high-achieving college students who elect to spend their summer vacation taking on eight hours a day of schoolwork. There was no difference in work ethic between us. If I spent more time studying than my classmates, that fact should not be taken as an accolade but as a marker of my inefficiency.

They had something over me, and that something was a culture, which is to say a suite of practices so ingrained as to be ritualistic. The scholastic achievers knew how to quickly memorize a poem in a language they did not understand. They knew that recopying a handout a few days before an exam helped them digest the information. They knew to bring a pencil, not a pen, to that exam. They knew that you could (with the professor's permission) record lectures and take pictures of the blackboard.

This culture of scholastic achievement had not been acquired yesterday. The same set of practices had allowed my classmates to succeed in high school, and had likely been reinforced by other scholastic achievers around them. I am sure many of them had parents who were scholastic high-achievers. This is how social capital reinforces itself and compounds. It is not merely one high-achieving child, but a flock of high-achieving children, each backed by high-achieving parents. I once talked to a woman who spoke German, English, and French and had done so since she was a child. How did this happen, I asked? "Everyone in my world spoke multiple languages," she explained. "It was just what you did."

There were five tiers of French students, starting with those who could barely speak a word and scaling upward to those who were pursuing a master's degree. I was in the second tier, meaning I could order a coffee, recount a story with some difficulty, write a short note (sans verb and gender agreement), and generally understand a French speaker provided he or she talked to me really slowly. The majority of people I interacted with spoke better, wrote better, read better, and heard better than me. There was no escape from my ineptitude. At every waking hour, someone said something to me that I did not understand. At every waking hour, I mangled some poor Frenchman's lovely language. For the entire summer, I lived by two words: "Désolé, encore."

Compared with my classmates on the second tier, my test scores were on the lower end. Each week, in my literature class, we were responsible for the recitation of some French poems (Baudelaire, Verlaine, Lamartine) from memory, and each day we had to recite a stanza. This sort of exercise may well be familiar to readers of *The Atlantic*, but the rituals required to master it were totally new to me. I had never been a high-achieving student. Indeed, during my 15 or so years in school, I was a remarkably low-achieving student.

The Joy of Learning French

There were years when I failed the majority of my classes. This was not a matter of my being better suited for the liberal arts than sciences. I was an English minor in college. I failed American Literature, British Literature, Humanities, and (voilà)

French. The record of failure did not end until I quit college to become a writer. My explanation for this record is unsatisfactory: I simply never saw the point of school. I loved the long process of understanding. In school, I often felt like I was doing something else.

Like many black children in this country, I did not have a culture of scholastic high achievement around me. There were very few adults around me who'd been great students and were subsequently rewarded for their studiousness. The phrase "Ivy League" was an empty abstraction to me. I mostly thought of school as a place one goes so as not to be eventually killed, drugged, or jailed. These observations cannot be disconnected from the country I call home, nor from the government to which I swear fealty.

For most of American history, it has been national policy to plunder the capital accumulated by black people—social or otherwise. It began with the prohibition against reading, proceeded to separate and wholly unequal schools, and continues to this very day in our tacit acceptance of segregation. When building capital, it helps to know the right people. One aim of American policy, historically, has been to ensure, [sic] that the "right people" are rarely black. Segregation then ensures that these rare exceptions are spread thin, and that the rest of us have no access to other "right people."

And so a white family born into the lower middle class can expect to live around a critical mass of people who are more affluent or worldly and thus see other things, be exposed to other practices and other cultures. A black family with a middle class salary can expect to live around a critical mass of poor people, and mostly see the same things they (and the poor people around them) are working hard to escape. This too compounds.

Now, in America, invocations of culture are mostly an exercise in awarding power an air of legitimacy. You can see this in the recent remarks by the president, where he turned a question about preserving Native American culture into a lecture on how we (blacks and Native Americans) should be more like the Jews and Asian Americans, who refrain from criticizing the intellectuals in their midst of "acting white." The entire charge rests on shaky social science and the obliteration of history. When Asian Americans and Jewish Americans—on American soil—endure the full brunt of white supremacist assault, perhaps a comparison might be in order.

But probably not. That is because fences are an essential element of human communities. The people who patrol these fences are generally unkind to those they find in violation. The phrase "getting above your raising" is little more than anxious working-class border patrolling. The term "white trash" is little more than anxious ruling-class border patrolling. I am neither an expert in the culture of Jewish Americans nor Asian Americans, but I would be shocked if they too were immune. Some years ago I profiled the rapper Jin. As the first Asian-American rapper to secure a major label contract, he often found himself enduring racist cracks from black rappers abroad and the prodding of fence-patrollers at home. "'Yo, what is this? You really think you're black, Jin?" he recalled his parents saying. "Bottom line—you're not black, Jin.'"

Pretending that black people are unique—or more ardent—in their fence-patrolling, and thus more parochial and anti-intellectual, serves to justify the current uses of American power. The American citizen is free to say, "Look at them, they criticize each other *for reading*!" and then go about his business. In that sense it is little different than raising the myth of "black on black crime" when asked about Ferguson.

I will confess to having very little experience with fence-patrolling, and virtually none with the idea that if you are holding a book, you are "acting white." The Baltimore of my youth was a place where white people rarely ventured. It would not have occurred to anyone I knew to associate reading with white people because very few of us knew any. And I read everything I could find: *A Wrinkle In Time, David Walker's*

Appeal, Dragon's of Autumn Twilight, Seize The Time, Deadly Bugs and Killer Insects, The Web of Spider-Man. I had a full set of Childcraft. I loved the volume *Make and Do.* I had a full set of World Book encyclopedias. I used to pick up the fat "P" edition, flip to a random page, and read for hours. When I was just 6 years old, my mother took me to the Enoch Pratt Free Library on Garrison Boulevard and enrolled me in a competition to see which child could read the most books. I read 24 that summer, far outdistancing the competition. My mother smiled. The librarian gave me candy. I was very proud.

For carrying books in black neighborhoods, in black schools, around black people, I was called many things—nerd, bright, doofus, Malcolm, Farrakhan, Mandela, sharp, smart, airhead. I was told that my "head was too far in the clouds." I was told that I was "going to do something one day." But I was never called white. The people who called me a nerd were black. The people who said I was going to "do something one day" were also black. There was no one else around me, and no one else in America then cared. This was not just true of me, it was true of most black children of that era who were then, and are now, the most segregated group in this country. Segregation meant many of us had to rely on traditions closer to home.

And at home I found a separate culture of intellectual achievement. This is the tradition of Carter G. Woodson, Frederick Douglass, and Malcolm X. It argues for education not simply as credentialism or certification, but as a profound act of auto-liberation. This was the culture of my childhood and it gave me some of the greatest thrills of my youth.

I was a boy haunted by questions: Why do the lilies close at night? Why does my father always say, "I can dig it"? And who really killed the dinosaurs? And why is my life so unlike everything I see on TV? That feeling—the not knowing, the longing for knowing, and the eventual answer—is love and youth to me. And I have always preferred libraries to classrooms because the wide open library is the ultimate venue for this theater. This culture was reinforced by my parents, and the politically conscious parents around me, and their politically conscious children. The culture was so strong that it could be regarded as a kind of social capital. It was so old that it could also be regarded as a legacy. This legacy is more responsible for my presence in these august pages than any other. That is because a good writer must ultimately be an autodidact and take a dim view of credentials. My culture failed to make me into a high-achieving student. It succeeded at making me into a writer.

I have never had much of an urge to brag about this. I have always known that in failing to become a scholastic achiever, I forfeited knowledge of certain things. (A mastery of Augustine comes to mind.) But what I did not understand was that I had also forfeited a culture, which is to say a tool kit, a set of pins and tumblers that might have unlocked the language which I so presently adore.

Scholastic achievement is sometimes demeaned as the useless memorization of facts. I suspect that it has more to offer than this. If you woke my French literature professor at 2 a.m., she could recite the deuxième strophe of Verlaine's "Il Pleure Dans Mon Coeur." I suspect this memorization, this holding of the work in her head, allowed her to analyze it and turn it over in ways I could only do with the text in front of me. More directly, there is no real way for an adult to learn French without some amount of memorization. French is a language that obeys its rules when it feels like it. There is no unwavering rule to tell you which nouns are masculine, or which verbs require a preposition. Memory is the only way through.

At Middlebury, I spent as much time as I could with the master's students, hovering right at the edge of overbearing. On average, I understood 30 percent of what was being said. This was, of course, the point. I wanted to be reminded of who I was. I wanted to be young again, to feel that old thrill of not knowing. It is the same feeling I had as a boy, wondering about the lilies and dinosaurs, listening to "The Bridge Is Over," wondering where in the world was Queens.

And I was ignorant. I felt as if someone had carried me off at night, taken me out to sea, and set me adrift in a life-raft. And the night was beautiful because it held all the things I would never know, and in that I saw my doom—the time when I could learn no more. Morning, noon, and evening, I sat on the terrace listening to the young master's students talk. They would recount their days, share their jokes, or pass on their complaints. They came from everywhere—San Francisco, Atlanta, Seattle, Boulder, Hackensack, Philadelphia, Kiev. And they loved all the things I so wanted to love, but had not made time to love—Baudelaire, Balzac, Rimbaud. I would listen and feel the night folding around me, and the ice-water of youth surging through me.

One afternoon, I was walking from lunch feeling battered by the language. I started talking with a young master in training. I told her I was having a tough time. She gave me some encouraging words in French from a famous author. I told her I didn't understand. She repeated them. I still didn't understand. She repeated them again. I shook my head, smiled, and walked away mildly frustrated because I understood every word she was saying but could not understand how it fit. It was as though someone had said, "He her walks swim plus that yesterday the fight." (This is how French often sounds to me.)

The next day, I sat at lunch with her and another young woman. I asked her to spell the quote out for me. I wrote the phrase down. I did not understand. The other young lady explained the function of the pronouns in the sentence. Suddenly I understood—and not just the meaning of the phrase. I understood something about the function of language, why being able to diagram sentences was important, why understanding partitives and collective nouns was important.

In my long voyage through this sea of language, that was my first sighting of land. I now knew how much I didn't know. The feeling of discovery and understanding that came from this was incredible. It was the first moment when I thought I might survive the sea.

My personal road to this great feeling, to these discoveries, to Middlebury, was not the normal one. I was raised among people skeptical of a canon that had long been skeptical of them. I needed some independent sense of myself, of my cultures and traditions, before I could take a mature look at the West. I wanted nothing to do with Locke because I knew that he wanted little to do with me. I saw no reason to learn French because it was the language of the plunderers of Haiti.

I had to be a nationalist before I could be a humanist. I had to come to understand that black people are not merely the victims of the West, but its architects. The philosophes started the sentence and Martin Luther King finished it. The greatest renditions of this country's greatest anthems are all sung by black people—Ray, Marvin, Whitney. That is neither biology nor a mistake. It is the necessary cosmopolitanism of a people, viewing America from the basement and thus forced to take their lessons when they get them—absorbing, reinterpreting, refining, creating.

Now it must never be concluded that an urge toward the cosmopolitan, toward true education, will make people stop hitting you. The inverse is more likely. In the early 19th century, the Cherokee Nation was told by the new Americans that if its members adopted their "civilized" ways, they would soon be respected as equals. This promise was deeply embedded in the early 19th century approach to this continent's indigenous nations.

"We will never do an unjust act towards you. on the contrary we wish you to live in peace, to increase in numbers, to learn to labor, as we do," Thomas Jefferson said. "In time you will be as we are; you will become one people with us; your blood will mix with ours; & will spread, with ours, over this great Island. Hold fast then, my Children, the Chain of friendship, which binds us together; & join us in keeping it forever bright & unbroken."

The Cherokee Nation—likely for their own reasons—embraced mission schools. Some of them converted to Christianity. Others intermarried. Others still enslaved blacks. They adopted a written Constitution, created a script for their language and published a newspaper, *The Cherokee Phoenix,* in English and Cherokee. Thus the Native Americans of that time showed themselves to be as able to integrate elements of the West with their own culture as any group of Asian or Jewish American. But the wolf has never much cared whether the sheep were cultured or not.

"The problem, from a white point of view," writes historian Daniel Walker Howe, "was that the success of these efforts to 'civilize the Indians' had not yielded the expected dividend in land sales. On the contrary, the more literate, prosperous, and politically organized the Cherokees made themselves, the more resolved they became to keep what remained of their land and improve it for their own benefit."

Cosmopolitanism, openness to other cultures, openness to education did not make the Cherokee pliant to American power; it gave them tools to resist. Realizing this, the United States dropped the veneer of "culture" and "civilization" and resorted to "Indian Removal," or The Trail of Tears. The plunder was celebrated in a popular song:

> All I want in this creation
> Is a pretty little wife and a big plantation
> Away up yonder in the Cherokee nation.

The Native Americans of this period found that America's talk of trading culture for rights was just a cover. In our time, it is common to urge young black children toward education so that they may be respectable or impress the "right people." But the "right people" remain unimpressed, and the credentials of black people, in a country rooted in white supremacy, must necessarily be less. That great powers are in the business of using "respectability" and "education" to ignore these discomfiting facts does not close the book. You can never fully know. But you can walk in the right direction.

The citizen is lost in the labyrinth constructed by his country, when in fact straight is the gate, and narrow must always be the way. When I left for Middlebury, I had just published an article arguing for reparations. People would often ask me what change I expected to come from it. But change had already come. I had gone further down the unending path of knowing, deeper into the night. I was rejecting mental enslavement. I was rejecting the lie.

I came to Middlebury in the spirit of the autodidactic, of auto-liberation, of writing, of Douglass and Malcolm X. I came in ignorance, and found I was more ignorant than I knew. Even there, I was much more comfortable in the library, thumbing through random histories in French, than I was in the classroom. It was not enough. It will not be enough. Sometimes you do need the master's tools to dismantle his house.

Reading the Genre

1. Coates writes what can be called a literacy narrative about his acquisition—and his struggles acquiring—literacy in French. The essay offers an analysis of French as an academic subject. What do you know about French that you didn't know before this essay began? Do you feel like Coates has helped you understand what it would take to learn the language?

2. If a literacy narrative has to balance the telling of a story with the analysis or exploration of literacy, does Coates achieve a balance between his focus on French and his focus on himself? How and when does he reveal personal details?

3. The most complicated part of this essay likely begins with the phrase "I had to be nationalist before I could be humanist." What does this mean for Coates? Do you agree? How could the opposite—that one must be humanist before they can be nationalist—also be true? How does this connect to your ability to learn?

4. WRITING: Think about your own experiences learning a second language or dialect (a dialect can be thought of as the common vocabulary, grammar, and speech patterns of a group of people). What was it like being an outsider? Think about your struggles and successes in expressing yourself. What conclusions can you draw about the process of learning a new language or dialect?

5. WRITING: Coates writes at length about the concept of "social capital." What is some of the "social capital" that you bring with you to school—the things that come naturally to you, that you were taught at an early age, or surrounded by—and what are some of the things that you have noticed you were or are unprepared for, surprised by, or find that you need to work harder at than your peers? In a short narrative, write about the experience of gaining some of this "social capital," and/or about the experience of finding it lacking.

COLLABORATIVE NARRATIVE   This collaborative narrative comes from the memoir *At the Broken Places: A Mother and Trans Son Pick Up the Pieces*. The entire book is written in this style, with Donald and Mary trading back and forth from chapter to chapter and section to section. Mary has written many other books of nonfiction and is a professor of English at Central Connecticut State University. Donald is a recent graduate of Emerson College and is just beginning a career as a writer, with essays appearing in publications including *Salon* and *PopMatters*.

DONALD COLLINS AND MARY COLLINS

We Call Back and Forth to Each Other About Things that Nearly Destroyed Us

My first major coming-out happened when I stood up at my dorm's Christmas party and said, "I'm trans." It also happened when I spoke to my mother in our kitchen. And it happened again when I finally created a Facebook at seventeen.

Much like R. Kelly's infamous thirty-three-chapter opera *Trapped in the Closet*, coming out is a process, with exhausting ups and downs, that continues to happen relentlessly.

◆ ◆ ◆

Non-trans people sometimes express a strain of entitlement that goes something like this: "I deserve to know if anyone I meet is transgender."

I'm trans. Being trans is a part of my identity. I'm also a writer, an amateur painter, and the proud owner of a used Ford Focus. The compulsion to "know" I'm trans wrongly assumes that this information is necessary for others to have, when most of the time it's not. The compulsion to "know" also propagates the idea that trans people are hiding something, that we are frauds or illusionists, that we are not *real*. Our gender is unfairly treated as if it were a costume that we must admit to wearing.

In her 1990 book, *Gender Trouble,* theorist Judith Butler famously asserted that gender identity is characterized by "a stylized repetition of acts through time." This is gender performativity theory, the idea that gender is a kind of behavioral consistency both in and of a system.

Butler herself was quick to point out that this doesn't mean we all have the empowering ability to constantly change our gender depending on what clothes we put on in the morning. As Sarah Salih explains in her essay on Butler, our "choices" surrounding our gender exist within a "regulatory frame." Rather than artists with infinite supplies, daily creating new and exciting works of gender, we're kind of stuck with paint-by-numbers.

Many scholars and thinkers have expanded on Butler's theory or challenged other, more rudimentary "performance" based theories. Julia Serano recalls her own experiences as a trans woman in doing so, asserting, "Many of us who have physically transitioned from one sex to the other understand that our perceived gender is typically not a product of our 'performance' (i.e., gender expression/ gender roles) but rather our physical appearance (in particular, our secondary sex characteristics)."

If you do not fit easily into a visual gender category, you are complicating someone's constant categorization of all nearby bodies. You are challenging the entire system of gender on which the viewer's identity is built. Oftentimes, onlookers may seek to fix this processing glitch by avoiding ("Don't stare, honey"), clarifying ("Are you a boy or a girl?"), or accosting ("What are *you* doing in this bathroom?"). They might just burn you with their laser eyes.

It's important to establish the weight of both sides when it comes to the compulsion to "know" and the decision to share. On one side, we have curiosity; on the other, we have a potential minefield. Many, if not most, trans people do not get to opt out of the minefield.

Coming-out scratches a variety of itches. It can be a personal deliverance or a medical or clerical necessity. The following are situations when I came out for one reason or another:

Coming out to a café cashier at a bus station to explain why the name on my credit card doesn't match my appearance.

Coming out to the bus driver a few minutes later to explain the same thing about my license.

Coming out to my tattooist, because I really liked her and it seemed chill.

Coming out to a new doctor in Hartford, Connecticut, and again when I move to Los Angeles.

Coming out at a party to the friend of a friend, whose own sibling is gender variant and who had some questions for me.

Coming out at two Departments of Motor Vehicles in one day trying to (unsuccessfully) get one of them to change my gender marker from "F" to "M."

Coming out in an essay to write about coming out.

There are many days when I don't come out to anyone. I just live my life, and some of the people in it know I'm trans and others don't. A lot of the time, sharing the fact that I'm trans is something I do to establish that I trust someone and want to know them better. Being "stealth" means I have to censor my stories, my history, and my stresses. I can most fully be myself by including "trans."

I'll admit that I often hate the moment when I tell people. I *feel* them look at me differently. I *feel* them explaining my behavior with this new information, or at least I *think* I feel it. I imagine them scrutinizing my body, my voice, even my hobbies. *Oh, that's why Donald bakes so much—he was raised as a girl!* I've had people tell me I have "women's hands" and that I stretch better after a workout because "women are more flexible."

Gender is a system maintained by a ruthless neighborhood watch (us). We constantly judge and disparage other people's bodies, both in and out of gender contexts. *Are they too fat? Are they too thin? Are they short? Do they have acne? Is it severe? Are they bald? Are their boobs too big or small?* I do it all the time in my own head, with the goal of not letting these runaway thoughts get legitimized by speaking them or acting on them. It's hard not to be obsessed with other people's bodies when you spend so much time obsessed with your own. And maybe that's why I sometimes hate that moment after I come out because it makes me feel so self-conscious about my own body and about the way I look at other people's.

My coming out: part two (the reckoning) happened my junior year of college. I pledged a fraternity called Phi Alpha Tau, came out as trans on cable news, and ultimately found myself in possession of $23,000. I'll start at the beginning.

By the fall of my junior year, I had been on testosterone for almost three years, my name was legally changed, and I lived in my own room on campus as an RA. My mother and I were on decent terms but shaky ground. She knew I was pursuing top surgery to flatten my chest, another physical alteration she couldn't get behind. I proceeded in the planning stage without her. We were both completely emotionally exhausted; I tried to just keep my own shit together and keep it far from her door.

I like to think of my experience joining Phi Alpha Tau as some kind of daytime movie special. It's a feel-good story; it's a cautionary tale; it's a melodrama and a buddy comedy.

Tau (pronounced "Tah") is a single-chapter fraternity dedicated to the "communicative arts," which includes film, TV, journalism, theater, music, marketing, and writing. Emerson College, thankfully, has no frat houses, so Tau's sense of community operates on the organization and commitment of its brothers alone. When I joined, our membership was around thirty.

I had never considered joining a fraternity before entering college, and I still can't fully comprehend I'm *in* a fraternity. Most people I meet can't either. They ask, "What *kind* of fraternity?"

My roommate pledged Tau his sophomore year. I became enamored with his new "brothers," realizing that many students I admired on campus were also members.

A friend and I went out for Tau the following winter. We submitted letters and resumes, were interviewed casually by individual brothers, and then attended a "smoker," a more formal interview process with the majority of the active brotherhood.

Fraternities are fundamentally exclusive organizations. They accept the people they want and turn away those they don't. At any college, especially a smallish one like Emerson, this rejection, however politely worded, hurts. Everyone knows if someone didn't get a "bid," the term that describes whether a fraternity wants you or not.

Tau is inclusive of a variety of personalities: hard partiers, quiet scholars, dedicated entrepreneurs, and brilliant performers. It's also known for being gay friendly, and when I sought entry, already had one trans member. But like any fraternity, Tau turns people away. To this day, my personal experience of unconditional support from the fraternity clashes with its status as an ultimately exclusive, conditional organization.

My motives for joining Tau were actually a jumble of contradictions. Fraternity life first appealed to me because it was separate from my "trans" life. It was a place where I could socialize like the extroverted college kid I wished I was and meet people from all different majors. Yet it was also a place where an only child and a trans guy could be called "brother." I needed validation *as a boy,* and it felt great when that validation came *from other boys.* I craved the feverish declarations of this family. That we all loved each other, that our homes were always open to each other, that we were available at all hours for brothers who needed us.

My mom and I still kept up a tentative correspondence. When I informed her I was pledging, she was surprised but supportive once I told her more about the fraternity. She always encouraged me to expand my social comfort zone and knew I would benefit from the kind of brotherly support Tau could offer.

My friend and I gratefully received and accepted bids. Our pledge class of ten convened a night later to begin the "new member process," a two-week, highly secretive ordeal. Fraternity members joke that pledging is "the most fun you don't want to have again." I will clarify that though I was not *always* having fun during this period, I was *never* hazed.

While pledging, we wore khakis, a collared shirt with tie, a blue blazer, and a fresh white carnation during "business hours" and evening meetings. For me, the most taxing part of it was the sheer amount of clothing layers I had to wear. I was still planning my top surgery and wearing binders to flatten my chest.

About a week into the process I received some bad news on this exact issue. My insurance claim for the surgery, a veritable thesis of paperwork, including proof of my name change, hormone therapy, and official letters of support from a counselor and endocrinologist, was denied.

Many doctors' offices that offer gender-confirming surgical procedures don't even entertain insurance claims because, historically, it's pretty futile. Only recently are tides turning. Since being "trans" is something that still has to be "diagnosed" to be legitimate in the eyes of insurers, it's frustrating when medical-care systems won't actually provide *care* for the diagnosis they force on you. It's beyond frustrating; it's a kind of demolition.

My doctor's office *did* work with insurance, and when it called to tell me the claim was denied, I was devastated. I was also shopping for neckties in an H&M, and so I hurried outside to cry on the curb. My pledge brother Alex reassured me, and we plodded slowly back to campus.

The sweat pooling on my back and ribs under all my layers of clothing stung with each step. I had been doing so well, trusting that all my discomfort would be over soon. Yet every day I had believed myself closer to top surgery, my rejected claim was sitting in a clerk's outbox. I possessed some savings, but out of pocket, the surgery was going to cost more than $8,000. I didn't have $8,000.

A few months earlier, I switched from my mother's insurance to my school's. She and I had both agreed to the terms. My mom didn't feel comfortable having her insurance cover the physical changes she was opposed to, and by having me move policies, we were able to remove at least one point of conflict from the list.

My school's policy covered hormone treatment, but its attitude toward GCS was vague. Emerson's health-center director was tireless in helping me, and together we pored over the policy to find some way to appeal.

I couldn't *really* share my claim defeat with my mother because I thought it might be a kind of victory to her—not that I was sad about it but because the medical system was preventing the same thing *she* wanted to prevent.

I missed my mom, who as a single parent and often self-employed writer/editor always had a kind of doggedness and resourcefulness in dealing with bureaucracy. She knows where to apply pressure and never forgets to follow up. Indeed, no matter how hard I tried to keep my "shit" from her door, there were days when I broke down and called her. I needed a ride somewhere or I needed help with a bill or I was just really depressed. These calls were our white flags, proof that our bond was intact.

My fraternity brothers were attentive and kind, but they were peers, not parents. It just so happened they were high-functioning peers. The insurance-claim debacle prompted me to come out to my pledge class, many of who did not know I was transgender. One of my pledge brothers, Dave, exhibited his characteristic gentility.

"I have no idea what that means," he told me earnestly. "Tell me about it."

I told them about it. The situation made its way to our pledgemaster (he who runs pledge) and then the active brotherhood.

I had no idea how far the information had carried. But by the meeting later that night, they had promised to help fund-raise so I could afford top surgery.

I graciously thanked them. *They're really nice,* I thought, *but who are they kidding?*

They certainly weren't kidding me. A central core of brothers set up a page and worked tirelessly to fund-raise toward the cost of my surgery. Within twenty-four hours they had almost $2,000.

Another of my brothers, Ben, a journalist worked for *Out* magazine at the time, conducted a short interview with me in response to the campaign. "Boston Fraternity Raises Money for Trans Brother" read the headline of the article.

Within another twenty-four hours, donations were pouring in from around the world.

I missed two days of work at my campus office job while I entertained media inquiries. Other RAs graciously covered my "on duty" nights at the dorm. I skipped some classes and fell asleep in others.

A national LGBTQ organization asked me to sign with them as a spokesperson. *Inside Edition* offered us $3,000 for our story if we would give them before-and-after pictures of me. Surgeons e-mailed me offering to do my surgery "free of cost." I said no to these, but agreed to other media inquiries. *HuffPost Live* had us on-air. We were on the front page of the *Boston Herald* and got a feature in the *Boston Globe* and a follow-up with *Out*.

Ours was the heartwarming story of the moment. We were rehabilitating the shattered respectability of fraternities, prompting an outpouring of love from "Greek" orgs and comments like "That's what a fraternity *should* be like." I was thrilled to bring such positive attention to my new brothers, and to the inconsistent state of trans health care. I was less clear about the attention directed toward my body and me.

On the first day of media, I called my mother to tell her firsthand what was happening. It was late. Next to me, my "big brother" Ryan mapped out a schedule to help me manage the next twenty-four hours. Homework, interview, food, interview, sleep, interview.

"You might see me on TV," I warned my mom.

Her voice was measured, brimming with concern for me, for herself. I can't remember our conversation, only a feeling. *Be careful.*

Like an outsize version of my coming-out at Loomis, this public stage represented a dramatic new step. I wasn't ready or willing to share everything. How could I talk about my family when things were still so muddy and difficult with them? How did I answer questions about my parent's reactions? How could I cast off my privacy but keep my mother's intact?

The answer was that I couldn't. But I didn't know it yet.

Within those first twenty-four hours, I wrote a thankful post about the fundraiser update on my Tumblr. I was stunned when other trans people reblogged it and a vocal minority disparaged me. Why was my surgery "free" while they were working overtime for theirs? *Lucky bastard!*

Others were mad I wouldn't share the wealth, and strangers e-mailed me asking for the money. Even those who passed along messages of support occasionally sent terse follow-ups because I wasn't getting back to them fast enough. A student posted anonymously on a public Emerson "confessional" Facebook page, accusing me of using donations to buy coffee at Starbucks. Transphobic forums and articles surfaced in response to the expanding list of articles. I read comments from people who made light of killing and raping me and people like me. I occupied pages of Google web and image searches. There would be no going back. It was the fastest, most brutal education I have ever received.

On day two I answered a phone call from my mother, in distress. She was concerned about the questions I would receive going forward.

"They'll want to know about me," she said. "They're going to ask about your family and where we are in all this."

She asked me to shut it down, and I readily agreed.

The boys were fully supportive of my decision. After nearly three days in the media spotlight, we had raised $23,308. My surgery was scheduled for the winter break, only weeks away.

"We accomplished what we set out to do," my brother Christian said.

He was right. They had helped me; I had helped myself. We pledged the excess funds to the Jim Collins Foundation (no relation), an organization that gives grants for gender-confirming surgeries to those in need. A storybook ending.

Within the next day or two, the insurance company "clarified" its position and agreed to cover my surgery.

My fraternity brothers and I all assumed this was a ploy to save face after the punishing media coverage, but we were discouraged by the college's PR department from publicly stating so. A few days later I was told that a lost memo had been found proving Emerson's insurance to be trans-inclusive. The policy had just never been updated correctly. My surgery would be covered, and future trans students would be saved the trouble of having to crowdsource their funds.

At first I was mortified. After all, we had just fund-raised $23,000 that I didn't actually need anymore. But then I realized: this is way better. We donated more than expected to the Jim Collins Foundation, and my medical care was rightly in the hands of a medical-care provider. Perhaps most importantly, this wouldn't happen again at Emerson.

On the home front, Mom and I both breathed easier, knowing *our* problems were back safe with us.

Later still, I learned that, through all this, my stepfather Andrew (who I call my dad because he took on that role) had made a series of calls to the college asking them to investigate the issue. It was his calls that prompted the paperwork search.

By agreeing to come out, be visible, and share my story, I achieved so much. My surgery was financed in full, the college's insurance policy was clarified to benefit others, and all the money I didn't need was going to a worthy charity.

So why did I feel so much anger and shame?

I felt I had sold out myself by agreeing to be "trans" for the camera. As much as I long to be social and fun, I'm also incredibly private. I enjoy being alone for long periods of time. I've never had the compulsion to go to a club or even to Disneyland. But it wasn't the media overkill that upset me; it was the sneaking suspicion that I was more manipulative and desperate for help than I had realized. Once the fundraiser took off, I quickly understood that if I played "trans" in all the right ways, people would help me get what I needed. And they did.

I *do* feel like I didn't earn an all-expenses-paid surgery, even though I sweated so hard for my physical and mental health progress. I *do* feel guilty and embarrassed about all the attention. And I *do* feel shitty and ungrateful for not being solely positive about all the amazing help I received. I love my fraternity, and I love my brothers. I was so hurt when those few trans people termed me a lucky bastard, but that's *exactly what I am.*

A woman in her sixties spills hot tea across my table in a bagel shop.

The conversation begins. Don't worry, I assure her.

We exchange simple introductions, then, for some reason, she asks the question: Do you have children?

Yes, a daughter, I say reflexively.

In the next millisecond I feel compromised, caught in some weird disclosure game I still haven't figured out how to navigate with integrity.

She has no children, she tells me.

Is my daughter in college?

Yes.

Then I shift the topic to bagels and the weather.

In the past I had a daughter, but now I have a transgender son. Just weeks prior to the spilt-tea incident, he (I use that pronoun with confidence at this point in the story) had a hysterectomy, the final step in his effort to make Donald's gender identity match his body. But in that random moment in that mundane space I was on autopilot, and in the primitive parts of my mind that allow me to speak without thinking, my daughter still resides.

After several years of practice, I know now not to weigh down the situation with the truth. I will not see that woman again. I do have a child. That child was in college at that time. I do not need to explain that I had a daughter but now have a son and they are one and the same person.

I am making up my own disclosure agreement as I go along, and I know that Donald has had to do the same.

In his case, now that he's had top surgery and takes hormones, he can more easily present as male anywhere he wants. Transgender people refer to this as going "stealth." When he worked in New York City as an intern for several organizations, his resume gave him away (if that's even the right phrase) a bit because of some guest-speaking assignments he listed on it. But his fellow interns never knew, even his housemates—five men in a jammed townhouse in Brooklyn—didn't know until he chose to tell them a week before he moved out.

Did it matter? Would anyone answer the woman in the bagel shop with phrases like "Yes, I have children, a daughter with cerebral palsy"? Or how about "Yes, I have a child, a gay son in college." So why do I feel deceptive when I say I have a daughter instead of saying I have a son? Why did I feel a touch of unease that Donald had not told his housemates that he is a trans man?

I could have felt positive about his discretion, the yin to disclosure's yang. Why make people feel uncomfortable about something that's really none of their business? It shouldn't impact the way they perceive you or treat you.

Donald himself has told me that there's nothing to "disclose," since that infers he has something to hide. While driving back from grabbing an iced coffee together, he surprised me with his level of anger about people online comparing the case of Rachel Dolezal, the now former president of the NAACP chapter in Spokane, Washington, who is a white woman who pretended to be black, with Bruce Jenner coming out as Caitlyn.

Dolezal lied and deceived to further herself, Donald argued, but Jenner sought to finally tell the truth. My trans son flushed red and tensed his shoulders while summarizing the way people online discussed parallels between the two stories. I told him to put his views in his essay, because I do not fully grasp his argument and hope I'll understand it better if he writes it down.

I do know that I'd be ashamed if I had a daughter who tried to pass as black and secured jobs and even college scholarships because of her ruse, but I am not ashamed that I have a transgender son. I am confused. I am afraid. I need to educate myself more about what that means for him. But I am awed by the fact that my child has the courage to engage in a journey toward self-realization that few people could ever think to undertake. I questioned physical steps he took at such an early age that even medical professionals argue about, but the feelings I have about that are not shame based.

When I look at the medical literature, with imposing titles like *Journal of Homosexuality,* about disclosure for anyone on the LGBTQ continuum, I hear conflicting messages.

Transgender people who *do not* disclose their status struggle more with depression and are more apt to harm themselves or even commit suicide.

Transgender people who *do* come out face a lot more harassment and bias, especially in rural areas. Of course, as an anxious mother I read "harassment" and think "violence" might be a better word.

Most transgender people come out to their family and friends but not their employer or coworkers.

And back and forth it goes. The discussion reminds me of the way the media talks about exercise—do short, intense workouts; no, take lots of short walks all day at a moderate pace; work out an hour each day; no, just thirty minutes three days a week is fine.

The answer must be arrived at on an individual basis.

For additional guidance I began exploring disclosure rules in a range of professions: When should a lawyer reveal that he knows his client has done something awful or tell a judge that he has a conflict of interest in a case? How about a psychiatrist who feels her client might turn violent? And, of course, the medical profession must weigh huge questions when it comes to whether or not to tell a cancer patient he has no chance, or a woman that her husband will not make it. When do you disclose these hard truths? *First, do no harm,* as the Hippocratic oath says. But which is more harmful: disclosure or discretion?

One summer while Donald was still in college I went to an island in New Hampshire with a boyfriend and his two young sons, both under age twelve. We spent a week in a cabin, with about thirty other people on the island with us, each in their own cabins, but we all united at meal time. My boyfriend's sons only knew Donald as my son. I didn't really think about it one way or another; it just happened naturally that way because when they saw Donald, they saw a man.

At one point I was chatting with a group of mothers while watching a camp volleyball game, and it came up that one of them had gone to my high school and we had some mutual friends. Since Donald had also attended my alma mater, Loomis, that also came up.

The woman's entire energy shifted as I stood there chatting idly about Donald. In that moment I knew that she knew our story, that our mutual friend must have talked about the journey Donald and I went on together while he was in high school, the hard times, the tough decisions, the first person in the school's 150-year history to come out as transgender.

Without hesitating, I brought up that Donnie was now in college and really enjoyed his school because it was very LGBTQ friendly and he is transgender. I let it slip in there like a glass of water on a hot summer day, meant to take the edge off, meant as a kind offering. And she took it without hesitation—open, friendly, and apparently relieved that I had chosen disclosure and done so with comfort and confidence.

But at the close of the conversation I felt that I had to tell her not to tell her young sons who played with my boyfriend's kids because they did not know and might find it all very confusing if they did.

I switched from disclosure to discretion in less than a minute.

Donald himself moved from being a young woman with a girlhood to a trans man with no boyhood in the span of about a year. This history further complicates the disclosure/discretion game. When should I reveal that I raised a daughter when I'm circulating with people who see me with a son? To never bring that up feels like a form of shunning, a death for something I loved above all else in my life. People might presume you simply switch the name and pronouns and get on it, but those who would say such glib things have never had to negate a past girlhood for the sake of a current manhood.

When Donald comes home to visit, I must remember to put away the photographs of J., the daughter he used to be. I have many albums stored in a cedar chest of baby pictures; my four-year-old girl in her Halloween costume, my eight-year-old girl playing in a blue boat at the lake, my twelve-year-old girl graduating middle school. But any image of his past life as a girl unsettles him, which, of course means that there is no childhood for Donald as a boy, no reference point for a young Donald versus an adult Donald.

◆ ◆ ◆

We moved from the South to New England when J. was fourteen, leaving behind nearly everyone who had ever known my child as a daughter and girl. The first time I returned to visit, I reflexively answered the question "So how is J.?" with pat replies. *Fine. Navigating a demanding high school. Volunteering at the theater.* In friends' minds, they were still adding to the narrative they knew as J., the golden-red-haired girl with the green eyes whom their daughters played with on the neighborhood trampoline.

But I knew that narrative had come to a full stop, like a period at the end of an incomplete sentence.

With each subsequent visit I started shutting down the narrative known as J. and building a new storyline known as Donald, my trans son. The people who cared about us did not get in the way of this shift, though the physical distance and this sudden, new timeline for a young man who was once a girl made it harder for most friends to follow along. Donald and I lost touch with almost all of them. When I visit the area now, even I sometimes have trouble believing that I ever lived the life of a mom with a daughter who used to play broomball in the cul de sac with me after school.

Dealing with the issue of J.'s transition should be easier when it comes to strangers who have no inkling of our past and present, but it is not, because for most of us there are only two gender categories. When my last book, *American Idle: A Journey Through Our Sedentary Culture,* came out, I traveled the country as a guest speaker for two years and invariably people would ask, "Do you have any children?" Yes, one, I'd say. "A boy or a girl?"

Think of all that is inferred by that simple question: You have a boy or a girl in diapers. You have a boy or a girl learning to walk. You have a boy or a girl who just braved his or her first day of school. You have a boy or a girl who plays on a sports team, loves an instrument, or embraces the theater.

You have a boy or a girl.

Sometimes I deflect the question, not out of shame or shyness, but simply because the situation doesn't call for any depth or true connection. I might say, "My Donnie is in college now," or something like that so I never directly say if I have a son or daughter. On occasion someone does retort, "So he's in school," with an emphasis on the pronoun.

More recently I have noticed that I give different answers depending on the time period the stranger asks about.

Yes, we used to summer at a lake in New Hampshire before my divorce, and J. loved to play on the rope swing or canoe with a friend to pick blueberries on the island.

Yes, J. deeply disliked the mind games girls played in middle school and stayed off online social sites like Facebook without being asked. She figured she'd be bullied and mocked.

Yes, J. has a childhood I can give you in story form.

Yes, Donnie is in college now and loves the city.

Yes, Donnie works so hard to help with the cost of college.

Yes, Donnie is funny, a fine student, has plenty of friends. He joined a fraternity that he loves.

Yes, a fraternity. In this new narrative line, J.'s story has ended and Donald's past has begun.

At the New Hampshire vacation camp, I brought up the fact that I have a trans son with a stranger because we had a mutual friend who knew our story, but I almost never do that. Peculiar things happen to people's body language when I move this directly to the truth. Most of the real feelings come through the face, the confusion in the eyes, the earnest effort not to react or seem judgmental or surprised. They really do not want to miss a beat and come across as transphobic. But I know I have made them uncomfortable, and many do not even truly know how they feel about such a turn of events in the conversation, in our society.

One of the most complex social groups I deal with is the distant relations I might hear from every two or three years, like a cousin in San Diego or New Haven. They send the Christmas Letter. They ask about J. They know she's getting older and must "be out of college now!" Sometimes they even call because they'll be in town. How's the family? Your mom? Your siblings? Your daughter?

I feel like shouting, "We've crossed into a different Gender Zone!" All of your saved Christmas letters from us tell you that I had a daughter, but that past is wrong. I was raising a trans child all along but just didn't know it.

These distant family relations hear the story, try to catch up, but slip up again and again. They still ask after J. They sometimes correct themselves, but it's all too hard to pin down, to give away a daughter's childhood and replace it with a trans man's present. Some manage to shift to the correct name but almost never to the correct pronoun.

My immediate family has fully embraced the transition story now after many rough years when some of us thought J. was moving too fast to become Donald and was too young to make such radical changes to her/his body. Some of us thought it was a passing phase; some accepted it immediately, in part because they weren't all that emotionally invested in J. to begin with, so they didn't feel they were losing anything.

My ninety-year-old mother wept when she heard that her beloved granddaughter wanted to be embraced as a grandson. For many months, my mom went through a strange period of grief, continuing to reach out and embrace J. as Donald but mourning the slipping away of all evidence of J. as a girl. The golden-red hair became a cropped buzz cut and the gift of a Vera Bradley bag got stowed in the closet.

It was as though in a matter of days she had held a funeral for one grandchild and then crafted a new memory book for a different grandchild. I was astounded at how smoothly she pulled this off, the eldest of the extended family, the one with the longest track record of loss (two husbands, most of her friends, several of her siblings) on a racetrack to a new space so she wouldn't lose her grandchild entirely.

My ninety-year-old mother was the first to bring Donald to buy clothes in the men's department.

My ninety-year-old mother was the first to tell me to my face without flinching that J. was never coming back and Donald was here to stay and I must accept it.

My ninety-year-old mother still talks about when J. was a child and visited her in Florida or lost to her at Scrabble or went to New York City to watch the Christmas show at Radio City Music Hall and bought a ten-dollar chocolate-covered strawberry at Rockefeller Center. One strawberry for ten dollars! They photographed it before eating it.

She shifts more easily than I do between such recollections of her beloved granddaughter's past and the reality of now. She has a wry quality about her whenever she talks about any of it, as though after nine decades it's not that she's seen everything, but that she has somehow weathered all that she has seen.

Just last year she disclosed to me that one of her sisters also has a transgender grandchild; my aunt's son's son became a woman named M.

I know that someplace in the future people will be more accepting of this entire process, the shifting gender continuum, and won't flinch when asked to overlook the fact that the man in front of them had a girlhood not a boyhood. But in these years of transition, and our growing but limited awareness about transgender people, in this window where my daughter, J., is still someone that many people knew even just a handful of years ago, I must move like water myself, flowing in this direction and that depending on the shape of the moment.

Among various professions, when it comes to disclosure, safety and context are everything, but even those measures change radically, especially when you look at how transgender people are treated globally. Even the most basic online search brings up color-coded charts and maps of the world that make it clear that most of Africa, India, and the Middle East consider sexual relations between two people of the same sex illegal. If I shift my focus to something more relevant to our family situation—gender expression—things muddy quickly.

Some countries that might put a person in prison for having homosexual relations, actually accept a person's right to change gender. But—and this is where I must step back and catch my breath—some of these same countries require people to have themselves sterilized before the government will acknowledge their new gender.

Require.

I felt marginalized when teachers, advisors, and counselors kept me out of the conversation about Donald's transition because he was sixteen, and they had no legal right to disclose anything to me, his mother. But at least I knew he was *choosing* his way to his new identity.

In such environments, a misstep along the line between disclosure and discretion could result in a person losing complete control over his or her own body. In India, for example, authorities would have *made* him shut down his ovaries.

Of course the US State Department and local registries of motor vehicles want full disclosure for official documents, such as a passport or driver's license, but the system hasn't caught up with Donald's reality. He's changed his name and presents as male, but he had to go through an incredible series of steps to finally shift from female-to-male on his driver's license. I know he'd probably be offended to know that I feel the state should take care with such things. Not that I would wish the state to deny an individual such rights to choose and shift, but I still feel some deliberation makes sense, especially for people under age twenty-five.

I must also acknowledge that trying to get a new gender designation all lined up on everything—Social Security, driver's license, passport—created bureaucratic inconsistencies in Donald's record that have made him a target for skittish public officials in our post-9/11 world.

Are you a man or a woman?

Somehow the answer to that question doesn't seem a matter of national security, and Donald feels targeted, feels sneaky, feels uncomfortable. When he has the choice, he opts for the bus.

To remind myself how prejudiced and off such inquiries must feel to Donald, I consider that if he were a lesbian, there would be no disconnect on his official identification, no new information to "disclose." Society and official agencies really do need to catch up. Perhaps Face-book's fifty-plus categories for gender aren't as farfetched as they feel to me. Perhaps agencies should just ask for gender identity, as many college applications do now, and let the person fill in what fits, or drop the question of gender entirely.

◆ ◆ ◆

I almost didn't write these essays, which disclose so much about what Donald and I think about what happened to our family as he went through his transition. I thought we could work it out, that we were that close. But the breaks between us started to feel permanent. The decision to use something we both love—writing—to truly divulge the full measure of our feelings engendered more compassion and empathy between us.

But is this more public conversation the right way to go? I felt cynical, even angry, when, in 2015, I heard that Bruce Jenner planned to talk about being transgender with Diane Sawyer on national television. *Right,* I thought, *he's eager for fame, money, and as much attention as possible.* I judged his decision to disclose with a ruthlessness that surprised me.

Then I watched the interview in May of that year, along with nearly a hundred million other people, and his sincerity came through. When Sawyer asked Jenner if he were a reporter what question he would have asked, he replied, "Are you going to be okay?" So Sawyer asked the question and, after a pregnant pause, Jenner answered it.

"I hope so," he said. "I feel like I'm going to be okay."

I felt teary-eyed with empathy.

But I was also struck by the interview with Jenner's former wife, Kris, which popped up on social media a few days after his interview. She wept while one of her daughters from the famous Kardashian clan reprimanded her for not accepting the situation.

So it's okay to disclose you're transgender, I thought as I watched, *but not okay for family members to disclose their grief over the person and relationship they've lost?* I've experienced the same sort of reprimanding looks and comments whenever I openly mourn the loss of my J.

Sometimes when we celebrate openness for a marginalized group, we wind up marginalizing someone else. The conversation around all of this continues to lack nuance and sophistication.

We all circulate within several social circles—family, friends, neighbors, coworkers—and when it comes to transgender rights, each circle can have conflicting social ground rules.

- Christian bakery owners don't want to be forced to craft wedding cakes for gay or transgender couples.
- The US Supreme Court rules that same-sex marriage is now legal in all fifty states.
- Employers in many states can still discriminate against transgender workers and refuse them employment.
- President Obama signed a law making it illegal to discriminate against transgender people employed by the federal government.
- Landlords in many states can refuse to lease to LGBTQ applicants.
- When Donald flies back to LA after visiting me at home, he can legally use a men's restroom in a Connecticut airport but not in North or South Carolina when he stops to catch a connecting flight.

I use bullets to capture the tennis ball—like bounce to all of this. One reason for the disconnect: We have few positive avenues for honest conversation. Everyone digs in with hard-and-fast points of view and shows little respect for the other side. We demonize each other.

Like some right-wing baker in Georgia, I deeply disagreed with my daughter's decision to change her name. I wept over the fact she would no long have my father's initials—JFC—and took on a name I had never even heard mentioned in our home. Now I see that the name was one of the first tools she had at her disposal to act on her need to alter her identity. I can still feel my sadness, the regret, but I dropped the judgment.

But I started with a value system handed down to me from generations of my family. My shift took time. I gave myself permission to work through my own transition in values and found it only here, in these essays, certainly not from the professional medical world. I entered into a conversation with myself because I could not find space to safely enter into that conversation anywhere else, except among some very close friends and family.

I still wrestle with the question, when does discretion tip into deceit? I had a mixed-race student who came to class for months with blue eyes and then suddenly came to class with brown. In an essay for the course she confessed that she idolized the white Barbie-doll ideal and had worn tinted contacts to make herself feel prettier.

We all hide things—hair color, eye color. Now we can add gender to the list.

The freer I feel about disclosing that I have a transgender son, no matter the social situation I'm in, the more discretion I show about flashing some of my darker feelings about the entire experience. Some of my closest friends and family were quick to start referring to Donald as my son when in conversation with me. I know they wanted to embrace me, him, and all of our changes without judgment, but the first few times that happened, I felt violated.

How dare you assume that I think I have a son, I thought, an irrational flash of rage that I later realized was really grief over the complete erasure of J.

How could I ever say I have a son when I never had a boy? It simply felt like a smoke-and-mirrors game. Each exchange demanded that I let go of a daughter I knew I had, a sacrifice I could not put into words.

Now I can say with confidence that I have a son, but I also tell people about my daughter's childhood whenever the conversation demands. My revised world view now includes a new gender continuum that can hold these two things in my mind at once. A grown man can have a girlhood.

As a transgender man, Donald has a right to actualize his own identity. As a mother, I also have a right to remember and cherish my baby girl. Those two lines can fit into the same paragraph and not destroy each other.

Reading the Genre

1. In Donald's section of this narrative, there is an emphasis on developing definitions for physical transitions, while in Mary's section, she spends time defining emotional transitions—though of course, the changes they both experience are physical *and* emotional. What are some of the key differences and similarities between the transitions that they experience and that they define for the reader?

2. Both Donald and Mary's sections of this essay make interesting and provocative jumps between thoughts and scenes. How do they manage these jumps so that the reader understands that the essay as a whole will have an unconventional pacing and organization? (See "Use physical devices for transitions," p. 394.)

3. WRITING: Don't worry, this prompt is not going to ask you to coauthor a personal narrative with a parent, friend, or family member. Instead, try writing a narrative in two parts. In the first part, write about a significant moment in your life and narrate it in the present tense, trying as carefully as you can to reflect on the actual events and feelings and responses that you had when this moment happened. Then, write about the same event again, but from your perspective now, adding in what you have come to learn and to know about this moment since it happened.

4. MULTIMODALITY—TATTOO ARTISTRY: Donald has a tattoo of a robin, and clearly the robin is a powerful metaphor in Donald's life. Imagine, and then draw or create, a series of tattoos that might have significance for you and for your life. Then write about what these tattoos mean to you, and what you would want people to see and to think if they saw the tattoos. Consider printing these as temporary tattoos—you can find lots of different methods for doing this if you look online.

Acknowledgments

Ta-Nehisi Coates, "Acting French," *Atlantic,* August 29, 2014. Copyright © 2014 The Atlantic Media Co., as first published in the *Atlantic Magazine.* All rights reserved. Distributed by Tribune Content Agency, LLC.

Teju Cole, "Finders Keepers," from *Known and Strange Things: Essays* by Teju Cole. Copyright © 2016 by Teju Cole. Used by permission of Random House, an imprint and division of Penguin Random House LLC. All rights reserved. Any third-party use of this material, outside of this publication, is prohibited. Interested parties must apply directly to Penguin Random House LLC for permission.

Mary Collins and Donald Collins, "We Call Back and Forth to Each Other about Things That Nearly Destroyed Us," editors' title for "Donald Has Something He Would Like to Tell the Class" by Donald Collins and "Disclosure" by Mary Collins, from *At the Broken Places: A Mother and Trans Son Pick Up the Pieces* by Mary Collins and Donald Collins. Copyright © 2017 by Mary Collins and Donald Collins. Reprinted by permission of Beacon Press, Boston.

Lacy Crawford, "Writing the Right College-Entrance Essay" (excerpt), *Wall Street Journal,* August 24, 2013. Reprinted with permission of the Wall Street Journal. Copyright © 2013 by Dow Jones & Company, Inc. All rights reserved worldwide. License number 4325380259634 and license number 4325380396658.

Clive Crook, excerpt from "John Kenneth Galbraith, Revisited." First published in the *Atlantic,* May 15, 2006. Copyright © 2006. Reprinted by permission of the author.

Matt Daniels, "Where New Slang Comes From," *The Pudding,* https://pudding.cool/2017/02/new-slang/. Copyright © 2017/. Reprinted by permission.

Lewis Dartnell, "Why Would Aliens Even Bother with Earth? The Pros and Cons of a Trip to the Planet We Call Home," originally published as "(Un)Welcome Visitors: Why Aliens Might Visit Us" in *Aliens: The World's Leading Scientists on the Search for Extraterrestrial Life,* edited and with an introduction by Jim Al-Khalili. Selection copyright © 2016 by Jim Al-Khalili. Essay copyright © 2016 by Lewis Dartnell. Reprinted by permission of Farrar, Straus and Giroux.

Philip DeLoria, "1831, March 5: The Cherokee Nation Decision." Reprinted by permission of the publisher from *A New Literary History of America,* edited by Greil Marcus and Werner Sollors, pp. 205–210. Cambridge, Mass.: The Belknap Press of Harvard University Press. Copyright © 2009 by the President and Fellows of Harvard College.

Emily Dickinson, "I felt a Funeral, in my Brain." Reprinted by permission of the publishers and the Trustees of Amherst College from *The Poems of Emily Dickinson,* edited by Thomas H. Johnson, Cambridge, Mass.: The Belknap Press of Harvard University Press. Copyright © 1951, 1955 by the President and Fellows of Harvard College. Copyright © renewed 1979, 1983 by the President and Fellows of Harvard College. Copyright © 1914, 1918, 1919, 1924, 1929, 1930, 1932, 1935, 1937, 1942 by Martha Dickinson Bianchi. Copyright © 1952, 1957, 1958, 1963, 1965 by Mary L. Hampson.

Daniel Engber, "Glutton Intolerance," from *Slate,* October 5, 2009. Copyright © 2009 The Slate Group. All rights reserved. Used by permission and protected by the Copyright Laws of the United States. The printing, copying, redistribution, or retransmission of this Content without express written permission is prohibited.

Joseph Epstein, excerpt from "Plagiary: It's Crawlin' All Over Me." Copyright © 2006 by Joseph Epstein. Originally published in the *Weekly Standard* (March 2006). Reprinted by permission of Georges Borchardt, Inc., on behalf of the author.

James P. Gannon, "America's Quiet Anger," *American Spectator,* March 30, 2010. Copyright © 2010. Reprinted by permission of the American Spectator.

Jake Romm, "Why That Catastrophic Pepsi Ad Was Actually a Resounding Success," *The Forward,* April 5, 2017, http://forward.com/culture/368310/why-that-catastrophic-pepsi-ad-was-actually-a-resounding-success/. Copyright © 2017. Reprinted by permission of The Forward.

"Safe at Any Speed" (excerpt), *Wall Street Journal,* July 7, 2006. Reprinted with permission of the Wall Street Journal. Copyright © 2006 by Dow Jones & Company, Inc. All rights reserved worldwide. License number 4325370960351 and license number 4325371228898.

David Sedaris, "Advice on What to Write About, When I Was Teaching." Excerpted from interview in *January* magazine, June 2000. Copyright © 2000 by David Sedaris. Reprinted by permission of Don Congdon Associates, Inc.

Steve Silberman, "Neurodiversity Rewires Conventional Thinking about Brains," *Wired,* April 16, 2013. Steve Silberman/Wired © Condé Nast. From Wired.com. All rights reserved. Reprinted by permission.

Zadie Smith, "*Their Eyes Were Watching God:* What Does *Soulful* Mean?," from *Changing My Mind: Occasional Essays* by Zadie Smith. Copyright © 2009 by Zadie Smith. Used by permission of Penguin Press, an imprint of Penguin Publishing Group, a division of Penguin Random House LLC, and by permission of Penguin Canada, a division of Penguin Random House Canada Limited. All rights reserved. Any third-party use of this material, outside of this publication, is prohibited. Interested parties must apply directly to Penguin Random House LLC for permission.

Susan Sontag, excerpt from "Notes on 'Camp,'" from *Against Interpretation* by Susan Sontag. Copyright © 1964, 1966, renewed 1994 by Susan Sontag. Reprinted by permission of Farrar, Straus & Giroux, LLC.

Eddo Stern, "Warcrack for the Hordes: Why Warcraft Pwns the World," *UCLA Game Lab,* 2009, http://games.ucla.edu/resource/warcrack-for-the-hordes-why-warcraft-pwns-the-world/. Copyright © 2009. Reprinted by permission of Eddo Stern.

Andrew Sullivan, "I Used to Be a Human Being." Originally published in *New York Magazine,* September 23, 2016. Copyright © 2016 Andrew Sullivan. Used by permission of The Wylie Agency LLC.

Michael Todd, "Is That Plastic in Your Trash a Hazard?," *Pacific Standard,* March 22, 2013, http://www.psmag.com/environment/could-that-plastic-in-your-trash-be-hazardous-54252/. Republished with permission of the Miller-McCune Center for Research, Media, and Public Policy; permission conveyed through Copyright Clearance Center, Inc.

Neil deGrasse Tyson, "The Cosmic Perspective," *Natural History,* April 2007. Copyright © 2007 Natural History Magazine, Inc. Reprinted by permission.

Leah Vann, "Bald Is NOT Beautiful," December 8, 2016. Reprinted by permission of the author.

Cat Vasko, "Grocery Store Economics: Why Are Rotisserie Chickens So Cheap?," *KCET,* March 4, 2014, https://www.kcet.org/food/grocery-store-economics-why-are-rotisserie-chickens-so-cheap. Copyright © 2014. Reprinted by permission.

Scott Walker, "What Do You Want to Be When You Grow Up?," May 15, 2017. Reprinted by permission of the author.

Joe Weisenthal, "Donald Trump, the First President of Our Post-Literate Age," *Bloomberg View,* November 29, 2016, https://www.bloomberg.com/view/articles/2016-11-29/donald-trump-the-first-president-of-our-post-literate-age. Used with the permission of Bloomberg L.P. Copyright © 2017. All rights reserved.

Index